THE PAPERS OF
THOMAS JEFFERSON

THE PAPERS OF
Thomas Jefferson

Volume 22
6 August 1791 to 31 December 1791

CHARLES T. CULLEN, EDITOR

EUGENE R. SHERIDAN, ASSOCIATE EDITOR

RUTH W. LESTER, ASSISTANT EDITOR

PRINCETON, NEW JERSEY
PRINCETON UNIVERSITY PRESS
1986

ACKNOWLEDGMENTS

As INDICATED in the first volume, this edition was made possible by a grant of $200,000 from the New York Times Company to Princeton University. Since this initial subvention, its continuance has been assured by additional contributions from the New York Times Company; by grants of the Ford Foundation, the Andrew W. Mellon Foundation, the J. Howard Pew Freedom Trust; and by other benefactions from the Charlotte Palmer Phillips Foundation, Time Inc., the Dyson Foundation, and from such loyal supporters of the enterprise as James Russell Wiggins, David K. E. Bruce, and B. Batmanghelidj. In common with other editions of historical documents, The Papers of Thomas Jefferson is a beneficiary of the good offices of the National Historical Publications and Records Commission, tendered in many useful forms through its officers and dedicated staff. For these and other indispensable aids generously given by librarians, archivists, scholars, and collectors of manuscripts, the Editors record their sincere gratitude.

FOREWORD

PUBLICATION of Jefferson's papers now continues under new direction that is firmly committed to maintaining the high editorial standards introduced to this edition at its inception. This commitment accompanies a belief that no two people edit documents the same way, nor should they try. Julian Boyd recognized this fact and even applauded it, hoping that new editors coming into the profession would further improve it, and believing that it is impossible to standardize scholarly activity.

Readers who have followed this edition will recognize some differences in the handling of essays and documents, although the intended modifications in design are few. Like some of the early volumes in this series, this one contains no extended historical essays. This reflects a conscious decision to focus editorial work on the documents themselves with a view toward more regular and frequent publication of Jefferson's papers, and thereby providing space for wider coverage in each volume. The Editors expect that some documents will address issues that require extended historical treatment, and in those cases essays will be written.

Increasingly in recent volumes, editorial essays introduced topics that were also illuminated by grouping and printing related documents together, several of which were printed out of chronological order. This "file folder" method of presenting edited documents within a comprehensive edition was one of Julian Boyd's contributions to modern editorial design, but it is now abandoned in favor of a strict chronological presentation. In a series of this size documents should be easily located, and the most widely recognized method of arranging documents is by chronological sequence. When a file folder system is frequently employed, the reader must understand the Editor's organizational logic in order to make full use of the edition. If editorial staffs change, so does the logic, and readers are increasingly ill-served.

Although a policy of printing documents in strict chronological order makes it somewhat more difficult for readers to cover the full range of some topics, the Editors of this edition have provided assistance by mentioning in their footnote annotation related documents that cover a single topic over an extended period of time. In addition, each volume of Jefferson's papers will henceforth contain a comprehensive index. Through the use of subject entries, the

Editors can lead readers to related documents even more fully and easily than was practicable under the file folder method. Readers can continue to approach Jefferson's papers topically, but those in search of a particular document can find it in strict chronological order without regard to the subject or the date of related documents. Moreover, adoption of a strict chronological method of presentation and the introduction of volume indexes go hand-in-hand with the decision to limit the number and size of editorial essays. The earlier design contributed to and perhaps even required the device of extended essays. The present Editors hope that any seeming loss to historical scholarship resulting from this change in policy will be made up for in articles and books written from the rich mine of information provided by the comprehensive publication of this seminal resource for studying our nation's history.

Most of this edition's established editorial method remains unchanged. The policy regarding historical annotation of documents remains as first described in Volume 1: "However tempting it is to any editor of Jefferson's papers to explore the multitudinous bypaths that his letters invariably point to; to attempt to assay the historical significance of each document in relation to its context; to identify or explain all persons, events, and places; to separate fact from rumor; to explain obsolete, technical, and regional terms; to trace literary quotations to their sources; or to furnish references to pertinent literature, &c.—such a procedure would prolong the editorial task indefinitely, if not postpone its completion altogether. The Editors construe their primary task as that of placing the whole body of Jefferson's writings in the hands of historians and of the public as expeditiously as can be done in view of the size and complexity of the undertaking and of the need for completeness and for scrupulous accuracy. Nevertheless, the policy decided upon with respect to annotation is that of providing a certain minimum basis of information essential to the understanding of each document. Though such a policy, ideally, admits a very wide latitude for interpretation, the editors in applying it will lay emphasis upon the words 'minimum' and 'essential.' "

In an effort to eliminate purely routine annotation, the Editors have used the index to assist in identifying persons mentioned in documents only by last name, and to clarify the identity of some who appeared first in earlier volumes. In Jefferson's letter to David Humphreys of 23 Aug. 1791, for example, the reference to "General Scott's success against the Indians" is not noted in the annotation, but the index contains an entry for "Scott, Charles: expedition against Indians" with the correct page reference, and a further check of the cumulative index (Volume 21) will reveal seventeen other references to that subject in earlier volumes. Likewise, when John Hamilton writes from Norfolk on 11 Oct. 1791, he is not identified in annotation to his letter, but the index to this volume and especially the cumulative index clearly indicate that he was the British consul in that Virginia port. Thus, the introduction of volume indexes enables the Editors to adhere more faithfully to their editorial policies, and readers should heed their advice to make use of them as an integral part of the edition.

Two documents require a note of explanation here. Editorial work on this volume has revealed new information that corrects or clarifies our view of both the Summary Journal of Public Letters (SJPL), which has been cited often as a source of important information, and the collection of Jefferson's notes that begins in August 1791 and is known as the "Anas."

Summary Journal of Public Letters. As indicated in Volume 18: 221 n. 1, the SJPL that covers Jefferson's tenure as Secretary of State was not compiled daily but was prepared sometime later "as a record of his chief public papers of the period." This is certainly true of the "six pages in TJ's hand" mentioned first in the Editorial Apparatus list of "Other Symbols and Abbreviations" in Volume 17 of this edition. These six pages follow the style of the SJPL, but it appears that Jefferson placed them in his Summary Journal of Letters (SJL) rather than in the SJPL, which was prepared by a clerk. The sheets lie between the page ending with his list of letters written on 25 Sep. 1789 and letters received on 22 Sep. 1789 and the one beginning with letters written on 30 Sep. 1789 and letters received on 26 Sep. 1789. Because this list contains only public documents, and regardless of its physical location, the Editors will continue to identify documents listed on these six pages as being part of the SJPL. The revised identification of the abbreviation in the Editorial Apparatus clarifies the distinction between the list in a clerk's hand and the supplementary file Jefferson prepared.

This reassessment of the SJL and the SJPL followed a detailed examination of these two journals when it was discovered that Jefferson had erred in recording on his supplemental list one document as belonging with two others. In the collection of papers now at the Library of Congress, Jefferson had placed three enclosures with a letter to Pierce Butler of 2 Dec. 1791; but one enclosure bears marginal references to events from 1792 and is written in a format different from the other two. The record entry reads:

[Dec.] 2. Th:J. to Pierce Butler:
   draught of Resolution of Senate for ransom and peace with
      Barbary.
   do.   of both houses.
   do.   of paragraph for bill on foreign intercourse.

An examination of other papers in the TJ Editorial Files revealed that the last mentioned enclosure—the one the Editors had questioned—was actually an enclosure to a letter to George Washington of 1 Dec. 1792. In organizing his papers for this period, Jefferson inadvertently placed a copy of this enclosure with copies of those to Pierce Butler of a year earlier and so listed them in his compilation of items covering his tenure as Secretary of State, the list that supplements the SJPL.

Evidence of when Jefferson might have prepared this supplemental list had eluded the Editors until an examination of these six pages in the Library of Congress revealed a clear watermark of 1800 on each piece of paper. Jefferson was still using some of this paper—as well as paper made in 1799 and 1801—as late as 19 March 1802 (see letters to Josef Yznardy and James Dinsmore in DLC). What is certain is that he could not have prepared this list of public letters prior to 1800, and, because it appears likely that preparation of it had a direct relationship to the preparation of at least the early documents in what has come to be known as the "Anas," a better idea of the dating of both emerges.

The Anas. The first document in the "Anas" is printed at 13 Aug. 1791 ("Notes of a Conversation with Alexander Hamilton"), and an extended editorial note to that document explains in full the collection's history and its evolution from the time Jefferson decided to compile his notes into a cohesive whole. The Editors believe that he first surveyed his papers from his tenure as Secretary of State, prepared the supplemental list described above, and then had the selected notes and memoranda bound together "by a binder who came into my cabinet, doing it under my own eye, and without the opportunity of reading a single paper" ("Explanations of the 3. volumes bound in Marbled paper," 4 Feb. 1818). This could easily have been done in 1801 or 1802, and if the list that supplements the SJPL was prepared in conjunction with this survey of his papers from that period, that is the most likely date.

FOREWORD

It was known in 1800 that John Marshall, the current Secretary of State, planned to write a history of the life of George Washington based on the former President's papers then in the possession of Bushrod Washington (see John Marshall to Caleb P. Wayne, 3 Oct. 1800, in Charles T. Cullen, ed., *The Papers of John Marshall* [Chapel Hill, N.C., 1984], IV, 314). It would have been characteristic of Thomas Jefferson to anticipate the interpretation that a staunch Federalist might give to the first administration and to organize his own papers in order to support what could be expected to represent a contrary view. The movement of the government's offices—and Jefferson's papers—from Philadelphia to Washington in 1800 also afforded an opportune time to survey his official papers from the period to be covered in Marshall's book. These suppositions reinforce the Editors' conclusion that Jefferson meant to include in the "Anas" only those documents covering his tenure as Secretary of State, and that editors of previous editions of his papers have erred in implying that he intended it to cover notes from his vice-presidency and presidency as well. Publication of these miscellaneous notes—many of them containing extremely important information—begins in this volume, and attention is called to the Editors' decision to publish them separately, as they were written. Readers should refer to the note at 13 Aug. 1791 for a more comprehensive explanation of the treatment of this material.

As a new group of editors begins to work together on this important enterprise, it is appropriate to renew sincere expressions of appreciation to the many librarians, archivists, and collectors who have provided valuable assistance, and to the Andrew W. Mellon Foundation, the J. Howard Pew Memorial Trust, Time Inc., the Dyson Foundation, the National Historical Publications and Records Commission, B. Batmanghelidj, and Frank Glass for their generous benefactions. The late Wilbourn S. Gibbs gave valuable assistance and encouragement to the Editor in his efforts to locate additional sources of financial support. We wish to express appreciation also to George H. Hoemann, J. Jefferson Looney, William G. Ray, Paul H. Smith, Mary A. Giunta, Sara Jackson, and Irma Jaffe for special assistance in preparing this volume.

CHARLES T. CULLEN

7 September 1985

GUIDE TO EDITORIAL APPARATUS

1. TEXTUAL DEVICES

The following devices are employed throughout the work to clarify the presentation of the text.

[...], [....]   One or two words missing and not conjecturable.

[...]¹, [....]¹   More than two words missing and not conjecturable; subjoined footnote estimates number of words missing.

[   ]   Number or part of a number missing or illegible.

[roman]   Conjectural reading for missing or illegible matter. A question mark follows when the reading is doubtful.

[*italic*]   Editorial comment inserted in the text.

⟨*italic*⟩   Matter deleted in the MS but restored in our text.

2. DESCRIPTIVE SYMBOLS

The following symbols are employed throughout the work to describe the various kinds of manuscript originals. When a series of versions is recorded, *the first to be recorded is the version used for the printed text.*

Dft   draft (usually a composition or rough draft; later drafts, when identifiable as such, are designated "2 Dft," &c.)

Dupl   duplicate

MS   manuscript (arbitrarily applied to most documents other than letters)

N   note, notes (memoranda, fragments, &c.)

PoC   polygraph copy

PrC   press copy

RC   recipient's copy

SC   stylograph copy

Tripl   triplicate

All manuscripts of the above types are assumed to be in the hand of the author of the document to which the descriptive symbol pertains. If not, that fact is stated. On the other hand, the following types of manuscripts are assumed *not* to be in the hand of the author, and exceptions will be noted:

FC   file copy (applied to all forms of retained copies, such as letter-book copies, clerk's copies, &c.)

Tr   transcript (applied to both contemporary and later copies; period of transcription, unless clear by implication, will be given when known)

3. LOCATION SYMBOLS

The locations of most documents printed in this edition from originals in private hands, from originals held by institutions outside the United States, and from printed sources are recorded in self-explanatory form in the descriptive note following each document. The location symbols BL and PRO are used for documents in the British Library and the Public Record Office in London, respectively. The locations of documents printed from originals held by public institutions in the United States are recorded by means of the symbols used in the National Union Catalog in the Library of Congress; (explanation of how these symbols are formed is given above, Vol. 1: xl). The symbols DLC and MHi by themselves will stand for the collections of Jefferson Papers proper in these repositories; when texts are drawn from other collections held by these two institutions, the names of the particular collections will be added. The list of symbols appearing in each volume is limited to the institutions represented by documents printed or referred to in that and previous volumes.

BL	British Library, London
CLSU	University of Southern California Library, Los Angeles
CLU	William Andrews Clark Memorial Library, University of California at Los Angeles
CSM	Colonial Society of Massachusetts, Boston
CSmH	Henry E. Huntington Library, San Marino, California
Ct	Connecticut State Library, Hartford
CtHi	Connecticut Historical Society, Hartford
CtY	Yale University Library
DeHi	Historical Society of Delaware, Wilmington
DLC	Library of Congress
DNA	The National Archives, with identifications of series (preceded by record group number) as follows:
	AL American Letters
	CD Consular Dispatches

DCI   Diplomatic and Consular Instructions
DCLB District of Columbia Letter Book
DD   Diplomatic Dispatches
DL   Domestic Letters
FL   Foreign Letters
LAR   Letters of Application and
         Recommendation
MLR Miscellaneous Letters Received
MTA Miscellaneous Treasury Accounts
NL   Notes from Legations
NWT Northwest Territory Papers
PC   Proceedings of Board of Commissioners
         for the District of Columbia
PCC   Papers of the Continental Congress
PDL   Printing and Distribution of the Laws
SDC   State Department Correspondence
SDR   A Record of the Reports of Thomas
         Jefferson, Secretary of State for the
         United States of America
SWT Southwest Territory Papers

G-Ar	Georgia Department of Archives and History, Atlanta
ICHi	Chicago Historical Society, Chicago
IHi	Illinois State Historical Library, Springfield
IMunS	St. Mary of the Lake Seminary, Mundelein, Illinois
InHi	Indiana Historical Society, Indianapolis
MB	Boston Public Library
MBA	Archives, State House, Boston
MBAt	Boston Athenæum
MdAA	Maryland Hall of Records, Annapolis
MdAN	U.S. Naval Academy Library, Annapolis
MdHi	Maryland Historical Society, Baltimore
MeHi	Maine Historical Society, Portland
MH	Harvard University Library
MHi	Massachusetts Historical Society, Boston
MHi:AM	Adams Manuscripts, Massachusetts Historical Society
MiU-C	William L. Clements Library, University of Michigan
MoSHi	Missouri Historical Society, St. Louis
MWA	American Antiquarian Society, Worcester, Massachusetts
NA	New York State Library, Albany

NBu	Buffalo Public Library, Buffalo, New York
NcD	Duke University Library
NcU	University of North Carolina Library, Chapel Hill
NhD	Dartmouth College Library
NhHi	New Hampshire Historical Society, Concord
NHi	New-York Historical Society, New York City
NjHi	New Jersey Historical Society, Newark
NjMoW	Morristown National Historical Park, Morristown, New Jersey
NjP	Princeton University Library
NK-Iselin	Letters to and from John Jay bearing this symbol are used by permission of the Estate of Eleanor Jay Iselin.
NN	New York Public Library, New York City
NNC	Columbia University Libraries
NNP	Pierpont Morgan Library, New York City
NNS	New York Society Library, New York City
O	Ohio State Library, Columbus
OCHP	Cincinnati Historical Society
OHi	Ohio Historical Society, Columbus
PBL	Lehigh University Library
PHC	Haverford College Library
PHi	Historical Society of Pennsylvania, Philadelphia
PHMC	Pennsylvania Historical and Museum Commission, Harrisburg
PP	Free Library, Philadelphia
PPAP	American Philosophical Society, Philadelphia
PPL	Library Company of Philadelphia
PRO	Public Record Office, London
PU	University of Pennsylvania Library
PWW	Washington and Jefferson College, Washington, Pennsylvania
RPA	Rhode Island Department of State, Providence
RPAB	Annmary Brown Memorial Library, Providence
RPB	Brown University Library
Vi	Virginia State Library, Richmond
Vi:USCC	Ended Cases, United States Circuit Court, Virginia State Library
ViHi	Virginia Historical Society, Richmond
ViRVal	Valentine Museum Library, Richmond
ViU	University of Virginia Library
ViU:McG	McGregor Library, University of Virginia
ViU:TJMF	Manuscripts deposited by the Thomas Jefferson

	Memorial Foundation in the University of Virginia Library
ViW	College of William and Mary Library
ViWC	Colonial Williamsburg, Inc.
VtMC	Middlebury College Library, Middlebury, Vermont
VtMS	Secretary of State, Montpelier, Vermont
WHi	State Historical Society of Wisconsin, Madison

4. OTHER SYMBOLS AND ABBREVIATIONS

The following symbols and abbreviations are commonly employed in the annotation throughout the work.

Second Series   The topical series to be published as part of this edition, comprising those materials which are best suited to a topical rather than a chronological arrangement (see Vol. 1: xv-xvi)

TJ   Thomas Jefferson

TJ Editorial Files   Photoduplicates and other editorial materials in the office of *The Papers of Thomas Jefferson*, Princeton University Library

TJ Papers   Jefferson Papers (applied to a collection of manuscripts when the precise location of a given document must be furnished, and always preceded by the symbol for the institutional repository; thus "DLC: TJ Papers, 4:628-9" represents a document in the Library of Congress, Jefferson Papers, volume 4, pages 628 and 629)

RG   Record Group (used in designating the location of documents in the National Archives)

SJL   Jefferson's "Summary Journal of Letters" written and received (in DLC: TJ Papers)

SJPL   "Summary Journal of Public Letters," an incomplete list of letters written by TJ from 16 Apr. 1784 to 31 Dec. 1793, with brief summaries, in an amanuensis' hand, supplemented by six pages in TJ's hand listing and summarizing official reports and communications by him as Secretary of State, 11 Oct. 1789 to 31 Dec. 1793 (in DLC: TJ Papers, Epistolary Record, 209-211, 514-559)

V   Ecu

f   Florin

£   Pound sterling or livre, depending upon context (in doubtful cases, a clarifying note will be given)

s   Shilling or sou (also expressed as /)

d   Penny or denier

₶   Livre Tournois

℔   Per (occasionally used for pro, pre)

5. SHORT TITLES

The following list includes only those short titles of works cited with great frequency, and therefore in very abbreviated form, throughout this edition. Since it is impossible to anticipate all the works to be cited in such very abbreviated form, the list is appropriately revised from volume to volume.

Adams, *Works*   Charles Francis Adams, ed., *The Works of John Adams*, Boston, 1850-1856, 10 vols.

Adams, *Diary*   L. H. Butterfield and others, eds., *Diary and Autobiography of John Adams*, Cambridge, Mass., 1961, 4 vols.

AHA   American Historical Association

AHR   *American Historical Review*, 1895-

Ammon, *Monroe*   Harry Ammon, *James Monroe*, New York, 1971

Annals   *Annals of the Congress of the United States: The Debates and Proceedings in the Congress of the United States . . . Compiled from Authentic Materials by Joseph Gales, Senior*, Washington, Gales & Seaton, 1834-1856, 42 vols. All editions are undependable and pagination varies from one printing to another. The edition cited here has this caption on both recto and verso pages: "History of Congress." Another printing, with the same titlepage, has "Gales & Seatons History" on verso and "of Debates in Congress" on recto pages. Those using the latter printing will need to employ the date or, where it is lacking, to add approximately 52 to the page numbers of *Annals* as cited in this volume.

ASP   *American State Papers: Documents, Legislative and Executive, of the Congress of the United States*, Washington, Gales & Seaton, 1832-1861, 38 vols.

Atlas of Amer. Hist.   James Truslow Adams and R. V. Coleman, eds., *Atlas of American History*, New York, 1943

Bear, *Family Letters*   Edwin M. Betts and James A. Bear, Jr., eds., *Family Letters of Thomas Jefferson*, Columbia, Missouri, 1966

Bemis, *Jay's Treaty*   Samuel Flagg Bemis, *Jay's Treaty: A Study in Commerce and Diplomacy*, rev. edn., New Haven, 1962

Bemis, *Pinckney's Treaty*   Samuel Flagg Bemis, *Pinckney's Treaty:*

America's Advantage from Europe's Distress, 1783-1800, rev. edn., New Haven, 1960

Betts, *Farm Book*   Edwin M. Betts, ed., *Thomas Jefferson's Farm Book*, Princeton, 1953

Betts, *Garden Book*   Edwin M. Betts, ed., *Thomas Jefferson's Garden Book, 1766-1824*, Philadelphia, 1944

Beveridge, *Marshall*   Albert J. Beveridge, *The Life of John Marshall*, Boston, 1916-1919, 4 vols.

Biog. Dir. Cong.   *Biographical Directory of the American Congress, 1774-1949*, Washington, 1950

B.M. Cat.   British Museum, *General Catalogue of Printed Books*, London, 1931-; also *The British Museum Catalogue of Printed Books, 1881-1900*, Ann Arbor, 1946

B.N. Cat.   Bibliothèque Nationale, *Catalogue général des livres imprimés. . . . Auteurs*, Paris, 1897-1955

Brant, *Madison*   Irving Brant, *James Madison*, Indianapolis, 1941-1961, 6 vols.

Bryan, *National Capital*   Wilhelmus Bogart Bryan, *A History of the National Capital*, New York, 1914-1916, 2 vols.

Burnett, *Letters of Members*   Edmund C. Burnett, ed., *Letters of Members of the Continental Congress*, Washington, 1921-1936, 8 vols.

Butterfield, *Rush*   L. H. Butterfield, ed., *Letters of Benjamin Rush*, Princeton, 1951, 2 vols.

Cal. Franklin Papers   I. Minis Hays, ed., *Calendar of the Papers of Benjamin Franklin in the Library of the American Philosophical Society*, Philadelphia, 1908, 6 vols.

Carter, *Terr. Papers*   Clarence E. Carter, ed., *The Territorial Papers of the United States*, Washington, 1934-1962, 26 vols.

Cutler, *Cutler*   William Parker Cutler, *Life, Journals, and Correspondence of Rev. Manasseh Cutler*, Cincinnati, 1888, 2 vols.

CVSP   William P. Palmer and others, eds., *Calendar of Virginia State Papers . . . Preserved in the Capitol at Richmond*, Richmond, 1875-1893, 11 vols.

DAB   Allen Johnson and Dumas Malone, eds., *Dictionary of American Biography*, New York, 1928-1936

DAE   Sir William A. Craigie and James Hulbert, eds., *A Dictionary of American English*, Chicago, 1938-1944

DAH   James Truslow Adams, ed., *Dictionary of American History*, New York, 1940, 5 vols., and index

DeConde, *Entangling Alliance*   Alexander DeConde, *Entangling*

Alliance; Politics & Diplomacy under George Washington, Durham, N.C., 1958

DNB   Leslie Stephen and Sidney Lee, eds., *Dictionary of National Biography*, 2d edn., New York, 1908-1909

Dumbauld, *Tourist*   Edward Dumbauld, *Thomas Jefferson American Tourist*, Norman, Oklahoma, 1946

Elliot's *Debates*   Jonathan Elliot, ed., *The Debates of the Several State Conventions on the Adoption of the Federal Constitution . . . together with the Journal of the Federal Convention*, 2d edn., Philadelphia, 1901, 5 vols.

Evans   Charles Evans, comp., *American Bibliography*, Chicago, 1903-1955

Fitzpatrick, *Writings*   John C. Fitzpatrick, ed., *The Writings of George Washington*, Washington, 1931-1944, 39 vols.

Ford   Paul Leicester Ford, ed., *The Writings of Thomas Jefferson*, New York, 1892-1899, 10 vols.

Freeman, *Washington*   Douglas Southall Freeman, *George Washington*, New York, 1948-1957, 6 vols.; 7th volume by John Alexander Carroll and Mary Wells Ashworth, New York, 1957

Fry-Jefferson Map   Dumas Malone, ed., *The Fry & Jefferson Map of Virginia and Maryland: A Facsimile of the First Edition*, Princeton, 1950

Gottschalk, *Lafayette, 1783-89*   Louis Gottschalk, *Lafayette between the American and the French Revolution (1783-1789)*, Chicago, 1950

Greely, *Public Documents*   Adolphus Washington Greely, ed., *Public Documents of the First Fourteen Congresses, 1789-1817: Papers Relating to Early Congressional Documents*, Washington, 1900

HAW   Henry A. Washington, ed., *The Writings of Thomas Jefferson*, New York, 1853-1854, 9 vols.

Hening   William Waller Hening, ed., *The Statutes at Large; Being a Collection of All the Laws of Virginia*, Richmond, 1809-1823, 13 vols.

Henry, *Henry*   William Wirt Henry, *Patrick Henry, Life, Correspondence and Speeches*, New York, 1891, 3 vols.

Humphreys, *Humphreys*   Frank Landon Humphreys, *Life and Times of David Humphreys*, New York, 1917, 2 vols.

Hunt, *Madison*   Gaillard Hunt, ed., *The Writings of James Madison*, New York, 1900-1910, 9 vols.

JCC   Worthington C. Ford and others, eds., *Journals of the Continental Congress, 1774-1789*, Washington, 1904-1937, 34 vols.

Jefferson Correspondence, Bixby   Worthington C. Ford, ed., *Thomas Jefferson Correspondence Printed from the Originals in the Collections of William K. Bixby*, Boston, 1916

Jenkins, *Records*   William Sumner Jenkins, ed., *Records of the States of the United States of America*, Library of Congress and University of North Carolina, microfilm, 1950

JEP   *Journal of the Executive Proceedings of the Senate of the United States ... to the Termination of the Nineteenth Congress*, Washington, 1828

JHD   *Journal of the House of Delegates of the Commonwealth of Virginia* (cited by session and date of publication)

JHR   *Journal of the House of Representatives of the United States*, Washington, Gales & Seaton, 1826, 9 vols.

JS   *Journal of the Senate of the United States*, Washington, Gales, 1820-1821, 5 vols.

JSH   *Journal of Southern History*, 1935-

Ketcham, *Madison*   Ralph Ketcham, *James Madison*, New York, 1971

Kimball, *Jefferson*   Marie Kimball, *Jefferson*, New York, 1943-1950, 3 vols.

King, *King*   C. R. King, ed., *The Life and Correspondence of Rufus King, Comprising His Letters, Private and Official, His Public Documents, and His Speeches, 1755-1827*, New York, 1894-1900, 6 vols.

L & B   Andrew A. Lipscomb and Albert E. Bergh, eds., *The Writings of Thomas Jefferson*, Washington, 1903-1904, 20 vols.

L.C. *Cat.*   *A Catalogue of Books Represented by the Library of Congress Printed Cards*, Ann Arbor, 1942-1946; also *Supplement*, 1948-1952

Library Catalogue, 1783   Jefferson's MS list of books owned or wanted in 1783 (original in Massachusetts Historical Society)

Library Catalogue, 1815   *Catalogue of the Library of the United States*, Washington, 1815

Library Catalogue, 1829   *Catalogue: President Jefferson's Library*, Washington, 1829

Loubat, *Medallic history*   J. F. Loubat, *The Medallic History of the United States of America, 1776-1876*, New York, 1878, 2 vols.

Maclay, *Journal*   Edgar S. Maclay, ed., *Journal of William Maclay, United States Senator from Pennsylvania, 1789-1791*, New York, 1890

Madison, *Letters and Other Writings*   James Madison, *Letters and Other Writings of James Madison*, Philadelphia, 1865, 4 vols.

Malone, *Jefferson*   Dumas Malone, *Jefferson and his Time*, Boston, 1948-1981, 6 vols.

Mason, *Papers*   Robert A. Rutland, ed., *Papers of George Mason, 1725-1792*, Chapel Hill, 1970, 3 vols.

Mathews, *Andrew Ellicott*   Catharine Van Cortlandt Mathews, *Andrew Ellicott, His Life and Letters*, New York, 1908

Mayo, *British Ministers*   Bernard Mayo, ed., "Instructions to the British Ministers to the United States 1791-1812," American Historical Association, *Annual Report*, 1936

Mays, *Pendleton*   David John Mays, ed., *Letters and Papers of Edmund Pendleton, 1734-1803*, Charlottesville, 1967, 2 vols.

Miller, *Hamilton*   John C. Miller, *Alexander Hamilton, Portrait in Paradox*, New York, 1959

Mitchell, *Hamilton*   Broadus Mitchell, *Alexander Hamilton*, New York, 1957-1962, 2 vols.

MVHR   *Mississippi Valley Historical Review*, 1914-1964

Notes, ed. Peden   William Peden, ed., *Notes on the State of Virginia*, Chapel Hill, 1955

NYHS, *Quar.*   New-York Historical Society *Quarterly*, 1917-

NYPL, *Bulletin*   New York Public Library *Bulletin*, 1897-

OED   Sir James Murray and others, eds., *A New English Dictionary on Historical Principles*, Oxford, 1888-1933

Padover, *National Capital*   Saul K. Padover, ed., *Thomas Jefferson and the National Capital*, Washington, 1946

Peterson, *Jefferson*   Merrill D. Peterson, *Thomas Jefferson and the New Nation*, New York, 1970

PMHB   *Pennsylvania Magazine of History and Biography*, 1877-

Randall, *Life*   Henry S. Randall, *The Life of Thomas Jefferson*, New York, 1858, 3 vols.

Randolph, *Domestic Life*   Sarah N. Randolph, *The Domestic Life of Thomas Jefferson, Compiled from Family Letters and Reminiscences by His Great-Granddaughter*, Cambridge, Mass., 1939

Rowland, *George Mason*   Kate Mason Rowland, *Life of George Mason, 1725-1792*, New York, 1892, 2 vols.

Rutland, *Madison*   William T. Hutchinson, William M.E. Rachal,

Robert A. Rutland and others, eds., *The Papers of James Madison*, Chicago and Charlottesville, 1962—, 14 vols.

Sabin   Joseph Sabin and others, comps., *Bibliotheca Americana. A Dictionary of Books Relating to America*, New York, 1868-1936

St. Clair, *Papers*   William Henry Smith, ed., *The St. Clair Papers. The Life and Public Services of Arthur St. Clair*, Cincinnati, 1882, 2 vols.

Setser, *Reciprocity*   Vernon G. Setser, *The Commercial Reciprocity Policy of the United States*, Philadelphia, 1937

Shipton-Mooney Index   Clifford K. Shipton and James E. Mooney, comps., *National Index of American Imprints through 1800, The Short-Title Evans*, [Worcester, Mass.], 1969, 2 vols.

Sowerby   E. Millicent Sowerby, comp., *Catalogue of the Library of Thomas Jefferson*, Washington, 1952-1959, 5 vols.

Sparks, *Morris*   Jared Sparks, *Life of Gouverneur Morris*, Boston, 1832, 3 vols.

Swem, *Index*   Earl G. Swem, comp., *Virginia Historical Index*, Roanoke, 1934-1936

Swem, "Va. Bibliog."   Earl G. Swem, comp., "A Bibliography of Virginia History," Virginia State Library, *Bulletin*, VIII (1915), X (1917), and XII (1919)

Syrett, *Hamilton*   Harold C. Syrett and others, eds., *The Papers of Alexander Hamilton*, New York, 1961-1979, 26 vols.

TJR   Thomas Jefferson Randolph, ed., *Memoir, Correspondence, and Miscellanies, from the Papers of Thomas Jefferson*, Charlottesville, 1829, 4 vols.

Tucker, *Life*   George Tucker, *The Life of Thomas Jefferson*, Philadelphia, 1837, 2 vols.

Turner, *CFM*   Frederick J. Turner, "Correspondence of French Ministers, 1791-1797," American Historical Association, *Annual Report*, 1903, II

U.S. Statutes at Large   Richard Peters, ed., *The Public Statutes at Large of the United States . . . 1789 to March 3, 1845*, Boston, 1855-1856, 8 vols.

Van Doren, *Franklin*   Carl Van Doren, *Benjamin Franklin*, New York, 1938

Van Doren, *Secret History*   Carl Van Doren, *Secret History of the American Revolution*, New York, 1941

VMHB   *Virginia Magazine of History and Biography*, 1893-

WMQ   *William and Mary Quarterly*, 1892-

CONTENTS

Foreword, vii
Guide to Editorial Apparatus, xiii
Illustrations, xxxvii

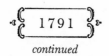

1791

continued

CONTENTS

CONTENTS

CONTENTS

CONTENTS

CONTENTS

CONTENTS

CONTENTS

CONTENTS

CONTENTS

CONTENTS

ILLUSTRATIONS

Following page 246

THOMAS JEFFERSON

Charles Willson Peale's celebrated portrait of Jefferson, painted in Philadelphia in December 1791, has had a checkered history. This work was regarded as a life portrait of Jefferson until 1944, when Fiske Kimball declared that it was actually an early copy by someone other than Peale. Kimball's opinion held sway for almost a decade until careful scientific analyses by Elizabeth Jones and Anne Clapp proved conclusively that this painting is indeed the original life portrait by Peale. But if the provenance of this work was once in doubt, there has never been any question about its iconographic significance. As the first portrait of Jefferson to be widely disseminated through prints before his election to the presidency, it had an immense impact on the American people's visual perception of the Virginia statesman (Alfred L. Bush, *The Life Portraits of Thomas Jefferson* [Charlottesville, Va., 1962], p. 31-3). (*Courtesy of Independence National Historical Park, Philadelphia*)

GEORGE HAMMOND (1763-1853)

Hammond, who arrived in Philadelphia in October 1791 as the first British minister to the United States, was the scion of an English country family and a graduate of Oxford. After serving as David Hartley's private secretary during the peace negotiations between America and Britain that brought the Revolutionary War to a close, Hammond held a series of minor diplomatic offices in Vienna, Copenhagen, and Madrid before being posted to the United States under the patronage of Lord Grenville. Charged by his government to prevent the passage of discriminatory legislation against British commerce and to discuss infractions of the Treaty of Peace, Hammond entered into a series of negotiations with Jefferson that ultimately failed to resolve the most outstanding points at issue between their respective nations.

Portrait painted by John Trumbull in 1792. (*Courtesy of Yale University Art Gallery*)

JEAN BAPTISTE TERNANT (1751-1816)

Ternant arrived in Philadelphia in August 1791 as Louis xvi's last minister to the United States. Unlike his British counterpart, Ternant brought an intimate knowledge of the new American nation to his task, having forsaken his lieutenancy in the Royal Corps of Engineers to join the Continental Army in 1778. Ternant served the American cause with distinction for almost five years, attaining the position of inspector of Continental forces in the Southern Department and rising to the rank of colonel. Though in general they worked together harmoniously, Ternant was disappointed by the reserve with which Jefferson treated him, thereby mistaking the Secretary of State's adherence to diplomatic niceties for personal aloofness.

Portrait painted by Charles Willson Peale in 1781. (*Courtesy of Independence National Historical Park, Philadelphia*)

ILLUSTRATIONS

THOMAS PINCKNEY (1750-1828)

The first American minister to Great Britain to be appointed under the new federal government, Pinckney was the offspring of a distinguished South Carolina family. He received a cosmopolitan education, studying in England at Westminster School, Oxford, and the Middle Temple and in France at the Royal Military Academy. After compiling a distinguished record of military service during the American Revolution, Pinckney practiced law and served as governor of his native state during the Confederation period. Some contemporaries took note of Pinckney's English education and concluded that his appointment as minister was an act of appeasement to Great Britain, but Washington strongly denied this, and Pinckney's own behavior in London was that of a vigorous defender of American national interests.

Portrait painted by John Trumbull in 1791. (*Courtesy of Yale University Art Gallery*)

GOUVERNEUR MORRIS (1752-1816)

Morris' nomination to succeed Jefferson as minister to France came as a distinct shock and surprise to the Secretary of State. Washington decided on this nomination without consulting Jefferson beforehand and remained adamant in the face of an effort by Jefferson to persuade him to dispatch Thomas Pinckney to Paris instead. Morris' nomination was a source of great unease to Jefferson because of the aristocratic New Yorker's well-known contempt for the French Revolution. But as soon as Jefferson realized that Washington was intent on submitting Morris' name to the Senate, he loyally refrained from any further opposition to the nomination.

Portrait painted by James Sharples in 1810. (*Courtesy of the National Portrait Gallery, Smithsonian Institution, Washington, D.C.*)

FIRST U.S. CENSUS, 1791

Title page and last page of the first publication of the Census of 1790 by Childs and Swaine of Philadelphia, entitled *Return of the Whole Number of Persons within the Several Districts of the United States* and consisting of 56 pages, the last bearing Jefferson's signature. (*Courtesy of Princeton University Library*)

WILLIAM TATHAM (1752-1819)

Tatham, the English-born son of an Anglican rector, was a man of many parts. After immigrating to Virginia at the age of seventeen, he worked as a clerk for merchants there and in the Tennessee country, mastered the elements of engineering and surveying, served as an Indian fighter in western North Carolina and as a volunteer cavalryman in Virginia during the Revolutionary War, and became a member of the North Carolina bar and state legislature during the Confederation period. Long interested in western exploration, Tatham was co-author in 1780 of the first history of Kentucky, a manuscript that was never published and has since been lost. Appointed state geographer of Virginia in 1789, Tatham was keenly interested at this time in enlisting Jefferson's support for two publication projects he never brought to fruition—a history and a topographical analysis of Virginia.

Portrait by Thomas Barrow. (*Courtesy of Hirschl & Adler Galleries, Inc., New York City*)

DAVID RITTENHOUSE (1732-1796)

This noted astronomer was the foremost American scientist of his age. Jefferson was an ardent admirer and close confidant of Rittenhouse, whose scientific achievements he proudly cited in *Notes on the State of Virginia* to refute European allegations about the degeneration of the human species in the New World. As Secretary of State, Jefferson regularly conferred with Rittenhouse when called upon to prepare state papers of a scientific nature, most notably in the case of his 1790 Report on Weights and Measures, but also with respect to the Report on Desalination of Sea Water printed in this volume.

Portrait by Charles Willson Peale in 1791 to commemorate Rittenhouse's election as president of the American Philosophical Society. (*Courtesy of the American Philosophical Society*)

ANAS

This 13 Aug. 1791 account of a conversation with Alexander Hamilton is the first entry in the work that has come to be known as Jefferson's "Anas." A miscellaneous collection of political anecdotes, gossip, and observations by Jefferson, it scandalized his critics and heartened his supporters when it was first published in 1829, and has been an important source for historians of the early national period ever since. Originally conceived by Jefferson to cover only his years as Secretary of State and to serve as a counterweight to the unabashedly pro-Federalist account of the party strife of the 1790s in John Marshall's *Life of George Washington*, 5 vols. (Philadelphia, 1805-1807), the Anas has been extended in scope by all previous editors of Jefferson's papers to include similar documents from his vice-presidential and presidential years as well. (*Courtesy of the Library of Congress*)

Volume 22

6 August 1791 to 31 December 1791

JEFFERSON CHRONOLOGY

1 7 4 3 • 1 8 2 6

1743.	Born at Shadwell, 13 Apr. (New Style).
1760.	Entered the College of William and Mary.
1762.	"quitted college."
1762-1767.	Self-education and preparation for law.
1769-1774.	Albemarle delegate to House of Burgesses.
1772.	Married Martha Wayles Skelton, 1 Jan.
1775-1776.	In Continental Congress.
1776.	Drafted Declaration of Independence.
1776-1779.	In Virginia House of Delegates.
1779.	Submitted Bill for Establishing Religious Freedom.
1779-1781.	Governor of Virginia.
1782.	His wife died, 6 Sep.
1783-1784.	In Continental Congress.
1784-1789.	In France as commissioner to negotiate commercial treaties and as minister plenipotentiary at Versailles.
1790-1793.	U.S. Secretary of State.
1797-1801.	Vice President of the United States.
1801-1809.	President of the United States.
1814-1826.	Established the University of Virginia.
1826.	Died at Monticello, 4 July.

VOLUME 22

6 August 1791 to 31 December 1791

12 Aug.	Receives new French minister.
2 Sep.	In company with James Madison, leaves Philadelphia for Monticello.
8 Sep.	Confers with D. C. Commissioners in Georgetown.
22 Oct.	Returns to Philadelphia.
24 Oct.	Report on census.
8 Nov.	Report on public lands.
21 Nov.	Report on desalination of sea water.
26 Nov.	Plan of commercial treaty with France.
29 Nov.	Begins negotiations with British minister.
2 Dec.	Resolutions on treaty with Algiers.
22 Dec.	Report on negotiations with Spain.

THE PAPERS OF
THOMAS JEFFERSON

◄〓〓〓〓〓►

From Charles Carter

[*Ludlow, ca. 6 Aug. 1791.*] Acknowledging with gratitude TJ's of 31 July. He neglected to mention the Bank of the United States. As TJ is fully informed of their powers, he can himself tell whether loan could be obtained on terms mentioned. A young Virginian studying under Dr. Barton says that he has added an entrance fee of £70 to the terms he took him on. This puts it totally out of his power to send his son to Philadelphia and he has decided to "put him into a Shop in Fredburg. for a Year, or perhaps two, to make him acquainted with medicine, and . . . lay the Ground work of his Education," after which he will send him to Edinburgh for two or three years as TJ advised. They hear many "Emigrants are coming over from Europe" and perhaps some may settle in Kentucky. A friend of his, Fr. Lewis, has 50,000 acres on Green River, a very rich tract of "second land," which he would sell as low as 6/8 per acre. If TJ could mention this, he would do "a very worthy man, a singular service." The excise law is taking place without the least confusion in this part of the State. Their only inconvenience is the want of small change. "All the Cut money is remitted to Britain," being bought at 1 pr Ct advance by merchants. He would like to know what TJ thinks they can expect for their wheat this year. Merchants now give only 4/. The crop is decreased by dry weather, but because of great quantity planted last year, what will come to market "will exceed any thing we ever had." Mrs. Carter joins in assurances of regard.

RC (MHi); 4 p.; endorsed by TJ as received 13 Aug. 1791 and so recorded in SJL.

The fees of DR. BARTON had been a topic of correspondence between TJ and Carter since May. TJ finally recommended EDINBURGH as "superior . . . for the study of physic, and also in point of economy" (Carter to TJ, 21 May 1791, and TJ to Carter, 10 and 31 July 1791).

From Tench Coxe

Augt. 6th. 1791

Mr. Coxe has the honor to inclose to the Secretary of State the account of all the payments for lands, which have been made to the United States prior to this day being Drs. 687,563 70/100.

The contract for land intended to have been made between the United States and Messrs. Flint and Parker, as will appear by reference to their letter of 18th. Octr. 1787 and to the resolution of Congress of the 22d of the same month, was not carried into execution, nor has any money been paid on that Account. It is represented as a project which the proposers abandoned before they took any step by which they became bound, and it is not perceived that it can be considered in any other light (see appendix to 12 Vol. Journ: of Congress, pages 226 and 227). The Survey of the tract on Lake Erie, included in the Cession of New York to the U.S. and since sold to Pennsylvania (See Congress's Journals 6th. June and 4th. Sept. 1788) has been completed. The Quantity of land proves to be 202,187 acres, agreeably to a return of survey, which accompanies this letter. That return however is so far deficient in the requisite notations of the length of some of the boundary lines, that a correct description of them cannot be made. This is very material and may give rise to questions of considerable importance hereafter. On the return of Mr. Ellicott from the Patowmac the field notes &ca. which have been requested are expected to be furnished to the Treasury.

The account for this purchase has been delayed first by the Vacancy in the Comptrollers office and afterwards in that of the Auditor. Some correspondence towards an adjustment of the demand has taken place between the Governor of Pennsylvania and the Secretary of the Treasury.

The contract proposed by Col. George Morgan was not completed, no money was paid, nor does there appear any reason to expect the object will be further pursued by him. The United states as it appears, possess nothing obligatory on Mr. Morgan.

The quantity of lands in the western Territory sold at new York is exactly 150,896 As. for which the whole purchase money has been received, as stated in the Registers account rendered herewith.

The resolution of Congress of 12th. Augt. 1790 appears applicable only to the purchase of the Ohio Company, that of the Scioto Association, and that of John C. Symmes and his Associates, called the Miami Company. The Survey of the Ohio Company's tract is among the papers transmitted on the 21 June and will be found complete, except the line which is required to coincide with the western boundary of the 17th. range of Townships, and that which is to run from the Northern termination of this line due East to the western boundary of the 7th. range of Townships. In the Month of May and again in August 1790 the Secretary of the Treasury wrote to the Deputies of the late Geographer to press their return of the surveys executed by them which they made at the Treasury in the Autumn of that year when one of them Israel Ludlow was further instructed to proceed agreeably to the approved resolution of Congress of the 12th. of August to execute all such parts of the Surveys of the lands comprized in the purchases abovementioned as were not given to him or his associate in orders by the late Geographer, or which were necessary to the complete execution of the intentions of the legislature.

Part of the lines of the Scioto company have been also run, and will be found among the papers transmitted on the 21st. June. The Survey will be completed by the running of the two lines mentioned under the head of the Ohio Company.

The lines of the Miami company remain to be run and were, as before mentioned, given in orders to Mr. Ludlow in the autumn of 1790, soon after the Resolution of Augt. on his arrival at the seat of Government, whither he had been previously directed to repair.

Letters from Mr. Ludlow the last of the 20th. May have been recd. by the Secretary of the Treasury informing him that the Indian hostilities have hitherto prevented his executing any part of the work except the survey of the South Boundary of the Miami tract, of which however he has not yet transmitted a return. A letter desiring that this return may be sent forward has been written to him.

There are some purchases which have been made by Individuals with what degree of regularity and effect remains to be determined, but which appear to merit inspection in taking a View of the Western Territory. The purchase of Illinois company, and the purchase of the Ouabache company now united under the two names of which a particular account can be given, so far as regards the claims and pretensions of the purchasers, by Judge Wilson, who is concerned in both. A report of a Committee of Congress on these claims will be found in the Journals Congress for 1781. A conference with the Attorney General appears highly expedient, he having had those claims under official Consideration. The two Yazou companies, the Grants and Contracts under N. Carolina within the Country now constituting the Government South of the Ohio, the lands reserved for the line of Virginia by that State, the Connecticut tract west of Pennsylvania, and the military rights acquired by service in the late war are objects that appear to merit examination. Mr. Coxe refrains from Remark upon them having no authentic information in either of the Cases but what is to be found in the journals and acts of Congress.

Dft (PHi: Tench Coxe Papers); with many interlineations and crossed out words. Not recorded in SJL.

Royal Flint, Joseph Parker, and George Morgan represented private land companies that sought to profit from the Continental Congress' policy of selling parts of the public domain to such institutions in order to help pay the public debt. In 1787 Flint and Parker sought a contract to purchase two tracts of land in the Illinois country totalling 3,000,000 acres, and in the following year Morgan applied for a contract to purchase 2,000,000 acres of land in the same territory. In both cases the applicants stressed their wish to encourage settlement on these tracts and at the same time wrest a share of the lucrative Indian trade from the English and the Spanish. But even though Congress was favorably disposed to each application, no contracts were ever signed (Flint and Parker to Continental Congress, 18 Oct. 1787; Report of Continental Board of Treasury, 22 Oct. 1787; Report of Continental Board of Treasury, 22 May 1788; Report of Committee of Continental Congress, 20 June 1788, in Carter, *Terr. Papers*, ii, 74-7, 109, 112-5; see also George Morgan to Continental Congress, 1 May 1788, DNA: RG 360, PCC).

On 4 Sep. 1788 the Continental Congress approved a contract signed by the Board of Treasury and the Pennsylvania delegates for that state's purchase of a portion of the public domain comprising slightly more than 200,000 acres and bounded by New York, Pennsylvania, and Lake Erie. Before this transaction could be completed, however, the Continental Congress was superseded by the new federal government. Pennsylvania finally acquired full possession of this tract in Jan. 1792 after Hamilton and Governor Mifflin reached agreement on the terms of payment in Nov. 1791 (Mifflin to Hamilton, 5 May 1791; Hamilton to Mifflin, 3, 10 June 1791, 22 Aug. 1791; Mifflin to Hamilton, 26 Sep. 1791, with enclosed opinion of Jared Ingersoll, 25 Sep. 1791; Hamilton to Mifflin, 28 Sep. 1791; Mifflin to Hamilton, 9 Nov. 1791, all in Syrett, *Hamilton*, viii, 325-6, 412, 458, ix, 92, 240-1, 245-6, 485; see

also Payson J. Treat, *The National Land System, 1785-1820* [New York, 1910], p. 63-4).

Congress' 12 Aug. 1790 resolve stated that "all surveys of land in the Western Territory, made under the direction of the late geographer, Thomas Hutchins, agreeable to contracts for part of the said lands made with the late board of treasury, be returned to, and perfected by, the Secretary of the Treasury, so as to complete the said contracts: and that the said secretary be, and is hereby, authorized to direct the making and completing any other surveys that remain to be made, so as to comply on the part of the United States with the several contracts aforesaid, in conformity to the terms thereof" (U.S. Statutes at Large, i, 187). Only two of the four letters from Hamilton to Deputy Surveyor Israel Ludlow mentioned by Coxe have been found (Hamilton to Ludlow, 13 May 1790, 20 Nov. 1790, Syrett, *Hamilton*, vi, 415, viii, 362 n. 2). None of Ludlow's letters to Hamilton has been located. The PAPERS Coxe transmitted to TJ on 21 June 1791 must have been dispatched without a covering letter, because there is no record of any letter of that date from Coxe to TJ. The validity of the Illinois and Wabash Company's land claims in the Illinois country was rejected in a committee report submitted to the Continental Congress on 3 Nov. 1781 (JCC, xxi, 1098, xxii, 230). U.S. Supreme Court Justice James Wilson and two other members of this company submitted a petition to the Senate in Dec. 1791 reaffirming the legality of their land titles, and they subsequently offered to surrender to the federal government their claims to the lands in question "on the proviso that the United States reconvey to the company one-fourth part of the said lands." But the Senate rejected this offer on the grounds that the Illinois and Wabash Company did not have a valid title to the lands it claimed (James Wilson, William Smith, and John Shee, Petition to Senate, 12 Dec. 1791; Report of Senate Committee, 26 Mch. 1792, ASP, *Public Lands*, i, 27).

TJ incorporated much of the information supplied by Coxe in his Report on Public Lands, 8 Nov. 1791.

From David Humphreys

Lisbon, 6 Aug. 1791. He has just received TJ's of 23 June, with gazettes for himself and dispatches for Carmichael. He has received TJ's of 11 Apr., but not that of 13 May.—TJ will learn from French papers, sent herewith, what they know about the late "tumult in Paris." Private accounts indicate the affair was much exaggerated. "The actual Period of the Revolution is however critical," and until the constitution is completed interesting events may happen every day.—There is a report here that new measures, dictated by jealousy, are being taken in Spain to prevent revolution there. An oath has been exacted of strangers and other conditions imposed, the particulars of which he is not fully possessed. Favoritism, imprudent and irritating, seems to increase. Since he last wrote he has not heard from Carmichael, and fears his health prevented.—"No political innovations happen here." The Queen will lay the first stone of a new convent at Mafra in a few days.—He thanks TJ for information about the Indian war and for observations on measures needed to be pursued by U.S.

RC (DNA: RG 59, DD); 2 p.; at head of text: "(No. 28.)"; endorsed by TJ as received 22 Oct. 1791 and so recorded in SJL. Tr (same).

From Juan Nepomuceno de Quesada

St. Augustine, 6 Aug. 1791. Replying to TJ's letter of 10 Mch. regarding the king's ruling on fugitive slaves in Spanish territory adjacent to the United States, he is sending his written opinion on the matter by James Seagrove.

RC (DNA: RG 59, MLR); 3 p.; endorsed by TJ as received 3 Oct. 1791 and so recorded in SJL.

Quesada's opinion on the matter was incorporated in his proclamation of 20 June 1791, which he sent to TJ and which appeared in the *National Gazette* on 17 Nov. 1791. Quesada simply decreed that im-migrants to Florida had to swear on oath that they were *bona fide* owners of the slaves accompanying them, hardly a resolution of the complicated matter of fugitives in his jurisdiction. This issue is discussed in Editorial Note and group of documents on the threat of disunion in the West, at 10 Mch. 1791. See also TJ to Governors of Georgia and South Carolina, 15 Dec. 1791.

From Benjamin Russell

Boston, 6 Aug. 1791. Enclosing account for publishing laws passed at the third session in the *Columbian Centinel.*

RC (DNA: RG 59, PDL); not recorded in SJL. Enclosure not found, but the amount was $37.87 for Russell as for other printers of laws passed at the third session of the First Congress (see Document VII, contingent expenses of the Department of State, 1790-1793, in group of documents on Department of State Personnel and Services, at 12 Aug. 1790).

To Arthur St. Clair

SIR   Philadelphia August 6th. 1791.

Your letter of May 25th. to the Secretary of the Treasury with the copies it enclosed of one of May 23d. to Judge Symmes and of his answer to you of the same day, having been referred to me, I have now the honor to enclose you a letter to Judge Symmes on the subject of the settlements made on the Lands of the United States between his upper line and the little Miami, by persons claiming titles from him, wherein I have desired from him an explanation of these proceedings.

Though it is the duty and determination of the Executive to see that no encroachments be made on the public Lands, yet as the settlers in this instance appear to have acted with good faith, you will be pleased to notify them that due attention will be paid to this circumstance, and in the mean time they are not to be disturbed.— I have the honor to be with great esteem Sir Your most obedient and most humble Servant,

PrC (DLC); in clerk's hand; lacks signature. FC (DNA: RG 360, DL).

Governor St. Clair's 25 May 1791 letter

to Hamilton and his enclosed correspondence with John Cleves Symmes are printed in Carter, *Terr. Papers*, II, 342-8.

To John Cleves Symmes

SIR   Philadelphia August 6th. 1791.

Copies of Governor St. Clair's Letter to you of May 23d. 1791, and of your answer of the same day to him, having been communicated to Government, it is perceived that sundry persons claiming titles under you have taken possession of Lands of the United States between the upper line of your Contract and the little Miami. As it is the duty and determination of the Executive to see that no encroachments be made on the public Lands, I am now to desire from you an explanation of these proceedings, and that it may be sent at as early a day as possible in order that your claim, if well founded, may not be prejudged in a Report on the subject of the Lands of the United States which is to be laid before Congress soon after they meet in October, and that such other proceedings may be had therein as shall be thought proper.—I am Sir Your most obt. & most hble. Servt.

PrC (DLC); in clerk's hand; lacks signature. FC (DNA: RG 360, DL).

Symmes, currently serving as a judge in the Northwest Territory, had acquired an interest in western settlement while he was a member of the Continental Congress in 1785-6 and spent the greater part of the last two and a half decades of his life developing a magnificent tract of land in the Ohio country that included the city of Cincinnati (DAB).

The judge and Governor St. Clair were involved in a dispute over the location of the eastern boundary of the former's tract in the Ohio country. In 1787 Symmes petitioned the Continental Congress for a grant of approximately 2,000,000 acres of land bounded on the west by the Great Miami river and on the east by the Little Miami river. The Continental Board of Treasury approved a contract with Symmes in the following year authorizing him to purchase 1,000,000 acres of land at 66½¢ an acre and setting the eastern boundary of the tract about fifteen miles west of the Little Miami. Before the tract was surveyed, however, Symmes made certain grants of land along the Little Miami that were beyond the limits specified by his contract with Congress. When Governor St. Clair called this transgression to his attention, Symmes defended himself by arguing that these grants were valid because the Board of Treasury

had allegedly failed to abide by the Continental Congress' intent to make the Little Miami the eastern limit of his purchase. In the end, Congress, acting in response to a petition from a recipient of one of the disputed grants, passed an act in April 1792 extending Symmes' tract to the Little Miami. The passage of this act was undoubtedly facilitated by the efforts of Elias Boudinot and Jonathan Dayton, two New Jersey congressmen who were business associates of Symmes (Symmes, Petition to Continental Congress, 29 Aug. 1787; St. Clair to Symmes, 23 May 1791; Symmes to St. Clair, 23 May 1791; St. Clair to Hamilton, 25 May 1791; Act to Ascertain Boundaries of Symmes' Purchase, 12 Apr. 1792; Symmes, Request for Alteration of Patent, 29 Sep. 1794, in Carter, *Terr. Papers*, II, 70-1, 342-8, 388-9, 492-5; see also Symmes to Dayton, 15 Aug. 1791; Symmes to Boudinot and Dayton, 25 Jan. 1792; Dayton to Symmes, May 6, 1792, in Beverley W. Bond, Jr., ed., *The Correspondence of John Cleves Symmes* [New York, 1926], p. 146-54, 159-62, 267-71).

Symmes replied to TJ in a letter of 17 Sep. 1791, recorded in SJL as received 23 Nov. 1791, but not found.

To Francis Eppes

DEAR SIR   Philadelphia Aug. 7. 1791.

A letter from Mazzei on the subject of Capt. Hylton's debt to him obliges me to ask from you what I am to say to him on that subject. You told me formerly you hoped to get some money into your hands, and that you would secure it. I wrote this to him, and he sollicits your patronage. Is there an insolvency in Captn. Hylton's affairs? If there is not, in whose hands is his property, and why cannot this debt be paid? Have you Mazzei's account? If you have I will thank you for a copy of it, as, if I possess one at all, it is mislaid so that I cannot find it.—Jack is pursuing a course of reading in law and it's kindred sciences with an assiduity which gives me perfect satisfaction. Nor does he shew any disposition to dissipate. I avoid extending his acquaintance, because I know it would lead to love or a neglect of study. His course will hold him a year or two more.—The incertainty in the time of the President's visit to Virginia, brings a like incertainty on mine. I shall endeavour to go as early in September as I can, because I must return early in October. Mrs. Eppes and yourself gave me a hope of a possibility of seeing you at Monticello. I need not tell you how happy this would make me; for I see no probability of visiting Eppington this time. The few moments I can pass in Virginia with the friends whom I love, is the only part of my existence on which I set any value.—The sale of[1] my tobacco here has not been advantageous. It costs me 7/ a hundred, by the time it gets here; which leaves less clear profit than Mr. Lewis was offered for it in Bedford. So that my payments this year will fall short. I am determined to sell property this winter to the whole amount of my bonds to Hanson, so as to clear my mind of that oppression. Present me most affectionately to Mrs. Eppes. Make her happy with assurances of the health and good conduct of her son. I do not know whether he has inherited the disposition to write many letters. Greet for me endearingly our friends of Hors-du monde. Adieu my dear Sir. Yours affectionately,   TH: JEFFERSON

PrC (ViU and MHi); the two leaves of this letter evidently became separated during one of the divisions of TJ's papers (see note 1).

On Mazzei's business with Hylton, see TJ to Mazzei, 2 Aug. 1791. The BONDS TO HANSON had troubled TJ for a long time. See their exchange of correspondence in Vol 20: 153-4, 326.

[1] The first page of PrC (ViU) ends at this point; PrC of the remainder of the letter is in MHi.

From Tobias Lear

[*Philadelphia*], *7 Aug. 1791*. He encloses a letter from the President to Thomas Johnson, with the request that it be sent with his commission and directed "to the care of the Postmaster at Baltimore as the most likely mean of their reaching their destination with safety and dispatch."—He also transmits a letter from Governor Blount to the Secretary of State and letters from the latter to Governor St. Clair and Judge Symmes which were submitted to the President.

RC (DLC); 2 p.; endorsed by TJ as from Washington with his "approbn. of lrs. to Sinclair and Symmes" and as received 7 Aug. 1791 (so recorded in SJL). PrC (DNA: RG 59, MLR). Tr (DNA: RG 59, SDC).

Enclosures: (1) Washington to Johnson, 7 Aug. 1791, regarding his appointment as Associate Justice of the U.S. Supreme Court; see Pendleton to TJ, 13 July 1791. (2) Blount to TJ, 17 July 1791. (3) TJ to St. Clair, 6 Aug. 1791. (4) TJ to Symmes, 6 Aug. 1791. TJ had submitted his letters to St. Clair and Symmes for the President's "perusal" (TJ to Washington, 7 Aug. 1791) and Lear avoided saying that they had been approved. TJ of course assumed approval, but took the unusual step of keeping Lear's letter in his personal files and noting that approbation had been given. In fact the entry in SJL recorded the letter as from the "President [T. Lear for him]."

To Thomas Mann Randolph, Jr.

DEAR SIR   Philadelphia Aug. 7. 1791

In my letter of July 24. I acknowleged the reciept of yours of the 7th. which is the last letter I have had from Monticello. I presume you will have seen in the Virginia papers an advertisement of Aug. Davies's on the subject of a post through Columbia and Charlottesville to Staunton. He writes me word he has no doubt of getting an undertaker to perform the ride once a week, so that I hope we shall get a more certain means of communication established with Richmond.

The President, who has been threatened with a very serious chirurgical complaint, like that he had in New York the year before last, has happily got over it with but a slight inconvenience. He does not go to Virginia till the beginning of October. I shall endeavor however to get away from hence early in September, if nothing arises to prevent it. Indeed I already am threatened with a very serious embarrassment. One of my carriage horses (the one you thought the handsomest) will, I think, in all probability die. His case is a lingering one, so that if he lives, he will not be in condition for a journey in time for me. As yet therefore I do not see how I am to get on. Mr. Madison, who goes with me, has a horse; but he is in the same condition. I will be obliged to you, if you have an opportunity, to have your eye on a good horse for me, a match for the other (Romulus) rather finer and larger than inferior either in size or form, and know the price for which he may be bought, if I should want him. This must depend on the condition in which I shall leave the sick horse, tho' I have scarce an expectation but that he will be dead, and consequently that I must buy another.—Our news from Europe indicate no changes there. France is going on steadily. England preparing for war, without the intention probably of making it. A decree of the National assembly of France, giving the rights of citizenship to the free people of colour of St. Domingo, has thrown that colony into a dangerous fermentation.—The Census is returned from all the states except Vermont, N. Jersey, Virginia and S. Carolina. Supplying the numbers of these by conjecture our whole numbers will be upwards of 3,800,000 inhabitants of every condition. Supposing that the omissions may have been of one in twenty, which is a moderate allowance, we may safely call ourselves four millions.—Present me affectionately to my daughters, who I hope are well, as well as the little one, and accept yourself assurances of the warm attachment of Dear Sir Your's sincerely,

TH: JEFFERSON

RC (DLC); addressed: "Thomas M. Randolph junr. esqr. Monticello." PrC (Harold J. Coolidge, Jr., Collection on deposit at ViU).

While TJ had written Randolph on 24 July 1791, he actually had acknowledged receipt of his OF THE 7TH. in a letter of 17 July 1791. He had written his daughter and son-in-law on 24 July, and significantly on that same day he wrote Augustine Davis about advertising for post riders from Richmond to the western sections of Virginia. His interest in hastening the carriage of mail between Philadelphia and Monticello, presently taking as many as two months, was as much motivation as the necessity of improving government correspondence with the Southwest Territory.

From Edward Rutledge

[*Charleston*], *7 Aug. 1791*. Introducing a "Gentleman of the Name of Harper" who is going northward for a short time chiefly on business. "He is however desirous of knowing, and being known to you; and I do not wonder at it. You owe the Trouble, which these Introductions occasion, to your Fame; which is the Result of your Understanding, and goodness. You will oblige me by shewing such Civilities as are in your Power, without imposing too much on yourself, from the Friendship which I know you entertain for me."

RC (DLC); 2 p.; endorsed by TJ as received 25 Aug. 1791 and so recorded in SJL. Entry in SJL identifies this letter as being "by Mr. Harper," thus proving that it was received four days after that which follows.

From Edward Rutledge

My dear Sir   [Charleston, 7 Aug. 1791]

There are Circumstances and Situations in Life which lead us into Measures we would wish to avoid, and we are at times obliged to yield to Requests which are against our Desires to grant. I have been placed to day precisely in that Condition. A young Man, who will deliver you a Letter of Introduction from me, appeared anxiously to wish it, and I could by no means refuse it. He is of the same profession with myself; we practice at the same Bar; and that alone is thought to give a Claim. However, after reflecting upon the Matter, as I think it possible, your auspicious Temper, and may I add, your Friendship and Attention to my Recommendation, may occasion you to commit yourself, I feel it my duty to apprize you of some Circumstances, and place you on your Guard. The Person I allude to, is carried to Philadelphia in fact by Business. He is a Proprietor of the Yazoo Company, and goes forward to advance their Plans. I very much suspect, they want some Information of the Views and Designs of Government; and as this young man has in him a Spirit of Intrigue; possesses a large Portion of Confidence; and is well acquainted with Mr. Hawkins of North-Carolina, who is a Senator from that State; he is the most fit Agent who can be employed. His requesting too a Letter to you, whom he spoke of, as being Secretary of Foreign Affairs; and having in truth no uncommon pretensions to an introduction from me—naturally led me to reflect, and inquire, and draw the Conclusions I have done. Under all these Circumstances, I thought it most adviseable to give the Letter which he has; and that you might not be imposed upon, either by that Letter, or by any other Introduction, I resolved to expose to your View every thing which was passing on my Mind on the Subject. I do not mean by these Observations to preclude him from the Civilities of a Gentleman—probably it may be as well to shew him some—but I mean to put you on your Guard, and place you beyond the reach of Surprize. And having done in this Affair, what is due to Friendship, I must request that you will in your turn put this Letter out of the Power of Accident, by throwing it into the Fire, after you shall have read it. I am the more naturally led to make this Request, because I strongly suspect from your Silence, that some accident has happen'd to a Letter of mine to you, which I wrote on the Subject, of the Views of Great Britain toward a Commercial Treaty with America, wherein I told you, the Grounds which led to think, such were her designs, and to which Letter I have never received an Answer. I hope however, I may be mistaken, and that your Attention to your important Duties, is the true Cause. Whilst on that Subject, let me tell you, that I have read with a mixture of Pleasure, and Anxiety, your Report on the Fishery. Alas my Friend I much fear that partial, local Interests, will defeat your honourable patriotic Designs, and that we are fated, to be for ever cursed, with temporary Expedients. General Pinckney and I are avowedly in favor of Mr. Maddison's System, with respect to the Tonnage. We have done every thing, and said every thing which has occur'd to us, to influence the opinion of our Friends; but I fear, to little purpose. Our Delegates are, to a Man, against it. I am at this time engaged in answering the Objections of Mr. Barnwell who succeeds Burke. He ardently wishes to think with us, but at present he does not. However, that he may have a Chance of changing his Mind, he has committed his Sentiments to Paper; and has requested me to answer them, and remove his strong doubts, if possible. He is a Gentleman of strong Understanding, and his Heart is better than his Head. Were he with us, he would be powerful. In addition to his other good Qualities, he has as strong an aversion to the

British as I have. I will take the Liberty of introducing Him to you, when he goes to Philadelphia, and I shall yet hope, you will be able to effect, what I fear I shall not be able to accomplish. But this is not my only fear. I fear that, a public avowal of our Sentiments when favourable to the Designs of Britain, will keep us for ever in a State of Humility—That she will exult in our timidity—that we shall never obtain from her what we are most justly entitled to— And that in the End all her Gifts will be like the Gifts of Desdemona's Father when he tells the Moor—

> I here do give thee that with all my Heart,
> Which, but that thou hast already, with all my Heart
> I would keep from thee.

I must now bid you Adieu. God bless you my dear Friend. May you succeed in your honourable and patriotic Designs, and may you long live to enjoy the Fruits of your Labor are the wishes of your very affectionate Hble. Servt.   ED: RUTLEDGE

RC (DLC); at head of text: "(Private)"; without date but obviously written immediately after Rutledge gave Robert Goodloe Harper his letter of introduction to TJ of this date; endorsed by TJ as received 21 Aug. 1791 and so recorded in SJL.

A LETTER OF MINE TO YOU: Rutledge to TJ, 20 June 1790. For additional information on Rutledge's views of commercial policy, which he shared with TJ and Charles Cotesworth PINCKNEY, see volume 18: 228

n. 27, and TJ to Rutledge, 25 Aug. 1791. Robert Gibbes BARNWELL, who had been elected to succeed Aedanus BURKE in the House of Representatives, was apparently impervious to Rutledge's efforts to convince him of the wisdom of Madisonian commercial policy, for he proved to be a staunch Federalist during his one term in Congress (N. Louise Bailey and Elizabeth I. Cooper, *Biographical Directory of the South Carolina House of Representatives, Volume III, 1775-1790* [Columbia, S.C., 1981], p. 53-5, 106).

To George Washington

Aug. 7. 1791.

Th: Jefferson has the honour to send for the President's perusal, his letters to Govr. Sinclair and Judge Symmes: as also letters received from the postmaster at Richmond on the subject of the two cross posts. He has gone further as to that towards the South Western territory, than Th: J's letter authorized, as he only submitted it to his enquiry and consideration whether a post along that rout could maintain itself. He has advertized it as if decided on. However there is doubtless time enough to correct the rout, if it be not what the President would wish.

RC (DNA: RG 59, MLR); endorsed by Lear. Not recorded in SJPL or SJL. Enclosures: (1) TJ to St. Clair, 6 Aug. 1791. (2) TJ to Symmes, 6 Aug. 1791. (3) Davis to TJ, 1 Aug. 1791.

Washington returned the letters to St. Clair and Symmes the same day (Lear to TJ, 7 Aug. 1791).

From Robert Adam

SIR   Providence. August. 8. 1791

Inclosed I have the Honour to transmit you a Copy of a New Work, of which I am the proprietor, and of which I have already lodged a Copy in the Office of the Clerk of the District Court agreeable to Law. I am Sir, with due Respect, Your Most Obedient And Most Hble Servt.,   ROBERT ADAM

RC (DNA: RG 59, MLR); endorsed by Remsen as received 16 Aug. 1791 but not recorded in SJL.

The enclosed NEW WORK was a new edition of Alexander McDonald's (1752?-1792) *The Youth's Assistant; being a plain, easy, and comprehensive guide to practical arithmetic: containing all the rules and examples necessary for such a work*, of which several editions were issued between 1785 and 1795. The copy enclosed with the above letter was that described in the copyright entry (DNA: RG 21, Records of the U.S.

District Court, Federal Records Center, Waltham, Mass.) and recorded in Evans No. 23521 as "Lately published" by Bennett Wheeler in Providence in 1791 (citing *United States Chronicle* for 22 Dec. 1791).

Robert Adam, with Thomas Collier, was printer of the weekly *Litchfield Monitor* in 1788-1789. The first edition of McDonald's *Youth's Assistant* was printed and sold by John Trumbull in Norwich in 1785 and the next by Adam's partner Thomas Collier at Litchfield in 1789 (Evans Nos. 19066 and 21928).

To Christopher Gore

SIR   Philadelphia Aug. 8. 1791.

Having understood that the legislature of Massachusets some time ago ratified some of the amendments proposed by Congress to the Constitution, I am now to beg the favour of you to procure me an authentic copy of their proceedings therein, certified under the great seal of the state, letting me know at the same time the office charges for the copy, seal &c. which shall be remitted you. The legislature of Massachusets having been the 10th. state which has ratified, makes up the threefourth of the legislatures whose ratification was to suffice. Consequently so much as they have approved, has become law, and it is proper that we should have it duly promulgated for the information of the judges, legislators, and citizens generally. I will thank you if this can be done without delay, as I am to leave this place about three weeks hence to be absent for some time. I have the honour to be with great regard Sir Your most obedient & most humble servt. TH: JEFFERSON

PrC (DLC); at foot of text: "Christopher Gore esq. Boston." FC (DNA: RG 360, DL).

It must have been about this time that TJ drew up in tabular form a record of votes by states on Amendments I through XII as proposed by Congress in 1789. Between 20 Nov. 1789 and 7 June 1790 New Jersey, Maryland, North Carolina, South Carolina, New Hampshire, Delaware, New York, Pennsylvania, and Rhode Island—in that order—had ratified Articles III through XII. On Amendment I, which prescribed the ratio of representation to population in the House of Representatives and which failed of adoption when the vote fell one state short of the three-fourths required, TJ's chart showed Delaware in the negative column as "silent." On Amendment II, which provided that no law varying the compensation of members of Congress should be effective until after an intervening election of Representatives and which also failed of adoption, his chart showed New Hampshire as opposed and Rhode Island, New York, New Jersey, and Pennsylvania as "silent." The chart recorded no actions for Massachusetts and Connecticut (Tabular MS, undated, in

DLC: TJ Papers, 234: 31910). TJ was mistaken in thinking that Massachusetts had ratified the Amendments. No act had passed the General Court of the Commonwealth because, as Gore informed TJ in responding to the above letter, the Senate had agreed to Amendments III through XII while rejecting I and II, the House had concurred except with respect to the Senate's approval of Amendment XII, and the resultant conference committee had not reported a bill (Gore to TJ, 18 Aug. 1791; RC in DNA: RG 11, Certificates of Ratification of the Constitution and Bill of Rights, M-338/1; endorsed by TJ as received 27 Aug. 1791 and so recorded in SJL). Ratifications by Vermont and Virginia followed on 3 Nov. 1791 and 15 Dec. 1791. TJ reported adoption of the last ten of the proposed twelve Amendments in his circular letter to governors of the states of 1 Mch. 1792, accompanied by the first printing of the Bill of Rights (see note to that circular). Massachusetts, Connecticut, and Georgia did not ratify the first ten Amendments until 1939 (Certificates of Ratification and correspondence between the governors of these states and Secretary of State Cordell Hull in same).

From Daniel L. Hylton

Richmond, 8 Aug. 1791. On return from Norfolk he found TJ's of 10th with bank note for 21.25 dollars, an unnecessary trouble to TJ since two days after writing he received £10 from Col. Lewis to pay shipping and other charges on tobacco. Lewis also left £100 to pay Dr. Currie part of an order TJ had drawn. If agreeable, he will pay Currie the amount of the note or apply it as TJ directs. Tobacco is still low. The prices TJ quotes in France would justify merchants giving a higher price, but "its not to be wonder'd at, when we have no other, but british Merchts. among us." He is told the late regulation in France almost prohibits export from England there. While he was at Norfolk a ship arrived from France for tobacco. He hopes it will be followed by many more. Official accounts of Scott's expedition must have reached TJ: he hopes "the little scourge they have received will be a check for some time." Mr. and Mrs. Williams, natives of Jamaica in America for her health, sailed ten days past for New York accompanied by Hylton's daughter Hetty. They may come to Philadelphia; if so, "any civility shewn them will confer an obligation on me."

RC (MHi); 2 p.; endorsed by TJ as received 18 Aug. 1791 and so recorded in SJL.

From James Madison

MY DEAR SIR   N. York Aug: 8. 1791.

I take the liberty of putting the inclosed into your hands that in case Col: Lee should have left Philada. the contents may find their way to Col: Fisher who is most interested in them. And I leave it open for the same purpose. The Attorney will be a fit channel in the event of Col: Lee's departure, for conveying the information.

You will find an allusion to some mysterious cause for a phænomenon in the stocks. It is surmized that the deferred debt is to be taken up at the next session, and some anticipated provision made for it. This may either be an invention of those who wish to sell: or it may be a reality imparted in confidence to the purchasers or smelt out by their sagacity. I have had a hint that something is intended and has dropt from ____ ____ which has led to this speculation. I am unwilling to credit the fact, untill I have further evidence, which I am in a train of getting if it exists. It is said that packet boats and expresses are again sent from this place to the Southern States, to buy up the paper of all sorts which has risen in the market here. These and other abuses make it a problem whether the system of the old paper under a bad Government, or of the new under a good one, be chargeable with the greater substantial injustice. The true difference seems to be that by the former the few were the victims to the many; by the latter the many to the few. It seems agreed on all hands now that the bank is a certain and gratuitous augmentation of the capitals subscribed, in a proportion of not less than 40 or 50 PerCt. and if the deferred debt should be immediately provided for in favor of the purchasers of it in the deferred shape, and since the unanimous vote that no change should be made in the funding system, my imagination will not attempt to set bounds to the daring depravity of the times. The stockjobbers will become the pretorian band of the Government, at once its tool and its tyrant; bribed by its largesses, and overawing it, by clamours and combinations.—Nothing new from abroad. I shall not be in Philada. till the close of the Week. Adieu Yrs. Mo: affy. Js. MADISON JR.

RC (DLC: Madison Papers); endorsed by TJ as received 11 Aug. 1791 and so recorded in SJL. The enclosure has not been found.

Henry Lee had asked Madison to obtain from New York physician Charles Mc-Knight a medical opinion of the condition of Daniel FISHER, who was then in Philadelphia undergoing treatment for a serious urinary affliction (Henry Lee to James Madison, 3 Aug. 1791, printed in Rutland, *Madison*, XIV, 63-5). For information on Fisher and other topics Madison addressed in the above letter, see same, XIV, 69-70.

From Joseph Fay

Bennington, 9 Aug. 1791. Has this day received TJ's of 16 June and cannot account for delay. The maple seed does not mature until Oct. and he will send them at that time. He has examined his young groves since TJ left there and finds "the young Maple very thrifty and numerous, by calculation nearly one thousand to the acre." He will plant an orchard in regular form next spring, hoping to encourage others if he succeeds.—He encloses one of their last papers. "Could I suppose your curiosity would be excited to receive them, and the *Quebec* paper (which I expect shortly) I should be happy to Enclose them to you weekly. . . . My compliments Most respectfully to Mr. Madison, which you will also please to accept your self."

RC (MHi); 2 p.; endorsed by TJ as received 16 Aug. 1791 but recorded erroneously under 15 Aug. in SJL. TJ's letter of 16 June 1791 has not been found and is not recorded in SJL. Fay's relationship with TJ is discussed in Vol. 20: 442-3.

From Moustier

Berlin, 9 Aug. 1791. He is infinitely appreciative of TJ's assurances that his conduct in the U.S. had won the approval of the President. His satisfaction is proportioned to his desire to deserve it. He had hoped that his presence in France at the time his ill health caused him to return would hasten the conclusion of arrangements he had undertaken with ardour to effect for mutual advantage "une union plus intime entre nos deux nations." But some major causes thwarted his wishes, though without slackening the efforts that he made up to the last moment to achieve his object.—He hopes nevertheless that his works will not be fruitless and that the seeds he planted will flourish. He so prepared things that his successor will find foundations for a work that he ardently desires, though the glory may be reserved for another. The one who replaces him is not less animated than himself by a desire "de cimenter une parfaite union entre les deux nations." He will rejoice infinitely at his success and if circumstances enable him to support him, he will demonstrate the sincerity of his affection for the U.S. and the wishes he was among the first of his compatriots to feel for their success and prosperity.—The token of the sentiments accorded him in the United States will be "infiniment agreable comme un temoignage du succès de mes efforts à les meriter."—The particular sentiments that TJ was kind enough to express are not less affecting for one, like himself, always desiring to merit the esteem and affection of those who are themselves capable of inspiring these sentiments, rather than seeking the banal plaudits of those as fickle and as thoughtless in their censure as in their praise.

RC (DLC); 4 p.; endorsed by TJ as received 6 Dec. 1791 and so recorded in SJL.

This effusive letter closed the corre-spondence with TJ who, because of Moustier's indiscreet and ineffective performance as minister to the United States, had been instrumental in having him recalled.

From William Short

DEAR SIR   Paris Aug. 9. 1791.

With the gazettes sent by the way of Havre, you will recieve the plan of the constitution as submitted to the assembly by the two committees appointed for that purpose. It is at full length in the Logographe, No. 102. Aug. 6. After being printed and distributed among the members, it was begun to be discussed yesterday. As it is for the most part a revision and new arrangement of the decrees really constitutional already passed, the assembly proceeded with much calm and expedition in their deliberations. Considerable progress was made yesterday, so that it is supposed the whole may be finished in ten days.

Out of the assembly the opinions are various with respect to this constitution—great defects are acknowleged to exist in all its parts. But the necessity of having some kind of government established strikes most people here so forcibly that they are impatient to have the experiment made on this such as it is. And indeed that is the only mode by which it can be judged of to the general conviction. Individuals may be convinced of its defects by reflexion and argument but it would seem that practical proof is indispensable for the nation. To me there appears insurmountable difficulties in the organisation of all its parts, legislative, administrative and judiciary, but I find so many others thinking so differently from me, that I conclude such variety of opinions can be brought to co-incide only by experience.

One great danger and difficulty however which strikes every body is that which arises from the King. The impossibility of keeping him a prisoner if he is to be charged with the government is manifest, and if at liberty great numbers are convinced and all suspect that he will take the first opportunity of retiring to the frontiers or out of the kingdom. This circumstance renders it impracticable to place the national confidence in the crown, where it is the more necessary

[19]

for the preservation of order and government, in proportion as the power it was formerly vested with is diminished. It is much to be apprehended that a government thus without either energy or confidence will not secure those advantages to such a country as France, which were expected from the recovery of liberty. Should anarchy and confusion take place, it is hard to say whether the impetuosity of the French character will admit of retrograde steps towards submission to law and government, and if not every body knows from the experience of other countries, where they lead to.

It seems certain that the Queen has written to her brother the Emperor to desire he will not interfere for the present in the affairs of France. She presents to him the personal dangers which will result to her family, and declares it her wish that things should be allowed to take their natural course. It is not yet known what effect this letter will produce. Whilst at Venise on his return to Vienna the Emperor expressed himself in such unaccustomed and unmeasured terms with respect to the arrestation of the Royal family as left little doubt that he would be for something violent. Since his arrival at Vienna it seems that he has become more calm, owing either to maturer reflexion or to Prince Kaunitz.

You will see in the papers the conclusion of the Diet of Ratisbon. The ministers of the electors of Bohemia, Brandenburg and Hanover were however in favor of continuing the negotiations amicably. As this gives the sentiments of the Emperor and King and Prussia it may be taken for granted they will prevail. Of course foreign interference by hostile measures will be delayed still for some time.

The King's brothers pushed on by the emigrants may perhaps not wait for them—they are impatient to make an entry into France and persuade themselves that great numbers would in that case flock to their standard. The greater part of one of the Irish Regiments in the French service has deserted and gone to join the emigrants, a circumstance which has roused their hopes and will confirm their opinion of the number of partisans they would find in the Kingdom. The army is in a state of indiscipline which is alarming. They express however much attachment to the national assembly, and much aversion for their officers who have abandoned them to join the emigrants. It is hard to say what would be the conduct of such an army in trying circumstances, but it seems to me that the assembly count too much on their patriotism.

The King of Sweden has left the frontiers of this country to return to Stockholm. His sentiments are more pronounced with respect to French affairs than those of any other crowned head. It is said he has ordered his Ambassador here not to communicate with M. de Montmorin and it has been for some time observed that he alone of all the corps diplomatique has withdrawn himself from the audiences of the minister. A letter is printed in some of the papers and particularly the gazette universelle of today, from the King to the Baron de Stael in which he gives him these orders and expresses himself with much violence respecting the Monarch's treatment. I observe that this letter is supposed true by several, but I cannot assert it, having not seen M. de Stael.

The conferences are renewed at Sistovie and there is no doubt peace will be the result. Russia however continues the war with vigour having lately gained two signal victories on the Danube and in the Cuban. The conferences of Sistovie and those carrying on at present at Vienna after having been begun with the Emperor in person in Italy seem to insure that Austria, Prussia and England will not engage in a military way. The Turk must of course make his peace as well as he can, and the terms offered by Russia, considering circumstances, are really moderate.

There seems a suspicion well enough founded that the active negotiations which have been for some time carrying on in the north are closely connected with a projected change in the system. It is known that the courts of Berlin and Vienna have long had desires that they have from time to time manifested with respect to the augmentation of their territory either by exchange or otherwise. Thorn and Dantzick are what the King of Prussia has particularly in view, and you know he failed in his late negotiation for that purpose with Poland. The Emperor wishes the exchange of the low countries for Bavaria. The King of Prussia desires also the exchange of two isolated principalities for Lusace, and the Elector of Saxony declines accepting the throne of Poland until the sentiments of those two monarchs are fully known. Out of this situation of affairs the idea has arisen of effecting by mutual services what they all desire. It seems now believed among the well informed here that the Emperor and King of Prussia will have soon a personal interview on these subjects. It will be happy for this country if they find sufficient employment for some time, either by their negotiations or their operations for supporting them, to lose sight of the French revolution. It is much to be feared however that the situation of affairs here will be in time too tempting not to induce foreign powers to interfere, if they can agree among themselves about the result of such an interference.

Spain has lately concluded the peace which has been so long

negotiating with Tunis. The Moors however continue the siege of Oran and force the Spanish government to pay serious attention to their possessions on that coast. Their jealousy against the foreigners settled in Spain has induced them to publish an edict of so rigorous a nature, that if executed, it will force them to leave the kingdom and be highly prejudicial to the commerce of that country.—I hear nothing from Mr. Carmichael and have nothing new to add respecting the business with which he is charged.

I have heard that a vessel lately arrived from N. Orleans at Havre, loaded with tobacco and other articles produced in Kentuckey. The vessel was American and navigated for the most part by American seamen under Spanish colours.

The English newspapers continue to speak of the hostile preparations of U.S. and Spain. The English Ambassador asked me about them some days ago, and seemed by his conversation very desirous to find out what I thought would be the consequences. It was evident that he thought it a matter well worth his enquiry. He spoke highly of the present arrangement of our finances, position of our credit &c.

It is printed in English newspapers that the Cherokees who have lately returned from England have rendered so favorable an account of their reception there that it was resolved to send others with the rarest productions of their country as a present to the King of England. This is taken, as it is said, from a letter written from N. Carolina on the 17th. of June.

It is reported here and I think it may be relied on, that the Dey of Algiers is dead, and that his first minister has succeeded to him without opposition. It is probably the same who our captives represented as being favorably disposed to the Americans.

The French governor at S. Domingo has of his own authority given an exequatur to our consul there. He is much condemned for it by the ministry who will annul his act as being contrary to his powers. They will however, as they tell me, express to him that he is to consider the consul as a person having the confidence of the government of the U.S. and of course to pay attention to his observations.

Drost has not yet had the articles drawn up of which I spoke to you. He agrees to go however on the terms mentioned. He insists on his time counting from his leaving Paris. He says it was what he understood when he spoke to M. Grand. He says also that it is the more just as he shall be obliged to superintend here the execution of the instruments, which, if made in America would of course entitle him to charge for the whole of the time employed. Here he only asks a small advance on their cost, and which with that will come much lower to the U.S. than if made by any other artist. On enquiry of the Abbe Rochon, I find that a *balancier* should cost 24,000₶. Drost stipulates that each, his services included, shall not exceed 22,000₶ and he hopes to be able to make them for 20,000₶. He will make three and if the U.S. do not chuse to have more than two at present he will take one for himself. He says however they will have occasion for three at least and that it would be best to make a greater number. I will thank you to give your instructions on this subject. He will be ready to go with the instruments in the spring.—I inclose a letter for the Secretary of the treasury and beg you to be persuaded of the sentiments of your most obedient servant,   W. SHORT

PrC (DLC: Short Papers); at head of text: "*No. 76.*" Tr (DNA: RG 59, DD). Recorded in SJL as received 6 Dec. 1791. Enclosure: Short to Hamilton, 8 Aug. 1791 (Syrett, *Hamilton*, IX, 20-3).

The CHEROKEE mission to England, led by the adventurer William Augustus Bowles, is discussed in David Humphreys to TJ, 4 Nov. 1790. See also TJ to George Hammond, 12 Dec. 1791. TJ's relationship to the French engraver Jean Pierre Droz is described in Editorial Note to report on copper coinage, 14 Apr. 1790.

From Ebenezer Stevens

New York, 9 Aug. 1791. He asks pardon for writing, but does so knowing TJ to be "a friend to Mechanical Operations."—He assisted Capt. John Stone in making the model of the Charles River Bridge, now in TJ's office. He supposes Stone's exclusive right died with him. Had he lived, he would have assisted Stevens in building two bridges in New Jersey "over first and second Rivers, between New Ark" and New York. Not having a copy of the plan, he asks TJ to let one of his clerks send it to him "and every Care shall be taken of it and Returnd Safe."—The President, Col. Hamilton, or Gen. Knox can give TJ his "Character if required."

RC (DNA: RG 59, MLR); 2 p.; endorsed by TJ as received 12 Aug. 1791 and so recorded in SJL.

Stevens (1752-1823) was a merchant whom Henry Knox appointed as agent for the War Department in 1794 to oversee the fortification of New York harbor (Syrett, *Hamilton*, XXI, 475-6. See also Mary-Jo Kline, ed., *Political Correspondence and Public Papers of Aaron Burr* [Princeton, 1983], I, 347-50).

From John Garland Jefferson

DEAR SIR [ca. 10 Aug. 1791]

I flattered myself before this to have received an answer to my last letter, which was written some days before the reception of your favor of Feb. 5; but I was disappointed in my expectation: I do not however consider your omission in not answering my letter, as the effect of neglect, but as an unavoidable consequence of your official duty, which required your attention in preference to every other object. I am fully sensible of the important truths contained in your last letter and shou'd illy merit your attention, or friendship, if I did not strictly conform to your advice. I consider myself under your direction, as well as protection, and mean, and wish, to be guided by you in other things besides the law.

I have finished Cokes instutes, and reports; I have also read Vaughan. I have perused with attention Gilbert's works, and have read some of them twice, from an impossibility of procuring others in time. My progress in history has been less considerable, as the time designated by you for the study of history is after candle light, and the season does not admit of that; so that the only time I have for the perusal of history, is a part of the time allowed by you to be necessary for recreation.

Vaughan in my judgment is an excellent reporter, his reasons clear, and solid, and his distinctions just, and acurate. The works of Gilbert, I think very good, and his evidence as far superior to any thing of that kind which I have seen: and his Baron, and feme I conceive is a very useful and necessary law.

Now permit me Sir, to call your attention to a design I have formed of returning to the neighbourhood of Monticello, if I can obtain your permission: for I determined previous to my going to that vicinity to live under your patronage, not to embark in any measure without your full approbation, and free consent. This is a resolution which I flatter myself I have not deviated from, and which I shall make it my care to observe. Policy seemed to suggest that it was prudent to leave Albemarle: policy now suggests that it is best to return. The difficulty of procuring books, renders it impractable to prosecute my study with that assiduity I cou'd wish: and every obstacle being removed which formerly impeded my improvement, and deprived me of the advantages which others possessed I think it my duty to embrace every opportunity of acquiring a degree of knowledge which may one day be beneficial.

Tho my father dyed in possession of a competent, and indeed a large fortune, the bad management of some of his executors, and the villainy of others, viz. those he left in North Carolina reduced his children to a state of indigence. My mother gave my elder brothers such an education as enabled them to support themselves decently in the mercantile line: and my Uncle Garland took me to his house, and gave me as good an education as his circumstances wou'd permit; and when he had done as much to serve me as his duty to himself, and family allow'd, as the last instance of his friendship he recommended me to your care; and you were so truly generous as to undertake that charge. But of this enough. Suffice it to say I will indeavour to merit the attention of you both.

Another reason which I will add to shew the expediency of the above mentioned design, is this: shou'd I again reside in Albemarle, by a prudent line of conduct, I may refute the objections of those who are not well disposed towards me, and convince the world that the malicius insinuations which have been infused into the minds of the people, are without foundation. These reasons I am persuaded, are sufficiently cogent to meet with your concurrence. I hope to see you in the fall, and shall be happy to receive a few lines from you whenever your business will permit. Believe to be dear Sir, with cordial esteem Your most grateful humble servant,

J. G. JEFFERSON

RC (ViU); undated; endorsed by TJ as received 20 Aug. 1791 and so recorded in SJL.

TJ had agreed to help Garland Jefferson the previous year and advised him in his reading (TJ to John Garland Jefferson, to Nicholas Lewis, and to James Monroe, 11 June 1790). Garland's LAST LETTER to TJ was 26 Feb. 1791. On the question of the MALICIUS INSINUATIONS about Garland Jefferson, see TJ to Martha Jefferson Carr, 7 Nov. 1790.

From Joshua Johnson

London, 10 Aug. 1791. He recognizes the justice of TJ's reasons given in his of 13 May for not acknowledging his regular communications, yet for want of information (particularly respecting American funds), he is placed in disagreeable situations. He was confident Congress would regulate the consular office at the last session. "Their omitting it has lessened the consequence of their Consuls, and produced continual Difficulties to the Execution of your Instructions. Yet my determination is to persevere at least until I see what the next Session will do." The picture TJ draws of American prosperity is "beyond pleasing." He hopes this will continue and induce the world to court her friendship.—There are varied opinions about the expeditions against the Indians. "Some insinuate that if you subdue them, your Arms will be employed otherways, and seem to dread the consequences. I tell them it is conceived in Delusion, our first wish is to be at Peace with all the world."

He was wrong in saying Hammond had been appointed "Minister to Congress." The matter is still in agitation and it is believed he will depart before long "tho' from the apparent fickleness of this Government, little Dependance can be placed on either their Actions, or Declarations . . . let them profess what they may, they are not well disposed towards us, and if I might venture to hint an opinion, it would be that Mr. Hammond should remain in America some Months before Congress sent any one to this Court. I am persuaded it would have a good effect and convince them that America is not so very anxious to form regulations with this Government, as the People generally believe they are. Indeed from all the observations I have to make, I do not consider them of that material consequence to America. A well regulated System of her own, would put our Mercantile, and Marine Affairs in such a train as would alarm those Interests in Britain, and induce the People to force the Ministry to court Congress to make such arrangements as they would reject at this Day.

"The pressing Seamen for the present, is suspended, and appearances would indicate a discharge of the Fleet; the people Seem very much dissatisfied with the needless Expences, and Distress given to Trade. Our Shipping has experienced too much of it, notwithstanding my unwearied Attention to them, indeed latterly it appeared to me that the Men on board the American Ships were frequently taken from wantoness by the Pressgangs. Within this Month, it has been discovered by some officer in the Service of the Revenue, that all American Vessels transporting Merchandize to the Islands of Guernsey and Jersey, are under an Act of Charles the 2nd. Reign, subject to Seizure, and in consequence of which, two Vessels after having delivered their Cargoes of Tobacco there, and proceeded to Liverpool, have been arrested, one other has since been arrested, on her Arrival at Guernsey, and notwithstanding I have by Memorial to the Lords of the Treasury clearly shewn that the Parties were ignorant of such an Act and that they were innocent in offending the Law, yet from the unfriendly Report of the Commissioners of the Customs, I fear they will be condemned. Several other Difficulties have been stated by the officers of the Customs, such as some of the American Vessels not being Navigated by two thirds American born Subjects, and others, that the Manifest of their Cargoes has not been conformable to an Act of Parliament. One Ship lays seized at Liverpool on Account of the former, and another at Greenock on Account of the latter."[1]

RC (DNA: RG 59, CD); 4 p.; in clerk's hand except for complimentary close and signature. FC (same); in Johnson's hand. Recorded in SJL as received 22 Oct. 1791.

[1] This paragraph, slightly altered, appeared in *Gazette of the United States*, 3 Nov. 1791.

From Joshua Johnson

SIR   London 10 August 1791

I beg that you will be pleased to make it Publicly known to the Citizens of the United States, that all the American Shipping carrying Tobaccos &ca. to the Ports of Guernsey and Jersey, are subject to Seizure, under an Act of Parliament in the Reign of Charles the Second, that they may govern themselves accordingly.—I have the honor to assure you that I am with the most perfect Respect Sir Your most Obedient & most Humble Servant,

JOSHUA JOHNSON

RC (DNA: RG 59, CD); in clerk's hand except for signature; "Thomas Jefferson Esqr." at foot of text. FC (same); in Johnson's hand. Recorded in SJL as received 22 Oct. 1791. Printed as above in *National Gazette*, 31 Oct. 1791.

To Henry Knox

DEAR SIR   Philadelphia August 10th. 1791.

I have now the honor to return you the Petition of Mr. Moultrie on behalf of the South Carolina Yazoo Company. Without noticing that some of the highest functions of sovereignty are assumed in the very papers which he annexes as his justification, I am of opinion that Government should firmly maintain this ground, that the Indians have a right to the occupation of their Lands independent of the States within whose chartered lines they happen to be; that until they cede them by Treaty or other transaction equivalent to a Treaty, no act of a State can give a right to such Lands; that neither under the present Constitution nor the antient Confederation had any State or person a right to Treat with the Indians without the consent of the General Government; that that consent has never been given to any Treaty for the cession of the Lands in question; that the Government is determined to exert all it's energy for the patronage and protection of the rights of the Indians, and the preservation of peace between the United States and them; and that if any settlements are made on Lands not ceded by them *without the previous consent of the United States*, the Government will think itself bound, not only to declare to the Indians that such settlements are without the authority or protection of the United States, but to remove them also by the public force.

It is in compliance with your request, my dear Sir, that I submit these ideas to you, to whom it belongs to give place to them or such others as your better judgement shall prefer in answer to Mr. Moultrie.—I have the honor to be with sentiments of the most sincere and respectful esteem Dear Sir Your most obedient and most humble Servant.

PrC (DLC); in clerk's hand; lacks signature. FC (DNA: RG 360, DL).

The PETITION from Alexander Moultrie, one of the directors of the South Carolina Yazoo Company, has not been found. For a fuller account of the grounds of TJ's opposition to the land claims of this company, see Opinion on Georgia Land Grants, 3 May 1790.

From Walter Boyd

Paris, *11 Aug. 1791*. When TJ considers importance to a young family settling in America of being known to him, he will pardon liberty taken in recommending his brother-in-law, Mr. Hemmings, to TJ's protection. They will attempt to settle in Maryland. He is too well acquainted with TJ's obliging disposition to doubt his readiness to render any service to them in his power.

RC (DLC); 2 p.; endorsed by TJ as received 5 Nov. 1791 and so recorded in SJL. TJ incorrectly endorsed the letter as being from "Wm. Boyd," rather than Walter Boyd, the English banker and principal member of the banking firm of Boyd, Ker & Co., with whom he had become acquainted during his mission to France.

Boyd's BROTHER-IN-LAW, Thomas Hemming, forwarded this letter to TJ from Georgetown (Hemming to TJ, 1 Nov. 1791).

From Nathaniel Burwell

Carter's Grove, *11 Aug. 1791*. In response to TJ's of 1st, he is sorry to report failure of scheme to sell timber for Paradise. Wilkinson says sales will be offset by cost of cutting and carrying to market.—Specie value of Paradise's paper is £968.5.6 1/3, of which all but £62.8 is in Virginia Loan Office Certificates. In final settlement, he would be obliged to TJ for information about value of these papers, but as he thinks they are included in the deed of trust to Dr. Bancroft and others in London, it would be proper for TJ to advise them and Paradise if he thinks it advisable to sell out.—Wilkinson manages plantations very well: his remittances will be as large as could be expected from the number of hands employed.—Burwell confesses he does not know how to act for Paradise. In 1788 he was appointed as his attorney and directed to pay Dr. Bancroft and Mr. Anderson £290 sterling per annum for his use and then to make reasonable arrangements with his creditors. But by a letter from Bancroft to Wilkinson last spring it appears the Doctor and others are appointed trustees of this same property. He therefore concluded he had no right to interfere. He is willing to do anything in his power for Paradise, but he does not see how "two different trusts can be carried on at one and the same time on the same Estate." He would appreciate having TJ's opinion by the 10th at Williamsburg or, if not, at Winchester by post via Alexandria.

RC (MHi); 2 p.; endorsed by TJ as received 20 Aug. 1791 and so recorded in SJL.

WILKINSON: probably the William Wilkinson, Jr., in Williamsburg whom Paradise wrote in 1789 about his affairs (Vol. 15:

270n). See TJ to John Paradise, 6 Jan. 1790, for TJ's uncharacteristically high opinion of this steward. Edward BANCROFT and William ANDERSON, both in London, had been involved in Paradise's financial affairs for years.

To William Blount

SIR   Philadelphia Aug. 12. 1791.

Your letter of July 17. to General Knox, having been referred to me by the president, as relating to a subject merely civil, I have the pleasure to inform you of his consent to the absence you therein ask from the 15th. of September to the 20th. of November. As it imports highly to the people within your government to conform to the articles of the treaty against hunting or settling on the Indian lands, I have no doubt you will see the necessity of duly promulgating before your departure these and such other parts of the treaty as are immediately interesting to them.

I avail myself of this occasion of acknoleging the reciept of your favor of July 17. addressed to myself, and of expressing my anxiety to recieve the ulterior information on the subject of the lands of the United States which you are so good as to promise me. Among other things it will be interesting to know whereabouts the Southern boundary of N. Carolina will be intersected by the North line of the Cherokees which is to go on till it meets the line crossing Houlston. Also to know what and where is Campbell's line spoken of in the treaties of Houlston and Hopewell, so that they may be delineated on the map.—I inclose you a paragraph from a newspaper on the subject of a Zachariah Coxe and others, which we hope to be without foundation. I have the honour to be with great esteem & respect Sir Your most obedt. humble servt.,   TH: JEFFERSON

PrC (DLC). FC (DNA: RG 360, DL).

Blount's 17 July 1791 letter to Secretary of War Knox is printed in Carter, *Terr. Papers*, IV, 70-1. Articles 8 and 9 of the 2 July 1791 Treaty of Holston between the United States and the Cherokee nation

forebade American citizens from HUNTING OR SETTLING on Cherokee land (same, p. 63). Blount left the task of providing TJ with the INFORMATION on public lands he requested to acting Governor Daniel Smith (Smith to TJ, 4 Oct. 1791).

Zachariah Cox, as head of the Tennessee

Company, was the recipient of one of the notorious Yazoo land grants from the state of Georgia in 1789. Cox came into conflict with the federal government when he announced plans in September 1790 to settle the Muscle Shoals area, which was recognized as Cherokee land by the Treaties of Hopewell and Holston. In order to preserve good relations with the Cherokees, Secretary of War Knox instructed Governor Blount to prevent this settlement. Blount had Cox and his associates indicted before the superior court of Washington District in the summer of 1791, but the grand jury, which was allegedly made up of settlers equally covetous of Cherokee lands, refrained from returning a true bill against them. Cox thereupon reiterated his plan to form a settlement at Muscle Shoals. But this plan, which seems to have been the source of TJ's concern, was frustrated by the opposition of the Creek chieftain, Alexander McGillivray, secretly aided and abetted by Blount (Isaac J. Cox, ed., "Documents Relating to Zachariah Cox," *Quarterly Publication of the Historical and Philosophical Society of Ohio*, VIII [1913], 31-4; Arthur P. Whitaker, "The Muscle Shoals Speculation, 1783-1789," MVHR, XIII [1926], 385 n. 47).

From Edward Church

Bordeaux, 12 Aug. 1791. Being greatly alarmed by what he learned on arrival, he expressed his fears in his of the 27th, sent by brig *Hetty*, Captn. Drinker, for Philadelphia.—This day his fears confirmed by letter from Carmichael, a copy of which he encloses. He is thereby arrested at the threshold, unable to advance or retreat. He cannot in any sense hold TJ responsible, but appeals to him as a fellow citizen: honored with public office, tempted by climate, having flattering prospect in trade at Bilbao, confiding in the justice of his country for annual compensation (far more acceptable because more certain than profits in trade), and having in pursuance of orders, duty, and inclination left home with his "last scanty gleanings," is now cast "or more properly *wrecked* on a foreign shore, with a Wife, four daughters, one Son, and other necessary dependants . . . without prospect or means of redress, except only, from *one* source." In this truly forlorn extremity he has written the President and TJ to extricate him and "devise some means of future employment and support." Friends known to TJ will freely give every possible satisfaction regarding his character and conduct: Wingate, Trumbull, Gerry, and others in Congress contemporary with him at "the University of Cambridge in . . . Massachusetts," as well as those in the highest offices in that state who knew his easy circumstances prior to the war. Since the peace he resided four years at Savannah and the Georgia delegation, particularly Gen. Wayne, will be voluntary sponsors of his character.—He entreats TJ to answer as early as possible, addressed care of Fenwick, with any letters the President may condescend to offer.

RC (DNA: RG 59, CD); 4 p.; endorsed by TJ as received 22 Oct. 1791 and so recorded in SJL. Tr (PHi); at head of text: "(Copy)"; unsigned. Enclosure: Carmichael to Church, Madrid, 4 Aug. 1791, informing him in response to his of the 20th that, by privileges accorded the Biscayners, no foreign consul is admitted at Bilbao; that, though sometimes attempted, the effort has always proved abortive; that he is extremely concerned for his situation; and that his brevity must be excused as he is "on the recovery from a dangerous Malady" (DNA: RG 59, CD). Another copy (missing) was transmitted in Tobias Lear to TJ, 9 Nov. 1791 (PrC in DNA: RG 59, MLR; FC in DNA: RG 59, SDC). On 8 Sep. 1791 Church, employing an amanuensis because he was recovering from a violent fever and still too weak to write, sent a duplicate of the above (RC in DNA: RG 59, CD; endorsed by TJ as received 24 Feb. 1792 and so recorded in SJL).

When the Spanish refused to allow him to serve as consul at Bilbao, Church remained in Bordeaux, and sought to curry favor with TJ by suggesting that the United States pay its debt to France in depreciated assignats. He also called upon his Harvard classmate, New Hampshire Senator Paine Wingate, to use his influence with the President to secure his appointment as consul

to Lisbon or Cadiz. The Senate approved Washington's nomination of Church as consul to Lisbon on 5 May 1792 (Church to TJ, 16 Dec. 1791, 1 Jan. 1792, 13 Apr. 1792; JEP, I, 121, 122). John L. Sibley and Clifford K. Shipton, in *Biographical Sketches of Graduates of Harvard University* (Cambridge and Boston, 1873-1975), XIV, 389-93, offer the most careful study of Church's career, although they erroneously state that he was so dissatisfied with his appointment as consul to Bilbao in 1790 that he remained in the United States and "campaigned for a better job" until he received the post in Lisbon.

From Delamotte

Le Havre, 12 Aug. 1791. He has little to add to what he wrote on the 25th, of which he encloses a copy. This goes by *Minerva*, Capt. Wood, together with public papers sent by Short and another by himself. *Le Jeune Eole* will bring a clock for TJ which he has just received and did not have time to put on *Minerva.*—TJ will see that the constitution has been presented to the King and it is said that he will accept it in good faith. If so, prices of colonial produce will fall and exchange will rise. They already talk in Paris of the return of important emigrants. If these events happen, he will notify TJ by *Le Jeune Eole* sailing at end of the month for Philadelphia and he will then be able to say "la revolution . . . est complette."—[P.S.] Prices of colonial produce: brown sugar, 80 to 90₶ per cwt.; coffee, 18 to 26s. per lb.; Virginia, Maryland, and Carolina tobacco of good quality, 38 to 42₶ per cwt.; of bad quality, 25 to 30₶, but little in demand.

RC (DNA: RG 59, CD); 5 p.; endorsed by TJ as received 22 Oct. 1791. Delamotte wrote on 24 Aug. that the *Minerva* had been delayed long enough to take on TJ's clock after all (TJ's customs statement dated 17 Oct. 1791 indicates the clock arrived on this ship. MS, owned by Forest Sweet, Sr., New York), adding that the ensuing days had offered no new news of the rev-

olution, except that the nation was alternately made to fear invasion by "une ligue des Princes d'Allemagne" and to hope that no one would invade. He also observed that successful American trade with the colonies had replaced French trade, further strengthening American credit in England (RC in DNA: RG 59, CD).

From J. P. P. Derieux

Charlottesville, 12 Aug. 1791. Knowing that TJ will be interested, he informs him of the good news in the last letter from Mde. Bellanger enclosed in his to Mr. Randolph, which informs him that M. Le Roy of Bordeaux had died and left him a legacy of 15,000₶. This makes him happy once more and he hopes the measures he will take will provide a solid establishment. In her letter of 14 Apr. Mde. Bellanger informed him she had written his uncle, M. Plumard at Nantes, to obtain this sum in the hands of the executor and dispatch it to him as soon as possible. At the request of the family, he sent a power of attorney to him, but it lacked the seal of the state. He has had a new one made and Mr. Randolph, who goes to Richmond tomorrow, will have the seal affixed.— He asks TJ to write a line to his uncle to point out the best and quickest way for him to receive the legacy, whether by a bill to TJ's order on Philadelphia or Richmond as he thinks best for safety and speed.—If, however, TJ thinks Fenwick at Bordeaux would be the most proper person, he offers full power of attorney for him to act, fearing the mishaps that might occur. He leaves open the letter to his uncle for TJ to read and to forward only if he thinks the measures taken are the best.—He asks TJ to inform Mazzei of his legacy. Mde. Bellanger, for reasons he will explain when he sees TJ, says that she did not mention it to him; that she sees little of him; that he appears entirely occupied "de ses Grandeurs, de ses Equipages et de ses domestiques." Mazzei's interest in Derieux and his family seems to diminish as his credit rises and if he is not yet at the crest, he will no doubt entirely forget them. He has written Mazzei several letters and he has not answered any in more than two years.—All his life he will be grateful to TJ for repeated good fortune coming to him, for he does not doubt that what TJ obtained for him from Mde. Bellanger and the steps taken by Fenwick were powerful inducements to persuade his kinsman to favor him. His gratitude is beyond measure. [P.S.] *Monticello, Sunday morning* [*14 Aug. 1791*]. He has just seen Mr. Randolph, who leaves at once for Richmond. On his advice about the best way to obtain the legacy, he has written to Mr. Fenwick and to the executor the two letters enclosed which are left open for TJ to read, in order to draw the sum directly from Bordeaux if his uncle had not obtained it or, if he had, to inform him. He therefore asks TJ to write to his uncle at Nantes about the safest and most prompt means of procuring the legacy.

RC (MHi); 4 p.; endorsed by TJ as received 27 Aug. 1791 and so recorded in SJL. The letters enclosed were from Derieux to his uncle at Nantes and to Joseph Fenwick at Bordeaux (not found).

Three days later Derieux wrote that the sudden departure of Randolph for Richmond had prevented him from enclosing in the above letter one for Mme. Plumard de Bellanger. He asked TJ to forward it by the first good occasion and, in case that for Fenwick had not gone off, to add to it that an inquiry at the residence of Le Roy would reveal the name of the executor. He added that he would await TJ's response "avec beaucoup d'impatience" (Derieux to TJ, 15 Aug. 1791; RC in MHi, endorsed by TJ as received 26 Aug. 1791 and so recorded in SJL).

To Jean Baptiste Ternant

Aug. 12. 1791.

The Secretary of state has the honour to inform the Minister of France that the President will recieve his letters of credence to-day at half after two: that this will be done in a room of private audience, without any ceremony whatever, or other person present than the Secretary of state, this being the usage which will be observed.

As the Secretary of state will be with the President before that hour on business, the Minister will find him there.

PrC (DLC). FC (DNA: RG 360, DL); at head of text: "To the Minister of France." Not recorded in SJL.

Upon Ternant's arrival in Philadelphia two days earlier, TJ had arranged at Ternant's request an unofficial visit with Washington which, in the minister's words, though "absolument etrangere aux affaires, de ma mission," was marked on the President's part by a display of "la cordiale intimé la plus flatteuse pour moi." Ternant was equally impressed by the republican simplicity with which his former commander received his LETTERS OF CREDENCE this day in the presence of TJ, reporting to the French foreign minister that "après avoir presenté mes lettres au Pres-

ident, sans lui avoir fait ni en avoir reçu aucun des complimens d'usage, il a paru mettre un peu de coté la dignité d'office, m'a fait asseoir auprès de lui, et a causé comme à la premiere entrevue de diverses choses etrangeres aux affaires, en ne laissant cependant echapper aucune occasion de me faire sentir tout le plaisir qu'il avoit à me voir Ministre du Roi près les Etats unis—Cet acceuil tout à fait amical du President, m'est d'un heureux présage pour l'avenir, et je trouve dans la maniere simple qu'il a adoptée pour la réception des Ministres publics quelques avantages relativement à une future mission d'Angleterre dont j'aurai l'honneur de vous parler dans ma depeche suivante" (Ternant to Montmorin, 13 Aug. 1791, Turner, CFM, p. 43-4).

The "Anas"

EDITORIAL NOTE

The following is the earliest document in the compilation made by TJ that has come to be known by the strange and perhaps ungrammatical title of "Anas." The work presents special problems because TJ apparently never gave it the title himself and because it has been published under that title in at least five editions since 1829, two of which differ in important particulars. It is necessary to examine the "Anas" in order to clarify as nearly as possible what it was, or is.

The origin of this work may be found in a long document TJ wrote in 1818 and which he headed "Explanations of the 3. volumes bound in Marbled paper." The volumes in question contained written opinions for the President, notes of meetings and conversations, and gossip—what TJ described as his "most secret communications, while in the office of state." These private snippets had been bound together "in a huge Quarto volume" probably between 1800 and 1802, when he rearranged his papers and prepared a supplement to his SJPL (see Foreword). He apparently had these notes rebound into three volumes later, most likely when he revised the collection and put it into the form he described in 1818 ("Explanations of the 3. volumes bound in Marbled paper," 4 Feb. 1818; and TJ to John Wayles Eppes, 25 Dec. 1809). In what editors of his papers have referred to variously as TJ's introduction or preface to the "Anas," he described his notetaking and the general contents of what he regarded as a distinct unit of his papers:

"In these three volumes will be found copies of the official opinions given in writing by me to General Washington while I was Secretary of State, with sometimes the documents belonging to the case. Some of these are the rough draughts, some press copies, some fair ones. In the earlier part of my acting in that office, I took no other note of the passing transactions; but after awhile I saw the importance of doing it in aid of my memory. Very often, therefore, I made memorandums on loose scraps of paper, taken out of my pocket in the moment and laid by to be copied fair at leisure, which, however, they hardly ever were. These scraps, therefore, ragged, rubbed, and scribbled as they were, I had bound with the others by a binder who came into my cabinet, doing it under my own eye, and without the opportunity of reading a single paper. At this day, after the lapse of twenty five years, or more, from their dates, I have given to the whole a calm revisal, when the passions of the time are passed away, and the reasons of the transactions act alone on the judgment. Some of the informations I had recorded are now cut out from the rest, because I have seen that they were incorrect or doubtful, or merely personal or private, with which we have nothing to do."

It is obvious, therefore, that TJ had prepared more notes than the number retained in these three volumes, but the focus of what remained is clear. He sought to offer counter-testimony to the highly partisan narrative of Washington's first administration given in the fifth volume of John Marshall's *Life of George Washington* (Philadelphia, 1805-1807, 5 vols.), which had become the standard history of the period. TJ accused Marshall of being a poor historian, of relying more on the letters *to* Washington than on those *by* him; that is, Marshall's treatment of TJ and the republicans came as much, or more, from documents emanating from such partisans as Alexander Hamilton as from those papers in Washington's hand, which, after all, constituted a small percentage of the whole.

TJ took no steps toward publishing this part of his notes, though his explanations implies that he thought it would be desirable. Three years after TJ's death, Thomas Jefferson Randolph published some of these papers at the end of his abbreviated collection, bestowing on them the title that has remained to identify this unusual and important group of miscellaneous notes (TJR, IV, 443-523; see also Joseph Carroll Vance, "Thomas Jefferson Randolph" [unpubl. Ph.D. diss., University of Virginia, 1957], p. 126-43, which does not mention the "Anas" but explains Randolph's desire for profits and his general policy of selection). "Anas" means a collection of memorable sayings or tabletalk, anecdotes, bits of information or gossip about persons (OED). The following year a second edition published in Boston corrected the grammar of the title, making it *Ana*, but subsequent editors have refused to accept it. Today the term is used primarily as a suffix, and what Randolph titled Jefferson's "Anas" we might call simply "Jeffersoniana."

Randolph's rendering is both more and less than what Jefferson addressed in his 1818 introduction to his revised collection of notes. Randolph began his version with TJ's "Explanations" of 4 Feb. 1818, although he excised from it some sharp but essential sentences that might be interpreted as reflecting on Washington but are actually directed at Marshall's use of Washington's papers. Moreover, he added some similar miscellaneous notes from TJ's tenure as Vice-President and President, documents that TJ did not intend to include in his 1818 compilation and which were not directly related to those described in his

"Explanations." This defective text was faithfully followed by Henry A. Washington in the "Congressional Edition" of TJ's papers (HAW, IX, 87-211), wherein Washington glossed over the expurgations and additions by stating: "the Editor has not felt himself at liberty to exclude the Anas from a publication professing to be a complete edition of the writings of Jefferson. They are accordingly inserted just in the form in which he left them after his last revisal," implying that his version corresponded to TJ's (same, p. 87).

Paul Leicester Ford was the first editor after Randolph to prepare a version of the "Anas" from original manuscripts. Although he restored what Randolph had excised from the material covering 1791-1793, he followed Randolph's example and included even more notes from the extended period 1797-1809, correcting some that had been misdated and inaccurately transcribed by TJ's grandson (Ford, I, 154-339). Ford's note of introduction did little to clarify his version: "The so-called Anas are the only portion of Jefferson's writings besides his Autobiography, which do not allow of chronological arrangment. Though commencing in 1791 and extending to 1806, with an 'Explanation' or preface added in 1818, they were intended by the author to constitute a unit. . . . With these 'loose scraps' Jefferson . . . evidently intended that certain of his official opinions, reports, and cabinet papers should be printed; but in the rebinding of his papers his arrangement was so changed, that it is no longer possible to print these papers as he intended. The portion here printed is therefore limited to his unofficial notes and memoranda of interviews and meetings, the remainder being placed with other papers of the same nature in their chronological position" (same, p. 154n).

In fact, Ford adds a degree of confusion here. Randolph had omitted the "official opinions, reports, and cabinet papers" referred to by TJ in his 1818 "Explanations," but his reason was merely to save space (TJR, IV, 443n). There can be no question that these documents were among the three manuscript volumes when he transcribed them. In a description of the papers he had deposited in the Department of State in 1848, Randolph noted: "The papers, documents, official correspondence, notes of transactions, while Secretary of State to Gen: Washington, are bound in three volumes of marbled paper, marked A. B. C." (Paul G. Sifton, "Introduction," *Index to the Thomas Jefferson Papers*, President's Papers Index Series [Washington, D. C., 1976], p. ix). These three quarto volumes composed Series IV in the Bureau of Rolls and Library at the Department of State, and must have been precisely what TJ "explained" in 1818. According to a manuscript index of that collection prepared by Worthington C. Ford, these three volumes remained intact as Series IV near the time they were transferred to the Library of Congress in 1904 and after Paul Leicester Ford had prepared his version of the "Anas." They were not taken out of their bindings and assimilated into the general collection until after their transfer to the Library of Congress in 1904 (Sifton, "Introduction," xiv; and St. George Sioussat to Lyman H. Butterfield, 1 Aug. 1947, TJ Editorial Files). What Ford meant by the "rebinding" and altered arrangement of the papers that made it impossible to reprint the "unit" TJ had intended is therefore unclear. And Ford's implication that TJ himself extended the compilation of 1818 to cover the period 1797 to 1806 seems unlikely because the later notes are irrelevant to TJ's purpose of countering Marshall's interpretation of Washington's first administration.

In a note to TJ's "Explanations," which both Randolph and Ford printed as the first document in their editions of the "Anas," Randolph stated: "These are the volumes containing the ANAS to the time that the Author retired from the office of Secretary of State." When Randolph reached the end of the material from those three volumes, he (or the printer) inserted a good amount of space and a short rule to separate the last 1793 entry (1 Dec.) from the first of 1797 (2 Mch.). Significantly, a similar space and rule separate the last note from his tenure as Vice-President (16 Feb. 1801) from the first as President (23 June 1801), suggesting that the documents from these two periods might have been bound in separate volumes, possibly among those found in Series V of the documents Randolph turned over to the State Department in 1848, described in 1897 as "Miscellaneous   16 vols 4° " (Sifton, "Introduction," xvi). Given TJ's description of the period covered by his "3. volumes bound in Marbled paper" and later archival records, it is unlikely that the three divisions of Randolph's "Anas" derive from TJ's arrangement of his notes in 1818. To TJ's original compilation Randolph added documents covering the period from 2 Mch. 1797 through 15 Apr. 1806, no doubt drawing from other notes taken by TJ during those years. This constituted the "Anas" from 1829 until 1892, when Paul L. Ford published his version with even more additions.

Ford's contention that it had become impossible to print the papers as TJ intended ignores TJ's implication in his "Explanations" that all he meant to include in the collection was material from his tenure as Secretary of State, not material through his terms as President. Though he titled that section of his first volume "Anas, 1791-1806," Ford included materials to 25 Feb. 1809. It seems most likely that Ford, and Randolph, found more than three volumes of miscellaneous notes among TJ's papers, and that each extended the coverage of what TJ had gathered into a distinct unit in 1818, Randolph by thirteen years and Ford by sixteen. Randolph gave no indication of why he ended the "Anas" at 1806, nor did Ford explain why he added three additional years or failed to alter the concluding date in his title. Both editors imply by their selection that they present what TJ compiled in 1818 when he wrote the document that opens the work. Yet, both omit the official documents and reports that TJ collected, the first arguing that he did so to save space, the second that subsequent rearrangement of TJ's papers made it impossible to know what TJ intended to include anyway. Ford's claim is unsubstantiated by any evidence, but this did not prevent him from publishing a more accurate and inclusive version of the "Anas" that Randolph first presented.

In 1903, two more versions of the "Anas" appeared, the first in yet another edition of TJ's papers, the second in a special edition of the "Anas" alone. A. A. Lipscomb and A. E. Bergh appear to have copied Washington's 1854 transcription (which was also Randolph's) verbatim up to a point. Their introduction to the "Anas" is almost identical to Washington's; they merely added: "The supplementary portion of the 'Anas' omitted from the Congressional Edition published in 1853, extends from 1797 to 1808, covering many interesting events of Jefferson's first and second Administrations while President of the United States" (L & B, I, 264). Their text through 15 Apr. 1806, where both Randolph and Washington ended, is the same expurgated version the early editors presented as the entire work. Thereafter, these editors follow the Ford edition but appear to have prepared a new transcription. Despite their claims to the contrary, these editors presented a version less complete and accurate than Ford's, and they clarified nothing about the "Anas," historically or archivally.

One might expect to find some answers to these questions in Franklin B. Sawvel's edition of *The Complete Anas of Thomas Jefferson* (New York, 1903). Actually, Sawvel's title is misleading because he added precious little to what Ford had published eleven years earlier. Sawvel's edition is identical to Ford's with only two exceptions: he inserted TJ's undated "Notes on the Vth vol of Marshall's life of Washington" at the end of the 4 Feb. 1818 "Explanations" and before the 13 Aug. 1791 entry; and he included Cabinet minutes from a meeting on the brigantine *Little Sarah*, 8 July 1793 (which Ford had noted in his version of the "Anas" would be found in its proper chronological order among the other papers). It is highly unlikely that Ford would have omitted from the "Anas" the notes on Marshall's biography or the 8 July 1793 Cabinet meeting minutes had they been in the bound manuscripts when he prepared his edition a few years earlier. Indeed, Sawvel stated that the earliest document in the "Anas" was that of 13 Aug. 1791, and he failed to explain how the notes on Marshall's biography came to be included.

Sawvel professed his aim to be "to bring together a complete edition of the *Anas* in a *single volume*" (emphasis added). He referred to the H. A. Washington edition (and by implication the Randolph edition) as containing "an incomplete and scattered arrangement," but said nothing of the Ford edition of the "Anas" that was identical to his own except for the two minor particulars (Sawvel, ed., *Complete Anas*, p. 9). What, then, did Sawvel use as evidence of what was supposed to be in a complete "anas"? He strongly implied that he was publishing the complete contents of the three quarto volumes explained by TJ in 1818; yet TJ repeated in closing his "Explanations" that his compilation of documents ended at "the moment . . . of my retiring from the administration," making it clear that he referred to Washington's administration rather than his own. Sawvel confounds us by stating that TJ's introduction "explains how and why they were put into the form in which they still exist in his own familiar hand-writing," adding: "In the revision [of 1818] he did not bring together into a separate order or folio these memoranda of conversations with his co-workers, colleagues and opposers, their personal opinions and utterances, with his own replies, inferences and suspicions; but allowed them to remain scattered through three large folios. These personal and private opinions, a sort of confidential diary, he named *Anas*, a meaningless and indefinite title. Hence one difficulty to the collector in determining what to admit and what not." Sawvel offers no evidence that it was TJ who named these notes "Anas," nor does he go further in explaining how he prepared what he termed the *Complete Anas*.

If we are to accept TJ's description in 1818, Randolph's inventory from his sale to the Department of State, and the librarian's identification of what Randolph sold to the department, the three volumes TJ addressed in his "Explanations" can pertain only to documents from his tenure as Secretary of State. Therefore, the "Anas," as we have come to know it in the forms published by Randolph, Washington, Ford, Lipscomb and Bergh, and Sawvel, does not correspond to a compilation made by TJ. Apparently, each of these editors (except Washington, who only copied Randolph) merely pulled together additional loose notes that TJ prepared after 1797, an indication that he continued the same pattern of notetaking he described for the period 1791-1793. Clearly, TJ regarded the special compilation he prepared in 1818—covering part of Washington's administration—as distinct from any other notes he might have saved (and even had bound) between 1797 and 1809, and clearly those notes existed in three quarto volumes from 1818 until they were transferred to the

Library of Congress in 1904. It was after that date, probably before 1920, that the miscellaneous documents—ana—were taken out of their bindings and scattered chronologically among the other papers (St. George L. Sioussat to Lyman H. Butterfield, 1 Aug. 1947, TJ Editorial Files). Thus the resulting archival crime was committed after all of the editors of the so-called "Anas" had published their different versions. Unfortunately we are left with no evidence of exactly what TJ had bound together and what he might have regarded as his own complete collection of "ana."

Primarily because these documents have been published under the title "Anas," the existence of such a work has become established, incorrectly, as TJ's own intended unit. All of TJ's loose notes comprise "ana" or "anas." Later publication of them as a distinct unit (one that continually expanded in one way or another) put together by TJ in 1818 has always been misleading inasmuch as he meant at that time to compile only those covering 1791-1793. If he added additional material to that compilation before his death in 1826, he made no reference to any supplement, and he did not revise the "Explanations" that covered the earliest material. With the foregoing observations in mind, TJ's notes that have appeared in the several published versions of the "Anas" will henceforth appear in their proper chronological place in the present edition of his papers, and their descriptive notes will contain the notation "included in the 'Anas.' "

Notes of a Conversation with Alexander Hamilton

Aug. 13. 1791.

Th:J mentioned to him a letter received from J. A. disavowing Publicola, and denying that he ever entertained a wish to bring this country under a hereditary executive or introduce an hereditary branch of legislature &c. See his letter. A. H. condemning Mr. A's writings and most particularly Davila, as having a tendency to weaken the present government, declared in substance as follows. 'I own it is my own opinion, tho' I do not publish it in Dan and Bersheba, that the present government is not that which will answer the ends of society, by giving stability and protection to it's rights, and that it will probably be found expedient to go into the British form. However, since we have undertaken the experiment, I am for giving it a fair course, whatever my expectations may be. The[1] success indeed so far is greater than I had expected, and therefore at present success seems more possible than it had done heretofore, and there are still other and other stages of improvement which, if the present does not succeed, may be tried and ought to be tried before we give up the republican form altogether,[2] for that mind must be really depraved which would not prefer the equality of political rights which is the foundation of pure republicanism, if it can be obtained consistently with order. Therefore whoever by his writings disturbs the present order of things, is really blameable, however pure his intentions may be, and he was sure Mr. Adams's were pure.'—This is the substance of a declaration made in much more lengthy terms, and which seemed to be more formal than usual for a conversation between two, and as if intended to qualify some less guarded expressions which had been dropped on former occasions.—Th:J has committed it to writing in the moment of A. H's leaving the room.

MS (DLC); entirely in TJ's hand; at head of text: "Notes of a conversation between A. Hamilton and Th:J." Entry in SJPL reads: "[Aug.] 13. Notes of conversation between A. Ham. and Th:J. on our constitution."

Hamilton was moved to make this guarded expression of support for republican government as a result of the controversy attendant upon TJ's endorsement of Thomas Paine's *Rights of Man*; see Editorial Note on Rights of Man, at 26 Apr. 1791. John Adams correctly denied authorship of the *Publicola* essays, which were written to rebut Paine's work, in the LETTER referred to by TJ. But he neglected to reveal that they came from the pen of his son, John Quincy Adams, one of whose aims was to defend the Vice-President against the charges of monarchism arising from the publication of the elder Adams' *Discourses on Davila* in the *Gazette of the United States* between April 1790 and April 1791 (see Adams to TJ, 29 July 1791, Vol. 20: 305-7).

¹ TJ first wrote "They are" but crossed it out.
² Word interlined, perhaps later.

To Christian Baehr

SIR   Philadelphia Aug. 14. 1791.
If either now or at any time hence you can find a superfine French cloth, of the very dark blue which you know I wear, I will be obliged to you to make and send me a coat of it. Furnish me also if you please a pair of black silk and a pair of black sattin breeches. I will take care, on receiving your accounts always to find an opportunity of remitting you the amount. I am Sir Your very humble servt.,

TH: JEFFERSON

PrC (MHi).

Christian Baehr was a New York tailor whom TJ had patronized while there and who of course had his measurements (Account Book, 12 July and 30 Aug. 1790). Two weeks after writing the above, TJ sent an additional order to Baehr: "When I wrote you lately desiring some clothes to be made, I omitted to desire a gilet and a pair of breeches of buff Casimir, a very light buff, not a yellow one. I leave this place for Virginia on the 2d. of Sep. and shall not return till the 24th. of Octob. when I shall be glad to recieve the several articles" (TJ to Baehr, 29 Aug. 1791; PrC in MHi). Early in 1792 TJ settled the account: "I inclose you herein a bank postnote for fifty one dollars sixty two cents, equal to £20-12-9 New York currency, the amount of the account you transmitted while I was in Virginia, and which following me there and back again has occasioned it's receipt to be delayed" (TJ to Baehr, 8 Jan. 1792; PrC in MHi).

To Sylvanus Bourne

Sir   Philadelphia Aug. 14. 1791.

My letter of May 13. acknoleged the reciept of your's of Nov. 30th. Since writing that, I have recieved yours of Apr. 29. and June 30. addressed to myself and July 14. to Mr. Remsen. As none of these acknolege mine of May 13. I now inclose you a duplicate of it, fearing the first has miscarried. In this you will find the sentiments of our government on the subject of your recognition. Subsequent circumstances have rendered it an object still less proper to be pressed. In the present divisions of that country, we wish to avoid every measure which may excite the jealousy of any party, being sincerely the friends and well-wishers of all. As to my writing to the Governor, as pressed in your letter of Apr. 29. it would be contrary to the usage established among nations and therefore cannot be done. We have recieved Consuls from France, England, Portugal, Sweden, with no other credential but their open commission; we have sent Consuls to most of the countries of Europe, with nothing more. There has never been an instance of a special letter demanded.

Tho' we have not recieved an authenticated copy of the Decree of the National assembly of France, extending the repeal of the law of Droit d'Aubaine by name to their colonies, yet we know it has been so extended, and doubt not that a notification thereof has been sent to the colonies, so as to relieve us from that oppression.

As Congress have not as yet allowed any emoluments to the Consuls of the U.S. and perhaps may not mean to do it, we do not expect that any of those gentlemen will think themselves confined to their residence a moment beyond their own convenience. These appointments are given to gentlemen who are satisfied to perform their duties in consideration of the respect and accidental advantages they may derive from them. When the consideration ceases to be sufficient, the government cannot insist on a continuance of services, because this would found claims which it does not mean to authorize. On these principles Mr. Skipwith has lately returned from Martinique; on the same, it is my duty to say that however satisfied we should be with a continuance of your services in St. Domingo, we cannot and do not ask them longer than convenient to yourself.— I have the honour to be with great regard Sir Your most obedt. humble servt,   TH: JEFFERSON

RC (CtY). PrC (DLC). FC (DNA: RG 59, DCI).

The National Assembly had resolved on 13 Apr. 1791 that a decree of the previous year abolishing the *droit d'aubaine* applied to the French colonies as well as France itself (*Archives Parlementaires*, xxv, 10). TJ had long contended that under the terms of the 1778 treaty of amity and commerce with France Americans in that country's colonies were not subject to the *droit d'aubaine*, which he denounced as a "fragment of barbarism" (TJ to William Short, 26 Aug. 1790). Bourne decided to resign his office in spite of these developments (Bourne to TJ, 10 Dec. 1791).

To William Channing

SIR   Philadelphia Aug. 14. 1791.

Your favor of July 27. came to my hands on the 7th. inst. only. I have now the honour to inclose you a post-bank note for forty five dollars the amount of your disbursements therein stated, and with my thanks for your past attention to the object of procuring the laws of your state, to accept your kind promise of continuing it in future till the collection can be completed.—I am with respect & esteem Sir Your most obedt. humble servt,   TH: JEFFERSON

PrC (MHi); at foot of text: "Mr. Channing. Newport." FC (DNA: RG 360, DL).

To Uriah Forrest

DEAR SIR   Philadelphia Aug. 14. 1791.

Mr. Coxe, the Assistant to the Secretary of the treasury purposing to take a tour of relaxation, and to visit George-town in the course of it, I take the liberty of introducing him to your acquaintance and good offices. His character and merit are too well known to need any commendations. Any services you can render him will be considered as conferring an obligation on Dear Sir Your most obedient & most humble servt,   TH: JEFFERSON

PrC (DLC). On this date TJ wrote an identical letter of introduction for Coxe to Benjamin Stoddert (PrC in MHi).

From Thomas Greenleaf

New York, 14 Aug. 1791. Encloses a copy of "Blessings of America" of which the notice of copyright had been inserted in the enclosed "paper four separate Weeks."

RC (DNA: RG 59, MLR); 2 p.; endorsed by Remsen as received 22 Aug. 1791 but not recorded in SJL. Enclosures: (1) William Linn's Fourth of July sermon, *The Blessings of America* (see note to Linn to TJ, 18 July 1791). (2) Copy of Greenleaf's

New-York Journal in which Linn's sermon was advertised.

Linn himself sent TJ a "volume" some weeks later to be copyrighted, which may have been *The Blessings of America* (Linn to TJ, 7 Oct. 1791; RC in DNA: RG 59, MLR; endorsed by TJ as received 10 Nov. 1791 and so recorded in SJL). Linn was incorrectly identified in Vol. 20: 706 as a one-time law student of Alexander Hamilton. Actually, he graduated from the College of New Jersey in 1772 and became a Presbyterian clergyman and schoolmaster, later changing to the Dutch Reformed Church and serving the Collegiate Church in New York City until 1805 (R. A. Harrison, *Princetonians: A Biographical Dictionary, 1769-75* [Princeton, 1980], p. 231-5). As indicated in Vol. 20, he was the clergyman who later opposed Jefferson's election to the presidency on religious grounds.

To John Harvie

DEAR SIR   Philadelphia Aug. 14. 1791.

Being charged with the preparation of a statement to Congress of all their lands North of the Ohio, it becomes necessary for me to know what quantity of lands was assigned to the Virginia Continental line on the South side of the Ohio, say on the Cumberland, in satisfaction of their claims of bounty lands against the Continent. If I can by any means come at this quantity, by deducting it from the sum total of bounty lands given to all the lines, which sum total I know, the residue will be exactly what the army is entitled to on the North side of the Ohio. I am in hopes your office can furnish me with this information, and am to ask the favor of you to have it enquired into. All I wish is the *sum total in toto* located by the Virginia *Continental line* South of the Ohio. I suppose your office can not inform me what was located for the same line North of the Ohio, and therefore I do not ask it. The fees of office for these researches be so good as to inform me of, and they shall be remitted you. As[1] your answer can not be here before my departure for Virginia, I shall be glad to recieve it there. If your office cannot furnish the information, and you know where it may be obtained, I shall consider it as a singular favor if you will be so good as to put it for me at once into it's right channel. I am with great esteem Dr Sir, Your sincere friend & humble servt,   TH: JEFFERSON

PrC (DLC).

[1] TJ first wrote "If" and then altered it to read as above.

To David Jameson

DEAR SIR   Philadelphia Aug. 14. 1791.

The loss of the records of our state during the time of my administration there, has left it without legal vouchers for the expenditure of the specific tax (I believe of the year 1780) which certainly was almost wholly applied to Continental uses. There remains no evidence but a bit of paper of which I send you a copy. What, in the copy, is in common writing, is in my hand in the original: what is scored in the copy, is in Mr. Blair's hand in the original: what is in red ink in the copy, is in Mr. Bush's hand in the original. All the marks, and dashes are also copied. Colo. Davies submitted it to me, expecting I might from memory furnish something additional: but I have nothing more than a general recollection. Knowing that you attended much to this business, and have been less bandied about since, I inclose you a copy, in hopes it will aid you in recollecting whatever you think may serve to decide what and how much was applied to Continental use, and what and how much to that of the state. If you will be so good as to give it a thorough consideration, and communicate to me what you recollect, perhaps it may recall things to my mind and enable me to bear some testimony in conjunction with you to this important paper.—I am happy in every occasion of renewing to you assurances of the ancient and unabated sentiments of esteem & respect of Dear Sir your affectionate friend and servant,   TH: JEFFERSON

PrC (DLC).

The enclosed copy of a BIT OF PAPER has not been found. Col. William DAVIES, the commissioner in charge of settling Virginia's accounts with the federal government, needed the information TJ requested about the specific tax in connection with his efforts to obtain reimbursement for the state's expenditures on Continental account during the Revolutionary War (CVSP, V, 226, 234-7, 254-5, 299-300, 392-3). Jameson had been a member of the Virginia Executive Council during TJ's tenure as governor.

To Martha Jefferson Randolph

MY DEAR DAUGHTER   Philadelphia Aug. 14. 1791.

Maria's letter of July 16. informs me you were all well then. However great my confidence is in the healthy air of Monticello, I am always happy to have my hopes confirmed by letter. The day of my departure is not yet fixed. I hope it will be earlier or later in the first week of September. I know not as yet how I am to get along, as one of my horses is in such a condition as to leave little hope of his life, and no possibility of his being in a condition to travel. I hope, before you recieve this, the articles sent by Capt Stratton will be come to hand.—The moment affording nothing new but what the gazettes will communicate, I have only to add my affections to Mr. Randolph & Maria, not forgetting the little one, and to yourself my dear Martha the warm love of Your's affectionately, TH: JEFFERSON

RC (NNP). PrC (Charles B. Eddy, Short Hills, New Jersey, 1955).

From William Tatham

[*Richmond*,] *15 Aug. 1791*. Mr. Ross and himself, in pursuance of TJ's proposals for a western post, dispatch his brother to "form Contracts and Arrangement to the North Fork of Holston agreable to your Plan." He has also set on foot a subscription among merchants, hoping "some Man of enterprize . . . may be dispos'd to engage in pushing the Matter as far as possible.—This will probably produce a Caravan, or Guard System of passing the Wilderness at given Periods." Nothing in his power will be wanting to assist Davis in what TJ wishes "to be establish'd for the good of the Union."—He encloses return from Kentucky. The hurry of this dispatch will apologize for his haste. "Horse &c. ready and to start to morrow morning." He will write fully by next post of his "several undertakings for the use of the community." P.S. The return will perfect the analysis sent Gen. Knox when added to the amendments in Col. Carrington's return.

RC (DLC); 4 p.; addressed: "Mr. Secretary Jefferson Philadelphia"; postmarked: "RICHMOND. AUG. 15" and "FREE"; endorsed by TJ as received 20 Aug. 1791 and so recorded in SJL.

Tatham and David Ross had responded to Augustine Davis' advertisement for establishing a post to the Southwest "towards the Holston Settlements," suggested by TJ in July (TJ to Davis, 24 July 1791; Davis to TJ, 1 Aug. 1791).

To Thomas Leiper

SIR   Philadelphia Aug. 16. 1791.

I must ask of you a note for 200 dollars in such form as may be negociated at the bank.

The marks and weights of the 4. hhds. of tobo. which you wished to know are as follows.

nett

TI. No. 1. 1223℔ ⎱
No. 2. 1150.   ⎰
No. 3. 1255   ⎱ delivd by the Thomas Capt. Stratton.
No. 4. <u>1250</u>   ⎰
       4878

As I propose to go to Virginia within a fortnight or three weeks, it is necessary for me to decide on my continuance in your house. Your assuring me that I should remain in the house, without paying more than Mr. Cassinove, certainly put me off my guard, and prevented my taking a lease when I might have had one. I thought I might as well wait for it till it should be known what would be the additional rent for the stable and bookroom.—Supposing this ground changed, you will certainly concieve on reflection that no prudent man can bind himself to so indefinite a proposition as yours of the other day, that I should agree to pay 6. per cent on the amount of account before that amount should be known, and be it what it would. Will you therefore be so good as to name the fixed sum, the lowest you mean to take for the house, stable, &c. that is to say for the whole tenement when finished? On consideration of which fixed sum I may[1] be able to say whether I can keep the house or not.— I am Sir Your very humble servt,   TH: JEFFERSON

PrC (CSmH); at foot of text: "Mr. Lie-per." See Leiper to TJ, 2 Aug. 1791, wherein the terms for leasing Leiper's house are stated.

MR. CASSINOVE: Théophile Cazenove.

[1] This word interlined in substitution for "shall," deleted.

To William Blount

SIR   Philadelphia Aug. 17. 1791.

I wrote you on the 12th. inst. to acknolege the reciept of your favor of July 17. addressed to me and of the reference to me of the one of the same date addressed to Genl. Knox and asking leave of absence for a time therein mentioned, and to inform you the President assented to such absence. I observed at the same time the necessity there would be to promulgate immediately such parts at least[1] of the treaty lately made with the Cherokees, as are interesting to our citizens.

I have now the honour to acknolege the reciept of your favor of July 27. by Mr. Macflorence and to return you my thanks for the papers accompanying it. On conversing with this gentleman, I find he cannot inform me whereabouts the S. Carolina Indian boundary, will strike the Southern boundary of N. Carolina, from which point you know the North line of your treaty is to set out and meet the line which crosses Holston. I will therefore still ask your information of this point.

I am in hopes we shall recieve your census in time to lay it before

Congress at their meeting.—I have the honour to be with great respect & esteem Sir Your most obedt & most humble servt,

TH: JEFFERSON

PrC (DLC). FC (DNA: RG 360, DL).

MACFLORENCE: James Cole Mountflorence, who asserted in a memoir that he had been sent to Philadelphia after TJ had asked Blount "to send him a person, possessed of the most extensive local, legal, and political knowledge of the country, from whom he might derive the necessary information for the elements of his report" (James C. Mountflorence, "A Short Sketch of the Public Life of Major J. C. Mountflorence," p. 6, enclosed in Mountflorence to James Monroe, 8 July 1817, DNA: RG 59, MLR). Blount's FAVOR OF JULY 27 might support Mountflorence's statement that he served TJ upon request, but TJ's failure to obtain from him needed information about the southern boundary belies the young man's assessment of his abilities. In recalling his early public career, Mountflorence described the cession of Tennessee as being tied closely to North Carolina's ratification of the U.S. Constitution. Having served as a delegate from Davidson County, he gave this account of the ratifying convention: "All the delegates from the district of Tennessee were instructed by their constituents to procure, at the same time, a cession of their country to Congress: the Blounts

had vast possessions in that district, and therefore felt an equal interest with us in carrying that point in the assembly of the State. The Legislature and the Convention met, in the same month, at Fayetteville: I laboured strenuously, in cooperation with the Blount-interest and with others, to accomplish the wish of my constituents; our joint efforts were crowned with success, the cession was voted, and I had the honor of being one of those to whom the formation of the Bill, which passed the House to that effect, was intrusted" (same, p. 5).

Since TJ's letter arrived in the Southwest Territory while Governor Blount was away on leave, acting Governor Daniel Smith replied to TJ's query about the eastern boundary of the Cherokee lands as defined by the Treaty of Holston (Smith to TJ, 4 Oct. 1791).

It may have been around this time that TJ made an abstract of article 4 of the Treaty of Holston defining the boundary between the Cherokees and the United States (MS in DLC: TJ Papers, 69:11900; endorsed by TJ: "Indians Cherokees. boundary by treaty of Holston").

[1] These two words interlined.

From David Humphreys

Lisbon, 17 Aug. 1791. Spanish decree against foreigners mentioned in his of 6th he has now seen in house of British consul, with a great company present. Though expressed in general terms, it seems aimed at French. Retailers, barbers, surgeons, shoemakers, &c. already there must take oath of allegiance to carry on trade. They are mainly French. Several diplomats are said to have protested to Florida Blanca. This act will probably drive some mechanics to U.S. if transportation can be found.

Events in other nations only too frequently confirm TJ's "observations on the precarious nature of our commerce with them." States General of Netherlands have just prohibited importation of tea by foreigners in their territories. He encloses resolution by vessel that should reach TJ earlier than any other and will forward duplicate by another tomorrow, since this may be of some consequence to American merchants. Merchants here are now shipping 20,000 chests of tea for Holland. English gazettes will inform him of great outrages of mob at Birmingham.—Peace is more confidently spoken of than ever, it being pretty obvious British fleet will not enter Baltic this year. After all the gasconading of the mediating powers, interests of Porte likely to be relinquished. In case of peace, not improbable Emperor and Kings of Prussia, Spain, and Sardinia will intervene in France. Meanwhile National Assembly are hastening completion of constitution and means of defense.

RC (DNA: RG 59, DD); 4 p.; at head of text: "(No. 29)"; endorsed by TJ as received 22 Oct. 1791 and so recorded in SJL. Tr (same). Note that this letter and one written the following day both arrived in Philadelphia at the same time.

From David Humphreys

Lisbon, 18 Aug. 1791. He writes chiefly to send duplicate of resolution of States General concerning tea.—Spanish decree respecting strangers so vague three different constructions said to have been given by Spanish ministry. Recently several foreign mechanics have applied to him about going to America and possibility of success there. On threshing harvest in Portugal, wheat crop is much smaller than anticipated, hence demand for wheat and corn from U.S. will increase. Harvest in some parts of France and Spain turned out indifferently.—When he ordered French gazettes, he did not know the expense. From French frontiers they pay same postage as letters, that for four sent herewith amounting to nearly 2 dollars. There is no other mode of obtaining them. He mentions this so TJ "may not be disappointed in the contingent expense." He will continue to "forward them to the Office of foreign Affairs" unless directed to the contrary.

RC (DNA: RG 59, DD); 3 p.; at head of text: "(No. 30)"; endorsed twice by TJ as received 22 Oct. 1791 and so recorded in SJL. Enclosure (in Dutch): "Extract uit het Register der Resolutien van de Hoog Moog: Herren Staaten Generaal der Vereenigde Nederlanden." Tr (same); erroneously dated 13 Aug. 1791. This letter and enclosure were printed in *National Gazette*, 3 Nov. 1791 (see Editorial Note on Jefferson, Freneau, and the founding of the *National Gazette*, Vol. 20: 743).

To Pierre Charles L'Enfant

SIR   Philadelphia. Aug. 18. 1791.

The President had understood for some time past that you were coming on to Philadelphia and New York, and therefore has delayed mentioning to you some matters which have occurred to him. Will you be so good as to inform me by return of post whether it is still your purpose to come this way, and when, that the President may thereon decide whether he will communicate his ideas by letter, or await your coming to do it by word? If you are detained by laying out the lots, you had better not await that, as a suggestion has been made here of arranging them in a particular manner which will probably make them more convenient to the purchasers, and more profitable to the sellers.—A person applied to me the other day on the subject of engraving a Map of the Federal territory. I observed to him that if yourself or Mr. Ellicot[1] chose to have this done, you would have the best right to it. Do either of you intend this? If you do I would suggest to you the idea of doing it on a square sheet to hang corner upwards thus ◈ The outlines being N.W. N.E. S.E. and S.W. the meridians will be vertical as they ought to be; the streets of the city will be horizontal and vertical, and near the center; the Patowmac and Eastern branch will be nearly so also; there will be no waste in the square sheet of paper. This is suggested merely for your consideration. I am with much esteem Sir your very humble servt,   Th: Jefferson

RC (DLC: Digges-L'Enfant-Morgan Papers); at foot of text: "Majr. Lenfant." PrC (DLC). FC (DNA: RG 360, DL).

Washington's concern over L'Enfant's delay in arriving and the significance of

TJ's suggestion that he held a private right to issue a map of the planned capital are discussed in Vol. 20: 33.

[1] L'Enfant wrote in the margin: "What right could this man have thereto."

To James Madison

My dear Sir   Philadelphia Aug. 18. 1791.

I have just now recieved your favor of the 16th. and tho late at night I scribble a line that it may go by the morning's post. I inclose you two letters which have been awaiting you here several days. Also a copy of the census which I had made out for you. What is in red ink is conjectural, the rest from the real returns. The return of Virginia is come in this day, seven hundred and forty odd thousand, of which 296,000 blacks, both exclusive of Kentucky.—Try to arrive here on Tuesday time enough (say by 4 a clock) to come and dine with E. Randolph, Ross &c. half a dozen in all en petite comité. I have been much pleased with my acquaintance with the last. He is a sensible merchant, an enemy to gambling and all tricks of finance.—My horse will certainly die from all accounts. He is out at pasture to see what fresh air and grass will do. Yours will be a fortunate aid. I have written to Mr. Randolph to look out for one to bring me back. I set out on Monday fortnight at the latest; but will try to be off some days sooner. I shall be obliged to meet the President at the sale at George town Octob. 17. All your acquaintances are perpetually asking if you are arrived. It has been the first question from the President every time I have seen him for this fortnight. If you had arrived before dinner to-day, I had strong charge to carry you there. Come on then and make us all happy. Adieu my dear friend. Yours affectionately,   TH: JEFFERSON

RC (DLC: Madison Papers); addressed: "James Madison esquire at Mr. Elsworth's Maiden lane New York"; franked; postmarked: "19AV" and "FREE." PrC (DLC). Madison's letter of 16 Aug. 1791, recorded in SJL as received 18 Aug., has not been found.

TJ had received CENSUS returns from every state but New Jersey, Pennsylvania, and South Carolina by this time (Report on Census, 24 Oct. 1791). The RETURN OF VIRGINIA came in Tobias Lear to TJ, 18 Aug. 1791 (RC in DNA: RG 59, MLR; FC in DNA: RG 59, SDC). ROSS: John Ross (1729-1800), a merchant-shipowner who had migrated to Pennsylvania from Scotland in 1767. Although he enjoyed great success in his business at this time, Ross died a debtor (Rutland, *Madison*, v, 204 n. 1).

From Benjamin Banneker

Maryland. Baltimore County. Near Ellicotts Lower Mills

SIR   August 19th: 1791

I am fully sensible of the greatness of that freedom which I take with you on the present occasion; a liberty which Seemed to me scarcely allowable, when I reflected on that distinguished, and dignifyed station in which you Stand; and the almost general prejudice and prepossession which is so prevailent in the world against those of my complexion.

I suppose it is a truth too well attested to you, to need a proof here, that we are a race of Beings who have long laboured under the abuse and censure of the world, that we have long been looked upon with an eye of contempt, and[1] that we have long been considered rather as brutish than human, and Scarcely capable of mental endowments.

Sir I hope I may Safely admit, in consequence of that report which hath reached me, that you are a man far less inflexible in Sentiments of this nature, than many others, that you are measurably friendly and well disposed toward us, and that you are willing and ready to Lend your aid and assistance to our relief from those many distresses and numerous calamities to which we are reduced.

Now Sir if this is founded in truth, I apprehend you will readily embrace every opportunity to eradicate that train of absurd and false ideas and oppinions which so generally prevails with respect to us, and that your Sentiments are concurrent with mine, which are that one universal Father hath given being to us all, and that he hath not only made us all of one flesh, but that he hath also without partiality afforded us all the Same Sensations, and endued us all with the same faculties, and that however variable we may be in Society or religion, however diversifyed in Situation or colour, we are all of the Same Family, and Stand in the Same relation to him.

Sir, if these are Sentiments of which you are fully persuaded, I hope you cannot but acknowledge, that it is the indispensible duty of those who maintain for themselves the rights of human nature, and who profess the obligations of Christianity, to extend their power and influence to the relief of every part of the human race, from whatever burthen or oppression they may unjustly labour under, and this I apprehend a full conviction of the truth and obligation of these principles should lead all to.

Sir, I have long been convinced, that if your love for your Selves, and for those inesteemable laws which preserve to you the rights of human nature, was founded on Sincerity, you could not but be Solicitous, that every Individual of whatsoever rank or distinction, might with you equally enjoy the blessings thereof, neither could you rest Satisfyed, short of the most active diffusion of your exertions, in order to their promotion from any State of degradation, to which the unjustifyable cruelty and barbarism of men may have reduced them.

Sir I freely and Chearfully acknowledge, that I am of the African race, and in that colour which is natural to them of the deepest dye,* and it is under a Sense of the most profound gratitude to the Supreme Ruler of the universe, that I now confess to you, that I am not under that State of tyrannical thraldom, and inhuman captivity, to which too many of my brethren are doomed; but that I have abundantly tasted of the fruition of those blessings which proceed from that free and unequalled liberty with which you are favoured and which I hope you will willingly allow you have received from the immediate hand of that Being, from whom proceedeth every good and perfect gift.

Sir, Suffer me to recall to your mind that time in which the Arms and tyranny of the British Crown were exerted with every powerful effort in order to reduce you to a State of Servitude, look back I intreat you on the variety of dangers to which you were exposed, reflect on that time in which every human aid appeared unavailable, and in which even hope and fortitude wore the aspect of inability to the Conflict, and you cannot but be led to a Serious and grateful Sense of your miraculous and providential preservation; you cannot but acknowledge, that the present freedom and tranquility which

*My Father was brought here a S[lav]e from Africa.[2]

you enjoy you have mercifully received, and that it is the peculiar blessing of Heaven.

This Sir, was a time in which you clearly saw into the injustice of a State of Slavery, and in which you had just apprehensions of the horrors of its condition, it was now Sir, that your abhorrence thereof was so excited, that you publickly held forth this true and invaluable doctrine, which is worthy to be recorded and remember'd in all Succeeding ages. "We hold these truths to be Self evident, that all men are created equal, and that they are endowed by their creator with certain unalienable rights, that among these are life, liberty, and the pursuit of happyness."

Here Sir, was a time in which your tender feelings for your selves had engaged you thus to declare, you were then impressed with proper ideas of the great valuation of liberty, and the free possession of those blessings to which you were entitled by nature; but Sir how pitiable is it to reflect, that altho you were so fully convinced of the benevolence of the Father of mankind, and of his equal and impartial distribution of those rights and privileges which he had conferred upon them, that you should at the Same time counteract his mercies, in detaining by fraud and violence so numerous a part of my brethren under groaning captivity and cruel oppression, that you should at the Same time be found guilty of that most criminal act, which you professedly detested in others, with respect to yourselves.

Sir, I suppose that your knowledge of the situation of my brethren is too extensive to need a recital here; neither shall I presume to prescribe methods by which they may be relieved; otherwise than by recommending to you and all others, to wean yourselves from these narrow prejudices which you have imbibed with respect to them, and as Job proposed to his friends "Put your Souls in their Souls stead," thus shall your hearts be enlarged with kindness and benevolence toward them, and thus shall you need neither the direction of myself or others in what manner to proceed herein.

And now, Sir, altho my Sympathy and affection for my brethren hath caused my enlargement thus far, I ardently hope that your candour and generosity will plead with you in my behalf, when I make known to you, that it was not originally my design; but that having taken up my pen in order to direct to you as a present, a copy of an Almanack which I have calculated for the Succeeding year, I was unexpectedly and unavoidably led thereto.

This calculation, Sir, is the production of my arduous Study in this my advanced Stage of life; for having long had unbounded desires to become acquainted with the Secrets of nature, I have had to gratify my curiosity herein thro my own assiduous application to Astronomical Study, in which I need not to recount to you the many difficulties and disadvantages which I have had to encounter.

And altho I had almost declined to make my calculation for the ensuing year, in consequence of that time which I had allotted therefor being taking up at the Federal Territory by the request of Mr. Andrew Ellicott, yet finding myself under Several engagements to printers of this state to whom I had communicated my design, on my return to my place of residence, I industriously apply'd myself thereto, which I hope I have accomplished with correctness and accuracy, a copy of which I have taken the liberty to direct to you, and which I humbly request you will favourably receive, and altho you may have the opportunity of perusing it after its publication, yet I chose to send it to you in manuscript previous thereto, that thereby you might not only have an earlier inspection, but that you might also view it in my own hand writing.—And now Sir, I shall conclude and Subscribe my Self with the most profound respect your most Obedient humble Servant,   BENJAMIN BANNEKER

NB any communication to me may be had by a direction to Mr. Elias Ellicott merchant in Baltimore Town.   B B

As an Essay of my calculation is put into the hand of Mr. Cruckshank of philadelphia, for publication I would wish that you might neither have this Almanack copy published nor give any printer an opportunity thereof, as it might tend to disappoint Mr. Joseph Cruckshank in his sale.[3]   B B

RC (MHi); at head of text: "Thomas Jefferson Secretary of State"; endorsed by TJ as received 26 Aug. 1791 and so recorded in SJL. Engraved facsimile from FC (PHC); in Banneker's hand; differs from RC in spelling, capitalization, punctuation, and other respects (see notes for some examples); at head of text: "Thomas Jefferson Secretary of State"; at foot of text: "Thomas Jefferson Secretary of State Philadelphia." The facsimile also includes the text of TJ's reply of 30 Aug. 1791 and has the following printed note at the foot of the text: "The Letters, from which this facsimile is taken, are in the hand writing of Banneker, who copied them into the volume of Manuscripts, in which they have been preserved. His house and manuscripts were burnt soon after his decease, except this book which was at a neighbor's at the time."

Banneker's accomplishments and the well-known exchange of letters between Banneker and TJ are described in Silvio A. Bedini, *The Life of Benjamin Banneker* (New York, 1972); see also Winthrop D. Jordan, *White over Black: American Attitudes Toward the Negro, 1550-1812* (Chapel Hill, N.C., 1968).

The history of TJ's changing attitudes toward Banneker reflects in miniature the contradiction in his views on the vexing issues of slavery and race relations in America. As revealed primarily in *Notes on the State of Virginia*, TJ firmly believed that slavery was a violation of the natural rights of man and hoped for its abolition. Yet he was equally convinced that blacks and whites could not peacefully coexist in freedom because of certain natural distinctions between them, such as color, temperament, and above all intellectual ability. He therefore argued that emancipation must be accompanied by colonization of the freed slaves beyond the limits of the United States.

In a widely read discussion that set the terms of debate on this issue in America for decades to come, TJ oscillated between ascribing black intellectual inferiority to the workings of nature and attributing it to the impact of slavery. Though at times he virtually suggested that blacks were intellectually inferior to whites by nature, in the end he left it to science to determine whether nature or environment was responsible for what he perceived to be a distressing absence of intellectual accomplishment among blacks, especially in the arts and sciences. "I advance it therefore as a suspicion only," he concluded, "that the blacks, whether originally a distinct race, or made distinct by time and circumstances, are inferior to the whites in the endowments both of body and mind" (Notes, ed. Peden, p. 137-43; Jordan, White over Black, p. 429-39). Benjamin Banneker was the first and only black man to challenge TJ's suspicion directly during his lifetime.

The eldest child of a free black couple who owned a tobacco farm in Baltimore County, Maryland, Banneker began to emerge from obscurity in 1788, the year after the publication of the first American edition of Notes on the State of Virginia. At that time Banneker, then in his fifty-seventh year, borrowed a set of astronomical instruments and four works on astronomy from George Ellicott, a member of a distinguished family of Quaker entrepreneurs who opposed slavery and operated a group of gristmills near Banneker's farm. Banneker applied himself to the study of astronomy and soon became so proficient in it that he conceived the idea of publishing an almanac in order to promote "the Cause of Humanity as many are of Opinion that Blacks are Void of Mental endowments" (Elias Ellicott to James Pemberton, 10 June 1791, PHi: Pennsylvania Abolition Society Papers). Encouraged by George Ellicott and his brother Elias, a member of the

Maryland Society for the Abolition of Slavery, Banneker prepared an ephemeris for the year 1791 that caught the attention of Major Andrew Ellicott, a cousin of the Ellicott brothers. He was so impressed by Banneker's mathematical achievement that he brought it to TJ's attention and, with TJ's approval, employed Banneker as an assistant during the preliminary survey of the Federal District early in 1791 (Joseph Townsend to James Pemberton, 28 Nov. 1790, PHi: Pennsylvania Abolition Society Papers; TJ to Condorcet, 30 Aug. 1791; Bedini, Banneker, p. 9-136).

Banneker soon won the support of several leading Quaker abolitionists in Maryland and Pennsylvania who were eager to take advantage of his scientific work to refute the growing belief in American society that blacks were intellectually inferior to whites by nature (Banneker to Andrew Ellicott, 6 May 1790; Joseph Townsend to James Pemberton, 14 and 28 Nov. 1790, all in PHi: Pennsylvania Abolition Society Papers; Bedini, Banneker, p. 94-102; Jordan, White over Black, p. 445-8). Buoyed by the prospect of further support from key figures in the Maryland and Pennsylvania antislavery movements, Banneker finished a second ephemeris in June 1791. Members of the Pennsylvania Society for the Abolition of Slavery recommended its publication in Philadelphia after David Rittenhouse, the foremost American scientist of the day, and William Waring, a noted Philadelphia astronomer, vouched for the accuracy of Banneker's work. It was thus against this background of careful and intense preparation that Banneker wrote the above letter and sent a copy of his ephemeris for 1792 to the man who was not only a distinguished statesman, scientist, and critic of slavery in his own right, but also the author of the recent pessimistic analysis of black intellectual capabilities (Elias Ellicott to James Pemberton, 10 June and 21 July 1791, PHi: Pennsylvania Abolition Society Papers; Notes, ed. Peden, p. 137-43; Bedini, Banneker, p. 137-52; Jordan, White over Black, p. 429-39, 455).

TJ's polite response was heartening to Banneker and his supporters. He expressed hope for the appearance of "such proofs as you exhibit" that nature had endowed blacks with "talents equal to those of the other colors of men" and that their apparent absence among blacks was only the result of "the degraded condition of their existence, both in Africa and America." He also informed Banneker that he was sending his ephemeris to Condorcet, the noted philosophe, ardent opponent of slavery, and secretary of the Académie Royal des Sciences in Paris, so that it could be used to redeem blacks "against the doubts which have been entertained of them" (TJ to Banneker, 30 Aug. 1791; see also TJ to Condorcet, 30 Aug. 1791, wherein TJ was more specific about the significance of Banneker's accomplishments).

At Banneker's suggestion and with the strong agreement of his Quaker supporters, the exchange of letters with TJ was published in 1792 in a variety of forms for the express purpose of advancing the antislavery cause by demonstrating that black failure to match the intellectual achievements of whites was the result of slavery rather than nature (Bedini, *Banneker*, p. 158, 163, 166-8, 183-8). But the correspondence soon became little more than a weapon in the hands of TJ's political enemies, who tried to use it to prove that he was a crypto-abolitionist. In the electoral campaigns of 1796 and 1800, southern Federalists cited his reply to Banneker as evidence that he favored "a speedy emancipation of the . . . slaves" (William Loughton Smith, *The Pretensions of Thomas Jefferson to the Presidency Examined* . . . [United States, 1796], p. 9-10 [Sowerby, No. 3174]; see also William Henry Desaussure, *Address to the Citizens of South Carolina, on the Approaching Election of President and Vice-President of the United States* [Charleston, S.C., 1800], p. 16 [Sowerby, No. 3228]; and Bedini, *Banneker*, p. 280-1). Even after TJ's reelection to the presidency, Thomas Green Fessenden, a Federalist satirist from New Hampshire, ridiculed TJ for allegedly abandoning the racial views set forth in *Notes on the State of Virginia* simply because of the "wonderful phenomenon of a Negro Almanac, (probably enough made by a white man)" (Thomas Green Fessenden, *Democracy Unveiled, or, Tyranny Stripped of the Garb of Patriotism*, 2 vols. [New York, 1805], II, 52n.).

TJ continued to think about Banneker. He might have first viewed Banneker's accomplishments as evidence of natural intellectual equality of blacks, but the absence of sufficient additional evidence and a later incorrect suspicion that Banneker had not worked independently led TJ to disparage Banneker's achievements (TJ to Condorcet, 30 Aug. 1791; TJ to Henri-Baptiste Grégoire, 25 Feb. 1809; and TJ to Joel Barlow, 8 Oct. 1809; Bedini, *Banneker*, p. 202-34; and Richard B. Davis, ed., *Jeffersonian America: Notes on the United States of America Collected in the Years 1805-6-7 and 11-12 by Sir Augustus John Foster, Bart.* [San Marino, Cal., 1954], p. 148-9). Nor can there be much doubt that he experienced increasing difficulty in reconciling his ownership of slaves with his libertarian political principles. Thus TJ was an early exemplar of the classic American dilemma of whether the equalitarian ideals of the Declaration of Independence were intended to apply to all members of American society or to whites only (see Jordan, *White over Black*, p. 429-81; David Brion Davis, *The Problem of Slavery in the Age of Revolution, 1770-1823* [New York, 1975], p. 169-84; and John C. Miller, *The Wolf by the Ears: Thomas Jefferson and Slavery* [New York, 1977], p. 3-103, for analyses of TJ's racial attitudes).

[1] Preceding thirteen words are missing from FC.
[2] This note is not in FC.
[3] The second postscript is not in FC.

From William Carmichael

SIR   Madrid 19th Augt 1791

Mr. Cassenave who means to establish a commercial house at Alexandria in your State will have the honor to present you this Letter. He is strongly recommended to me by the House of Messrs.

Drouillet Capital Banquers here and who have always been disposed to render me and every American who has come hither every service pecuniary or friendly in their Power. I flatter myself that you will favor this Gentleman and his Partner with your kind Notice. They are perfect Strangers in our Country but they go there with the fixed Determination of becoming usefull Citizens with a Capital (as I am Informed) which may be advantageously employed in the Extension of our Commerce. From the knowledge which I have of your Liberal Manner of thinking, I have taken the Liberty of giving Mr. Cassenave this Letter and have the honor to be with the highest Esteem & respect Your Most Obedt & Hle. Sert,

WM. CARMICHAEL

RC (DLC); endorsed by TJ as received 19 Nov. 1791 and so recorded in SJL.

Despite Carmichael's claims that he wrote regularly to TJ, this private letter and an official dispatch of 24 Jan. 1791 are the only letters TJ received during his tenure as Secretary of State from the American chargé d'affaires in Spain, with the exception of those Carmichael later wrote in conjunction with William Short during their joint mission to Spain. In light of this abysmal record, it is not surprising that TJ subsequently requested Short to "communicate to me confidentially the true character of Carmichael, his history at Madrid &c." (TJ to Short, 18 Mch. 1792). Samuel G. Coe, *The Mission of William Carmichael to Spain* (Baltimore, 1928), p. 110, suggests that Carmichael's dispatches to TJ were intercepted, though he fails to identify the culprit.

From C. W. F. Dumas

The Hague, 19 Aug. 1791. While waiting for the National Assembly to act on all of the articles of the French constitution, he encloses documents concerning the pacification in the North. He will see in them the arguments of Britain and Prussia answered by the Empress of Russia, who has more spirit than the cabinets of those two powers combined. Her request for the bust of Fox, to be placed between those of Demosthenes and Cicero because by his eloquence he turned his nation from a war which had neither rhyme nor reason, is a sharp and characteristic touch which will please neither Pitt nor his cousin Grenville.

FC (Dumas Letter Book, Rijksarchief, The Hague; photostats in DLC); 2 p.; at head of text: "No. 81." Recorded in SJL as received 27 Oct. 1791.

From David Rittenhouse

DR. SIR   [ca. 20 Aug. 1791]

If we consider the same thing in the manner following we shall immediately perceive that the proposition is not new. Since the hole in the vessel may be of any size it may be equal to the intire bottom. The vessel then becomes a Cylinder and the problem is reduced to this, To find the lenghth of a perpendicular Cylinder in which a fluid will descend from the top to the bottom in a given time—that is, the space thro' which a heavy body descends in the Same time, which brings it immediately to the Case of a Pendulum. Yours &c.

D. R.

RC (DLC); addressed: "Mr. Jefferson"; undated, but endorsed by TJ as received 20 Aug. [1791] and so recorded in SJL.

No communication from TJ to Rittenhouse to which the above was a response has been found, but clearly the two were again discussing the use of the rod pendulum as a unit of measure as they had done the previous summer when TJ was preparing his report on weights and measures. This renewed discussion may have been prompted by TJ's having received from Condorcet on 19 July 1791 the report of the Academy of Sciences recommending a unit of measure of which he thoroughly disapproved (see note to Condorcet to TJ, at 3 May 1791, and TJ to Condorcet, 30 Aug. 1791).

To Mary Jefferson

My dear Maria   Philadelphia Aug. 21. 1791.

Your letter of July 10. is the last news I have from Monticello. The time of my setting out for that place is now fixed to some time in the first week of September, so that I hope to be there between the 10th. and 15th. My horse is still in such a condition as to give little hopes of his living: so that I expect to be under a necessity of buying one when I come to Virginia as I informed Mr. Randolph in my last letter to him. I am in hopes therefore he will have fixed his eye on some one for me, if I should be obliged to buy. In the mean time as Mr. Madison comes with me, he has a horse which will help us on to Virginia.—Kiss little Anne for me and tell her to be putting on her best looks. My best affections to Mr. Randolph, your sister, and yourself. Adieu My dear Maria.

Th: Jefferson

RC (ViU); addressed: "Miss Maria Jefferson Monticello." PrC (ViU). Mary's letter of the 10th is printed at 16 July 1791 (see text and note there).

From James Cole Mountflorence

Sir   Sunday 21st. August 1791

A Coachee sets off from this City on Tuesday for Staunton; I think it would be a convenient and quick Conveyance for Dispatches to Governor Blount, especially as Mr. Peter Heiskell of Staunton is directed to transmit to Capt. Craig, Abington, Washington County Virginia all Letters and Packets which may come to his hands directed to Govr. Blount, by the Travellers from that part of the Country to Kentucke, And I am told that there is not a Week at this time of the Year, without Some opportunity of that Kind from Staunton.

Mr. Bidwell the Owner of the Carriage, opposite the State house desires that all Letters and Packets should be left at his house to-morrow Evening.—I have the Honer to be with high Respect Sir Your most obedient and most humble Servant,

J. C. MOUNTFLORENCE

RC (DNA: RG 59, MLR); endorsed by TJ as received 21 Aug. 1791 and so recorded in SJL. Another letter from Mountflorence, 25 Aug. 1791, recorded in SJL as received 26 Aug. 1791, has not been found.

From George Washington

DEAR SIR   Sunday. 21st. August

At eight o'clock A:M tomorrow, I set out for Mr. Powells farm, to see the operation of Colo. Anderson's threshing machine.—I Breakfast, you know, at half past Seven; if it is convenient to take that in your way, I should be glad to see you at it.

When you have read the enclosed letters I will converse with you on the subject of them.—I am always yours,

GO: WASHINGTON

RC (DLC); addressed: "Mr. Jefferson"; endorsed by TJ as received 21 Aug. 1791 and so recorded in SJL.

POWELL: Samuel Powell (1731-1793), a friend of Washington's and president of Philadelphia's agricultural society, lived on Third Street between Spruce and Walnut in Philadelphia, but kept a farm on the Schuylkill River just across the Market Street bridge. TJ accompanied Washington to that place to see demonstrated Alexander ANDERSON'S THRESHING MACHINE (Arthur Young, ed., *Annals of Agriculture & Other Useful Arts* [London, 1792], XVII, 206-8; TJ's Account Book, 22 Aug. 1791). The ENCLOSED LETTERS have not been identified, but probably had to do with the subject of TJ's letter to Thomas Harwood of the following day, printed below.

To William Blount

SIR   Philadelphia Aug. 22. 1791.

Tho' I had the honour of writing to you by post on the 12th. and 17th. of Aug. to inform you of the President's consent to the absence

[57]

you desired, yet as it is interesting to you to recieve it in time, and a good private conveyance now occurs I avail myself of it to repeat the same thing.

I have written to the postmaster of Richmond, to desire he will endeavor to establish a post from that place to your government, and stated to him the plan on which it may lawfully be done. He gives me hopes of accomplishing it.

Since Majr. Mountflorence's arrival I have had time to go through the papers you were so kind as to send me by him.

The only articles for which I have occasion still to trouble you are the claims of the guards, chaincarriers, masters and hunters who attended Shelby, and others in laying out military bounties, and the Preemption rights of the first settlers of Davidson county. These I shall hope still to recieve from you in time before the meeting of Congress, as well as your Census.—I have the honor to be with great esteem Sir Your most obedient & most humble servt.,

TH: JEFFERSON

PrC (DLC). FC (DNA: RG 360, DL).

TJ's letter to the POSTMASTER OF RICH-MOND was the one he wrote to Augustine Davis on 24 July 1791. For the claims of Isaac SHELBY of Kentucky, see Report on Public Lands, 8 Nov. 1791.

To Thomas Harwood

SIR   Philadelphia Aug. 22. 1791.

The Commissioners for the public buildings at George town inform the President that they are in want of a sum of money for the objects of their appointment, and that they suppose you will accept his draught for the first instalment of the money granted by the state of Maryland. The President being unwilling to make any draught but on a certainty of it's acceptance, I am to ask the favor of your information whether, from the circumstances of the funds, you find yourself in a condition to accept his draught for the first instalment or for any, and what, smaller sum.—I have the honor to be with great respect Sir Your most obedt. & most humble servt,

TH: JEFFERSON

PrC (DLC); at foot of text: "Mr. Harwood. Treasurer of Maryland." FC (DNA: RG 360, DL). Recorded through error in SJL as written 21 Aug. 1791. See Commissioners to Washington, 2 Aug. 1791 (DNA: RG 42).

From David Humphreys

Lisbon, 22 Aug. 1791. Reports say a courier has arrived today from Paris with news King of France has declined to accept the constitution, because, though it might be very good, he was deprived of all counsel and could not act on it.—King of Sweden is said to have written very spirited letter to National Assembly, declaring Fersen acted on his orders to effect escape of King. Thus royalty finds an "interest in supporting Royalty, as it has existed for ages." It has for some days been whispered that 2 million crowns, brought in fleet from Brazil, sent from Portugal to support anti-revolutionists. Now spoken of with confidence but he gives this as reports, not ascertained facts. But several persons have been arrested in Lisbon, some Frenchmen included, for "speaking too freely in favour of the French Revolution." Not known where they are confined.—"Spain appears most agitated." Said to be 100,000 French there. But it is known military preparations are going on, a detail of which happened under his own eye: Many people of Galicia seek employment in Portugal subject to being recalled or on condition of returning at specified period. A Spanish servant in Portugal several years, with him seven months, is now ordered home to serve in militia. He goes immediately to avoid forfeiting "a little patrimony."

RC (DNA: RG 59, DD); 4 p.; at head of text: "(No. 31)"; endorsed by TJ as received 22 Oct. 1791 and so recorded in SJL. Tr (same).

From James Maury

Liverpool, 22 Aug. 1791. In response to his application to the Treasury in behalf of vessels mentioned in his last letter, he has received and encloses their decision.—[P.S.] *9 Sep. 1791.* Morning's post brings *London Gazette* with information dated at Petersburg 17 Aug. of signing of preliminaries of peace between emissaries of Empress and King of Sweden, the only condition being that the *status quo ante* form the basis of the negotiation. Ratifications were to be exchanged in six days.

RC (DNA: RG 59, CD); 2 p.; endorsed by TJ as received 22 Oct. 1791 and so recorded in SJL. Enclosure: Letter informing Maury that the Commissioners of the Treasury, on advice of the Commissioners of the Customs concerning the ship *Hope* and the brigantine *Janet*, then under seizure for landing cargoes at Guernsey in violation of 12 Charles II, ch. 18, sect. 3, had ordered their release provided reasonable satisfaction was made to the seizing officers; that this was done because the petitioners had pled ignorance of the law and evidently no fraud was intended; but that Maury should make it known to all owners and masters of American vessels that the law would be strictly enforced in future (Charles Long to James Maury, 13 Aug. 1791; Tr in DNA: RG 59, CD).

From Thomas Mann Randolph, Jr.

DEAR SIR   Tuckaho' August 22. 1791.

I can give you no account of the objects of our mutual affection later than the 15. of this month when I left every thing well at Monticello. I came down principally to give my vote in the County of Henrico to my Father who is candidate for a place vacant in the Senate of Virginia. I had made a disagreeable mistake with respect to the day of the election and should have returned immediately if he had not expressed a wish for me to wait, the affair being so uncertain that one Voice may be of consequence.

He appears not so much disposed to part with Edgehill as he was the last year. From Colo. Harveys representations the value of it has risen considerably in his Estimation. Having conversed with the Steward on the Subject I concluded that the terms of last year would not be accepted and offered 1600 £ for the land alone, to be discharged by 3 annual payments with Interest at 5 per Cent from the date of the bonds; the Stock &c to be valued and paid for in the course of 2 or 3 months. This I believe will be accepted, but I shall take care to enter into no obligation which your disapprobation shall not cancell.

I inclose to you some letters of M. De Rieux relating to a legacy lately left him in France. He gave me a power of Attorney for M. De Rieux of Nantz desiring that I would get the Seal of the State affixed to it and transmitt it to you with the letters, but he had neglected to have it attested and I had passed over the defect, not being accustomed to attend to such things. I shall send it on by the post of the 30. August and must request the favor of you in M. De Rieuxs name to leave directions concerning it, as I have hopes that before it arrives you will have set out for Virginia. The letters are sent open as they were delivered to me.

Your Stores are yet at Mr. Browns where I have determined to let them lie (as they are not in the way) untill I can have them carried up by a Waggon from Monticello, which Colo. Lewis says it will be very convenient to send down immediately.

I have just read your letter to Patsy of the 14. and am rendered extremely happy by being informed that you are to set out so soon.[1] I expect to arrive at Monticello on the 26. with the pleasing news.— I am Dear Sir your most affectionate friend & devoted Servt.,

                                              T. M. RANDOLPH.

RC (ViU). Recorded in SJL as received from "Richd." 27 Aug. 1791.

The ELECTION to replace Turner South-all in the Virginia Senate was apparently not as uncertain as Randolph feared. His father won handily. See James Currie to TJ, 26 Aug. 1791.

[1] Randolph first wrote "immediately," but corrected it to read as above.

From Thomas FitzSimons

SIR   Augt. 23, 1791

Your Report Appears so Correct that Nothing Important Occurred to me to Add to it. The few Observations I have made are of very Little Consequence. One of the Great Evils experienced by the Americans in their intercourse with Great Britain is on Account of the Seamen. The line of Naturalization drawn by the British exclude a Great No. of the persons employd in our Navigation and indeed Little Regard is paid at times when they are Impressing even to those Who are Actually Citizens according to their own Construction. If any Commercial Negotiation should take place with that Nation, this Subject would merit particular attention, because the delay to Ships by Haveing their men Impressed would be Grievious, and Seamen Knowing they would be Subject to that hardship would demand Very high Wages.

I have not been able to find any person Sufficiently Acquainted with the Commerce of Denmark to give me any information on that head but I will Continue my Inquiry, and Communicate any I may Receive.—I am Respectfy Sir Yr. Mo Hble Servt,

THOS. FITZSIMONS

RC (DLC); endorsed by TJ as received 24 Aug. 1791 and so recorded in SJL. Enclosure: Notes on commercial regulations of Spain, Portugal, Great Britain, and the Netherlands affecting American trade (undated MS in FitzSimons' hand, except for additions by TJ, in DLC: TJ Papers, 65: 11313).

FitzSimons, a member of Congress from Pennsylvania who was also a trustee of the Bank of North America, compiled his OBSERVATIONS on European commercial regulations after reading TJ's comprehensive report on American trade, which TJ was planning to submit to Congress during its forthcoming session but which he delayed presenting until shortly before his retirement as Secretary of State (see Report on Commerce, 16 Dec. 1793). There is no evidence to indicate when TJ submitted a text of this report to FitzSimons.

To David Humphreys

DEAR SIR   Philadelphia Aug. 23. 1791.

I recieved yesterday your favors of June 7. No. 21. and June 17. No. 22. Mr. Barclay will have delivered you my two letters of May 13. and July 13.

Since his departure no remarkeable events have taken place. He would convey to you the official information of General Scott's success against the Indians. A second party somewhat stronger is now gone against them.

Nearly the whole of the states have now returned their census. I send you the result, which as far as founded on actual returns is written in black ink, and the numbers not actually returned, yet pretty well known, are written in red ink. Making a very small allowance for omissions, we are upwards of four millions; and we know in fact that the omissions have been very great.—Our crop of wheat is very abundant, and of the best quality ever known. There has been an extraordinary drought, prevailing most to the North of this. The crop of Hay here is short, and calamitously so further North. We have lately had the most copious rains, which will recover the Indian corn and tobacco. A spirit of gambling in the public paper has lately seised too many of our citizens. Commerce, manufactures, the arts and agriculture will suffer from it if not checked. Many are ruined by it; but I fear that ruin will be no more a correction in this case than in common gaming. We cannot immediately foresee how it will terminate.

Colo. Ternant is arrived here as Minister plenipotentiary from France.—I shall soon be able to send you another newspaper written in a contrary spirit to that of Fenno. Freneau is come here to set up a National gazette, to be published twice a week, and on whig principles. The two papers will shew you both sides of our politics.

Being about to set out for Virginia in a few days, it will probably be two months before I shall again have the pleasure of writing to you. The President will go to Mount Vernon within three or four weeks.

You will recieve herewith your newspapers as usual and a parcel for Mr. Carmichael.—I am with great & sincere esteem Dear Sir Your most obedt. & most humble servt.,   TH: JEFFERSON

P.S. Your favor of May 17. No. 19. is this moment recieved.

RC (A.S.W. Rosenbach, Philadelphia, 1946); addressed, in Remsen's hand; endorsed. PrC (DLC). FC (DNA: RG 59, DCI). Enclosed census not found.

To George Washington

The Secretary of State has had under consideration the Official Communications from the Secretary of the Territory of the United States North-West of the River Ohio, from January 1st. to June

30th. 1791 inclusive: and thereupon REPORTS to the President, that none of the said Communications appear to require any thing to be done on the part of the Government of the United States; that they contain indeed the titles of several acts passed by the territorial Legislature, but the acts themselves not being yet communicated, no opinion can be given on them.   TH: JEFFERSON

Aug. 23. 1791

RC (DNA: RG 59, MLR); in clerk's hand except for date and signature which have been excised and are supplied from PrC (DLC). Dft (DLC); TJ added date and following note at foot of text: "to be copied fair for signature." FC (DNA: RG 59, SDR). An entry in SJPL under 21 Aug. 1791 shows that TJ drafted his "Report . . . on proceedings of N.W. territory" on that date.

On 1 July 1791 Winthrop Sargent transmitted to Washington a copy of the "Official Communications from the Secretary of the Territory . . . Northwest of the River Ohio from Jany the 1st 1791 to June 30th inclusive," to which was appended a list of six Acts passed by the legislature on 22 and 29 June, as follows: "1st. a Law supplementary to a 'Law respecting Crimes and Punishments.' 2d. a Law for the Punishment of Persons tearing or de-

facing Publications set up by Authority. 3d. a Law creating the Office of Clerk of the Legislature. 4th. A Law for rendering authentic as Evidence in the Courts of this Territory the public Acts &ca. of the Courts in the united States. 5th. a Law for abolishing the Distinction between the Crimes of Murder and petit Treason. 6th. a Law regulating the Enclosures of grounds." Sargent noted that the texts of these Acts could not be copied from the records in time to be transmitted with his communication to the President (Tr of Proceedings in DNA: RG 59, NWT; M-470/1; text printed in Carter, *Terr. Papers*, III, 334-47). Lear transmitted Sargent's report to TJ with Washington's request that "if there is anything contained therein, which requires the agency or attention of the President the Secretary . . . report it to him" (Lear to TJ, 18 Aug. 1791; PrC in DNA: RG 59, SDC).

To William Carmichael

SIR   Philadelphia Aug. 24. 1791.

Your letter of Jan. 24. is still the only one recieved from you within the period so often mentioned. Mine to you of the present year have been of Mar. 12. and 17. Apr. 11. May 16. and June 23. I have lately preferred sending my letters for you to Colo. Humphreys, in hopes he might find means of conveying them to you. The subjects of those of the 12. and 17th. of March are still pressed on you, and especially the first, the great object of which cannot be delayed without consequences which both nations should deprecate.

Mr. Jaudenes arrived here some time ago, and has been recieved as joint Commissioner with Mr. Viar. The concurring interests of Spain and this country certainly require the presence of able and discreet ministers.

The crop of wheat of the present year has surpassed all expectation as to quantity, and is of fine quality. Other articles of agriculture will suffer more by an extraordinary drought.

I inclose you a copy of our census, which so far as it is written in black ink is founded on actual returns, what is in red ink being conjectural, but very near the truth. Making very small allowance for omissions which we know to have been very great, we may safely say we are above four millions.

Our first expedition, against the Indians, under General Scott, has been completely succesful; he having killed thirty odd, taken fifty odd, and burnt three towns. A second expedition against them has commenced and we expect daily the result.

The public credit continues firm. The domestic debt funded at six percent is 12½ per cent above par. A spirit however of gambling in our public paper has seised on too many of our citizens, and we fear it will check our commerce, arts, manufactures and agriculture, unless stopped.

Newspapers for you as usual accompany this, addressed to the care of Colo. Humphreys.—I am with great esteem Sir Your most obedt. & most humble servt.,   TH: JEFFERSON

PrC (DLC). FC (DNA: RG 59, DCI).

TJ's letter to Carmichael of 12 Mch. instructed him to urge Spain to recognize the United States' right to navigate the Mississippi and is printed as Document VI in group of documents on the threat of dis-

union in the West, 10 Mch. 1791. His letter of 17 Mch. directed Carmichael to suggest that the Spanish government adopt a navigation act aimed at Great Britain and is printed as Document III in group of documents on the search for a European concert on navigation law, 15 Mch. 1791.

To Thomas Leiper

SIR   Philadelphia Aug. 24. 1791.

I have determined to agree to give you 250£. for your house and tenement in my possession as proposed in your letter of the 16th. on condition that you lease it to me for seven years with a right in me to relinquish it at any time after the expiration of the first year on giving you three months previous notice: the new lease to begin as to the bookroom and stable when they are delivered to me, on the terms you mention, and as to the entire tenement the 7th. day of January next, when the present lease expires. Your immediate answer will oblige Sir Your humble servt.,   TH: JEFFERSON

P.S. I never proposed to med[dle] with any thing but the inside finishing of the Garden house. You were to cover it, put doors and windows so as to complete the hull and this is what I now shall expect.

PrC (MHi). Leiper's letter of 16 Aug. 1791, recorded in SJL as received the same day, has not been found. Leiper replied to the above at once, evidently complying with the terms TJ insisted on; his letter of 24 Aug. 1791 is recorded in SJL as received that day, but that letter also is missing.

From Thomas Newton, Jr.

Norfolk, 24 Aug. 1791. The justices there desire to know how to "proceed when call'd on by the British Consul for Warrants to Apprehend Sea Men who quit their Ships, and whether they have power to Commit them to Gaol or send them on board their Ships." Some think they have no power to do it, others that it should be done. This day a Capt. Stuport brought in a seaman who had not signed articles. The consul consulted the justices, and the greater part thought the man not bound to proceed. Some of the ship's crew proved on oath before the consul that he had agreed to come in the ship from Jamaica and proceed back again, and the justices therefore would have nothing to do with it. "On this, Mr. Hamilton Issued out his Authority to the Capt: who brought some of his men on Shore and Violently seized the Sailor, and was Carrying him Off, but he made his escape . . . and run into my House, where they pursued him and endeavor'd to drag him Out. Not being at home at the time, I was sent for, and found a Croud about my Doors, with Capt. Stuport, his Boatswain and Others after the Sailor who was in the House. The Capt: offered me the Authority he had from the Consul. I wou'd have nothing to do with it, and told him I knew of no Authority that the Consul had to Issue Warrants and Seize men on our Lands." He told the sailor, which he regrets, that he was not under his protection and to leave the house. He did so and made a momentary escape but soon publicly appeared on the streets. He desires TJ's opinion, which will govern them in future, "so that we shall not infringe the privileges of a Consul and that he may not invade the rights of the Land." Events of the sort happen daily, so he asks for TJ's instructions "as it will be a Means of promoting harmony and good Order, when each know their Duty."

RC (DNA: RG 59, MLR); 4 p.; endorsed by TJ as received 1 Sep. 1791 and so recorded in SJL.

TJ reaffirmed the traditional view on the status of consuls under the law of nations in his response of 8 Sep. 1791. For information on Newton, one of Norfolk's most prominent leaders, see "Newton of Norfolk," VMHB, XXX (1922), 87.

From Nathaniel Randolph

Hopewell, New Jersey, 24 Aug. 1791. Having for some time had an inclination to come to Philadelphia concerning "any place in either of the Departments over which you preside," he has conferred with his friends, particularly the bearer, Dr. Rogers, whom he hopes TJ will confer with on the subject.—"I have likewise indulged myself with some incouragement from your Excellency's Interest; although the short acquaintance you had with me; from the length of time since, must be almost eradicated, should it you may perhaps remember the plan of the western Expedition, which was laid in Virginia, against Detroit in Sept. 80, to have been carried into execution, in conjunction, with Pensilvania in 81, which fell through after the principle part of the expence was accumulated."

RC (DLC: Washington Papers); 2 p.; addressed: "His Excellency Thomas Jefferson Secretary of State Philadelphia Handed by Doct. Rogers." Endorsed by TJ as received 2 Nov. 1791 and so recorded in SJL.

Randolph had served as a purchasing agent during the 1780 western expedition while TJ was governor of Virginia (Randolph to TJ, 22 and 27 Nov. 1780).

From William Short

DEAR SIR   Paris August 24. 1791.

The assembly have continued since my last deliberating on the plan of constitution submitted to them. They have made no material alterations, but have referred two or three questions to be decided after the others—one of them is that for augmenting the property of electors and abolishing the *marc d'argent* hitherto decreed for the members of the legislature—and another is the condition of the Princes of the blood, viz. the rights they are to enjoy as members of the society. Some are for leaving them the title of Prince and excluding them from the rights of citizens as being dangerous in popular assemblies. No body knows how these questions will be decided. The doubt will be soon removed however as it is supposed the finishing hand will be put to them in the course of the week.

The committees have not yet decided in what manner the constitution shall be presented to the King so as to obtain his free acceptation. For some time it was said that his intention was to refuse it, but that opinion seems now to have given place to another, that he will accept it, but will abandon it as soon as an opportunity presents itself. The enemies of the constitution, as well the aristocrats as the republicans, as they are termed, propagate this opinion.

Nothing further has transpired with respect to the intentions of foreign courts relative to the affairs of this country. There are various proofs of their malevolences. The inferior princes of Germany particularly shew a disposition to proceed to hostilities and to draw after them the more influential, but the more powerful electors have in the diet voted for a continuance of negotiation. Their proceedings in this business will of course be rendered subordinate to their more immediate and more leading interests. It is no longer doubted that the Northern Christian powers will preserve peace among themselves—of course no obstacle from the Turkish war—but active negotiations are carried on at Vienna which seem to indicate some change in the general system of the Empire. The Prussian negotiator there is in the highest favor and it is thought the present moment will be siezed on for rounding and squaring their possessions to their wishes. The result cannot yet be known but it is manifest that the several European powers have an anxious eye on them. Denmark and Sweden, particularly the last, without any symptoms of war keep up a state of armament that indicates some hidden plan or fear. Poland also is preparing for defence, and the Elector of Saxony delays his decision with respect to the crown offered him. I cannot say what part Spain does or may take in this business, though I suppose the curtain will be soon raised so as to shew it. Until then it would be rash to pronounce what will be the result of a state of negotiation, the activity, duration and mysterys of which have few examples in the annals of Europe.

You will no doubt learn from Mr. Carmichael what regards Spain in particular. It seems the dispositions of that court with respect to the Mississipi business have gone through several changes, as far as I can judge from the correspondence of M. de Montmorin. In the beginning he informed me that they had shewn a much more favorable disposition than he had expected. They afterwards seemed disposed to reject all kind of negotiation on the principle of our pretensions being *exagerées*, and lately again (this is the last account) discover a propensity to listen to terms so as to give hopes that the affair may be terminated amicably to the wishes of the United States. This is only a vague account of the posture of the business of Madrid, but I am persuaded it is all that M. de Montmorin knows of it. I still continue in my former opinion that his disposition to serve the U.S. in this instance may be relied on. His influence of course will have been diminished by the late unfortunate event of the King's flight from Paris and the proceedings consequent thereto.—I hope the Government of the U.S. will have influence enough on the western inhabitants to prevent them for the present from proceeding to extremities, as I cannot doubt, whatever may be the event of negotiation at this moment at Madrid, the development of their resources and the manifestation of their firm resolution to obtain an acknowlegement of their rights will in a very short time induce the Spanish cabinet to subscribe to an act which is not only just but necessary. So long as the ministry remains here the same we shall have the aid of their friendly interposition. You will easily conceive that in the present crisis it is impossible to say how long they will remain, or what changes will take place, this depending on the issue of the revolution.

A person has lately arrived here from Kentuckey. He is a Frenchman settled there. He reports that the navigation of the Mississipi is now allowed our inhabitants without any kind of restriction and that he saw great numbers of large boats load to go down the river. A brother of the English minister here (Lord Ed. Fitzgerald) travelled from Canada along our western frontiers and went down the Mississipi to New-Orleans. He is now in Paris and tells me that whilst there he saw several of the inhabitants of Kentuckey who came down the river with their productions, that he was once in particular a witness to a dispute between some of them and the Governor who insisted on their paying a duty on these articles, that they refused it and succeeded in their refusal. I mention this merely as accidental perhaps inaccurate information. I suppose you recieve more authentic from the Americans resident there. I learn from him that there are several well informed and particularly a Mr. Jones, brother to the Physician of that name at Philadelphia.

The[1] report mentioned in my last of the death of the Dey of Algiers was soon after fully confirmed, as well as the peaceable nomination of his successor. I learn by the French consul that he is the same, who whilst minister discovered more favorable dispositions than the others to the American prisoners. He thinks this would be a favorable moment for attempting their redemption. He observes it would have been at all times practicable by proper measures, viz. by authorizing some Consul or commercial house established at Algiers to effect it, leaving them at liberty to chuse the suitable moment, and fixing the sum beyond which they could not go, authorizing them at the same time, to draw for it, on the agreement being concluded. He supposes that for the 14. captives who remain the sum should be fixed at 200,000.₶ tournois all expences included and says it is possible that 150,000.₶ might suffice, the agents employed exerting themselves of course to reduce it as much as possible for the interest of their employers. He seems to be persuaded there is no other mode of succeeding but this, which he agrees is subject to objections arising from the great confidence necessary to be placed in the agents employed. He adds also that the character and dispositions of the present Dey are much more liberal than those of the last, and of course that this is the favorable moment for the U.S. to make a permanent arrangement with that regency for the safety of their flag. This negotiation he thinks should be carried on in the same manner with the other. He cannot however form a conjecture of what that would cost.

I have had a good deal of accidental conversation also lately with M. Pujet who has the direction of the consular department in the marine. He is I believe, known to you, and is a man of a good reputation and understanding and is particularly acquainted with the relations between this country and the Barbary powers. He insists that France pays no tribute to the Dey of Algiers, nor England nor Spain. He agrees that Holland (I think) and some others do, and says that the difference is perfectly understood at Algiers between nations that are tributary and those that are not, and also that all Christian powers are obliged to make pecuniary sacrifices to secure peace there. Those of France consist 1. in the establishment of a consul at Algiers, whose salary and expences amount to about 25,000.₶ p ann., and 2. in presents which are made from time to time to the officers of government in order to settle differences which accidentally arise between French vessels or citizens and the cruisers or regency of Algiers. These amount to from 70, to 80,000₶ annually, and are as he assures me the only expences paid regularly. The large sums which I mentioned to you some time ago to have been paid by M. de Senneville, for the renewal of the treaty, he denies altogether to have been for that purpose, or to have been as considerable as I supposed them. He says they were to satisfy the regency for a vessel they lost on the coast of France and also for one delivered up to Naples after having been taken by an Algerine cruiser.

Mr. Pujet says the U.S. would be wrong to put themselves on the footing of a tributary power as it insures more contempt than safety at Algiers. He supposes their consular establishment and annual accidental presents would cost as much as those stated above for France, notwithstanding their commerce is so much more inconsiderable; as this would not be calculated by the officers of the regency. He does not know to what amount presents would be necessary for securing the peace in the beginning.—There are some honorary expences to which France and other European powers are sometimes subjected from which the U.S. would be exempted, such as at present the furnishing a vessel to carry the new Dey's ambassador to Constantinople to obtain the investiture of his place. This mark of distinction is accorded to France and is considered as a proof of the Dey's favorable dispositions to this country.

Should it be possible to obtain a peace of Algiers it would be of little service without one could be secured also with Tunis and Tripoli, each of which would cost the same to the U.S. The establishment at Tunis costs more to France as there is much more of the parade and luxury of a court there than at Algiers.

I observed to M. Pujet that such powers as were at peace with these piratical states would probably put as many obstacles as possible in the way of others obtaining it and that the U.S. might perhaps meet with some difficulties on that account. He agreed that this policy did prevail. He thought however that France would in the new order of things abandon it, and would aid the U.S. in obtaining a peace. He added that he did not see how our free entrance into the Mediterranean could be against the interests of France as we were not a carrying power, and said that for his part so far as it depended on him he would certainly contribute all in his power to serve the interests of the U.S. in this instance.—I have thought it well to communicate these things to you that you might judge how far they deserve weight in an attempt to redeem our unhappy captives or to secure a permanent peace.

Letters have been just recieved from the Governor of S. Domingo as late as the beginning of July. The decree of May 15. respecting the *gens de couleur* had arrived there and thrown every thing into confusion. The governor apprehends serious disorders that it will not be in his power to suppress. The inhabitants shew marks of much discontentment with the national assembly and particularly those who had adhered formerly to their decrees and took side against the assembly of St. Marc. The reports and private letters go much farther and say that it was determined to have no further connexion with France and that deputies were sent to Jamaica for assistance. The city of Bordeaux is become particularly obnoxious to them for having offered to send their *garde nationale* to the islands to enforce this decree of the assembly. The assembly had directed commissaries to be sent out to carry this decree. Notwithstanding the time which has elapsed they have not yet set out, and such is the present organisation of the government that the assembly cannot find out on whom to place the non-execution of their intentions. The colonial committee have the Governor's letter now under consideration and are in a few days to make their report on it.

The National assembly have new modelled their post office, and in fixing the price of postage have augmented that on letters for the U.S.

Drost has not yet had the articles of agreement drawn up because he wishes to concert them with Mr. Grand. He tells me to assure you he may be counted on for the spring. I think he is probably of a dilatory turn from what has been lately told me, but further information is much in favor of his moral character, and the money he struck in England for Messrs. Bolton &c. shews his talents. I communicate in my letter to the Secretary of treasury herein inclosed some of his observations with respect to the subject of a mint. On further consideration he declines engaging at all in the assaying part. He tells me he finds he shall be less adequate to teach it than he hoped, as mentioned in a former letter. It will be indispensable he says to have a person on purpose. One may be procured here on easy terms. I shall make enquiry for such an one but will not engage him until I hear further from you as there is full time from what Mr. Drost tells me. I will thank you therefore to say in what manner you would chuse him to be engaged as to time, and as near as you can, what kind of terms you have a view to.

I am informed with certainty that the English ministry lately made Mr. Walpole their envoy extraordinary (I believe at Munich) the offer of going to America in the same character. He took time to consider of it and at length declined it. It is said now they intend to send as minister plenipotentiary Mr. Hammond who has lately returned from Spain where he was Secretary to the embassy.

This letter incloses a memorial for the State of So. Carolina to which the memorialists hope an answer will be given. I have promised them to forward it. You will recieve also by the same conveyance the usual gazettes which will go to Havre by the diligence.

You gave me reason to hope in your last letter of May 10. that you would write in future by the French and English packets. They have arrived however as late as those of June and July without bringing me any letter. The Secretary of the Treasury wrote by the French packet of July. It is important that I should be able to meet the questions which are asked me about the Mississipi business, and also about the Indian hostilities to which much more importance is given here than I can suppose they deserve. Having no authentic information there are many things originating probably in the English newspapers that I cannot venture to contradict flatly, and a bare denial or expression of doubt about them is taken of course as a confirmation of them by those who take it for granted I must be informed and would assert the contrary if they were not true.—I beg you to be persuaded of the attachment & respect of Dear Sir, your most obedient humble servant,   W: SHORT

PrC of missing RC (DLC: Short Papers); at head of text: "No. 77." Tr (DNA: RG 59, DD). Recorded in SJL as received 6 Dec. 1791. Enclosure: Short to Hamilton, 23 Aug. 1791 (PrC in DLC: Short Papers; printed in Syrett, *Hamilton*, IX, 97).

The Spanish government had decided in 1788 to lure settlers to Louisiana and West Florida and to loosen the ties that bound the West to the union by opening the NAVIGATION OF THE MISSISSIPI to American frontiersmen, subject to the payment of a duty to Spain (Arthur Whitaker, *The Spanish-American Frontier: 1783-1795* [Boston, 1927], p. 101-2).

The National Assembly's DECREE OF MAY 15. extended the franchise to all properly qualified blacks and mulattoes in the French colonies born of free parents, and promised not to change the political status of the far greater number of other blacks and mulattoes without prior consultation with the colonial assemblies (*Archives Parlementaires*, XXVI, 95). This decree encountered strong opposition among French West Indian planters, weakened the legitimacy of metropolitan authority in the islands, and was an important link in the chain of events leading to the great slave revolts on Saint-Domingue.

Secretary of the Treasury Hamilton's letter to Short of 30 June 1791 is printed in Syrett, *Hamilton*, VIII, 519.

[1] Following five paragraphs excerpted and sent to John Adams for the Senate with TJ's letter of 9 Dec. 1791.

To Sir John Sinclair

DEAR SIR   Philadelphia Aug. 24. 1791.

I am to acknolege the reciept of your two favors of Dec. 25. and May 14. with the pamphlets which accompanied them, and to return you my thanks for them. The Corn law, I percieve, has not passed in the form you expected. My wishes on that subject were nearer yours than you imagined. We both in fact desired the same thing for different reasons, respecting the interests of our respective countries, and therefore justifiable in both. You wished the bill so moulded as to encourage strongly your national agriculture. The clause for warehousing foreign corn tended to lessen the confidence of the farmer in the demand for his corn. I wished the clause omitted that our corn might pass directly to the country of the consumer, and save us the loss of an intermediate deposit, which it can illy bear.— That no commercial arrangements between Gr. Britain and the U.S. have taken place, as you wish should be done, cannot be imputed to us. The proposition has surely been often enough made; perhaps too often. It is a happy circumstance in human affairs that evils which are not cured in one way, will cure themselves in some other.— We are now under the first impression of the news of the king's flight from Paris, and his recapture. It would be unfortunate were it in the power of any one man to defeat the issue of so beautiful a revolution. I hope and trust it is not, and that for the good of suffering humanity all over the earth, that revolution will be established and spread thro' the whole world.—I shall always be happy my dear Sir to hear of your health & happiness, being with sentiments of the most cordial esteem and respect Dear Sir your most obedt. humble servt,

                                        TH: JEFFERSON

I send you a small pamphlet on the subject of our commerce written by a very judicious hand.

PrC (DLC). RC sold by Charles Hamilton, Auction No. 102, 30 Jan. 1977 and reproduced in facsimile.

TJ was relieved because Parliament had passed the CORN LAW without a clause allowing American wheat imported into Great Britain by British ships to be stored without charge in British warehouses (see TJ to Charles Carroll, 4 Apr. 1791, and notes). The SMALL PAMPHLET TJ enclosed with this letter was Tench Coxe, *A Brief Examination of Lord Sheffield's Observations*

on the Commerce of the United States (Philadelphia, 1791), which was a rebuttal of Sheffield's celebrated defense of the British mercantile system. By thus expressing his approval of Coxe's pamphlet, which criticized British restrictions on American commerce and called for the passage of legislation to encourage the development of American manufacturing, TJ undoubtedly hoped the threat of American retaliation might help secure commercial concessions from the British government.

From Joel Barlow

SIR   London 25 Aug. 1791

I should not take the liberty of commending to your notice and protection my excellent friends Mr. and Mrs. St. John were it not that their merit entitles them to more than I can otherwise do for them. Mr. St. John transfers a considerable property to our country with an intention to devote that and himself wholly to Agriculture, of which his accurate intelligence in every part of rural œconomy and mechanics renders him one of the first ornaments.

I have recommended to his enquiry the neighborhood of the Potowmac as an inviting part of the country to settle in. Your advice may be essentially useful to him in this particular. If he were admitted a member of the Philosophical and agricultural societies of Philadelphia it might be a means of making his knowledge and abilities more useful to himself and others.—I have the honor to be Sir with great respect your obet. servt.,   J. BARLOW

RC (NNP); endorsed by TJ as received 24 Oct. 1791 and so recorded in SJL. Both in endorsement and in SJL TJ recorded the letter as from "John Barlow," but altered the endorsement to read correctly.

To Edward Rutledge

MY DEAR SIR   Philadelphia Aug. 25. 1791.

I have recieved your favor of the 7th. by Mr. Harper, and that also by Mr. Butler. I thank you for both, and shall duly respect both. I find by the last that, not your letter on the subject of British commerce, but mine in answer to it has miscarried. Yours was dated June 20. 1790. was recieved July 2. and answered July 4. I send

you a copy of the answer, which will read now like an old almanac,
but it will shew you I am incapable of neglecting any thing which
comes from you. The measures therein spoken of as in contemplation
for the purpose of bringing Gr. Brit. to reason, vanished in a reference of the subject to me to report on our commerce and navigation, generally, to the next session of Congress. I have little hope
that the result will be any thing more than to turn the left cheek to
him who has smitten the right. We have to encounter not only the
prejudices in favor of England, but those against the Eastern states
whose ships in the opinion of some will overrun our land. I have
been sorry to see that your state has been over-jealous of the measures
proposed on this subject, and which really tend to relieve them from
the effects of British broils. I wish you may be able to convert Mr.
Barnwell, because you think him worth converting. Whether you
do or not, your opinion of him will make me sollicitous for his
acquaintance, because I love the good, and respect freedom of opinion.—What do you think of this scrip-pomany? Ships are lying idle
at the wharfs, buildings are stopped, capitals withdrawn from commerce, manufactures, arts and agriculture, to be employed in gambling, and the tide of public prosperity almost unparraleled in any
country, is arrested in it's course, and suppressed by the rage of
getting rich in a day. No mortal can tell where this will stop. For
the spirit of gaming, when once it has seised a subject, is incurable.
The taylor who has made thousands in one day, tho' he has lost
them the next, can never again be content with the slow and moderate earnings of his needle. Nothing can exceed the public felicity,
if our papers are to be believed, because our papers are under the
orders of the scrip-men. I imagine however we shall shortly hear
that all the cash has quitted the extremities of the nation, and accumulated here. That produce, and property fall to half price there,
and the same things rise to double price here: that the cash accumulated and stagnated here, as soon as the bank paper gets out,
will find it's vent into foreign countries, and instead of this solid
medium which we might have kept for nothing, we shall have a
paper one for the use of which we are to pay these gamesters 15.
per cent per annum as they say. Would to god yourself, Genl.
Pinkney, Majr. Pinkney would come forward and aid us with your
efforts. You are all known, respected, wished for: but you refuse
yourselves to every thing. What is to become of us, my dear friend,
if the vine and the fig-tree withdraw, and leave us to the bramble
and thorn?—You will have heard before this reaches you, of the
peril into which the French revolution is brought by the flight of
their king. Such are the fruits of that form of government which

heaps importance on Ideots, and which the tories of the present day are trying to preach into our favour. I still hope the French revolution will issue happily. I feel that the permanence of our own leans in some degree on that; and that a failure there would be a powerful argument to prove there must be a failure here.— We have been told that a British minister would be sent out to us this summer. I suspect this depends on the event of peace or war. In the latter case they will probably send one: but they have no serious view of treating or fulfilling treaties. Adieu my dear Sir Your's affectionately,

TH: JEFFERSON

RC (PHi); endorsed. PrC (DLC).

TJ's efforts to enlist the support of the Pinckney brothers for the Republican cause were doomed to failure. Gen. Charles Cotesworth Pinckney and Maj. Thomas Pinckney eventually became staunch Federalists. Indeed, Gen. Pinckney was the Federalist presidential candidate in 1804 and 1808 and Maj. Pinckney was the party's vice-presidential candidate in 1796. Ironically, Thomas Pinckney did COME FORWARD, but not as TJ had hoped. In November 1791 Washington decided to nominate him minister to Great Britain without having consulted TJ (see TJ to Thomas Pinckney, 6 Nov. 1791).

To Nathaniel Burwell

DEAR SIR   Philadelphia Aug. 26. 1791.

I am favoured with yours of the 11th. inst. and am happy to be able to explain the appearance of a double employment of trustees[1] in the affairs of Mr. Paradise. This is what was at first arranged, while I was in Europe. It was necessary to have trustees in London who might receive the proceeds of Mr. Paradise's estate and pay it to his creditors, and to whom the creditors might apply. Dr. Bancroft and one or two others were appointed by mutual con[sent] of parties. But it was necessary also to have a trustee in Virginia into whose hands the estate might be delivered, free from the disposal of Mr. Paradise, except the part of the profits allowed for his subsistence. You were in like manner appointed by general consent for this,[2] and it rests with you to do all authorita[tive] acts concerning the estate here, and the remittance to England.

On mature consideration and consultation with persons here more knowing than myself[2] in the public stocks, it appears clearly for Mr. Paradise's interest to subscribe his public paper to the loan opened by the general government. Immediately on this being done four ninths of it will be at 6. per cent and can be sold @ about 22/6 the pound, two ninths will be at three per cent and would sell now @ 12/6 in the pound and three ninths will be at 6. per cent from about

8. years hence, and might now be sold for about 12/6 the pound: so that the whole would fetch about 17/ the pound. However I should not think it adviseable to sell till orders can be recieved, and I write to Mr. Paradise on this subject this day. But the subscription I think adviseable, because it cannot be done after the last day of the next month, the law having fixed that term for closing the loan. Were that term to be passed over the chance will be lost for ever, and it is very incertain what would become of the debt. I venture to suggest this matter, Sir, for your consideration, having no right to meddle in it, otherwise than as the friend of Mr. Paradise, and as the measure I would take were it to depend on my opinion.—I have the honour to be with great esteem Dr. Sir Your most obedt. & most hble servt.,   TH: JEFFERSON

PrC (MHi).

THE LOAN OPENED BY THE GENERAL GOVERNMENT: The act of 4 Aug. 1790 approving a plan for the federal assumption of state debts established a deadline of 30 Sep. 1791, but later extended it to 1 Mch. 1793 (U.S. Statutes at Large, I, 138-44, 281-3; and E. James Ferguson, *The Power*

of the Purse: A History of American Public Finance, 1776-1790 [Chapel Hill, N.C., 1961], p. 306-25).

[1] This word interlined in substitution for "agents," deleted.

[2] Preceding two words inserted above the line.

From James Currie

Richmond, 26 Aug. 1791. He acknowledged TJ's polite and friendly letter and wrote again by Lewis Burwell. Now writes at request of Col. Harvie to say that he received TJ's letter about "some papers (respecting lands) to be obtained from Colo. N. Lewis" before setting off with other James River Canal Commissioners to examine the river "and try to let out the clearing a part of it . . . in which they failed." On his way he saw Lewis who promised to send papers but they have not come to hand. About 16 days ago Harvie was seized "dangerously ill with a Bilious peripneumony and has been in the most imminent danger indeed." He is now barely able to sit up and has received TJ's other letter about lands granted Virginia Line on Ohio, which will be attended to the instant he can perform any sort of business. "All the rest of his family are well as likewise Colo. Randolph and his Lady, your son and his Lady with her family all are well. He was down here on Monday visiting his estate. Colo. Randolph [of] Tuckahoe and Meriwether were Candidates for . . . Colo. Southalls place as Senator. Colo. Randolph was elected by a very great Majority."

RC (DLC); 3 p.; addressed: "The Hble. Thomas Jefferson Esq. Secretary of State Philadelphia"; postmarked: "RICHMOND Aug 26" and "FREE"; endorsed by TJ as received 1 Sep. 1791 and so recorded in SJL.

TJ's letter to John Harvie about SOME PAPERS is probably that of 7 Apr. 1791. The OTHER LETTER to Harvie is that of 14 Aug. 1791.

From Alexander Hamilton

Philadelphia Aug. 26. 91

The Secretary of the Treasury presents his respects to the Secretary of State. He returns the draft of Ratification with some alterations to conform more accurately to the fact which are submitted. The Secretary of State will recollect that there is another loan (the contract for which was also forwarded to him) concluded by Messrs. Willinks & Van Staphorsts and of which likewise a Ratification is desired. To possess the Secretary of State fully of the nature of the powers and course of the transactions in both cases, the drafts of the powers as well to the Commissioners as to Mr. Short are sent herewith. When the Secretary of State has done with them he will please to return them.

RC (DLC); endorsed by TJ as received 26 Aug. 1791 and so recorded in SJL. Enclosures: (1) Hamilton to Willink, Van Staphorst & Hubbard, 28 Aug. 1790 (printed in Syrett, *Hamilton*, VI, 580-5). (2) Hamilton to William Short, 1 Sep. 1790 (printed in same, VII, 6-15).

The instruments of RATIFICATION pertained to two loans that were negotiated in the Netherlands in order to help the United States pay its foreign debt. The first loan,

which was negotiated by Willink, Van Staphorst & Hubbard in January 1790, was for 3,000,000 florins, and the second, which was negotiated by William Short in conjunction with this firm in March 1791, was for 2,500,000 florins. Texts of the ratifications of both loans, signed by Washington and dated 1 Sep. 1791, are in DLC: Washington Papers; the ratification of the first loan is printed in Fitzpatrick, *Writings*, XXXI, 353-4.

To James Madison

Th:J. TO J.M.   Friday Aug. 26.

Will you come and sit an hour before dinner to-day? Also take soup with me tomorrow?

Since writing the above the President has been here, and left L'Enfant's plan, with a wish that you and I would examine it together immediately, as to certain matters, and let him know the result. As the plan is very large, will you walk up and examine it here?

RC (DLC); addressed: "Mr. Madison." Not recorded in SJL.

L'ENFANT'S PLAN: the map that L'Enfant later took back to the federal district and

refused to make available for engraving (see Editorial Note on fixing the seat of government, Vol. 20: 33-41; and TJ to Commissioners, 28 Aug. 1791).

To John Paradise

Tho' the incessant drudgery of my office puts it out of my power to write letters of mere correspond[ence], yet I do not permit them to suspend the offices of friendship, where these may affect the interests of my friends. You have in the funds of Virginia in loan office certificates reduced to specie value £985-17-6½ and in final settlement £62-8. These are of the description allowed by the general government to be transferred to their funds, if subscribed to them before the last day of next month. If so transferred, four ninths of them would now sell for about 22/6 the pound, or would bear an interest of 6. per cent paid regularly: two ninths would bear an interest of 3. per cent paid regularly, and sell for 12/6 the pound: the other three ninths will bear an interest of 6 percent after about 8. years hence, and would now sell for 12/6 the pound. I wrote to Mr. Burwell to know if any orders were given him on this subject, and he answers me in the negative. Supposing that this has proceeded from your being unable at such a distance to judge of the expediency of transferring the debt from the state to the General government, I have taken the liberty this day to advise him to do it, because if not done before the last day of next month it can never be done afterwards. Observe that since Congress has said it would assume all these debts, where the parties should chuse it, the states have repealed their provision for paiment, and the moment the time is out for transferring them, their value will sink to nothing almost. Tho' I advise Mr. Burwell to transfer them to the funds of the United states, so as to secure them, yet I advise him also to let them lie there, and not to sell them till orders from England: because I do not foresee any loss from waiting a while for orders. I would certainly advise powers to be given to him to sell the 6. per cents, when he finds a favorable occasion; I believe they may rise to 24/ the pound, which will be making them nearly as much sterling as they are currency. This might enable a remittance immediately to your creditors of about 500£. It might be well to authorize him also to do as to the 3. per cents, and the deferred part, what occurrences shall render expedient. It is impossible to foresee what may happen, and therefore power had better be given where there may be a full reliance in the discretion of the person.

Be so good as to present my respects to Mrs. Paradise, to convey to her my acknowlegement of the reciept of her favor of Mar. 1. and to pray her to consider this as intended for her as well as yourself.

I am with the greatest esteem of her & yourself Dear Sir Your friend & servt.,   TH: JEFFERSON

PrC (DLC).

To John Ross

DEAR SIR   Philadelphia Aug. 26. 1791.

The inclosed extracts from a report I am preparing for Congress, and composing a general statement of our commerce, I have formed from such notes and knowlege as I have gathered up thro' life. But I cannot confide in them myself without submitting them to the correction of those who are acquainted with the subject practically. Will you do me the favor to go over them with attention, fact by fact, and with a pen in your hand note on a separate paper, ever so briefly and roughly, such facts as you think mistaken, or doubtful, or omitted? You will in this confer on me a great obligation, and I am ashamed to be obliged to ask it soon. The head of Denmark you will percieve is entirely blank. I happen to have nothing of that subject. If you can give me information therein, or point out the person who can I will thank you.—I am with great esteem Dear Sir, Your most obedt. hble. servt.,   TH: JEFFERSON

PrC (DLC). Recorded in SJL as written to "Ross ⟨David⟩ John." Ross had served Congress as a purchasing agent in France during the Revolutionary War ("Memoir of John Ross, Merchant, of Philadelphia," PMHB, XXIII [1899], 77-85). Enclosure not found.

From William Tatham

DEAR SIR   [Before 26 Aug. 1791]

I will make no appology for this intrusion on the first hours of your leisure; for you are no stranger to my zeal in the service of that Country, to whose prosperity you have devoted your own labours. It is therefore proper to consult You in what concerns the National wellfare; and certainly it is of great moment to bring speedily forward, the arrearages of Virginia on the score of its History; Geography; and common concerns.

I therefore take the liberty of inclosing to You the Titles of the several Works on which I am now preparing matter, as I have arrang'd them in the minutes and materials which I have collected together since I had the pleasure of seeing You. I will refer to them

in their order, and make such observations, or requests as occur.
1st. "The History of Virginia &c, in a large Quarto or Folio."—
This must be a Work of very considerable magnitude and will
require abilities very far superior to mine, aided by public Countenance; and more than their *luke warm* inducements towards furnishing requisites from the several Quarters where Individuals are
possess'd of Personal knowledge or manuscript Materials. I believe
You have seen the Plan of my circular Letter of February 1790,
whenever this has been answer'd, it has serv'd a good purpose, and
some of the few returns which have come to hand are valuable. The
Plan is well calculated to obtain the end of modern particulars: but
fails in the distinction between an *indifferent*, and a *spirited* recco-
mendation from the Legislature.

I have to notice under this head that my necessary enquiries in
pursuit of Geographical knowledge, lead me unavoidable into a Feild
of Historical acquisition; and an intimate acquaintance with the
several Reccords. Eighteen Months spent in such researches, necessarily furnishes a desultory collection of Minutes, and transcripts:
these thro' a carefull arrangement have produc'd the several Works
specified in the list; and a System is now attended to by giving
every Paper its proper file and entry in my office.

When we consider the imperfection of what is yet publish'd
(taking Smith's and Stith's Histories to 1624, which is only the
commencement of our Reccords: for those in the Land Office go no
farther back than 1623.) when we find Beverlys History reaching
only to 1710, and Keiths (Which I have not yet seen) no later than
1725 perhaps all of them imperfect: It wou'd be allmost criminal to
omit some perpetuation of our observations, least some unforseen
accident added to the destruction of Time, and havock of the late
War, shou'd erradicate the remaining Vestiges of our Chronological
essentials. But this[1] kind of perpetuation will be much lighter Evidence to posterity, if it comes thro' any but official hands: And hence
I wou'd ask (tho' perhaps I ought not, after the President has reccomended my own Plan;) whether it would not be better to put
this Work, and the finishing of my large Map on a public footing?
In this case I wou'd chearfully resign what is allready done on such
terms as are reasonable; and apply Myself under their direction and
support to the execution of both which wou'd probably reach greater
perfection, than is in the power of an individual to do otherwise.—
Shou'd You however think this mode either improper, or impracticable, I cou'd wish an Able Partner in the historical part; such as
Mr. Hazzard (to whom I have touch'd this subject) or some Gentle-

man whom you cou'd reccomend as a proper Person to finish the fair Copy for the Press: for the rough materials, and maps wou'd fall to my share; and the Lanscapes, Portraits and other drawings can be executed here; unless better Artists shou'd offer else where.
2d. "A Concise History of Virginia."

This I purpose to compleat on my own Account, as my Minutes in the other Branches will need but little addition to furnish a pocket Volume.

3d. "The Traveller's Guide thro' the State of Virginia and Strangers Instructor in Common concerns."

I am now engag'd on this (as I cannot proceed with the Maps till my Room is plaister'd and finish'd; and am oblig'd to use one at present, too small and dark to admit of my Materials in that undertaking). I flatter myself this will be an usefull Book, and that it will be mostly ready for publication by the meeting of the Assembly: possibly addittions may be made during their sitting, for which I shall have time by Candle light. A dificulty will then arrise as to the printing, and I am at a loss to know how this might be done in Philadelphia: for the presses here will be engag'd at that time; and even when they are at leisure are tedious; extravagant; and incorrect.

It will be my chief study to select usefull matter, and confine myself to simple Facts, wholy disengag'd from the Chimerical opinion of mere fancyfull Historians. The arrangements I have made are A Concise Sketch from the first discovery of Virga. to the present time.

A Short View of the present State Government with the Charters; Constitutions; Officers; Comissions; Oaths; duties &c.

The same as to the Federal Departments within the District of Virginia.

A Compleat View of the several Counties, (includg. Kentuckie) each under their proper Head.

Common Concerns; Mercantile and Maritime concerns; and other matters under their proper Heads, with the Laws on each selected from our New Revisal on a plan something like Mercers abridgement.

The Roads and Stages thro' the State, and as far as practicable thro the other States to the Southward and Westward.

Tables of Coins; Weights; Measures; Duties; Fees &c. &c. with a Collection of Treaties; Charters &c., an abridg'd collection of the Laws of Congress where they respect us: with such other desultory Matter as may from time to time occur.—I will be thankfull for any light You may throw on these subjects either as to what may be improper or what may be addittionaly usefull; and shall be glad to know if I have your permission to extract from your Notes, in the way Mr. Mercer has done.

4th. "A Topographical Analysis of the United States of America &c."

As I have allready sent a Copy of this to Genl. Knox (tho' that will not be perfect till the addittions of the Returns I have lately receivd from Kentuckie &c. are added.) I suppose You have seen it. A Compleat Copy is now in Mr. Nicholsons hands; and as soon as he has printed it I shall furnish the Federal and State offices with Copies for public use. I take the liberty here of asking your Opinion, and the Attorney Generalls as it comes within his official province, whether the Law Authorizes entering the Copy for the United States by filing the Title when the first sheet (*Virginia*) which comprehends the Whole System is compleated? or whether the other States can only be enterd as they are respectively compleated. This is a matter in dispute between the Clerk of the Federal Court and myself; and I have taken care to compleat the entery for the Copy Right of Virginia, and to deposit the one for the United States subject to the Attorny Gls opinion, at the Clerk's request.

My own opinion is that the Law contemplates three several objects, to wit a Security to those whose Works were in esse at the passing of the Act—"A priviledge to those who had been at the pains of searching foreign Countries for valuable Works, with intent to reprint them here" and "an inducement to litterary Invention amongst our own Citizens"—I comprehend the Analysis to be of the last Class; and that the compleat Invention entitles me to enter the Copy Right by a deposit of the Title &c.: for if the law is otherwise its purposes are easily defeated when a person supposing it to reward the multiplicity of Labour shall catch the Invention from a Sight of my Copy, or Minutes; and being possess'd of more Money and power than myself shall run away with the execution of 13/14ths. of my intention in spite of my endeavours; and notwithstanding my sacrifices to the object.

Lastly. On the subject of the Maps, The smaller one is that which You reccomended to me at Richmond; and is now nearly compleated as to the Virginia part notwithstanding the disapointments I have experienc'd among the members of Assembly who had promis'd me County Surveys; and the necessity of giving place to the Workmen engag'd on the Capitol: But as to the large map it will need pecuniary assistance from some Quarter.—The difficulties stated last Session of Assembly, were various on this subject; Some thought the Work ought to be aided, but aided by Congress and not by the Individual State. Others objected to the Term Southern Division, as one calculated to favour a seperate confederacy and lastly a *personal* dislike on the part of Govr. Harrison; the narrow mindedness of the old Squire; and extreme prudence of John Clarke, with the Restlessness of the House after the disagreable News from General Harmars Troops, beat down all the oratory of Mr. Henry and Colo. Lee; and left me to shift as well as I coud.—I have persevered thus far without help: but as the meeting of the assembly is again approaching and it will most likely be out of my power to be in Philadelphia before that time, I know of no better way than to solicit your attention towards some mode of reccomending the Several Works to public Notice and aid of either Congress or the individual State. Your private opinions on this subject (if an official step is improper) may greatly influence the tone of the Legislature.

If any new Maps or Authorities occur to You I will thank You to suggest them. I reccolect a map of Albemarle said to be at Monticello, this woud be usefull to me: but I did not think it proper to ask it of Mr. Randolph without your permission. There are allso several maps which I find it difficult to command. Of these are Churchmans Map of the Peninsula between delaware and Chesapeak; Doctr. Williamsons draft of the Cession Lands; a manuscript of Gl. Seviers said to be left with Yourself or Gl. Knox; but the General writes me he does not remember to have seen it; (this contains the Ten[nessee] and Cherokie Country); Barkers Map of Kentuckie if it is publish'd; Colol. Morgan of the Jerseys promis'd to transmit me further new materials; several New Maps of the Fedl. Lands &c. over the Ohio. If all or any of these or others, are in Your power, I will thank You to lend them, and will promise to take the greatest care to return them in safety. Indeed there is such a difficulty in procuring Geographical materials; and so little care taken of those collected on public account that I have wish'd Your advice whether some plan cou'd not be adapted to our situation by constituting an Office here for the Southern department of the Geographer and obliging the respective County Surveyors to transmit the Surveys of their County as a duty in office, for I find these and many others which have necessarily been once fil'd in the Capitol are now entirely missing. I will particularize Mason and Dixons Line; Byrd and Dandridges; Fry and Jeffersons; Dolensons; Christian and Prestons; Campbells Cherokee Boundary; Thompsons Survey of the Inland Navigation of James River to the falls of Kanhawa &c.

These Instances (which must have cost the State some thousand Pounds) occurrd to me at the last Session of Assembly; and I prepar'd a Bill on this subject offering to do the Buisiness for Nothing while I stay here: but tho' every one saw the necessity of some such arrangement as woud furnish this kind of information with certainty, yet the Creation of a New office was a Bugbear; and the generality seemd to think it ought to be task'd on the Clerk of Council as an addittional duty of his office which wou'd in my opinion put us in no better condition on this head.

I inclose a copy of the Census and Strength of Kentuckie, by which the Analysis sent Gl. Knox can be amended if he is not allready furnish'd with the same particulars.

I have to request Your information on the best mode of publishing in France such of my productions as You conceive usefull to Government; and on what plan such publication will be made advantageous to myself: for as I shall necessarily visit France for the Completion of my maps, it wou'd not be amiss to have money laid in there from Sales of the Analysis &c.

I have sent my Brother to Governor Blount on the Western Post and other Buisiness. Genl. Knox's last dispatches under Cover to Nicholson were forwarded by Him. He is Authorized by Mr. Davis to make Contracts agreable to Your directions but I think he will not succeed on this Journey; I have made Some Estimates from my knowledge of both Routs, and their dependencies. I think a Capital of 1000£ will be necessary. The proportion of this that will be sunk in the Annual expenditures will risque too much for one Years contract only; and the two posts at least as far as Columbia will interfere because the Routs will then come within 4 miles and generally ten at Most. Woud it not be better that the post shou'd continue in one to Columbia running a two Horse Stage as far as Staunton and Lynchburgh, the last of which I understand has 14 Stores and some of the Merchants are anxious to encourage this but backwards otherwise. If Government wou'd give up these posts for three years, I think I cou'd bring about the following establishment.
From Richmond to Columbia
A Two Horse Stage once a Week.
The Same from Columbia to Lynchburgh and Staunton
From Lynchburgh to Bottetourt Court House a Single Horse and Mail once in Four Weeks.
From Bottetourt to Abingdon at Washington Court House, a Horse and Mail once a Month.

From Abingdon to Ross's Iron Works and thence a tour thro Govr. Blounts Territory, a Single Horse and Mail Monthly

The Kentuckie Post being subject to Contingencies must pass the Wilderness thro different Roads; consequently Ross's Iron Works near the Long Island will be the Western Office of this Rout.

The Rout From Staunton by Bath and Lewisburgh towards the Mouth of Kanhawa may be establishd on a Simular footing and during the fall Season a Stage may pass to the Springs.—I will consider this subject more fully and if any thing more Occurs shall take the liberty of mentioning it, as Mr. Davis seems to wish my assistance where the Country is known to me.

While I am on this subject, it occurs to me that I experience great difficulty from the postage of information &c. in Works that are of a public nature—wou'd it not be just and practicable to establish some mode of Franking those which concern my Works and confind thereto in strictness are of public concern. I am Dear Sir Yr. Obt. H. Servt., WM. TATHAM

P.S. I feel at a loss for the proper Address to Officers of the Federal Government—for the [Former Reverence] which we espouse warmly on our own principles seems to hold distinction in a dishonorable point of View.

RC (ViU); undated, but endorsed by TJ as received on 26 Aug. 1791 and so recorded in SJL.

Tatham's FIRST SHEET of his "A Topographical Analysis of the United States of America &c."—that dealing with Virginia—was soon disseminated with a printed letter dated 3 Sep. 1791 (RC in DLC: TJ Papers, 66: 11507; endorsed by TJ as received 3 Oct. 1791 and so recorded in SJL; Sowerby, No. 3159). No response by TJ

has been found, but someone managed to INFLUENCE THE TONE OF THE LEGISLATURE, which provided for a lottery to aid Tatham's work at its fall 1791 session (*Virginia Gazette, and General Advertiser* [Richmond], 28 Dec. 1791; and Hening, XIII, 318). Tatham never finished his planned series of maps, however.

[1] Tatham orginally began this sentence with "This," then altered it to read as above.

From Thomas Harwood

Annapolis, 27 Aug. 1791. Acknowledging TJ's of 22d, he is extremely sorry to say he is not at liberty to make any advance for the public buildings until 1 Jan. next, when he expects "the Funds will be productive." He has so informed the commissioners.

RC (DLC: District of Columbia Papers); 2 p.; endorsed by TJ as received 30 Aug. 1791 and so recorded in SJL.

From Harry Innes

Sir   Kentucky August 27th. 1791

I did myself the pleasure of acknowledging your favor by Mr.
Brown in June. His leaving the District to return to Philadelphia
presents so favorable an opportunity of writing again, that I cannot
omit it and am encouraged by your invitation to a correspondence.

Your ideas of the impropriety of attacking the Indians by Regular
armaments I think will be justly verified by comparing the bad
success of Genl. Harmar last fall to the very great, which hath
attended the Expeditions of General's Scott and Wilkinson this
summer. The first you are before this informed of; the second hath
been almost as successful. Wilkinson, hath destroyed the principal
Town of the Ouioctanon Tribe and one Kicapoo Town, cut down
about 400 Acres of corn in the Milk, took 35 prisoners, released
one Captive and kiled 7 Warriors (1 Squaw and a child by accident),
with the loss of two men kiled and 1 wounded slightly in the hand.
Harmars loss in men was great, and the expence of the Campaign
at least 130000 Dol.—the injury to the Savages very inconsiderable.
The expence of Scotts and Wilkinson's Expeditions will not exceed
42000 Dol.—These two last expeditions will I hope restore the
Credit of the Kentucky Militia, and I am confident that if Government would pursue this mode of attacking the Indians by detach-
ments on Horseback it will have the desired effect and compel them
to peace. It fills them with Terror and keeps them watching at
home.

The people of Kentucky are all turned Politicians, from the highest in Office to the Peasant. The Peasantry are perfectly mad—
extraordinary prejudices and without foundation have arisen against
the present Officers of Government, the Lawyers and the Men of
Fortune. They say *plain honest Farmers* are the only men who ought
to be elected to form our Constitution. What will be the end of these
prejudices it is difficult to say. They have given a very serious alarm
to every thinking man, who are determined to watch and court the
temper of the people.

As the time is not very distant when our District is to come into
existence as a member of the Union, I beg leave to request you to
appropriate some of your leisure moments to answer the following
Quaeries—What kind of an Executive is most eligible for a State
Government, a Chief Magistrate only, or one with a Council—
Which is the most eligible mode of choosing a Senate, by Commissioners, or by the People—Whether is it best to have a Court of

Chancery separate or as the old Genl. Court of Virga. and as the Fœdral Courts now are—Whether Elections of the Legislature ought to be annual or biennial—Whether the Chief Magistrate ought to be re-elected after the expiration of his Election, or ought there to be a certain period of exception.

It is my wish to collect the sentiments of Gentlemen of abilities and experience on these questions previous to the formation of our Government, as in our infant Country we have very few characters, who have turned their attention to these important subjects. I have therefore ventured sir to ask your Opinion on them, under a confidence that it will not be withholden, when you reflect that it may tend to the general good of mankind. Without any other appology I am with very great respect Dr Sir your mo. ob. Servt.,

HARRY INNES

We are extremely anxious to be informed of the Answer given by the Co. of Spain to the demand of the Navigation of the Mississippi, so far as may be consistent and agreable to you.

RC (DLC); endorsed by TJ as received 22 Oct. 1791 and so recorded in SJL.

Innes had actually acknowledged TJ's

FAVOR in a letter of 30 May 1791. No evidence of TJ's responding to Innes' QUAERIES about the projected Kentucky constitution has been found.

From John Ross

DEAR SIR   Philadelphia Saturday 27 August 1791.

I shoud take pleasure in communicating any information in my power Respecting the Commerce of a favourable prospect to America, but find I can add nothing to what you have already obtained. Nor can I say much of the Danish Trade, having had but little intercourse with Denmark in my commercial pursutes.

Their Trade in that Kingdom depend principally on India, their own West India Islands and on Iceland, and are Supplyed with the Articles proper for carrying on this Trade from different parts of Europe. England Supplys a great part, in their Manufactorys, and with the chiefe part of the only Article of American produce Required by them, vizt. Tobacco.—Iceland Supplys a great proportion of their Oyle and Fish, and as to Rice there is no great consumpt nor demand at any of the Danish markets in Europe, except at Altona, and occasionally in the Dutchy of Holstain.—American Shipping were employed before the War to carry their West India Produce to Coppenhagen and if I am not mistaken coud be sold in that Kingdom Subject to a trifling duty. But whether any alterations may have been made since, to encourage their own Navigation, is what I cannot venture to say with certainty. They Build many fine Shipping and employ a great Number in the *line of Freight from Altona* and other Ports.

I think Mr. Campbell who is here at present from Denmark, and looks forward to the appointment of Consul for that Nation, will be a proper person to give you the information you wish on this Subject. With real Respect and Esteem I have the honor to be Dear Sir Your very obedt Servant, JNO. ROSS

P.S. The Danes Receive favourably all articles of Commerce from this Country Subject to the Sound Dutys imposed on all Nations, and these dutys are imposed on every Article that passes the Sound in a certain degree, whither introduced to the Danish Markets or not.—The Revenue of the Kingdom depending in a great degree on this toll. J.R.

RC (DLC); endorsed by TJ as received 26 Aug. 1791 and so recorded in SJL, both entries being in error. On the ap- pointment of a CONSUL for Denmark, see Report on Appointment of Consul at Co- penhagen, 10 Jan. 1792.

To Commissioners of the Federal District

GENTLEMEN Philadelphia Aug. 28. 1791.

Your joint letter of the 2d. inst. to the President, as also Mr. Carrol's separate letters of the 5th. and 15th. have been duly re- cieved. Major Lenfant also having arrived here and laid his plan of the Federal city before the President, he was pleased to desire a conference of certain persons, in his presence, on these several sub- jects. It is the opinion of the President, in consequence thereof, that an immediate meeting of the Commissioners at George town is requisite, that certain measures may be decided on and put into a course of preparation for a commencement of sale on the 17th. of Octob. as advertised. As Mr. Madison and myself, who were present at the conferences, propose to pass through George town on our way to Virginia, the President supposes that our attendance at the meeting of the Commissioners might be of service to them, as we could communicate to them the sentiments developed at the con- ferences here and approved by the President, under whatever point of view they may have occasion to know them. The circumstances of time and distance oblige me to take the liberty of proposing the day of meeting, and to say that we will be in George town on the evening of the seventh or morning of the 8th. of the next month, in time to attend any meeting of the commissioners on that day, and in hopes they may be able in the course of it to make all the use of us they may think proper, so that we may pursue our journey the next day. To that meeting therefore the answers to the several letters before mentioned are referred.

This letter is addressed externally to Mr. Carrol only with a requisition to the postmaster at George town to send it to him by express, under the hope that he will by expresses to the other gentlemen take timely measures for the proposed meeting on the 8th.—I have the honour to be with sentiments of the highest respect & esteem Gentlemen Your most obedt. & most humble servt.,

TH: JEFFERSON

PrC (DLC); at foot of text: "Messrs. Johnson, Stewart and Carrol." FC (DNA: RG 360, DL). Tr (DNA: RG 42 DCLB). The Commissioners' JOINT LETTER TO THE PRESIDENT is in DNA: RG 42, wherein they made mention of "advice from the Governor of the low state of the Treasury of Virginia." This advice was dated 25 July 1791 and was answered by the Commissioners on 2 Aug., in which they wrote: "We are now so circumstanced that we must in a little time pay about six thousand Dollars nor can it be omitted without discrediting the undertaking. Unwilling as we are to add to difficulties, we can but take the chance of a better state of the Treasury and have drawn on you in favour of William Deakin, our Treasurer for six thousand Dollars, and begg that if it can be done it may be honor'd; if it cannot we shall be under the necessity to raise the money if we can by private Credit; for in this stage the business would be very much hurt by a want of punctuality" (Tr in Vi in hand of Samuel Coleman). On this day TJ wrote separately to George Walker as follows: "I have it in charge from the President of the United States to acknolege his receipt of your letter of the 15th. inst. and to ask the favor of you to call on me at Georgetown on the 8th. of the next month for the answer to it" (PrC in DLC).

Queries for D. C. Commissioners

[ca. 28 Aug. 1791]

Will circumstances render a postponement of the sale of lots in the Federal City advisable?—If not

Not adviseable?

2. Where ought they to be made

Left to be considered ultimately on the spot, the general opinion being only that the leading interests be accomodated.

3. Will it in that case, or even without it, be necessary or prudent to attempt to borrow money to carry on the difft. works in the City?

Doubtful if a loan can be *proposed* without previous legislative authority, or *filled* till a sale shall have settled something like the value of the lots which are to secure repaiment.

The ready money paiment increased to one fourth.

Whether ought the building of a bridge over the Eastern branch to be attempted—the Canal set about—and Mr. Peter's propo[si]sion with respect to wharves gone into *now*—or postponed until our funds are better ascertained and become productive?—

Must wait for money.
The property of reclaimed lands to be considered of.

At what time can the several Proprietors claim, with propriety, payment for the public squares wch. is marked upon their respective tracts?—

Whenever the money shall have been raised by the sale of their own lands.

Ought there to be any wood houses in the town?

No.

7. What sort of Brick or Stone Houses should be built—and of what height—especially on the principal Streets or Avenues?

Liberty as to advancing or withdrawing the front, but some limits as to height would be desireable.

No house wall higher than 35. feet in any part of the town; none lower than that on any of the avenues.

When ought the public buildings to be begun, and in what manner had the materials best be provided?—

The digging earth for bricks this fall is indispensable. Provisions of other materials to depend on the funds.

How ought they to be promulgated, so as to draw plans from skilful architects? And what would be the best mode of carrying on the Work?

By advertisement of a medal or other reward for the best plan. See a sketch or specimen of advertisement.

Ought not Stoups and projections of every sort and kind into the streets to be prohibited *absolutely*?—

No incroachments to be permitted.

11. What compromise can be made with the Lot holders in Hamburgh and Carrollsburgh by which the plan of the Federal City may be preserved?

A liberal compromise will be better than discontents, or disputed titles.

Ought not the several Land holders to be called upon to ascertain their respective boundaries previous to the Sale of Lots?

Certainly they ought.

13. Would it not be advisable to have the Federal district as laid out (comprehending the plan of the Town), engraved in one piece?

It would.
To be done; but whether by the Commrs. or artists, to be considered of.

[14] Names of streets, alphabetically one way, and numerically the other. The former divided into North and South letters, the latter East and West numbers from the Capitol.

[15] Lots with springs on them to be appropriated to the public, if practicable without much discontent; and the springs not to be sold again.

[16] The public squares to be left blank, except that for the Capitol, and the other for the Executive department which are to be considered as appropriated at present. All other particular appropriations of squares to remain till they are respectively wanted.

[17] Soundings of Eastern branch to be taken in time for the engraving.

[18] Post road through the city. Will see to it immediately.

19 Name of city and territory. City of Washington and territory of Columbia.

[20] Meeting of President and Commrs. on afternoon of Oct. 16.

RC (DLC: Washington Papers); enclosed in TJ to George Washington, 8 Sep. 1791, which see.

The queries through 13 were written by Washington in one column on or before 28 Aug. 1791. Notes 14 through 20 were set down by TJ at the conferences he and Madison had with Washington sometime between then and 8 Sep. 1791. TJ's letter to Washington of 8 Sep. 1791 suggests the answers were written by TJ prior to the meeting with the D.C. Commissioners that day and that they agreed with those answers while suggesting some additions. The notes of the Commissioner's meeting states, however, that the "queries were presented by the Secretary of State to the Commissioners and the answers thereto . . . were given and adopted" (Padover, *National Capital*, p. 70. See also Editorial Note on fixing the seat of government, Vol. 20: 38-40).

To Thomas Mann Randolph, Jr.

DEAR SIR   Philadelphia Aug. 28. 1791.

I have just now recieved your two favors of the 22d. with the information, always welcome to me, of the health of our family. Mr. Derieux's letters will go by a vessel which sails on Saturday next, consequently before his power of Attorney arrives, nor can I leave any directions to forward it, as the letter inclosing it cannot be described to the chief clerk of the office so as to authorize him to open it. Of course it will come back again to me at Monticello, for which place I set out on the 3d. of the month. I am to meet the Commissioners of the public buildings at George town on the 8th. and may possibly be at Mr. Madison's in Orange the 11th. I should be very glad if a pair of good steady waggon horses could be sent to me there on that day, as the road from thence is very hilly, my horses will be jaded and I shall there drop the horse of my companion Mr. Madison which will help us on so far. The doubt is whether you may recieve this in time, tho I hope you will.—The papers will convey to you the event of the king of France's attempt to escape.— I have a letter for Mr. Derieux, but I think it safer to reserve and take it with me. Kiss the girls for me and assure of my love. Your's Dear Sir affectionately, TH: JEFFERSON

RC (DLC); addressed: "Thomas Mann Randolph junr. esq. Monticello." PrC (MHi). In his haste to dispatch the letter, TJ may have intended but failed to acknowledge Randolph's letter of 9 Aug. 1791 (recorded by TJ in SJL as received 24 Aug. 1791, but not found) as well as that OF THE 22D.; only one letter from Randolph of the latter date is recorded in SJL or known to exist.

To James Brown

SIR   Philadelphia Aug. 29. 1791.
By the sloop Polly capt. Heath I the other day forwarded to your address a small box containing putty, which be so good as to send for me to Monticello. I am Sir Your very humble servt.,
TH: JEFFERSON

PrC (MHi).

To Joshua Johnson

SIR   Philadelphia Aug. 29. 1791.
I have now to acknolege the reciept of your several favours of Mar. 26. and 27. Apr. 4. and 18. and May 31.

Your conduct with respect to Mr. Purdie is perfectly approved, as the papers you sent on his subject shew it was not a case on which the government should commit itself: nor would they have thought of doing it, if the papers they had before recieved had not been of a very different import. We would chuse never to commit ourselves but when we are so clearly in the right as to admit no doubt.[1]

I thank you for the statements of the Whale fisheries. With respect to the Cod fishery, as you say it would cost dear, I will decline asking it: for tho' those statements are desireable at a moderate expence, they are not of a nature to justify me in procuring them at a great one. The paper indeed which you mention in your letter of Apr. 18. would be worth a good deal. I should not think 50. or 100 guineas mispent in getting the whole original,[2] from what I know already of it. However I expect it cannot be obtained.

With respect to your enquiries on the subject of Consuls, vice-consuls and Agents, you will observe that the system of the U.S. is different from that of other nations. We[3] appoint only native citizens Consuls. Where a port is important enough to merit a consular appointment, if there is a deserving native there, he is named Consul; if none, we[3] name a merchant of the place vice consul, notifying him that whenever a citizen settles there, he will be named Consul, and that during his residence the functions of the Vice consul will cease, but revive again on his departure. In the mean time the Vice consul of one port and it's vicinities has no dependance on the Consul of another. Each acts independantly in his department, which extends to all places within the same allegiance nearer to him than to any other consul or vice consul. Each may appoint agents within their department, who are to correspond with themselves. In France we have three Consuls (natives) and several vice consuls (Frenchmen). In England yourself and Mr. Maury are consuls, Mr. Auldjo is a vice consul. In Ireland Mr. Knox is consul. Each has his determinate and independant jurisdiction. This account of our system will answer your enquiries, and shew you that you may appoint agents under yourself in all ports nearer to you than to either Mr. Maury or Mr. Auldjo.

I received also the sequel of your account down to Mar. 31. all of which I find properly chargeable, the former balance being first corrected according to my letter on that subject. I must beg the favour of you to make out your account annually only, because I find it very difficult to get small bills of exchange: and I will propose the 30th. day of June to terminate the annual account, because that is the day of the year on which all the accounts within my department must be brought to a balance, the grant of money being annually for the year from July 1. to June 30. inclusive.

I inclose you a letter from the President to Mr. Young with whom he has a correspondence, and I am to ask the favor of you to let Mr. Young know that you will in future be the channel of correspondence and convey letters and packages mutually. Whatever expences of postage or transportation may occur in that correspondence, be so good as to pay, and make a separate annual statement of it, and it shall be remitted with the public balance. It is necessary to separate it from the public account because it concerns the President only and not my department.

I recieve regularly the papers you forward, tho' I have not noted them by the dates.—I am with great esteem Dear Sir Your most obedt. humble servt.,·   TH: JEFFERSON

RC (DNA: RG 59, CD); addressed: "Joshua Johnson esquire London"; endorsed as received 8 Oct. 1791, as answered 6 Apr. 1792, and as delivered "ⱳ the Mary Capt. McKinsey." PrC (DLC). FC (DNA: RG 59, DCI).

Johnson's role in the case of MR. PURDIE is discussed in Editorial Note and group of documents on the impressment of Hugh Purdie, and others, 17 July 1790. The PAPER of which TJ requested Johnson to procure a copy was Lord Hawkesbury's *A Report of the Lords of the Committee of Privy Council, appointed for all Matters of Trade and Foreign Plantations, on the American Trade. 28th January 1791*, a vigorous defense of British mercantilism which opposed any significant commercial concessions to the U.S. and spoke optimistically of the formation of a pro-British party in the Senate (see Editorial Note and group of documents on commercial and diplomatic relations with Great Britain, 11 Dec. 1790). TJ had just received a lengthy summary of this document from Tench Coxe, who had received it in turn from William Temple Franklin, and was naturally eager

to obtain a copy of the full text (see Coxe to TJ, 27 Aug. 1791, Vol. 18: 268). As TJ feared, Johnson could not procure a copy of Hawkesbury's report (Johnson to TJ, 6 Apr. 1792).

In his 15 Aug. 1791 letter to the noted English agricultural writer Arthur Young, Washington acknowledged receipt of the latest issue of Young's *Annals of Agriculture and Other Useful Arts* and a bag of Chicorium Intybus grass and promised that he would soon provide the information requested by Young "with respect to the prices of Lands, Stock, Grain, [and] amount of taxes" in the U.S. (Fitzpatrick, *Writings*, XXXI, 339-41). Washington was responding to a 25 Jan. letter from Young that had arrived on 30 July in which Young stated that he was thinking of moving to America because of the heavy burden of taxation in England (DLC: Washington Papers).

¹ This sentence added prior to posting.
² Preceding three words substituted for "it," deleted.
³ This word substituted for "they," deleted.

To Thomas Johnson

SIR   Philadelphia Aug. 29. 1791.

The President having recieved a joint letter of the Commissioners on the subject of regulations, and two separate letters from Mr. Carrol on other subjects, as also Majr. Lenfant's plan these have been the subjects of conferences held at his desire and in his presence. He has concluded an immediate meeting of the Commissioners necessary, to take preliminary measures preparatory to a commencement of sale on the day appointed. As Mr. Madison and myself, who were at those conferences shall be passing thro' Georgetown on our way to Virginia, he wished the meeting of the Commissioners could be so timed as to enable us to communicate to them the ideas

developed at the conferences and approved by the President, supposing we might be able to resolve any doubts of the Commissioners
on those subjects in whatever points of view they might present
themselves. We shall be in Georgetown the evening of the 7th. or
morning of the 8th. of the next month in time for attending the
Commissioners on that day, and in hopes they may in the course of
it make all the use of us they may desire, so that we may pursue
our journey the next morning. Time and distance have obliged me
to take the liberty of proposing the day. A letter to the joint Commissioners is gone to George town, and I write this separate one to
you viâ Baltimore to multiply the chances of your recieving it in
time. I am with great & sincere esteem Dear Sir Your most obedt.
humble servt.,   TH: JEFFERSON

PrC (DLC). This was written at the request of the President (Washington to TJ, 29
Aug. 1791).

To David Ross

SIR   Philadelphia Aug. 29. 1791.
   The time of my departure for Virginia being now fixed on the
2d. or 3d of the ensuing month, I am able to say I shall arrive about
the 13th. at Monticello where I shall be happy to find a letter from
you which may enable us to have our difference of opinion decided.
My stay in Virginia will not be of more than three or four weeks,
and it will not be in my power to leave my own house. I am with
great esteem Sir Your most obedt. humble servt.,
                                                       TH: JEFFERSON

PrC (DLC). On TJ's DIFFERENCE OF OPINION with Ross, see TJ's letter to him of 6
May 1791.

To William Short

DEAR SIR   Philadelphia Aug. 29. 1791.
   I am to acknolege the receipt of your No. 67. June 6. 68. June
10. 69. June 22. 70. June 26. 71. June 29. the three last by the
British packet. My last to you was of July 28. by a vessel bound to
Havre. This goes to the same port, because accompanied by newspapers. It will be the last I shall write you these two months, as I
am to set out for Virginia the next week. I now inclose you a copy

of my letter of Mar. 12. to Mr. Carmichael which you say was not in that of the same date to you. There was no paper to accompany it but St. Marie's, which you say you recieved.—I inclose you also a copy of our census written in black ink so far as we have actual returns, and supplied by conjecture in red ink where we have no returns. But the conjectures are known to be very near the truth. Making very small allowance for omissions which we know to have been very great, we are certainly above 4. millions, probably about 4,100,000.—There[1] is a vessel now lying in Philadelphia, advertising to receive emigrants to Louisiana gratis, on account of the Spanish government. Be so good as to mention this to M. de Montmorin, who will be a judge what we must feel under so impudent a transaction.—You observe that if Drost does not come you have not been authorized to engage another coiner. If he does not come, there will probably be one engaged here. If he comes, I should think him a safe hand to send the diplomatic dye by, as also all the dyes of our medals, which may be used here for striking off what shall be wanting hereafter. But I would not have them trusted at sea but from April to October inclusive. Should you not send them by Drost, Havre will be the best route. I have not spoken with the Secretary of the treasury yet on the subject of the presses, but believe you may safely consider two presses as sufficient for us, and agree for no more without a further request.

The decree of the National assembly relative to tobo. carried in French or American ships is likely to have such an effect in our ports as to render it impossible to conjecture what may or may not be done. It is impossible to let it go on without a vigorous correction. If that should be administered on our part, it will produce irritation on both sides, and lessen that disposition which we feel cordially to concur in a treaty which shall melt the two nations as to commercial matters into one as nearly as possible. It is extremely desireable that the National assembly should[2] themselves correct the decree by a repeal founded on the expectation of an arrangement.

We have as yet no news of the event of our second expedition against the Indians.—I am with great & sincere esteem Dear Sir, your friend & servant,   TH: JEFFERSON

PrC (DLC). FC (DNA: RG 59, DCI), lacking marginal note mentioned in note 1 below.

TJ's critically important LETTER OF MAR. 12 to William Carmichael instructed him to take advantage of the seizure of a clerk of Joseph St. Marie by Spanish officials east of the Mississippi in territory claimed by the United States to urge the government of Spain to recognize the United States' right of navigation on this vital waterway (printed as Document VI in group of documents on the threat of disunion in the

West, 10 Mch. 1791). The National Assembly's 1 Mch. 1791 decree RELATIVE TO TOBO. levied a discriminatory duty of 25₶ per quintal on tobacco imported into France in American ships (*Archives Parlementaires*, XXIII, 595).

The invitation of the Spanish government to pay emigrants' passage to LOUISIANA represented a change in policy from that announced in Nov. 1790. See TJ to George Washington, 2 Apr. 1791, for a more expansive account of TJ's view of invitations to U.S. citizens to emigrate to Spanish territories.

¹ TJ wrote in the margin: "[Se]e inclos[ed] paper," no doubt referring to those mentioned above.

² TJ first wrote and then deleted "do it itself."

From George Washington

DEAR SIR   Monday Morning August 29th. 1791

The enclosed for Mr. Young, I pray you to put under cover to Mr. Johnson—the other for Mr. Vaughan may go in like manner, or otherwise, as you may think best;—both however by the Packet.

The letter for Mr. Carroll I also return—besides which, were you to write a line or two to Mr. Johnson, addressed to the care of the Postmaster in Baltimore, *it might be* a mean of giving him earlier notice of the intended meeting.—The Plan of Carrollsburgh sent me by D. Carroll it will be necesary for you to take along with you. To settle something with respect to *that* place and Hambg. which will not interfere with the genl. Plan is difficult, but essential.— There are other Papers also which it may be useful for you to have.— Mode of improving, Regulations &ca. &ca. will be subjects to occupy your thoughts upon.—I am always Yours,

GO: WASHINGTON

RC (DLC); addressed: "Mr. Jefferson"; endorsed by TJ as received 29 Aug. 1791 and so recorded in SJL.

On letter to Arthur YOUNG, see TJ to Joshua Johnson, 29 Aug. 1791; that for

VAUGHAN was Washington to Samuel Vaughan, 25 Aug. 1791, acknowledging Vaughan's of 10 May 1791 from London (DLC: Washington Papers). The letter for Daniel CARROLL was TJ to Commissioners of the Federal District, 28 Aug. 1791.

To Benjamin Banneker

SIR   Philadelphia Aug. 30. 1791.

I thank you sincerely for your letter of the 19th. instant and for the Almanac it contained. No body wishes more than I do to see such proofs as you exhibit, that nature has given to our black brethren, talents equal to those of the other colours of men, and that the appearance of a want of them is owing merely to the degraded condition of their existence both in Africa and America. I can add with truth that no body wishes more ardently to see a good system commenced for raising the condition both of their body and mind to what it ought to be, as fast as the imbecillity of their present existence, and other circumstances which cannot be neglected, will admit.—I have taken the liberty of sending your almanac to Monsieur de Condorcet, Secretary of the Academy of sciences at Paris, and member of the Philanthropic society because I considered it as a document to which your whole colour had a right for their justification against the doubts which have been entertained of them. I am with great esteem, Sir Your most obedt. humble servt.,

Th: Jefferson

PrC (DLC); at foot of text: "Mr. Benjamin Banneker near Ellicot's lower mills. Baltimore county." Engraved facsimile of Tr in Banneker's hand (PHC).

To Condorcet

Dear Sir Philadelphia Aug. 30. 1791.

I am to acknolege the reciept of your favor on the subject of the element of measure adopted by France. Candor obliges me to confess that it is not what I would have approved. It is liable to the inexactitude of mensuration as to that part of the quadrant of the earth which is to be measured, that is to say as to one tenth of the quadrant, and as to the remaining nine tenths they are to be calculated on conjectural data, presuming the figure of the earth which has not yet been proved. It is liable too to the objection that no nation but your own can come at it; because yours is the only nation within which a meridian can be found of such extent crossing the 45th. degree and terminating at both ends in a level. We may certainly say then that this measure is uncatholic, and I would rather have seen you depart from Catholicism in your religion than in your Philosophy.

I am happy to be able to inform you that we have now in the United States a negro, the son of a black man born in Africa, and of a black woman born in the United States, who is a very respectable Mathematician. I procured him to be employed under one of our chief directors in laying out the new federal city on the Patowmac, and in the intervals of his leisure, while on that work, he made an Almanac for the next year, which he sent me in his own handwriting, and which I inclose to you. I have seen very elegant solutions of Geometrical problems by him. Add to this that he is a very worthy

[98]

and respectable member of society. He is a free man. I shall be delighted to see these instances of moral eminence so multiplied as to prove that the want of talents observed in them is merely the effect of their degraded condition, and not proceeding from any difference in the structure of the parts on which intellect depends.

I am looking ardently to the completion of the glorious work in which your country is engaged. I view the general condition of Europe as hanging on the success or failure of France. Having set such an example of philosophical arrangement within, I hope it will be extended without your limits also, to your dependants and to your friends in every part of the earth.—Present my affectionate respects to Madame de Condorcet, and accept yourself assurance of the sentiments of esteem & attachment with which I have the honour to be Dear Sir Your most obedt & most humble servt,

TH: JEFFERSON

PrC (DLC); at foot of first page of text: "M. de Condorcet."

The FAVOR in question is Condorcet's 3 May 1791 letter to TJ and an enclosed report on a unit of measure by the French Academy of Sciences (see also Editorial Note and group of documents on report on weights and measures, at 4 July 1790). Benjamin Banneker was of course the NEGRO mentioned by TJ. For a discussion of the possibility that Condorcet may not have received this letter or its enclosure, see Silvio A. Bedini, *The Life of Benjamin Banneker* (New York, 1972), p. 161-2.

To James Currie

DEAR SIR   Philadelphia Aug. 30. 1791.

Being to set out for Monticello in two or three days, I have only to acknolege the receipt of your favor of July 25. and to inform you that a judgment will be very soon obtained in your case. In a conversation I had with Mr. Morris, to engage him to favor your interests as far as he could with justice, he assured me he had settled with Dr. Griffin, and that the balance due was about £4500. for which ballance his bonds had by mutual consent been lodged in a third hand as security for Dr. Griffin's performing certain conditions, which he said he was sure he would never perform, and therefore he considered himself as clear of all demands. He would not name to me either the conditions, or the hand in which the bonds are. Considering them therefore as only meant to be concealed, I have desired Mr. Barton (the lawyer) to draw forth this deposit if possible, by his interrogatories, and to have the bonds changed, in the hands where they shall be found, with your demand after Mr. Morris's shall be satisfied.—A thousand letters to write oblige me to conclude here with assurances of the esteem of Dear Sir Your friend & servt,

TH: JEFFERSON

PrC (MHi).

John Tayloe Griffin had come to Philadelphia in April hoping to recover debts owed him by Robert Morris in order to satisfy those he owed James Currie. William Barton soon reported progress in his legal efforts to recover Currie's debt (Currie to TJ, 13 Apr. 1791; TJ to Currie, 10 July 1791; and Barton to TJ, 1 Sep. 1791).

To Delamotte

SIR   Philadelphia Aug. 30. 1791.

I am now to acknolege the reciept of your favors of Feb. 9. Mar. 25. and Apr. 24. as also of the several packages of wine, carriages, &c. which came safe to hand, and for your care of which be pleased to accept my thanks.

I am sensible of the difficulties to which our Consuls are exposed by the applications of sailors calling themselves American. Tho the difference of dialect between the Irish and Scotch and the Americans is sensible to the ear of a native, it is not to that of a foreigner, however well he understands the language, and between the American and English (unless of particular provinces) there is no difference sensible even to a native. Among hundreds of applications to me at Paris, nine tenths were Irish, whom I readily discovered, the residue I think were English: and I believe not a single instance of a Scotchman or American. The sobriety and order of the two last preserve them from want. You will find it necessary therefore to be extremely on your guard, against these applications. The bill of expences for Huls is much beyond those aids which I should think myself authorised to have advanced habitually, until the law shall make express provision for that purpose. I must therefore recommend to you to hazard only small sums in future, until our legislature shall lay down more precise rules for my government.

The difference of duty on tobo. carried to France in French and American bottoms has excited great uneasiness. We presume the National assembly must have been hurried into the measure without being allowed time to reflect on it's consequences. A moment's consideration must convince any body that no nation upon earth ever submitted to so enormous an assault on the transportation of their own produce. Retaliation, to be equal, will have the air of extreme severity and hostility. Such would be an *additional tonnage* of 12₶-10s. the ton burthen on all *French* ships entering our ports. Yet this would but exactly balance an *additional duty* of 6₶-5s the hogshead of tobo. brought in *American ships* entering in the ports of France. I hope either that the National assembly will repeal the measure, or the proposed treaty be so hastened as to get this matter out of the way before it shall be necessary for the ensuing legislature to act on it. Their measure, and our retaliation on it which is unavoidable, will very illy prepare the minds of both parties for a liberal treaty. My confidence in the friendly dispositions of the National assembly, and in the sincerity of what they have expressed on the subject, induce me to impute it to surprize altogether, and to hope it will be repealed before time shall be given to take it up here.—I have the honour to be with great esteem, Sir, Your most obedient humble servt.,   TH: JEFFERSON

PrC (DLC). FC (DNA: RG 59, DCI).

The PROPOSED TREATY refers to the National Assembly's 2 June 1791 decree requesting Louis XVI to negotiate a new treaty of commerce between France and the United States (*Archives Parlementaires*, XXVI, 710).

To James Duane

DEAR SIR   Philadelphia Aug. 30. 1791.

The bearer hereof, Mr. Osmont, is a young gentleman who was very particularly recommended to me from France, and who very particularly deserved it as he is a young man of extraordinary merit and talents. I take the liberty of asking your advice to him in the following case wherein I am not sufficiently informed to counsel him. A Frenchman of the name of Le tonnelier, who was connected with Penet in the Oneida country, and claimed a part of the lands given there by the Indians to Penet, or to Penet and him, went to France where he offered them for sale. Mr. Osmont had just then received from his ruined parents their blessing and what guineas they could raise, to go abroad to seek his fortune. He determined to come to America, and was persuaded by Le tonnelier to take his lands and give him his money. He did so, and this money enabled Le Tonnelier to run off from his creditors, without having made a regular conveyance to Mr. Osmont, who now wishes to be advised whether he might hope for success were he [*to*] undertake the trouble and expence of going to the Oneida country to seek after the land. On this subject my own inability to advise him makes me ask for him the charity of your information. I am with great esteem Dr. Sir Your most obedt. humble servt.,   TH: JEFFERSON

RC (NHi); addressed: "The honourable James Duane New York favored by Mr. Osmond."; endorsed. PrC (DLC). TJ's efforts on behalf of Louis Osmont are discussed in note to TJ to Osmont, 10 July 1791.

To C. W. F. Dumas

DEAR SIR   Philadelphia Aug. 30. 1791.
I am to acknolege the reciept of your favors of Jan. 23 Feb. 15. Apr. 8. and May 24. with the intelligence they contained, and the regular transmission of the Leyden gazette by the British packet.

A course of tranquil prosperity leaves me nothing to detail to you. The crops of the earth are again promising, public credit remains high, and a general content prevailing thro the states. A first expedition against the Indians this summer has been succesful, having ended in killing 30 odd, capturing 50. odd, and burning 3 towns. A second is gone against them. These we hope will suffice to induce them to accept our peace and protection, which is all we ask of them. You will wonder they should need to be beaten into this. It is the effect of insinuations from our neighbors.

I shall hope, before the meeting of Congress, to recieve your account brought down to the 30th. of June last past, as I am to lay before Congress a statement of the accounts of my department to that day in every year.—I am with very great & sincere esteem Dear Sir Your most obedt. & most humble servt.,   TH: JEFFERSON

PrC (DLC). FC (DNA: RG 59, DCI).

To Joseph Fay

SIR   Philadelphia Aug. 30. 1791.
I am to acknolege the receipt of your favor of the 9th. inst. and to thank you for your attention to my request of the Maple seed. Every thing seems to tend towards drawing the value of that tree into public notice. The rise in the price of West India sugars, short crops, new embarrasments which may arise in the way of our getting them, will oblige us to try to do without them.

The Bennington paper has been desired to be forwarded to me

regularly. The Quebec paper would indeed be a most valuable acquisition to me. If you can be instrumental towards it's being sent to me regularly, I should be extremely glad of it. The cost of it should be annually discharged with that of the Bennington paper.

We have no news yet of the event of our second expedition against the Indians.—The king of France's flight and recapture is the subject of universal attention at present. I have still entire confidence in the result of that revolution, and that it will enable republicanism to hold a firm countenance here and prove to the world that man can be governed by reason more effectually than by rods and chains. But should it fail, he would be a coward indeed who would give up his liberty for f[ear] of losing it.—I am with great esteem, Dear Sir your most obedt. humble servt.,   Th: Jefferson

PrC (DLC).

To Joseph Fenwick

Sir   Philadelphia Aug. 30. 1791.
The object of the present is principally to acknolege the receipt of your favors of Feb. 10. Mar. 22. 29. and Apr. 26. and the cases of wine forwarded for the President and myself, for your care of which be pleased to accept my thanks. I hope you have drawn on Mr. Short for the balance of 143₶-9s due to you.

The difference of 6₶-5s duty on tobo. carried in French and American bottoms makes an extreme impression here. Notwithstanding the dispositions expressed by the National assembly to treat on a friendly footing, I fear a retaliation will be thought indispensable, which if equivalent to their duty on our vessels will have the appearance of hostility. An *additional tonnage* of 12₶-10s the ton burthen on all *French ships* entering the ports of the U.S. would be but equivalent to an *additional duty* of 6₶-5s the hogshead on all tobo. carried in *American ships* into the ports of France. I take for granted the National assembly were surprised into the measure by persons whose avarice blinded them to the consequences, and hope it will be repealed before our legislature shall be obliged to act on it. Such an attack on our carriage of our own productions, and such a retaliation would illy prepare the minds of the two nations for a liberal treaty as wished for by the real friends of both.

I trouble you again in the affairs of my neighbor M. de Rieux, whose letters I leave open for your perusal, as they will explain their object, together with the one addressed to yourself. I must ask the favor of you to advise Mr. Plumard de Rieux of Nantes as to the best mode of remitting the money hither, as that will be much better known to you on the spot, than to me at this distance.—I am with great esteem Dear Sir Your most obedt. humble servt.,

TH: JEFFERSON

P.S. I will beg of you to procure the speediest remittance possible to M. de Rieux of Virginia as I know him to be in pressing distress.

PrC (DLC). FC (DNA: RG 59, DCI).

To James Maury

DEAR SIR   Philadelphia Aug. 30. 1791.

I am to acknolege the reciept of your favor of the 23d. of June, and of the copy of the Corn law, which was the first information I had of it's passage, and is now the only information of it's form.

You observe that some masters of vessels refuse to comply with your requisitions to furnish the particulars of your reports. To this we are obliged to submit until the legislature shall go thro their Consular bill and decide whether they will oblige the masters or not to render accounts.

The crops of wheat in America have been remarkeably fine. A drought about the time of harvest and since that, has afflicted certain parts of the country beyond any thing known since the year 1755. Albemarle is among the most suffering parts. Corn is there now at 20/. There have been fine rains lately which will recover the tobo. in some degree, but the corn was past recovery.—I am with great & sincere esteem, Dear Sir Your friend & servt.,

TH: JEFFERSON

RC (ViU); addressed: "Mr. James Maury Mercht. Liverpool," and in another hand: "᭭ Alexander Capt. Coffin"; stamped "LIVERPOOL SHIP"; endorsed in part: "recieved the 24 Octr. and 10 Novr." PrC (DLC). FC (DNA: RG 59, DCI).

To Gouverneur Morris

DEAR SIR   Philadelphia Aug. 30. 1791.

My letter of July 26. covered my first of exchange for a thousand dollars; and tho that went by so sure an opportunity as to leave little doubt of it's receipt, yet for greater security I inclose a second.

The tranquillity of our country leaves us nothing to relate which may interest a mind surrounded by such bruyant scenes as yours. No matter; I will still tell you the charming tho' homespun news, that our crops of wheat have been abundant and of superior quality; that very great tho partial drough[ts] have destroyed the crops of hay to the North and corn to the South, that the late rains may recover the tobo. to a midling crop, and that the feilds of rice are promising.

I informed you in my last of the success of our first expedition against the Indians. A second is gone against them the result of which is not yet known. Our public credit is good. But the abundance of paper has produced a spirit of gambling in the funds which has laid up our ships at the wharves as too slow instruments of profit, and has even disarmed the hand of the taylor of his needle and thimble. They say the evil will cure itself. I wish it may. But I have rarely seen a gamester cured even by the disasters of his vocation.—Some new indications of the ideas with which the British cabinet are coming into treaty confirm your opinions, which I knew to be right, but the Anglomany of some would not permit them to accede to. Adieu my dear Sir Your affectionate humble servt.,

TH: JEFFERSON

PrC (DLC). FC (DNA: RG 59, DCI). To SJL entry for this letter TJ noted: "[dupl. xcha.]." BRUYANT: French word for "noisy," a reference to the din of London.

From William Short

DEAR SIR   Paris Aug. 30. 1791.

I wrote to you very fully six days ago by the way of Havre—this letter will be sent to London to be forwarded by the English packet which sails next week—it incloses one for the secretary of the treasury.

The assembly have at length completed their *charte constitutionelle*. In abolishing the requisite formerly decreed for *members of the legislature* they have augmented somewhat that of *electors*. Still it is so inconsiderable as not to exclude from that body men who are poor enough to be dependent for their subsistance or that of their families, on those who are rich enough to purchase their votes— this is with reason considered as a great defect in the constitution. In abolishing all titles of nobility the assembly have preserved that of *Prince* for the members of the Royal family—they are excluded however from any of the places which depend on the choice of the people. The Duke of Orleans and his friends opposed the decree with all their force. He declared he was ready to resign all the rights attached to the members of the Royal family rather than be deprived of those of a French citizen. This like all the other efforts which he has made during the present revolution, only served to expose him to the sarcasms and contempt of his enemies.

It was expected that the committees would to day propose the mode of offering the constitution to the Kings acceptance. It seems however that they intend first to fix the manner of reforming the constitution by conventions—that subject is made the order of to day—the mode of acceptance will probably be proposed in the course of the week. The opinion at present is that the King will accept the constitution making some observations on the parts which he considers defective. By one of those vicissitudes which takes place in the course of revolutions the three members who formerly were the demagogues of the assembly (A. Lameth, Duport and Barnave) have now lost all their favor and gained in some measure the confidence of the King and Queen—there is no doubt that they have secret communications. This triumvirate resolved to risk every thing to attain the ministry, have removed all the obstacles, except the decree of the assembly which excludes its members. They have attempted in vain to have it repealed—it is now said that they have prevailed on the King to include this among the alterations he will ask. The assembly however being aware of the motive and being constant in the sentiment of jealousy of their own members and particularly violent at this moment in the hatred of these three, will certainly reject any proposals for changing this decree. The certainty of this may perhaps also prevent their being made. It seems certain however that this triumvirate has been too long accustomed to rule and are of dispositions too active in intrigue to allow themselves to be condemned to nullity for two years, without making every effort to prevent it.

The King remains in the same state of confinement as yet. He receives any of the French nation that he pleases, and as well as the Queen, has always a great number who go to pay their court. The *corps diplomatique* are not admitted, they all go to M. de Montmorin's except the Swedish Ambassador. The assembly have decreed that the King's guard shall consist of 1200 men of his own choice, to be paid out of the civil list—they reserve to themselves however the right of organising the corps. Until that is done he will of course be guarded by those who are not of his choice.

The elections for the next assembly are going on. The members will assemble here in the course of the next month and probably displace their predecessors in the early part of October. The clubs which are dispersed throughout the Kingdom, and who have under the pretence of watching the several *fonctionaires publics* arrogated to themselves all the powers of government, will control the elections in most places. It is feared therefore that the next assembly will be composed of many violent, exagerated and bad men. As the general opinion however is that they are to have some limits to their powers, it may be hoped that they will not trespass all bounds in usurping the exercise of all the branches of government; and if so, they will not cause the present assembly to be regretted as its members seem to flatter themselves.

The intelligence which continues to arrive from S. Domingo increases the alarms here. It is probably much exagerated by the different parties for different purposes, but is in reality bad enough. The troops there have taken side with the white inhabitants who are unanimously against the decree in favor of the *gens de couleur*. The commissaries intended to be sent there so long ago have resigned—others named have set out—whilst at Brest the assembly determined (a few days ago) that their departure should be suspended until the colonial committee should have made their report on the late troubles. It is said they sailed before this determination could be announced to them. This is the more unfortunate as they will go with orders to enforce the decree of May 15. and it is probable the assembly will either repeal or modify it. The colonial committee however are so much divided on this subject that several of its members have quitted it.

Nothing new has taken place in the political state of Europe since my last. I then announced to you the certainty of peace in the North among the Christian powers. The Turks abandoned by those who have hitherto kept the countenance of supporting them, must necessarily subscribe to the conditions offered by the Empress of Russia. The principal is the cession of the territory on the Russian side of the Dniester. The late successes of the Imperial arms do not admit of the Crimea being brought into question. Mr. Pitt will probably have an advantageous treaty of commerce to present to the next Parliament as a compensation for the late expences of arming ostensibly against that power. The British arms have been more successful in Asia than their negotiations in Europe. The last advices from that quarter shew that the capital of Tippo Saib is in peril. It was expected that Lord Cornwallis would soon force him to a general action which could not fail to be fatal.

Spain has hopes of some respite on the coast of Africa by the interposition of the new Dey of Algiers. The seige of Oran it is said is suspended. The pride of the Spanish cabinet does not permit them to abandon their possessions on that coast, which certainly occasion much more expence than they are worth. The edict lately made with respect to foreigners, designed principally against the French, is so difficult of execution and productive of so much inconvenience that explanatory amendments have become necessary. They have been published two or three times successively. The edict occasions much injury and discontent among some parts of the community. It will probably fall into desuetude.

The gazettes will be sent as usual by the way of Havre. In them you will see a state of the French commerce for the years of 88 and 89. It is formed by the committee of commerce and has been laid before the assembly to shew that the revolution has not an unfavorable influence, even in the midst of its disorders, on the commercial operations of this country. I beg you to remain fully persuaded of the sentiments[1] of respect & affection with which you have ever known me to be, Dear Sir, Your friend & servant,

W. SHORT

PrC (DLC: Short Papers); at head of text: "No. 78." Tr (DNA: RG 59, DD). Recorded in SJL as received 22 Oct. 1791. Enclosure: Short to Hamilton, 30 Aug. 1791, announcing that "the bankers at Amsterdam have in consequence of my letters to them had a loan contracted for in behalf of the U.S. for six millions of guilders" (PrC in DLC: Short Papers; printed in Syrett, *Hamilton*, IX, 128).

In an effort to prevent the dissemination of revolutionary propaganda by foreigners residing in Spain, the Spanish government issued a royal EDICT on 20 July 1791 which required foreign residents to become subjects of the King of Spain or else leave the country (Richard Herr, *The Eighteenth-Century Revolution in Spain* [Princeton, 1958], p. 256-7).

[1] PrC ends here; remainder of closing is added from Tr.

From Joseph Fenwick

SIR Bordeaux 31 August 1791.

The foregoing is a copy of my last respects covering a report of the vessels that entered and cleared from this port the first six months of the present year, copy of which is also inclosed.

The political situation of France is at present an obstacle to the commercial intercourse with America. The difficulty of procuring specie, its high price, the very low exchange with the neighbouring Countries, and the incertitude of the Government are circumstances that opperate against the Americans and tend to discourage many from resorting to the french markets with their produce. The late bad crops of wine and very high price of Brandy (the principal export to America) also contribute. I hope in a little time things will be permanently established. The Constitution will soon be presented to the King and on his disposition toward it, will depend the tranquillity and credit of the Country. If he accepts freely, all will probably go well, but if he rejects it, it is to be feared the Country will be plunged into a greater state of incertitude, division, and discredit, than it has been since the begining of the Revolution. There is very little doubt but the King will accept, yet the National Assembly seem to be preparing for a refusal, by augmenting their Troops on the frontiers and providing against an invasion.

I could wish it was possible to engage all American Sailors that come out of the Country to be provided with a certificate of their Citizenship, and that there was a law to oblige each vessel to take home two or three men that might be in real distress in foreign ports, or that the Consuls were furnished with some funds and directions to aid them. I have been obliged in several instances to make advances to releive such as were in actual want, and to procure them a passage home; which I hope the United States will repay. I have and shall avoid as much as possible going into any expence on their account, but there are instances when necessity and humanity require it. With the greatest respect & consideration I have the honor to be Sir Your most obedient & most humble Servant,

JOSEPH FENWICK

RC (DNA: RG 59, CD). Recorded in SJL as received 3 Nov. 1791. Dupl (same); in another hand; at head of text: "Copy"; endorsed by TJ as received 10 Mch. 1792.

To Alexander Hamilton

Aug. 31. 1791.

Th: Jefferson presents his respectful compliments to the Secretary of the Treasury and incloses him the proposed letter to the Minister of France, in which however he shall be glad to make any modifications of expression to accomodate it more perfectly to the ideas of the Secretary of the Treasury. It will be necessary to shew it in it's ultimate form to the President before it be sent.

PrC (DLC). Not recorded in SJL. PRO-POSED LETTER: Draft of TJ's letter to Ternant, 31 Aug. 1791. For description of text of enclosure and alteration made at Hamilton's suggestion, see note 1 to TJ to Ter-nant, 1 Sep. 1791. See also Hamilton to TJ, 31 Aug. 1791 and Editorial Note to group of documents on American debt to France, at 10 Apr. 1791.

From Alexander Hamilton

[Philadelphia, 31 Aug. 1791]

Mr. Hamilton presents his compliments to the Secretary of State. He would think the turn of expression on the whole safer, if instead of what follows the words "depreciated medium" the following was substituted—"and that in the final liquidation of the payments, which shall have been made, due regard will be had for[1] an equitable allowance for the circumstance of depreciation."

Under 31 Aug. 1791 TJ recorded in SJPL receipt of an undated letter from Hamilton of which no holograph has been found. The above is reprinted from John C. Hamilton, ed., *The Works of Alexander Hamilton* (New York, 1851), IV, 240. Hamilton's texts were not always accurately presented by this editor, as may be seen on the same page wherein he quotes the draft of TJ's letter to Ternant without exactness. However, the modification which Hamilton proposed was incorporated in TJ's text in the form given above, with a single unimportant change (see note 1). Whether this was an error of the editor or a choice of a word preferred by TJ cannot be determined.

[1] In TJ to Ternant, 1 Sep. 1791, "to" is employed.

From David Humphreys

Lisbon, 31 Aug. 1791. The enclosed papers reveal that the report of Louis XVI's rejection of the French constitution, mentioned in his last letter, is premature. The Gazettes from France that arrived tardily yesterday were probably delayed in Spain. The Gazettes of Leyden forwarded with this letter were delivered by sea to save postal expenses. The two English packets that arrived here late last week brought few letters and some newspapers containing a note from Burgess to the master of Lloyd's Coffee House proving that "the British Ministry believe a Peace in the North will certainly be effected."—French affairs continue to arouse widespread interest. He is the only member of the diplomatic corps, with the possible exception of the minister from Prussia, who is not an enemy to the French Revolution. It is difficult for him to become acquainted with other members of the diplomatic corps because it is almost impossible to avoid the subjects of "Revolution and Politics" in conversation. He cannot conceal his own opinions and thinks it indiscreet to endeavor to try to change the opinions of others.—The Papal nuncio, the most respected member of the diplomatic corps, spoke well of him in private letters to one of the professors at Mafra. Last week he spent a day with the nuncio, the secretary of the Inquisition, and several other ecclesiastical dignitaries "at a beautiful Quinta belonging to the Fathers of Mafra, which is very near this City." During this visit the nuncio received foreign letters by special courier but nothing important occurred. "I cultivate the friendship of this Class of Society the rather, because I have found many extremely worthy Characters among them, because they are capable of making in proper places impressions much to the advantage of my Country, and because on occasions their friendly influence might possibly be very useful to us. In truth it is fashionable among them to speak well of the United States."—At first M. Chalons, the French ambassador, treated him politely, thinking he was an Englishman. Since then he has had little contact with Chalons and none at all with the Dukes of Luxembourg and Coigny, the latter of whom resides with the ambassador. Chalons has been especially friendly with the Margrave of Anspach.—In his letter of 7 June he mentioned that the Chevalier de Caämona, the Spanish chargé d'affaires, was interested in a diplomatic appointment to America, and he had since tried to use him to influence the Spanish ministry to negotiate with the U.S. Caämona has now lost interest, having been appointed minister to Switzerland. Yesterday he visited him on the eve of his departure but was unable to engage him in political conversation.—All the English here have been attentive and polite to him. "In short Persons of no nation have been more so." He lent "the Federalist, Gazettes, and other publications" to several English gentlemen who were eager to learn more about the United States.—There is no truth to the report in one of the enclosed papers that English ships carrying fish lately arrived here. He is authorized to say that not one vessel with new fish has yet arrived.

RC (DNA: RG 59, DD); 4 p.; at head of text: "(No. 32)"; endorsed by TJ as received 25 Oct. 1791 and so recorded in SJL. Tr (same).

To John Paul Jones

DEAR SIR   Philadelphia Aug. 31. 1791.

I am to acknolege the receipt of your favor of Mar. 20 with the several papers it inclosed, which were duly communicated to the President. No proof was necessary to satisfy us here of your good conduct every where. In answer to your request to obtain and transmit the proper authority of the U.S. for your retaining the order of St. Anne conferred on you by the Empress, I can only say that the Executive of our government are not authorized either to grant or refuse the permission you ask, and consequently cannot take on themselves to do it. Whether the legislature would undertake to do it or not, I cannot say. In general there is an aversion to meddle with any thing of that kind here, and the event would be so doubtful that the Executive would not commit themselves by making the proposition to the legislature.

Our new constitution works well, and gives general satisfaction. Public credit is high. We have made a successful expedition against the Indians this summer, and another is gone against them, which we hope will induce them to peace. A census of our numbers taken this summer, gives us reason to believe we are about 4,100,000 of all ages and sexes. A state of tranquil prosperity furnishing no particular and interesting events to communicate to you, I have only to add assurances of the constant esteem & attachment of Dear Sir your most obedt. humble servt.,   TH: JEFFERSON

PrC (DLC); at foot of text: "Admiral Paul Jones." Tr (DNA: RG 59, DCI).

Jones had received the ORDER OF ST. ANNE from Catherine the Great in 1788 as a result of his service with the Russian Black Sea fleet during the Battle of Liman against the Turks (Jones to Potemkin, 13 July 1788, F. A. Golder, *John Paul Jones in Russia* [New York, 1927], p. 109-10).

To Thomas Leiper

SIR   Philadelphia Aug. 31. 1791.

On bringing together my accounts before my departure I find I have occasion for about 50. or 100. dollars more, and should therefore be glad of a note from you to be discounted at the bank for so much.

I expect about half a dozen hhds. of tobo. more by captain Stratton during my absence, which please to receive and pay the expences of.—I am Sir Your very humble servt.,   TH: JEFFERSON

PrC (ViU).

To Pierre Charles L'Enfant

Wednesday Aug. 31.

Th: Jefferson presents his compliments to Majr. Lenfant, and begs the favor of him to come and take a dinner with him and Mr. Madison alone tomorrow at half after three, as they wish to converse with him before their departure on several matters relative to George town.

RC (DLC: Digges-L'Enfant-Morgan Papers). Not recorded in SJL.

From Peyton Short

SIR   Indian-Queen Augst. 31. 1791

I am a brother of Mr. W. Short, the Gentleman whom you have so long honored with your friendship and patronage.—My great Anxiety to obtain some intelligence respecting him, induces me to impose so far on your goodness of heart as beg the favor of you to acquaint me with the latest Advices you have received from him.

Has he ever forwarded to your Cover any Letters for me?—Will you suffer me to leave with you a few lines to be transmitted him by the first safe Conveyance?

I shall, tomorrow, set off for Virga. If you have any Commands in that quarter, should be happy to be honored with them.—I am, Sir, respectfully Yrs. &c., PEYTON SHORT

RC (MHi); endorsed by TJ as received 31 Aug. 1791 and so recorded in SJL.

From William Short

DEAR SIR Paris August 31. 1791.

I had the honor of writing to you yesterday by the English packet. This inclosing a letter for the Secretary of the treasury, will be delivered to you by a M. de Barth, son to the person of that name who is gone to settle in the western country. I have not seen him, but have promised his brother who seems to be a worthy to introduce the bearer to you.

You will see in the gazettes sent, as low down as this date, that an embarkation of troops took place in Spain in July, and that from the state of provisions on board it was conjectured they were for some part of the gulph of Mexico. I know nothing further of this matter but suppose it probable. You will have been informed of it, if true, by Mr. Carmichael.

Count de Mercy has gone to England. It is said he is to remain there eight or ten days only. Blumendorf takes so much pains here to convince every body that the object of his journey is merely to examine the English mode of agriculture that I am fully convinced that it is not the true one. It is certain that the affairs of France have been presented to the consideration of the principal powers of Europe by the Emperor, and particularly to that of England and Prussia. I know not whether their ideas are brought to any common center on this subject and it will be probably difficult. Yet when we consider the influence which Kings Nobility and Clergy have in Europe, and that they consider the French revolution as in some degree personal against them, joined to the inviting situation of French affairs, both here and in their islands, it is impossible to say what effects and prodigies of union may be brought about against them. The issue of Count de Mercy's journey to England will perhaps give some better grounds of conjecture.

I know not whether the malevolence of England still continues the same against the U.S., but should suppose it probable at least at St. James's. If so it would be possible that that court engaging in a cruisade with other powers against the French revolution might have a disposition to make use of so good an opportunity of seeking some revenge of us. I have no reason whatever for suspecting it, yet it seems so natural that that country should see with a jealous eye our present prosperity and particularly our increasing navigation and must naturally have so much desire to check that part of our growth that some act against our fisheries or against the carrying branch of our commerce would seem to me not absolutely impossible. The apprehensions entertained of the U.S. by the European powers having colonies in the islands would make them well enough satisfied, it seems to me, with any step that should tend to prevent our having a navy.—I mention these circumstances, as you will easily see Sir, as being merely conjectures founded on other conjectures. All may be groundless perhaps but it is not amiss to be aware of them.

You will learn from the Secretary of the Treasury the probability of the U.S. being able to make loans in London. I sent him in my letter of the 23d. inst. a copy of Mr. A. Donald's letter to me on that subject. Not knowing Mr. Donald myself and having heard you speak of him as being long and well acquainted with him, I have referred him to you to say how far his authority is to be relied on. I am with the sincerest affection & regard, Dear Sir, your friend & servant,   W: SHORT

P.S. I inclose you a state of the Nantucket fishery at Dunkirk for the years 88. and 89. I have not been able yet to get that of L'Orient.— I lately sent to the bankers at Amsterdam the amount of the articles which you direct them to charge to the *department of State*. I find there are some trifles omitted. I mention this because the account I shall send you will differ to this amount from that you will probably have received from them before I could put them right.

PrC (DLC: Short Papers); at head of text: "No. 79." Tr (DNA: RG 59, DD). Recorded in SJL as received 28 Oct. 1791. The enclosed letter was Short to Hamilton, 31 Aug. 1791 (printed in Syrett, *Hamilton*, IX, 132-6).

Legal Opinion of Edmund Randolph

[Philadelphia, ca. Aug. 1791]

The question is, whether any punishment can be inflicted on persons, treating with the Indian tribes, within the limits of the United States, for lands, lying within those limits; the preemption of which is vested in the United States?

The constitution is the basis of fœderal power.

This power, so far as the subject of Indians is concerned, relates

1. To the regulation of commerce with the Indian tribes.
2. To the exclusive right of making treaties.
3. To the right of preemption in lands.

1. Even if the act, supposed in the question, were really an infraction of the right to regulate commerce, there could be no penalty, unless the law prescribed it.

Accordingly a law of the second session enters into such a case, but only forfeits the merchandize carried into the Indian country. No other law affects it.

2. Without an existing law, no treaty, or compact made by an individual of our nation with the sovereign of another, and not partaking of a treasonable quality, is punishable.

It seems indeed to be an assumption of the sovereignty of the United States in this respect.

But the compact being in the name of an individual, does virtually disclaim any assumption of public authority. If it be void, the United States cannot be deprived of their rights.

It may be indecent and impertinent for a citizen thus to behave. But where no law is, no crime is.

3. As to the right of preemption.

No man has a right to purchase my land from my tenant.

But if he does purchase, I cannot sue him on the supposition of damages, arising from the mere act of purchase.

Nor could the United States sue the purchaser of the right of preemption, since the purchase itself is void, and their interest cannot be prejudiced by any purchase, which an individual can make.

Far less would the purchaser be indictable.

But it undoubtedly is in the power of congress, to regulate commerce with the Indians in any manner to guard the right of making treaties, by forbidding the citizens to meddle under a penalty, and to provide a security to their preemption by passing adequate laws.

Until this shall be done, I conceive that this commerce is protected by no law, but the act above mentioned; that an interference in the article of treaties has no penalty, denounced against it; and that the fœderal property, like that of individuals, must depend upon existing laws.

It may perhaps be proper, if the testimony be strong, to warn all persons by proclamation that the rights of government will be inforced; and possibly a monitory message to the Indians might have a good affect. (signed) EDM: RANDOLPH

Extract from Edmund Randolph to George Washington, 12 Sep. 1791 (DLC: Washington Papers).

The provenance of this document is necessarily a matter of conjecture. No evidence has been found to indicate what prompted TJ to request this legal opinion from Randolph, TJ left no record of when he received it, the original text has not been found, and the opinion itself is written in such general terms that it is impossible to be completely certain of the specific occasion for it. Nevertheless, it seems likely that Randolph drafted this opinion in response to the efforts made by Zachariah Cox and his associates in the Tennessee Yazoo Company in the spring and summer of 1791 to create a settlement at Muscle Shoals. TJ expressed concern about Cox's activities to the governor of the Southwest Territory in August 1791, and Washington echoed this concern in a letter to Randolph written two months later, laying special emphasis on the opposition of various Southwestern tribes to Cox's scheme (TJ to William Blount, 12 Aug. 1791; Washington to Randolph, 10 Oct. 1791, Fitzpatrick, *Writings*, XXXI, 386-7). If this surmise is correct, TJ probably asked Randolph for an opinion on the legal ramifications of Cox's actions at about the same time that he wrote to Governor Blount, which means that the opinion itself could have been written at any time after 12 Aug. but before 2 Sep. 1791, the date TJ left Philadelphia for Monticello. The LAW OF THE SECOND SESSION was the 22 July 1790 act of Congress regulating trade and intercourse with the Indians (*Annals*, II, 2301-3).

From William Barton

[*Philadelphia*], *1 Sep. 1791*. The suit of Currie v. Griffin, an action of attachment, was begun at the July term of the Pennsylvania Supreme Court and the sheriff has now attached the goods of Isaac Hazlehurst, Matthew McConnell, William Shannon, Richard and James Potter, and Robert Morris as garnishees. Currie will be entitled to judgment at the January term of court and interrogatories may then be filed which will require them to confess any property of Griffin they may possess or know of. "If the Garnishees . . . should refuse to appear and make such disclosure, it will be taken *pro concesso*, that they have in their hands Goods, or Monies &c. of the Defendant; and Execution will go, accordingly, against them. This mode of procedure . . . is in virtue of an Act of our Legislature passed in Septr. 1789." He knows that lawyers do not normally charge for their services, but he asks that Currie be informed that "about forty dollars may be deemed a reasonable fee. I do not, however, wish it may be viewed as *a Charge*."

RC (DLC); 3 p.; endorsed by TJ as received 1 Sep. 1791 and so recorded in SJL. TJ had the $40 FEE paid to Barton immediately (Memorandum for Henry Remsen, Jr., 2 Sep. 1791).

From George Clymer

SIR   Thursday Sept. 1.

I have obtained from a gentleman much engaged in the trade to the Danish west Indies, the inclosed list of duties, but can learn little of the home regulations, scarcely any intercourse subsisting between Denmark and America.—It is said that Governor Walterstroff is returned to Santa Croix from Denmark, with a new sett of colonial regulations, favourable to the Island trade, by which a trade also favourable to the United states is understood, but they were not published when the last vessel sailed.—Another gentleman will endeavour to get for me the national code. I am Sir Your most obt st,   GEO CLYMER

RC (DLC); endorsed by TJ as received 1 Sep. 1791 and so recorded in SJL. Enclosure not found.

To Madame de Rausan

à Philadelphie ce 1er. 7bre. 1791.

J'ai bien reçu, Madame, les vins de Rauzan, que vous avez eu la bonté de m'envoyer, en bon etat, et sans qu'il y avoit rien de cassé; et j'en suis tout-à-fait content. J'ai l'honneur de vous en demander actuellement un envoi de cinq cens bouteilles de l'année 1785. *en bouteilles*, et de deux barriques de 250 bouteilles chacun, de la recolte de l'année 1790. *en futaille*: et je vous prie de vouloir bien faire passer le tout a Monsr. Fenwick, qui vous en fera payer le montant.— J'ai l'honneur d'etre avec des sentiments tres respectueux Madame, Votre tres humble et tres obeisst. serviteur,   TH: JEFFERSON

PrC (MHi); at foot of text: "Madame Briet de Rausan, locataire au convent de Notre dame, rue Dutra, à Bordeaux."

Henry Remsen, Jr. to Tobias Lear

SIR   September 1st. 1791.

The power or commission from the President of the United States to the Secretary of the Treasury to borrow money, I will do myself the honor of sending you a copy of tomorrow, as we shall be wholly employed this day in completing several pieces of business that require finishing before Mr. Jefferson sets out.—The powers from the Secretary of the Treasury to Mr. Short, and to Messrs. Willinks, Van Staphorsts and Hubbard, founded on the power to him, have been sent to Mr. Jefferson for perusal and but returned to the Secretary of the Treasury.

The bearer will wait for the Commissions now sent, which, with the ratified Contracts, will be transmitted to the Secretary of the Treasury this afternoon.—I have the honor to be &ca,

H. REMSEN JUNR.

FC (DNA: RG 59, SDC).

To William Short

DEAR SIR   Philadelphia Sep. 1. 1791.

Finding it necessary to send to Bordeaux for my year's stock of wine, I inclose herein a bill of exchange of Mr. John Vaughan of this place on Messieurs Le Coulteux & co. for a thousand livres Tournois. Besides this, being in the moment of my departure for Virginia, I leave my letter open with a friend to put into it another bill of £40. sterling on London, which a broker is now in quest of for me. I make them payable to you, because if you will be so good as to negociate them, it will save a good deal of time, which would be lost by their going to Bordeaux and back again, and I have therefore, in the inclosed, mentioned it to Mr. Fenwick, to whom I must ask you to write a line.

The most ingenious workman in America, Mr. Leslie, a watchmaker, being the same to whom we are indebted for the idea of the rod-pendulum as an Unit of measure, has desired me to endeavor to get some workmen for him, to wit, a good movement maker, a finisher, and casemaker, used to gold and silver work. He will advance the expences of their passage from Paris to Philadelphia, and when they arrive here, he will expect them to work for him exclusively, till they shall have reimbursed him his advances, and the money for their subsistance which may be necessary in the mean time, he allowing them the Paris price for their work by the peice.— I am in hopes you can get such men without any other trouble than speaking to Mayer or Chanterot. Should they not be able to bear their own expences from Paris to Havre, be so good as to pay them on my account and reimburse yourself from my funds. Their passage from Havre to this place may be paid here.

I inclose you a letter from your brother who arrived here yesterday, and went off to-day. He wrote me a line on his arrival, which I received just as I was setting out to dine in the country. I immediately wrote to ask him to come and dine with me to-day, but his hurry prevented him; so that he is gone without my seeing him. I am, my dear Sir, with constant affection your sincere friend & servt,

TH: JEFFERSON

PrC (MHi); at head of text: "Private."

TJ's letter of this date to FENWICK, recorded in SJL, has not been found, but TJ's accounts for 1 Sep. 1791 indicate he was asking Fenwick to use the £40 bill of exchange to pay for wine he had purchased. According to another entry under the same date, the bill on John Vaughan was to buy for Henry Knox 250 bottles of 1785 wine and a "cask of equal quality of 1790. from Mde. de Rauzan." On the following day,

TJ purchased from Robert LESLIE an odometer, no doubt for use on the journey to Virginia that began on that day (TJ's Account Book, 2 Sep. 1791, MS in NN; immediately following this entry TJ kept a journal of the trip, marking the miles and recording information about the terrain). The invitation to Peyton Short TO COME AND DINE, not recorded in SJL, is missing. See Memorandum for Henry Remsen, Jr., 2 Sep. 1791.

From Daniel Smith

Southwest Territory, 1 Sep. 1791. Enclosing proceedings of Gov. Blount. Suggests official seal be prepared for Gov. Blount at public expense to replace private one thus far used in the territory.

RC (DNA: RG 59, SWT, M-471/1); 2 p.; endorsed by TJ as received 23 Oct. 1791 and so recorded in SJL. Enclosure: Journal of Executive Proceedings of the

Southwest Territory, 7 Mch.-26 July 1791 (same; in Smith's hand; full text in Carter, *Terr. Papers*, IV, 443-6). Tr (DNA: RG 76, Yazoo Land Claims).

To Jean Baptiste Ternant

SIR   Philadelphia. Sep. 1. 1791.

I have communicated to the President what passed between us the other day on the subject of the paiments made to France by the United States in the assignats of that country, since they have lost their par with gold and silver: and after conferences, by his instruction, with the Secretary of the Treasury, I am authorised to assure you that the government of the United States have no idea of paying their debt in a depreciated medium, and that[1] in the final liquidation of the payments, which shall have been made, due regard will be had to an equitable allowance for the circumstance of depreciation.— I have the honor to be with sentiments of the most perfect esteem & respect Sir Your most obedt. And most humble servt.,

TH: JEFFERSON

PrC (DLC); at foot of text: "Monsieur de Ternant, M. P. de France." FC (DNA: RG 360, DL). Dft (DLC: Madison Papers); dated 31 Aug. 1791, but text is identical with the above except for the important change suggested by Hamilton and accepted by TJ (see note 1 below). Dft contains no indication of the alteration proposed and may or may not be the text that TJ submitted to Hamilton. The fact that Dft is in the Madison Papers suggests that TJ conferred with Madison on the subject either before or after incorporating Hamilton's amendment in the final text as approved by Washington.

On the matter under discussion, see Editorial Note and group of documents on the American debt to France, at 10 Apr. 1791.

[1] From this point on in TJ's draft the text reads: ". . . they will take measures for making their payments in their just value, avoiding all benefit from depreciation, and only desiring on their part to be guarded against any unjust loss from the circumstances of mere exchange." On Hamilton's advice TJ deleted this passage and caused the final text to read as above.

From Francis Eppes

DR SIR   Richmond September 2d. 91

Your favour the 8th. of August I have recd I wish it was in my power to say somthing certain about Mazzeis claim against Capt. Hyltons Estate. It ought certainly to be paid. I never had his account and wish you coud assertain its amount. Every thing in my power shall be done to have settle'd whilst you are in Virginia. I have no part of the Estate in my hands having given in an account of my administration and given up all the bonds in my possession to Ralph Hylton to collect. I shall see him shortly and will inquire what prospects he has for collection. The Estate is by no means insolvent.

Betsy and my self wou'd most willingly meet you at the mountain were it possible. She on the twenty fourth of last added a fine girl to the Family, which will put it out of her power to move any distance from home this Winter. As soon as I hear of your arrival will do my self the pleasure of waiting on you if you find it impossible to pay a Visit to Eppington. We shall be happy in seeing Mr. and Mrs. Randolph and Polly with you. Your account of Jack gives me great pleasure. I hope he will at all times make it his Study to do as you would have. He will in that case avoid love and dissipation two things which woud effectually put an end to every thing like study and improvement and of course destroy the purpos of his leaving his own country.

Jack in his last letter mentiond you wish'd to have thirty pounds sterling annually laid out in Books. That sum can be lodged in Philadelphia at any moment you please. I have the promis of bills on that place for whatever will be necessary for Books or other purposses. Against I see you will thank if can fix what sum will be necessary for both those purposses. I am with best wishes for yourself & all with you Dr. Sir Your Friend, FRANS. EPPES

RC (ViU); endorsed by TJ as received 17 Sep. 1791 and so recorded in SJL.

TJ's FAVOUR THE 8TH. OF AUGUST was actually dated the 7th.

Memorandum for Henry Remsen, Jr.

[2 Sep. 1791]

Mr. Remsen will be so good as to get the bill of excha. for 40.£ sterl. on London from Mr. Franks in time to put into Mr. Short's letter, and to endorse to Mr. Franks the check on the bank for 186⅔ Dollars which I leave with him.[1]

——

Put Mr. Short's letters under cover to M. la Motte.

——

To pay Herbst & Lex 115D. 80C[2] as soon as he shall have received my quarter's salary, and take in my order given them.

——

I leave in the bank about 80 or 90 dollars, over which as well as my salary, I leave a power with Mr. Remsen.[3]

——

Furnish Mr. Eppes what money he may have occasion for.[4]

——

After I shall be gone, give Ducomb the 6. dollars I leave with Mr. Remsen, and his certificate and discharge him. If he asks the reason, he may be told that I do not find that he understands house business well enough.

——

Pay Francis 6. Dollars the 1st. day of October.

——

Answer any other expences for my house or affairs, which Mr. Remsen may judge necessary. I have great confidence in the discretion of Petit and Francis, and in any applications of this kind they may make to Mr. Remsen. My horses particularly will have occasion for provender.[5]

——

The balance now in the bank will cover the above purposes. As soon after my quarter's salary is recieved, as the stable loft shall be in readiness, to recieve hay, I shall be obliged to Mr. Remsen to

[121]

purchase five ton of good clover hay for me: as also 18. cords of oak wood for the kitchen, and 9 cords of beach or ash, for the house.[6]

As also to pay Mr. Barton 40. dollars for Dr. Currie.[7]

Beach's and Fenno's newspapers to be sent to me till the 15th. inst. and all letters, not appearing to cover newspapers and other large packets.

Open Mr. Short's letters which come before the President's departure, and if they are written 'private' at the head seal them up again: if not, then communicate them to the President, and afterwards send them to me.[8]

MS (DLC); undated; at head of text: "Memorandums"; entirely in TJ's hand except for (1) endorsement by Remsen reading: "Mr. Jeffersons direction's Septemr. 2d. 1791" and (2) marginal notations in Remsen's hand as indicated below. Not recorded in SJL.

The bill of exchange TJ ordered obtained from Isaac FRANKS, a Philadelphia broker, was to be sent to Short who was told to give it to Joseph Fenwick to pay for wine TJ had purchased (TJ to William Short, 1 Sep. 1791). HERBST & LEX were grocers on Market Street in Philadelphia (Philadelphia Directory, 1791). DUCOMB: Philippe Ducombe had begun working for TJ in April, perhaps in response to the following advertisement TJ placed in the Philadelphia General Advertiser in January and February 1791: "Wanted, A Genteel Servant, Who can shave and dress well, attend a gentleman on horseback, wait at table, and be well recommended. Enquire at Market-street, No. 274." Obviously, Ducombe failed to meet TJ's expectations. TJ personally discharged another servant, Jacob, who had worked for him since July, just prior to leaving for Virginia (Account

Book, 1 July, and 2 Sep. 1791, MS in NN; see TJ to Andrew Ellicott, 15 Sep. 1791, for related information). The fee for BARTON is discussed in William Barton to TJ, 1 Sep. 1791.

[1] In the margin to the left of this and the following two paragraphs, Remsen indicated that the task had been "done."

[2] The "D." and "C", written above the amounts, have been lowered to the line and placed after the figures to which they apply.

[3] Remsen wrote in the margin: "This money has not been touched."

[4] Remsen noted in the margin of this and the following four paragraphs that he had done the task.

[5] In addition to writing "Do." [Ditto] in the margin, Remsen also wrote "No. 6" next to this paragraph.

[6] Remsen wrote in the margin: "The hay purchased is the best clover," and "Bought 8 3/4 cords ash, 15 1/2 do..Oak."

[7] Remsen noted in the margin that he had done this and the following request.

[8] Remsen wrote in the margin: "None arrived before the Remsens departed and of course none were opened."

From Stephen Cathalan, Jr.

Marseilles, 4 Sep. 1791. Acknowledges receipt of TJ's letter of 13 May and its pleasing account of American affairs.—He hopes that France will soon enjoy internal tranquillity. "Matters are now at a critical Period. The constitution will be presented very soon to the King. He must be rendered at a full Liberty to accept it Legaly. It appears that the rational of the Nal. Assy. and of the Nation, has now the Majority, and that all will end well; but if unfortunately the Factious abusing of the Blindness of the People, were to succeed in their Plan, France would be totaly distroyed by Factions. . . . In the next Month the result will be known. It is expected with anxiety."—His exequatur has been returned from Paris "without any alteration as you will observe by the Inclosed Copy of a letter from the Minister of Marine" and he has been "lawfully acknowledged by the admiralty of the Place; and all the other administrative Powers." French officials and foreign consuls "are greatly Satisfied to [see] the U. S. reppresented here, but they all regret that any american vessels appears in the harbour, on account [of] the algerians."—The English brig *Favorite*, Capt. Smith, arrived from Philadelphia 10 Sep. [Aug.?] with a cargo of tobacco and staves, but the tobacco could only be sold for reexport because it was not brought under French or American colors. The price of brandy has risen throughout France because of the "Poor Prospect of the Crop of wine"; it costs £50₶ p. ql. Brut at Cette and might rise to £60₶., and only costs £42₶ here because of imports from Naples and Trieste. Good tobacco is selling from £42₶ to £45₶., and good Virginia tobacco would fetch £48 to 50₶ p. ql. Marc. Whale oil sells for £36₶. p. ql. of 90 ℔. English, and there is none in town. Carolina indigo is £5₶. to 6₶.15 p. ℔. Because of a rise in wheat prices caused by "a very meedling" French crop good American wheat would obtain at least £38₶ to 39₶. p. charge and superior fine flour £40 to 42₶. per Bushel. Indian corn sells for £17₶ to 18₶. per charge and Carolina rice £16₶. to 17₶. p. ql. No dried rice has yet appeared. He encloses news of Algiers.

RC (DNA: RG 59, CD); 2 p. Recorded in SJL as received 10 Feb. 1792. Enclosures: (1) Letter from Thevenard, Minister of Marine, to M. Lejean, Deputy to the National Assembly, Paris, 15 July 1791 (Tr by Lejean [?] in DNA: RG 59, CD, where it is filed with the above letter from Cathalan). (2) For THE NEWS ON ALGIERS AFFAIRS, see the following enclosure.

ENCLOSURE

Algier's affair

Marseilles the 4th. September [1791]

By Two Letters that I have received from algiers the 13th. and 26th. Last July, from Capn. Richd. obrian American Captive in that Place, I am Informed that—

"the 12th. July 1791—a 6 1/2 A M. this day departed this Life Mahomet Pacha Dey of algiers, and was Immediately succeeded by the addi Hasnagi or Prime Minister, now hassan Pacha.

I have reason to think that U. S. will more easily obtain a Peace with the present dey, than the Former as he always Seemed Inclinable to Serve the Americans. I hope his present exalted Station will not errace from his Memory his former Friendly Sentiments toward the Americans.

And Perhaps the Present Dey will be more favourable towards the Ransom of Captives than the Former. Other Changes will take Place in this Government, these Particulars please to Communicate to U. S. He was the only one of the Ministry that was in Favor of the Americans when M. Lamb was in algiers in 1786."

July 26th.

"Several Slaves a few days Past have been redeemed on Moderate Terms, one was priced at 1500 Sequins and was redeemed at 755 Sequins, a Sailor Priced at 1000 Sequins was redeemed at 600, the first Cost. So I hope the Present Dey will make Some abbatment on the Ransom of the present 13 American Victims. We are dayly Experiencing the Fruits of Independance and Liberty.

If there had been any positive orders in algiers Relative to our Ransom, a more favorable opportunity Could offer the present we Might be got of perhaps as reasonable Terms as other Captives, but I have my Fears that also this favorable opportunity which offers towards obtaining Peace and our Release, will Pass unnoticed by our humane countryman in Europe.

The Same time I cannot Say Positively if there will be any abatment relative to our Ransom, and as to orders to have our Ransom assertained, I must observe to you that it is not Customary; the only way is for Some Persons to be Empowered to redeem us on the Best terms they Can; we have been most cruelly treated and neglected by our Country and not the Least assurance of Liberty given us, Kept in this tormenting state of Suspense to make us feel Slavery too fold.

I presume the Portugeise will Immediately be trying for a Peace, redeeming now their Su[bjects?]. If they Succeed, America will experience Fatal consequences.

The Peste has broke out at Trunison a City in the Western Province of the Regency. Should it reach algiers it may occasion Some abbatment to be made in our Ransom by reducing our present number to 1/2.

The Dey has renewed the Treaties of Peace and tribute, with all the Christian nations he is at Peace with; a few days Past, the Dean's [Dane's] Annual Tribute arived, 400 Barrels of the Powder Brought by the Deans is returned.

You mention that the British Consul Should be Kept Ignorant relative to American affairs, I readily agree with you; the English, Spanish, and Perhaps the Chamber of Commerce of Marseilles will do everything to Bafle the Americans in obtaining a Peace with this Regency."

I have Judged proper to transcribe as above the Letters of Capn. obrien, deducting only from the Said the repetitions, and Some too strong expressions (caused by the desespired Situation of that Poor men and his Brothers Sufferers) against the american administration, for not having taken measures for their Liberty; which I beg you to forgive considering the deplorable life they are Supporting.

On the Contrary I Earnestly entreat you, Sir, to use all your endeavours towards Congress to obtain a Sum of Money, for the redemption of these Captives, with which the Person Employed by Congress, will treat for the Best advantage their Redemption, and Immediately after, Lay the foundation of a Lasting treaty of Peace if he is Empowered to do it; the advantages of such a treaty is Known enough; If you will confide me Such important affair, I will go myself to Algiers and do everything to Succeed; but as Great advantages for U. S. will arise by trading on their own vessels in the Mediteranean, if such treaty can't take place on acceptable terms, my avice would be to feet the soonest Possible Two small Frigates to protect your Flag in the Mediteranean, in cruising on the Coast of Barbary and distroy their Cruisers; I am Sure that Two American Frigates well manned, [would] do more against these Pirates, than all the Marine of Maltha, Naples, Genoa, and Rome, and Giving to Europe an example of what are ablest Americans in their undertaking, would at Such time Shew to the algerians that their Interest to be in Peace with the U. S.

I have not answered to Capn. Obrien, not knowing what I can Say him to Comfort him; nor I will do nothing further on that affair but on your Positive Orders.   STEPHEN CATHALAN JUNR.

MS (DNA: RG 59, CD); at head of text: "To Thos. Jefferson Esqr. Secretary of State."

For a discussion of the shift in American foreign policy resulting from the succession of a new DEY OF ALGIERS, see note to TJ to Pierce Butler, 2 Dec. 1791.

From William Short

DEAR SIR   Paris Sep. 4. 1791.

The Assembly decreed three days ago that a deputation should be named to present the constitution to the King, that he should be *prié* to give such orders as he should judge proper for the guard and the dignity of his person, and finally that if he adhered to the wishes of the nation in adopting the constitution, he should be *prié* to settle the formality with which he should solemnly pronounce his acceptation in presence of the National Assembly. As it was apprehended that the King would wish for some changes in the constitution and would make observations in consequence of it, it was decreed at the same time that the constitution when completed should not suffer any alteration. It was completed yesterday in all its details as to conventions.

In consequence of this decree a deputation of sixty members of the Assembly went last night at nine o'clock to the King's appartment, and presented him the constitution. M. Thouret, as their organ, addressed him in the following terms: "Sire, L'Assemblee Nationale nous a chargés de presenter a l'acceptation de Votre Majesté l'acte constitutionel qui consacre les droits imprescriptibles du peuple Francois, qui regenere le Gouvernement et qui assure la veritable dignité du trone."

The King (appearing well satisfied with the deputation and on the whole composed and tranquil in his manner and with an air of sincerity) replied: "Messieurs—J'examenerai la constitution que l'Assemblee Nationale vous a chargés de me présenter; je lui ferai connoitre ma resolution dans le delai le plus court que puisse exiger l'examen d'un objet aussi important: je me suis determiné à demeurer à Paris: je donnerai au commandant de la garde nationale parisienne les ordres que je croirai convenables pour le service de ma garde."

He will probably pronounce his acceptation in a few days. But as it is evident that he is not freer in this acceptation than in the sanction of the laws against which he protested, it is much to be feared that the nation at large will have no confidence in this adhesion. Such a government without confidence, which is its essence, is nothing more than a state of anarchy and will be productive I fear of much misfortune.

The conduct of the King's brothers, who are of course believed to act in concert with him, though probably without reason, would of itself destroy all the national confidence in the monarch. They are openly at the head of the emigrants whose avowed plan is to enter the Kingdom in arms, as soon as they become sufficiently strong. The Count D'Artois is gone to Vienna, it is generally believed, to excite the Emperor to declare himself with respect to the french affairs, or to press him for the succours with which the emigrants have been some time flattered, with the intention probably of granting them or not according to circumstances.

The National Assembly have by a decree declared the right of the nation to change the constitution, but at the same time recommended it to be exercised seldom. If three Legislatures successively recommend a change, the fourth is to be considered as a convention. This has been judged a more peaceable mode of reforming the constitution than that by periodical conventions.

Nothing has transpired with respect to the situation of S. Domingo since my last. The report of the commissaries having sailed, as mentioned formerly, was groundless. Their departure is suspended of course until the colonial committee shall have made their report. It is so much divided in opinion that it will be difficult for them to agree on any thing. Several of the members have quitted it on that account.

The elections for the new Legislature continue to go on peaceably throughout the kingdom. Such as have already taken place shew more moderation than was expected except in the southern provinces, where those who possess the most exaggerated principles have for the most part been chosen.

The articles of peace signed between the Emperor and Turk are now published. The *statu quo* of the commencement of the war is very little deviated from. I observe that the article by which the Porte guarantees the Austrian flag against the piratical states is renewed.—You will see by the Leyden gazette inclosed an account of the negotiation between the Empress and the allied powers at Petersburg.

I learned from the Venetian ambassador last night that he had a few hours before seen in the hands of the Spanish Ambassador a formal manifest and declaration of war just received from Madrid, of that Court against the Emperor of Morocco. There have been for a long time bickerings between them, and ill usage of Spanish subjects on the part of the Emperor.—This war will probably be confined to the increase of the garrison of Ceuta and to cruises by sea. It will however be injurious to the Spanish commerce and augment the present expences of that Government and after all will probably end by a purchased peace. I am with sincerity & affection, Dear Sir, your friend & servant,   W. Short.

Tr (DNA: RG 59, DD). PrC (DLC: Short Papers; at head of text: "*No. 80*"; at foot of text: "Thomas Jefferson Secretary of State, Philadelphia"; badly faded. Recorded in SJL as received 28 Oct. 1791.

From Henry Skipwith

Dear Sir   Hors du Monde September 4th. 1791.

Your ideas (conveyed by letter 6th May) respecting our critical situation as the Representatives of Mr. Wayles, were truly comfortable, as they were coincident with my wishes, and dispel a little of the gloom which has but too long hovered over our matters.— Yesterday for the first time at the District court of P. Edward, I ventured to shew your letter to a friend of mine truly eminent in the Law. He observed *your Law* was uncontrovertable, and that from his knowledge of navigation and the African businiss, it was impossible that Mr. Wayles letter of the 14th of May could arrive previously to Farell & Jones's engagements on Acct. of the Guineaman—and consequently that such engagements were not the effect of this letter. Enclosed you have Ronalds and Marshalls opinion procured some time since.—A Subpœna in Chancery was a few days served on me, at the suit of Thomas Wigan Exr. of James Bevins decd. late of Bristol, to appear in Richmond before the Judges of the United states 22d. of November next.—This is a matter you are too well acquainted with for me to make a single comment.—However there is certainly some irregularity in this process, for to say nothing of myself and wifes being mentioned in the process before you, Mr. Eppes and wife are intirely omitted.—Paul Carrington Jnr. (Lawyer) mentioned to me yesterday, a matter which Mr. Isaac Coles Exr. of Waltr. Coles deceased some years since touched upon to Mr. Eppes and myself, to wit, a Debt due from Benjamin Harrison late deceased to his Testator—£400 and long interest. Mr. Carrington tells me he understands he fashionably died insolvent.—As the Payers of British debts into our Treasury under the Sequestration law have become exceedingly sanguine, and this important question is to be determined this Fall I take the liberty to enclose you a duplicate of the instrument of writing copied by you at the request of Hansen and which he signed, previously to my entering in conjunction with you and Mr. Eppes, into any engagement for a payment of our respective parts of Mr. Wayles's debt to Farell & Jones.—I am induced to this Sir because should the payments into the Treasury be established, my remedy I suppose must be in Chancery and lest this instrument (which you know was drawn up by myself) should be deemed somewhat inexpressive of my open and avowed intention by it, I must however unwillingly (in justice to a distressed family) call upon you to declare the circumstances relative to this matter, all of which happened in your own house and which must be recent in your memory.—I am emboldened to hope you will not be reluctant in this matter, as believe me! my dear Sir! nothing but your influence and my respect for you, could possibly have induced me to commit an act which I had often sworn never to do, and which since has given me more uneasiness than all the misfortunes which God in his vengeance has poured upon my devoted head.—For fear of yours and Mr. Eppes's death, I must endeavour by some means to perpetuate your testimony and his; but how this can be done previously to the determination of the grand question and a suit brought upon one of my Bonds, I know not.— I have annexed to the enclosed Instrument, a few interrogatories, which Mr. Eppes has seriously examined and which he says he is ready whenever called on to answer in the Affirmative.—Mrs. Skipwith who is in better health than she has been for many months, joins me in the warmest wishes for your health and happiness and hopes much to see you this Fall.—I am Dear Sir Your affectionate friend,

HENRY SKIPWITH

RC (DLC); addressed: "Thomas Jefferson Esqr."; endorsed by TJ as received 3 Oct. 1791 and so recorded in SJL. Enclosure: Agreement by Richard Hanson regarding Skipwith's payment of £4,000 into the Virginia treasury under the sequestration law (see note below).

For RONALDS AND MARSHALLS OPINION of 1 Apr. 1791, see note at Skipwith to TJ, 7 Apr. 1791. Skipwith's INSTRUMENT which he had DRAWN UP BY MYSELF was incorrectly identified earlier in this edition as having been drafted by TJ. The INTER-ROGATORIES written at the bottom of the enclosed copy of the agreement (and printed in Vol. 15) are in Skipwith's hand and must be assigned the date of this letter rather than one contemporary with the Feb. 1790 compromise worked out at Monticello among Eppes, Skipwith, and TJ concerning the Wayles debt. See Editorial Note on the debt to Farrell & Jones and the slave ship *The Prince of Wales* in Vol. 15: 645-7.

From William Short

DEAR SIR   Paris Sep. 5. 1791

I informed you in my letter of yesterday that the *acte constitutionel* had been presented to the King the evening before, by a deputation of the assembly, and that he had answered that he would examine it and make known his determination as soon as so important a subject admitted of.—The organ of the deputation, M. Thouret, in informing the assembly yesterday morning of this circumstance added "Le Roi a montré un air constamment satisfait.—Parce que nous avons vu, par ce que nous avons entendu, tout pronostique que l'achevement de la constitution sera aussi le terme de la revolution."

There seems no doubt entertained by any body of the King's acceptance. It will probably take place in a few days. It remains still to be seen whether that will inspire the confidence and give that energy to government which alone can secure the tranquillity and safety that are the true objects of a free constitution. The contrary is much to be feared. It remains still to be decided by what passage the country is to get out of the state of anarchy in which it has been for so long a time past, and which from its own nature cannot last.—I still think that a nation as enlightened as this assembled to consult on its own affairs cannot fail in time to establish that order of things which is most conformable to its real interests and happiness, and as this is certainly a well organized, free and efficient government it is hard to believe they would not at length attain such an one if left to themselves.

Foreign interference however seems to become every day more probable. The reception of the Count D'Artois at Vienna, and the interview which was to take place between the Emperor and King of Prussia in the latter part of the last month, one of the objects of which were the affairs of France, leaves no doubt as to the dispositions of those courts to interfere.—There will be difficulty perhaps when they come to agree on the means of execution. They will probably begin by negotiation making the violated rights of the German Princes in Alsace, the pretext of their interference, as I formerly mentioned to you. A short time must now inevitably remove the veil which has so long covered the designs of several european cabinets with mystery.

I omitted mentioning that immediately on the King's answer to the deputation of the assembly, the sentinels placed in his appartment and that of the Queen in consequence of the decree for suspending the Royal functions, were removed.—He gave his orders to the commandant generale, and every thing was put on the same footing as before his departure.—Yesterday the courts of the palace and garden of the Thuilleries which have been kept shut from the time of the King's arrestation were opened to the public. The walks were immediately filled and presented the air of what you were always accustomed to see, and in general the streets and environs of Paris, to the astonishment of every thinking observer, continues to present the same appearance of contentment, gaiety and security which existed before the revolution and which might be expected under the reign of order and permanent peace.—I am with the sentiments of respect & affection, of which I hope You will never doubt, Dear Sir, Your friend & servant, W: SHORT

PrC (DLC: Short Papers); at head of text: " *No. 81*"; at foot of text: "Thomas Jefferson Secretary of State Philadelphia." Tr (DNA: RG 59, DD). Recorded in SJL as received 7 Dec. 1791.

From David Hartley

DEAR SIR   Bath September 6 1791

May I beg the favour of you to give me your assistance officially, and as an old friend, towards obtaining letters patent in the united states of America, for the improvement of one of the most universal and important manufactures for the uses of life, that can exist in any country in the world; I mean the manufacture of all edged instruments of steel; than which none is more extensive or important, in every use and convenience of human life. The papers annexed to this letter will explain this point fully to you. I have letters patent for the sole and exclusive right of the invention in this Country.

I have a copy now before me of the American act for granting letters patent, and have endeavored to accomodate my application to the terms of that act. The specification annexed is the same upon which the letters patent in this Country have been granted. I have endeavored to explain the principle, and the application of the principle which constitutes the invention, in the most precise, and scientific, and intelligible terms; by which any intelligent workman, or adept person in the art and manufacture of steel, may be able to apply and use the same hereafter. If the petition, or any other branch of the application should be defective, according to the mode of your country, I will beg the favour of you to give me proper instructions, by which I may transmitt any amended or more formal application. Our friend Mr. Hammond, now minister to your Country, and whom you will recollect to have known at Paris, will do me the favour to negotiate the correspondence and I heartily wish both to him and to you, the most cordial and unanimous negotiations, in all other points whatsoever, which may contribute to the happiness, peace and prosperity of our two Countries. I beg to be most sincerely and kindly remembered to all my friends, both diplomatic and personal, in your country. I am Dear Sir with the greatest respect ever most sincerely yours,   D. HARTLEY

RC (DLC); at foot of text: "To The Honble. Thos. Jefferson Esqr. &c. &c. &c."; endorsed by TJ as received 11 Nov. 1791 and so recorded in SJL.

On 24 Feb. 1792 a PATENT was granted to David Hartley for his invention for "Hardening and tempering steel" (*List of Patents Granted . . . from April 10, 1790, to December 31, 1836* [Washington, 1872]).

From James Brown

SIR   Richmond 7th. Septr 1791.

I have your favor of the 20t.[1] ulto. and shall attend to the Box of Putty ℔ Sloop Polly Cap Heth, the articles you forwarded some time ago still remain with me, Mr. Randolph, who was here, ten days ago, desired they might remain till he sent a waggon for them.— I propose making a Shipmt. of Tobacco for France but am alarmed at the proceedings in that Kingdom. Should a Civil War ensue private property would be in danger.—I should be glade of your opinion on this head when you can Spare a moment from more urgent Business.—I am with Respect Sir Your Obt. Hble. Ser.,

                                              JAMES BROWN

RC (MHi); endorsed by TJ as received 3 Oct. 1791 and so recorded in SJL.

[1] Thus in MS; should be 29th.

From William Knox

Cork, 7 Sep. 1791. A recent trip to England on private business has prevented him from sending the shipping return requested by TJ. As soon as he arrives in Dublin he will send one to TJ covering arrivals from 1 Jan. to the present. "Mr. Nepean under Secretary of State for the Home Department of Great Britain informed me previous to my leaving London that Mr. Hammond would certainly be the person who would go to America as the Representative of England; this Gentleman is about thirty five years of age, and has been employed as Secretary of Legation to several Courts, the last of which was Spain, from whence he lately returned to solicit the appointment to America. He is appointed by the interest of the Duke of Leeds."—He recommends that in any commercial agreement with Great Britain the U.S. seek permission to have American produce reshipped from Ireland to London, Liverpool or Bristol so as to avoid being adversely affected by temporary surpluses of American goods in the Irish market.—Merchants here involved in the provisions trade complain of the loss of their traditional markets, particularly in the French West Indies, to American competition.—He has received TJ's letter of 13 May and is pleased by its favorable account of conditions in the U.S.—He hopes that during the forthcoming session of Congress provision will be made for the remuneration of consuls as he is unable to support himself in office strictly on the basis of his private income.

RC (DNA: RG 59, CD); 4 p.; at head of text: "No. 3"; at foot of text: "Honble. Thomas Jefferson Secretary of State"; endorsed by TJ as received 5 Nov. 1791 and so recorded in SJL.

TJ had requested a semi-annual shipping return of all American ships dropping anchor in consul's ports in his circular to American consuls, 26 Aug. 1790.

From Thomas Auldjo

Cowes, 8 Sep. 1791. Nothing of commercial importance has occurred here since his letter of 8 July last. Americans enjoy every advantage and attention they can expect.—British armaments have been reduced to peacetime levels "since the Allied Courts have come to an agreement with Russia about terms of peace to be proposed to the Porte for the termination of the War."—The Secretary of State still has not decided upon the ratification of his commission, but the issue will be decided when Lord Grenville returns to London. Apparently the delay is caused by their reluctance to approve consuls at new locations.

RC (DNA: RG 59, CD); 2 p.; endorsed by TJ as received 22 Oct. 1791 and so recorded in SJL.

The difficulty with Auldjo's COMMISSION is explained in note to Auldjo to TJ, 4 Nov. 1790, but see also Auldjo to TJ, 7 Nov. 1790, and Documents II and IV in group

of documents on consular problems at 20 Feb. 1791. The decision to accommodate the British government's wish to have him appointed to another post had not reached Auldjo when he wrote the above letter, but on 2 Nov. 1791 he wrote TJ that "his Britannick Majesty has been pleased to acknowledge the Commission which Congress has honoured me with for the port of Poole and in consequence I shall now be enabled to enter upon the dutys of my office which I shall hope to fulfill with honor to myself and advantage to America" (RC in DNA: RG 59, CD; endorsed by TJ as received 16 Jan. 1792 and so recorded in SJL).

From Sylvanus Bourne

SIR   Cape François Sept. 8th. 1791.

I duly received the letter you did me the honour to write me of Augt. 14th. covering a duplicate of yours of May 13th. which I acknowledged the receipt of, in a letter dated July 5th that must probably have reached you before this.

Prior to the receipt of your last I had concluded upon embarking for America soon as every prospect of obtaining a reception here had ceased. Particulars, I shall at present waive, expecting before long the pleasure of seeing you at Philadelphia.

I am unhappy to learn of the Kings defection and attempt to quit France as it must involve a good Cause in still greater difficulties, destroy confidence and create confusion. I hope however that the Genius of Liberty will finally triumph over all embarrassments and firmly place herself in that Throne which the King has seen fit to relinquish.

A new and alarming Catastrophe hath assailed this devoted Island. About the 23d. of Augst. an insurrection among the negroes took place at Lembay about 3 or 4 Leagues distant and from thence to Lemonade, being about 10 Leagues they have burned and laid waste all the Plantations. Their whole plan is marked with bitter resentment for former injuries and the cry of "les droits de l'homme" is echoed thro their Camp. They still continue their depredations and Government, for want of regular troops is unable to act offensively against them, and I fear it will be a long contest, and ruinous to the property of the Island. The City is now a perfect Garrison Pallisaded all around and Cannon mounted at every avenue.

The noble plain which fronts this City and which perhaps had not a parallel on the Globe for the rich luxuriance of its soil, elegance of its Buildings and the various decorations of art that the highly cultivated taste of its opulent possessors had given to it, is now again but a barren waste. All which gave pleasure to the eye, has been subject to a general conflagration. Here we have a lively instance of the baneful effects of Slavery, and I wish that America might add another laurel to her wreath of Fame, by leading the way to a general emancipation.

In respect to my resolution to return home, Be assured my Respected Sir, that it is far from being my choice as I had placed sanguine hopes on my present essay, but not experiencing even the most distant of those advantages belonging to my official station which you allude to, it is not in my power to tarry. I have no other prospect at all, have expended considerable money and received no income. Under these disagreable circumstances I must ask the favor of your kind notice of me in case any situation under Govt. occurs to your mind which you may think me capable of filling with propriety and you will confer an essential obligation on him whose only ambition is to find himself so situated that he may with ease fulfill every duty of Life incumbent on him and who has the honour to be with the greatest Respect Your Obt. devoted Servt,

SYLVA. BOURNE

RC (DLC: Washington Papers); endorsed by TJ as received 22 Oct. 1791 and so recorded in SJL.

Bourne's LETTER of 5 July 1791 has not been found and is not recorded in SJL.

To Thomas Newton, Jr.

DEAR SIR   George town Sep. 8. 1791.

I was in the moment of my departure from Philadelphia for Virginia when I recieved your favor enquiring how far the law of nations is to govern in proceedings respecting foreign Consuls.

The law of nations does not of itself extend to Consuls at all. They are not of the diplomatic class of characters to which alone that law extends of right. Convention indeed may give it to them, and sometimes has done so: but in that case the Convention can[1] be produced. In ours with France, it is expressly declared that Consuls shall not have the privileges of that law, and we have no convention with any other nation.

Congress have had before them a bill on the subject of consuls, but have not as yet passed it. Their code then furnishes no law to govern these cases.

Consequently *they are to be decided by the State laws alone*. Some of these, I know, have given certain privileges to Consuls; and I think those of Virginia did at one time. Of the extent and continuance of those laws, you are a better judge than I am.

Independantly of law, Consuls are to be considered as distinguished foreigners, dignified by a commission from their sovereign, and specially recommended by him to the respect of the nation with whom they reside. They are subject to the laws of the land indeed precisely as other foreigners are, a convention, where there is one, making a part of the laws of the land: but[2] if at any time their conduct should render it necessary to assert the authority of the laws over them the rigour of those laws should be tempered by our respect for their sovereign as far as the case will admit. This moderate and respectful treatment towards foreign Consuls it is my duty to recommend and press on our citizens, because I ask it for their good, towards our own consuls, from the people with whom they reside.

In what I have said I beg leave to be understood as laying down general principles only, and not as applying them to the facts which may have arisen. Before such application, those facts should be heard from all whom they interest. You, who have so heard them, will be able to make the application yourself, and that, not only in the present, but in future cases.

Dft (DLC); written by TJ on verso of address cover on which is written in an unidentified hand: "[Thom]as Jefferson Esquire Secretary of State Philadelphia." FC (DNA: RG 360, DL). Tr (DNA: RG 60, T326/1).

Under the terms of Virginia law, the master of a British vessel could apply to a justice of the peace for a warrant to apprehend a deserting British seaman and return him to his ship, or a British consul could request the governor to order sheriffs, constables, or militia officers to cooperate with the master in achieving these goals. But in the case in question the British consul in Norfolk, John Hamilton, after first having appealed in vain for assistance from some local justices, had exceeded his authority under the laws of Virginia by personally authorizing the master of a British merchant vessel to seize a British mariner who had deserted his ship (Newton to TJ, 24 Aug. 1791; Hening, x, 202-3).

In laying down GENERAL PRINCIPLES ONLY, TJ had the support of three well-known authorities—Abraham de Wicquefort, Emmerich de Vattel, and Wyndham Beawes—among whom only Vattel argued that consuls "must be accorded, to a certain extent, the protection of the Law of Nations" because they bore a commission from their sovereign and were received by the local sovereign (Wicquefort, *The Embassador and his Functions* [London, 1716], p. 40; Vattel, *The Law of Nations or the Principles of Natural Law* [Washington, D.C., 1916], p. 124; Beawes, *Lex Mercatori a Rediviva* [London, 1752], p. 260; Sowerby, Nos. 1411, 1428, 2101).

In 1793 TJ reiterated his belief in the inapplicability of the law of nations to consuls, and successive attorneys general and secretaries of state reaffirmed this principle during the next half-century. Under the impact of the nation's increasing interest in international trade, however, the State Department issued new consular regulations in 1856 and 1881 that finally placed consuls under the protection of international law (TJ to Christopher Gore, 2 Sep. 1793; Irvin Stewart, *Consular Privileges and Immunities* [New York, 1926], p. 23-33).

[1] This word interlined in Dft in substitution for "must," deleted.

[2] At this point TJ first wrote in Dft "but in the application of those laws to them, their rigor should be tempered, as far as the case will admit, by our respect for their sovereign, even where his Consul may have so acted as to forfeit his right to personal respect"; then deleted, interlined, and otherwise altered to obtain the reading: "if at any time . . . the case will admit."

To George Washington

SIR   Georgetown Sep. 8. 1791.

We were detained on the road by the rains so that we did not arrive here till yesterday about two oclock. As soon as horses could be got ready, we set out and rode till dark, examining chiefly the grounds newly laid open, which we found much superior to what we had imagined. We have passed this day in consultation with the Commissioners, who having deliberated on every article contained in our paper, and preadmonished that it was your desire that they should decide freely on their own view of things, concurred unanimously in, I believe, every point with what had been thought best in Philadelphia. They decided also the following additional matters.

Quere 2. Lots to be sold in four places, viz, on the Eastern branch, near the Capitol, near the President's house, and in the angle between the river and Rock creek.

3. The ready money payment at the sale to be increased to one fourth, and so advertized immediately. They will send advertisements to some printer in every state.

7. The houses in the avenues to be *exactly* 35 feet high, that is to say their walls. None to be higher in any other part of the town, but may be lower.

11. The compromise stated to you by Mr. Johnson has put this matter out of all dispute.

13. The map to be engraved on account of the Commissioners, and the sales of them for the public benefit.

19. They have named the City and the territory, the latter after Columbus.

Tomorrow they meet to take measures for carrying into execution all the several matters contained in the paper which I have the honor to return to you, as I believe you have no copy of it.—Mr. Madison and myself propose to pursue our journey in the morning. Four days more will bring me to my own house.—We were told in Baltimore that that place was becoming better humored towards this, and found it better that the government should be here than in Philadelphia.—I have the honor to be with sentiments of the highest respect & attachment Sir Your most obedt. & most humble servt.,

TH: JEFFERSON

RC (DLC: Washington Papers); addressed: "The President of the United States Philadelphia"; postmarked: "GEO. TOWN. SEP. 9" and "FREE"; endorsed by Washington. In recording this letter in SJL, TJ noted: "[no copy]." Enclosure: Queries for D. C. Commissioners, ca. 28 Aug. 1791 (printed above). See Editorial Note on fixing the seat of government, Vol. 20: 32-9.

From Willing, Morris & Swanwick

DEAR SIR   Philada. Septr. 8. 1791.

In Letters that we have Received from some very Respectable Houses in Europe with whom we have the honour to Correspond we have been Requested to solicit two Appointments of Consulships from the United States abroad. We can not Refuse to our Friends our solicitations with you on the Subject any more than our assurances of our firm belief that the offices will be deservedly filled should they succeed in the appointment. It will Remain with you Sir to decide on the Question—and we shall be much obliged to you if you will be pleased to favour us with your Opinion thereon. The Gentlemen Named to us are William Douglas Brodie Esqr. to be Consul for Malaga, John Ross Esqr. to be Consul for Gibraltar.

If any thing can be done to serve these Gentn. or either of them in this way We shall be happy to know it and to be made acquainted whether any and what other Steps are proper to be taken by us to succeed on this Occasion.—With very great Respect for you we have the honour to Remain sincerely Sir Your most obed hble servt,

WILLING MORRIS & SWANWICK

RC (DLC: Washington Papers); in hand of John Swanwick; endorsed by TJ as received 20 Sep. 1791 and so recorded in SJL.

From Henry Remsen, Jr.

DEAR SIR   Philadelphia September 9th. 1791

The letters [an]d gazettes have been regularly forwarded agreeably to your directions. Among those now sent is a letter from Judge Chipman, which, from it's being under a kind of flying seal and the information I received from the bearer of it, Mr. Tichenor an intimate friend of Mr. Chipman, I took the liberty of opening. You will be surprised to find, Sir, that the duplicate commission you sent in a letter to the Judge the 22d. June last has miscarried as well as the first. To relieve the anxiety and embarrassment of Judge Chipman, which Mr. Tichenor represented as very great from not having heard from you at all, since his appointment was announced in the newspapers, I thought it would be proper to make out a triplicate commission. Mr. Lear informed me it was the President's opinion, when he signed it, that it ought to go directly to Mr. Chipman, instead of being first sent to you, especially as a principal part of Mr. Tichenor's business in coming here, was to see you concerning it. I therefore delivered it to Mr. Tichenor myself, with a short letter for the Judge, mentioning the transmission of a duplicate commission the 22d. of June, which was the next day after you received his letter of the 10th. of May, whereby you was informed the first had not come to hand.

The singularity of this case will justify a request I shall make at the General Post Office, which I trust will meet your approbation, that an official enquiry may be made of the cause of the miscarriage of your second letter. Crosby does not recollect the delivery of it particularly at the post office here; but says he is confident he has always put into the Office the letters given him for the purpose, and has never lost one.

Mr. Eppes is very well. From what Mr. Ogden and others tell me, I shall think it advisable to procure your hay as soon as possible; and have requested Mr. Leiper to have the new stable loft prepared for it's reception by monday, the 12th. instant. It is scarce, and will probably be as high as £10 pr. ton before the cold weather sets in.— I have the honor to be with the greatest respect, Dr. Sir Your obliged & obedient Servt., HENRY REMSEN JUNR

P.S. The draft or press copy of your letter of June 22d. to Judge Chipman, is among your own papers, or else I should have sent a duplicate of it.

RC (DLC); endorsed by TJ as received 22 Sep. 1791 and so recorded in SJL.

The letter from JUDGE CHIPMAN was of 28 Aug. 1791 (recorded by TJ in SJL as received 22 Sep. 1791, but now missing). Remsen erred in thinking TJ had sent a duplicate commission to Chipman on 22D. JUNE LAST. It was actually transmitted in TJ to Nathaniel Chipman, 14 July 1791, which see for a note describing the difficulty Chipman experienced in obtaining his commission as a federal district judge for Vermont.

From David Humphreys

Lisbon, 10 Sep. 1791. He has just received a letter of the 19th ulto. from Carmichael delivered by Mr. Milne, who visited the President at Mount Vernon in 1779. Carmichael has sent his dispatches to America and complains of ill health. Milne said that he was "emaciated and weakened by the late attacks of the Cholic which he has suffered."—The wavering policy of Spain manifests itself in the many explanations occasioned by the royal cedula of 20 July concerning foreigners. "Mr. Milne informs that the French who were resident in Spain have been principally intended and affected by it: that it had however been extended in its operation to others: that Lord St. Helens had made strenuous remonstrances respecting three English Merchants of Alicant who had been imprisoned in consequence of it, and that the Compte de Florida Blanca had promised every possible satisfaction: that more than fourteen thousand

Passports had been obtained for Strangers to leave Madrid before he came away: that the system of favoritism and Queen-politics are worse than ever: that general irritation against the government prevails: that the Persons employed in the government seem to have lost their reason; and that the measures adopted by them to prevent a Revolution appear entirely calculated to accelerate it."—He forwards the French papers received since his letter of 31 Aug. and reports that the English packet is momentarily expected. Lord Shrewsbury, who just arrived in his yacht, notes that the fleet was being disarmed when he left England.—He has no further news about peace in the north. The Empress of Russia has forestalled the plans of the mediating powers. "The Minister of Prussia just now remarked to me, that Prussia and England having disarmed, without definitive arrangements between Russia and the Porte, he thinks the fairest concurrence of circumstances that could possibly have happened invites the Empress to prosecute her conquests to Constantinople itself.—Indeed, it should seem, that hardly any thing but her moderation can prevent it."— Yesterday he received a letter from Thomas Barclay notifying him of Barclay's arrival in Oporto and General Scott's success against the Indians. The news respecting Scott was particularly welcome because reports of the Indian war have been greatly magnified to discourage European emigration to America.— The Queen is at Mafra and the country itself is undergoing a process of gradual amelioration. But a long drought has produced a shortage of wine and fruit, though salt is still abundant. The temperature has been unusually intense and there has not been a single rain or thunder shower this summer.

RC (DNA: RG 59, DD); 4 p.; at head of text: "(No. 33)"; endorsed by TJ as received 17 Nov. 1791 and so recorded in SJL. Tr (same).

From Ezra L'Hommedieu

SIR   Southold Long Island Sept. 10. 1791.

Since I saw you at this Place I have received from Colo: Sylvester Dering of Shelter Island some Observations he had made on the wheat Insect commonly called the hessian fly, which I send you herewith inclosed with some Stubble of the yellow bearded wheat (as little subject to Injury by the Insect as any we have). By carefully examining this Stubble, by opening the Straw near the Roots and first Joints you will find many of the Insects in their chrysolis State still alive and their Inclosure or Case very Tender. This Stubble was taken from the field in the beginning of Harvest: how long it will be before the Insect comes to perfection if kept in a cool place from the sun is uncertain: but by this Experiment it is easy to see that the Insect might be brought from Germany to New York or carried from us to Europe in the Straw or Stubble but not in the wheat except by much trouble and by design. Yesterday I compared a number of the Insects taken directly from the Stubble in the field with a number that had been taken from Stubble in the same field about a month before and put in a Glass covered with Lawn (in order to observe the Time of the fly coming out) and found them to be in equal forwardness to leave their Chrysalis State. You will find one of the Straws of the Stubble I send tied round with a peice of Twine; just below the Twine you will observe a small hole and at the bottom of the same the Place where the Insect come to Maturity, and being disincumbered from its case and not being able to force its way between the Stalk and Leaf eats through the Leaf. We find many such Straws in our Stubble. The holes I believe were made by the Insect deposited last fall while the leaf was yet tender. How the Insect will extricate itself from its confinement which now remain in the Stubble I shall particularly observe. Altho the yellow bearded wheat and the red bald wheat are not supposed by our Farmers in general to be injured by the Insect yet I make no doubt but the Crop is less by some Bushels in the Acre by the obstruction in the Circulation of the Stalk made by the Insect. If this wheat is sown in poor Land the Stalk will be in proportion feeble and the crop greatly injured. In Guilford this year the same wheat was greatly hurt altho the Land was good owing to the uncommon Number of the Insect there. If wheat was the only vegitable by which these Insects are preserved it would be easy to distroy them by distroying the stubble by burning or otherwise, but I have reason to believe that other vegitables answer for their support but none so well perhaps as wheat.

I have lately received a Letter from Doctor Samuel Mitchell of Queens County (Long Island) who informs me that he is favoured with a Letter from Sir Joseph Banks President of the royal society of London upon the subject of the wheat Insect, who assures him it does not exist in England and he has no reason to beleive its existance in any part of Germany. If the Insect leave the Stubble this fall, it will then be past a Doubt (admitting Colo Derings observations) that the fly is produced in the spring and in the fall, but not three Times in a Year as I supposed to be the case when I saw you and in which he was mistaken. I shall always be happy in giving you every Information I may receive on this Subject or which my own Observations may afford and am with great Esteem & Respect Sir Your most Obedient Servt., EZRA L'HOMMEDIEU

RC (DLC); endorsed by TJ as received 22 Oct. 1791 and so recorded in SJL. Enclosure: "Colo. Dering's Observations on the wheat Insect" (same).

TJ had encountered COLO: SYLVESTER DERING, whom he described as "particularly serious in his observations on" THE HESSIAN FLY during his northern tour the previous spring. See Editorial Note and documents on the northern journey of Jefferson and Madison, at 21 May 1791.

From Tubeuf

MONSIEUR   à Richmond ce 10 Septembre 1791.

Un des avantages que j'attendais d'une létre que M. le Mis. dela Fayette m'a remise, par laquelle il veut bien me recomander a vous, etait de vous la présenter moimême, de vous exposer le Plan de l'Entreprise que je vais faire, sur les bords du clinch. Une traversée de 85 jours, du hâvre de Graces ici, moitié plus longue que je ne l'avais compté, ne me laisse pas disposer d'un instant, et me presse de me rendre a ma destination, distante encore d'ici de plus de 300 milles, afin d'arriver assez tôt, pour pouvoir y préparer un abri, contre les rigueurs de l'hiver a 35 personnes que j'ai déterminées a venir avec moi y former des Etablissemens. C'est sous ce point de vue que j'ai acheté, sur les bords du clinch, dans le Comté de Russel, cinquante cinq mille acres de terre, a raison de neuf livres tournois l'acre, dont je vais en ce moment en faire ocuper cinq mille acres, par huit familles de mes Parents et de mes amis, composées de 13 Maîtres, et de 22 Domestiques et Ouvriers. Si mon premier Etablissement prospère, ainsi que me le font esperer les facilités et l'encouragement que le Gouvernement de Virginie nous donne, les honeurs dont il nous comble, plusieurs émigrations françoises, plus considérables que celleci, se sont proposées de venir nous joindre, au Printemps prochain, et je vais dès ce moment les y disposer. Daignez, je vous prie, Monsieur, favoriser mon Entreprise, m'eclairer de vos lumieres, et m'aider de vos Conseils pour la faire réussir, et pour que je puisse la rendre utile et agréable à l'Etat. Nous portons avec nous tous les moyens que j'ai cru nécéssaires pour la former.

Je vous demande, Monsieur, la permission d'aller moimême vous en rendre compte, et de vous remétre la létre de M. le Mis. delaFayette, aussitôt qu'il me sera possible de perdre, pendant quelques jours, ma petite Colonie de vue, sans inquiétude et sans inconvénient.— Je suis avec le plus profond respect Monsieur Votre très humble et très obeissant Serviteur,   DE TUBEUF

RC (MoSHi); at foot of text: "chez le Colonel Tatham, au Capitole: à Richmond"; addressed: "Thomas Jefferson Esqr. Secretary for Foreign Affairs &c Monticello Virginia, or in Philadelphia"; endorsed as received 20 Sep. 1791 and so recorded in SJL. Enclosure not found.

Tubeuf, a French industrialist who immigrated with his family, eighteen other adventurers, and thirty servants after the failure of his coal mines in Normandy, also wrote an identical letter to George Washington on this date (DLC: Washington Papers). Tubeuf failed to attract many more French emigrants to his frontier settlement in Russell County, despite Virginia's generous assistance with finances, military protection against Indians, and clearing the wilderness. In 1795 he and his family were murdered by a gang of robbers (CSVP, VI, 112-3, 484, VIII, 241-2, 250-1, 365, 415-6; see also Marcel Rouff, *Tubeuf, un grand industriel français au* XVIIIe *siècle* [Paris, 1922]). The LETRE QUE M. LE MIS. DELA FAYETTE wrote to TJ introducing Tubeuf has not been found.

One of Tubeuf's companions wrote TJ three days later that he had a letter for him from Lafayette, but it has not been found nor did TJ record receipt of a letter from Lafayette in SJL that could be one brought to Virginia by the Frenchman (Fr. Hardy to TJ, 13 Sep. 1791, RC in DLC; endorsed by TJ as received 14 Apr. 1792 and so recorded in SJL).

From Joshua Johnson

SIR   London 12 September 1791

I had the Honor to write you on the 10th. Ultimo, which Letters went by the America Captn. Mackay, via New York, and which I now confirm, since then I am deprived of the pleasure of any of your much respected Favors.

I now inclose you Copies of Mr. Long's (Joint Secretary to the Treasury) Letters to me, in Answer to mine on the Subject of the Seizure of the Hope, and Janet at Liverpool, which the Lords of the Treasury have ordered to be liberated on Compensation being made to the seizing officers. Their Lordships have also directed the liberation of the Thomas, Captn. Vickery at Guernsey but are determined to condemn all offenders hereafter.

Mr. Hammond has at length obtained his Appointment, and Embarked in the last Packet for America. People here seem very sanguine that on his Appearance, Congress will be so much pleased that they will readily come into any Measures this Court shall ask, and that great Commercial Advantages will be granted to Britain by the United States, and that a Treaty Offensive and Defensive will be concluded; I pretend not to be capable of judging, but it strikes me that it would be as well to move slowly, and consider very well before the United States bind themselves in any thing, nor should they be too hasty in sending an Envoy in return to this Court.

You will pardon the Ideas I have taken the Liberty of throwing out, and believe me always Sir Your most Obedient and most Humble Servant,   JOSHUA JOHNSON

RC (DNA: RG 59, CD); in clerk's hand except for signature; at foot of text: "Thomas Jefferson Esqr. Secretary of State for the Department of State"; endorsed as received 29 Nov. 1791 and so recorded in SJL. Dft (same). Enclosures: (1) Charles Long to Johnson, Treasury Chambers, 1 Aug. 1791, informing him that his letter transmitting "petitions of Captns. Fendel and Griffith was transmitted to the Commissioners of the Customs on the 5th of last month," together with some papers received from Brownlow, owner of the *Janet*, sent to the board on 12 July; and that no answer had been received, but in response to Johnson's recent letter he had written to the secretary of customs "to desire as speedy a report as possible." (2) Long to Johnson, Treasury Chambers, 18 Aug. 1791, informing him that the Lords Commissioners of the Treasury, on the report of Commissioners of the Customs on the American ship *Hope* and the brig *Janet* charged with landing their cargoes at Guernsey "contrary to the Provisions of an Act of 12 Chas. 2 chap. 18; sect: 3," had concluded on the petitioners' plea of ignorance that no fraud was intended, that they had issued warrant for release of the vessels, and that "their lordships desire you will make it known . . . that the said Act will be strictly enforced in future" (Tr of both texts in DNA: RG 59, CD).

From James Swan

Paris 12th. Septr. 1791.
SIR   Rue de Montmorency No. 63.

It will give you much satisfaction to know, the Success that has attended an essay of Boston Salted Beef and pork. I ordered a barrel of each sort of these articles to be sent me last December. They were Ship'd from Boston to Rochelle, from thence to Havre and from Havre here. All these Shipments and reShipments took up about nine months, when the Commissaries named by the Minister of Marine, at my request, examined and inspected each sort, which they unanimously found excellent in quality and perfectly well preserv'd. The Certificats from the french and american Consuls determin'd the age of the different Shipments. The delay was long and distressful, as I fear'd the loss of their qualities, and in effect one had lost its pickle and was spoilt, which appear'd more favorable than if all had been in good order. Here is the report as communicated to me by M. de Verdan de la Crenne, Chairman of the Commissioners and an officer in the navy of a very high rank "Je crois (4 Sepr.) pouvoir (sans indiscretion) vous dire que le proces verbal que nous avons arreté, et que sera remis au ministre le 6. ou 7e. Court, est tout à l'avantage des Salaisons que nous avons fait cuire et que nous avons trouvées tres bonnes; et quoique notre mision fut bornée à examiner la qualité et bonté de ces Salaisons, nous avons cependant cru pouvoir ajouter, que nous pensions qu'il seroit utile au Gouvernement de traiter pour les Salaisons avec les Etats-Unis d'Amerique, au moins, pour la fourniture des rationnaires dans les Colonies, et pour les suppliments en Salaisons à envoyer pour les Batimens qui y sont stationés."

Thus at last the door is opened for the introduction of our meats, which I have so long labour'd for; and as I ought to receive a part of the benefit I shall be obliged to you, not to make it Known publickly, untill our bargain shall be made here, as it might bring a competition injurious to those who have had this trouble, and no ways advantagous to the United States; and besides as many Americans will be interested, as will be necessary to the proper Execution. To lodge the funds and to assure the Government some french Compagnies will be interested, who have it in their power to do the one and the other.

I have, by reason of the loss on the paper money, got a Suspension of my Timber Contract untill such time as I shall judge it convenient to fullfill it.—I am very respectfully & with much esteem Sir Your mo. obed. & v. humble, JAMES SWAN

RC (DNA: RG 59, MLR); at foot of text: "Mr. Jefferson Minister for foreign affairs at Philadelphia." Recorded in SJL as received 10 Feb. 1792.

From James Maury

Liverpool, 14 Sep. 1791. He last wrote to TJ on 22 Aug.—British ports are closed to foreign wheat, and in this district many American vessels have experienced difficulties primarily because of "excess of spirits." All but three of them have been released without great expence, though not without injury to their owners. The brig *Betsey*, commanded by Captain Salter of Portsmouth, New Hampshire, was not allowed to enter the Clyde for six weeks because of the "tonnage and where built being omitted in the Manifest and the affidavit thereto being made before a Justice of the peace instead of the British Deputy Consul altho' it was afterwards certified by said Deputy Consul."—These particulars should be made public to avoid similar inconveniences in future.

RC (DNA: RG 59, CD); 3 p.; endorsed by TJ as received 26 Nov. 1791 and so recorded in SJL; at foot of text TJ wrote in pencil: "the names may be published"; on verso he added, also in pencil: "send a copy to Fenno and a press copy to Freneau." Enclosure: Tr of Board of Customs to Collector and Comptroller of Liverpool undated, calling attention to strict enforcement of section of 1660 Navigation Act forbidding American vessels to ship American goods to Jersey and Guernsey. Most of the letter and all of the enclosure were printed in *National Gazette*, 1 Dec. 1791, "By Authority."

From William Short

DEAR SIR Paris Sep. 14. 1791

I have the honor to inclose and forward you by the way of England a copy of the King's letter sent yesterday to the national assembly announcing his acceptance of the constitution, and his intention of going to day to solemnize that acceptation in the assembly. He accordingly went today and took the oath required. The Queen also was present in a lodge adjoining the assembly room. This circumstance though apparently indifferent acquires some importance from the manner in which it is considered by the two parties. As she was not expected to be present—as she had never been there before and of course was at liberty to have absented herself, this volunteer step is considered by them as a proof of her decision to unite with the assembly. The most remarkable members of what is called the *cote droit* were not present at the ceremony of the King's oath, and that party may now be considered as containing his most inveterate enemies.

The real friends to order and to the re-establishment of the monarchy on constitutional principles desired to conduct this ceremony in such a manner as to give the King perfect satisfaction and to endeavour to attach him as much as possible to the present order of things. A circumstance however occasioned by a misunderstanding is thought to have very much hurt his feelings. It was determined before his arrival that the assembly should receive him standing and be seated whilst he repeated the oath. His speech was short and contained the oath which was taken only by the King's repeating it. As soon as the assembly found that he was pronouncing the oath they seated themselves abruptly and the President followed their example, so that the King was left standing alone. He stopped his speech and took his seat also and then proceeded. Those who are much better acquainted with his countenance than I am say that it discovered a wrath and discontentment which makes them fear that this circumstance will have left a deep and disagreeable impression. I was very near him and well situated for observing his countenance. It appeared to me to shew rather surprize and embarassment than anger, and I can hardly suppose that an accident of that kind surrounded with such momentous concerns can have any lasting influence, and particularly as both he and the Queen received the loudest applauses after the oath was taken both from the assembly and the people on their passage.

The President's answer also to the King seemed to displease generally, either from its matter or the manner in which it was pronounced. It is thought to have been much too dogmatic.

You will see by the King's letter that he desired an amnesty for those prosecuted on account of the revolution. M. de la fayette immediately moved that this should be adopted and it was done in the midst of the applauses of all present. These circumstances give a favorable appearance to the present moment. Much will depend on the conduct of the King and the future legislature. I fear however that events will occur either at home or abroad which they will not be able to controul by the force of the constitution as it remains at present.

The garde nationale of Paris is to be organized differently and commanded alternately by one of the six *chefs de division*. This gives M. de la fayette what he has long desired, an opportunity of quitting it immediately on the constitution being completed.

The next legislature will succeed this about the end of the month. The assembly previous to the King's arrival this morning decreed that Avignon and the Comtat should be incorporated with France conformably to the desire of its inhabitants. The colonial committee have not yet made their report.—I have the honor to assure you of the sentiments of affection and attachment with which I am, Dear Sir, your sincere friend & humble servant,   W. SHORT

PrC (DLC: Short Papers); at head of text: "*No. 82*"; lacks part of complimentary close and signature which have been supplied from Tr (DNA: RG 59, DD). Re- corded in SJL as received 6 Dec. 1791. Enclosure: Louis XVI to National Assembly, 13 Sep. 1791 (Tr in same).

From Edward Stevens

Culpeper Court House, 14 Sep. 1791. Thanking TJ for his of the 10th, he acknowledges his gratitude to him and to President Washington for offering him an appointment. Perplexed over whether to accept, he apologizes for explaining himself. "But from the Knowledge I have of your disposition, I find myself under no restraint to take up so much of your time, as to give a small Sketch of the reasoning within myself on the Occasion. If I accept of the appointment now offered, I am concerned whether I am sufficiently capable of the task. It will open such an extensive field, I fear I may be lost. It not only requires capacity of mind, but perhaps much more bodily activity than I am possesed of. And there must after all be a considerable Portion entrusted to others who from the wide bounds to act in, be so much out of my view, that disgrace as well as ruin might be brought down on my head very undeservingly." In the end he declines the offer. He regrets not seeing TJ and "our friend Mr. Maddison" as they passed through the area.

RC (MHi); 2 p.; endorsed by TJ as received 16 Sep. 1791 and so recorded in SJL.

TJ's letter to Stevens of 10 Sep. 1791 has not been found. It is uncertain what office Stevens was declining, but most likely it was that of excise inspector, a position he finally accepted the following March (JEP, I, 102, 111).

To Augustine Davis

SIR   Monticello Sep. 15. 1791.

I shall be very glad if we can get the matter of the two cross posts arranged while I am here which will be till the 10th. of Octob. It has occurred that there might be a saving were you to make the same post do for both as far as Columbia, and there branch off through Charlottesville on the North and New London on the South. I shall be glad to hear from you from time to time on the subject during my stay. Colo. Pickering being not yet at Philadelphia when I came away, I had no opportunity to confer with him on this subject, but spoke with the President the morning of my departure, who wished me to get it done while I am here. I am Sir Your humble servt.,   TH: JEFFERSON

PrC (MHi).

To Andrew Ellicott

SIR   Monticello Sep. 15. 1791.

Having been struck with the conduct of the boy (Billy) who attends at Mr. Shuter's, I mentioned it to Mr. Madison who added to mine his own opinion and knolege of him, and as I wanted a house servant, he said he thought it possible that it might be worth my while to give what it would be worth Mr. Shuter's while to take for him. Having turned the subject in my mind since, I have concluded to ask your aid in the matter, as you are on the spot. If Mr. Shuter would part with the boy, and the latter would be willing to go and live with me in Philadelphia I would willingly give Mr. Shuter fifty dollars a year for him. This mode would suit me best. But if he will not do this, and will let me have him, paying the same hire in advance all at once, at the delivery of the boy, I would agree to do even this tho it would not be convenient, and it would throw on me the risk of his life &c. I should mean to clothe him in addition. Will you be so good as to try this negociation for me, not letting Mr. Shuter know who it is for, till the matter is agreed, because I would not excite a suspicion in him that I wish to withdraw a servant from him or any body, of which I am incapable; and because it might raise his terms. If he shall be found willing it will be necessary to obtain the consent of the boy. To serve where he may fit himself for the best places, and in such a town as Philadelphia where new prospects and chances of doing something for himself may open upon him, may be inducements for him. And thus the interests of all the three parties may be promoted. If the matter is agreed I would take him along with me when I return. Pardon my troubling you with this affair, which I would not have done but that you are in the house and can find apt occasions of opening the matter in some of your daily conversations with Mr. Shuter.—I am with great esteem, Sir Your most obedt. humble servt., TH: JEFFERSON

PrC (MHi); at foot of text: "Mr. Ellicot." On TJ's need for a house servant, see Memorandum for Henry Remsen, Jr., 2 Sep. 1791.

To Adam Lindsay

SIR   Monticello Sep. 15. 1791.

Your kindness in offering to execute any little matters for me in your place, will perhaps induce me to trouble you annually, during my residence in Philadelphia for the two articles of Myrtle wax candles, and Hughes's crab cyder, which can be got no where else. I will now ask the favor of you to procure for me, in the proper seasons 250. ℔ of myrtle wax candles, moulded, and of the largest size you can find, and 4. casks (say 120. gallons) of the best Hughes's crab cyder. The latter I would not wish unless it be really fine. Whenever procured, be so good as to forward them to Philadelphia, and the moment you inform me of their cost, I will remit you a bank post note for the money from Philadelphia, to which place I shall be returned by the 25th. of October. I must beg your pardon for this trouble and add assurances of the esteem & regard of Sir Your very humble servt.,   TH: JEFFERSON

PrC (MHi).

To James Lyle

DEAR SIR   Monticello Sep. 15. 1791.

When I was in Virginia the last year, I took the liberty of solliciting you to furnish me a copy of the account of my father's estate from his death Aug. 17. 1757. till I came of age which was Apr. 2. 1764. at which time I believe the account commences which you furnished Mr. Nicholas. These two accounts are necessary for the settlement of many others; but peculiarly so for that of Dr. Walker relative to an article of £200. now become £500 which it is necessary for me to decypher. If this is ready let me beg the favor of it by Mr. Randolph who is the bearer of this. If it is not ready, I must repeat my prayers to have it got ready, as I am extremely anxious to finish this matter of Dr. Walker's, and every delay which arises on my coming to Virginia, of course puts it off a year, since I come but once a year, and can look into it here alone.

I wrote you formerly of the credit to the last of this month which I had been obliged to give on the sale of my crop of tobo. On my return to Philadelphia in October, you will hear from me as to the payment I can make you out of it, and my other provision for you. I am with great esteem Dear Sir your affectionate humble servt.,

TH: JEFFERSON

PrC (CSmH).

See TJ to James Lyle, 16 Oct. and 3 Nov. 1790 for letters about TJ's FATHER's ESTATE. It is uncertain what letter TJ wrote Lyle about credit on the sale of his TO-BACCO. Many letters between them are now missing, suggesting that TJ turned them over to someone, perhaps, or otherwise separated them from his other papers. Lyle's response of 28 Sep. 1791 is quoted in TJ to Francis Walker, 6 Oct. 1791.

From C. W. F. Dumas

[*Amsterdam*], *17 Sep. 1791*. Has just received the happy and important news that on the 13th the king accepted the Constitution, without protest, as it was presented to him, and that he would go the next day before the Assembly to solemnly confirm his acceptance. Dumas has been at Amsterdam for a few days with friends and will remain here until the end of the month. He has delayed sending this packet until he could mention this great event with certainty. Now two powers in the world have a true constitution. May the public happiness induce all the others to likewise reform themselves, so that the sarcasm of the old poet Ennius might no longer apply to them: "*Stolidum, Genus Æacidarum, Bellipotentes sunt magi quam Sapientipotentes.*" The English and "les Anglomanes" here report that a Mr. Hammond is going to conclude a treaty in America of offensive and defensive alliance between Britain and the United States, with great advantages for the latter, in order to punish Russia for not allowing itself to be influenced and controlled. P.S. *19 Sep.* Will learn tomorrow evening how the solemn appearance of the king went at the National Assembly. P.S. *20 Sep.* A vessel ready to lift anchor makes it necessary to close before the arrival of letters from France tonight, but the acceptance is no longer doubted. He will immediately write on returning to The Hague next week.

FC (Dumas Letter Book, Rijksarchief, The Hague; photostats in DLC); 2 p., in French; at head of text: "No. 82." Recorded in SJL as received 6 Mch. 1792.

From William Blount

"Territory of the United States of America south of the river Ohio," 19 Sep. 1791. Enclosing a census of the territory showing 35,691 inhabitants, 3,417 of whom are slaves.—"The heads of families very generally were opposed to giving in their numbers fearing a General Assembly would shortly be the consequence. Hence it may be fairly inferred that the numbers are not exaggerated and to this cause may be attributed the delay in compleating the Returns."—A few districts have yet to report but he forwards the "imperfect" report now before leaving to visit his family in North Carolina. The missing count, probably about 1,500 souls, will be sent as soon as it is received.—Judge Anderson arrived prior to the meeting of the district court on 15 Aug. and "his conduct both as a Judge and a man has met the approbation and applause of people in general." [P.S.] The census returns are too bulky to be forwarded now.

RC (DNA: RG 59, SWT, M-471/1); 2 p.; endorsed by TJ as received 22 Oct. 1791 and so recorded in SJL. Enclosure: "Schedule of the whole number of persons in the territory of the United States of America, South of the River Ohio, as taken on the last Saturday of July 1791, by the Captains of the Militia within the limits of their respective districts"; not found, but see text printed in *Return of the Whole Number of Persons within the Several Districts of the United States* (Philadelphia: Childs and Swaine, 1791), p. 56; and Carter, *Terr. Papers,* IV, 80-1.

From Joseph Fay

SIR   Bennington September 20th 1791

I had the honor of your letter of the 30th ult. I omitted sending by the last post in Expectation of receiving the Quebec papers. I have established a corrispondence with several public characters in that Province, by which meanes I expect daily to receive them Regularly, no time will be lost in forwarding them to you, free of expence.—I enclose you several of our last papers, but they are filled with Inteligence which you have been long acquainted with, excepting some little occurency of the State.

Soon after you and Mr. Madison left this, I obtained Mr. Payne on the rights of Man, which led me to reflect on the conversation which passed between us, relative to the Constitution of G. Britain. I am now happy in an opportunity to *retract*[1] from the sentiments which I then expressed in favour of it; Mr. Payne has in a *Masterly* Manner pointed out the defects of British Government, and plainly shewn that they have no Constitution, and reflected great light to the world relative to the Natural rights of Man; I hope the happy day is hastening when the Nations of the Earth will be *regenarated* and once more partake of the Natural rights of Man.—France *to be sure* has made a Great Stride towards it, and I think the flight of their King will *facilitate* the establishment of a parminent Government; The wisdom with which the National Assembly conducted on the occasion, and the firmness with which the body of the Nation entered into new Resolutions to support their *freedom* will secure them against the envasions of other Powers. The revolution in *Poland*, the Fire which has kindled in *Spain*, and the apprehensions which the Uropeon *Monarchs* are under from the spread of the same spirit of freedom will engross their Attension to their own safety, which will leave France in Peace.

We sensibly feel the Good effects of our efficient Government in America. No power on Earth abounds with such Plenty of every Comfort of Life, and we have Nothing to fear from the invasions of *foreign Powers*. Canada will be ready to join in our Government as soon as they can be useful to us. At Present they are making wide and extensive settlements at the Expence of Great Britain, from which I calculate, that America is drawing from them (at least) a Million a year. I am acquainted with a Number of principle people who went from this Country during the War, and are settling on the St. Lawrence river and the western lakes, and with whom I hold a Corrispondence, and from whom I learn that they are wishing to participate in the American advantages of Commerce, and they own themselves pleased with our free Government.

I shall not forget your Maple seed. I have been very particular in writing my friends in Canada to encourage the Manufactoring of sugar as being a Most Valuable object.—I shall be happy to hear from you at all times when your Leisure will permit, and receive early information of the Politicks of the day.—I have the honor to be Dr. Sir with Sentiments of friendship & esteem your Most Obedient and very Humble servant,   JOSEPH FAY

RC (DLC); endorsed by TJ as received 22 Oct. 1791 and so recorded in SJL.

¹ Substituted for "recind," deleted.

From John Harvie

DR SIR   Richmond Septr 20th. 1791

Your Letter of August the 14th. came to my hands at a time when I was two much Indisposed to pay any Attention to its Contents, and upon now looking into it, I am sorry to find that the Land Office can furnish you with no Information of the Quantity of Land located for the Virginia Continental Line on the South Side of the Ohio, the Warrants of Survey issuing from this Office being General, not distinguishing the Lands set apart to Satisfy the Military Bountys that lye on the South, from those that lye on the North Side of the Ohio.

Colo. Anderson the principal Surveyor for the Continental Line who lives at the Falls of the Ohio, only can give Information of the Quantity of Land Actually located in his Office on the different sides of that River. Recollecting that the Executive had Obtained a Report from the principal Surveyor and Superintending officers of the State and Continental Line in the Year 1788. on the Subject of the Military Lands, I Conceive that these Reports may throw some light upon your Enquirys, wherefore I have procured the Originals from the Clerk of the Council and now transmit you Copys of them.—I have also thought it might be Useful to Subjoin two Letters of Governor Randolphs on the same Subject, the One Addressed to the President of Congress, the other to the Virginia Delegates. My principal View in sending you a Copy of these Letters is to show the Light in which the Interference of Congress with our Military Rights has been Considered by the Governing Authority of this State. Notwithstanding the force and in my Judgment propriety of the Reasoning in these Letters Congress in Repealing their Resolution Complained of passed a Law in the Year 1790 which has deranged the whole System of the Military Survey and Suspended every Effective Operation towards its Completion. The 2nd and 3rd Sec. of their Law requiring a Statement from the Secretary of War of the persons Intitled to Military Bountys and the Aggregate amount due the whole Line which is to govern the future Survey renders Nugatory and Void the Land Warrants which have already issued under the Inspection and Direction of the Chief Magistrate here. The 4th Sec: requires a General Survey to be made, Entred in a Book and Certifyd by the Superintendants before a Return shall be made to the Secretary of State, whereby a few persons withholding the Necessary Advances for Fees and Contingent expences may delay all others at their pleasure. Sec: the 5th. Directs all Grants to issue in the Name of the person who was Originally Intitled to such Bounty, Although an Assignment of those Rights have been Sanctiond and Authorizd by the Laws of this State, Warrants issued in the Names of the Assignees, and a fund raisd by a tax upon such Assignd Rights for the Maintenance and Support of the Superintending Officers and paying in part the Contingent expences of the Survey. If Title should now issue to the Original Owners, how are the Assignees to Acquire the Legal Estate, must they Seek it in Chancery. If so, in many Instances they had better at once quietly resign it. I beg your pardon Sir for troubling you upon this Subject, but the Statement that you are about to make, Specializing as I Suppose it will, the Quantity of Land due the Continental Line of this State on the North West side of the Ohio, I Conjecture the design is to have such Quantity Allotted to the Line agreably to the Spirit, Mode and principles of the aforementioned Law, which I not only Consider as a Violation of private Right, but as an Infraction in the terms of Cession, as Virginia intended certainly to retain the power of Granting her Military Bountys in what Manner and Form she thought proper upon the Reservd Lands, before any part of them should be Relinquished to Congress. Under this Idea I have Uniformly received Surveys into this Office made on the North west Side of the Ohio, and have issued Grants upon them in the Course of Regular Application. If this Law of Congress Continues in force without some Modification to the Convenience and Rights of our Citizens the Legislature of this State will certainly make it the Subject of Serious Remonstrance, for it is two Humiliating for them passively to Submit to the Violation of Rights Sanctiond and Guaranteed by their repeated Acts. I had till this day flatterd myself with a hope that I might be able to pay you a Visit of a day or two whilst you were at Monticello but an Unforeseen Circumstance will I fear deprive me of that pleasure. The little Land affair between you and me may be Settled at any time we meet, or Submitted to the Arbitration you propose upon Colo. Lewis furnishing me with the Copys of your Orders of Council and the Entrys. As I have Wrote but little since my Sickness, this long Letter has quite fatigued me. Permit me therefore to Assure you that I am Dr Sir with most perfect Esteem Yr. Most Obt. & Oblidgd Servt,

JNO. HARVIE

It may not be amiss to Observe that our General assembly have from time to time given to many Meritorious Officers Bounty Lands, who were not Strickly Intitled to them under the General Law. These not being known to the Secretary of War will make a deficiency in his Report.—Warrants for Military Bounty Lands have issued from the Land Office of this State to the amount of 4,075,000 Acres Including both State and Continental Line.

RC (MHi); addressed: "Thomas Jefferson Esqr. Monticello"; endorsed twice by TJ as received 26 Sep. 1791 and so recorded in SJL.

Harvie was exercised by a little-noticed conflict between state and national authority in the new American nation. During the American Revolution Virginia offered generous land bounties to its state and Continental officers and soldiers, setting aside an extensive tract in western Kentucky for those who were eligible for the bounties and creating a Land Office to administer the bounty system. Then, when Virginia ceded its claims to the Northwest Territory, one of the conditions of the act of cession accepted by the Continental Congress in 1784 stipulated that if the quantity of good land in the area Virginia had reserved southeast of the Ohio River proved to be insufficient, the state reserved the right to make up this deficiency northwest of the Ohio between the Scioto and Little Miami rivers. As soon as the sufficiency of good land southeast of the Ohio appeared doubtful, Virginia began to lay out land for the veterans between the Scioto and the Little Miami. This alarmed the Continental Congress, which was concerned that Virginia might claim more land in that area than the veterans were justly entitled to, and led that body to resolve on 17 July 1788 that all "locations and surveys" made by Virginia northwest of the Ohio were invalid "until the said deficiency, if any, on the south east side of the Ohio shall be ascertained and stated to Congress" (JCC, XXXIV, 333-4; William Grayson to James Madison, 31 Aug. 1787, Rutland, *Madison*, X, 159). Governor Randolph immediately protested that this resolution violated Virginia's retained right to grant lands to Continental veterans above the Ohio. Soon thereafter, however, the state prudently submitted a preliminary statement on the deficiency of bounty lands below the Ohio as requested by the Continental Congress (Edmund Randolph to Virginia Delegates, 4 Aug. 1788, Rutland, *Madison*, XI, 221-4; Edmund Randolph to President of Continental Congress, 4 Aug. 1788, ASP, *Public Lands*, I, 6; Report of Superintendents for the Continental Line, 17 Nov. 1788, same, p. 6-7). Nevertheless, the offending resolve continued to remain in force, pending the compilation of a definitive statement on this issue by the state, until it was finally repealed by an act passed by the federal Congress in August 1790 that also prescribed the procedures for granting lands to Virginia veterans northwest of the Ohio, which Harvie criticized in this letter as yet another infringement of Virginia's authority by the national government (Carter, *Terr. Papers*, II, 296-8). In response to complaints from Virginia military officers and the state legislature, Congress passed an act in 1794 that made it less onerous than before for Virginia Continental veterans to obtain bounty lands between the Scioto and the Little Miami (Resolve of Virginia General Assembly, 20-22 Dec. 1790, ASP, *Public Lands*, I, 17; Petition of Virginia Officers to Virginia General Assembly, [ante 20 Dec. 1790], same, p. 18; *Annals*, IV, 1474-5).

The LITTLE LAND AFFAIR involved a dispute between TJ and Harvie over the boundary of TJ's Edgehill estate (TJ to John Harvie, Jr., 7 Apr. 1791).

From Joseph Atkinson

SIR   Stateburg So Carolina Sepr 21st. 1791

Being inform'd that there has been Orders by official Authority, for some Enquiries to be made, whether any Manufactories are establish'd in this State? what Progress are already made in them? and whether there is any probable Prospect of their being carried on to any Advantage? I was peculiarly pleas'd with the Information from the satisfaction it afforded me (as a warm Advocate for extending general Benefits to my Country) in reflecting that Characters are appointed at the Head of Departments in the general Government, so attentive in investigating the Situation of distant States and so Assiduous in wishing to promote such Establishments

as with Attention and the fostering Care of public Notice promise
to become gen'rally useful and to be nearly of equal Benefit to ev'ry
Branch of the Federal Union as the promotion of Agriculture and
superior to that of Commerce; as by giving the best Encouragement
to Industry, forming the early Manners of the numerous Youth,
supplying the Wants of the Citizens generally with those Articles
which with ev'ry Dissadvantage we are now oblig'd to take from
Foreigners, afford constant Employment to the Poor, give general
Circulation of Cash amongst ourselves, add increasing Strength to
Government and will prove a continual Source of Independence to
the federal States; And notwistanding, it has hitherto been the prevailing Opinion and has been industriously propogated from partial
Views, that the southern States from the Manners of their Inhabitants, their Situation and Climate, have and ever wou'd be hostile
to Manufactories of ev'ry Kind, yet Experience and Observation
(especially since the Introduction of mechanical Improvements into
this Country) have of late convinc'd me that under ev'ry Difficulty
arising from Prejudice, local Situation, or the Habits of the People,
Manufactories once establish'd and properly encourag'd, may be
carried on even in the Southern States, at a Distance from the
Metropolis to a considerable Extent beneficial to the Undertaker
and highly advantageous to the Community; A small Attempt of
that Kind by an ingenious Mechanic lately arriv'd from North Britain has been made at the high Hills Santee near this place, situated
in a healthy and most plentiful part of this State, but unhappily
most of the Inhabitants have not been accustom'd to Labor and
Industry. Yet under ev'ry Dissadvantage of Prejudice in the People
with very few Resources except his own Application and diligent
Attention, has erected and work'd Jennies, Carding, Slabbing and
spinning Machines of the newest English Contruction and equal in
their Execution to any of the like Size made in Europe, and with
the trifling Assistance only of a few Negroes, he was supplied with
by two Gentlemen in the Neighbourhood, and without any pecuniary Advances whatever, now employs them, and is carrying on
the Manufactory of Cotton, and I am told on Enquiry without Loss
to himself; but for want of Hands to Labor, and some additional
Encouragement, he has not had it in his Power to render it so
beneficial to himself, as a Work of such Ingenuity and Consequence
and the giving up all his Time and Attention to it realy merits; and
tho' he had an Offer soon after he began the Attempt in this State
of three Hundred Guineas to be paid him in Charleston as an Inducement to remove to a distant Country where he shou'd find

constant Employment and Support, yet he had the Resolution to refuse the Offer from a Motive of Honor, and Predilection to this Country, and has under ev'ry Difficulty which he encounter'd and which will ever attend all new Systems of Invention and Improvement by indefaticable Industry and Application alone been enabled in little more than twelve Months to finish and give Employment to a Carding Machine which can finish and turn of 50 Weight Cotton Rolls ready prepar'd for Spinning, by the work of one Negroe only, but if work'd by Water or Horses can finish from 70 to 80 lb. clean rolls daily. A Slabbing Machine (the first and I am told the only one introduc'd into America) with 30 Spindles which takes of the Rolls from the carding Machine and prepares them for Spinning fine Thread on the spinning Machines, capable with one grown Negroe and two small Boys or Girls about 10 or 12 years old of turning of 40 lb. course Thread daily. Four Spinning Machines containing 84 Spindles each, ev'ry one of which, with the Labor of one Negroe Wench and the Assistance of one Girl about 12 years old to two Machines to join the Threads when broke, is capable of Spinning daily 6 lb. of very fine or 8 lb. of courser Thread proper for making Muslins, Handkerchiefs, Dimothys, Jeans, Thicksets, Corduroys, Velvets, Velverets, Royal Ribbs, Manchester Stripes, Cottons for printing or any other Kind of cotton Manufactory useful and proper for the Climate and which are usually imported to a very large Amount annually into the united States. These with the Addition of four other spinning Machines might be conducted with the Expence of one white person to superintend the whole, and the Labor of 11 or 12 Grown Negroes and seven or eight Boys and Girls for ten to 12 years of Age wou'd produce on an Average 50 lb. Thread daily, which Thread I am inform'd will manufacture 200 yards of any of these enumerated Articles and give constant Employment to 25 or 30 Weavers, and the Thread if sold at the moderate price of 2/6 pr Lb. will amount annually to about two Thousand pounds but with the Addition of proper Workmen to Weave, Bleach, dye, dress, and finish the same for Sale wou'd Amount at the low Average price of two Shillings and Sixpence per Yard to Seven Thousand five Hundred pounds yearly and upwards and which cou'd in the like proportion without any other Inconvenience than an Increase of Capital and additional Employment of Labourers and Workmen be enlarg'd to equal any Demand for Consumption this Country might require and wou'd be a real Saving to the States of such an annual Sum as is now constantly remitted to Foreigners for the purchase of such Articles as might be procured at Home, give Circulation of Cash among ourselves, be the Means of disengaging the Country from the Difficulties and Incumbrances they now labor under from accumulating Debts and their Dependance on foreign Countries for Supplies. As I have taken some pains in making Enquiries into the Nature and Practicability of conducting a Manufactory in this State I find that under ev'ry Discouragment of the first Attempt to introduce a regular System of Industry, by instructing Youth very early in the Habits of learning useful Branches of Manufactories, concentering one general Plan of carrying on a Factory unsuitable to the former Habits and Disposition of the Inhabitants and generally seems impracticable or at least not worth Attention and Support, and which Opinion has been studiously supported by importing Merchants who since the Revolution have had a very serious and alarming Influence over the Minds of the greatest part of the Citizens who were most active in and lost the greatest part of their Property by the Revolution, yet by constant Care and Attention to that Business this valuable Artizan with the want of proper Conveniences in Buildings proper to accomodate a Factory and other Support necessary for the Undertaking, his Machines have been kept employ'd and he has at constant Work about eight Weavers and a Stocking Loom and has already manufactured above 2000 Yards of Cloth of different Kinds, and weaves on an Average about 10 pair Stockings weekly but for want of being able to extend his Plan has been oblig'd to refuse employing a Number of Weavers lately arriv'd from Europe who have apply'd to him for Work and who to be in Numbers settled in this Country unemploy'd, yet from the Hope he still flatters himself with, of being able ultimately to succeed in the Design of rendering it beneficial to himself, useful to the public, and of overcoming fix'd Rooted prejudices, he has undertaken to invite over from Europe the necessary Artificers wanting to compleat his Design, viz. Bleacher, Dyer, Callico Printer and Dresser, who are shortly to arrive, and then he doubts not to finish his Goods for Sale as cheap and in as neat and workmanlike a Manner as any of the Kind imported. He has further endeavour'd to extend the Benefits of his Knowledge in these useful Machines to save Labor in the manufactoring Line by introducing under his Inspection and Patronage the like Machines for carrying on those Branches of cotton Manufactory at or near Lands Ford on the Catawba River in York County near the No. Carolina Line and will promote, as far as his Abilities will allow, the Establishment of those Manufactories in the different Remote Parts of this State where Clothing of ev'ry Kind except at very dear Rates and under great

Dissadvantages owing to the Distance and Difficulty of transporting their Produce to Market; and will supply Machines on reasonable Contracts (and instruct the Inhabitants in the Use of them) to any person or persons who will apply to him for them; And as many if not most of the Articles necesary for Spinning, dyeing and Dressing may be cultivated and rais'd in the State, large Quantities of Goods may be manufactor'd at Home with little Expence and Labor, take of few or none of the grown Inhabitants from improving and cultivating their Land in farming and Agriculture, be the means of finding a ready Market at Home for many Articles they have not yet thought of cultivating. Children from 10 to 15 years old who are now brought up by their parents in Habits of Idleness may find beneficial Employment and by adding their Mite to the Maintenance of a large Family, be instructed in useful Trades and be thro' Life a continual Source of Advantage to them and their growing Families, thereby rendering us independent of foreign Nations for any real Convenience of Life, promote general Industry and give Strength, Riches and Stability of every Part of the Union. Many course Articles for private Consumption I understand have since the War been manufactur'd by individuals in the remote parts of the State under many Dissadvantages and at very dear Rates on Account of the Scarcity of Artificers and the consequent high Prices of Labor from those Wants, but from the best Information I have been able to obtain, this is the first Attempt to introduce a Plan on general Principles of establishing a Factory for supplying the Citizens at large: New Systems have ever met with Opposition and liable to many Difficulties, but it's highly reasonable to suppose that by promoting and encouraging the Introduction of new Inventions to supply the purpose of personal Labor, and if by that Assistance, Experience proves that one Man can perform the Labor of twenty, I think there can be no doubt that in an infant Country like this, when once properly establish'd, its Value and Usefulness to the States will rapidly increase, Artificers of every kind will be induc'd to emigrate from foreign Nations and settle in a Country where constant Employment will be given and a better price for their Labor afforded them than they can receive elsewhere, where Taxes are low, Provisions cheap, the conveniences of Life abundant, valuable Freeholds easily acquir'd, and from the Nature and fix'd principles of our republican Government, wherein ev'ry industrious Citizen has a constitutional right to take his Share in it's Organization, themselves and their Posterity will remain free from the Fetters of Tyranny, Oppression and Bigotry. History informs us that the Netherlands and Flanders not many Ages ago were the great Imporiums for Manufactures of all Kinds which Great Britain imported with great Loss to her Revenue, and England at that Time like America now exported her staple Commodities to those Countries to be manufactored for her Use and continued so 'till the Oppression and Superstition of the spanish Task Masters brought the poor industrious Artificers to such a State of Vassalage and Slavery as compell'd them to seek an Asylum in a Land of more Liberality and Freedom, where under the protection and with the fostering Hand of royal and parliamentary Aid, with prospects then less flattering than America can now boast of, they acquir'd a settled Establishment that has ever since been gradually improving and by increasing the Value of ev'ry kind of property in that Country, multiplying her Inhabitants, civilizing her Subjects by learning them useful Habits of Industry and increasing the Circulation of Cash amongst them, has been the principal Cause of raising Great Britain to her present State of Grandeur and Opulence, and from a small Beginning has in little more than a Century brought Manufactories to that State of Excellence and Perfection as to be deservedly the Admiration of the whole World.

As you Sir are plac'd in a public Station in the federal Government, I have taken the Liberty of troubling you with these Remarks on the Policy of encouraging ev'ry improv'd Method of Carrying on manufactories so much wanted in America; shou'd any Thing of the Kind come under public Consideration, and you shou'd think that any Thing can be collected from the Observations I have made serviceable to the Community, you are at Liberty to make what Use of them you think proper. My Knowledge of the Business extends very little further than from Information which I have taken some pain to collect from the best of Motives, that of public Utility, and I hope you will believe that I am with Regard Sir your most Obt. Hble Servt,
JOS. ATKINSON

RC (DNA: RG 59, MLR); endorsed by TJ as received 26 Nov. 1791 and so recorded in SJL.

Joseph Atkinson was a Charleston merchant and shipyard owner who had served in the South Carolina Senate from 1782 to 1786. Atkinson's enthusiasm for promoting the economic development of South Carolina led him to play a leading role in various enterprises that were designed to encourage the creation of a canal system and foster the growth of iron manufacturing in that state (Emily B. Reynolds and Joan R. Faunt, comps., *Biographical Directory of the Senate of the State of South Carolina 1776-1964* [Columbia, S.C., 1964], p. 175). The ORDERS BY OFFICIAL AUTHORITY, FOR SOME ENQUIRIES came from Alexander Hamilton who, in preparation for his Report on Manufactures, had requested the information about domestic manufacturing to which Atkinson refers (Hamilton's circular letter to Supervisors of the Revenue, 22 June 1791, Syrett, *Hamilton*, VIII, 497-8). It is curious that Atkinson addressed his remarks to TJ instead of responding directly to Hamilton.

To James Wilson

SIR   Monticello Sep. 21. 1791.

Colo. Lewis tells me you had proposed to come to this neighborhood to make a settlement of the business of mine in your hands,
and that it would be convenient to you to fix on the time when I
should be at home. He writes you on this subject. I shall be here
about a fortnight longer, and am very anxious this settlement should
be as much sooner as possible that I may have the more time afterwards to arrange other matters which cannot be done till I know
the exact state of this. The bearer is sent express to carry you these
letters and will bring us the notification of the day we may expect
to see you, if you will be so good as to fix it.—I am Sir with much
esteem Your most obedt. humble servt.,   TH: JEFFERSON

Tr (ViU). Wilson's reply, dated at
Buckingham 23 Sep. 1791, is recorded in
SJL as received 24 Sep. 1791, but has not
been found. THE BEARER: Tom Shackle-
ford (d. 1801), one of the slaves inherited
from John Wayles, for whom TJ paid
"ferrge. to Wilson's 1/3" (Account Book,
21 Sep. 1791).

From William Short

DEAR SIR   Paris Septr. 22. 1791.

Since the King's solemn acceptation of the constitution mentioned to you in my last he seems to have taken much pains to shew
that it was his free choice. The day of the constitution being proclaimed throughout Paris agreeably to the decree of the assembly,
the chateau and garden of the Thuilleries and the Champs-Elysees
were illuminated at the King's expence. He went in the course of
the evening with his family to visit the illuminations and recieved
the loudest applauses from all quarters; two days ago he went also
with the Queen and family to the opera. This circumstance seems
to have given uncommon pleasure, as it is not only the first time
they have been to a theatre since the revolution, but the first time
the King was ever at the opera in Paris.

These external marks of adhesion have so displeased those who
are here of the aristocratical party that they have almost entirely
abandoned the court.—On the contrary those of the courtiers who
had for some time absented themselves on account of the active part
they took in the revolution have now returned there. The King and
Queen are apparently well satisfied with this circumstance and treat
them with marked civility. Time alone can shew whether the King
will be able by such measures and by his future conduct to obtain

the confidence of the nation in his acceptation of the constitution. For my own part I am well persuaded that at this moment he is fully determined to act up to his professions as he was also at the time of his going to the assembly in February 1790.—But should future events be different from those he expected and should an opportunity present itself of flying from them it can hardly be supposed that it will not be made use of again.

At present the King sees or thinks he sees order and tranquillity restored by his acceptance—in his refusal he sees personal danger to himself and family, and even if he should be able to escape, he sees the necessity of reconquering the Kingdom under the auspices as it were of his brother. Of course his own power passed into his hands, a circumstance highly displeasing to the Queen and which it is supposed decides her to shew so perfect an adhesion to the assembly. Should the King be deceived in his expectations, should the next legislature be domineered by factions in or out of the assembly, and following the example of their predecessors attempt to take the exercise of the functions of government into their hands and thus continue the state of anarchy, which is too much to be apprehended from the nature of the constitution and the present disposition of men's minds, he may then prefer the alternative however disagreeable of putting himself under the protection of his brother and of foreign aid.

The interview between the Emperor and King of Prussia took place at Pilnitz. Their own affairs were probably the principal object of the interview, but the Count D'Artois being present and having had two private and long conferences with them shews that the affairs of France also were taken into consideration. Nothing certain has transpired of the result. A declaration which you will see in the newspapers sent by the way of Havre has been published as having been signed by the Emperor and King of Prussia and delivered to the Count D'Artois. There is no official certainty of its truth but seems generally to be considered as true, as well as letters addressed to the King by the Princes in order to engage him to refuse the constitution. The principal argument is drawn from the certainty of relief from abroad and his being in a state of captivity.

The assembly have determined to put an end to their session the last day of this month. It is thought there will be then a sufficient number of the new house to proceed to business. The elections are going on throughout the Kingdom and it is apprehended that a great number of the members of the next assembly will have very exaggerated and dangerous principles.

The intelligence from the islands continues to be obscure and contradictory. It may be considered as certain however that the decree of the 15th of May gives general dissatisfaction. It is yet uncertain whether this assembly will recede.

The papers will have informed you of the peace between the Empress of Russia and the Turk.

The minister of marine (M. Thevenard) has resigned on account of ill health. M. de Bougainville destined to succeed him declines. Other changes in the ministry are expected to take place soon.

You will be informed by Mr. Swan of an examination lately made of some American beef and pork, by commissaries appointed by the minister and who have made the most favorable report of it.

I recieved yesterday a packet by the way of Havre of which the postage cost 60₶. It contained only two books for the consulate of Rouen and Bordeaux. As I am sure it was not your intention that it should come in this manner I have thought it proper to mention it to you that you may in future have marked on the cover of such packets that they are books or papers, which would exempt them from being considered as letters and subjected to that postage. I recieved this morning from M. de la Motte a small packet marked No. 1. containing two newspapers. He tells me he has received others to my address which he shall send by the first private conveyance. I suppose it possible there may be a letter from you among them. The last I have had the honor of recieving from you was dated May 10. Yours most respectfully,   W. Short

PrC (DLC: Short Papers); at head of text: "No. 83"; at foot of text: "Thomas Jefferson Secretary of State Philadelphia." Tr (DNA: RG 59, DD). Recorded in SJL as received 26 Dec. 1791.

In response to Louis xvi's and Marie Antoinette's flight to Varennes and their subsequent apprehension by French authorities, Emperor Leopold II, the queen's brother, and Frederick William II of Prussia met at Pilnitz in Saxony and on 27 Aug. 1791 issued their celebrated DECLARATION in which they stated that the situation of Louis was a matter of concern to all the sovereigns of Europe and asserted that they were willing to intervene in French affairs in order to restore him to his rightful authority, provided they were joined by the other great powers of Europe (L. G. Wickham Legg, ed., *Select Documents Illustrative of the History of the French Revolution: The Constituent Assembly*, 2 vols. [London, 1905], II, 127). Although Leopold knew when he approved this artfully contrived proviso that most of the other European powers then had no wish to intervene in France, the Declaration of Pilnitz was nevertheless viewed by many Frenchmen as a clear harbinger of foreign intervention in opposition to their revolution. This impression was merely strengthened by the issuance on 10 Sep. 1791 of two LETTERS ADDRESSED TO THE KING signed by five prominent *émigré* leaders—the first by the Comte d'Artois and the Comte de Provence and the second by the Prince de Condé, the Duc de Bourbon, and the Duc d'Enghien—that urged Louis to reject the French Constitution and declared that the great powers stood ready to intervene in his behalf (same, p. 128-37). The Declaration of Pilnitz even raised apprehensions among republican circles in America, with the *National Gazette* warning its readers, for example, that this document indicated

a settled resolve on the part of the Holy
Roman Emperor and the King of Prussia
"to restore the liberty of the King, and the
splendor of the French Monarchy; and that
for this purpose they undertake to act with
mutual accord, in employing the forces

necessary for this important purpose" (*National Gazette*, 12 Dec. 1791).

Delamotte's SMALL PACKET was sent in
Delamotte to Short, 20 Sep. 1791 (DLC:
Short Papers).

From David Humphreys

Lisbon, 23 Sep. 1791. Despite Thomas Barclay's arrival in Oporto, he still
has not received the letters Barclay brought from America for him.—Two
British packets and a cutter from England with dispatches for Mr. Walpole
have arrived since his letter of the 10th instant. Peace has been concluded
between the Emperor and the Porte, and peace will soon follow between the
Empress and the Porte, "unless the latter shall consent to be abandoned by the
Mediating Powers, whose Ministers have agreed upon the terms with the
former. The Empress will then have terminated the war in as favorable a manner
as she could have desired."—The recent interview between the Emperor, the
King of Prussia and the Elector of Saxony is supposed to have concerned Poland
and given offense to Russia. Letters delivered to the Margrave of Anspach by
the last packet indicate that Russia, Austria, and Prussia have agreed that no
branch of their royal families should marry the heiress of the Polish throne. He
learned last night from the Swedish agent that the King of Sweden was going
to St. Petersburg.—There are many different rumors about Louis XVI's acceptance of the French constitution and the attitude of the other European
powers toward France. The Duke of Alafoñes told him on Sunday that the
Queen had heard nothing from France about the constitution. The Prussian
minister informed him the night before last that the king had approved the
constitution. But yesterday he could not ascertain from the Papal nuncio or
the Spanish chargé d'affaires the basis for the report of the king's acceptance,
and today none of the Gazettes just received from France contain anything
bearing on this question.—The Portuguese minister to the United States,
[Cypriano Ribeiro] Freire, is about to leave London for America.—The Spanish
government has announced a new prohibition "concerning French publications
and manuscripts."—P.S. Barclay has arrived in the Tagus, but the letters he
brought with him have still not been received.

RC (DNA: RG 59, DD); 4 p.; at head
of text: "(No. 34)"; at foot of text: "The
Secretary of State"; endorsed by TJ as received 1 Dec. 1791 and so recorded in SJL.
Tr (same).

On 16 Sep. 1791 the Spanish government, eager to prevent the spread of revolutionary ideas among its subjects, reaffirmed its 1790 prohibition of the
importation or publication of any books,
papers, or objects pertaining to the French
Revolution (Richard Herr, *The Eighteenth
Century Revolution in Spain* [Princeton,
1958], p. 254-5).

From John Skey Eustace

SIR   Bordeaux 24th. September 1791

I do myself the Honor of transmitting for your Excellency's Acceptance the best Edition I have been able to select of the french Constitution as solemnly ratified by the Monarch on the 14th. Instant, together with the Act of general Amnesty passed by the national assembly the Day following on a particular recommendation of the King contained in his Letter of the 13th. which is declaratory of his subsequent Sanction. This Letter is annexed to the Constitution. I have added however a loose Copy which has just been sent me by a municipal officer of my Acquaintance.

Your Excellency will observe by the Deliberation of the Municipality of Bordeaux on the 17th. the very prompt and magnificent Manner in which this Event has been announced and celebrated with us. As the first commercial City of the Kingdom and the most extensively connected with the french Colonies the late troubles in Saint Domingo and Guadeloupe had spread a general Alarm through every Branch of the mercantile and manufacturing Interests, the late Decree, however, which secures to the Colonial Assemblies the Right of suspending a former one respecting the People of Colour has re-established for the Moment our wonted Tranquility and Confidence of which the best Testimonies are the immediate Rise in the Exchange with foreign Nations and the consequent Appreciation of their paper Currency. This Decree, Sir, I have also the Honor of transmitting for your Excellency's Perusal.

I trust, Sir, that my Character and my Duty as an American will be admitted as sufficient Motives for the Liberty I have taken. The immense Distance of the Capital from the sea-Ports of the Kingdom and the Infrequency of direct Opportunities to Philadelphia suggested to me the Propriety of transmitting to your Excellency by the most immediate Conveyance an authentic Document of this important Event. I had hoped for the Honor of handing it to your Excellency but being obliged to retard my Departure from hence till the 10th. of October in a Ship bound to Savannah in Georgia some Months will necessarily elapse before I visit Philadelphia.— Permit me to assure you, Sir, that I have the honour to be, with the most unfeigned Consideration, your Excellency's most obedient and most humble Servant,   JOHN SKEY EUSTACE

RC (DNA: RG 59, MLR); endorsed by TJ as received 10 Mch. 1792 and so recorded in SJL.

Information on Eustace, a political adventurer who had been wandering in Europe, may be found in Dunmore to Sir William Howe, 2 Dec. 1775, William J. Van Schreeven et al., eds., *Revolutionary Virginia: The Road to Independence*, 7 vols. (Charlottesville, 1973-1983), v, 39; and Lee Kennet, "John Skey Eustace and the French Revolution," *The American Society Legion of Honor Magazine*, XLV (1974), 29-43. By the time TJ received Eustace's letter most of the documents enclosed in it had been printed in America. The 17 Nov. 1791 issue of the *National Gazette* published Louis XVI's 13 Sep. 1791 letter to the National Assembly announcing his acceptance of the French constitution, and Peter Stewart and Willam Young both published texts of the constitution itself in pamphlets entitled *The French Constitution Revised, Amended, and Finally Decreed by the National Assembly* (Philadelphia, 1791). Eustace also wrote a brief letter to TJ on 26 Sep. 1791, transmitting "the enclosed Deliberation of the Municipality of Bordeaux for the Publication of the Constitution which was made yesterday with all the Pomp and Magnificence prescribed by that act and suited to the Occasion" (RC in DNA: RG 59, MLR; endorsed by TJ as received 10 Mch. 1792 and so recorded in SJL).

To Nicholas Lewis

DEAR SIR   Monticello Sep. 24. 1791.

I now return you the bonds of Woodson & Lewis and Lewis & Ware, as also Woodson's note, and a statement of Lewis's debt for the rent of Elkhill. Calculating the interest on each of them to the last day of this month, they stand thus.

	Principal		Interest		Whole amount
Woodson & Lewis on their bond	£172–17–7	+	£22–17–0	=	£215–14– 7
Woodson. On his note	6– 7–0	+	1– 7–3	=	7–14– 3
(Lewis & Ware on their bond	100– 6–8½	+	24–18–3	=	125– 4–11½
Lewis for rent	112– 0–0	+	7– 4–0	=	119– 4– 0
Amounting in the whole to					467–17– 9½
Deduct P.F. Trent's order, and your debt to R.L. suppose					215
There will remain due the last day of this month about					252–17– 9½

It will be necessary for you to give a very particular explanation to Mr. Pope as to the claim for Elkhill, as an exact idea of it will decide what kind of writ he takes out: also to caution him not to take it out till you are satisfied the 4th. year is expired. I shall be obliged to you to inform me the exact sum you are to stop for me on account of your brother's estate, and whether you are to allow to R.L. interest on it, and from what time. The bearer will bring the books and papers we spoke of. I am with great esteem Dear Sir your friend & servt,   TH: JEFFERSON

PrC (CSmH).

The action TJ took regarding LEWIS's DEBT is explained in TJ to Robert Lewis and TJ to Robert Lewis, Jr., 5 Oct. 1791.

MR. POPE: Nathaniel Pope, an attorney who lived in Hanover County.

From Joseph Fenwick

Bordeaux, 25 Sep. 1791. "The political situation of this country is now likely to take a favorable turn and faith and tranquility will I hope succeed fear and incertitude." The King unequivocally sanctioned the Constitution on the 14th and the 30th is fixed for the Legislature to replace the National Convention. All persecutions for revolutionary actions have ceased and a general amnesty is decreed, giving hope for union and stability to the Constitution. However, equipment of 97,000 militia is going on. The "quota, 2000 and odd of this Department, will march in a few days for the southern frontiers." There are no maritime preparations, the English fleet is actually disarming, the fear of war is ended, and "The rumour of a league on the Continent against France can be nothing more than a chimera."

"Exchange is rising a little and specie coming into circulation tho' yet at an advance of 5 @ 15 ⅌ Ct. As confidence gains it will become more abundant which will operate in favor of the intercourse with America heretofore greatly interrupted by the low exchange and rarity of specie. Was exchange near par this Country would now pay 10 @ 20 ⅌ ct. higher for Tobacco, Rice, Indigo and Grain than any of its neighbours." This year, because of short crops, considerable grain would be taken in all of southern France. "The want of knowledge in America of the french manufactures, the inability and reluctance among the manufacturers to giving *foreign* credits, prevent an exchange of commodities." Unless government measures promoting mutual exchange are taken, he fears it will never come about. If Congress should establish arsenals and take clothing and supplies for the Indian trade, it would promote use of French manufactures. The "coarse woollens and fancy stuffs of Carcasson, Montpellier, Toulouse, and Montauban" are well adapted for this purpose and are cheaper than those of England. "The Linens also of Flanders, Brittany and Tourenne might be put in competition with those of England and Ireland. The trade in the Levant also offers many articles of exchange," as peace on much better terms may be made with the present Dey of Algiers.

He hopes Congress will establish duties and regulations for the consular officers. Fees and perplexities saved for American vessels in French ports by transferring their business and disputes from the Admiralty courts, always tedious and expensive, would pay a living to the consuls without adding to costs.

RC (DNA: RG 59, CD); 2 p. Recorded in SJL as received 14 Jan. 1792. Extracts printed in *National Gazette,* 16 Jan. 1792, along with Fenwick to TJ, 28 Oct. 1791. Enclosures: (1) Dupl of Fenwick to TJ, 31 Aug. 1791. (2) Fenwick to Short, 28 July 1791, stating that he has been asked by French merchants whether vessels bringing in tobacco after touching English ports are English, in which case they would be denied the right to unload their cargoes; that he has asked whether vessels touching in foreign ports without unloading would forfeit the right to sell their cargoes for consumption in France—a question which has been referred to Paris; that he has perhaps construed the decree too rigidly, advising that tobacco and oil could only be imported direct from America; that he believes touching in England would not benefit real American traders but only help preserve the English monopoly on American trade; that commercial privileges without reciprocal advantages cannot last and the fewer shackles on commerce, the more it will prosper; that he does not doubt all the tobacco then held there is English property, one of the ships being English "under the Cloak of American papers"; and that he will not be displeased if their cargoes are denied French consumption. At the close of the letter to Short, Fenwick added a note to TJ explaining that a complaint to Short from an English merchant in London caused him to give the details lest he should be censured and his conduct be misrepresented in America; that it had since been decided at Paris "that no Tobacco expedited for a foreign port, or having touched in one (except thro' necessity) shall be admitted in france for the Consumption of Country," a decision he feels is not a disadvantage to trade between France and America (Tr in clerk's hand, except for signature and note in Fenwick's; DNA: RG 59, CD).

From William Short

DEAR SIR   Paris Septr. 25. 1791.

I informed you in my last that it was uncertain what measures the national assembly would take with respect to their decree of May relative to the islands. The colonial committee have since made their report on that subject and the assembly adopted yesterday the decree which you will see in the paper inclosed, with a slight alteration in the 3d. and 4th. articles limiting the time of the provisory execution of the laws made in the colonies.

For some time past this subject has been that which has excited the greatest degree of acrimony in the opposite parties of the assembly. Both sides have made use of fabricated addresses, alarms and exaggerated reports to carry their point. Those who were in favor of supporting the decree of May, finding that several who had then voted for it had changed their opinions in consequence of the effect it had produced at S. Domingo, used every effort to adjourn the question of its repeal to the next legislature.—It was contended on the other hand that in order to quiet the colonies it was necessary to make a constitutional decree on this subject so as to put it out of the power of a future legislature to change it. How far future legislatures will consider this binding on them will depend on future circumstances. If they desire to change the decree they will argue as several of the members of the assembly did on this question— that they are no longer, agreeably to their own declaration, a *pouvoir constituant*.

No hostile manoeuvres seem to be preparing as yet against this country in consequence of the interview at Pilnitz. They will of course depend on the situation of internal affairs here. A few of the emigrants have returned, but a much greater number of disaffected persons continue to leave the kingdom, some merely from weariness of the present state of anarchy, and others with an intention of joining those who project plans of entering the kingdom in an hostile manner. It is expected the King will soon take some open and decisive measure with respect to his brothers and the powers who permit the emigrants to assemble openly and make hostile preparations on their territory.

You will have heard of the death of M. de la Luzerne in England. The dyes for the medal destined for him have been retarded in a most unexpected manner on account of the engraver being employed here in the new coinage. Previous to the death of M. de la Luzerne I explained to him the cause of this delay and sent him a letter from the engraver on the subject which he answered by a desire that the national work should be first performed. The dyes were since completed, but unfortunately one of them failed, as often happens, in the hardening. The engraver is now employed in repairing this evil and says it will be done in two or three weeks. I suppose it so certain that this medal should be given to M. de la Luzerne's representative, that as soon as it is ready I shall mention the subject to M. de Montmorin and follow his advice respecting it.

I have sent by the way of Havre to your address a box containing the usual papers and several books on the subject of mint of coinage for the Secretary of the treasury. I will thank you to mention to him also that I wrote to him by that port the day before yesterday, as I fear by a letter since received from thence that it may be detained there some time. This will go by the way of England, and will carry assurances of the respect & attachment with which I am, Dear Sir, your's affectionately,   W SHORT

PrC (DLC: Short Papers); at head of text: "*No. 84*"; at foot of text: "Thomas Jefferson Secretary of State, Philadelphia." Tr (DNA: RG 59, DD). Recorded in SJL as received 7 Dec. 1791.

In response to rising discontent among French West Indian planters and strong protests from French merchants involved in the colonial trade, the National Assembly on 24 Sep. 1791 rescinded its DECREE OF MAY 15 1791, granting the franchise to some "gens de couleur" in the colonies, and authorized the local colonial assemblies to determine the status of free blacks and mulattoes (*Archives Parlementaires*, XXXI, 282, 288). TJ's efforts to have a diplomatic MEDAL made in honor of the Chevalier de La Luzerne are discussed in Editorial Note and group of documents on Jefferson's policy concerning presents to foreign diplomats, 20 Apr. 1790.

The papers sent to Hamilton are Short to Hamilton, 23 Sep. 1791; and Willink, Van Staphorst, and Hubbard to Short, 8 Sep. and 16 Sep. 1791 (all printed in Syrett, *Hamilton*, IX, 226-35).

To James Brown

DEAR SIR   Monticello Sep. 27. 1791.

I was in hopes, when you were in this neighborhood, I should have had the pleasure of seeing you. Besides the gratification as a friend, I was anxious to settle our account. I gave to Mr. Donald the only list of the tobacco sold him which I possessed, and tho I had left directions to procure me another from the Lynchburg warehouse, it has not yet been done. From a general recollection of the amount, as well as a general idea of the monies and goods furnished, I know I had an expectation when I left Virginia in Octob. 1790. that the balance was sensibly in my favor. But I have so constantly experienced deception in my own favor in those general ideas that I confide little in them. I will thank you to furnish me the account.— I must beg the favor of you to send me by Mr. Randolph a small memorandum of muslin, dimity and shoes he has for my younger daughter who is going to Philadelphia with me: and 40. or 50. dollars cash for my travelling expences back, for a collection here has entirely failed on which I had counted for getting back. If you are in my debt, these furnitures will be in payment: if I am in yours, they shall be returned to you by a post banknote the day after my arrival in Philadelphia, and the balance on your books shall be paid of wheat now on hand. It will be equal to me to send you an order on the bank of Philadelphia for the amount of the muslin &c and money desired by Mr. Randolph as soon as the amount is known to me, as also whether it will be a payment or an advance: but I suppose I shall be at Philadelphia myself before any order I can send you after Mr. Randolph's return can go to Philadelphia by the way of Richmond. I am with great esteem Dr. Sir your most obedt. humble servt.,   TH: JEFFERSON

RC (NN).

The COLLECTION TJ had counted on while at Monticello was most likely that from the rent of Elkhill. See TJ to Nicholas Lewis, 24 Sep. 1791; and TJ to Robert Lewis, Jr., 5 Oct. 1791.

From David Humphreys

Lisbon, 27 Sep. 1791. Barclay arrived on the evening of the 23d instant and delivered TJ's dispatches of 13 May, 13 July and 26 July. These letters were the first to inform him of Barclay's mission to Morocco, a letter on this subject from Barclay in Philadelphia having failed to arrive.—On the 24th instant he gave the Compte de Rhode, the Prussian minister to Portugal, a letter for

William Carmichael on the subject of the prisoners in Algiers, a copy of which is enclosed. Despite the bitter complaints of the prisoners about the failure of the U.S. to secure their release, contained in late letters he has accidentally seen from Captain O'Bryen, he thinks it would be better for him to continue to negotiate through Carmichael rather than opening a direct correspondence with them. It would only subject him to "a torrent of pathetic and severe complaints, the source of which it would not be possible for me to remove," and lead the captors to demand a higher ransom.—He has conferred with Mr. Bulkeley about the money to be drawn from Holland for the subsistence of the Algerian captives, and Bulkeley promises no difficulty. Though disinclined to handle public money lest he make an honest mistake and fall under popular suspicion of mishandling public funds, "I will endeavour to have the business done in so clear a manner, and with such vouchers, as that I may have a right to *ask* and *receive* a definitive settlement of all the pecuniary concerns between the Public and myself, the *moment* they shall be completed. And I have to request as the last and greatest favour I can expect from your office, that you will be so kind as to facilitate my endeavours for the accomplishment of this object."—He suspects that the French Gazettes he expected to receive by the weekly post have been detained in Spain. He encloses several issues of the Leyden papers and has forwarded TJ's dispatches to Carmichael by the Compte de Rhode.—P.S. He will forward a copy of his letter no. 19, which describes his reception by the Queen, if he learns that TJ has not received the original.

RC (DNA: RG 59, DD); 4 p.; at head of text: "(No. 35)"; at foot of text: "The Secretary of State &c. &c. &c."; endorsed by TJ as received 6 Dec. 1791 and so recorded in SJL. Tr (same). Enclosure: Humphreys to Carmichael, 24 Sep. 1791, directing him to ascertain the disbursements made for the subsistence of the American captives in Algiers "by the Spanish Consul or others," so that he could arrange for the settlement of those accounts.

From Augustine Davis

Sir   Richmond Sept. 28th. 1791

I was honored with your favor of the 15th. inst this day, which was handed to me by a Mr. Carr, with two other letters for the mail, which will be forwarded to morrow.

I have been in daily expectation, for some time past, of having the Cross Post from this to Staunton fixed, but have been disappointed by the person failing to procure his securities. David Ross, Esq. and Major Langham, of Columbia, have recommended another person for the place, and have promised to render him every Assistance, in order that the business may be regularly performed; and I expect that in the course of 5 or 6 days to make a final close of the Contract.

With respect to the South Western post to go by Lynchburg rather than New London, has been mentioned to me by several gentlemen living at Lynchburg as more advantageous, it being a place of considerable trade and that the letters to and from Lynchburg would be greater, which induced me to conclude to fix it in that manner, when it shall be in my [power] to make the Contract, but as yet no person has offered for the place.

I am greatly obliged, Sir, for your mentioning that it has occurred to you that there may be a saving were the same post to do both as far as Columbia, which Idea had also struck me, and which I shall observe when it is in my power to make the Contract for the South Western Cross Post.

Accompany this are several letters addressed to your Excellency received from the Northward; all which I wish safe to hand. And have the Honor to be, Sir, yr Most Humble Servt,

AUGUSTINE DAVIS

RC (DLC); endorsed by TJ as received 3 Oct. 1791 and so recorded in SJL. Judging from entry in SJL, the letters enclosed by Davis were the following: (1) Johnson to TJ, 2 July 1791. (2) Maury to TJ, 12 July 1791. (3) Clark to TJ, 29 June 1791.

From William Short

DEAR SIR.   Paris Sep. 29. 1791.

I recieved two days ago from Havre your letter of the 28th. of July together with the newspapers and books for the consulates accompanying it.

I am sorry that the circumstance mentioned in the second and third page of that letter continues still in force. My letters will have explained to you how it was brought about by the personal interests and designs of some and the unparalleled ignorance of the greater number. Time and experience will correct it and the person who resides here now and he who may reside here then will probably be blamed for the one and commended for the other, and equally unjustly in both cases. In this distribution I shall have as little right to be satisfied as in the favors of fortune in general. You will probably soon after the date of your letter have recieved what was intended as a corrective of these errors. I wish much to know what may be thought of it on your side of the water. I have previously communicated my opinion respecting it. It is a subject which will require additional prudence and caution at present on account of the situation of affairs on this side.

What you mention in the third page of your letter as being complained of because misunderstood was often cited and was made an engine in the hands of the designing: but it was often also and fully explained to them. Nothing however can resist ultimately the constant efforts of a few artful men operating under the active principle of personal interest on a numerous and tumultuous body.

I was rendered happy by the cyphered part of your letter because it shews that I had not mistaken the sentiments which I was sure would prevail in America. I felt this with so much conviction that I have never failed whenever proper to assert it and to enforce it by arguments drawn as well from the nature of our government, and the character of our citizens in general, as the known dispositions of those who are now, and the probable dispositions of those who may hereafter arrive at the administration of affairs. The person to whom you allude has proper sentiments and the dispositions to be desired on this occasion. His influence however has much declined and in this instance would be less than in any other. Still it may be always counted on as far as it will go.

The assembly is to end its session to-morrow, and their successors of whom a great number have arrived, are to assemble the day after. It is already buzzed about that there is a party among them who will be against taking the oath prescribed for supporting the constitution; on the principle that they have full powers to alter it. I hardly think however that the oath will be objected to in the lump and from the start, although it is highly probable that it will be set aside in detail in the long run.

I shall send you by the way of Havre a report made by the committee of finance and adopted by the assembly, on the state of their finances before the revolution, during the assembly, and what it will be in future. It presents very flattering prospects but few people view them through the same medium.

The commissaries intended to be sent to S. Domingo are to set out immediately with instructions conformable to the decree for repealing that of the 15th. of May as already mentioned to you. They are to carry also an act of general amnesty for all the French islands. Opinions are divided here between those who think that the islanders from gratitude for the repeal of this decree will readily submit to strict commercial regulations, and those who think on the other hand that having thus found out a means of obtaining what they desire their pretensions will augment in proportion to the facility of realizing them.

I have been waiting for some time to get from London an account of postage due there in order to draw up my account to the beginning of July. I shall not wait longer for it and will send you this account exclusive of that article by the way of Havre, from whence a vessel sails without fail as I learn in the beginning of the month. It will arrive nearly as soon that way as by the English packet which carries this letter, and I have preferred that conveyance.—I have the honor to add assurances of the sentiments of attachment which I hope you will readily believe in your friend & servant,   W: SHORT

PrC (DLC: Short Papers); at head of text: "*No. 85*"; at foot of text: "Thomas Jefferson Secretary of State, Philadelphia." Tr (DNA: RG 59, DD). Recorded in SJL as received 27 Dec. 1791.

The CIRCUMSTANCES alluded to by Short were the discriminatory measures against American commerce adopted earlier in the year by the National Assembly, especially the imposition of a prohibitive duty on tobacco brought to France in American ships (TJ to Short, 28 July 1791). Short described his efforts to undo these measures in his letter to TJ of 6 June 1791. The

MISUNDERSTOOD subject mentioned by Short was the tonnage act passed by Congress in 1790, which the French contended was discriminatory with respect to their shipping (see Editorial Note and group of documents on representation by France against the tonnage acts, at 13 Dec. 1790). Short rejoiced in the CYPHERED section of TJ's letter of 28 July 1791 because it strongly denied that the United States had any designs on the French West Indies other than a wish to trade with them. Lafayette was the person through whom TJ wanted Short to convey this sentiment to the French government.

From William Short

DEAR SIR   Paris Sep. 29. 1791

My late private letters to you have been of July 7. (bis) and 17.— I received two days ago yours of July 28. inclosing a bill of exchange for £131.5 stlg. which shall be placed to your credit in the hands of V. Staphorst & Hubbard as has been already the balance remaining here in your favor.—I will send you by the way of Havre in a few days the continuation of our private account. In it you will see the amount of the Champagne wine and I will inform you also of the value in specie here of your bill of exchange.—My public account will go at the same time and I shall be much obliged to you to alter it or modify it in any manner you may judge proper.— I will see if any thing can be done with Barrois but I doubt it. The letters inclosed in yours have been forwarded to their several addresses, except that to Paine.—That to Gouv. Morris was delivered with my own hand.—A Person in whose skill I have confidence is to chuse the vanilla and it shall be forwarded to you immediately by the way of Havre.—I was happy to hear of my brother through you. American like he never lets me hear from him himself. Still I hope you will be civil and kind to him for my sake if he should

[173]

come to Philadelphia as I love him most tenderly knowing his real worth and merit. If R.H.L. should resign I should desire my conditional congé still more. My last private letters will have explained to you my ideas on this subject. Notwithstanding I then said so much of myself still I should repeat it here, if the hour of the post did not absolutely preclude me.—A letter from America informs me that the delay in the appointment of the minister here is supposed to proceed from your endeavouring to prevail on Madison to accept it and his hesitating and taking time to consider. As the person who writes me is a great friend of yours as well as mine I should have supposed what he said well founded if your letter did not prevent it.—If Madison doubts I should wish him to remain in America even if I were not interested because I am sure he may be more useful there and that he will find the ground here different from what he may expect.—It is supposed here that Mr. Ammond carries out in his pocket the commission of Minister Plenipotentiary and of course that one will be appointed for London. Genl. Schuyler it is thought will stand foremost for this place as I am told by an American here.

I received two days ago a letter from the Sec. of the treasury of Aug. 1. It gave me infinite pleasure on account of the satisfaction which it expresses relative to my conduct and he tells me that '*all are satisfied with* my *prudence and judgment.*' I feel that I stood in need of approbation, because in a business of that kind which has so many sorts of delicacy attending it, silence would have been painful. It is the kind of business which of all others it is the most disagreeable to meddle with and particularly when one acts alone. It is this consideration which would have made me excuse myself from it if it had been possible, and which made me, having undertaken it, act with additional rigour with the agents at Amsterdam.— That has brought on a difference of opinion betwixt us on a point which they propose referring to the Sec. of the treasury, and which I shall accept readily as it will place the decision where I desired it. I have kept him regularly informed of this circumstance and am sure he will be satisfied with it. I am much pleased with the favorable manner in which he has several times expressed himself of my conduct and hope he will have no reason to change. I am exceedingly sorry for the circumstances mentioned in the cyphered part of your private letter. I hope that experience will correct opinions which would otherwise be really dangerous. Adieu my dear Sir & believe me unalterably your affectionate friend & servant,   W: SHORT

I shall wait with much anxiety to learn what is done with respect to the appointment here and would be very glad to know if it were possible the causes of the unexpected delay in this appointment the two last sessions. I cannot help in spite of myself auguring sometimes favorably from it for myself. I see so few and (indeed no one) to whom the ground here would not be entirely new that I cannot find out the causes of preference, especially when I consider the usages of other countries even where difference in rank and birth has such weight.—I should be much obliged to you to send me the Journals of congress as well as the acts of each session. I have never received any part of the journals of the senate.—If I am to stay here the winter I should be glad also to have a suit of the best American cloth which I could wear here to court.

RC (DLC); at head of text: "*Private*"; endorsed by TJ as received 27 Dec. 1791 and so recorded in SJL. PrC (PHi).

TJ's INCLOSED letters to Gouverneur Morris and Thomas Paine were dated 26 July 1791 and 29 July 1791, the latter printed as Document XI in Editorial Note and group of documents on *Rights of Man*, at 26 Apr. 1791.

R.H.L.: Richard Henry Lee reportedly was about to resign from the U.S. Senate because of ill health. Short had expressed interest in becoming Lee's successor, but long before he actually left the Senate in

October 1792, Short was appointed minister to The Hague and joint commissioner with William Carmichael to negotiate a treaty with Spain.

The DIFFERENCE OF OPINION between Short and Willink, Van Staphorst, and Hubbard hinged on the question of whether the firm was entitled to a commission of 4% or 4½% on a 6,000,000 guilder loan it had recently negotiated for the United States. Short favored the lower figure, but Hamilton subsequently decided that the higher commission was proper (Mitchell, *Hamilton*, II, 128-33).

From Harry Innes

D R SIR   Kentucky September 30th. 1791

Impressed with an idea of the necessity and great utility which would result to government by uniting the views and interests of the Inhabitants of Kentucky with those on the North West side of the Ohio, and adopting some measures for reconciling existing jars between the Fœdral Troops and the people of this District, I take the liberty of suggesting to you an opinion on the Subject, with the hope that if we should concur in sentiment, you will be pleased to make such communications thereon as you may judge expedient.

What hath been the cause of the Division in the views of the people of Kentucky and those on the other side of the Ohio I cannot assign a reason for, but so it is prejudices exist which make us view each other as strangers, with very jealous eyes. The prejudices of the Military, and against them can in part be accounted for. The

Officers and soldiers who first descended the Ohio came with violent prejudices against the inhabitants of this District, viewing them in the character of Barbarians inhabiting a Wilderness without control. This idea, added to the imprudencies we often see men guilty of invested with power, supported by an armed force, and far removed from the supreme head, have caused jars between the Military and the Citizens of Kentucky, which hath been increased on the part of the people from a belief, that their general conduct hath been grossly misrepresented to Government thro' that channel.

There is no measure so likely to produce an union between the settlers on the two sides of the Ohio and destroy the existing prejudices against the Military as one or two appointments to be made from the District of influential characters in the Army, whose Estates would remain in Kentucky; it would cause an exertion in those Officers to banish discord and to desiminate the seeds of Harmony and unanimity. Such Officers would have but one interest and it would become essentially necessary to their own ease, happiness and duty also to lead all parties to center at one point. It would be an inducement to the Militia to march out with chearfulness when caled for, whose tardiness on a late call of Genl. St. Clair's had almost frustrated the views of Government for the present campaign. They will march it is true, but more like slaves than soldiers who are anxious to reap Laurels by their valour. Under this circumstance they are not to be relied on.

From a conviction of the good effects which would result from such a measure, and as the opportunity is now offering for such an accomodation by the resignation of Genl. Harmar, and that intended by and by of Genl. St. Clair, I am induced from a consideration of promoting the public good and also prompted by my friendship for Genl. James Wilkinson to solicit your interest for a command in his favor in the Fœdral Army, who is well acquainted with the views, interests, and dispositions of the Western people, who possesses very much the confidence of the people of Kentucky and who possesses Talents well adapted to bring about that reconciliation of parties, which would greatly contribute towards effecting the views of Government in the Western Country.

As Genl. Wilkinson was once honored with the rank of Brig. Genl. in the Army of the U. states he would still hope for a command equal thereto. If that cannot be obtained he would accept of a Regiment.

Pardon me sir for this intrusion upon your time and more important business. Nothing but a conviction of the benefits which

Government would derive by such a measure and a wish at the same time of promoting the inclinations of my intimate friend could have induced me there to.—I have the honor to be Dr. sir your mo. ob. servt.,   HARRY INNES

RC (DLC); addressed: "The Honble Thomas Jefferson Esq. Philadelphia"; endorsed by TJ as received 26 Oct. 1791 and so recorded in SJL.

Four days before Innes' letter reached TJ, Washington issued a commission to James Wilkinson to serve as Lieutenant Colonel Commandant of the Second Regiment. The Senate approved this appointment on 2 Nov. 1791. Wilkinson was also recommended for the appointment by two of his other Kentucky political allies, John Brown and George Nicholas (George Nicholas to Madison, 16 Sep. 1791, Rutland, *Madison*, xiv, 75-6; commission for Wilkinson, 22 Oct. 1791, facsimile reproduced in James R. Jacobs, *Tarnished Warrior: Major-General James Wilkinson* [New York, 1938], p. 114; JEP, i, 86, 88). See also George Muter to TJ, 17 Nov. 1791.

From Joshua Johnson

SIR   London 30 September 1791

I had the Honor to write you on the 12 Inst. by the Zephyr, Capt. Crombie, via Annapolis, to which I pray your reference.—We have nothing of a political nature stirring worth your attention: the King and his followers are still at Weymouth.—The general opinion is, that the Parliament will not meet 'till after Christmas to do Business; then, the Minister will face them, and give his reasons for the expensive Armament. The discharging the Ships of War, has thrown a number of our poor Countrymen loose on the World, who cannot get any employ, and who are in the most wretched starving situation; the trouble I experienced during the warmest time of pressing Men, is nothing to be compared to the present; as a Mans feelings, and Humanity is continually put to the rack, from the number of Objects who present themselves to him; at present there is but one American Ship in Port, so that I have not the Power to get them home by that means; and indeed if there were a Number here, I cannot generally applaud the Commander's humanity; for some have been wanton enough to demand from them, three to six Guineas ℘ Man, and the Man work his passage; however there are but few will take them without their Victuals being laid in; and as for the English Commanders, they will take none, alledging, that they may have what they please of their own Country, who will continue the Voyage; when Americans would be sure to run away on their arrival in their own Country; at this time I have many on my hands; particularly a Capt. MClemmey of Baltimore, who is insane, and whom

I have put to farm into a Poor House @ 4s/ ℔ week, untill I can find an American Captain who will take him home; I mention those matters that you may be enabled to represent them to Congress; who I trust will make provision for my reimbursement, and their future support under such circumstances. Inclosed I transmit you the quarterly Account of the inward, and outward Entries of all the American ships at the Port of London, ending this day; I also hand you inclosed, an Account of the Seamen, Citizens of the United States of America, which I protected during the last armamt. I kept no Account of those which I protected last year as I expected Congress would at their last session, have pointed out forms, and directions for the Consular Office.—I beg, Sir, that you will be pleased to lay those Papers before the President of the United States, from which (independent of the many matters which are constantly falling on me to do for the service of the Public) he may judge of the compensation the Public ought to make me for the past, and allow for the future, and urge Congress to pass an Act for that purpose.

It will probably be urged by some that the appointment may throw advantages into my hands, equivalent to the trouble; should any such reasoning be offered; I am ready to Swear, that I have never been benefitted by one single Commission (except a small one from Coll. Humphreys) and that my loss in undertaking the execution of the office, has by far exceeded any benefits; indeed my situation is different from any other. I am appointed to a place where every Merchant in America has his Correspondent, and who will not remove his Business so long as he does it well; but if the Captain of his Ship is arrested by a Seaman; or he gets into any Scrape, it falls on me to protect, and extricate him; whilst the Merchant is freed from any trouble, and is reaping the advantages of American favors.—Inclosed I hand you, my quarterly Account of Disbursements, and which leaves a Balance due me, from the Public of £42.1.5 which I doubt not, you will find right, and which pray note in conformity.

I mean to make duplicates of my applications to the Lords of the Treasury; the Lords of the Admiralty, and the Commissioners of the Customs, with the answers, and forward them to you ere long.— I am, with the greatest regard, and esteem, Sir, Your very obedient, & most Humble Servant,   JOSHUA JOHNSON

RC (DNA: RG 59, CD); in clerk's hand except for signature. Enclosure: financial accounts, 1 July-30 Sep. 1791; list of ships not found. FC (same); in Johnson's hand. Recorded in SJL as received 7 Dec. 1791.

From George Twyman

WORTHY SIR   [ca. 30 Sep. 1791]
The very great enequality in our Circumstances, But more in knowledg, Education, and preferment, makes it indisputable that you Can hope, or expect, any Sattisfaction from any Conversation that might be between us. And a Bare Sight of each-other must be full as little.—And although I have not Before now been to see you, yet I must say it is not for want of a Due Respect.—For being so sensible of your abillities, and my own weakness, am Bound to Conclude that my Confined thoughts to, and ingagements in, Domestick affairs, Can add nothing to your noble and Exalted minde.— What has attached my affections to you, I leve you to Judge, for I count no man my Superiour but as he Excels in Virtues, and none inferiour but for the Contrary.—However for the present, interest as wel as sattisfaction, induces me to make you a Visit, which I intend Shall be on monday, next.—And be the Case as it may, I shall be Sattisfied only to be inrol'd, and rather know, That I am your friend, which will better appear if ever it should be wanted.— In reasonable Service,   GEORGE TWYMAN

RC (MHi); addressed: "Mr. Thomas Jefferson Esqr. Albemarle per favour Mrs. Marks"; endorsed by TJ as received 30 Sep. 1791 and so recorded in SJL.

From C. W. F. Dumas

[*The Hague*], *1 Oct. 1791.* The King's acceptance of "la Constitution des françois" has strengthened the monarchy and ensured the future happiness of France. The replacement of the Legislative by the Constituent Assembly also bodes well for the progress of the revolution in France.—The news from the Netherlands is of quite a different nature. The money for the forced loan of 25th last no longer exists. Thirty million florins have been used to assist "la Compagnie des Indes orientales." The whereabouts of the other fifty million florins is unknown. As a result, taxes on wine, coffee, tea, tobacco, servants, horses, and crossing gates will be raised in the province of Holland.—The reports of a combination of the great powers of Europe against France are not to be taken seriously; "en bon françois, elles voudroient ce qu'elles ne peuvent."—*9 Oct.* Nothing is known about the new legislature in France except that it began by examining credentials.—P.S. *11 Oct.* The assembly in France "s'est déclarée législative, sans s'arroger rien de constituant." It precipitously passed and then revoked a decree on royal ceremonial. The "fugitifs" are more to be pitied than feared.

FC (Dumas Letter Book, Rijksarchief, The Hague; photostats in DLC); 3 p.; at head of text: "No. 83". It is not certain that TJ ever received this letter and its enclo-

sure. In his next letter to Dumas, he reported that he had received "Nos. 84. 85.

86. 87. and one of Sep 17. without a No."
(TJ to Dumas, 3 June 1792).

From David Humphreys

Lisbon, 1 Oct. 1791. He does not know when he will have another opportunity of directly forwarding letters to America as the last American vessel in the harbor has been sold and converted into a Portuguese ship. Taking advantage of the British packets, he announces that Louis xvi has accepted the French constitution and that acts of oblivion, recommended by the king and proposed to the National Assembly by Lafayette, will be adopted to generate acceptance of the new order.—Count Potocki, a Polish nobleman TJ may remember seeing in France at Madame d'Houdetot's, has just returned from Morocco with useful information for Thomas Barclay. The new Emperor will require more than twice the amount of money as his predecessors for negotiations, though Potocki thinks the United States will have less difficulty than other powers in treating with him. The Emperor is besieging Ceuta but will probably not capture the garrison. At Potocki's behest, Barclay will go from hence to Gibraltar and from thence to Tangier. Barclay knows the present governor of Tangier from his former mission to Morocco. "The reigning Emperor has beheaded most of the Persons who were about the Court in his father's time."—Something will be lost in the exchange between this place and Holland, "but the business shall be done as advantageously as possible, and Mr. Barclay's departure facilitated with all the Dispatch the nature of the circumstances will allow."

RC (DNA: RG 59, DD); 2 p.; at head of text: "(No. 36)"; at foot of text: "The Secretary of State"; endorsed by TJ as received 16 Jan. 1792 and so recorded in SJL. Tr (same).

From Fulwar Skipwith

DEAR SIR   Richmond 1 Octor. 1791

For some time back I had been looking forward to the agreeable event of your arrival at Monticello that there above all other places I might have the pleasure of paying you my respects in person. This satisfaction I am now compelled to defer untill your return to Philadelphia, being called to Norfolk by some little business of such urgency as will not indulge me with delay.

The same reasons which have led me to return from M/que I find by a letter lately received from Hispaniola have induced Mr. Bourne the Consul for the U States there to take up the resolution of leaving Cape François. That island seems to be overwhelmed in fresh troubles—'tis said that the negroes throughout are in insurrection and threaten destruction to the whites. No accounts however have I yet seen that in my opinion ought to be confided in or that lead me into a satisfactory knowledge of the nature of their disputes. M/que remains in peace, but its ports are shut against our flour. With the highest Respect and Esteem I remain my dear Sir Your mo ob Servant, FULWAR SKIPWITH

RC (DNA: RG 59, CD); endorsed by TJ as received 4 Oct. 1791 and so recorded in SJL. On Sylvanus Bourne's intention to resign his consulship, see Bourne to TJ, 10 and 29 Dec. 1791.

From Joseph Fenwick

SIR   Bordeaux 2d october 1791.

The inclosed letter was too late for the Vessel from Bayonne. I have Since Seen the Executors of Mr. Le Roi who have confirmed to me the legacy of 15.000₶ left to your neigbour Mr. De Rieux payable in 6, 12 and 18 months after his Death. The first payment is now Due and will be paid to the Attorney of Mr. de Rieux on demand. You can dispose of me in the remittance of the legacy to Virginia. Mr. Le Roy also left each of Mr. De Rieux's brothers 15,000.₶—I have the Honor to be Sir your most obt & most hble Servt.,   JOSEPH FENWICK

RC (MHi); endorsed by TJ as received 14 Jan. 1792 and so recorded in SJL. Dupl (missing) recorded in SJL as received 24 Feb. 1792.

The INCLOSED letter (missing) probably contained news of Derieux's legacy, which the latter had learned of from another source in August (Derieux to TJ, 12 Aug. 1791). See TJ to Fenwick, 24 Mch. 1791, for an explanation of Derieux's financial difficulties and attempts to obtain help from his family in France.

From William Short

DEAR SIR   Paris Octob. 2. 1791.

An end was put to the session of the national assembly the day before yesterday by the speech of the King and the answer of the President which I have the honor of inclosing you. There has been no instance perhaps where His Majesty has been more sincerely satisfied with the reception he met with from the public than that day.—The assembly room was crowded with people of all classes and all seemed to vie with each other in demonstrations of their attachment ⟨to the King⟩. He was much affected himself by these marks of affection and was moved in such a manner as to shed tears;

which changing the tone of his voice produced the same effect on the greater part of those present. Every sentence was interrupted by clapping of hands and cries of *Vive le Roi* as well from the assembly as the galleries.

The members of the legislature assembled yesterday morning, and formed themselves into divisions for the verification of their powers, and adjourned to this morning when they met again and a sufficient number being verified they formed themselves into an house. They are to meet to-morrow to chuse their proper officers and the day after the King is to go and open the session. No judgment as yet can be formed of the line in which they will march.

No answer has as yet been recieved from foreign courts to the King's notification of his acceptation of the constitution. The Princes continue to act as during the King's confinement and affect to consider him still in a state of captivity.—The encouragement and pressing invitations they hold out to emigrants induce great numbers still to go and join them daily. All here are anxious to see what measures the King will have taken with respect to those who are so nearly connected with him and who say they act in his name.

M. de Montmorin determines to realize an intention he has for some time had of retiring from the ministry. The place is offered to M. de Moustier and an express has been sent to him to Berlin. It is uncertain whether he will accept under present circumstances. This appointment is not yet known to the public so that I cannot say what effect it will produce on them. I fear however a bad one as he is considered by those who know him as decidedly an enemy to the present order of things. He has some bitter enemies among the most exagerated and dangerous members of the assembly who I am persuaded will exert themselves on all occasions to prevent his acquiring their confidence, which will be more than ever essential to the ministry now in order to prevent the assembly and its committees taking the administration into their hands.

I will write to you more fully respecting this appointment in my letter which goes by the way of Havre. This is sent by the way of England—I have the honor to be with accustomed sentiments Dear Sir, your affectionate friend & servant,   W: SHORT

PrC (DLC: Short Papers); at head of text: "*No. 86*"; at foot of text: "Thomas Jefferson Secretary of State, Philadelphia." Tr (DNA: RG 59, DD). Recorded in SJL as received 26 Dec. 1791.

From James Currie

Richmond, 3 Oct. 1791. He has learned from Colo. Randolph that TJ's visit to Monticello will be too brief to afford him time to pay his respects and extend personal thanks for TJ's assistance in helping him recover the debt John Griffin owes him. Griffin wrote him from Baltimore on 15 Sept., complaining of "the infamous conduct of those to whom he had confided his principal affairs and mentions particularly the name of one gentleman." Griffin asks him to be patient and he will repay his debt in time. Currie has "no faith in what he now says or writes," however, and asks TJ to resume his efforts to recover the debt when he returns to Philadelphia. He may come there himself "in the course of the ensuing Winter" on important business, and he will call upon TJ then. A visit to Mrs. Eppes "tother day" found her ill with "a Bilious fever," though he thinks she has since improved. Francis Eppes mentioned visiting Monticello if his wife continued improving. Mrs. Currie sends her compliments.

RC (DLC); 2 p.; endorsed by TJ as received 6 Oct. 1791 and so recorded in SJL. Robert Morris was the ONE GENTLEMAN named by Griffin. See TJ to Currie, 30 Aug. 1791.

From Gouverneur Morris

DEAR SIR   Paris 3 October 1791

I am favored with yours of the twenty sixth of July for which I pray you to accept my thanks. I mentioned to you from London that Mr. Walpole had been offered the Place of Envoy extraordinary to the United States which he had refused. I took Care to avoid any sort of Intercourse with the Government while I was there and of Course could not possess any minute Information worthy of your Notice. I avoided also seeing any of the Chiefs of Opposition lest some Conclusions of a disagreable Nature should be drawn from that Circumstance. Of Course it was not untill my Arrival in this City that I learnt (from the british Embassador here) what had been done. Mr. Hammond was sent for from Spain and passed thro this City while I was in London. I do not know whether he is gone out, if not you have long since I suppose received the Communication of his Appointment. The Plan seems to have been that which I long since mentioned viz the sending out a Minister with Letters of Credence in his Pocket to be delivered when you shall appoint to this Court.

From a Variety of small Circumstances I am convinced that the british Cabinet begins very seriously to consider its Situation in Respect to us. The rapid Rise of our Credit, the wise Decisions of our Courts, the general Peace and Order which prevail, and the gradual Display of our Population wealth and Industry, produce very great Effect upon their Minds. Let me add that the calm Dignity of those who are at the Head of Affairs has a considerable Influence. Events confirm me in the Opinions which I formed from an attentive Consideration of the Subject, and I think we may calculate almost with Certainty on forming a good Treaty with that Country as soon as they shall determine to form *any* Treaty; and untill that Time I agree fully with you that Attempts on our Part should be such only as to justify to the World that Conduct which it becomes us to pursue. I know that among the many whose Duty or Occupation it may be to consider this Subject there must be a Variety of Opinions because Dispositions Differ, because Prejudices exist, because Interests sway, in a Word because Men are Men; but Time will set his Seal of Truth on that which is right.

FC (NNC); in Morris' hand. Recorded in SJL as received 20 Dec. 1791.

From David Jameson

DEAR SIR   York Virginia Octob. 4. 1791

I was honoured with your letter of the 14th. of August, and am truly sorry it is not in my power to throw any light on the subject. I made it my business to see Mr. John Browne and Mr. John Pierce in hope that by a free conversation with them something might be thought of that would give aid to the business, but they assured me every thing that came to their knowledge they had communicated to Col. Davis. Mr. Brown you may remember was Commissary at the time; and Mr. Pierce was afterwards employed by the Executive to call on all the Commissioners in the different Counties for their Accounts and Vouchers. Mr. Pierce and Mr. Brown told me Col. Finnie (through whose hands many of the supplies passed as Contl. Q. Master) had delivered to Col. Davis his Accounts and Vouchers. And I cannot suppose but Col. Davis got from Mr. A. Blair every information *he* could give him. I am pretty certain that a great portion of the articles collected under the specific tax Law were expended for Continental purposes, but I have not a paper or Memo. now by me that will enable me to speak with any degree of preciseness on this important subject. I have been sick for upwards of three weeks, and am still so weak I find it difficult to write.—It will always give me great pleasure if my services can in any manner be made agreable to you, being with sincere Esteem Dear Sir Your Affectionate and Obedt humbl Servt,   DAVID JAMESON

RC (DLC); endorsed by TJ as received 22 Oct. 1791 and so recorded in SJL.

From Daniel Smith

Southwest Territory, 4 Oct. 1791. Letter of 12 Aug. to William Blount is received in his absence.—Provides answers to questions TJ asked relating to boundaries of Indian claims.—Rumors that Zachariah Cox has established a settlement on the Tennessee River are untrue. The Chickasaws permitted him to set up a post solely to trade with them. His acquittal by the Superior Court has encouraged others to think they can settle in that territory contrary to law. He has published a proclamation forbidding such incursions into the territory and enjoining those already there from aiding them.

RC (DNA: RG 59, SWT M-471/1; full text in Carter, *Terr. Papers*, IV, 83-4); 2 p.; endorsed by TJ as received 24 Oct. 1791 and so recorded in SJL.

To Francis Eppes

DEAR SIR   Monticello Oct. 5. 1791.

I was in hopes to have seen you here till Mr. Randolph arriving last night from Richmond, informed me Mrs. Eppes was unwell. I hope it has not been serious and that this will find her in that good health I wish her ever to enjoy. I set out four days hence with Polly for Philadelphia. I am following your example in taking measures to clear myself of Hanson at once as far as bonds will do it. These will be ready this winter, and very possibly I may come to Virginia in the spring to take such a clearance from him as our agreement entitles me to.

I cannot find Mazzei's account against Hylton. I imagine Mr. Blair has it. I thought I recollected pretty certainly his giving you a copy of it.

When I went away last year, I left a memorandum with Mr. Lewis to pay you the £19-6-10 you had been so good as to lay out for Polly, out of the money to be received from Woodson & Lewis on their bond, which they had promised to pay immediately. They have not paid a shilling since, which has prevented Mr. Lewis's reimbursing you. I have ordered suits against them, but this does

[185]

not concern you. I will furnish Jack with that sum in Philadelphia, so you may consider it as if you had made him that remittance.

I think it would be well to import about £30. sterling's[1] worth of books for Jack annually. Otherwise, when the time comes of his wanting them, it will be so heavy a job that it will be put off from time to time, and perhaps be never done, and he will go on bungling thro' life for want of them. The order should go to Europe in April, that the books may come in before the winter. In a winter passage books always get injured, or ruined.

A thousand things crowding on me oblige me to conclude with expressions of my warm affection to Mrs. Eppes yourself and family. Adieu my dear Sir Your's sincerely, TH: JEFFERSON

P.S. Mr. Skipwith writes me that Wigan the administrator of Bevins has brought suit against us. I do not recollect the nature or amount of the debt. Will you be so good as to inform me of the sum, how due and on what evidence, and who and where is the agent. Where a debt is just I think it best to transact it amicably with the creditor.

RC (DLC). PrC (MHi); consisting of the first page only (see note 1).

[1] First page of RC and PrC ends here; second page of PrC missing.

To Robert Lewis

DEAR SIR   Monticello Octob. 5. 1791.

It is with a great deal of pain that I have found myself under a necessity of having suits brought against two persons so nearly connected with yourself and Mrs. Lewis as your son Robert and Capt. S. Woodson. You know that I was left burthened with a great debt for Mr. Wayles's estate, and in scuffling to pay what I could of that, I suffered my own accounts to accumulate. My attornies found it necessary in 1785. to sell negroes to answer these demands, and to rent out the lands at Elkhill on which these negroes had been working. Messrs. Woodson & Lewis purchased negroes, and the latter rented Elkhill. A large sum is still due on their joint bond for the negroes, and not a shilling has been paid for rent after four year's occupation of the place. As long as my creditors could be kept quiet, I have indulged these gentlemen from no earthly motive but their connection with you. Theirs are the only debts which have not been either paid or called for long ago. At length I am sued, and I cannot think of selling more of my property merely to indulge those who have already been indulged six years. Had my stay here been long enough to have written to them and got answers, I would have waited. But I set out for Philadelphia in four days, and have therefore put my demands against them into the hand of Mr. Pope. I could not go away without expressing to yourself and Mrs. Lewis the uneasiness this has given me. But I am sure you are both so reasonable as to see in my past indulgence too real a proof of my attachment to you to doubt the sincere & antient friendship of Dear Sir your friend & servt, TH: JEFFERSON

PrC (MHi).

To Robert Lewis, Jr.

SIR Monticello Oct. 5. 1791.

My principal object with respect to Elkhill being to sell it, I do not propose to subject it to any lease which might disappoint me of a purchaser. If you think proper to continue the occupation as lessee at will as you have heretofore done and on the same terms, I consent to it. But I shall expect the rent of the year to be paid with the produce of the year, and think it but fair to observe to you that after a reasonable time for selling your crop, I shall not fail to exact the rent. Four years occupation already and not a shilling paid have proved to me the necessity of the disagreeable means I have been forced into of demanding my rent by a suit. Mr. Pope is instructed to do this, and you will be pleased to settle with him for the past. Colo. N. Lewis tells me he will pay me for you the sum of £22-9-11½ which therefore I am willing to take in his hands. He allows no interest on it.—I am Sir your humble servt,

TH: JEFFERSON

PrC (MHi).

To Henry Skipwith

DEAR SIR Monticello Oct. 5. 1791.

I am favoured with yours of Sep. 4. which comes to me here. In the suit you mention to be brought by Bevins's exr. against you and myself, the order of the names is not even an irregularity. The omission of Mr. and Mrs. Eppes is more material, and if he will not amend his writ by consent, we ought to oblige him to do it by plea.

I will beg the favor of you to have my appearance entered with your own, and think we should do well to avail ourselves of no cavils or checks which might indispose the plaintiff to reasonable indulgencies. Where does Mr. Wigan live? Or who acts for him here? Will not an accomodation be prudent and practicable? What is the amount? It is all out of my head.

With respect to the queries you propose on the subject of the paper signed between Mr. Hanson and yourself I shall always be ready to answer them. The whole transaction appeared to me thus. You refused to sign our general agreement but with a salvo of the benefit of your paiment into the treasury. Hanson refused to admit the salvo, each with equal positiveness. This suspended our treaty till after several trials you could form a paper in such terms as in your opinion saved your paiment, and in his did not. The paper being formed, both signed it, with meanings directly opposite, and each confiding in his own view and understanding of the instrument. So that each thinking himself safe in signing it, the accomodation as to Mr. Eppes and myself was no longer obstructed.

You mention a debt of the late Ben. Harrison to Coles, but do not say whether it concerns us. Was Mr. Wayles security for it? If he was, I am clear, in all cases of his securityships, for taking every benefit which the law allows us: for in these cases it is nothing more than a struggle between two parties who shall avoid a loss which is unjust on both. The act of limitations would certainly save us even in the case of a bond, which must be more than 20 years old. After that time, Chancery will presume it paid, and in any event quiet a security. If we are concerned, take care that no fault in pleading should bring on us a new liability.

I wish my stay in Virginia would have permitted me to visit Hors du monde and Eppington. But I now set out within four days. I am taking measures for putting into Mr. Hanson's hands bonds enough to clear me. I think it possible this may bring me to Virginia in the Spring. If so, I shall see you somewhere, and possibly at Hors du monde. I am happy to hear that Mrs. Skipwith is got better. God bless her and all of you. Adieu my dear Sir Your's affectionately,

TH: JEFFERSON

PrC (CSmH).

From James Yard

St. Croix, 5 Oct. 1791. He encloses an account of the annual imports and exports of St. Croix and St. Thomas and a list of duties on imports from America. The former is not entirely accurate. The quantity of imported Indian meal is probably one fourth and that of imported lumber one third less than the figures given in the enclosed account, "as permission to export Sugars is granted only to Such persons as import Lumber, Cattle and coarse provisions for Negroes, and even in that Case only to one Half the Value of Such Articles, paying besides a Duty of 7 1/2 ℔Ct." Imports of superfine flour and rye meal are at least 1,000 barrels less than the official figures because both of these products are subject to a duty of 10 ℔ct. Many people have turned to smuggling sugar because of the high duty on it and the difficulty of obtaining permission to ship it.—He expects to learn by the end of the year of the Danish government's attitude toward his consular appointment and in the meantime has had many opportunities to be of service to his countrymen.

RC (DNA: RG 59, CD); 2 p. Recorded in SJL as received 1 Nov. 1791.

To David Meade Randolph

SIR   Monticello Oct. 6. 1791
The office of Marshal for the district of Virginia being now to be newly filled, on the appointment of Colo. Carrington to the department of the Excise, I take the liberty of asking whether it would be acceptable to you. If you authorize me to say so to the President, the appointment will be given to you. It's duties are as yet scarcely sketched out, by the federal legislature. By turning to the act of the first session of Congress, chap. 20. sect. 27. &c. you will see what has been prescribed and provided for that officer hitherto. As I shall be in Philadelphia before any answer of your's can reach me, I must beg the favor of you to direct it to that place.—I have the honor to be with great respect Sir Your most obedient humble servt,
                                                                          TH: JEFFERSON

PrC (DLC).

From William Short

DEAR SIR   Paris Octob. 6. 1791.
I inclose you at present my account with the U.S. from July 1. 90. to July 1. 91.—A balance as you will see remained due to me at that date of 4146. florins of which 1846. were due on the account

[189]

of the year before. This shews that the whole of my salary is not expended which arises from two circumstances. 1. That I had for a long time no house rent to pay, and 2. that I have not augmented my expences in proportion to the augmentation of my salary for the last year. The uncertainty of the time I should remain prevented me from forming so extensive an establishment as I should have done if I had been permanently fixed and in this I conformed to usage. Besides my expences being born whilst I was in Holland increases the balance 1116. florins more than I had expected. In consequence of your last letter of July 28. I have charged those expences which I did not know before that I should be authorized to do. You will find four accounts annexed to the general account of Dr. and Cr. They contain the details of articles announced in general terms in the general account. The vouchers of the account that is to say the receipts for such articles as admit of receipts, remain in my hands. They may be thought necessary in the final settlement of the account, but still I did not know whether I should risk them lest they should be lost and as they are the only proofs I have. I do not know what is the usage in such cases. If you desire that they should be sent I will thank you to say so and it shall be done immediately. Should any part of the account require explanation I hope you will ask it also, and I renew here my request to you to arrange it in any manner you may judge proper as mentioned in your last. The reciepts for my tavern expences and carriage hire at Amsterdam are lost, because I did not know that I should have occasion for them. The charges made therefore are taken from my journal where they were entered in proportion as paid and conformably to the reciepts then given. If necessary I can have the reciepts renewed I imagine, as the books of the tavern and carriage hires will shew them. The carriage hire will be found moderate, as I did not keep one constantly, finding it as well in the manner things were there to take one only the days I went out. I charge the wages of my valet de place in consequence of your letter as I kept one constantly the whole time. My travelling servant desired that instead of paying his tavern expences I would augment his wages as is the usage which I did. I charge therefore this augmentation instead of the tavern expences which I should otherwise have had to charge.

I recieved in your last letter the bill of exchange you indorsed me for £131.5/. sterlg. I send it to Messrs. V. Staphorst & Hubbard to be kept at your disposition. Previous to this there was a balance for you in their hands remitted from hence as formerly mentioned to you. The value of the bill at Paris is 4742₶. 15s in assignats and

3436₶ in specie according to the present rate of agio and exchange.

I do not send you the continuation of your private account to this day because Mr.¹ Grand has not made out the one he promises me daily. Immediately on recieving it it shall be forwarded to you, which may be perhaps before this leaves Havre. In the mean time I can inform you that Mr. Grand paid for the champagne wine 1680. livres, and that de la Motte paid on the same as follows: Transportation to Havre and duty in Rouen on four

	₶ s.	
hampers champaign wine	203.5.6	
Laboures and porterage of do.	6.8	226₶.18
Duty outre on do.	17.4.6	

You will recieve in the gazettes sent the 50. batons de Vanilla you desired. It cost 20. sous the baton. It was chosen by Mde. de Flahaut who says it may be relied on as excellent. Besides Piebot seemed so well satisfied with your remembrance, that I am persuaded he has given only the best in hopes of a continuance of your practice.

I observe that you pass over in silence a great many of the articles contained in my several letters, and in that case I suppose nothing further is to be done on them and shall therefore not send the *proces verbaux* of the national assembly which I asked you about in one of my letters of which you acknowlege the reciept.

I have already mentioned to you that an express was sent to Berlin to offer the department of foreign affairs to De Moustier. It is not yet known whether he will accept. The appointment astonishes all those who are informed of it, as he had expressed himself hostile to the present order of things. It arises principally I believe from an opinion of his having talents, firmness and courage. Some of the members of the former assembly who were for a long time called the *enragés* and who true to the end supported the monarchical system, as Lameth, Duport, and Barnave, with whom De Moustier was indirectly connected, have probably had some influence on this appointment by their advice. M. de Montmorin will probably remain in the council.

I imagine that this appointment will not please generally in America. So far as relates to our business with Spain it may probably be considered as a misfortune, or at least it would certainly have been more agreeable, and more safe, to have had it in the hands of M. de Montmorin. Still I think there are reasons which will prevent his acting in opposition to what he knows to be the public opinion of the U.S. on this question, not from affection to America for that it would be unsafe to count on with any minister, but from a desire to keep the U.S. in the balance of the house of Bourbon. His old plan with respect to France acquiring territory on the Mississippi he will find it difficult if not impossible to gain a taste for here. The nation have so much to do at home and in its own neighbourhood that it will be impossible to bring them to think of an acquisition of this kind at present. Should De Moustier be for reviving the system however I think he will endeavour to bribe us into a connivance by offering the navigation of the river in hopes of restricting it hereafter. It is possible also that having the plan still at heart and finding the moment unfavourable he may underhandedly endeavour to prevent the cabinet of Madrid granting what we want now in order to be able thereafter to induce us to aid in its execution in order to obtain of France (or the promise of it) what we now ask of Spain.

There are other subjects in which I think the appointment of De Moustier will not be disadvantageous to the U.S. Although he may be as it has been often said, personally ill disposed towards the U.S., yet it is certain that he has a better idea of their rising greatness and the necessity of favoring close connexions with them than any minister that could be appointed. Another truth of which he is fully convinced also is that commercial connexions are the only basis which can be relied on for those of a political nature with the U.S. After his return from America I had several conversations with him on these subjects and his sentiments appeared then to be what we should wish. It is impossible to say however how far a change of place may bring on a change of opinions and whether M. de Moustier minister of foreign affairs and M. de Moustier desiring to be employed somewhere or other, may be the same. I spoke to you of him in my letters last year. He was then a great advocate for a liberal treaty of commerce being formed, and he told me more than once, after he was named for Berlin, that if one was to be negotiated he would wish to be sent for and that he would return to Paris for that purpose. He desired I would mention this to M. de Montmorin. He shewed me also as I mentioned to you in my letter of Oct. 27. 90. what he had written to Mr. Necker on the subject of augmenting the commerce of France with the U.S. and Mr. Necker's answer.

On the whole if a treaty of commerce is to be formed I should think it not a misfortune that it should be done with De Moustier, for this reason only that his knowlege of the rising force of the U.S. will have convinced him of the importance of being friendly allies to them and because he is well persuaded that proper commercial connexions are the only solid basis of such an alliance.

Whether this is the proper time to form such a treaty with France is another question which will merit very great attention, and which cannot be decided in this moment on account of the present situation of this government. The constitution is formed on paper but it has not yet been put in practice. Doubts exist every where among thinking people whether it can be carried into execution, and if not by what means a change will be effected. In such a situation it may be doubted whether administration can be brought to give proper attention to the negotiation of a treaty of commerce, and also how far such a treaty would be considered as valid, if a total change of the present order of things were effected by any means from abroad. Although this is not probable yet it is impossible not to take it into the account. A proper judgment of its weight can be formed only with time.

Under these circumstances as it will be necessary I suppose to take some measure at least ostensible in consequence of the decree of the assembly and the instructions carried out by Ternant on this subject, might it not be well to authorize the Minister residing here to prepare this treaty and in conjunction with him who may reside at London or elsewhere in Europe, to conclude it? (I take it for granted that the U.S. will prefer appointing two or three persons in all cases to conclude treaties of commerce on account of the separate interests of the separate states. This would be more satisfactory to all parties and particularly the agents employed for such purposes.) If this mode were adopted the U.S. will have done all that can be expected of them by this country, no useless effort will have been made, and no favorable opportunity, if such an one should present itself, will have been lost.

Should this mode be judged proper and should I continue here (which I must own I cannot help entertaining hopes of after so long a delay and other considerations often mentioned to you) I should hope to receive from you very full instructions on this subject. I should certainly use every effort in the preparatory steps, but on all accounts should desire to be joined by one or more for the conclusion of the business. Under these circumstances I confess I should be happy to be employed in a business where I should have hopes of being useful to my country, being persuaded that proper commercial connexions with France on liberal principles would be highly advantageous to both countries.

You will see in the *gazette universelle of Oct. 4.* an article respecting

Morris which I should not have mentioned if it had not been published, although perhaps I ought to have done it, as I think it probable he holds out an idea here that if he is not appointed as minister, it will be because he does not chuse it. That would seem to render it my duty to inform you in what light he is considered at this place. With respect to the article abovementioned I do not observe that it has made any very great impression, because such a variety of matter and particularly calumny appears in the gazettes that it is readily forgotten. But his aristocratical principles, his contempt of the French revolution and of the French nation expressed in all societies without reserve, and his dogmatizing manner and assumed superiority has exposed him generally to ill will and often to ridicule. For some time he was a favorite among the aristocratic party, but even that is now worn off, and as the French have no measure in their expressions of people they dislike they say of Morris the most disagreeable things, many of which I know he does not deserve, but it produces the same effect. As he is engaged in commercial affairs it is in that way they attack him. He told me himself of a report which circulated here, that he was an enemy to the revolution because under the ancient system he had an exclusive contract with the ministry &c. As he is a very active talking forward man and goes about a good deal he has established generally and particularly in the corps diplomatique who see him at the Count de Montmorin's that he is *un intrigant.* I have really taken pains to wipe off this opinion with several who have told me they considered him in that light, because I was persuaded he did not deserve it, and that it was his vanity alone that made him act in a manner which gave him that appearance. It will be impossible however to check that opinion when it comes to be generally known. It is now generally believed that he sent to the King the observations as mentioned in the *gazette universelle* with a plan of conduct. A foreigner who thus meddles in the affairs of a country with which he has nothing to do, and particularly in opposition to the public opinion does it at his peril and risk and cannot blame those who attach the seal of intrigue and design to such conduct, and particularly when he is a volunteer. Morris says that his plan was received with favor but rejected by fear. I know however with certainty that the letter of the King on his acceptation was concerted at M. de Montmorin's and written by a former friend of Mirabeau employed by M. de Montmorin for that purpose. I know not by what channel Morris sent his proposition as there are ten thousand private ways of conveying such things, but I think it must have been far from agreeable to M. de Montmorin, being in opposition to the plan he proposed and supported. This letter will go by a private hand to Havre, its contents particularly the latter part are only between you and me. I should not have said any thing on the subject but for the reasons abovementioned. I have really thought it my duty to shew, as is the case, that if there is any idea of appointing Mr. Morris here (which I rather suppose he gives out sometimes though he always says the contrary to me and confines himself to say he *fears* he shall be appointed to London) that there are reasons against it which deserve to be weighed and which can have been observed only here.—Adieu my dear Sir and believe me Your friend & servant,

W: SHORT

RC (DLC: TJ Papers, 66: 11538 [first two pages]; 63: 10947-9 [final six pages]); partly in code, with interlinear decoding in TJ's hand; at head of text: *"Private"*; endorsed by TJ as received 10 Feb. 1792 and so recorded in SJL. PrC (DLC: Short Papers).

[1] From this point, at the beginning of the third page in the manuscript, TJ marked an X through the remainder of this and the next two paragraphs.

To Tubeuf

SIR   Monticello Octob. 6. 1791.

I am honored with your favor of Sep. 11. and should have been much pleased to recieve you personally, had the cares with which you are charged permitted it. I congratulate my own country on the acquisition of so many good people from yours; and sincerely wish that in your particular case the advantages may be reciprocal. I have seen enough to be always in fear that strangers may not find their situation here as satisfactory as they may have been made to expect. I desire much that this fear may be groundless as to you and those who have come with you, and shall be happy in every occasion of proving to you my wishes for the prosperity of your enterprize, and the sentiments of esteem & regard with which I have the honor to be Sir Your most obedient & most humble servt,

TH: JEFFERSON

PrC (DLC).

To Francis Walker

Sir   Monticello Oct. 6. 1791.

When last in Virginia I wrote pressingly to Mr. Lyle to have my father's estate's account copied from the books of Kippen & co. from his death to the commencement of the account he had furnished Mr. Nicholas. On my arrival here now, I wrote to him for the account in hopes it was ready. I just now recieve his answer in these words. 'Manchester Sep. 28. 1791. Dear Sir, I am favored this morning with your letter dated the 15th. It gives me pain that you have been obliged to write me again on the subject of the £200. I have no clerk with me, but I will immediately employ one to draw up the estate's account from 1757. I have the books to look out for, for the first five years. As you will be gone to Philadelphia, I will so soon as tis finished forward it to you there.' Thus the settlement of this matter is postponed for another year, however anxious I am to see it settled, because should any accident happen to me, no one will bestow equal attention on it. Mr. Lyle is without any doubt of establishing the article of £200 of 1766. Aug. 31. and as to that of £199-18-1 of 1761. March (and not of £200 as stated in Dr. Walker's acct.) since I last wrote you on the subject, I have found, in corroboration of Dr. Walker's books, the account book of Mr. Harvie, where in two different places he states the same payment. The one is in[1] the estate's account with Dr. Walker, entered in Mr. Harvie's own handwriting in these words '1762. To cash in account with Mr. McCaul £199-18-1' and again in a settled account with McCaul in these words '1762. Dec. 25. By cash paid per orders from Thomas Walker £199-18s-1d.' I should suspect that in Dr. Walker's account the date of the year 1762 is omitted 1. because Mr. Harvie charges it in 1762. 2. because the March which followed Apr. 1761. must have been March 1762. Mr. Harvie's entry in McCaul's account 'cash paid *by orders* from T. Walker,' renders it probable the money was drawn by different orders from McCaul, and accounts for Mr. Lyle's not having been able to find the single sum of £200 at that date. Still the books of Dr. Walker and of Mr. Harvie establish the charge of 1761. 1762. and Mr. Lyle will establish that of 1766. Aug. 31. in date as well as sum. I hope he will enable me in my next visit to Virginia to see the question finally settled. I have the honor to be with great esteem Dear Sir Your most obedt. humble servt.,   Th: Jefferson

RC (DLC: Rives Papers); addressed: "Francis Walker esquire at Castlehill"; endorsed. PrC (ViU: Edgehill-Randolph Papers; MHi); see note 1.

Lyle's letter of 28 Sep. 1791, recorded in SJL as received 3 Oct. 1791, has not been found.

[1] The first page of the document ends here. Page one of the PrC is at ViU; page two is at MHi.

To James Wilson

SIR   Monticello Oct. 6. 1791.

Colo. Nicholas Lewis has communicated to me the account you inclosed him of your transactions in my affairs and I am happy to find them drawn so near to a close. There appear to me two corrections however to be made in the account. The first respects the article of £9-5-7 which had been charged in the account of Richardson & Scruggs's bonds which you had rendered before in these words '1786 Nov. to cash pd. Cum. Sheriff £9-5s-7d.' consequently it should not be charged again in the last account which respects only the bonds of Austin, James, Carter, and Randolph. Another correction respects Mr. Randolph's bond, on which, allowing the credits claimed by Mr. Randolph, the balance will be £81-19-9 instead of £70-16-3 as credited in your account. For thus I state it.

		£ s d	£
1785. Feb. 1.	Mr. Randolph's bond		105
	By Randolph & Cary's acct.	31–18–3	
	4. years interest on do.	6– 7–8	38– 5–11
			66–14– 1
	Int. on £66–14–1 to Sep. 1789. 4y. 7m.		15– 5– 8
			81–19– 9

I suppose the following therefore to be a true statement of our account at present.

	£
Mr. Wilson to Th:J. Dr. to balance as per acct. rendd. Sep. 1791.	6– 7–2
To a sum twice charged	9– 5–7
To short allowance for Randolph's bond	11– 3–6
	26–16–3

The[1] articles left blank in your account on both sides may produce some small alteration. Whatever the real balance is, I will be obliged to you to pay it to Mr. Dobson to whom I shall send an order on you, not for any specific sum, but for the balance whatever it may be.

I propose this summer to make a sale which will probably give a great deal more of this business to be done. I believe you will be pretty much in the center of it, and I shall be happy to put the bonds into hands so diligent.—I am with great esteem Sir Your very humble servt.,

TH: JEFFERSON

PrC (MHi); incomplete (see note 1). Tr (ViU); in a 19th century hand.

The ACCOUNT from Wilson has not been found, but a related document is "Memo. of Accounts delivered James Wilson to Collect for Th: Jefferson," ca. 1791 (MS in MHi), which contains the following:

Abner Witt	£ 3.16.11
Leonard Price	2.10.
Th. Turpin	7.15

Jo. Cabbell	3. 7. 3
Isaac Cole	5
Saml. Gay	2.17. 9
Wm. Allegre	1.10
James Pleasants	3.18
John Fry	8
John Coles	10
Wm. Cabbell	7.12. 3
Alex. Fretwell	2.12. 6

[1] PrC ends here; remaining text supplied from Tr.

To John Bolling

DEAR SIR   Monticello Oct. 7. 1791.

I should have been extremely gratified could my stay in Virginia have permitted me to have paid you a visit in Chesterfeild, and it would have been some compensation for the want of that power, had my sister's visit to this place happened to fall in with mine. In the ensuing spring I think it possible that business may call me into your neighborhood, in which case I shall most assuredly have the pleasure of seeing yourself and family.

I wrote you from hence the last year, inclosing a statement of your account with my mother's estate &c. I am recently called on by James Lyle for a debt due from that estate to Kippen & co. amounting with interest now to about £180. The great sums I am already in advance beyond the value of all my mother's assets, and the amount of other debts I am pressed to pay have obliged me to authorize Mr. Lyle to recieve what was due to my mother. Of this nature was the chief part of your balance, amounting on the 6th. of March 1790. to £52-19-8 according to the account I then enclosed you, for which sum I have therefore given him an order on you. I would not have done it to any person who would have been troublesome to you, which I know he will not be; and I hope you will not think it unkind in me to have lessened as much as I could this demand for my mother when I inform you that for the balance[1] of that demand, and of others which I cannot otherwise answer I find myself obliged this winter to make a very considerable sale of negroes in addition to the sales of land I have already made and shall further make.—Present my best love to my sister and the family and be assured of the sincere affection of Dear Sir Your friend & servt,

TH: JEFFERSON

PrC (MHi); consisting only of first page, second page being in ViU (see note 1).

[1] PrC in MHi ends here; remainder of letter is among fragments of the Edgehill-Randolph papers in ViU.

TJ's letter of THE LAST YEAR was TJ to Bolling, 6 Mch. 1790.

To Andrew Donald

SIR
Monticello Oct. 7. 1791.

When I left Virginia the last year, I left with Colo. Nicholas Lewis instructions to pay you for Wm. & James Donald & co. £27-3-9 with interest from Apr. 19. 1791.[1] out of some money due to me on bond and for rents from Robert Lewis and Samuel Woodson, of which they had promised prompt payment. They paid not a shilling which prevented Colo. Lewis from doing as I had desired. I have put my demands against those persons into the hands of Mr. Pope an attorney, who has brought suits against them in the Richmond District court. Both the persons are wealthy, and I now inclose you an order on Mr. Pope for the money as soon as he shall recieve it, which being the surest and speediest resource in my power, will, I hope, prove satisfactory to you. I am with great esteem Sir Your most obedt. humble servt,
TH: JEFFERSON

PrC (CSmH). Enclosure: Order addressed "N. Pope esq. Atty. at law," in TJ's hand, signed, and dated 7 Oct. 1791, directing Pope to pay Andrew Donald for William and James Donald & Co. £27 3s. 9d. "currency with interest thereon from the 19th. of April 1783. of the monies for which you have brought suits for me against Robert Lewis & Samuel Woodson when you shall have recieved so much thereof" (PrC at foot of foregoing in CSmH; Tr in ViU).

[1] Thus in MS; 1783 intended.

To James Lyle

DEAR SIR
Monticello Octob. 7. 1791.

In your letter of Oct. 23. 1790. you informed me there was a balance due to Kippen & co. from my mother of £126-9-5. currency before the beginning of the war. This letter having been delivered me just as I was setting out for Philadelphia I informed you I could give no answer to it till I should come here this present fall. I have now had time to examine papers on that subject and find no reason to doubt the demand. I have greatly overpaid the assets of that estate which have come to my hands, even counting at their full value negroes in which the testatrix had only a life estate. Yet as I paid all demands against her during her life, and believe that on view of that she had credit and quiet from the merchants with whom she dealt, I am willing to assume this debt also to be paid with interest from Apr. 19. 1783. the year after my last instalment shall be due to Henderson McCaul & co. that is to say on the 19th. of July 1796. to which, on receiving your agreement to it, I will oblige myself in due form.

There remains due from me on my bond to Harvie & co. assigned to Henderson McCaul & co. the balance, according to my statement of £54-5-6 with interest from Apr. 19. 1783. amounting now to about £77 or £78. You will oblige me if you will collect the inclosed order from Mr. Bolling for £52-19-8 and interest from Mar. 6. 1790. and place it to the[1] credit of that balance. I rendered an account to Mr. Bolling the last year, and write to him now on the subject.

Your letter of Sep. 28. is duly recieved, and I shall be thankful for the copy of the account therein promised. I am extremely anxious on that matter, being assured that if any accident happens to me before it is finally settled, no one else will take so much trouble to settle it rightly as I shall do.

I set out for Philada. within three or four days, from which place you shall hear from me again.—I am with great esteem Dear Sir Your friend & servt, TH: JEFFERSON

PrC (CSmH); consisting of first page only, the second page being in MHi (see note 1). Enclosure: Order on "Mr. John Bolling Chesterfeild" in favor of James Lyle for £52 19s. 8d. "current money of Virginia with interest thereon from the 6th day of March 1790, being the balance that day due from you to me according to an account then rendered you" (PrC at foot of foregoing in MHi).

Lyle's letter of 28 Sep. 1791, recorded in SJL as received 3 Oct. 1791, has not been found, although it is quoted in TJ to Francis Walker, 6 Oct. 1791. A letter from Lyle, perhaps in response to this, of 28 Nov. 1791 is recorded in SJL as received 10 Dec. 1791, but it also is missing. A portion of it is quoted in TJ to Thomas Mann Randolph, 18 Dec. 1791, however.

[1] First page of PrC in CSmH ends here; remainder of letter taken from fragment in MHi.

To Nathaniel Pope

SIR   Monticello Octob. 7. 1791.

Colo. Nicholas Lewis having declined the care of my affairs, I
have been obliged so to arrange them as that much more attention
to them falls on myself, and particularly as to the direction of the
collection and payment of my debts: and as my occupations at Philadelphia permit me to come here but once a year, I am obliged
while here to take arrangements for the year following. It is for this
reason I am obliged to point out at this time what is to be done
with the monies due from Robert Lewis and Samuel Woodson when
you shall have recovered and recieved them. Having to pay to Mr.
James Strange of Richmond for Donald Scott & co. £97-14-6¾ and
to Andrew Donald of Osborne's for Wm. & James Donald & co.
£27-3-9. both current money and with interest from Apr. 19. 1791.[1]
I have this day inclosed orders on you in favor of these gentlemen
for those sums and shall give Mr. Dobson an order for the balance
charges being first deducted, when you shall have collected the
money, which I hope you will do with all the expedition the law
will admit. I am in hopes you received Colo. Lewis's letter in time
to stop the suit against Lewis and Ware, as it was found that the
order on them in favor of Trents had been larger than he had
imagined, and, if paid, must have taken the whole balance. Any
letters you may be pleased to favor me with will come safely by post
to Philadelphia. I am Sir, with great esteem your mo. obedt. humble
servt,   TH: JEFFERSON

PrC (CSmH).

[1] Thus in MS; 1783 intended.

From Edward Rutledge

MY DEAR SIR   Charleston October 7th: 1791.

I had the Pleasure of receiving some days ago your Letter of the
25th. August, and now take the Liberty of introducing to your
acquaintance my Friend Barnwell, who wishes much to be known
to you, and who deserves to be gratified in what he wishes. I have
already given you his Character. I told you in my last that, he had
given me his Sentiments respecting the carrying Trade, in writing,
and that I was then preparing to answer what I could by no means
approve; a task in my Opinion not very difficult. But easy as it is,

I have been prevented hitherto from doing it, as I could wish, by the multiplicity of my professional Business, and the constant and dangerous illness of my wife, who occupies every Moment of my Leisure, and indeed many days that, my clients conceive, should be devoted to their Affairs. He however who has many Duties to discharge, finds it often difficult, and sometimes impossible, to discharge them with punctuality; in such Cases, we must select the most important, and trust to the good nature of others, to be excused from the rest. Under the Circumstances of my Domestic Affairs, it is impossible for me my dear Friend to quit my native Home. But [you] must not from thence be led to believe, that I dedicate no portion of my time to the Service of my Country. Far otherwise. In the small Circle of my own State, I take my full Share in her public Measures, and contribute my best Endeavors, to advance her Interest, and preserve her Tranquillity. This, you may rely upon it, was an arduous Undertaking, when we reflect on the distracted and impoverished State we were left in, at the close of the war; the almost total want of Subordination to any Government, and the different and discordant Interests which it had become necessary to reconcile. Every one therefore, my good Sir, to the Station in which he can be most useful. I was once a field officer. I am now a Subaltern in Politics; but I aim at doing my Duty, and I am *almost* contented. Yet not altogether. I often pant to be in Congress, were it but for one Vote. I glow with Resentment when I think that, at this moment, we suffer our old Enemies to keep up an armed Force, within the acknowledged Limits of our States; and not only so, but give to that people as many Advantages in Commerce as we do to those, who were, and are our Friends. And why? Because we are afraid that Great Britain will lay restrictions on our Commerce! Because she may take Umbrage! Ah! my dear Friend, if the Sentiments which are now current had prevailed in the years 1775, 6, and 7, the Lovers of Liberty would have died on a Gibbet, or perished in a wilderness, and the rest of our Fellow Citizens would have been hewers of Wood, and Drawers of Water for the most insolent set of Beings that today inhabit the Earth. My Friend Izard for whom I have a very great Esteem, says that on this Subject I am "Mad." I wish to God, he, and his Colleague had a little of my Madness; the more especially as they must all admit, that there is Method in it. Barnwell is much in Sentiment with me in inclination altogether. He wishes to be convinced, and has promised to shew you the Letter which he wrote me. As he is full of Candor he did himself propose it, and if when you become acquainted with him, you will give him an opportunity of doing it, I shall thank you. I am mortified when wise men, and good men go wrong: but when Men of this description are my Friends, and go wrong in essentials, we are afflicted, as well as mortified.

I find by the Public Prints that the King of France is resolved, not to be handed down to Posterity, as the Restorer of the Liberties of his Country. Should he regain his Personal Freedom, I shall tremble for the Nation, over which he has presided: as I am convinced, there is not a crown'd head in Europe, that would not strain every nerve to reinstate the Claims of arbitrary Power, in his Person. Adieu for the present my dear Friend and be assured that I am ever your affectionate, ED: RUTLEDGE.

RC (DLC); endorsed by TJ as received 2 Nov. 1791 and so recorded in SJL. Pierce Butler was the Senate COLLEAGUE of Ralph Izard to whom Rutledge refers.

To James Strange

SIR   Monticello Octob. 7. 1791.

Since my return to this place I have examined my papers relative to the demands stated in your letter of July 10. I find nothing against those of £16-11-3 due from my mother to Donald Scott & co. at their Charlottesville store, and £19-6-5¼ from myself to the same company on dealings with Buchanan and McDowell, which therefore I will undertake to pay with interest from the 19th. of April 1783.—As to the demand of £131-16-18 from the same company for my own dealings with Richard Anderson in their Charlottesville store, I find a credit of £70. Sep. 24. 1775. and some smaller ones omitted. That transaction was as follows: Henry Mullins was to pay me £170. by order of Colo. Skipwith. His tobacco being in the hands of Mr. Anderson, he authorized me to call on him for that sum, and I desired Mr. Anderson to pay £30. of it to Dr. Walker, £70 to R. Harvie & co. and to apply £70. the residue to the credit of my account in his store, which he assumed to do. Desirous afterwards of having a written acknolegement I applied to Mr. Anderson who gave me one in these words. 'Sir I was to have paid one hundred and seventy pounds for Henry Mullins in October 1775. so that if you will give him credit on his bond for that sum, I will be answerable to Mr. Harvie and Doctr. Walker for your orders in favor of them payable at the same time. I am Sir your mo. obedt. Richd. Anderson. 28th. April 1777. To Thos. Jefferson esq.' The original paper is in my possession and shall be shewn to yourself or any other person applying to me at this place. The credit can moreover be fully established by Henry Mullins in Goochland, and I dare say that on turning to his account in your books you will find him debited that sum on my account. I must further ask the favor of you to turn to the account of Harvie & co. and see whether their part of it was duly entered to their credit, and to inform me, as I am bound to see that it is so. This account then should stand thus.

Donald Scott & co. for dealings with Richard Anderson Dr.

1772. July 13.	To cash of Wm. Michie for counsel	£1– 0– 0
1773. Sep. 25.	To do. of Richd. Woolfolk for do.	1– 0– 0
1774. Aug. 31.	To do. of Thos. Garth	63– 0– 0
1775. Sep. 24.	To R. Anderson's assumpsit for H. Mullins to Dr. W.	30– 0– 0
	to R. Harvie & co.	70– 0– 0
	to credit of my acct. with him	70– 0– 0
1778.	To balance of his bond for £155 (£95–9–3 pd. to Minor)	59–10– 9
	Balance due to Donald Scott & co.	61–16–16½
	Cr.	356– 9– 1½
1777. Aug. 31.	By amount of acct. to this day as pr. acct. rendd.	256– 9– 1½
	By assumpsit of R. Anderson for them to Dr. Walker	30– 0– 0
	By do. do. Harvie & co.	70– 0– 0
		356– 9– 1½

And our whole account will stand thus.
Th:J. to Donald Scott & co. on sundry accts. Dr.

To balance on dealings with Richd. Anderson	61–16–16½
To do. on do. with Buchanan & McDowel	19– 6– 5¼
To do. for Jane Jefferson	16–11– 3
	97–14– 6¾

for which[1]

PrC (CSmH); consisting of first two pages only; third page missing. Enclosure: Order on Nathaniel Pope, in TJ's hand, signed, dated 7 Oct. 1791, in favor of James Strange for £97 14s. 6 3/4d. "currency with interest from the 19th. of April 1783." to be paid out of "monies for which you have brought suits for me against Robert Lewis & Samuel Woodson when you shall have recieved so much thereof" (PrC in ViU).

TJ received and recorded in SJL on 17 Nov. 1791 a letter of 10 Nov. 1791 from Strange, possibly his reply to this, which has not been found.

[1] Second page ends here.

From William Short

DEAR SIR   Paris Octob. 9. 1791.

The King postponed going to open the assembly until the day before yesterday. He then went and delivered the speech which you will find in the gazette inclosed. It was well received by all the spectators and by much the greater part of the members of the assembly.

During the two days that passed between the assembly's being formed and the King's going there some circumstances passed which merit attention as indicative of the opinion of Paris which must always have much influence on that of the Kingdom in general. The assembly passed a decree changing the ceremonial adopted by their predecessors for receiving the King. By it he was to have a fauteil in the assembly without *fleurs de lys* &c. This decree was astonishingly ill recieved by the people out of doors and particularly the crowds in the *Palais Royale*. They considered it as designed to disgust the King who has lately become popular and their expressions of discontentment were so loud that the assembly the next morning repealed it. Such of the members as had supported the decree are considered for the most part as disturbers of the peace and many of them have been insulted by the garde nationale. As one of these scenes took place in the assembly room a few minutes before the session commenced it was denounced to the assembly. The officer of the garde nationale who had offered the insult desired to be heard at the bar of the house in his justification, which was allowed and thus the matter ended.

The King was firmly decided not to go to the assembly if the decree had not been repealed. This shews that he counts sufficiently on the garde nationale and people of Paris, to act independently of and balance the assembly. If confined within proper bounds this will be a great advantage for the constitution in limiting the transgressions of the assembly.

They are now engaged in forming their plan of proceeding and will name committees as the former assembly did. The several ministers are to tender them an account of the present state of their departments which will comprehend the internal and external affairs of the Kingdom. This will take place in eight or ten days. M. de Montmorin informed them in general terms that answers had not yet been received to the King's notification to the several powers of his acceptance of the constitution and determination to support it.

The Princes continue to act as before this acceptance and hold out to their followers certain hopes of foreign interference. Numbers of the nobility, clergy and other discontented go and join them in consequence thereof. The Empress of Russia has made them a present of money; some say two millions of livres, but there are many reasons to believe that it is less. This as well as the other marks of her support were during the imprisonment of the King. Time alone can shew what changes in the dispositions of foreign cabinets will be effected by the change in the King's situation.

The Marquis de la fayette resigned yesterday his command of the garde nationale. I inclose you a letter which he addressed to them on the occasion. They are now to be commanded alternately by the six commandants of division. He goes this morning to Chavelle where he will stay some days and from thence go to his estate in Auvergne to spend there the winter unless called away by a command in the army.

I inclosed you in my letter of the 6th inst. (private) sent by the way of Havre my account from July 1. 90. to July 1. 91.—I omitted in that letter to explain the article of 700₶ 10s. paid for printing and distributing the pamphlet on tobacco. I explained it in one of my letters I think from Amsterdam.—Before going there I authorised Brissot de Warville who was then supposed to have much influence on Mirabeau, to distribute to the members of the assembly a *feuille volante* when the subject of tobacco should come on in order to explain it to them.—Under that authorisation and against my intention he had a pamphlet printed and distributed 2000 copies. As I was then absent I did not know of it until it was too late and of course I thought it better to repay his disbursements than to object to them in that stage of the business.

Whilst the assembly were deliberating on the reform of their mint several propositions were submitted to them and among the rest those which you will see in the memoire inclosed of which I have had a copy taken. They were made by Bolton of Birmingham. I know not why he refused to join his name, but he exacted secrecy of the committee. His plan was not adopted. I have learned lately that Drost and he differed. They speak ill of each other and Bolton particularly of Drost's machine although Drost says it is used by him (Bolton) in the copper he has struck.—Drost assures me he shall be ready to go the next spring. I find him however exceedingly dilatory.

I have this moment recieved a packet from you containing four news papers, the latest of the 13th. of August, without any letter.

The packet was sent to me by the penny post. I know not how it came to Paris.—I am my dear Sir, most affectionately, yours,

W: SHORT

P.S. I send you the plan of public instruction reported to the national assembly and a valuable work on the balance of French commerce taken from authentic and official papers. I think they are proper for public use and are destined for your department or that of the treasury as you may see fit. You will have received also with the last newspapers a pamphlet on the commerce of the French islands.

PrC (DLC: Short Papers); at head of text: *"No. 87"*; at foot of text: "Thomas Jefferson Secretary of State, Philadelphia." Tr (DNA: RG 59, DD). Recorded in SJL as received 20 Dec. 1791.

From William Tatham

DEAR SIR   Capitol in Richmond 9th. Oct. 1791

I am just inform'd that You will certainly be at Alexandria the 17th. Inst. on the business of the federal City, and the hopes I had entertain'd of seeing You here is vanishd. It wou'd have given me great pleasure to have consulted You on my several objects in pursuit of general utility: as it is; and the Virginia Assembly so near at hand, your knowledge of my singular situation will plead a pardon for reminding you, how usefull Your attention to my two last Letters may prove, if You are not too much incomoded with public concerns before You leave Potowmack.

My Brother has done every thing possible about the S. Western Post; He is not yet returnd, but I collect from a Copy of His Journal that the Subscriptions are between Eighty and a hundred pounds; I am nevertheless persuaded that Post [will] not be establish'd without Government will give it to the Contractors for three Years instead of one. On these Grounds I beleive I can establish it.—I am Dr. sir Yr. Obt. Hb servt,   WM TATHAM

RC (MiU-C); endorsed by TJ as received 18 Oct. 1791 and so recorded in SJL. Tatham's TWO LAST LETTERS were 26 Aug. and 3 Sep. 1791.

To the Rev. Matthew Maury

DEAR SIR   Monticello Oct. 10. 1791.

Finding that the amount of the account (£22-13) which you left with me is such as that I can pay it in Philadelphia, and that this will be more speedy than any resource I can refer it to here, I have determined to remit it from thence. This I can do by sending a bank post bill to your brother at Fredericksburg, at which place it shall be by the last day of this month. The collector of the port is bound to pay the cash for those bills which renders them the usual and sure means of remittance from Philadelphia to the different states. At any time therefore after the last day of this month you may safely instruct your brother what to do with that sum.

There will then be arrearages of subscription, Dabney's board &c. for the present year, and entrance for the next, amounting as I conjecture to about fifty two or three pounds which the person whom Colo. Lewis shall employ to recieve my business from him, will be directed to pay out of monies, which I think he cannot fail to recieve within a moderate time, so as I hope to prevent your suffering any inconvenience. Mr. Lewis will be so good as to express to him my anxiety that he pay it at the earliest moment possible. I am with great & sincere esteem Dear Sir Your affectionate friend & servt,

TH: JEFFERSON

PrC (CSmH).

TJ paid Maury $75 on 25 Oct. 1791, the day after he received from Henry Remsen an accounting of the State Department expenses that indicated he was paid $875, one-fourth his annual salary, on 5 Oct. 1791 (Henry Remsen, Jr., to TJ, 24 Oct. 1791, RC in DLC).

From Thomas Bell

DEAR SIR   [Charlottesville] 11th. Oct. 1791

A Mr. Franklin is expected in Town this evening, who formerly was Overseer at the Mountain.

It has been hinted to me that he would Suit, as manager for you perhaps, better than some that has been Mentioned. Colo. Lewis— although he may not mention him—can give you his Character better than I can. And whether Franklin would undertake the business, or no, can't say. You will excuse my mentioning him, as I am no ways interested except for your Interest.—I am Sir with respect your most ob. Srt.,   THO BELL

RC (DLC). Endorsed by TJ and recorded in SJL as received 11 Oct. 1791.

Bernard FRANKLIN served as TJ's overseer from 1788 to 1790. His name appears

in accounts for 1794, 1795, 1800, and 1801,
but it is uncertain what relationship the
two men had during that time (Betts, *Farm
Book*, p. 149, 517).

From John Hamilton

SIR   Norfolk Octr. 11th. 1791.
Hearing of your arrival in the flourishing State of Virginia, I take
the earliest opportunity to congratulate you on the very agreeable
excursion which I understand you have recently made to the Eastern
States, and to assure you that I most sincerely rejoice on being
informed that you are in good health.

As Great Britain and America have not yet entered into a Convention for the purpose of defining and establishing the functions
and Privileges of their respective Consuls it seems a matter of doubt,
with some people, whether Consuls recognized and acting by permission have the same powers as those appointed in Virtue of a
Convention; while others are of opinion that those Recognized and
Admitted have more extensive privileges than if they were confined
to Articles established by a Convention for their particular Government, because, where there is no Convention the Laws and Customs
of Nations and of Merchants, must be the Rule of their Conduct.

It is my most earnest wish to avoid Altercation, and not to extend
the Consular powers in any case whatever, beyond it's proper limits,
and would therefore esteem it a very great favor to be honored with
your Opinion how far You concieve those powers extend? Whether
Consuls Recognized and Admitted (where there is no Convention)
are to be guided by the Laws and Customs of Nations and Merchants? And in what cases amenable to the Laws of the Country in
which they reside. I have the honor to be, with the greatest Respect
& Esteem, Sir, Your most Obedt. & most Hble Servant,

JNO: HAMILTON

RC (DNA: RG 59, CD); endorsed by TJ as received 24 Oct. 1791 and so recorded
in SJL.

To John Garland Jefferson

Dear Sir   Monticello Oct. 11. 1791.
A little before my departure from Philadelphia I received your
letter expressing a wish to remove into this neighborhood that you

might be convenient to the books which are to be read. I am told your present situation is favorable for study; and I doubt whether in this neighborhood your mind would not be more disturbed and withdrawn from it by a revival of matters which if let alone, will sink into oblivion; and as Peter Carr assures me the books are forwarded regularly and in good time for yourself and Sam Carr I imagine you are now less anxious on this subject. Colo. Lewis retiring from the management of my affairs himself, has undertaken to employ some one to take care of them. I imagined it would be more agreeable to you to have a fixed sum of money deposited somewhere for your maintenance, and under your own command, than to be obliged to write to the manager for every little want. I have therefore directed that he should lodge the sum of £50. in the hands of the merchant to whom he sells the crop of wheat, and give you notice in what hands it is. This I presume will suffice for a year's boarding, clothes and all other expences, to be counted from the first day of this month, and at this time next year a like provision shall be made for you for another year. Any thing due for board before the 1st. day of this month shall be paid up exclusive of the allowance for this present year.—I cannot deny myself the pleasure of mentioning to you the satisfaction I recieve from the accounts given me of your assiduity in your studies and your advancement in them. You live in a country where talents, learning, and honesty are so much called for that every man who possesses these may be what he pleases. Can there be a higher inducement to acquire them at every possible expence of time and labour?—With respect to the old subject of uneasiness which arose in this neighborhood, be assured that no impression unfavourable to you remains on my mind. On this head quiet yourself most thoroughly; and rest satisfied that no one feels a more lively interest in the success you may hereafter have in the world, than I do. I repeat again that this may be what you please, because it will depend on your learning and integrity, which are in your own power. I shall always be happy to hear from you, tho it will not be in my power to answer always, as you must be sensible from the nature of my vocations. I am with perfect attachment Dear Sir Your affectionate friend & servt,

TH: JEFFERSON

PrC (MHi).

To Nicholas Lewis

DEAR SIR   Monticello Oct. 11. 1791.

I omitted to mention in my memorandum about the sale that if any ready money should be recieved, about £70. of it should be paid to Dr. Currie, and the residue, as far as £300. to Dobson. It is not probable so much will be received, if any, therefore it would be useless to say that any further sum should be paid to Hanson.

Mr. Tom Cobbs applied to me to-day about 2. hhds. of tobo. carried down by Phill and no more heard of. I desired him first to see what Ballow would say about it, who would be answerable if he did not use due diligence in enquiring into it. I since learn that Ballow is dead, and therefore unless neglect on his part could be more clearly proved than is probable, any attempts against him would be useless, and would be unjust too if he were not really negligent in the matter, because he could not be understood to warrant the honesty of my driver. Therefore I suppose the loss is to fall on me, and have to beg of you to compromise it on the best terms you can with Mr. Cobbs. No payment can be made on the subject till Christmas twelvemonth. I am with great esteem Dr. Sir your's sincerely,   TH: JEFFERSON

PrC (CSmH).

Cobb's inquiry into tobacco carried to Richmond in 1786 and apparently lost led to a suit against TJ for the value thereof

(Account Book, 6 June 1796; see also TJ to Thomas Mann Randolph, Jr., 7 Feb. and 11 Apr. 1796). Charles BALLOW had served as a steward at the time of the delivery.

To Anderson Bryan

SIR   Monticello Oct. 12. 1791

The constant absence from the [. . .] I am now held, requires that I should [unburden?] myself from all [. . .] and particularly from all [. . . .] other responsibilities of that mat[ter?] Therefore on Thursday [. . .], [. . . .] [re]lease me from my securityship [. . .] of which I thought it right to [. . .] that you may [be?] there to [defend?], [. . . .] necessary [for your interests], [. . .] and [. . . .]. I am Your   TH: JEFFERSON

PrC (DLC); badly faded. Not recorded in SJL.

This is the last letter TJ wrote before leaving Monticello to return to Philadel-

phia, and it is the last correspondence between TJ and Bryan, the surveyor of Albemarle county for whom TJ had become security, and who had performed TJ's surveying without fees. Bryan's work was particularly important in TJ's dispute with John Harvie (TJ to Bryan, 6 Jan. 1790). Although much of this letter is illegible, it appears that TJ was now taking steps to end his role as security for Bryan.

From William Short

DEAR SIR   Paris Octob. 14: 1791

Drost called on me yesterday and after some hesitation told me that several circumstances had taken place in his private affairs which rendered it necessary that he should decline going to America. I was as you may readily concieve much astonished at such an announce, and the more so as two days before he had repeated to me what he had before told me twenty times that he should be ready to go out in the spring. I suppose now that the fact is that he has never been absolutely decided in his own mind and for that reason always delayed on various pretexts forming the contract. Hitherto when I have pushed him, which was very often, to lose no time in executing the machines which were to be made here, he always answered that he had several articles to complete first, but that he had already begun the models and other necessary preliminaries and would certainly be ready as soon as the season would permit his undertaking the voyage.

On my observing to him that his conduct appeared to me far from delicate, that I had written to you as authorized by him that you might count on his going and that it was probable arrangements would have been taken in consequence thereof, he seemed somewhat hurt, and said that if I learned from you that that was the case that he would consent to go. Whether this was merely a palliative or not I cannot say. He said however that he would write me a letter today confirmably thereto. Should it be recieved before the departure of this letter it shall be forwarded to you. He went further and said that he should continue to have two *balanciers* made on his own account and that if you insisted on his going he would yield them to the U.S. and set out. It would be unsafe however I fear to count on him.

He has an intention at present of treating the French revolution in a series of medals and thinks he shall soon make a large fortune by this means. Should his speculation fail he may be more disposed to go to America, unless indeed his declining it at present proceeds from a consciousness that his machine will not answer for striking money, although perfect for striking medals. This as I have informed you is insisted on by Dupré the engraver here and by Bolton also. So long as Drost shewed an intention of going to establish a mint on that principle, and on the condition of not being paid until the work was executed it was not allowed to doubt of his own conviction at least, but I own since his declining it in this abrupt manner it is impossible not to suspect some uncertainty.

Mr. Gautier of the house of Grand had told me that Drost could not be depended on he feared for such an undertaking, and that at any rate it would be necessary to deal with him with much caution. He had collected this opinion from Bolton and his friends. I mentioned the circumstance to Mr. Grand who said he did not know Drost well enough to answer for him, but advised me to mention to him what had come to my knowlege with respect to his machine having not answered at Birmingham. I did it and Drost expressed his thanks to me for this opportunity of explaining to me his difference with Bolton. He shewed me many papers and among the rest an arbitration and an agreement in consequence thereof by which Bolton was to pay him a certain sum of money for his time. All this did not prove the success of his machine and I had only his word that it was made use of by Bolton and Bolton's denial of it. However as you had directed me to employ him and as he was to be paid only after the work was completed I determined to prosecute the measure, and particularly as he then said if I had any doubts of his ability to execute the engagement he was willing it should stop there, and as Mr. Grand seemed to think that under those circumstances there would be no risk in treating with him.

I sent you in my last a copy of Bolton's proposals for striking the copper coin of this country. It will be perhaps found well to contract with him for striking the same for the U.S. as that must be the most pressing, the gold and silver of other countries having course with us. He will strike the copper at Birmingham at a very low rate, or will make an establishment for it in the U.S. Drost tells me that whilst he was in England Bolton was in treaty for that purpose either with the U.S. or some citizen thereof. I shall let him know through Mr. Gautier that Drost does not go to America so that he may make overtures directly to you for establishing a mint in America on the principle proposed in his memorial sent you, viz. for a given sum, or for striking at Birmingham and furnishing by contract the copper coin of which the U.S. may have immediate need. Should you persist however in preferring Drost, and he bind himself by the letter mentioned above then you will be so good as to give me your orders thereon. It will be necessary at the same time to give some idea of the extent to which this undertaking is to be carried that Drost may know how many *balanciers* and what other instruments may be requisite. He thinks nine or ten will be necessary, being the smallest number in the smallest of the several *hotels de monnoye* in France.

I am exceedingly sorry for this disappointment and the delay which will ensue in consequence thereof, in a business so interesting to the credit and dignity of the U.S. as the having their own coin. I should be particularly so at Drost's not going if his conduct did not inspire some doubts with respect to the plan which he proposes, and which as yet has not been reduced to real practice in the coinage of large sums of money as far as we know of.

The assembly have as yet done nothing of an interesting nature. They are still engaged in forming the rules of the house.

Some of the couriers who had been sent with the notification of the King's acceptation of the constitution have returned and brought congratulatory answers, particularly from London and the Hague. The French Ambassador at Vienna who during the King's imprisonment had been desired to withold himself from court has again made his appearance there and been recieved. The Swedish Ambassador by order of his master had during that time witheld himself from the public eye. He now appears at the Thuilleries.

The conjectures with respect to the interview at Pilnitz continue to vary, which shews that certainty is not yet attained.

Spain has already concluded a truce with the Emperor of Morocco as it is said, occasioned by the brother of the latter rebelling at the head of a considerable force. It is said also that Spain has ceded Oran to the Bey of Mascara. These hostilities obliged Spain to put on foot a considerable force which the present situation of affairs on that coast leaves at their free disposal.

The Marquis de la fayette has set out for Auvergne. The garde nationale and citizens of Paris intend petitioning the assembly to indemnify him for the expences incurred in support of the revolution.

This letter will be sent by the way of Havre and inclose one which I have just recieved from Lyons. I suppose it proper to send it to you.—I am with sentiments of unalterable attachment Dear Sir your affectionate friend & servant,   W: SHORT

PrC (DLC: Short Papers); at head of text: "No. 88."; at foot of text: "Thomas Jefferson Secretary of State Philadelphia." Tr (DNA: RG 59, DD); enclosure: Droz to Short, 14 Oct. 1791. Recorded in SJL as received 10 Feb. 1792. For information on the relationship between Jean Pierre Droz and Matthew Boulton, see note at TJ to John Jay, 1 Feb. 1787.

From Delamotte

Le Havre, 15 Oct. 1791. Nothing interesting has happened since his last letter of 24 Aug. except for the king's acceptance of the constitution. The king apparently acted in good faith as England and the Emperor solemnly recognized his act. The nation is so attached to the "dernieres résolutions" of the National Assembly that this induced the king to accept the constitution and has prevented the growth of republicanism in the Legislative Assembly.—The opening of a new dock that holds 120 ships and plans to build another one the same size in three years have improved the prospects for American trade with Le Havre. Despite the difference in tobacco duties and the prohibition of foreign vessels, the city remains a promising market for American tobacco, ash, rice, flour, grain, salted meat, and timber. Europe is deeply impressed by the recent American loan in Holland and by the general state of American finances.—The harvest has been disappointing. Nantes, Bordeaux, and Bayonne have to import grain and cheese from abroad. England opened her ports fifteen days ago, but America can also profit from this situation.—He is pleased to receive Remsen's letter of 2 Aug. and the collection of American laws.

RC (DNA: RG 59, CD); 2 p.; in French; recorded in SJL as received 10 Feb. 1792. TJ wrote in the margin by the last paragraph: "This passage to be translated & given to Mr. Freneau." The passage related to the poor harvest and the need for American imports. See *National Gazette*, 13 Feb. 1792.

From Peyton Short

DEAR SIR   Richmond 15th. Octr. 1791

Will you be so good as to excuse my troubling you with another Letter to my Brother. I have frequently written to him through other Channels and he complains of never hearing from [me.] If I could be permitted to enclose my Letters to you and you would not consider it an inconvenience to forward them with your packets to Paris, I should be certain of their reaching him, and esteem such an Act of friendship as the greatest obligation that could be confered on Yr. most Obt. Sert,   PEYTON SHORT

RC (MHi); addressed: "Mr. Thomas Jefferson Secry. of State, Philadelphia"; endorsed by TJ as received 26 Oct. 1791 and so recorded in SJL.

From William Short

DEAR SIR   Paris Octob. 15. 1791.

I now inclose you a note of your account with me as furnished by Mr. Grand which will shew you the balance you have at Amsterdam. This is independent of the bill of exchange which I have sent to Messrs. Staphorst & Hubbard to be kept at your disposal as formerly mentioned to you.

As Ternant has arrived I suppose it certain the appointment of Minister here will take place during this session of Congress. This of course will be the last time I shall ever mention to you a subject about which I have already importuned you a great deal too much. I have therefore less scruple in mentioning to you at present that from the letter of the Sec. of the treasury to me, it appears that he does not chuse to place the affair of our loans here in other hands than mine, or even join others to me as I had requested on account of the delicacy of the business. His letter shewed also that the President had the same sentiments with himself. If therefore it is not known that I would accept any other place than this here, it is possible they would not name another person minister here, at least until that point were ascertained—as they may suppose the affair of our loans the most important branch of our immediate concerns on this side of the Atlantic, and seem to think, probably because I have already been employed in it, that I am the most proper for this business. Under these circumstances I should imagine it possible that a desire that I should prosecute the business would have weight with them in leaving me here, particularly if they did not know they could command my services in this line by employing me elsewhere. I mention this to you that you may arrange it if you think proper and in any manner you may judge best for me. I will add only one circumstance more and then beg you a thousand pardons for all this trouble, importunity and perhaps impertinence. It is that if you should think in a couple of years from hence or if it should be then thought by any other that it would be better for any other person to come here I would willingly at that time withdraw. It is possible that it may be thought best to keep me here as minister one or two years under the present circumstances of this country and that after that time it may be best to send another. Of this I cannot judge, and as it might be thought disagreeable to appoint a person for only two years, I mention this merely to shew that I will of myself remove any difficulty of that kind. Of choice I think should desire to retire at that time.—After all I own to you I am ashamed of all my letters written to you on these subjects, and as their purpose is now at an end, and as they were never destined for any other eye, and further as no other person could enter into the true spirit of them but yourself, and would even certainly take up an improper idea from them not knowing that what I write to you I consider as written to myself, and as nothing but fire can put out of all doubt their being one day exposed to other eyes since you are exposed like all to the bills of mortality, I close here all the prayers and intreaties which I have made to you on these subjects by one general one, that you would commit to the flames all my letters relative thereto, and beg you to remain firmly persuaded of the unalterable affection of your friend & servant,   W: SHORT

P.S. Your friends here and particularly the la Rochefoucauld family are much pleased by your recollection of them. I beg you not to forget Mde. D'Enville's commission about seed &c. of which you have already mentioned the receipt by my former letter.

RC (DLC); at head of text: "*Private*"; endorsed by TJ as received 10 Feb. 1792 and so recorded in SJL. PrC (DLC: Short Papers). The letter from Secretary of the Treasury Hamilton mentioned by Short was that of 1 Aug. 1791 (Syrett, *Hamilton*, IX, 1-3).

From William Short

DEAR SIR   Paris Octob. 15. 1791

I wrote to you yesterday by the way of Havre to inform you that Drost had suddenly and unexpectedly informed me that certain changes in his affairs had rendered it necessary that he should abandon the idea of going to America. This is merely to inform you by the way of England, referring you to my letter of yesterday for further particulars, of this abrupt change.—He now proposes in addition to what I then mentioned to undertake the business but with the privilege of remaining in Paris himself and sending another to execute his plans in Philadelphia. It is for you to determine whether such a mode will suit you. He says his presence on the spot is by no means necessary.—He mentioned to me further yesterday evening that he was in treaty with a foreign court to make one of his *balanciers* at Paris and sell them his art. And I think it probable that this with his other schemes mentioned to you yesterday may have determined him to remain here; perhaps also an aversion to a sea voyage which he has frequently expressed may have some weight. I can only repeat here what I mentioned yesterday of my mortification at this disappointment. It may however turn out only a delay, and in that case it will be in some measure compensated by the greater degree of certainty acquired as to the practical success of Drost's machine should the foreign court of which he speaks reduce it to experiment in actual coinage.

The *courier* sent to De Moustier has returned. It is said he refuses. I suppose it may be considered as certain that he has not absolutely accepted. However as he was to leave Berlin for Paris a few days after receiving the courier I rather think he means to examine the ground first, and will accept afterwards. This delay may be because he thinks such a caution necessary or with a design to make a greater merit of his acceptance in appearing to yield to intreaty.

The answer of Spain to the King's notification of his acceptation of the constitution consists simply in a communication of the Count de Florida Blanca to French chargé des affaires, when he asked an audience for that purpose. The communication imported that His C.M. having been previously averted that such a notification he (the Count) could immediately give the chargé des affaires the answer viz. that His C.M. had by no means as yet a sufficient moral conviction of the liberty of His M.C.M. to be able to appreciate such a notification, but that he His C.M. was desirous and well disposed to acquire proofs thereof.—I have nothing further to add to my letter of yesterday & beg you to be persuaded of the sentiments of attachment & Affection with which I am Dear Sir Your friend & Servant, W: SHORT

PrC (DLC: Short Papers); at head of text: "*No. 89*"; at foot of text: "Thomas Jefferson Secretary of State Philadelphia"; lacks part of complimentary close and signature, which are supplied from Tr (DNA: RG 59, DD). Recorded in SJL as received 13 Mch. 1792.

From David Humphreys

Lisbon, 16 Oct. 1791. Since his last letter of 1 Oct. he has received TJ's dispatches of 23 Aug. He is grateful for the American publications TJ sent him and will forward those intended for William Carmichael.—He is impressed by "the mild Government and prosperous state of Portugal." Since his arrival in the country there has been only one execution, and that involved a fratricide. Otherwise he has not heard of a single assassination or robbery in Lisbon or throughout the kingdom. He attributes these improvements to "the extreme mildness of the Queen and particularly her reluctance to consent to sanguinary punishments." Despite the misgivings of advocates of harsh punishment for criminals, banishment has turned out to be more effective than executions in deterring crime.—There has also been a dramatic reversal of Portugal's balance of trade with England. In the past an English packet commonly brought from 50 to 100,000 moidores to England. But recently Portugal has exported no gold to England, and within the last month two English packets and a merchant vessel have actually brought gold here. This change has occurred as a result of a declining volume of imports as well as an increasing volume of exports. The growth of Portuguese manufactures of woolens, glass, hats, and leather goods, which can be attributed to the wise policies of the Marquis de Pombal, has greatly lessened the country's dependence on imports, "particularly of coarse woolens for the colonies." At the same time "Cotton, Sugar, and some other productions from the Colonies" have enabled Portugal significantly to increase its export trade. "The late vast demand for Cotton in England has operated more powerfully towards this change than almost all the other articles together." There has also been a marked growth in exports of wine to England. Last year Oporto shipped 48,000 pipes of wine to England, as compared to 25 to 30,000 pipes in the past.—Barclay has purchased almost all the articles he plans to take to Morocco but has been unable to find passage to Gibraltar.

RC (DNA: RG 59, DD); 4 p.; at head of text: "(No. 37)"; at foot of text: "The Secretary of State"; endorsed by TJ as received 10 Dec. 1791 and so recorded in SJL. Tr (same).

From Augustine Davis

SIR   Post Office, Richmond, October 17th. 1791

I had the honor to write your Excellency when at Monticello in this state, on the subject of the Establishment of a Cross Post from this to Staunton, informing that I expected in a few days from that date to complete the Contract, which was done the 8th. instant, except to executing the Bond, which cannot be effected until David Ross, Esqr. returns to this place, who is one of the Undertaker's securities, and is to be here in the course of the present month. The Contract is to take place the 15th. of next month, by which time I flatter myself I shall be able to get the Bond signed by Mr. Ross and returned to your Excellency.

I have lately seen several gentlemen from the South Western Country, and from the conversation had with them on the establishment of a Cross post to that part of the country, they think there is but little probability of any person in those parts undertaking it, and seem to signify that whoever does undertake it must be a loser.—I have the Honor to be Sir yr Excellency's Most Obt Sert,

AUGUSTINE DAVIS

RC (DLC); endorsed by TJ as received 24 Oct. 1791 and so recorded in SJL.

From David Meade Randolph

SIR   Richmond 17th October 1791

I have to acknowledge the receipt of your very kind letter of the 6th. instant.—The appointment I shall accept, if upon a recommendation to the president, he shall so far honor me by his approbation. The duties thereof I shall make it a point to regard, and execute them with the utmost of my abilities. Among the many motives to a faithful acquittal of the trust, there shall be none more urgent than to support and justify your choice.—I have the honor to be your obliged Huml. Sert.,   D M RANDOLPH

RC (DLC); endorsed by TJ as received 24 Oct. 1791 and so recorded in SJL. TJ forwarded Randolph's commission as U.S. marshal for Virginia on 27 Oct. 1791 (Tr in DNA: RG 360, DL) which Meade acknowledged receipt of on 7 Nov. 1791 (RC in DLC: TJ Papers, 67: 11785; endorsed by TJ as received 15 Nov. 1791 and so recorded in SJL). In the latter, Meade informed TJ that he had decided to delay assuming office until the next meeting of the court to enable his predecessor, Edward Carrington, to put his office in order.

To Mary Jefferson

MY DEAR MARIA   Tuesday morning Oct. 18.
Mr. Giles carries your trunk to Baltimore where he will see you tonight. Take out of it whatever you may want before you get to Philadelphia and leave the trunk with Mr. Grant and I will call on him for it. The weather is so bad that perhaps I may not be able to overtake you in the morning as I had hoped: but I shall if possible. Adieu my dear Maria. Yours affectionately,   TH: JEFFERSON

RC (ViU); addressed: "Miss Maria Jefferson." Not recorded in SJL.

From Uriah Forrest

DEAR SIR   Geo Town 19 Oct 1791
The enclosed list of the sale of Lots, will give you all the information to be had, respecting the Proceedings since you left here— Only that the Commissioners have discontinued the sale. I beleive all, except the four Lots noted, are really sold. Mr. Gilchrist I beleive had no intention of buying when he came. I am not well acquainted with him. He is the Agent of some English Houses, though not very strong ones. Mr. Cabot bought for a Mr. Walker of this place, except one Lot. Pearce will buy to-morrow or the next day, if he can agree with the Commissioners at private sale thirty or forty Lots.—I wish very much, that the Commissioners, and the others, who have superintendance in this business, may Harmonize, but I very much fear it will not be sufficiently the case to prevent incon-

venience, if not injury. I write in great haste lest the Office should be shut.—I am dear Sir With all Consideration & Respect, Your very obliged & Obedt hble Sert.,   URIAH FORREST

RC (MHi); endorsed by TJ as received 24 Oct. 1791 and so recorded in SJL.

Forrest's enclosed list of the first sale of lots in the Federal District, which had begun on 17 Oct. 1791, has not been found. Forrest, William Pearce, and George Walker were all substantial landowners in Georgetown, Md., the first two of whom had agreed several months before to cede the property they owned there for the use of the Federal District (Agreement of Forrest, Pearce and others, 30 Mch. 1791, Columbia Historical Society, *Records*, XXXV-XXXVI [1935], 44-6). Francis Cabot, who had recently settled in Georgetown, was the brother of Massachusetts Senator George Cabot.

From James Brown

DEAR SIR   Richmond 21 Octbo 91
I beg leave to trouble you with Extracts from two letters lately recd. from Mr. Short. On rect. of your answer I will take Measures to arrange the Business as you may recommend. For my own part, tho' a considerable Stock holder I am much a Stranger which plan is most adviseable for Mr. Shorts interest.

I hope you found the Account sent you free from Error. My absence from home prevented me writing you at that Period.—With much respect I am Sir Your Obt: Hl: St,   JAMES BROWN

RC (MHi); endorsed by TJ as received 27 Oct. 1791 and so recorded in SJL. Enclosures: extracts of William Short to James Brown, 27 July 1791 and 14 Aug. 1791, in which he asks Brown to consult with TJ and then to invest his 3% and 6% stock in the Bank of the U.S.

From William Short

DEAR SIR   La Rocheguyon Oct. 22. 1791
I have just recieved at this place where I have come to spend a few days, a letter from M. de Moustier, from which it would appear that he has persisted since his arrival in Paris, in his determination to decline the department of foreign affairs. He tells me that Brissot de Warville is one of the causes of his declining, being persuaded that from the credit which he seems to enjoy at present he, de Moustier, could not expect to render real service. I am not fully convinced however that he will not accept if still sollicited, and I think he will be sollicited, from the real embarassment in finding a proper person to fill the place.

Dispositions abroad appear pacific since the notification of the King's acceptation. The continuance of these dispositions will depend of course upon the internal situation of affairs here. The assembly have as yet done nothing. Not a single decree has been passed. Day after day is passed in vain extravagant declamation, and in recieving addresses and petitions by deputations who are admitted at the bar and who flatter the assembly in the most ridiculous manner. This circumstance joined to the personal want of consideration of almost all the members, exposes the assembly to popular disrespect and to the assaults of a weapon, ridicule, which in no country is more powerful than in this.

Notwithstanding the little hopes of foreign succour emigrants continue in great numbers to go and join the Princes. In many provinces not a man of the nobility able to bear arms remains and many of them carry their whole families with them. An idea prevails among them that they are dishonored if they remain in France, and that only those who go to join the Princes will be considered as noble after the counter revolution which they consider as certain. The assembly are now deliberating on the means of preventing emigrations and punishing the emigrants. If they adopt violent measures the King will probably refuse his sanction.

The price of bread has risen considerably in Paris and threatens still to rise. This is produced by several causes—the obstacles put to the free circulation of grain in every department and the low waters of the Seine occasioned by the excessive drought, and the depreciation of the assignats which begins to be percieved in the price of all articles. It is much to be apprehended that this will occasion disorder in Paris during the winter.

I mentioned to you that the Marquis de la fayette had gone to Auvergne. The municipality of Paris have voted him a golden medal, and the statue of Genl. Washington in marble to be executed by Houdon, "Pour etre placée dans celui de ses domaines (de la fayette) qu'il designera, afin qu'il ait toujours devant ses yeux son ami et celui qu'il a si glorieusement imité." They determined at the same time that this vote should be placed on the bust of M. de la fayette, given to the municipality by the state of Virginia. I suppose of course you will mention this to the President, to whom I do not take the liberty to communicate it directly not having the honor to be in correspondence with him.

I recieved the day before I left Paris the letters of introduction given by the President and yourself to Mr. Horry of So. Carolina for me eighteen months ago. He has come to spend a short time at

Paris and I hope you will both be assured of my readiness to follow your desires contained in those letters. I was uncertain whether I should have made use of the opportunity thus furnished me of writing to the President, but the consideration of his multiplied occupations, as well as respect for himself and his time made me suppose it would be most proper not to break in on it by a letter.—I am desired by the old Dutchess D'Enville, and the Duke and Dutchess de la Rochefoucauld to recall them to your memory often and to assure you of their real attachment. I beg you to count also on the sincere affection & profound respect of your friend & servant,

W: SHORT

RC (DLC); at head of text: "*Private*"; at foot of text: "Thos. Jefferson Secretary of State Philadelphia"; endorsed by TJ as received 10 Feb. 1792 and so recorded in SJL. FC (DLC: Short Papers); at head of text: "(Copy)"; in Short's hand; text varies slightly in phraseology from RC.

TJ's letter introducing Daniel HORRY was that of 24 Apr. 1790. Washington's was written two days later (Washington to Short, 26 Apr. 1790; DLC: Washington Papers).

From Archibald Stuart

DR SIR   Staunton Octr. 22d. 1791

The objections to our State Government are so generally felt, that I am convinced its reformation will shortly be attempted; in that event I feel some anxiety for the Consequence should we be deprived of the Aid of Our absent Citizens. Are we to Expect the Assistance of yourself and Mr. Madison upon such an Occasion and if so, when could it most conveniently be afforded?

I must now express the pleasure I have felt that Agricola did not, nor could not produce a necessity for your appearing in the news papers. It was an event I dreaded as distressing to your feelings. Tho you might by that means have chastized so unprovoked and impertinent an Attack you have more effectually done it by silent contempt.

It will afford you no pleasure to be informed that the supposed Author is as much despised throughout the Circle of my Acquaintance as his greatest enemy could wish and that this is generally the Case I suspect will shortly appear.

I have not considered nor do I understand the principles of the Bank lately established by congress but am told that it is confessedly opposed to the principles of the government and that the expediency of the Measure was contrasted with and out weighed constitutional Objections. I hope this is not true as I cannot conceive the men of the present day are so daring as to offer such an insult to a free people. The Antis exclaim against the principles of your Collonial establishments as they are called as aristocratic and oppressive and altho they are the Germe of the old are generally ascribed to the New government. The Excise scheme tho unpopular is going quietly into operation in this quarter.

I feel interested in the establishment of cross posts throughout this state and particularly that a post office should be established at this place altho the whole of the Expence might not at first be defrayed from the profits of the establishment I conceive this would not long be the Case and perhaps a small and temporary sacrifice to the Objects it presents us with might not be inexpedient.—Fare well, I wish you health & happiness,   ARCHD. STUART

RC (MoSHi); endorsed by TJ as received 4 Nov. 1791 and so recorded in SJL; on verso TJ made in pencil the following notes for his reply of 23 Dec. 1791: "Exec. responsible—no Council
Exec. respect permanence
                       indepdce
Legis. respect by permanence
                       small number
Eql. represtn.
Senate better chosen."

Stuart's mention of OBJECTIONS TO OUR STATE GOVERNMENT is representative of the division between parties that was intensifying in Virginia. His analysis of the sentiment for reform is optimistic, reflecting perhaps the intense concern of those living in the western parts of the state over defense of the frontier and the apparent inability of the government to protect them.

Talk of revision of the state's constitution continued from 1776 until a convention finally met in 1829. See TJ to Stuart, 23 Dec. 1791; and TJ to James Madison, 17 Oct. 1792, and John Beckley to James Madison, 17 Oct. 1792 (printed in Rutland, *Madison*, XIV, 385-6). See also Richard R. Beeman, *The Old Dominion and the New Nation, 1788-1801* (Lexington, Ky., 1972), p. 90-118; and Norman K. Risjord, *Chesapeake Politics, 1781-1800* (New York, 1978), p. 501. The well-known "Publicola" essays of 1791 by John Quincy Adams were answered by someone using the name AGRICOLA in *Dunlap's American Daily Advertiser* (Philadelphia), 5 and 9 July 1791, and these articles were reprinted in Richmond newspapers (*Virginia Gazette & General Advertiser*, 20 July 1791, and *Virginia Gazette & Public Advertiser*, 30 July 1791).

From James McHenry

Fayetteville, Md., 23 Oct. 1791. The recurrence of an indisposition that might be cured by a sea voyage has interested him in the possibility of a foreign appointment.—The prospect of war between France and other European powers, "and the claims for succours she may bring forward under the 11th article of the treaty of Alliance, in case of being attacked," makes it necessary for the U.S. to appoint a minister to The Hague. Such a minister would also be in a position to advance U.S. commercial interests and negotiate advantageous loans for the U.S. government. In support of his pretensions to this appointment, he refers TJ to his service in the Continental Army, the public offices he held after the war, and TJ's knowledge of his personal talents. In addition to the restoration of his health, a foreign appointment would also enable him to pursue "certain literary researches" that would be more difficult to complete in the U.S.—He has not written to the President about this matter, being willing to entrust it to TJ's care, and wishes it to be understood that "I do not desire an appointment of this kind should Mr. Maddison or any other person of his abilities be disposed to embrace it."—The day after seeing TJ he met with Mr. Sterett and discussed the ignorance of Murray, Sheridan &c. about U.S. commercial relations with Great Britain. He urged Sterett to apprise these and other members of the Maryland congressional delegation of "the true interest of the commercial part of the State and of the United States," and is confident that he will act accordingly.

RC (NNSotheby); 2 p.; at head of text: "(private)"; endorsed by TJ as received 25 Oct. 1791 and so recorded in SJL.

McHenry, recently elected to the Maryland Senate, also solicited Alexander Hamilton's support for his effort to become U.S. minister to The Hague. He decided to serve in the Maryland Senate after receiving no support for his pretensions from the Secretaries of State or Treasury (Syrett, *Hamilton*, IX, 386, 454, 510-1).

To George Washington

Octob. 23. 1791.

Th: Jefferson has the honour to subjoin the alteration he suggested in the last paragraph of the President's speech.

Having read Colo. Humphreys' letters after Mr. Short's he had been led into an erroneous arrangement of the facts they state. Colo. Humphreys' letter mentioning the king's refusal of the constitution is of Aug. 22. while it appears by Mr. Short's letter of Aug. 30. that it had not yet been presented to him, and that it was believed he would ratify it.

A provision for the sale of the vacant lands of the United states is particularly urged[1] by the important considerations that they are pledged as a fund for reimbursing the public debt; that, if timely and judiciously applied, they may save the necessity of burthening our citizens with new taxes for the extinguishment of the principal; and that being free to[2] pay annually but a limited proportion of that principal, time lost in beginning the payments cannot be recovered however productive the resource may prove in eve[nt].

PrC (DLC). Not recorded in SJL, but entry in SJPL reads: "Oct. 23. Paragraph for speech to Congr." Washington included the last paragraph of this letter in his annual message to Congress on 25 Oct. 1791, with the alterations noted below.

[1] At this point Washington inserted "among other reasons" in the text of his 25 Oct. 1791 address to Congress (Fitzpatrick, *Writings*, XXXI, 403).

[2] Washington substituted the following for the remainder of this sentence: "discharge the principal but in a limited proportion no opportunity ought to be lost for availing the public of its right" (same, p. 404).

From Francis Eppes

DR. SIR   Eppington October 24th. 1791

I find myself much mortified at not being able to see you whilst in Virginia. Mrs. Eppes's ill health was only cause. After being much weakend by lying in she got violent cold which brought on a fever that lasted ten days and was very nigh carrying off. She has at length got quite clear of all complaints and is gathering strengh fast.

I wrote you from Richmond the first of September and again by Martin early in this month. No answer has yet come to hand to either of them. In my last I informd you of having purchasd a Jenny of the Malta breed from Mrs. Bolling. The price £20. If convenient and agreeable to you will thank you either to direct Colo. Lewis to remit the money, or if more agreeable you may furnish Jack with it and I will pay Mrs. Bolling. I also request you woud give me your opinion respecting the sum necessary for Jacks annual expenditures including books and all other expences. I am sorry to be so troublesome but hope when you recollect Jacks inexperience you will excuse it. Mr. Skipwiths sale is over. He has made a very good one considering the fall of Tobacco. Their average was fifty three or four pounds. I am with every wish for your health & happiness Dr Sir Your Friend,   FRANS. EPPES

RC (ViU); endorsed by TJ as received 27 Nov. 1791 and so recorded in SJL. Eppes letter of the FIRST OF SEPTEMBER was actually that of 2 Sep. 1791. His letter BY MARTIN was likely that of 2 Oct. 1791 (missing), recorded by TJ in SJL as received 10 Nov. 1791. See TJ to Eppes, 13 Nov. 1791.

SCHEDULE *of the whole number of* PERSONS *within the several Districts of the* UNITED STATES, *taken according to* "An Act providing for the Enumeration of the Inhabitants of the United States;" *passed March the 1st*, 1790.

STRICTS.	Free white Males of sixteen years and upwards, including heads of families.	Free white Males under sixteen years.	Free white Females including heads of families.	All other free persons.	Slaves.	Total.
Vermont	22,135[1]	22,328	40,505	255[2]	16	85,539
New-Hampshire	36,086	34,851	70,160	630	158	141,885
Maine	24,384	24,748	46,870	538	NONE	96,540
Massachusetts	95,453	87,289	190,582	5,463	NONE	378,787
Rhode-Island	16,019	15,799	32,652	3,407	948	68,825
Connecticut	60,523	54,403	117,448	2,808	2,764	237,946
New-York	83,700	78,122	152,320	4,654	21,324	340,120
New-Jersey	45,251	41,416	83,287	2,762	11,423[3]	184,139
Pennsylvania	110,788	106,948	206,363	6,537	3,787[4]	434,373
Delaware	11,783	12,143	22,384	3,899	8,887	59,094
Maryland	55,915	51,339	101,395	8,043	103,036	319,728
Virginia	110,936	116,135	215,046	12,866	292,627	747,610
Kentucky	15,154	17,057	28,922	114	12,430	73,677
North-Carolina	69,988	77,506	140,710	4,975	100,572	393,751
South-Carolina	–	–	–	–	–	–[5]
Georgia	13,103	14,044	25,739	398	29,264	82,548[6]

	Free white Males of twenty-one years and upwards, including heads of families.	Free white Males under twenty-one years of age.	Free white Females including heads of families.	All other Persons.	Slaves.	Total.
. Western Territory	6,271	10,277	15,365	361	3,417	35,691
. Do.	–	–	–	–	–	–[7]

Truly stated from the original Returns deposited in the Office of the Secretary of State.   TH: JEFFERSON.

October 24, 1791.
*This return was not signed by the marshal, but was enclosed and referred to in a letter written and signed by him.

MS not found; text taken from first printed copy by Childs and Swaine, 1791, consisting of 56 pages, the last page bearing TJ's signature; delayed returns from South Carolina have been tipped in as page 54, dated 5 Feb. 1792, showing a total of 249,073 persons (copy in NjP: Rare Books). Tr (DNA: RG 59, MLR); copy of MS prepared some time after 5 Feb. 1792 with significant differences described in textual notes below.

These returns had been arriving at the President's office all summer and were normally transferred to the Secretary of State upon receipt (Tobias Lear to TJ [Connecticut, Delaware, Georgia, and districts of Kentucky and Maine], 12 July 1791], RC in DNA: RG 59, MLR; FC in DNA: RG 59, SDC; Lear to TJ [Maryland, New York, North Carolina], 5 Aug. 1791; RC and FC in same; Lear to TJ [Rhode Island], 6 Aug. 1791, RC and FC in same;

Lear to TJ [Virginia], 18 Aug. 1791, RC and FC in same; Lear to TJ [New Jersey], 20 Aug. 1791, RC and FC in same; Lear to TJ [Pennsylvania], 22 Aug. 1791, RC and FC in same; and William Blount to TJ [Southwest Territory], 19 Sep. 1791). South Carolina requested and was granted an extension by an act of Congress adopted on 2 Nov. 1791. Washington sent the final return from South Carolina, dated 5 Feb. 1792, to Congress on 3 Mch. 1792 (JHR, I, 446-7, 526; JS, I, 336-7, 404).

TJ sent this summary to the President, who announced the completion of the census "excepting in one instance in which the return has been informal, and another in which it has been omitted or miscarried" in his annual message to Congress on 25 Oct. 1791, the day after the session began.

He transmitted the summary to Congress two days later (Fitzpatrick, *Writings*, XXXI, 400, 407; JHR, I, 437; and JS, I, 329-30).

[1] In Tr: 22,435.
[2] In Tr: 252.
[3] In Tr: 11,453.
[4] In Tr: 3,737.
[5] The Tr includes the figures for South Carolina as follows: 35,576, 37,722, 66,880, 1,801, 107,094, and 249,073.
[6] In Tr after this figure in this column a total is calculated as follows: "3,893,635, from below 42,691, 3,936,326."
[7] The Tr contains "supposed total 7,000" at this point. Judging from Washington's comment in his annual message, the original MS TJ submitted to him probably had contained this figure as well.

From John Trumbull

DEAR SIR   Phila Oct 24th 1791

I had not forgotten my promise, tho' it was made so long since.

The first days of liesure which I enjoyed among my friends in Connecticut, were devotd to render this little picture more worthy of your acceptance than it was when you saw it.—I wish it were now a more valuable testimony than it is of the Gratitude and Esteem of D sir Your obliged friend & Servant,   JNO. TRUMBULL

RC in Collection of Jonathan T. Isham, Newport, R.I., 1975 (Tr by Irma B. Jaffe, Fordham University); endorsed by TJ as received 24 Oct. 1791 and so recorded in SJL. The LITTLE PICTURE was what TJ called the "premiere ébauche" of Trum-

bull's sketch of "The Surrender of Lord Cornwallis at Yorktown" (Irma B. Jaffe, *John Trumbull: Patriot-Artist of the American Revolution* [Boston, 1975], p. 319; and TJ's Catalogue of Paintings at Monticello, ViU).

From Willink, Van Staphorst & Hubbard

SIR   Amsterdam 24 October 1791.

We are honored with your favors of 13 May, 13 July and 5 August, To the contents of all which we have paid utmost attention. Your Remittances

[228]

ƒ99000   for the department of State } are in good order,
ƒ32175   for the Fund of 3 March 1791 }
and to your Credit under their respective Heads.

Whenever Coll: Humphreys shall draw on the Latter, his Bills will be discharged to debit of the Fund of 3 March 1791, as far as it will extend; and those He will draw for discharge of the arrears due and for the Maintenance of the Captives at Algiers, to the general account for the department of State.

We inclose you,

Your acct. currt. for the Department of State up to 30 June last, the Balance whereon due by us Hd. Cy. ƒ70670.3.8 is to Credit of a New Account for this Department; Upon which you will perceive by a Note at foot we have already paid Hd. cy. ƒ11179.1.8.

Besides which there is further drawn on us

Bƒ2800 by Mr. Carmichael.
  "2200 in   800 hard Dolls. @110 Ex) by Coll: Humphreys.
  "5450 in 2000 do.   109 Ex)

which will be regularly charged to your account for the Department of State.—We are Respectfully Sir Your most Obedient and very humble Servants,   WILHEM & JAN WILLINK
                    N. & J. VAN STAPHORST & HUBBARD

RC (DLC); addressed: "To the Honble Thomas Jefferson Esqr. Secretary of State Philadelphia ⅌ The Morning Star Capt. Kermit"; postmarked: "[NEW Y]ORK MARCH 6" and "FREE"; endorsed by TJ as received 7 Mch. 1792 but recorded in SJL under 6 Mch. 1792.

ENCLOSURE

Statement of Account with the United States

DR: TH: JEFFERSON ESQR: SECY: OF STATE TO THE UNITED STATES OF AMERICA CR:

1791			1791	
April 30.	To sundry Drafts Money furnished from the 1st: July 1790 till the 30 Apl. 1791 as ⅌ note	ƒ26467.11.8	June 10.	By your Remittce. in a draft of Saml. Meredith Esqr. of 19. March 10/d sight to your order on our Selves No. 210. ƒ99000.
May 5	To 1 draft of D. Humphreys Esqr: order J. Bulkeley &			

Son B. ƒ1331.5 Ago.

₩ 1331. 5.

June 29 To 1 do. of Wm.
Short Esqr: order
Grand & Co.
Bo. ƒ529.14. Ag. 1/2
₩Ct. 531.

30 To balance which we
carry to new Acct: 70670. 3.8

ƒ99000.

Since are paid by us the following Drafts

July   25. 1 of D. Humphreys 20 May
@ 2. Us. order J.
Bulkeley & S: Bo. ƒ5275. ag. 1₩   ƒ5327.15.

29. 1 of Wm: Short 18. July
10/d order Grand &
Co.   Bo. ƒ223.15. ag. 1₩   226.

Augt: 10. 1 of do. 4 June 10/d order
Grand and Co.   298. 6.8   298. 6.8

12. 1 of do. 5 July do.   222.10. @ 1₩   224.14.8

1 au do. C.W.F. Dumas
order N. & J.V.
Staphst & Hubbard   296.14.

Septr: 1. 1 of D. Humphreys 1 July a
Us. order J. Bulkeley
& Son   Bo. ƒ3990. 1.8 ⅞ pct.   4024.19.8

1 of Wm: Short 18 Augt.
10/d. order Grand &
Compy.   Bo. ƒ220.   ⅞

Octr: 6. 1. of do: 20 Septr. 10/d. do: 553. 2.8 1₩   558.13.8

ƒ11179. 1.8

Errors Excepted
Amsterdam. the 30. June 1791
WM: JN: WILLINK
N. & J. VAN STAPHORST &
HUBBARD.

Note of sundry drafts and money furnished to the following from the 1. July 1790 till the 30. April 1791 for which the formerly Account Currt: sent to the United States are debited, for which amount or by Specifications hereunder we credit the Account of the United States, and transfer on that of Th: Jefferson Esqr. Secretary of State vizt.

1790. Wm: Short

1	draft	7. Augt: 10/d	Bo. ƒ556.10. Ago.	¼ ₩ ct:	ƒ557.18.
1	do.	3 Sept:	445. 5.	½	447.10.
1	do:	7 Octr.	271.18.8.	⅛	272. 5.8
1	do:	22 Septr:	1328.17.	"	1330.10.
1	do.	3 Novr.	354. 2.	@ 99½	352. 7.

1 do. 13 "		859. 6.			859. 6.	
Money paid him					2199. 5.	
Money paid him					8131.14.	
1791. 1 draft 31 March		704.7.			704. 7.	
1 do. 7 April		612.			612.	
					ƒ15467. 2.8	

Of which we deduct the sums disbursed by him on public Account vizt. for sundry disbursements including the expenses of his Journey here and Salary of his Secretary £175. 1.   ƒ2491.14.

1 assign. of £76.10.						
5 ℔Ct. loss 3.16.6	72.13.6				91. 6.	2583.
	£247.14.6 @ 44. ago. ½ ℔.					ƒ12884. 2.8
790. Wm: Carmichael						
1 draft 22 April	1½ Us Bo. ƒ2800 ago.		⅜ ℔.	ƒ2810.10.		
1 do. 12 July	do.	2180. 2	¼	2185.11.		
1 do. do.	do.	619.18.	99½ ℔.	616.16.		
791 1 do. 29 Novr: 1790	9%¼ do.	1400.	1 ℔.	1414.		
1 do. 31 Jany.	1½ Us.	2800.	99¾	2793.	9819.17.	
790. C.W.F. Dumas						
1 Assign.				ƒ1625.		
1 do.				297.		
791 1 do.				216.12.		
1 do.				1625.	3763.12.	
					ƒ26467.11.8	

PrC (DLC). Tr (DNA: RG 59, DL). FC (DLC: Washington Papers). TJ enclosed the above account with his letter to Washington of 7 Mch. 1792.

To James Brown

DEAR SIR   Philadelphia Octob. 25. 1791.

I recieved by Mr. Randolph the sum you were so kind as to send by him, which I presume to have been 50. dollars not having weighed it, and I have now the pleasure to return you that sum in a bank post-bill. I left directions that as soon as our wheat shall be sold, the sum of fifty pounds Virginia currency be paid to you on account. I am with great esteem Dear Sir Your most obedt. humble servt,

TH: JEFFERSON

RC (NNP); addressed: "Mr. James Brown Mercht Richmond"; franked; postmarked "26 oc" and "FREE"; endorsed. PrC (MHi).

To J. P. P. Derieux

DEAR SIR   Philadelphia Oct. 25. 1791.

I have the pleasure to inclose you a letter which I found on my arrival here. I find one also of July 8. from Mr. Fenwick our Consul at Bordeaux in which is the following passage. 'Mr. Le Roy has been absent all this summer from Bordeaux. He is now in Paris and expected to return in course of a month or two. Immediately on his arrival I will wait on him in person with the letter you covered and communicate the details you was pleased to enter into concerning your neighbor Mr. de Rieux, and sincerely hope they may have the desired effect, which from his circumstances and situation, being a wealthy batchelor, there is some reason to expect. No attention on my part shall be spared to interest him in favor of Mr. de Rieux.'

My letters inform me that the affairs of France are going on solidly well. The election of the new legislature was to be completed in September, and to meet the 15th. instant. They are probably now in session. Assignats current at from 8. to 20. per cent below par.

Be pleased to present my compliments to Mrs. de Rieux and to accept assurances of the esteem with which I am Dear Sir Your most obedient hble servt,   TH: JEFFERSON

PrC (DLC). Fenwick's letter to TJ of 8 July 1791, recorded in SJL as received 22 Oct. 1791, has not been found.

To the Rev. Matthew Maury

DR. SIR   Philadelphia Oct. 25. 1791.

I have now the satisfaction to inclose you a bank post-bill for seventy five dollars and a half as I informed you I would in my letter from Monticello. I inclose this letter to you open, under cover to your brother at Fredericksburg, that he may get at the bill, recieve the money from the nearest collector of the U.S. and dispose of it according to such directions as you shall in the meantime have lodged with him. I am with great & sincere esteem Dear Sir Your friend & servt.,   TH: JEFFERSON

PrC (ViU: Edgehill-Randolph Papers); at foot of text: "The revd. Matthew Maury." TJ had written Maury from Monticello on 10 Oct. 1791.

To Thomas Mann Randolph, Jr.

DEAR SIR   Philadelphia Oct. 25. 1791.

The first part of our journey was pleasant, except some hair-breadth escapes which our new horse occasioned us in going down hills the first day or two, after which he behaved better, and came through the journey preserving the fierceness of his spirit to the last. I believe he will make me a valuable horse. Mrs. Washington took possession of Maria at Vernon and only restored her to me here. It was fortunate enough as we had to travel through five days of a North East storm, having learned at Mount Vernon that Congress were to meet on the 24th. instead of the 31st. as I had thought. We got here only on the 22d. The sales at George town were few, but good. They averaged about 2400. dollars the acre. Maria is immersed in new acquaintances; but particularly happy with Nelly Custis, and particularly attended to by Mrs. Washington. She will enter with Mrs. Pine a few days hence.

Congress met to-day. The President's speech ran on the following subjects.—The Indians.—A land law. Militia law. Post office. Weights and measures. Navigation and commerce.—The English minister, Mr. Hammond is arrived. Affairs in France are going on well. Their new legislature is probably now sitting. I imagine a general peace has taken place through Europe.—Present my warm affections to my daughter and kiss little Anne for me. Adieu my dear Sir Your's affectionately,   TH: JEFFERSON

RC (DLC); addressed: "Mr. Thomas M. Randolph junr. esq. Monticello. By the Richmond post"; franked. PrC (DLC: TJ Papers, 69:11954); mutilated so that about a fourth of text is lost, including dateline, and mistakenly filed under 24 Nov. 1791.

NELLY CUSTIS: Eleanor Parke Custis (1779-1852), a granddaughter of the Washington's who lived with them much of the time because her father (John Parke Custis) died in 1781 and her mother (Eleanor "Nelly" Calvert) was ill (Donald Jackson and Dorothy Twohig, eds., *The Diaries of George Washington* [Charlottesville, 1978], IV, 109; Rutland, *Madison*, XIV, 56). Mary PINE, widow of artist Robert Edge Pine, operated a boarding school near TJ's house in Philadelphia until the end of May 1792 when she closed it to return to England (Robert G. Stewart, *Robert Edge Pine* [Washington, D.C., 1979], p. 25-6, 35-7; TJ to Thomas Mann Randolph, 1 June 1792).

From C. W. F. Dumas

The Hague, 26 Oct. 1791. The Provincial States have passed a resolution opposing the Stadtholder's decision to return the 5,000 German troops who had been used to help suppress the revolution. The Stadtholder has tried unsuccessfully to induce the Regents to overturn this resolution.—The States General is still considering East Indian affairs. The governor general of Batavia has resigned, and the governor and second treasury officer of the Cape of Good Hope have returned to answer charges of financial irregularities. The Stadtholder is also concerned about the East India Company.—*1 Nov*. He has learned that tomorrow a bookseller will be flogged in Amsterdam for selling a libelous publication against the Stadtholder. Today he witnessed the arrest of a bookseller for publicly selling *Memoires pour servir a l' histoire de la revolution des Provinces-Unies, par Mandrillon*, a work containing original correspondence pertaining to the suppression of the revolution.—*4 Nov*. Yesterday, by order of the court of Holland and the local magistracy, every house in the city was illuminated in honor of the marriage of the young hereditary prince to a Prussian princess. But the marriage evoked little enthusiasm among the populace.—*5 Nov*. The Provincial States will definitely dismiss the German troops in January or February and replace them with less expensive forces. Zeeland will do the same, but the other provinces probably will not.—*10 Nov*. He has procured "3 Exemplaires du Livre, dont j'en joins 1 à ce paquet-ci, et l'autre au duplicata." He forgoes writing at length about European affairs since the enclosed papers will show that the monarchical and aristocratic opponents of the French Revolution are nothing more than "une cohue de disparates."

FC (Dumas Letter Book, Rijksarchief, The Hague; photostats in DLC); in French; 4 p. At head of text: "No. 84"; recorded in SJL as received 5 Apr. 1792.

To George Hammond

Oct. 26. 1791.

Mr. Jefferson has the honor of presenting his compliments to Mr. Hammond, of expressing his regrets that he happened to be from home when Mr. Hammond did him the honor of calling on him, and was equally unlucky in not finding him at home when he waited on him on Monday. Being informed by Mr. Bond that Mr. Hammond is charged with a public mission to the government of the United States, relative to which some previous explanations might be proper, Mr. Jefferson has the honor to assure Mr. Hammond he shall be ready to recieve any communications and enter into explanations either formally or informally as Mr. Hammond shall chuse, and at any time suitable to him. He recollects with pleasure his acquaintance with Mr. Hammond in Paris, and shall be happy in every opportunity of rendering him such offices and attentions as may be acceptable to him.

PrC (DLC). FC (DNA: RG 360, DL).

George Hammond, who had arrived in Philadelphia on 20 Oct. 1791, two days before TJ returned, was the first British minister plenipotentiary to the United States. He came armed with instructions from Grenville to discuss the controversies surrounding implementation of the Treaty of Paris, to consider the U.S. proposals for a commercial treaty with Britain, to offer British mediation to resolve the conflict between the United States and the western Indians, and to oppose adoption of any congressional legislation that might be injurious to British trade and navigation. Hammond's dealings with TJ were sin-gularly devoid of any substantive diplomatic agreements, in no small part because of the clandestine interference of the Secretary of the Treasury in many of the ongoing negotiations between the British minister and the Secretary of State (DNB; Leslie Reade, " 'George III to the United States Sendeth Greeting . . .,' " *History Today*, VIII [1958], 770-80; Charles R. Ritcheson, *Aftermath of Revolution: British Policy Toward the United States, 1783-1795* [Dallas, Texas, 1969], p. 123-44; Editorial Note to group of documents on commercial and diplomatic relations with Great Britain, Vol. 18: 252-4, 258, 276-83; Grenville to Hammond, 1 and 2 Sep. 1791, Mayo, *British Ministers*, 13-19).

From George Hammond

26th. October 1791.

Mr. Hammond presents his most respectful Compliments to Mr. Jefferson, and begs leave to assure him that he has felt equal regret with him at the circumstances, which have hitherto prevented their meeting. In conformity to Mr. Jefferson's obliging proposal Mr. Hammond will have the honor of waiting on him tomorrow, at any hour that he will have the goodness to appoint.

Mr. Hammond is extremely flattered by Mr. Jefferson's kind recollection of him at Paris, and fully sensible, as he ought to be, of the value of his polite and friendly offers.

RC (DNA: RG 59, NL); endorsed by TJ as received 26 Oct. 1791 and so recorded in SJL. Tr (same).

The President to the House of Representatives

GENTLEMEN OF THE
HOUSE OF REPRESENTATIVES   Oct. 26. 1791.

I have recieved from the Governor of North Carolina a copy of an act of the General assembly of that state authorizing him to convey to the U.S. the right and jurisdiction of the sd. state over one acre of land in Occacock island and ten acres on the Cape island within the sd. state, for the purpose of erecting lighthouses thereon, together with the deed of the Governor in pursuance thereof, and the original conveyances made to the state by the individual proprietors, which original conveyances contain conditions that the light house on Occacock shall be built before the 1st. day of January 1801. and that on the Cape island before the 8th. day of Octob. 1800. And I have caused these several papers to be deposited in the office of the Secretary of state.

PrC (DLC), entirely in TJ's hand. In lower left corner, TJ wrote "Oct. 26. 1791 Th. J." Not recorded in SJL, but entry in SJPL reads: "[Oct.] 26. Message cession by N. Cara. for lighthouses at Ocacoke and Cape isld."

Washington used this text in a message he submitted to Congress on 27 Oct. 1791 that also dealt with the first U.S. census and a report by Attorney General Randolph "respecting certain persons who are said to have fled from justice out of the State of Pennsylvania into that of Virginia" (Fitzpatrick, *Writings*, XXXI, 406-7). In a letter of 27 Oct. 1791, Tobias Lear transmitted to TJ authenticated copies of acts of the North Carolina legislature pertaining to the building of lighthouses as well as the use of state jails by federal officials, an act of the Pennsylvania legislature ratifying the first amendment, and an act of the New Hampshire legislature relating to lighthouses (RC in DNA: RG 59, MLR; not endorsed and not recorded in SJL; Dupl in same, SDC).

From Delamotte

Le Havre, 27 Oct. 1791. Praises behavior of American ship captains and crews in Le Havre.—Encloses copy of "d'une observation maritime" received by way of some Catholic priests in Baltimore. It will be helpful if the document's contents can be verified.—In 1785 *Le Compere Mat*[. . .] left Le Havre for Baltimore commanded by Lieutenant d'Elivet and accompanied by his son. The ship arrived safely in Baltimore, but d'Elivet's wife has since had no word from them. He asks TJ to ascertain whether they are dead so that "la femme abandonnée" can claim her inheritance.—Virginia tobacco is selling for 34 to 40 livres per quintal and rice for 27 to 28 livres. "Ce sont de hauts prix assurement."[P.S.] All of France is dismayed by the recent arrival of news of the "désastre de St. Domingue."

RC (DNA: RG 59, CD); 4 p.; in French; endorsed by TJ as received 10 Feb. 1792 and so recorded in SJL.

The enclosure was Pierre Douville's "Observation importante sur le Banc de Nantucket," an attempt to clarify the size and location of the Nantucket shoal. TJ wrote on the letter "for Mr. Freneau To be published and the name and quality of the writer subjoined." A translation of the portion of Delamotte's letter relating to Virginia tobacco prices appeared in the 13 Feb. 1792 *National Gazette* with an abbreviated version of Douville's "Observation." A brief sketch of Douville may be found in André Lasseray, *Les français sous les treize étoiles*, 2 vols. (Macon and Paris, 1935), I, 187.

From Thomas Pleasants, Jr.

DEAR SIR   Raleigh 27th. Ocr. 1791.

Your Letter of the 17th. Inst., which Came by yesterdays Mail, is a fresh and flattering proof, of your kind attention, and regard to me. And tho' the place, that you have put within my power, would probably make me independent and happy for Life, yet such is my Situation that I Cannot with propriety accept it. In an unpropitious moment, I was led into an extensive plan of business, the burthen of settling which, has in a great measure fallen upon me and which, for many years past, has occupied the greater part of my time, and been a Continual source of trouble and anxiety, and may the Cause of future difficulties and distress: but I cannot at present withdraw myself from it, with Honour and Credit.

I am still at a loss to know how it will terminate, but I would fain hope in a manner that will leave me sufficient to begin again, with which, and a good name, which I trust has Continued unsullied; I flatter myself that I may yet be able to do a little business with Credit and Reputation, which I Confess would be More agreeable to me than the drudgery of office. It however may turn out otherwise and therefore it Cannot but afford me Consolation to think, that I have in you a friend to whom I may look up, should there be occasion. But whatever may be my Situation, I shall ever entertain the most lively sense of your friendship.—And With Sincere regard & Esteem, I am, Your obliged friend & Mo obt. Hble St.,   THOMAS PLEASANTS JR

Your opinion, whether Congress will during their present Session, Countervail the Extra duty lately imposed by the National assembly of France, upon Tobacco imported in American Bottoms, Will oblige, Yrs.,   T.P.

RC (MHi); endorsed by TJ as received 3 Nov. 1791 and so recorded in SJL.

TJ's 17 Oct. 1791 letter to Pleasants, a Virginia merchant and planter, has not been found, nor is it recorded in SJL. The office TJ offered to Pleasants may have been that of surveyor of the port of West Point, Va., to which Washington nominated Alexander Moore eight days after TJ received this letter (JEP, I, 89).

From Louis Alexandre

Bayonne, 28 Oct. 1791. Two years ago he wrote a letter to TJ describing the opposition to continuation of American free port privileges at Bayonne. Now the opponents of these privileges want to persuade the French government to abolish them on the grounds that they are detrimental to French manufacturing.—The municipal government of Bayonne favors these privileges.—He asks TJ, "Comme vous êtes dans ce moment President du Congré," to prevail on Congress to address "l'assemblée Nationale" in favor of continuing Bayonne's free port status.—[P.S.] A copy of this letter is in another port. "Sy j'avois conu votre residence, il y a longtems que je vous en aurois fait Part."—He has recently sold a cargo of tobacco, flour, rice, and salt beef from Philadelphia and desires more cargoes from there.

RC (DNA: RG 59, MLR); 4 p.; in French; in another hand, except signature and postscript which apparently were written later when Alexandre realized TJ was in Philadelphia; at head of text: "Duplicatta"; endorsed by TJ as received 20 Mch. 1792 and so recorded in SJL. Dupl (same); in Alexandre's hand; at foot of text: "A Monsieur Jefferson President du Congre a NYork"; lacks postscript.

Alexandre's previous letter to TJ was that of 5 June 1789. He wrote again to TJ on 29 Nov. 1791, reiterating that it would be unwise of the Legislative Assembly to abolish American free port privileges at Bayonne and stating mistakenly that "les troupes et Secours que vous allies Envoyer au Cap St. Domingue" especially entitled the United States to enjoy these privileges (RC in DNA: RG 59, MLR; endorsed by TJ as received 28 Mch. 1792 and so recorded in SJL; Dupl in same).

From Thomas Barclay

Lisbon, 28 Oct. 1791. He is waiting to find passage on a ship to Gibraltar or any part of the Mediterranean but this is difficult because any ship arriving in Italy from Gibraltar must be quarantined for ten days. He hopes nevertheless to proceed on his mission in a week. "At present I need only observe that the character of the present Emperor is very different from that of his predecessor, that every article fit to carry with me is one third dearer here than in either France or England, and that the proceeds of the bills will fall considerably short of the estimate, owing to all the foreign exchange being much in favor of this Country."

RC (DNA: RG 59, CD); 2 p.; endorsed by TJ as received 21 Jan. 1792 and so recorded in SJL. John Barclay informed TJ that his brother had written on 3 Sep. of his arrival in Oporto in good health, and that he "would proceed to Lisbon by the first Conveyance" (John Barclay to TJ, 24 Oct. 1791; endorsed by TJ as received the same day and so recorded in SJL; RC in DNA: RG 59, MLR).

From Joseph Fenwick

Bordeaux, 28 Oct. 1791. A citizen of New York, Mrs. Ollivier, married a Frenchman in 1786 and subsequently came with him to Bordeaux where she has lived since. Mr. Ollivier died last summer, leaving her without children, a will, or a marriage contract. French law entitles her to the proportion of his estate equal to what the law allows in the country in which they were married. With apologies for the burden of such a request, he asks for certified information on what inheritance New York would allow.

RC (DNA: RG 59, CD); 2 p.; endorsed by TJ as received 14 Jan. 1792 and so recorded in SJL.

From Joseph Fenwick

Bordeaux, 28 Oct. 1791. He encloses a copy of his letter by the Wilmington Packet, Capt. Andrews. Peace in Europe seems secure. The national militia mentioned in his last letter have been quartered in neighboring towns instead of marching to the frontiers.—He acknowledges receipt of the laws of the U.S. for the use of his consulate, and he notes that on 3 Mch. Congress repealed the section of a 1789 act for the collection of import duties setting the value of the rix dollar. Since Congress apparently acted in response to the depreciation of that coin in Denmark, it should take similar action with respect to the livre tournois. Otherwise American duties on French products will be at least 20 ℔Cent higher than those of other countries because since 1 May the value of the livre tournois has been less than 15 1/2 cents in comparison with the Spanish milled dollar and less than 8 pence sterling in comparison with the pound sterling.

Tr (DNA: RG 59, CD); 1 p.; at head of text: "Copy." Recorded in SJL as received 14 Jan. 1792. Extract printed in *National Gazette*, 16 Jan. 1792, together with extracts of Fenwick to TJ, 25 Sep. 1791.

From David Humphreys

Lisbon, 28 Oct. 1791. He calls TJ's attention to the following extracts from a 22 Aug. 1791 letter from Captain [Richard] O'Bryen in Algiers to a commercial house here.

Washington has drawn Congress' attention to their plight, but the American captives in Algiers are still in slavery and have no assurance of regaining their freedom. Nevertheless he is confident that Congress will instruct "their ambassadors or Agents in Europe" to effect the captives' release.—On 25 July the Spanish clergy freed two "public Slaves" in return for the payment of a ransom of 2,700 dollars to the new Dey of Algiers—2,300 dollars less than the ransom demanded by his predecessor. The present Dey is willing to ransom all current slaves but hopes that his cruisers will capture others. The Dey's moderation with respect to ransom is probably calculated to lessen the dread of seamen at the prospect of capture by Algerine corsairs. If anyone in Algiers had been authorized to redeem the thirteen remaining American captives, they could have been freed for less than has been hitherto demanded for their ransom. A review of past efforts to redeem the captives and conclude peace with Algiers is necessary for appraising present prospects of achieving these goals.

Mr. Lamb made a regular bargain with the Regency for our release for 16800 Sequins but he failed to keep his word. Messrs. Bushara & Dininio negotiated our ransom for 16525 Sequins, and to make the agreement official, they had the bargain recorded in the Regency Books, a precaution he thinks carries little weight with the present Dey.—"It is a matter of indifference to the Algerines whether those persons that have had our redemption ascertained

[239]

were empowered by Congress, the Ambassadors in Europe, or their Agents. The Algerines well-knowing that any enquiries that are made proceed from some American in Office that has been empowered by the fountain head.— Monsr. Parret being authorised by Monsr. Cathalan of Marseilles to sound the Regency relative to a peace with America and to ascertain in a faint manner our redemption: the Regency well knew that these orders to make these enquiries came originally from Congress. For common sense will dictate to any rational Being that no Persons particularly in Algiers would propose any thing relative to the making of a peace without first being empowered by some superior Authority: and of course every thing that has been said or done by Mr. Lamb, Bushara and Dininio, and lastly by Monsr. Parret, this Regency considers that all originated in Congress.—I will now tell you candidly, Sirs, that all these enquiries that have been made relative to the peace and towards our release have been in general prejudicial to the U.S. It shews the enemies of America the views and weakness of our American Government; and whoever is authorised or empowered to come to Algiers should be fully empowered so as to bribe or palm the Algerine Ministry. And if peace can be obtained, it may nearly be concluded in a few days: or fully empower some person to act so as to lay the foundation of the peace and after the principal points are arranged, then let the American Ambassador come and put a finishing hand to the negociation.—A Person high in Office (Vice President) wrote us five years ago that our redemption concerned the peace. He will now find that the peace concerns our redemption: for would any one that knows any thing of this Country suppose that the sum asked for our release would be an inducement to this Regency to make a peace with the U.S. And as our redemption has been three different times ascertained and so many uncustomary enquiries made and so often talked of to the Algerine Ministry; the present Dey, then prime Minister, has said, that if the Americans did not keep to their word and agreement on this affair, that there was no great dependence to be put upon them in affairs of more importance.—I assure you, Sirs, that the favorable opinion we have always tried to imbibe in those people seems to be rapidly on the decline: There have been so many enquiries and such shuffling work and all come to nothing. And I have my fears, that those favorable opportunities that the U.S. had of making a peace with this dreaded and respected Regency are irrecoverably lost.—Should the Portuguese try to obtain a peace with the Regency and succeed, the Algerines will have all the Atlantic Ocean free to cruze in, and then, Sirs, what would be the fatal consequences to the American Commerce, what would be the alarm?—The U.S., in my opinion, may obtain a peace with this Regency for the sum of 60 or 70 thousand pounds Sterlg: that is if the affair is well managed and our redemption and all expences included. That is, if the affair is well managed and by giving maritime Stores and a few light Cruisers, it would not cost 100,000 Dollars. Any peace bought with Money is by no means on a sure and lasting basis: for those people only think of the money, while counting it into the Treasury and by paying every two years. A certain quantity of Tar, Pitch, Turpentine, Masts, Plank and Scantling would be the only means of keeping a peace, for it is not the sum given for the peace that those people consider, it is the annual Tribute they receive that secures the peace."

Mahomet Pashaw, Dey of Algiers, died on 12 July and was immediately succeeded by the prime minister, Hassan Pashaw. The new Dey soon renewed peace with all the powers represented in Algiers save Spain, informing the Spanish consul that he would renew no peace with Spain until the problem of Oran was settled. Spain has decided to relinquish Oran to Algiers and has instructed the governor of Oran to notify the Bey of Mascara of this decision.— It is impossible to conclude peace between Algiers and the U.S. through "the present Channel of Marseilles . . . as all that are concerned in the affair are Agents and Creatures of the Chamber of Commerce of Marseilles . . . and the French will never help the U.S. to be a Sharer of those valuable branches of Mediterranean Commerce."—He has been obliged to become indebted to Jews in Algiers in order to buy the necessaries of life and hopes that the U.S. ambassador to Lisbon will honor him and his fellow captives with a few lines.

Humphreys has been thus copious in quoting from this letter to give TJ an accurate account of the most recent intelligence from Algiers. He has instructed the commercial house mentioned above to inform Captain O'Bryen that the American minister in Lisbon has nothing to say respecting the redemption of the captives and thinks it would be unwise for him to correspond with them but that measures are being taken by an American in Spain to pay their debts and provide for their subsistence. He plans to write again to William Carmichael about subsistence for the captives and to find some other channel of relief for them in the event Carmichael fails to send a timely reply.—The arrival of a Russian courier from Petersburgh has occasioned speculation that the Empress wants to borrow money from the Queen. Barclay is ready to depart but has not been able to find passage for Gibraltar.—P.S. He is unable to explain why he failed to receive any newspaper by the English packet.

RC (DNA: RG 59, DD); 12 p.; at head of text: "(No. 38)"; at foot of text: "The Secretary of State"; endorsed by TJ as received 21 Jan. 1792 and so recorded in SJL. Tr (same).

From George Hammond

SIR   Philadelphia 30th October 1791

As I am apprehensive that, in the short conversation, which I had with you yesterday at General Knox's, I may have been misunderstood, I take the liberty of communicating to you in writing, the substance of what I then stated, as well as what I meant to have added, had I not been unwilling to trespass farther, at that time, on your attention.

With respect to the manner of presenting the credentials, with which I am charged by my Court, I have no other instructions, than those that I had the honor of mentioning to you on Thursday last. The interpretation of them, and any modification of them, which I may think it expedient to adopt, are necessarily left to my own discretion.

I hope, Sir, you will do me the justice to believe that I am not much inclined to magnify trifles, or to assign too great a degree of importance to matters of mere ceremony. In the present instance, I should consider your assurance of the disposition and determination of this government, to nominate a Minister to England, as a sufficient justification for me to present my credentials without delay, if my hesitation could have arisen from even the most remote doubt of the existence of that disposition. But the real point of etiquette, consistent with the dignity of both our Countries, appears to me to be this—that, although a strict conformity, in regard to time, in the respective appointment of Ministers by the two Governments, is rendered impossible by the circumstance of my prior arrival at the place of my destination, yet (and in this opinion I flatter myself you will concur with me) it is still in some measure practicable that the *nomination* of a Minister by this government may *ostensibly* keep pace with my *actual appearance* in a diplomatic character. The mode prescribed in my instruction (of delivering my letters of credence, "whenever I shall be informed that a Gentleman has been actually *invested* with a ministerial character to my Court, similar to mine, or has been *nominated* for that purpose") seems to me exactly to meet this notion.

I must however, Sir, desire you to be persuaded that I am not solicitous to accelerate my public reception, and that I am perfectly willing to wait any time that may suit the President's convenience. Whenever his Excellency shall have made his election—should it fall upon any Gentleman in the vicinity of this state, a few days, perhaps hours, would be sufficient, to learn his acceptance or refusal of the station offered him, and to afford the opportunity of making such a communication to me, as might enable me to comply literally with my instructions.—But should the case occur, which you, Sir, have suggested, of the President's proposing the appointment to a Gentleman, who may be at a considerable distance from the seat of government, I shall, in that case, conceive myself fully justified in departing from my instructions so far, as to present my credentials, upon receiving an assurance, that the President has offered to a Gentleman, at a distance, a ministerial appointment to my Court, similar to that, with which I am invested in this Country.

I shall not enlarge farther upon this subject than to desire you, Sir, not to consider this letter as a formal communication, but rather as a friendly exposition of those sentiments, which I have before stated in conversation, and which I have thrown into this form, in order that we may clearly understand each other.—I have the honor to be, with great truth and respect, Sir, Your most obedient, humble Servant, GEO. HAMMOND.

RC (DNA: RG 59, NL); at foot of text: "Honble Mr. Jefferson"; endorsed by TJ as received 30 Oct. 1791 and so recorded in SJL. Tr (same).

This minor contretemps over the presentation of Hammond's diplomatic credentials foreshadowed the often frustrating relationship TJ enjoyed with the British minister throughout the remainder of his tenure as Secretary of State. Soon after his arrival in Philadelphia on Oct. 21, Hammond informed TJ through Phineas Bond, the British consul, that he had been instructed by his government to delay presenting his credentials to the President until an American minister to Great Britain had either been nominated or appointed. TJ assured Bond that the President intended to nominate such a minister as soon as possible and repeated this assurance dur-

ing a personal meeting with Hammond at the home of Secretary of War Knox the day before this letter was written. But TJ's assurances were not enough for the punctilious Hammond. Hammond waited until TJ officially notified him on 10 Nov. that Washington had selected a nominee for the post of minister to the Court of St. James and then presented his credentials to the President on the following day, at which time, he later reported, "The President received me with the utmost politeness and respect, and assured me that I should find, not only in himself, but in every description of persons in this country, the sincerest alacrity to meet those friendly dispositions, which his Majesty has been pleased to express" (Hammond to Grenville, 23 Oct., 1, 16 Nov. 1791, PRO: FO 4/11, f. 93-4, 100-1, 142-3).

From James Brown

DEAR SIR   Richmond 31st. Octbo 1791

I did myself the Honor of writing you a few days ago to which I crave your reference. I am this night favored with your letter of the 25t. covering a Bank Bill for Fifty Dollars which is to your Credit. I observe the further paiments alloted for me which is well. The inclosed or annexed Copy of a letter from Mr. Short has just got to hand. I beg you will write me as soon as possible what you think I had best do, that an immediate investment take place should you recommend it.—With much Respect & great consideration I am Sir your Obet: Hl: Srt,   JAMES BROWN

RC (MHi); endorsed by TJ as received 5 Nov. 1791; addressed: "Thos. Jefferson Esq. Secretary of State Philadelphia"; postmarked: "RICHMOND, OCT. 31." and "FREE." The entry in SJL records receipt of a letter from James Brown dated "Paris Aug. 31"— a transference of the place and date of the letter from Short enclosed in Brown's.

Brown's letter of A FEW DAYS AGO was that of 21 Oct. 1791. In the copy of the letter Brown ANNEXED to this dated at Paris 31 Aug. 1791, Short wrote him about investing his 6% and 3% stock "should Mr.

Jefferson advise it." He gave Brown instructions for reimbursing himself for the expence, and added: "I learn that the whole of the Stock was Subscribed to the Bank the first day of its being opened. If so, I suppose many must have subscribed with a view to speculate by selling their subscriptions. In that case I know not what to advise, perhaps they may be forced to sell at the rate of the Subscription. If they are sold higher I should be unwilling to go too largely in them but will ask the favor of you to consult with my friend Mr. Jefferson and act for the best."

From Francis Eppes

Dr Sir   Richmond October 31st. 1791

Receiving a letter this Evening from Jack in which he expresses much anxiety for his Mama's health I have taken the liberty of inclosing a letter for him in one to you. I have writen three letters befor this and have recd. no answer to either. I shall be much obliged when you have leasure if you will answer them all. I have the pleasure to inform you that Betsey is once more in a fair way to be well having no complaint except weakness. I am with every wish for your health & happiness Dr Sir Your Friend,   FRANS. EPPES

PS. Give our love to Polly. We have this day been informd she is with you.   F E

RC (ViU); endorsed by TJ as received 5 Nov. 1791 and so recorded in SJL.

From Tench Coxe

                                                              Novr. 1. 1791

Mr. Coxe has the honor to inform the Secretary of State that he has just discovered a Monsr. Hallet, who is said to be a very excellent Draughtsman. He lives at a Mr. Savery's a hatter at the Corner of 3d. and arch Streets. Mr. Hallet does not speak English, but the writing can be added by a Clerk.

RC (DNA: RG 59, MLR); endorsed by clerk as received the same day.

Hallet was employed not long after by the Department of State, as their records show he was paid 100 dollars on December 13, 1791, for "two drafts of the federal town" (Vol. 17: 367).

From Jonathan N. Havens
and Sylvester Dering

Sir   Shelter Island Novr. 1st: 1791

We have not the honour of a personal acquaintance, but have presumed to adress this Letter to you at the request of Mr. L. Hommedieu of Southold, by whom we have been informed, that it would be very agreeable to you to receive every possible information respecting the hessian fly; that as a member of the agricultural society of Pensylvania you were in a more particular manner desirous of gaining that information; and that, when he saw you at Southold in the month of June last, he had mentioned our names to you in conversing on that subject. By him we have been encouraged to hope, that if we were to transmit to you an account of our observations on that insect, we might possibly drop some useful hint, or say something which might throw further light on so interesting a subject; and were assured, that if we should be particular in describing its various transformations, and in giving a relation of the various times in which it has prevailed in our part of the country, the account would not be the less agreeable. This intended communication has been delayed until this time, to afford an opportunity of making further observations during the last summer, and examining whether the opinions we had heretofore entertained concerning its nature were in any great degree erroneous; and to see whether further discoveries might not be made which would be useful. When it first made its appearance in our part of the country, if we had apprehended that any of our observations on its nature would have ever extended beyond the sphere of our personal acquaintance, we should without doubt have been more diligent in our inquiries; but as all our experiments and observations were then made merely to gratify private curiosity, or to throw light on the subject in common conversation, we did not pay so much attention to it as its importance required. We reside near each other, and are well acquainted with each other's observations and opinions on this subject, and have united in writing a single letter to avoid a repetition of the same ideas and sentiments.

The hessian fly was first perceived on Shelter Island, and the adjacent parts of Long Island, a little before the harvest of the year eighty six, and in its progress through the country appeared to come from the westward; and in the fall of the same season it was found in great plenty in the green wheat, and did most injury to that which had been most early sown. At this time the nature of the insect, and its varous transformations, were with us very little understood. In the winter following it was currently reported that the fly was to be found in great plenty in the wheat in sheaf; from whence it was concluded that it must have some immediate connection with, or dependence upon the wheat in grain, either for food or for the preservation of its species. This led us into a careful examination of that kind of insect which was affirmed to be the hessian fly; and we found it in the first place to bear a very great resemblance to a booklouse, in shape, agility, and colour; and as it grew larger it appeared gradually to turn brown, and to have wings, but not to undergo any regular transformation; and at last it became a small black fly.

We could discover no other insect except this which could be imagined to be the hessian fly; and this we had no doubt might have been easily discovered before if the wheat had been examined: it was sufficiently evident, both from its shape, and every other attending circumstance, that it could have no relation to, or connection with, the insect discovered in the field; and in this opinion we were abundantly confirmed by all our succeeding observations. In the spring of the year eighty seven, the insect in the field, which was the real hessian fly, increased very fast in the green wheat and at the ensuing harvest many fields were almost wholly destroyed; and in the fall of the same season the wheat again suffered as great injury as before, and the harvest of the year eighty eight was cut off almost universally. The kinds of wheat then in use were the red balled, and summer wheat; both of these were equally affected; rye tho' less affected in general was in many places much injured; and what appeared most singular was, that a piece of summer barley belonging to Mr. Dering, was about that time wholly cut off. After so general a destruction of wheat for two successive harvests rye was in general sown, except in some instances where the bearded wheat had been obtained, and at the ensuing harvest in the year eighty nine the insect appeared to be gone; and in the fall of this year the several kinds of bearded wheat were pretty generally introduced, and the harvest next following, which was in the year ninety, was in general very good, and very few of the insect were to be seen. This gave great encouragement to farmers and induced them to suppose, that the raising of bearded wheat alone without any other precaution, would prove an effectual remedy against the hessian fly; but notwithstanding the use of this, the fly has again increased in the present year so as to be found in great plenty in many places, which we suppose must be occassioned by our sowing our wheat early; a circumstance very necessary to be attended to with us, that the wheat may obtain a good growth before the cold weather, and be less liable to be injured by the winter. In the two years abovementioned, in which the fly proved so generally destructive to wheat, we made a variety of experiments and observations with a view to ascertain its nature, and method of propagation; and have again had an opportunity of renewing our observations with more particular attention since its increase in the present year; and the result of our inquiries is this; that the hessian fly is a species of insect which has no direct dependence upon the wheat in grain, either for food, or in any other manner for its preservation, but is in the winter season a chrysalis, and remains in the field on the green wheat without suffering any

Thomas Jefferson

Jean Baptiste Ternant

George Hammond

Gouverneur Morris

Thomas Pinckney

RETURN

OF THE WHOLE

NUMBER OF PERSONS

WITHIN THE

SEVERAL DISTRICTS

OF THE

UNITED STATES,

ACCORDING TO

"AN ACT PROVIDING FOR THE ENUMERATION OF THE INHABITANTS OF THE UNITED STATES;"

PASSED MARCH THE FIRST,

ONE THOUSAND SEVEN HUNDRED AND NINETY-ONE.

———————

PHILADELPHIA:
PRINTED BY CHILDS AND SWAINE.

M,DCC,XCI.

First Census, 1791, Title Page

Schedule of the whole number of perſons in the territory of the United States of America, South of the River Ohio, as taken on the laſt Saturday of July 1791, by the Captains of the Militia within the limits of their reſpective diſtricts.

		Free white males of 21 years and upwards, including heads of families.	Free white males under 21 years.	Free white females including heads of families.	All other perſons.	Slaves.	Total of each county.	Total of each diſtrict.
WASHINGTON DISTRICT.								
Counties.	Waſhington	1009	1792	2524	12	535	5872	
	Sullivan	806	1242	1995	107	297	4447	
	Greene	1293	2374	3580	40	454	7741	
	Hawkins	1204	1970	2921	68	807	6970	
	South of Fr. Broad	681	1082	1627	66	163	3619	
MERO DISTRICT.								28649
Counties.	Davidſon	639	855	1288	18	659	3459	
	Sumner	404	582	854	8	348	2196	
	Tenneſſee	235	380	576	42	154	1387	
								7042
		6271	10277	15365	361	3417		35691

Note. There are ſeveral Captains who have not as yet returned the Schedules of the numbers of their diſtricts, namely : In Greene County, three—in Davidſon, one—and South of French-Broad, one diſtrict.

September 19*th*, 1791.

W^m: BLOUNT.

By the Governor,

DANIEL SMITH, *Secretary.*

First Census, 1791, Last Page

William Tatham

David Rittenhouse

Aug. 13. 1791. Notes of a conversn between A. Hamilton & Th:J.

Th:J. mentioned to him a lre recd from J. A. disavowing Publicola, & denying that he ever entertd. a wish to bring this country under a heriditary executive, or introduce an hereditary branch of legislature &c. see his lre. A. H. condemning mrs A's writings & most particularly Davila, as having a tendency to weaken the present govmt declared in substance as follows. 'I own it is my own opn, tho' I donot publish it in Dan & Bersheba, that the present govmt is not that which will answer the ends of society by giving stability & protection to it's rights, and that it will probably be found expedient to go into the British form. however, since we have undertaken the experiment, I am for giving it a fair course, whatever my expectns may be. the success indeed so far is greater than I had expected, & therefore at present success seems more possible than it had done heretofore, & there are still other & other stages of improvemt which, if the present does not succeed, may be tried & ought to be tried before we give up the republican form altogether for that mind must be really depraved which would not prefer the equality of political rights which is the foundn of pure republicanism, if it can be obtained consistently with order. therefore whoever by his writings disturbs the present order of things, is really blameable, however pure his intentns may be, & he was sure mr Adams's were pure.' this is the substance of a declaration made in much more lengthy terms, & which seemed to be more formal than usual for a private converson between two, & as if intended to qualify some less guarded expressions which had been dropped on former occasions. Th:J. has committed it to writing in the moment of A. H's leaving the room.

11414

62-28

apparent injury from frost or snow, and is transformed into a fly as soon as the weather becomes warm enough in the spring. The period of time in which this transformation is made will begin more or less early according as the season may be more or less forward, and generally continues according to our observations about three weeks: in the year eighty seven we observed it to begin about the sixteenth of april, and end about the first of may; and this we think may be considered as the usual time of its commencement and continuance in our climate. The fly disengages itself from the wheat, by boring a small round hole through its brown case, and through the leaf of the wheat just opposite to the place where it is lodged, and comes forth wrapt in a thin white skin, which it soon breaks, and is then at liberty; and this hole is to be seen in the stubble as long as it remains entire. Very soon after the fly comes out, it is prepared to spread itself every where in the field where it has lain during the winter, or to take its flight to more distant places in search of wheat on which to lay its nits or maggots; and it is at this time that it has an opportunity of going on the summer wheat, which would otherwise escape without being injured. The great variety in the time of its first becoming a fly in the spring, produces the like variety in the time of its laying the maggot on the wheat, but this we suppose may be generally placed between the twentieth of april and the tenth of may; and this period of time like the former must necessarily be regulated by the season; and may perhaps be affected by bad weather and unfavourable winds, which may benumb the fly, or prevent it from taking its flight. The maggot is always found between the inside of the lowest part of the leaf, and the outside of the part which forms the stalk or straw, to which it closely adheres, and is generally, as near the root as possible; but to this there are some few exceptions for it is sometimes, tho' very rarely, to be found a little above some of the upper joints. It appears at first like a very small white nit or egg; and as it grows larger becomes a sluggish, and almost inanimate maggot, or worm, of a white colour, and capable of very little perceivable motion. This is properly the first state or mode of existence with the insect, and is that in which it destroys the wheat; and altho' it appears at first to resemble a nit or egg, yet we are inclined to suppose that the fly is viviparous, for we never could discover that any transformation took place from a nit to a maggot. In this state the proper and most natural food of the insect is the sap or juice of that kind of green wheat which has the most delicate straw, and next to this may be ranked the several kinds of wheat whose straw is more firm and solid, and last of all rye and barley: some have affirmed that they have been found on oats, but of this we have no certain knowledge. The maggot obtains the juice altogether by suction, and has no means or faculty of corroding or consuming the solid part of the straw, and as it grows larger its whole body indents the straw, and prevents the rise of the sap, and the grain either falls down or perishes before it has grown to be of any considerable height. The size of the maggot when grown, and the time necessary to compleat its growth, depend in a considerable degree on the quantity of nourishment it may obtain from the grain, and the number of them that may happen to be on one straw; and this time according to our observations is somewhere between four and six weeks, and their growth will generally be compleated in the first part of June: but here the several causes of variety before mentioned conspire to render this time so various that some will be transformed into a chrysalis, whilst others are small, and this circumstance has led many skilful observers to suppose that there are two compleat generations of the insect before harvest. As soon as the maggot has obtained its growth it is transformed into a chrysalis of a dark brown colour, this is the second state or mode of existence which the insect assumes, and is that in which it is mostly observed: in this state it is found in the time of harvest, and when the wheat is gathered remains in the stubble until it undergoes its transformation into a fly; excepting those few which are sometimes in the upper joints, these must necessarily be gathered with the wheat and must always go with the straw, because they adhere too closely to it to [be] beaten or threshed off without being destroyed. The time of their continuance in this state appears to be regulated very much by their enjoying that particular degree of heat and moisture, which is most agreeable to their constitution: if they are removed into the house, and kept dry, and in the shade, they continue longer a chrysalis, than if they remain in their natural situation in the field: cold and wet affect them no otherwise than to continue them in the same state, and prevent their transformation into a fly, as long as they remain in that situation; but of heat they can endure but a small degree, beyond that which is natural for them in the summer seasons and will perish on being exposed to the rays of a hot sun, in such manner as to become very dry, and have all their natural moisture exhaled. Those and various other circumstances render it difficult to ascertain with precision the length of time that they continue a chrysalis during the summer season, but we conclude from our observations that it is not less than two months; and may be prolonged to a much longer time by any of the causes before mentioned.

The several causes of variety in the time of their continuing in this state, together with the various times in which they are first formed into a chrysalis in the month of June, conspire to render the period of time in which they make their next transformation, much longer than any of the other periods of time in which they make their several transformations: we think it begins in many instances as soon as the twenty fifth of August, and continues in a greater or less degree through the whole month of September, but by far the greater part are without doubt transformed into a fly in the first part of this month. A reflection here naturally arises, that nature appears to have fixt this transformation, to commence with, and continue through, the whole of that season of the year which is most proper for sowing wheat. The fly is the third and last state of the insect, and compleats what we term one generation: it resembles the moscheto in almost every respect, except that it is much smaller, and has a short bill: it never preys upon the wheat and very probably requires no other nourishment than what it may obtain from dew, or moisture: it is of so delicate a texture as to be injured and destroyed by the slightest accident: and soon after it becomes a fly, it again lays the maggot on the wheat sown in the fall; and if this is not sown soon enough so as to be up at the time the fly requires it, the maggot will be in great measure lost, and the species reduced to an inconsiderable number. The length of time in which it naturally continues a fly is very difficult to ascertain, but is without doubt very short. In the fall of the year the maggot generally proves more destructive to wheat than in the spring, and before cold weather is transformed into a chrysalis, in which state it is prepared to remain during the winter, without any apparent injury from frost, snow, or wet, and in the spring again becomes a fly, which compleats two generations of the insect in one year. It is probable that many, reasoning from analogy, will doubt the reality of this transformation into a fly in the fall, and will suppose that there can be but one compleat generation of the insect in one year: but in support of this we will mention one of our experiments; we gathered a number of the chrysalis from the wheat about the middle of last June, and kept them in the house in a dry place, and out of the sun, and where they could not be molested; and a number of these were transformed into a fly between the tenth, and the thirteenth of September; and besides these a number of others gathered from the stubble after harvest, and placed in the same situation, became a fly about the same time: the remainder of those, which were not transformed at that time, still continue in the same state; this we impute to their being too cold and dry to make their transformation. Since the first of September we have examined the stubble as often as once or twice in a week, and have found them to diminish in number, but that there are still some remaining; from whence we conclude that this transformation in the fall will be in some degree partial; and that many of those, which become a chrysalis late in the month of June, will remain in that state for so long time, that the weather will become too cold for them to make their transformation in the fall; and then they must necessarily continue in that state through the winter, until the weather becomes warm enough in the spring. To this we may add, that if we suppose but one generation in a year, it must follow; that the chrysalis which is formed in June will without exception continue through the winter, and be disposed by nature to be transformed into a fly at the same time with the chrysalis formed in the fall; and that the fly which comes out in the spring will live through the whole summer, and become prolific a second time in the same season; but these are consequences which appear improbable, and difficult to reconcile to phænomena. In the course of all our examinations into the nature of the insect, we have taken the most pains to determine these three points; whether it has any connection with the wheat in grain; whether it is a chrysalis in the time of harvest, and remains in that state in the stubble for any considerable time afterwards; and whether it is transformed into a fly in the fall of the year: with respect to the first of these points, we think it may be considered as clearly decided in the negative, that the insect has no dependence upon the wheat in grain, either for food, or as a place in which to deposit any nit or egg for the preservation of the species: and with respect to the two last, we think, there can be no doubt but that they must be considered as decided in the affirmative.

Of all the various methods which have been proposed to the public for preventing the injurious effects of this insect, that of raising the different sorts of bearded wheat has best succeeded. This kind of wheat, having a more solid straw, resists the impressions made by the body of the insect, and in great measure prevents the injury which arises from stopping the rise of the sap; and very possibly there may be some peculiar quality in this sap, which may render it in some measure disagreeable to the constitution of the insect; but experience shews, that even this sort will not succeed, unless it be attended with the circumstance of being sowed late. Whether any preference ought to be given to any one of the different sorts which have a more firm and solid straw, we have had, during the last year, an opportunity of making one fair experiment; in a field belonging to one of us, were sown three different sorts of wheat, contiguous to each other, and all at the same time; the white bearded; the yellow bearded; and the great red balled, or red-chaff wheat; of these three sorts, the red-chaff was by far the most injured; and the yellow bearded, which lay adjoining to it, least of all.

We will here take the liberty of suggesting a method of destroying them, which has frequently occured to our minds, and which we have not heard mentioned by others; and that is to destroy the stubble of grain soon after harvest. This idea naturally occured on discovering that the insect is then a chrysalis and remains so for some time afterwards. Whether this would be best affected by burning or other wise; and whether the wheat in this case ought not to be cut with the sickle, rather than mowed or cradled; whether the cost that would attend it would not overbalance the advantage; and whether the aid of government might not be necessary to render it uniform and general, are points to be taken into consideration in determining whether any thing of this kind would be feasible, and which we shall not now pretend to discuss: but if the stubble of wheat were to be universally burnt, turned over with the plough, or other wise destroyed soon after harvest, and this were to be done for several years together; we have little doubt in our minds but that it would prove an effectual means of destroying the species: for it is not very probable that the species would be continued long on rye, more especially, as that can be sown much later than wheat without injury from the winter; and the stubble of rye might, if necessary, be as easily destroyed as that of wheat: and if in aid of this, the best sort of bearded wheat were to be used, and that to be sown as late as possible consistent with a good crop, it would be still more likely to succeed.

It has been a received opinion in the country, that they will stay only three years in a place and then be gone; but experience shows that this cannot be true, and we can see no reason why the species should not continue as long as it can find proper food for subsistence. With respect to the probability of their being imported from any foreign country we shall make only one remark, that by our experiments in the last summer it appears, that they may be removed from their natural situation in the field, and be kept alive long enough to be carried across the Atlantic; from which circumstance it appears possible that they might have been imported in straw or stubble. It has been generally remarked, that in spreading over the country, they go between twenty and thirty miles in a year, but as they are a fly twice in the same season, it appears probable, that the fly itself never goes much farther than twelve or fifteen miles. All abstract reasoning and theory on subjects of this nature ought no doubt to be consistent with phænomena, and yield to the test of experiment; if therefore it should appear evident from the experiments and observation of others, that we are wrong in our opinions concerning the nature of this insect, we shall with pleasure stand corrected. A great many particulars respecting our experiments, and the various appearances of the insect, might have been mentioned; but to have given a particular detail of these, would have exceeded the intended bounds of this letter. We are with the greatest respect your most obedient humble Servants,

JONATHAN N. HAVENS
SYLVESTER DERING

RC (DLC); recorded in SJL as received 1 Dec. 1791. Signed but undated covering letter reads: "Sir, Enclosed we have the honour of presenting you an account of the hessian fly. We reside at Shelter Island in the county of Suffolk, and State of New York, about six miles from Mr. L'hommedieu's. With the greatest respect we are yours &c." (RC in DLC: TJ Papers, 67: 11707; franked; endorsed: "Recd. and forwarded by Sir your mo. obedt. Servt., David Gelston").

From Thomas Hemming

SIR   George Town 1 November 1791

I take the liberty of sending you the enclosed letter from my Brother in law Mr. Boyd of Paris, transmitted to me at this time, from my being unfortunately deprived by death of the advice and protection of his brother who has resided twenty five years in this part of the World, and if your Excellency will pardon my intruding on your patience for a few minutes I will relate the nature of my situation. Mr. A. Boyd after this long absence from his Brother by whom he was much beloved, paid him a visit last Winter and during his residence with him, in consequence of the solicitation of him and Mrs. Boyd promised to take myself and family to America, as his Children and that we should remain under his roof, till he could by some means point out a mode of my procuring myself a comfortable subsistance, which he assured me by industry and a small sum of money might easily be done. With these views we prepared to embark with him for this Country, and for that purpose expended a considerable part of the small pittance of which I was possessed for household furniture &c.—Filled with the most flattering expectations of prosperity and happiness we left our native Country, but unaccompanied by him, as some accident prevented his joining the Ship: this however we deemed only a trivial misfortune, thinking ourselves certain of his presence by the next Vessel that sailed, which on our arrival here we expected with the utmost anxiety and impatience but alas! when she did arrive all our fair hopes and expectations were blasted by letters informing us that he departed this life about ten days after we left England: Thus deprived of a relation under whose patronage and direction I had assured myself of success, I find myself in a strange country to whose Inhabitants and manners I am almost a Stranger without a friend on whose advice I can depend in what manner it be best for me to proceed.—Should your Excellency happen to have time from your more weighty and important concerns, to bestow a little Instruction on a Young Man who would exert himself with the utmost assiduity and industry by any means to maintain himself and family it would be received as a very great obligation by Sir Your Excellency's Most obedient humble Servant, THOMAS HEMMING

RC (MHi); at foot of text: "Please to direct to the care of Robert Peter Esqr."; endorsed by TJ as received 5 Nov. 1791 and so recorded in SJL.

The enclosed letter was Walter Boyd to

TJ, 11 Aug. 1790. Archibald Boyd must have left his home in Bladensburg, Md., to visit his brother in Paris soon after his meetings with TJ in the spring of 1790. See TJ to Walter Boyd, 6 Apr. 1790, and Boyd to TJ, 1 Mch. 1792.

From Archibald McCalester

SIR   Belville Novr. 1st. 1791.

I was going to beg your permission to recall a pleasure, which is the honor I had of being known to you at Monticello, when with the late Colonel Bland, we placed the British Troops under the Convention of Saratoga, at Charlottesville—and in the succeeding campaign to the Southward. Tho' the distance of time, and change of circumstance, with the Multiplicity of important affairs which your Excellency has been engaged in since, leave little room to hope that I retain the honor of a place in your memory; thus situated, I beg leave to observe, that I entered the Army early in the late War, as an Officer in the Maryland line, and at the Peace, I married and settled in Carolina, where I have since resided as a Rice Planter.

I hope you will pardon my being thus particular with respect to my self, which became necessary to introduce a request that I beg leave to make your Excellency, and in confering which, you will oblidge and lay me under the highest obligation.

The Lady with whom I am united, has an only Son, a most promising youth twelve years of age. He is now at the Acadamy in New Jersey, and as soon as he is perfect in the Classicks it is our wish to send him to the best Seminary in Europe, where he would most likely receive a liberal Education, with the least risque of bad morals.

I would not wish to send him to England, (which has been the Custom of this Country) because an American ought not to imbibe English prejudices, but would prefer some part of France or Switzerland; Where he might receive a liberal Education, better suited to this Country.

As I am sure no one can give such good information on the Subject as your Excellency, I have taken the liberty to request you will please to favor me with a line of advice on the Occasion. If, from the momentous affairs which engage the time of your Excellency, an instant can be spared to advise me which of the Colleges in France you would recommend, please to direct it to No. 23. Hassell Street Charleston, South Carolina.

Since I wrote the above another matter has occurred; The British Troops that ravaged the Carolinas, carried off Twenty eight Negroes from my Plantation, and a number more from an Estate to which I am an Executor. Several of my Negroes were after the Peace at Birch Town in Nova Scotia; but I never could reclaim them, as the British would not give them up.—Query, are not the British bound to pay for them, and is there any possibility of obtaining Payment?

I am induced to mention my claim at this time as I have been informed since I sat down to write that the British Court are sending out a Mr. Hammond with a view to negotiate a Treaty of Offensive and Defensive Alliance with the United States, which the[y] vainly hope to effect, through what the[y] hold out as commercial advantages to this Country. I do not know that the above is a fact, but I think it probable, and if such overtures are made, I may be allowed to hope, that the United States will reject such a connection with disdain.—As a Nation, it is a misfortune that we speak the English Language:—and there is no advantage we could receive from them, would compensate for the deadly blow such a league would strike at the Spirit of Independance, and National Character so essential to our prosperity as a Nation.

The United States and the Russian Empire possess the natural Seeds, which must ere long subvert the *British empire of the Occean.* The Federal Goverment, and the Possessions which Russia has just obtained from the Turks on the Black-Sea, will soon ripen those

Seeds to the ruin of the British Navigation. At this prospect they are now alarmed, and are setting every engine at work to keep the current of our Commerce, which has but too long centered in their Ports.

While the British Executive hold the latch of their Ports with one hand, the[y] are exerting the other to spoil our Trade, and prevent our Vessells going elsewhere.

As the British Court now wish a Commercial Treaty, and are anxious to secure us in the Consumption of their Manufactures the[y] ought as an introduction to it, to open their West India Ports for the sale of our Lumber and Provisions—reduce their excessive Duties on our Rice, Tobacco, &c. and guarantee the neutrality of the Algiers Confederacy with respect to the American Flag. These are a few of the many concessions which the[y] ought to make as an equivallant for the immence advantages the[y] receive from our Trade with them.

If my warm wishes do not carry me too far, I think the period is not distant, when the United States will not thank the British for such concessions.—Indeed, I trust that the period will soon arrive when the American Flag will display its stripes with lustre in the numerous Ports up the Mediterranean, even into Assia. And through this Channel a considerable part of our Trade with India, and even China itself, will more advantageously come.

These are the effusions of a heart warm with good wishes for the prosperity of my native Country, as such, I hope you will pardon them.—I have the honor to be, with much respect your Excellency's Most Obedient Servant,   A. McCALESTER

RC (ViW); addressed: "His Excellency Thomas Jefferson Esquire Secretary of State Philadelphia"; endorsed by TJ as received 20 Dec. 1791 and so recorded in SJL.

TJ favored McCalester with A LINE OF ADVICE regarding European universities for his stepson, James Hasell Ancrum, on 22 Dec. 1791.

From Edmund Randolph

DEAR SIR   Philadelphia November 2. 1791.

I took the liberty of mentioning to you the other day the application, which Mr. Telles's friends had made, for his appointment to the office of consul in Lisbon, and which they wished me to assist. On recollecting, what passed between us, I suspect that I was not clearly understood in my statement of Mr. Telles's situation. He can never sue the court or any individual of Lisbon. His suit is in England, and against English subjects. So that he cannot be in danger of irritating any man in or out of power in Portugal. His creditors here have not only borne the most ample testimony to his worth, but have given him so full a discharge, that he will not be obstructed in the execution of any consular function. And, altho' he now appears in the character of a man, stripped of his fortune, his unequivocal expectations of more than 2,000£. per annum from two of his aged relations there, will put him in a condition to answer any trust, which the mercantile interest may choose to repose him.

I have been induced to trouble you with this letter, from a persuasion, that in my former conversations with you on this subject, I have not been so explicit, as I now am. Mr. Telles is a stranger to me, except from the recommendation of many virtuous men in this city. Neither for him nor any other, should I hold myself justified, to make private friendship a ground for soliciting from a public officer an act, which respects his public duty. But for any man I would undertake to represent facts; and if they tend, as in the present instance, to remove the obstacles, which stand in the way of a deserving, tho' unfortunate man; I confess, that his promotion would be a real gratification to my feelings.—I am dear sir with truth yr. friend & serv: EDM: RANDOLPH

RC (DLC: Washington Papers); endorsed by TJ as received 2 Nov. 1791 and so recorded in SJL.

Randolph was undoubtedly correct in estimating John Telles as "a deserving, tho' unfortunate man." But if in his presentation of facts he meant to include the assurance that Telles had no intention of pursuing his case at Lisbon, he had been imposed upon by the friends promoting Telles' candidacy for the consulate there. One of the principal reasons the MERCANTILE INTEREST had advanced for his appointment was that Telles' influence at the court of Portugal and in commercial circles there would enable him to recover his losses more quickly than through the English courts (see Editorial Note and documents on consular problems, at 21 Feb. 1791).

From Elizabeth Carter

DEAR SIR   Frederickbg Academy November the 3d. 1791

I take the liberty once more, to beg your friendship for my eldest Son Walker Randolph Carter, who is now on his way in the Packet for Philadelphia, to live with Mr. Hunter a Coachmaker, who takes him for two years without fee. I am in hopes I shall be able to cloath him decently and allow him a little pocket money. All I have to ask of you is, that you will be so good to give him your advice and countenance. He has a tolerable education, but fear he may loose what he has learned, unless some friendly person, will sometimes put him in mind of the bad consequences that will attend his not reading all leasure hours. Any Books you will think propper to recommend and lend, I make no doubt he will be thankfull for, as I can asure you, as I told you in a former letter, that his disposion is very placid, but rather to diffidently backward to go through this life with out the encouragement of a friend, as such I flatter myself you will be. The Atorney has procured the place for him and make no doubt will act a friendly part, but a parents tender feelings woud have all the world look with their eyes on their Children, which must plead my excuse, for now soliciting your attention to my Child, who is in a strange place, at so great a distance from his parents. Mr. Carter has written to several of our Country Gentlemen on this subject, who I hope will all have an eye to the conduct of our Son, and advise him whenever they see Occation. Our Second Son Charles Landon we have placed with a Phisician in this Town, to get acquented with medecine, after which, if our finances will allow, we shall send him to Edenburg. I shoud have preferd Philadelphia, coud we have fixed him there without paying so enormous an admistion fee. After beging your forgivness for this intrution will subscribe myself your obedient & much oblig'd,

Eliza Carter

RC (MHi); endorsed by TJ as received 8 Nov. 1791 and so recorded in SJL.

Mrs. Carter had written TJ a former letter about her eldest son on 19 Sep.

1790 (Vol. 17: 552n). the atorney: Edmund Randolph. Regarding the training of Charles and Elizabeth Carter's second son, see TJ to Carter, 31 July 1791.

From Samuel Smith

Sir   Baltimore 5th. Novr. 1791.

In behalf of myself and the gentlemen concerned in the sloop Jane and cargo, I beg leave to enclose you the Captain and people's protest, which will fully shew you the insult done to the american flag, and they still continue to detain the property. I also return your obliging letter to Mr. Skipwith who had left Martinique before it arrived there.

The purport of the present is to request the favor of you to State the situation of this business to the French Minister, and to request him to write to those in authority at Martinique to make restitution. We have employed a gentleman by the name of Thomas Darlington who will leave this in a few days for Martinique, and there act in conjunction with Mr. George Patterson Merchant of that Island, for the recovery of the property. If the French Minister will write, we wish the names of those gentlemen to be mentioned by him, as the persons employed by the sufferers. Your immediate answer will very much oblige your obedient huml. Servt.,   SAML. SMITH

Tr (DNA: RG 360, DL); includes enclosure. Recorded in SJL as received 7 Nov. 1791. See TJ to Ternant, 16 Nov. 1791. The OBLIGING LETTER was TJ to Fulwar Skipwith, 24 June 1791, regarding the SLOOP JANE.

To William Carmichael

SIR   Philadelphia Nov. 6. 1791.
My last letter to you was of the 24th. of August. A gentleman going from hence to Cadiz will be the bearer of this, and of the newspapers to the present date, and will take care that the letter be got safe to you if the papers cannot.

Mr. Mangnal, at length tired out with his useless sollicitations at this office, to obtain redress from the court of Spain for the loss of the Dover Cutter, has laid the matter before Congress, and the Senate have desired me to report thereon to them. I am sorry to know nothing more of the subject than that letter after letter has been written to you thereon, and that the office is in possession of nothing more than acknolegements of your receipt of some of them so long ago as Aug. 1786. and still to add that your letter of Jan. 24. 1791. is the only one received of later date than May 6. 1789. You certainly will not wonder if the receipt of but one letter in two years and an half inspires a considerable degree of impatience. I have learnt thro' a circuitous channel that the court of Madrid is at length disposed to yield our right of navigating the Missisipi. I sincerely wish it may be the case, and that this act of justice may be made known before the delay of it produces any thing intemperate from our Western inhabitants.

Congress is now in session. You will see in the papers herewith sent the several weighty matters laid before them in the President's speech. The session will probably continue through the winter. I shall sincerely rejoice to receive from you not only a satisfactory explanation of the reasons why we recieve no letters, but grounds to hope that it will be otherwise in future.—I have the honour to be with great esteem Sir Your most obedt. & most humble servt.,
                                                    TH: JEFFERSON

PrC (DLC). FC (DNA: RG 59, DCI).

TJ had instructed Carmichael to take up the case of John Mangnall and the *Dover* with the Spanish government in his letter to Carmichael of 11 Apr. 1791, continuing a series of such instructions that had begun with John Jay (see Jay to Carmichael, 14 Mch. 1786, 24 Nov. 1786, 14 May 1787, 23 Sep. 1788, 24 Nov. 1788, DNA: RG 360, FL). TJ's report to the Senate on Mangnall's case is at 14 Nov. 1791.

TJ had recently learned from William Short that the French foreign minister, Montmorin, had been told of Spain's willingness to recognize the right of the United States to navigate the Mississippi (see Short to TJ, 20 July 1791). But it was not until 6 Sep. 1791 that the Spanish government actually issued a formal order to Viar and Jaudenes, who were then serving as its agents in the United States, instructing them to notify the American government of Spain's wish to negotiate a settlement of this issue. Viar and Jaudenes did not receive the order until December 1791, at which time they promptly brought it to TJ's attention (see TJ to Washington, 22 Dec. 1791; and Arthur P. Whitaker, *The Spanish-American Frontier: 1783-1795* [Boston, 1927], p. 148-9).

To Francis Eppes

DEAR SIR   Philadelphia Nov. 6. 1791

I received last night yours of Oct. 31. complaining that you had written three letters before that, to me, which remained unanswered. Be assured my dear Sir that in the last seven months, I had received but your letter of Sep. 2. This I answered from Monticello Octob. 6. and I hope is come to hand before this. I therein asked the favor of you to inform me of the nature and amount of the demand of Bevins's administrator, and who and where his agent was, which I must still ask of you.

Jack is well, and is just finishing his first reading of Coke Littleton. He continues assiduous, and to shew so many other good qualities as may justly fill your hearts with comfort. He will attend courses in Natural history and Anatomy this winter, so as to interfere little with his law reading.

You will have seen by the President's speech the mass of weighty matter presented to the view of Congress. Maria is well and wishes to join me in affectionate respects to Mrs. Eppes and the family. Adieu my dear Sir Your affectionate friend & servt.,

TH: JEFFERSON

Tr (ViU). TJ's answer to Eppes' letter of SEP. 2 was actually dated 5 Oct. 1791. See TJ to Eppes, 13 Nov. 1791.

To Thomas Mifflin

SIR   Philadelphia Nov. 6. 1791.

I am honoured with your favor of yesterday on the subject of the laws of the U.S. furnished to you from my office. I would with pleasure add a third copy, but that, your Excellency will percieve, on turning to the act of Congress which establishes my department, that that has fixed the number of copies of the laws to be furnished by me to the Executives of the states, and of course that the Treasury department could not pass my accounts but by the rule there prescribed. Otherwise the propriety of sending a third copy is too obvious to have produced a moment's hesitation.—I have the honour to be with the greatest respect & esteem Your Excellency's most obedt & most humble servt,   TH: JEFFERSON

PrC (DLC); at foot of text: "H. E. Governour Mifflin." FC (DNA: RG 360, DL). In his FAVOR OF YESTERDAY Mifflin had asked for a third copy of the laws to enable him to give copies to each house of the state legislature and to retain a copy for the executive office (FC in PHMC: Mifflin Adm. Papers).

From Gouverneur Morris

DEAR SIR   Paris 6 Novr. 1791

I take the Liberty of writing this Letter to make you acquainted with the Bearer of it Monsieur de Cormeré Brother to the late Monsieur de Favras. Mr. de Cormeré has been in the finance of this Country and is well acquainted with that Subject. He has lately published a short Work on the Relations of Commerce proper for the french Islands of which I have sent you a Copy. He is now going to S. Domingo in which Country I understand that he means to pitch his Tent. His Connections with the leading Characters there and his Habits of Industrious Investigation will I am perswaded bring him into the Possession of many particulars which will be amusing if not interesting to you, and I have thought it my Duty to put him in that Channel of Communication which appears to me under all Circumstances the most proper.

FC (DLC: Gouverneur Morris Papers); in Morris' hand. Not recorded in SJL.

The pamphlet by Guillaume François, Baron Mahy de Cormeré, mentioned by Morris, was entitled *Observations sur les colonies Françoises de l'Amerique* (Paris, 1791). See Sowerby, No. 2593.

Morris' letter conceals far more than it reveals about his relations with Cormeré, whose brother, the Marquis de Favras, had been executed in 1790 for conspiring to help the royal family escape from Paris. Cormeré and Morris had recently been involved in an abortive scheme to persuade the National Assembly to approve a liberal plan of self-government for the French West Indies in order to pave the way for their eventual independence and closer commercial relations with the United States. Undaunted by this setback, Cormeré, with Morris' knowledge and approval, was about to set sail for Saint-Domingue with yet another plan for promoting the independence of that island (Beatrix C. Davenport, ed., *A Diary of the French Revolution*, 2 vols. [Boston, 1939], II, 233, 241, 298, 299). In addition to bringing Cormeré to TJ's attention, Morris also wrote a letter of recommendation for him to Robert Morris, which reads in part: "His [Cormeré's] Plans are vast but Time only can tell whether they be practicable. . . . Mr. de Cormere will open himself fully to you and propose among political Objects some Plans of business. . . . I shall give him an Introduction to Mr. Jefferson which may serve meerly to bring them together and the Interviews with him will be on such Subjects as may have been previously concerted with you" (Morris to Robert Morris, 6 Nov. 1791, DLC: Gouverneur Morris Papers). There is no evidence that TJ ever met with Cormeré, the exact nature of whose plan to free Saint-Domingue from French rule is still a mystery. In any case, it seems doubtful that Cormeré would have met with TJ's favor, given TJ's expressed concern that an independent Saint-Domingue would fall under British influence (see TJ to William Short, 24 Nov. 1791).

To Thomas Pinckney

SIR   Philadelphia Nov. 6. 1791.

The mission of a Minister Plenipotentiary to the court of London being now to take place, the President of the United States is desirous of availing the public of your services in that office. I have it in charge therefore from him to ask whether it will be agreeable that he should nominate you for that purpose to the Senate. We know that higher motives will alone influence your mind in the acceptance of this charge. Yet it is proper at the same time to inform you that as a provision for your expences in the exercise of it, an Outfit of 9000. Dollars is allowed, and an annual salary to the same amount payable quarterly. On recieving your permission, the necessary orders, for these sums, together with your credentials, shall be forwarded to you, and it would be expected that you should proceed on the mission as soon as you can have made those arrangements for your private affairs which such an absence may render indispensable. Let me only ask the favor of you to give me an immediate answer, and by duplicate, by sea and post, that we may have the benefit of both chances for recieving it as early as possible.— Tho' I have not the honor of a personal acquaintance with you, yet I beg you to be assured that I feel all that anxiety for your entrance on this important mission which a thorough conviction of your fitness for it can inspire; and that in it's relations with my office, I shall always endeavor to render it as agreeable to you as possible.— I have the honour to be &c.,   TH: JEFFERSON

PrC (DLC); lacks part of complimentary close and signature, which are supplied from Tr (DNA: RG 360, DL); caption on latter reads: "To Major Thomas Pinckney."

As soon as it became apparent during the summer of 1791 that Great Britain was about to send an officially accredited diplomatic representative to the United States a number of aspirants for the post of minister to the Court of St. James appeared. William Knox, U.S. consul in Dublin, Charles Cotesworth Pinckney, governor of South Carolina, and William Stephens Smith, the former secretary to the American legation in London, were among the most active in seeking the appointment (William Knox to Henry Knox, 18 July 1791 and 3 Aug. 1791, MHi: Knox Papers; Pinckney to Madison, 6 Aug. 1791, Rutland, *Madison*, xiv, 66-8; and Smith to John Adams, 21 Oct. 1791, with enclosed letter from Smith to Washington of the same date, MHi: AM). But there is no evidence that their contacts ever brought these candidates to the attention of Washington, perhaps because of the belief that Gouverneur Morris "stands very high in the opinion of the Presidt." and was destined to be nominated minister to Great Britain (Edward Rutledge, Jr., to William Short, 3 Aug. 1791, DLC: Short Papers).

George Hammond's arrival in Philadelphia late in October 1791 finally prompted Washington to select the first American minister to London and other European capitals since the adoption of the Constitution. The appointments began with a private consultation between the President and the Secretary of State over Washington's choices for the more important posts. Without consulting beforehand with any member of his administration, Washington met with TJ on 6 Nov. and unexpectedly informed him that he intended to nominate Thomas Pinckney minister to Great Britain. It is likely that he also mentioned a preference for Gouverneur Morris if Pinckney were to decline, and indicated he might appoint Morris minister to France if Pinckney accepted. TJ had no objections to giving Pinckney a major diplomatic appointment, but Morris' well known hostility to the French Revolution rendered him undesirable as minister to France in TJ's view.

Accordingly, he tried to persuade the President to send Pinckney to Paris. In drafting the present letter to Pinckney after their meeting, TJ, hoping that Washington was still open to persuasion, left a blank space after the words "to the court of" and transmitted the letter to the President with a promise to fill in the blank "when you shall have made up your mind on it" (TJ to Washington, 6 Nov. 1791; TJ to William Short, 9 Nov. 1791). The subject was again discussed when he met with Washington two days later and suggested that it would be more fitting to send Pinckney to Paris and Morris to London. But Washington, refusing to be swayed by his Secretary of State, returned the Pinckney letter to TJ the next day with instructions to insert London in the blank (Washington to TJ, 9 Nov. 1791, RC in DLC; endorsed as received 9 Nov. 1791 but not recorded in SJL). TJ promptly complied and forwarded the letter to South Carolina with a brief note addressed to "The Post Master at Charleston," requesting swift and sure conveyance to Pinckney (PrC in DLC; FC in DNA: RG 360, DL). The postmaster replied that he had received this letter on 26 Nov. 1791 and forwarded it immediately, and he now sent Pinckney's reply of 29 Nov. 1791 (Thomas Hall to TJ, 30 Nov. 1791, RC in DNA: RG 59, MLR; endorsed by TJ as received 14 Dec. 1791 and so recorded in SJL).

TJ's efforts to prevent Gouverneur Morris' nomination as minister to France had led him to advise Washington to consider William Short for that crucial diplomatic post, but the President did nothing more than agree to nominate him minister to the Netherlands in the event Morris was dispatched to Paris (TJ to Short, 9 Nov. 1791). The issue was settled when, on 14 Dec. 1791, TJ received a letter from Pinckney announcing his willingness to represent the United States at the Court of St. James. TJ prepared a list of three appointments on 21 Dec. 1791 (Nominations of ministers to France, Great Britain, and Netherlands, 21 Dec. 1791, PrC in DLC), and the next day Washington submitted to the Senate his nominations of Pinckney as minister to Great Britain, of Morris as minister to France, and of Short as minister to The Hague (see Pinckney to TJ, 29 Nov. 1791; JEP, I, 92). Having failed to prevent

Morris' nomination, TJ suppressed his doubts about the New Yorker's fitness to represent the American government in France and dutifully supported all three of the President's nominees in the face of sometimes strong senatorial opposition (see TJ to Short, 3 Jan. 1792; TJ to the Senate, 4 Jan. 1792; TJ to Pinckney, 17 Jan. 1792).

Although Pinckney's nomination excited little public comment when it was made, it later became a matter of political controversy. In 1799 Tench Coxe, who by then had become a bitter opponent of the Federalists, arranged for the publication in the Philadelphia *Aurora* of a letter John Adams had written to him in May 1792 which expressed suspicion that the British had unduly influenced Pinckney's appointment. While Republicans cited this letter as incontrovertible evidence of Federalist subservience to Great Britain, Washington indignantly denied the substance of Adams' allegation, Pinckney incorrectly denounced the letter as a forgery, and Hamilton cited it in his famous pamphlet attack on Adams during the election of 1800 as irrefutable proof of his contention that Adams was unfit to serve as President (Fitzpatrick, *Writings*, xxxvii, 428-9; Syrett, *Hamilton*, xxv, 110 n. 23, 198-204; Jacob E. Cooke, *Tench Coxe and the Early Republic* [Chapel Hill, 1978], p. 358-60, 378-9). Thus, in a consummate stroke of irony, Washington's appointment of Pinckney, which in one respect had been intended to strengthen the bonds of union by giving South Carolina her proper share of federal patronage, served in the end to exacerbate the fatal schism among Federalists that played so large a role in bringing about TJ's election in 1800.

To George Washington

SIR   Nov. 6. 1791.

I have the honour to inclose you a draught of a letter to Governor Pinkney, and to observe that I suppose it to be proper that there should, on fit occasions, be a direct correspondence between the President of the U.S. and the Governors of the states; and that it will probably be grateful to them to recieve from the President answers to the letters they address to him. The correspondence with them on ordinary business may still be kept up by the Secretary of state in his own name.

I inclose also a letter to Majr. Pinckney with a blank to be filled up when you shall have made up your mind on it.

I have conferred with Mr. M. on the idea of the Commissioners of the federal town proceeding to make private sales of the lots and he thinks it adviseable.—I cannot but repeat that if the surveyors will begin on the river, laying off the lots from Rock creek to the Eastern branch, and go on, a-breast, in that way from the river towards the back part of the town, they may pass the avenue from the President's house to the Capitol before the Spring, and as soon as they shall have passed it a public sale may take place without injustice to either the Georgetown or Carrolsburg interest. Will not the present afford you a proper occasion of assuring the Commissioners that you leave every thing respecting L'Enfant to them? I have the honor to be with the most sincere respect, Sir, Your most obedt. humble servt,   TH: JEFFERSON

RC (DNA: RG 59, MLR); addressed: "The President of the U.S."; endorsed by Washington: "From Thoms. Jefferson Esqr. 6th. Novr. 1791.—Opinion on the propriety of the President of the U.S. corrisponding with the Governors of the Individual States and on the Sale of Lots in the Federal City." PrC (DLC). Tr (DNA: RG 59, SDC). FC (DNA: RG 360, DL). Noted in SJPL. Enclosures: (1) draft of George Washington to Charles Pinckney, 6 Nov. 1791. (2) TJ to Thomas Pinckney, 6 Nov. 1791.

TJ's DRAUGHT reply to Charles Pinck-

ney's 18 Aug. and 20 Sep. 1791 letters to Washington dealt primarily with the governor's request for aid to Saint-Domingue and is printed, with several alterations, at 8 Nov. 1791 in Fitzpatrick, *Writings*, XXXI, 412-3. Pinckney's letters to Washington are quoted in Editorial Note on threat of disunion in the West, 10 Mch. 1791 (Vol. 19: 433-4). Washington addressed the issue raised in Pinckney's 18 Aug. 1791 letter by enclosing a copy of TJ's letter to him of 7 Nov. 1791, as TJ had suggested.

Regarding BLANK TO BE FILLED UP in the enclosed letter to Thomas Pinckney, see note to preceding letter.

From Seth Jenkins

SIR   Hudson Nov. 7. 1791

This will be handed you by Mr. Cotton Gelston of this place, whom I have taken the Liberty of introducing to your acquaintance.

His business is to obtain a Patent for Mr. Benjamin Folger, for securing an important discovery he hath made in manufacturing Whale Oil—the particulars of which discovery will be communicated to you by Mr. Gelston.

From the information I have had, and the experiments Mr. Folger has made, I am fully convinced that the discovery is entirely new, and a very important one, and that it will prove highly beneficial to the United States.—I am very respectfully Sir Your Mo: Obed: Servt,   SETH JENKINS

RC (DNA: RG 59, MLR); endorsed by TJ as received 15 Nov. 1791 and so recorded in SJL.

Jenkins, a whaling captain based in Hudson, N.Y., had met TJ during his northern tour with James Madison in May

and June 1791 (TJ to Jenkins, 21 June 1791). BENJAMIN FOLGER was granted a patent on 2 Jan. 1792 for his process for "Cleansing whale oil" (*List of Patents Granted . . . from April 10, 1790, to December 31, 1836* [Washington, 1872]).

From Gouverneur Morris

DEAR SIR   Paris 7 Novr. 1791.

Enclosed you will find some Hints relative to Coins Currency Weights and Measures. The Consideration of those Things has occurred to me at different Intervals for the last twenty Years of my Life, and I have frequently determined to begin a pretty extensive Enquiry and as frequently abandoned the Idea. Indeed my other occupations will not afford the Time. You who have thought on the Subject know by Experience that it consumes a great Deal.

Any thing which has the Air of a System is I know very apt to disgust, and that too in the same Proportion that the System Maker is attached to his Work. In Respect to the Object now in Question, there are few Men who will give themselves the Trouble to go thro the laborious Calculations which are needful to a due Understanding of it. I shall not be at all surprizd therefore if the enclosed Paper should have no other Effect than to occupy Part of a pigeon Hole in your Office; and truly it is owing to my Belief that such will be its fate, that you have not received it many Months ago, for it is now above a Year since it was written in detached Pieces.

In copying it, the other Day, an Idea occurred to me which may I think be well worth pursuing in America. Whatever may be the Road Measure adopted by the United States, they will of Course cause the Roads when properly laid out to be marked by Mile Stones. Now I think it would be very useful to mark on each Road the Degrees and Quarter Degrees of Latitude. This will involve but little Expence and when coupled with tolerable Road Maps will fix with considerable Precision both the latitude and longitude of every Part of the Country. I need not give you the Reasons, because I am sure they will present themselves to your Mind as it were intuitively.

I will not make this Letter long because the enclosed Paper will be sufficiently tiresome. I would otherwise detail my Reasons for being of Opinion that the Adoption of Weights Measures and Money on an easy and uniform Plan is an Object of very great Importance to America. Much more so than to most other Countries. Every Man is called by our Constitution to share in the Government. A Knowlege of Statics is therefore in some Measure necessary to every American Citizen, and the obtaining of this Knowlege will be greatly facilitated by the Establishment of a Currency which gives the Means of conceiving immediately the Value of any Sum of foreign Money of a Measure which gives the same Means as to Distances and the Surfaces of Countries and lastly of a Weight which (combined with the Currency) gives at the same Time an easy Mode for Conversion of foreign Weights. But I must conclude. Accept the Assurances of my Esteem &ca.

FC (DLC: Gouverneur Morris Papers); in Morris' hand. Recorded in SJL as received 14 Apr. 1792. Enclosure not found.

Apparently TJ's reaction to Morris' notes on COINS CURRENCY WEIGHTS AND MEASURES was as he suspected. About a year later, Morris sent a copy of this letter to Alexander Hamilton with the comment that TJ "never acknowledged" it or "some other Communications at the same Epoch" (Morris to Hamilton, 24 Oct. 1792, in Syrett, *Hamilton*, XII, 617-8).

To George Washington

SIR   Philadelphia November 7th. 1791.

I have duly considered the letter you were pleased to refer to me, of the 18th. of August from his Excellency Governor Pinckney to yourself, together with the draught of one proposed to be written by him to the Governor of Florida claiming the redelivery of certain fugitives from justice who have been received in that Country. The inconveniencies of such a receptacle for debtors and malefactors in the neighbourhood of the Southern States are obvious and great; and I wish the remedy were as certain and short as the letter seems to suppose.

The delivery of fugitives from one Country to another as practised by several Nations is in consequence of conventions settled between them, defining precisely the cases wherein such deliveries shall take place. I know that such conventions exist between France and Spain, France and Sardinia, France and Germany, France and the United Netherlands, between the several Sovereigns constituting the Germanic Body, and I believe very generally between co-terminous States on the Continent of Europe. England has no such Convention with any nation, and their laws have given no power to their Executive to surrender fugitives of any description; they are accordingly constantly refused, and hence England has been the asylum of the Paolis, the La Mottes, the Calonnes, in short of the most atrocious offenders as well as the most innocent victims, who have been able to get there.

The laws of the United States like those of England receive every fugitive, and no authority has been given to our Executives to deliver them up. In the case of Longchamp a subject of France, a formal demand was made by the Minister of France and was refused. He had indeed committed an offence within the United States but he was not demanded as a criminal but as a subject.

The French Government has shewn great anxiety to have such a convention with the United States, as might authorise them to demand their Subjects coming here; they got a clause in the Consular Convention signed by Dr. Franklin and the Count de Vergennes, giving their Consuls a right to take and send back Captains of Vessels, Mariners, and *passengers*. Congress saw the extent of the word *passengers* and refused to ratify the Convention; a new one was therefore formed, omitting that word. In fact, however desirable it be that the perpetrators of crimes, acknowledged to be such by all mankind, should be delivered up to punishment, yet it is extremely difficult to draw the line between those and acts rendered criminal by tyrannical laws only, hence the first step always is a convention defining the cases where a surrender shall take place.

If then the United States could not deliver up to Governor Quesada a fugitive from the Laws of his Government, we cannot claim as a right the delivery of fugitives from us: and it is worthy consideration whether the demand proposed to be made in Governor Pinckney's letter, should it be complied with by the other party, might not commit us disagreeably, perhaps dishonorably in event; for I do not think we can take for granted that the legislature of the United States will establish a Convention for the mutual delivery of fugitives, and without a reasonable certainty that they will, I think we ought not to give Governor Quesada any grounds to expect that in a similar case we would redeliver fugitives from his Government.—I have the honor to be with the most profound respect and attachment Sir Your Most obedient and most humble Servant,

TH: JEFFERSON

RC (DNA: RG 59, MLR); in clerk's hand, except for signature; endorsed by Lear. PrC (DLC). FC (DNA: RG 59, DL). Tr (DNA: RG 59, SDC).

The letter OF THE 18TH. OF AUGUST was Pinckney to Washington, enclosing transcript of Pinckney to Quesada, 18 Aug. 1791 (DNA: RG 59, MLR). Pinckney's letter to the Spanish governor of East Florida requested the return of two fugitives who were wanted in South Carolina for counterfeiting state securities, and suggested that compliance with this request would induce the federal government to agree in future to Spanish demands for the extradition of fugitives from justice in East Florida. See Editorial Note to group of documents on threat of disunion in the west, Vol. 19: 430-6, which, however, incorrectly states that Pinckney actually sent his drafted letter to Quesada. Washington transmitted TJ's present letter to Pinckney along with a covering letter of 8 Nov. 1791 that was largely drafted by TJ (Fitzpatrick, *Writings*, XXXI, 412-3; see also note to TJ to Washington, 6 Nov. 1791).

TJ's letter evoked a long and spirited response from Pinckney which said in part: "The Constitution having very properly delegated the management of all our foreign concerns to the General Government I considered it as my Duty not to have any intercourse of consequence with a foreign power or its dependencies without your knowledge and concurrence. It was for this purpose the draught was submitted and as Mr. Jefferson appears to differ in opinion with me, the respect I have for his experience of public affairs and his knowledge of the Usages of Nations is such that I immediately directed the Attorney General not to transmit the application, and shall rely on the firmness and exertions of the General Government to relieve us from one of the most serious and growing inconveniences under which our laws at present labour" (Pinckney to Washington, 8 Jan. 1792, DNA: RG 59, MLR). Pinckney's

plea for an extradition agreement between the United States and Spain was not in vain (See TJ to Washington, 22 Mch. 1792; Washington to TJ, 25 Mch. 1792; TJ to Pinckney, 1 Apr. 1792; TJ to Carmichael and Short, with enclosure, 24 Apr. 1792).

The controversy arising out of the 1784 assault by Charles Julien, Chevalier de LONGCHAMPS, on François Barbé de Marbois, the French chargé d'affaires in Philadelphia, is dealt with in note to Charles Thomson to TJ, 18 June 1784. The reasons for the Continental Congress' rejection of the CONSULAR CONVENTION of 1784 between France and the United States are analyzed in Editorial Note to group of documents on the consular convention of 1788, Vol. 14: 67-77.

From William Prince

Flushing Novr. 8th 1791
Bot. of Wm. Prince—

The following trees—

No.						
1	60	Sugar Maple trees	at	1/	3–	0–0
2	6	Cranberry trees		2/	0–	12–0
3	3	Balsam Poplar		1/6	0–	4–6
4	6	Venetian Sumach		1/6	0–	9–0
5	8	Burré Pears		1/6	0–	12–0
6	4	Brignole Plumbs			0–	6–0
7	4	Red Roman Nectarine	⎫	1/6	0–	6–0
8	4	Large early Apricot				
9	4	Brussels do.				
10	4	Roman do.	⎬ 40 trees at 1/6		3–	0–0
11	4	Yellow Roman Nectarine				
12	4	Green Nutmeg Peach				
13	4	Yellow October Clingne.				
14	12	Esopus Spitzenburgh apple				
15	4	Large early harvest apple	⎭			
16	2	Moss rose		3/1	0–	6–0
17	2	Rosa mundi		2/	0–	4–0
18	2	Monthly rose		2/	0–	4–0
19	2	Large Provence rose		1/6	0–	3–0
20	2	Musk rose		2/	0–	4–0

21	2	Primrose	1/	0– 2–0
22	2	White rose	1/	0– 2–0
23	2	Thornless rose	1/	0– 2–0
24	2	Cinnamon rose	1/	0– 2–0
25	2	Yellow rose	1/6	0– 3–0
27	3	Hemlock Spruce	1/6	0– 4–6
28	3	Silver firr	1/6	0– 4–6
29	6	Monthly	0/6d	0– 3–0
30	3	Balsam of Peru	1/6	0– 4–6
32	12	Filbud trees	1/6	0–18–0
31	6	Rhododendrons	1/6	0– 9–0
		Matts the trees are Packed in		0– 6–0
		Carting		0– 1–0
				£12–12–0

Given in No. 33—1 Lemon Clingstone
              the largest & best of *Peaches*—
The above trees are in four Bundles
some cuttings of Yellow Willow
tyed to one of the Bundles of trees—

RC (DLC); noted by Prince on verso: "List of trees for Mr. Jefferson Care of Mr. James Brown Mercht. *Richmond*"; recorded in SJL as received 24 Nov. 1791 but erroneously indicated as written 22 Nov. 1791.

At the time TJ ordered these trees (see TJ to Prince, 6 July 1791), he prepared a working list, on the back of which he penned planting instructions. He anticipated receiving 80 sugar maples and noted that they should be planted at Monticello "below lower Roundabout at N. End. 30 f. apart." The fruit trees were "to be planted in the vacant places of the same kind of fruit trees in the orchard. Where there are no vacancies of the same kind, they may be planted in those of any other kind." The madeira walnuts he wanted "among the trees on the S.W. slope of the hill from the kitchen towards the grove, or in open places in the grove." Fir trees were to be planted "in a clump in a vacant space of the grove where I have planted some lilacs." He wanted the balsam poplars, yellow willows, and Carolina kidney bean (which Prince failed to send) trees placed "in the vacancies of the 4 clumps at the corners of the house or round the level or on the S.W. slope." Sumacs and rhododendrons should be "among the clumps of trees, or on the slope"; bush cranberries "in a row next above the vines"; filberts "in the room of the square of figs, which may be dug up"; all the roses "round the clumps of lilacs in front of the house"; and the honey suckle "at the roots of the weeping willows" (MS from Roger W. Barrett, Kenilworth, Illinois, 1947).

From William Short

DEAR SIR   Paris Nov. 8. 1791.

I mentioned to you in a former letter that the several ministers were to lay before the assembly a state of their respective departments. M. de Montmorin performed this task some days ago and at the same time added that it was the last communication he should have with them as minister of foreign affairs, His Majesty having at length accepted his resignation. The state he presented shewed in general that there was no appearance of hostile intentions from abroad at this moment. You will find it at full length in the gazettes of the beginning of this month sent by the way of Havre.

M. de Montmorin has as yet no successor. M. de Moustier persisted in declining this post and is now in hopes of being appointed Ambassador to London. M. de Ségur, after much intreaty, had agreed to accept the place, but the day before he was to take the oath of office the ministers were so indecently treated in the assembly that he withdrew his word and wrote to the King to be excused. Since then several people have been successively talked of, but it is probable no one is yet decided on, and there will be much difficulty in finding a person to accept a place which has been thus refused.

You will find also in the gazettes the state of the marine department. It is favorable as to the number and condition of the vessels but desperate on account of the spirit of insubordination which prevails in the ports and among the sailors in general.

On the whole it is too true that the horizon here blackens daily. In most of the departments serious and alarming troubles are taking place on account of the expulsion of the curates who refused the oath prescribed last year. Many of the peasantry deluded by them forget the advantages they hoped from the revolution which they now consider can be purchased only at the price of their salvation. These and other disorders contribute to prevent the payment of taxes which from their nature and mode of perception would probably have been illy paid even in times of calm and prosperity. This monthly deficit is supplied of course from the *caisse de l'extraordinaire*, viz., the funds appropriated to the redemption of the assignats now go to the support of government—hence a continuance of their depreciation and consequently a nominal and even a real rise in the price of all articles. Bread is that which is the most alarming and gives serious apprehensions for Paris this winter. Government being without force to protect the free circulation of grain gives an additional rise to this article in many places. The emigrants continue to go in great numbers to join the Princes, at first they were only nobles and ecclesiastics, at present the discontented of the commons follow the example. They are in great numbers on account of the inhuman suppression without indemnity of the employments by which they and their families were supported. These emigrants suffer cruelly from want of money, but foreign powers will probably furnish them clandestinely merely for their support. Notwithstanding all this, if it were possible for the present government to acquire a sufficient degree of force to protect the persons and property of the citizens and insure the payment of taxes many of the emigrants would return and submit, but the number of those who lose all hopes of such an issue increases daily.

It is much to be apprehended that the commercial class of citizens who have been hitherto much in favor of the revolution will become discontented on account of the situation of their affairs in the West Indies and the Mediterranean. You must be acquainted with the former better than we are here. Reports are probably much exagerated but the West India merchants express serious apprehensions of the destruction of that branch of commerce on account of the disorders prevailing at S. Domingo and the inability of France at present to protect the inhabitants and proprietors against the insurrection of their slaves. It is said that intelligence was recieved yesterday from the Governor of S. Domingo, but I am not certain of it. If not the only accounts here are those which come by the way of England, and by a private vessel to Bordeaux. They were vague and differed from each other. Troops however are to be immediately sent to S. Domingo. The English Ambassador here sent a letter to the minister of foreign affairs informing him that the Governor of Jamaica had allowed the inhabitants of S. Domingo to purchase provisions there and had sent them arms of which they were in need to protect themselves against the revolted slaves. The assembly immediately voted their thanks to the English nation.

In the mediterranean there are apprehensions of danger from the Dey of Algiers. The minister of marine has informed the assembly that the Dey on coming to the head of affairs had at first discovered favorable dispositions to France and desired a frigate should be furnished him to carry his ambassador to Constantinople. Before its arrival at Algiers the Dey's patience was exhausted, he accepted the frigate from Spain, threatened the French consul with imprisonment and gave such other marks of hostile intentions that the King has thought proper, as the minister informed the assembly, to order a small armament to protect the French commerce in the Levant. He has taken measures at the same time for calming this ill humour in the Dey by pecuniary negotiations. Several of the members of the assembly murmured at this part of the communication, and were for the nation wiping off at one blow the stain of so long a tribute paid by the ancient government. The commercial part of the assembly will probably over-rule this movement and support the attempt to purchase the continuance of peace with the Regency. As the Dey in reply to the French consul, among other things said the French were no longer what they were formerly, that there was at present no King in France &c. it is supposed that Spain has had influence in this unexpected step. It will very soon be known now whether France is to be added to those powers who will in time combine to protect their commerce by force of arms from these pirates who would have ceased long ago if they had not been alimented by the infamous policy of some of the European governments. The minister informed the assembly that the last negotiation with this regency had cost France 800,000ℓt. I mentioned this to you formerly as near as I could then come at it.

A person from New York of the name of Vail called on me yesterday and desired me to remind you of his having spoken with you last winter on the subject of appointing a consul at L'Orient. As he is now settled there he wishes to obtain that appointment. I know nothing further of him.

I shall go to Amsterdam in the course of this month to sign the bonds of the late loan and to have another opened probably at a reduced rate of interest. The situation of affairs and particularly of the ministry in this country renders my presence here by no means essential. I inferred from your letter and that of the Secretary of the treasury that it was expected I should go to Amsterdam to prosecute the business of the loans there. Arrangements might be very well taken however so as to transact it in future from hence without any detriment to the U.S. My absence from Paris will not be considerable but I shall inform you of it with more precision from Amsterdam. I beg you to remain fully persuaded of the sincere attachment with which I shall ever be, Dear Sir, your friend & servant,

W Short

P.S. Nov. 9. The minister of the marine has communicated to the assembly official accounts at length recieved from the Governor of S. Domingo. They come by the way of Jamaica, and confirm fully the revolt of the negroes. Many of them were killed, and the rest put to flight. Still the alarm was such that he mentions having applied for succour to the Spaniards, the Governor of Jamaica and the President of the U.S. Private accounts of a later date say that the insurrection has ceased. Still two ships of the line with troops are to be immediately sent there. The minister applied yesterday for the necessary funds for this purpose. The alarm here with respect to their colonies still continues, a thousand different conjectures are made with respect to this insurrection. Those who consider themselves the most clear sighted think they see a general plan of independence supported by England who will have an interest in emancipating her own colonies, provided she can at the same time open the ports of all the others in America. De Moustier is of this number. I heard him offer a wager of three to one a few days ago at M. de Montmorin's that the independence of S. Domingo was now declared. The more reasonable considered his offer as a mark of unreasonable extravagance. This letter goes by the French packet. It incloses one to the Secretary of the treasury.

PrC (DLC: Short Papers); at head of text: "No. 90"; at foot of text: "Thomas Jefferson Secretary of State, Philadelphia"; recorded in SJL as received 29 Feb. 1792. Tr (DNA: RG 59, DD). Enclosure: Short to Hamilton, 8 Nov. 1791 (printed in Syrett, *Hamilton*, IX, 479-80).

TJ failed to recommend a consular appointment for the New York merchant Aaron Vail during his tenure as Secretary of State. As President, however, he appointed Vail commercial agent at Lorient in 1803.

From John Street

Lisbon, 8 Nov. 1791. Acknowledges receipt of TJ's letter of 13 May. He is late in writing because the government of Portugal had refused to confirm his commission. "The objection was, that, as I was born in the Portugues Dominions I was a Subject to her Faithful Majesty, therefore she would not Confirm my Commission untill the United States should aknowledge in her the same right to nominate, in like manner, Citizens of the said States."—He overcame this objection by pointing out to Secretary of Foreign Affairs Pinto that "notwithstanding I was born in Fayal, I was of an English family, and had been educated in the United States of America, and there naturalized, that I could not be considered, but as a Citizen of the said States." Pinto notified him that his commission would be confirmed if he signed a declaration renouncing all the rights and privileges of a Portuguese subject. He immediately wrote and signed such a declaration and was proud to be "a Citizen of a Republic, which already makes, in the History of the Nations, the mos shining figure."—He offers to serve the United States as consul general for Portugal. In the event he is appointed to that office his cousin, Joseph Street d'Arriaga, whose wealth, alliances, and character make him a respected figure at the Portuguese court, has promised "not only his house, and the participation of his property to support the dignity and respect due to that imploiment, but his advises and Counsels whenever it may be wanted."—Colonel Humphreys in Lisbon and John Telles in Philadelphia can both attest that "you will find my interest compatible with that of the States."

RC (DNA: RG 59, CD); 4 p.; endorsed by TJ as received 21 Mch. 1792 and so recorded in SJL. Street had been appointed vice-consul at Fayal in July 1790 (Vol. 17: 251, 319).

To George Washington

Sir   Philadelphia Nov. 8. 1791.

I have now the honour to inclose you a report on the lands of the U.S. within the North Western and South Western territories, unclaimed either by Indians, or by citizens of these states.

In order to make the estimate of their quantity and situation, as desired by the legislature, it appeared necessary first to delineate the Indian boundaries which circumscribe those territories, and then to present a statement of all claims of citizens within the same; from whence results the residuary unclaimed mass, whereon any land law the legislature may think proper to pass, may operate immediately, and without obstruction.

I have not presumed to decide on the merits of the several claims, nor consequently to investigate them minutely. This will only be proper, when such of them as may be thought doubtful, if there should be any such, shall be taken up for final decision.—I have the honour to be with sentiments of the most perfect respect and attachment, Sir, Your most obedient & most humble servt,

Th: Jefferson

RC (DNA: RG 59, MLR); docketed: "Report of the Secretary of State on the quantity and situation of Lands belonging to the U.S. in the N.W. and S.W. Territories. Novr. 8th: 1791." Tr (DNA: RG 59, SDC). Tr (DNA: RG 59, SDR).

ENCLOSURE

Report on Public Lands

The Secretary of State, to whom was referred by the President of the United States, the resolution of Congress requesting the President "to cause an estimate to be laid before Congress at their next session, of the quantity and situation of the lands not claimed by the Indians, nor granted to, nor claimed by, any citizens of the United States within the territory ceded to the United States by the state of North Carolina, and within the territory of the United States north west of the river Ohio," makes thereon the following Report.

South-Western Territory.

THE territory ceded by the State of North Carolina to the United States, by deed bearing date the 25th. day of February 1790, is bounded as follows, to wit: Beginning in the boundary between Virginia and North Carolina, that is to say, in the parallel of Latitude 36½ degrees north from the Equator, on the extreme height of the stone mountain, where the said boundary or parallel intersects it, and running thence along the said extreme height to the place where Wataugo river breaks through it; thence a direct course to the top of the yellow mountain, where Bright's road crosses the same; thence along the ridge of the said mountain between the waters of Doe river and the waters of Rock creek, to the place where the road crosses the Iron mountain; from thence along the extreme height of said mountain to where Nolichuckey river runs through the same; thence to the top of the Bald mountain; thence along the extreme height of the said mountain to the painted rock on French Broad river; thence along the highest ridge of the said mountain to the place where it is called the Great Iron or Smoaky mountain; thence along the extreme height of the said mountain to the place where it is called Unaka mountain, between the Indian towns of Cowee and Old Chota; thence along the main ridge of the said mountain to the southern boundary of the said State of North Carolina, that is to say, to the parallel of Latitude 35 degrees north from the Equator; thence westwardly along the said boundary or parallel to the middle of the river Missisippi; thence up the middle of the said river to where it is intersected by the first mentioned parallel of 36½ degrees; thence along the said parallel to the Beginning: which tract of country is a degree and a half of Latitude from North to South, and about 360 miles in general, from East to West, as nearly as maybe estimated from such maps as exist of that country.

Indian Claims.

THE Indians having claims within the said tract of country, are, the Cherokees and Chickasaws, whose boundaries are settled by the treaties of Hopewell, concluded with the Cherokees on the 28th. day of November 1785, and with the Chickasaws, on the 10th. day of January 1786, and by the treaty of Holston concluded with the Cherokees, July 2d. 1791. These treaties acknowledge to the said Indians all the lands westward and southward of the following lines, to wit: Beginning in the boundary between South and North Carolina where the South Carolina Indian boundary strikes the same; thence North to a point from which a line is to be extended to the river Clinch, that shall pass the Holston at the ridge which divides the waters running into Little river from those running into the Tannissee; thence up the river Clinch to Campbell's line, and along the same to the top of the Cumberland mountain; thence in a direct course towards the Cumberland river, where the Kentucky road crosses it, as far as the Virginia line, or parallel aforesaid of 36½ degrees; thence Westwardly or Eastwardly, as the case shall be, along the said line or parallel, to the point thereof, which is due North East from another point to be taken on the dividing ridge of Cumberland and Duck rivers 40 miles from Nashville; thence South-west to the point last mentioned on the said dividing ridge, and along the said dividing ridge north-westwardly to where it is intersected by the said Virginia line, or parallel of 36½ degrees. So that there remained to the United States the right of pre-emption of the lands westward and southward of the said lines, and the absolute right to those northward thereof, that is to say; to one parcel to the Eastward, somewhat triangular, comprehending the counties of Sullivan and Washington, and parts of those of Greene and Hawkins, running about 150 miles from East to West on the Virginia boundary as its base, and between 80 and 90 miles from north to South, where broadest;[1] and containing, as may be conjectured, without pretending to accuracy, between seven and eight thousand[2] square miles, or about five millions of acres: and to one other parcel to the Westward, somewhat triangular also, comprehending parts of the counties of Sumner, Davidson, and Tannissee, the base whereof extends about 150 miles also from East to West on the same Virginia line, and its height from North to South about 55 miles,[3] and so may comprehend about four thousand square miles, or upwards of two and a half millions of Acres of land.[4]

Claims of Citizens.

WITHIN these triangles, however, are the following claims of citizens reserved by the deed of cession, and consequently forming exception to the rights of the United States.

I. Appropriations by the State of North Carolina for their Continental and State Officers and Soldiers.

II. Grants, and titles to grants vested in Individuals by the laws of the State.

III. Entries made[5] in Armstrong's office, under an Act of that State of 1783, for the redemption of specie and other Certificates.

Military Bounties.

THE claims covered by the first reservation are,

1st. The bounties in land given by the said State of North Carolina to their continental line, in addition to those given by Congress: These[6] were to be located within a district bounded northwardly by the Virginia line, and southwardly by a line parallel thereto, and fifty five miles distant: Westwardly, by the Tannissee, and eastwardly by the meridian of the intersection of the Virginia line and Cumberland river. Grants have accordingly issued for 1,239,498 Acres, and warrants for the further quantity of 1,549,726 Acres, making together 2,789,224 Acres.[7] It is to be noted, that the Southwestern and Southeastern Angles of this district, constituting, perhaps, a fourth or a fifth of the whole, are south of the lines established by the treaties of Hopewell and Holston, and, consequently in a country wherein the Indian title is acknowledged and guaranteed by the United States. No information is received of the exact proportion of the locations made within these angles.[8]

2nd. Bounties in Land to Evans's battalion raised for State purposes: these were to be taken West of the Cumberland mountain. The locations are not yet made.[9]

Entries and Grants.

THE second reservation covers the following claims. 1st. Lands for the Surveyor General's fees for laying out the military bounties, to be located in the military district. The grants already issued on this Account, amount to 30,203 Acres.[10]

Commissioners.

2nd. Grants[11] to Isaac Shelby, Anthony Bledsoe, and Absalom Tatum, commissioners for laying out the military bounties; and to guards, chain carriers, markers, and hunters, who attended them, already issued to the amount of 65,932 Acres, located in the Military district.[12]

Washington County.

3d. Entries in Washington county,[13] amounting to 746,362½ Acres, for 214,549¾ of which grants have already issued. Of the remaining 531,812¾ Acres, a considerable proportion were declared void by the laws of the State,[14] and were particularly excluded from the cover of the reservation in the deed of cession by this clause in it, to wit: "Provided that nothing herein contained shall extend, or be construed to extend to the making good any entry or entries, or any grant or grants heretofore declared void by any Act or Acts of the General Assembly of this State." Still[15] it is to be considered, that many of these persons have settled and improved the lands, are willing, as is said, to comply with such conditions as shall be required of other purchasers, form a strong barrier on the new frontier acquired by the treaty of Holston, and are, therefore, Objects meriting the consideration of the Legislature.

Sullivan County.

4th. Entries in Sullivan county, amounting to 240,624 Acres, for 173,332 Acres of which grants have already

Pre-emptions.

Henderson.

Martin & Wilson.

General Greene.

Armstrong's office.

issued. Of the remaining entries, many are certified void; and others understood to be lapsed, or otherwise voidable, under the laws of the State.[16]

5th. Certain Pre-emption rights granted to the first settlers of Davidson county[17] on Cumberland river, amounting to 309,760 Acres.

6th. A grant of 200,000 Acres to Richard Henderson and others on Powel's and Clinch's rivers, extending up Powel's river in a breadth of not less than four miles, and down Clinch's from their junction in a breadth not less than twelve miles; A great part of this is within the Indian territory.

AMONG the grants of the State, now under recapitulation, as forming exceptions out of the absolute rights of the United States are not to be reckoned here two grants of 2000 Acres each to Alexander Martin, and David Wilson, adjacent to the lands allotted to the officers and soldiers; nor a grant of 25,000 Acres on Duck river to the late Major General Greene; because they are wholly within the Indian territory, as acknowleged by the treaties of Hopewell and Holston.

THE extent of the third reservation, in favor of entries made in Armstrong's office, is not yet entirely known, nor can be 'till the 20th. of December 1792, the last day given for perfecting them. The sum of certificates, however, which had been paid for these warrants into the Treasury of the State, before the 20th. day of May 1790, reaches in all probability, near to their whole amount. This was £373,649.6.5. Currency of that State, and at the price of ten pounds the hundred Acres, established by law, shews that Warrants had issued for 3,736,493 Acres. For 1,762,660 of these grants have passed, which appear to have been located partly in the counties of Greene and Hawkins, and partly in the country from thence to the Missisippi, as divided into Eastern, middle, and Western districts. Almost the whole of these locations are within the Indian territory. Besides the Warrants paid for as before mentioned, it is known that there are some others outstanding, and not paid for; but perhaps, these need not be taken into account, as payment of them has been disputed on the ground that the lands, being within the Indian territory, cannot now be delivered to the holders of the Warrants.[18]

ON a review of all the reservations, after making such conjectural allowance as our information authorizes, for the proportion of them which may be within the Indian boundaries, it appears probable, that they[19] cover all the ceded lands susceptible of culture, and cleared of the Indian title, that is to say; all the habitable parts of the two triangles beforementioned, excepting only the lands south of French Broad and Big Pidgeon rivers. These were part of the tract appropriated by the laws of the State to the use of the Indians, whose title being purchased at the late treaty of Holston, they are now free to be disposed of by the United States, and are probably, the only lands open to their disposal within this South Western territory, which can excite the attention of purchasers. They are supposed to amount to about 300,000 Acres, and we are told that three hundred families have already set down upon them without right or license.

North Western territory.

THE territory of the United States northwest of the Ohio, is bounded on the south by that river, on the East by Pennsylvania; on the north and West by the lines which divide the United States from the dominions of Great Britain and Spain.

Claims of Indians.

THE part of this territory occupied by Indians, is north and West of the following lines established with the Wiandots, Delawares, Chippawas and Ottawas, by the treaty of Fort McIntosh, and, with the Shawanese, by that of the Great Miami, to wit: Beginning at the mouth of the Cayahoga, and running up the river to the Portage between that and the Tuscaroras branch of the Muskingum; then down the said branch to the forks at the crossing place above Fort Lawrence; then Westwardly towards the portage of the Big Miami, to the main branch of that river; then down the Miami to the fork of that river next below the old fort which was taken by the French in 1752; thence due West to the river de la Panse, and down that river to the Wabash. So far the lines are precisely defined, and the whole country Southward of these lines, and eastward of the Wabash, cleared of the claims of those Indians, as it is also of those of the Poutiwatimas and Sacs, by the treaty of Muskingum. How far on the other side of the Wabash, the Southern boundary of the Indians has been defined, we know not. It is only understood, in general, that their title to the lower country between that river and the Illinois, has been formerly extinguished by the French, while in their possession. As to that country then, and what lies still beyond the Illinois, it would seem expedient that nothing be done, 'till a fair ascertainment of boundary can take place, by mutual consent between us and the Indians interested.

THE country within the Wabash, the Indian line before described, the Pennsylvania line, and the Ohio, contains, on a loose estimate, about 55,000 square miles, or 35 millions of Acres.

Antient Companies.

DURING the British government, great numbers of persons had formed themselves into companies, under different names, such as the Ohio, the Wabache, the Illinois, the Missisippi, or Vandalia companies, and had covered, with their applications, a great part of this territory.[20] Some of them had obtained orders on certain conditions, which having never been fulfilled, their titles were never completed by grants. Others were only in a state of negociation, when the British authority was discontinued. Some of these claims, being already under a special reference, by order of Congress,[21] and all of them probably falling under the operation of the same principles, they will not be noticed in the present report.

Claims of Citizens.

THE Claims of citizens to be here stated, will be

ist. Those reserved by the States in their deeds of cession.

iind. Those which have arisen under the government of the United States themselves.

Connecticut.

UNDER the first head presents itself the tract of country from the completion of the 41st. degree to 42°.2′ of North Latitude, and extending from the Pennsylvania line before mentioned 120 miles westward, not mentioned in the deed of Connecticut,[22] while all the country westward thereof was mentioned to be ceded. About two and a half millions of Acres of this, may perhaps, be without the Indian lines beforementioned.

French at Kaskaskias &c.

2nd. A reservation in the deed of Virginia of the possessions and titles of the French and Canadian Inhabitants, and other settlers of the Kaskaskias, St. Vincents, and the neighbouring Villages, who had professed themselves citizens of Virginia; which rights have been settled by an Act of the last session of Congress, intituled "An Act for granting lands to the Inhabitants and settlers at Vincennes and the Illinois country in the territory North-West of the Ohio, and for confirming them in their possessions." These lands are in the neighbourhood of the several villages.

Clarke's Regiment.

3. A reservation in the same deed of a quantity, not exceeding 150,000 Acres of land, for General George Rogers Clarke, and the officers and soldiers of his regiment, who were at the reduction of Kaskaskias, and St. Vincents: to be laid off, in such place on the North-West side of the Ohio, as a majority of the officers should choose. They chose they should be laid off on the river adjacent to the rapids, which, accordingly, has been done.

4. A reservation in the same deed, of lands between the Scioto and Little Miami, to make up to the Virginia

Virginia Line.

troops, on continental establishment, the quantity which the good lands in their Southern allotment, might fall short of the[23] bounties[24] given them by the laws of that State. By a statement of the 16th. of September, 1788, it appears that 724,045⅔ Acres had been surveyed for them on the South-eastern side of the Ohio; that 1,395,385⅓ Acres had been surveyed on the north-western side; that Warrants for 649,649 Acres more, to be laid off on the same side of the river, were in the hands of the surveyor, and it was supposed there might still be some few warrants not yet presented: so that this reservation may be stated at 2,045,034⅓ Acres, or perhaps, some small matter more.[25]

II. The claims of individual citizens, derived from the United States themselves, are the following.

Continental Army.

1. Those of the Continental army, founded on the resolutions of Congress, of September 16th. 1776, August 12th. and September 30th. 1780, and fixed by the Ordinance of May 20th. 1785; the resolution of October 22d. 1787, and the supplementary Ordinance of July 9th. 1788, in the seven ranges of townships; Beginning at a point on the Ohio, due north from the Western termination of a line then lately run as the Southern boundary of Pennsylvania: or, in a second tract of a million of Acres, bounded East by the seventh range of the said townships; south, by the lands of Cutler and Sargent; North, by an extension of the northern boundary of the said townships, and going towards the West so far as to include the above quantity: or lastly, in a third tract of country, Beginning at the mouth of the Ohio, and running up the Missisippi, to the river au Vause; thence up the same 'till it meets a West line from the mouth of the little Wabash; thence along that line to the Great Wabash; thence down the same, and the Ohio to the Beginning. The sum total of the said military claims is 1,851,800 Acres.[26]

Purchasers at New-York.

2. Those of the Individuals who made purchases of land at New York, within the said seven ranges of townships, according to the Resolutions of Congress of April 21st. 1787, and the supplementary ordinance of July 9th. 1788, which claims amount to 150,896 Acres.

3. The purchase of one million and a half Acres of land by Cutler and Sargent, on behalf of certain individuals, associated under the name of the Ohio company. This begins where the Ohio is intersected by the Western boundary of the seventh range of townships, and runs due North on that boundary 1306 chains and 25 links; thence due West to the Western

Ohio Company.

boundary of the seventeenth range of townships; thence due South to the Ohio, and up that river to the Beginning; the whole area containing 1,781,760 Acres of land, whereof 281,760 Acres, consisting of various lots and townships, are reserved to the United States.

4: The purchase by the same Cutler and Sargent on behalf also of themselves and others. This begins at the North-eastern angle of the tract of their purchase before described, and runs due north to the northern boundary of the tenth township from the Ohio; thence due West to the Scioto; thence down the same, and up the Ohio to the south-western angle of the said purchase before described, and along the Western and Northern boundaries thereof to the Beginning; the whole area containing 4,901,480 Acres of land; out of which, however, five lots, to wit: Nos: 8. 11. 16. 26. and 29. of every township, of six miles square, are retained by the United States, and out of the whole are retained the three townships of Gnadenhutten, Schoenbrun, and Salem, and certain lands around them, as will be hereafter mentioned.

5. The purchase of John Cleves Symmes, bounded on the West by the Great Miami; on the South by the Ohio; on the East by a line, which is to begin on the bank of the Ohio, twenty miles from the mouth of the Great Miami, as measured along the several courses of the Ohio, and to run parallel with the general course of the said Great Miami: and on the North[27] by an East and West line, so run as to include a million of acres in the whole area, whereof five lots, numbered as beforementioned, are reserved out of every township by the United States.

IT is suggested that this purchaser, under colour of a first and larger proposition to the Board of Treasury which was never closed (but pending that proposition) sold sundry parcels of land, between his eastern boundary beforementioned, and the little Miami, and that the purchasers have settled thereon. If these suggestions prove true, the settlers will, perhaps, be thought to merit the favor of the Legislature, as purchasers for valuable consideration, and without notice of the defect of title.[28]

THE contracts for lands, which were at one time under consideration with Messieurs Flint and Parker, and with Colonel Morgan, were never so far prosecuted as to bring either party under any obligation. All proceedings thereon were discontinued at a very early stage, and it is supposed that no further views exist with any party. These, therefore, are not to be enumerated among existing claims.

Scioto Company.

Symmes.

Flint & Parker.
Morgan.

6. THREE townships were reserved by the Ordinance of May 20th. 1785, adjacent to Lake Érie, for refugees from Canada and Nova Scotia, and for other purposes, according to resolutions of Congress made, or to be made on that subject. These would of course contain 69,120 Acres.

Canadian Refugees.

7. THE same Ordinance of May. 20th. 1785, appropriated the three towns of Gnadenhutten, Schoenbrun, and Salem on the Muskingum, for the Christian Indians formerly settled there, or the remains of that society, with the grounds round about them, and the quantity of the said circumjacent grounds, for each of the said towns was determined by the resolution of Congress of September 3d. 1788, to be so much as, with the plat of it's respective town, should make up 4,000 Acres; so that the three towns and their circumjacent lands were to amount to twelve thousand Acres. This reservation was accordingly made out of the larger purchase of Cutler and Sargent, which comprehended them. The Indians, however, for whom the reservation was made, have chosen to emigrate beyond the limits of the United States, so that the lands reserved for them still remain to the United States.[29]

Christian Indians.

ON the whole it appears that the United States may rightfully dispose of all the lands between the Wabash, the Ohio, Pennsylvania,[30] the forty first parallel of Latitude,[31] and the Indian lines described in the treaties of the great Miami and Fort McIntosh, with exceptions only of the[32] rights saved by the deed of cession of Virginia, and of all rights legally derived from the Government of the United States, and supposing the parts south of the Indian lines to contain as before conjectured, about thirty five millions of Acres, and that the claims of citizens, before enumerated, may amount to between thirteen and fourteen millions,[33] there remain at the disposal of the United States, upwards of twenty one millions[34] of Acres in this Northwestern quarter.

AND 'though the want of actual surveys of some parts, and of a general delineation of the whole on paper, so as to exhibit to the eye the locations, forms, and relative positions of the rights before described, may prevent our forming a well defined idea of them at this distance, yet, on the spot, these difficulties exist but in a small degree; the individuals there employed in the details of buying, selling, and locating, possess local informations of the parts which concern them, so as to be able to keep clear of each others rights: or if, in some instances, a conflict of claims should arise

Connecticut about	2,500,000
Kaskaskians &c. abt.	100,000
Clarke's Regiment	150,000
Virginia Line	2,045,034
Continental Army	1,851,300
Purchasers at N. York	150,896
Ohio Company	1,500,000
Scioto Coy.³¹⁄₃₆ of 4,901,480. . .12,000 }	4,208,720
Symmes	1,000,000
	13,506,450
	35,000,000
	21,493,550

from any Want of certainty in their definition, a local judge will doubtless be provided to decide them without delay, at least provisionally. Time, instead of clearing up these incertainties, will cloud them the more, by the death or removal of Witnesses, the disappearance of lines and marks, change of parties, and other casualties.   TH: JEFFERSON
                                        Secretary of state
                                        Nov. 8. 1791.

MS (DNA: RG 59, MLR); in a clerk's hand, except signature and date. PrC (DLC); on verso in clerk's hand: "Recorded and examined," signed by TJ. Dft (DLC); endorsed on verso: "Western lands." Tr (DNA: RG 59, SDR).

This report must be viewed within the context of the reconsideration of the land policies of the Confederation Congress that took place at both the executive and the legislative levels of the federal government during Washington's administrations. Congressman Thomas Scott of Pennsylvania first brought this issue to public attention in a speech delivered to the House of Representatives in 1789. Noting that federal land sales in the public domain had ceased upon the dissolution of the Board of Treasury, the agency in charge of selling public land under the Confederation, Scott pointed out that many of the tracts sold under the Confederation had still not been surveyed because of the recent death of Thomas Hutchins, the geographer of the United States, and warned that western settlers would fall under the influence of Spain unless the federal government took steps to provide them with proper titles to their lands. In order to promote the settlement of the public domain and at the same time raise revenue for the payment of the national debt, Scott recommended the creation of a Land Office in the Northwest Territory, but his proposal failed to win House approval.

The House reconsidered this issue in January of the following year, at which time it requested Alexander Hamilton to prepare a comprehensive report on the disposition of the public domain. Hamilton completed his report in July 1790, and five months later the House turned its attention to his suggestions for encouraging the sale and settlement of western lands. After much debate over such thorny issues as the terms of purchase, the preferred pattern of settlement, the extinction of Indian land titles, and the competing interests of settlers and speculators, the House approved a Land Office Bill in February 1791 that was heavily influenced by Hamilton's report. But the Senate postponed consideration of the bill until the next session of Congress and instead passed a resolution on 1 Mch. 1791, in which the House subsequently concurred, asking the President to provide Congress with a report on land claims in the Northwest and Southwest Territories—a task Washington promptly assigned to TJ (*Annals*, I, 629-31, 665-6, II, 1876-84; JHR, I, 42, 48, 64-5, 69, 142-3, 148, 347-9, 354, 374-5, 377, 379-81, 400, 403; JS, I, 270-3, 277, 289, 294-5, 306; Report on Public Lands, 20 July 1790, Syrett, *Hamilton*, VI, 502-6).

TJ welcomed the opportunity to prepare this report for diplomatic as well as ideological reasons. He was convinced that the westward flow of American settlement would eventually resolve the boundary dispute in the southwest between Spain and the United States in favor of the latter, and he also believed that westward expansion would guarantee the predominance for generations to come of the agrarian social order upon which his hopes for the future of republicanism in the United States so greatly rested (TJ to Washington, 2 Apr. 1791; Drew R. McCoy, *The Elusive Republic: Political Economy in Jeffersonian America* [Chapel Hill, N.C., 1980], p. 13-6). Inspired by these convictions, TJ prepared this report with his usual care and efficiency. He solicited information about southwestern land claims from William Blount, the governor of the Southwest Territory, and Alexander Martin, the governor of North Carolina, whose state's land cession of 1790 had brought the territory into being. For information about northwestern claims he turned to Arthur St. Clair, the governor of the Northwest Territory, Tench Coxe, the indefatigable assistant Secretary of the Treasury, and John Harvie, the head of the Virginia Land Office. In addition, he personally examined relevant records in the archives of the Continental Congress and the Department of State.

TJ completed the draft of the report by the early part of October 1791 and then revised it after receiving "a large book" from Secretary of State James Glasgow of North Carolina recording all of that state's land claims in the Southwest Territory (Tobias Lear to Washington, 14 Oct. 1791, DLC: Washington Papers. Glasgow's letter of 3 Sep. 1791, recorded in SJL as received 3 Oct. 1791, has not been found). The resultant report, which contained the most comprehensive account to date of the state of the public domain, was submitted to Congress on 10 Nov. 1791. Despite TJ's labors, however, Congress took no action on his report. The arrival one month later of news of St. Clair's shattering defeat apparently convinced a majority of that body that subduing the western tribes would have to take precedence over formulating a new policy respecting the sale of public lands. It was not until 1796—after Anthony Wayne's victory over the western tribes at Fallen Timbers in 1794 and the conclusion of the Treaty of Grenville with them in 1795—that Congress passed a Land Office Act which led to the resumption of the sale of federal land in the public domain. This act reflected TJ's influence only insofar as it was confined to the Northwest Territory, TJ's report having made clear that very little unclaimed land remained in the Southwest Territory (Arthur St. Clair's Report to TJ, 10 Feb. 1791, Carter, *Terr. Papers*, II, 323-37; St. Clair to TJ, 19 Mch. 1791; TJ to Alexander Martin, 10 May, 2 July 1791; William Blount to TJ, 17, 27 July 1791; Tench Coxe to TJ, 6 Aug. 1791; TJ to John Harvie, 14 Aug. 1791; TJ to William Blount, 17 Aug. 1791; John Harvie to TJ, 20 Sep. 1791; Payson J. Treat, *The National Land System 1785-1820* [New York, 1910], p. 66-79; Malcom J. Rohrbaugh, *The Land Office Business: The Settlement and Administration of American Public Lands, 1789-1837* [New York, 1968], p. 3-26).

TJ's report had a more immediate impact on foreign affairs, for it was instrumental in persuading the British government to abandon its efforts to create a neutral Indian barrier state between the United States and Canada. After being instructed to pursue this goal by his superiors in the spring of 1792, George Hammond quickly ascertained that TJ, Hamilton, and Henry Knox were all opposed to the projected barrier state because it would weaken American control over the western Indians, undermine the "right and jurisdiction" the federal government assumed over lands occupied by the Indians, and require the cession of territory claimed by the United States. TJ's report on public lands forcibly impressed the second and third objections on Hammond—and through him eventually on the British government as well—as he indicated in a report to the British foreign minister: "With respect to the second point—In my last conference with Mr. Jefferson, I took the liberty of adverting to his report, 'on the quantity and situation of the lands not claimed by the Indians, nor granted to, nor claimed by, any citizens within the territory of the United States' (a copy of which I had the honor of enclosing in my dispatch No. 5 of last year) and requested him to inform me of the claims, which the United States asserted over the soil and internal regulation of the Indians occupying lands within the American territory. Mr. Jefferson replied that the nature of the sovereignty of the United States was not yet precisely defined, but that in regard to the soil they claimed the right of pre-emption, by which the Indians were understood to be precluded from disposing of any part of their land except with the consent of the United States—that in respect to the internal regulation of the Indians the United States have not hitherto exercised any other jurisdiction over them than that of prohibiting them from allowing any person to inhabit their country, who were not provided with licenses from the government of the United States. On the validity or justice of these arguments it is unnecessary for me to make any comment, but your Lordship will perceive from them that as this government asserts this sort of paramount sovereignty over the soil actually occupied by the Indians, it would naturally regard any grant of that soil in perpetuity not only as a dereliction of right, but also as a sacrifice of a part of its territory" (Hammond to Grenville, 8 June 1792,

PRO: FO 4/15, f. 288-92; see also Bemis, *Jay's Treaty*, p. 109-33).

[1] Preceding two words substituted in Dft for "to a point in the mountains dividing the South Western territory from the state of North Carolina," deleted.

[2] TJ first wrote in Dft "about 6000," but altered it to read as above.

[3] In Dft TJ first wrote: "may be between 40 and 50 miles," and then altered it to read as above.

[4] TJ revised these figures and manner of expressing them several times in Dft before settling on the above text.

[5] At this point in Dft TJ wrote and then deleted: "in lieu of double locations ⟨of⟩ for specie or other certificates."

[6] At this point in Dft TJ first wrote and then deleted: "amounted to   acres." Next to this in the margin in Dft TJ first wrote and then deleted: "Govr Martin to send statement."

[7] Preceding sentence interlined in Dft. At this point TJ noted in the margin of Dft: "see Glasgow's return."

[8] In the margin at this point TJ first wrote and then deleted: "perhaps Govr. Martin may distinguish them."

[9] Next to this paragraph in Dft TJ wrote: "Govr. Martin to furnish statemt."

[10] In margin of Dft next to this paragraph TJ first wrote and then deleted: "[see Blount's lre.; how to estimate amount, when the military locations shall be known]." At end of paragraph he wrote in margin: "Glasgow's return."

[11] At this point in Dft TJ first wrote and then deleted: "of 500 acres each."

[12] At this point TJ first wrote and then deleted in the margin of Dft: "Govr Blount to send statemt." Below this he then wrote: "Glasgow's return."

[13] At this point in MS and PrC of Tr, the clerk wrote, "and partly in the Counties of Greene and Hawkins," but it was then deleted. In Dft, TJ first wrote and then deleted at this point: "an authentic list whereof amounting in the whole to 746,362½ acres has been furnished to the Secretary of State," and noting in margin: "Glasgow's return. The grants in Washington amount to 214,549¾."

[14] In Dft, TJ first wrote "but it is said a considerable proportion of these were without legal right," but then altered it to

read as above, noting in margin: "informn. by Majr. Mountflorence & also Govr. Blount."

[15] Remainder of paragraph added in Dft, partly in margin.

[16] In margin of Dft, TJ wrote "Glasgow's return. The grants in Sullivan amount to 173,332 acres," and revised his Dft from "Entries in Sullivan county; an authentic list whereof, amounting in the whole to 240,624 acres, has been also furnished to the Secretary of state" to read as above.

[17] In Dft TJ first wrote remainder of paragraph as follows: "[supposed to be about 500 rights of 640 acres each, and consequently amounting to about 320,000 acres.]" He noted in margin "Govr. Blount to send list," but deleted that and substituted "Mr. Hawkins." He finally noted in margin: "Glasgow's return."

[18] This paragraph reads as follows in Dft: "The claims under the third reservation amount to 1,762,660¼ acres, and have been located in the counties of Greene and Hawkins, and in the country from thence to the Missisipi as divided into an Eastern, Middle and Western district by the laws of the state. Almost the whole of these are within the Indian territory."

A second variant, which is on a detached sheet in DLC: TJ Papers, 59: 10146, reads as follows: "The extent of the IIId reservn in favor of entries made in Armstrong's office is not yet entirely known. ⟨£373,649.6.5. in certificates @ £10. the hundred acres having been pd. into their treasury before the 20th. day of May 1790⟩. The best indication of their amount which has been yet obtained is the sum of certificates pd into the treasury of the state for these warrts. which on the 20th day of May 1790 amounted to 373,649-6-5. and at the price £10 the hundred acres establd by law gives 3,736,493 acres for 1,762,660 of this grant have been already issued, which appears to have been located partly in the counties of Greene and Hawkins and partly in the country from thence to the Missisipi as divided into Eastern, middle, and Western districts. Almost the whole are within the Indian territory. Besides the warrts. pd for acres before mentd. it is known that there are others outstanding which have not yet been pd for. But it is also doubted whether these need be taken into the acct. as payment of them has been refused on the ground that the lands being within the Indn. territory cannot now be delivered to the ⟨claimants⟩ holders."

[19] This sentence in TJ's Dft reads as follows to this point: "Upon the whole the reservations probably." In the second variant (DLC: TJ Papers, 59: 10146), TJ wrote: "On a review of all the reservns., making such conjecturable allowance as our information authorizes, it appears probable that they cover all."

TJ added the following table of figures in the margin of Dft next to these paragraphs:

"214,549 3/4 in Washington
172,332   in Sullivan

1,762,660 1/2	in Greene, Hawkins and the 3 district
2,150,542.	Glasgow's returns according to the explanation of Mr Hawkins
Military	2,789,224
Evans—about	150,000
Surveyor-Genl	30,203
Commissioners	65,932
Washington	746,362
Sullivan	240,624
Preemptions	309,760
Henderson	200,000
Armstrong	3,736,493
	8,268,598
Martin and Wilson	4,000
Genl Greene	25,000"

The following table appears on the second variant text in DLC: TJ Papers, 59: 10146.

		Warrts	grants
"Washington		746,362 1/2	214,549 3/4
Sullivan		240,624	173,332
Armstrong	{ Greene Hawkins Eastern Middle Western" }	3,736,493	1,762,660

[20] At this point in Dft TJ noted in the margin: "might it not be well to shew this paragraph to E. R. [Edmund Randolph] who has probably accurate knowledge of the no. and nature of these L[ands] and the several paragraphs relating to Indian boundaries to Genl Knox?"

[21] At this point in Dft TJ noted in the margin: "to the Secretary of the Treasury who has consulted the Atty Genl. thereon."

[22] At this point in Dft TJ noted in the margin: "Is this reservation a *claim of Citizens*—or only made for the *State?*"

[23] In Dft, TJ first wrote "legal bounties," but altered it to read as above.

[24] At this point in Dft TJ originally wrote: "given to the Virginia troops on Continental establishment. The act of Congress of Aug. 10 1790 for enabling the sd officers and soldiers to obtain titles has directed the mode of ascertaining the quantity and location of these lands. Tho no regular return has been made of the proceedings herein, as directed by that law, yet we are able to say that   acres in the Southern allotment having been located in part of their bounties, they will be entitled under this reservation only to   acres on the North West side of the Ohio, as the whole amount of that bounty was 181,450 acres."

[25] At this point in Dft TJ noted in the margin: "possible that land in the [Southern] allotment not located [was] adjudged good."

[26] In Dft, TJ first wrote: "is 1,670,350 acres, deduction made of 184,650 acres the proportion of the Virga line," and then altered it to read as above.

[27] In Dft, TJ first wrote and then revised: "Northern boundary."

[28] At this point in Dft TJ noted in the margin: "ought not the purchase money to be paid to the U.S. by the Settlers when from them—and by Symms recd by him"

[29] In Dft, TJ first wrote then marked for deletion the following paragraph at this point: "On the whole the U.S. have a right to dispose of in the Southwestern territory 'all the lands Southward of the Southern boundary of Virginia, and Northward of the Indian lines described in the treaties concluded with the Cherokees and Chickasaws at Hopewell and Holston, with an exception of all rights saved by the deed of cession of N. Carolina.' Supposing the part North of the Indian lines to contain about seven and a half millions of acres as before conjectured, and the several claims of citizens before enumeratd. on both sides the Indian lines to amount to   acres, yet till

it be known what proportion of these lies on each side those lines, it can only be said that the U.S. have more than _____ acres to be disposed of on this quarter at present."

In the margin of Dft TJ entered the following table of figures next to this deleted paragraph:

"Military bounties	2,789,224
Evans's battalion	150,000
Surveyor genl	30,203
Shelby and others ⎱ Guards &c ⎰	65,932
Washington entries	746,362¼
Sullivan do	240,624
Preemption rights	309,760
Henderson	200,000
Armstrong's office	1,163,554
Genl. Greene	25,000

Martin and Wilson	4,000
	5,724,769
	7,500,000
	1,775,230"

See also note 19 above.

[30] In Dft, TJ first wrote "the Western boundary of Pennsylva.," then altered it to read as above.

[31] In Dft, TJ first wrote this phrase: "the Eastern boundary of the lands mentioned to be ceded in the deed of Connecticut."

[32] Preceding three words substituted in Dft for "of all," deleted.

[33] In Dft TJ first wrote: "sixteen and seventeen millions of acres," and then altered it to read as above.

[34] In Dft, TJ first wrote "about eighteen or nineteen" but altered it to read as above.

To William Short

Philadelphia Nov. 9. 1791.

Thomas Pinckny of S. Carolina has this day the offer of the mission to London as minister Pleni. When we know whether he accepts, or not wch. will not be these six weeks, the nomination of a minister pleni. for Paris and a minister resident for the Hague will be made. The former is in suspence between yourself and another. If you do not have that you will have the latter. There was never a symptom by which I could form a guess on this subject til three days ago. Nobody here will know a word of it these six weeks. Hearing a vessel in this port was just hoisting sail for Havre I avail myself of it to give you the information which you are to keep secret til it may be openly communicated. Adieu.

RC (ViW); entirely in code except for dateline, with interlinear decoding in Short's hand; endorsed by Short as received 17 Jan. 1792. PrC (DLC). Entry in SJL records this letter as "private." This letter was not posted until 25 Nov. 1791. See TJ to Short at that date.

Short correctly surmised that Gouverneur Morris was the other candidate under consideration for the post of minister to France (Short to TJ, 24 Jan. 1792).

To Samuel Smith

SIR   Philadelphia Nov. 9. 1791.

I have duly recieved your favor of the 5th. on the subject of the sloop Jane, which it was impossible to dispatch with the celerity you expected. It was necessary to copy the papers to communicate them to the French minister, and the copies are not yet ready. In the mean time I have seen Mr. Skipwith, who being to pass through Baltimore, I am persuaded his information to you will be thought important. I have therefore prevailed on him to call on you. If in consequence of his communications, you should prefer applying at Paris, it will be necessary for you to engage some person there to make application for you, and I will write to Mr. Short to support it. [He cannot be the person who is to go through the details of sollicitation.] If you still determine to try the matter at Martinique, I will endeavor to get aid for you from the French minister. I shall await your answer, and am with much esteem Sir Your most obedt & most humble servt, TH: JEFFERSON

PrC (DLC); brackets in MS. FC (DNA: RG 360, DL).

To Lord Wycombe

Nov. 9. 1791.

Th: Jefferson has the honour of presenting his respectful and affectionate compliments to Ld. Wycombe and of asking the favor of him immediately on his arrival in Charleston to have the goodness to send the inclosed letter to the Post-office. He knows how troublesome it is to travellers to have to think of letters, and therefore apologizes by the importance of the one inclosed, and the probability of it's going so much quicker by water than by post.

Th:J. regrets that constant occupation has put it out of his power to see as much of Ld. Wycombe as he would have wished during his short stay here; he should with great pleasure have contributed his mite towards possessing him of all that information relative to this country, which he knows to be the object of Ld. Wycombe's travels. He shall always be happy to hear of him, and from him, and bids him an affectionate adieu, with sincere wishes for prosperous and speedy passages to him.

PrC (DLC).

Wycombe replied immediately, thanking TJ for his kind remarks and assuring him that he would properly handle the INCLOSED LETTER of 6 Nov. offering Thomas Pinckney the appointment of minister to Great Britain (Wycombe to TJ, 9 Nov. 1791, RC in MHi; addressed: "To Mr. Jefferson &c. &c. &c."; endorsed by TJ as received 9 Nov. 1791, but not recorded in SJL). The young English nobleman was currently touring the United States, being "upon no Political Errand whatever," his father assured Washington, "but singly from the desire natural to his Age of seeing all he can," in which endeavor, Lansdowne was certain, he "can meet with no conversation which will not confirm him in those Principles of Freedom which have constituted my Happiness thro' Life" (Lansdowne to Washington, 4 July 1791, DLC: Washington Papers; see also TJ to Wycombe, 25 July 1789).

To David Campbell

SIR   Philadelphia Nov. 10. 1791.

I have now the pleasure to inclose you a catalogue of books on the scale you mentioned to me. I would advise you to establish your correspondence with some bookseller in Dublin, from whence such of them as have been printed there will cost you not two thirds, and the law books not one third of what they will in London.

I thank you, Sir, for the compliment you have been pleased to pay me in the naming of your son. Nobody is more sensible than myself of the little pretension I have to distinctions of that kind; but there is the greater cause of being thankful for them.—I have the honor to be with great esteem, Sir your most obedt. humble servt,

TH: JEFFERSON

PrC (MHi); at foot of text: "Judge Campbell." TJ recorded in SJL receipt of a letter from Campbell of 3 Nov. 1791, now missing.

Campbell, a judge in the Southwest Territory, was currently visiting in Philadel-phia. The enclosed CATALOGUE OF BOOKS (missing), might have been the Lackington's Catalogue from which TJ ordered books about two weeks later, showing no reluctance to pay London prices himself (TJ to Alexander Donald, 23 Nov. 1791).

From James Maury

Liverpool, 10 Nov. 1791. Since his of 14 Sep. he has received TJ's of 30 Aug. 1791, and now attends to it. "The Irregularity of the Masters of our Vessels, as I have mentioned before, prevented my furnishing the particulars you required." Trade with this port increases greatly, ninety-six American vessels having sailed from here this year. Only half that number have left other ports in his district. A "most Accurate Account" of the whole number will be forthcoming at the end of the year. "From this Sketch you will readily percieve that whenever I shall have the Consular act, the Duties of the office will require a considerable degree of Attention."—He notes the difference between what constitutes citizenship in the U.S. and in this country. A subject of this country is still regarded a citizen here even though he had lived in U.S. territory since the peace and been regarded a citizen of the U.S. "Many persons of this Description" own American vessels here, and lately the legality of such ownerships has been questioned.—"Our Vessells continue (in a Manner) the sole Carriers of the produce of this Country to theirs. The prosperous State of our Funds have occasioned great Speculations in them by the monied Men here. The ports of this Kingdom continue shut to foreign wheat. Tobaccoe is rather a better Article than it has been."

RC (DNA: RG 59, CD); 3 p. FC (James Maury Letterbook, Miss Aileen Carroll Maury, Maplewood, New Jersey, 1968); in Maury's hand; note at foot of text indicates RC went by *Ceres* and its duplicate by *Fortitude*.

To George Washington

Philadelphia Nov. 10. 1791.

I have duly examined the inclosed papers relating to the purchase by judge Symmes of the lands on the Great Miami, and think it will be proper to lay them before the legislature. They will thereby see the foundation of the larger claim of this purchaser mentioned in the report I have had the honour of presenting to you, and also the expediency of providing some speedy and regular mode of deciding this and other questions of a like nature which might arise hereafter, and obstruct for a considerable time the proceedings relative to the public lands.—I have the honour to be with the most profound respect & attachment, Sir, Your most obedient & most humble servt, TH: JEFFERSON

PrC (DLC); at foot of text: "The President of the U.S." FC (DNA: RG 360, DL).

Washington followed TJ's advice and submitted "Sundry papers relating to the purchase by Judge Symmes, of the lands on the Great Miami" to Congress, which received them on 14 Nov. 1791 (JHR, I, 453; JS, I, 340). On John Cleves Symmes' land grant in the Ohio country, see TJ to Symmes, 6 Aug. 1791. See also TJ's Report on Public Lands, 8 Nov. 1791.

To James Madison

Nov. 11. 1791.

In my report on How's case, where I state that it should go to the President, it will become a question with the house Whether they shall refer it to the President themselves, or give it back to the Petitioner, and let him so address it, as he ought to have done at first. I think the latter proper, 1. because it is a case belonging purely to the Executive. 2. the Legislature should never shew itself in a matter with a foreign nation, but where the case is very serious and they mean to commit the nation on it's issue. 3. because if they indulge individuals in handing through the legislature their applications to the executive, all applicants will be glad to avail themselves of the weight of so powerful a sollicitor. Similar attempts have been repeatedly made by individuals to get the President to hand in their petitions to the legislature, which he has constantly refused. It seems proper that every person should address himself directly to the department to which the constitution has allotted his case; and that the proper answer to such from any other department is, that 'it is not to us that the constitution has assigned the transaction of this business.'—I suggest these things to you, that if they appear to you to be right, this kind of business may in the first instance be turned into it's proper channel.

RC (DLC: Madison Papers); at head of text: "Th:J. to J.M." PrC (DLC). TJ's report on the case of William How is printed at 14 Nov. 1791.

From Daniel L. Hylton

DEAR SIR   Richmond Virga. Novr. 12th. 1791

Colo. Morgan has just given a call and informs me of his intention in seting of for the Northwd. in an hour and is obligeing enough to take charge of this letter. I wrote you 8th. of Augt. last by post, since have not had the pleasure of a line from you and as I wish to know if you reced. 2 Hhds tobo. by Capt. Stratton, he had taken from Manchester Whouse, supposeing from the Marks belonging to you, on examination of Mr. Balls books whose Whouse some of your tobo. had been lodg'd through mistake, found one of the 2 Hhds he had taken the property of yr. son in law Mr. Randolph in consequence, agreed to replace it with one of yours which came down afterwards. The Capt. not having left bills of lading for these 2 Hhds am at a loss to know if ever reced. by you, tho have no doubt if arriv'd safe they have been delivered. The last tobo. of yours that came down, was in shocking order having got wet on its way and scarcely a stave left to two of the hhds. Was therefore compel'd to have New Hhds and repack'd, of course swell'd the expences to more then I cou'd wishd.—I shd. have written you long before, but was in daily expectation after hearing you was at Monticello we shd. have the pleasure of a Vissit from you. The money lodgd with me by Colo. Lewis and the bank note reced from you is more than necessary to defray the expences of the tobo. As their will be a balance left in my hands, be pleasd to say how you will have it apply'd, whether, as mention'd in my former letter or any other manner you'll direct. Mrs. Hylton joins with me in wishing you every happiness & am Dr Sir Your Fd. & St,

DANL. L. HYLTON

P.S. I wd. have transmitted the Acct. by this conveyance, the inspectors being out of the way I cou'd not obtain the acct. tho will do it in a few days.

RC (MHi); endorsed by TJ as received 13 Dec. 1791 and so recorded in SJL.

From James Cole Mountflorence

[*Philadelphia*], *12 Nov. 1791*. Proposes leaving on 16 or 17 Nov. for Richmond and North Carolina, where he will see Gov. Blount and the Governor of North Carolina at Newbern. Offers to deliver dispatches to them.—After staying no longer than ten days, he will sail for France and spend about a month in Paris, "after which I will return with the greatest dispatch to the Territory South of the Ohio." Offers to carry letters to France and asks for letters of introduction to use there.

RC (DNA: RG 59, MLR); 2 p.; endorsed by TJ as received 12 Nov. 1791 and so recorded in SJL. A letter Mountflorence had written to TJ on 4 Nov. 1791, recorded in SJL as received 5 Nov. 1791, has not been found.

To Francis Eppes

DEAR SIR   Philadelphia Nov. 13. 1791.

I wrote you the last week, since which I have received yours of Oct. 2. and Nov. 3d. informing me that mine of the 5th. of Oct. was come to hand. I thank you for the purchase of the Jenny, and I will furnish the price here to Jack; as it seems useless for you to be sending £20. here, and me sending £20. to you. My extreme wish is to put immediately the Jenny to a Jack of as pure a breed as possible, in order to get one for myself. What is become of Mazzei's? or is there any of his breed to be got at? I shall be obliged to you for[1]

I shall pay my own British debts, but I shall not pay the debts of others if I can help it. I understand there has been some irregularity in the bringing Bevins's suit. As it is not our own debt, I should be for taking advantage of the irregularity to abate or delay it. In event however I take for granted we shall each provide for our third so as to prevent his levying all on one. Polly is well and writes to her aunt. Jack is well also and well employed. My love to Mrs. Eppes and the young ones. Your's Dear Sir affectionly.

TH: JEFFERSON

Tr (ViU: Edgehill-Randolph Papers); in a 19th century hand; as indicated in note below, one or more pages from this letter were missing when the transcript was made. Eppes' letter to TJ of 2 Oct. 1791 is recorded in SJL as received 10 Nov. 1791, but has not been found.

[1] The transcript breaks here, followed by a large gap, after which it resumes.

To Ebenezer Hazard

Nov. 13. 1791.

Th: Jefferson sends to Mr. Hazard the papers he spoke of. He presumes Mr. Hazard has a copy of the grant to Ld. Fairfax, an important paper to Virginia. If he has not Th:J. has the substance of it faithfully extracted. He will thank Mr. Hazard to return such of these papers as he shall not print.

RC (PHi). Not recorded in SJL.

THE PAPERS TJ was sending—which unfortunately cannot be further identified—were intended for Hazard's famous *Historical Collections; consisting of State papers, and other authentic documents; intended as materials for an history of the United States of America*, 2 vols. (Philadelphia, 1792-1794).

To Martha Jefferson Randolph

MY DEAR MARTHA   Philadelphia Nov. 13. 1791.

Maria and myself are waiting with impatience to hear that Mr. Randolph and yourself and dear little Anne are well. We now write alternately, once a week, so that the correspondence is become more equal. I now inclose to Mr. Randolph Freneau's paper instead of Bache's on account of the bulk of the latter which, being a daily paper, was too much for the post. And Freneau's two papers contain more good matter than Bache's six. He will see that the affairs of the French West Indies are in a desperate state. A second set of deputies has arrived here to ask succours. Abundance of women and children come here to avoid danger. The men are not permitted to come. I should not wonder to see some of your friends among them.—We expect hourly the arrival of Capt. Stratton, by whom the clothes for the house servants shall be sent. To forward them by any other vessel, is risking their miscarriage. Maria is fixed at Mrs. Pine's, and perfectly at home. She has made young friends enough to keep herself in a bustle with them, and she has been honored with the visits of Mrs. Adams, Mrs. Randolph, Mrs. Rittenhouse, Sarjeant, Waters, Davies &c., so that she is quite familiar with[1] Philadelphia. Present my sincere attachment to Mr. Randolph and kiss Anne for us. Adieu my dear, dear daughter. Your's affectionately,   TH: JEFFERSON

RC (NNP). PrC (Dr. Robert H. Kean, Alexandria, Va., 1945).

[1] These two words interlined for another, marked out and illegible.

To Hugh Williamson

DEAR SIR   Nov. 13. 1791.

On considering the subject of the clause you wished to have introduced in the inclosed bill, I found it more difficult than I had on first view imagined. Will you make the first trial against the patentee conclusive against all others who might be interested to contest his patent? If you do, he will always have a collusive suit brought against himself at once. Or will you give every one a right to bring actions separately? If you do, besides running him down with the expences and vexations of law suits, you will be sure to find some jury in the long run, who from motives of partiality or ignorance, will find a verdict against him, tho' a hundred should have been before found in his favour. I really believe that less evil will follow from leaving him to bring suits against those who invade his right. If however you can get over the difficulty and will drop me a line, I will try to prepare a clause, tho' I am sure you will put your own ideas into form better than any body else can.—Your's with sincere esteem,   TH: JEFFERSON

PrC (DLC); at foot of text: "Dr. Williamson."

Congressman Williamson of North Carolina was chairman of a committee appointed on 28 Oct. 1791 "to prepare and bring in a bill or bills to amend the act, entitled 'An act to promote the progress of useful arts' " (JHR, I, 444). For further information on TJ's interest in reform of the U.S. patent system, see Bill to promote the Progress of the useful Arts, 1 Dec. 1791.

Report on Petition of William How

The Secretary of State, to whom was referred, by the House of Representatives, the Petition of William How, praying Satisfaction from the United States, for a Debt due to him in Nova Scotia, and whereon Judgment has been rendered against him, contrary to existing Treaties, as he supposes, with Instruction to examine the same, and report his Opinion thereupon to the House, has had the same under Consideration, and thereupon

REPORTS

That if the Facts be justly stated in the Petition, Indemnification is to be sought from a foreign Nation, and, therefore, that the Case is a proper one to be addressed to the President of the United States.

That, when in that Channel, if it shall be found, after advising with Counsel at Law, that the Verdict or Judgment rendered in the said Case, is Inconsistent with Treaty, it will become a proper Subject of Representation to the Court of London, and of Indemnification from them to the Party.

That to this Interposition the Petitioner will, in that Case, be entitled, but not to any Reimbursement from the United States directly. Th: Jefferson
Nov. 14. 1791.

PrC (DLC); in clerk's hand, except for date and signature; on verso in clerk's hand: "Recorded and Examined." FC (DNA: RG 59, SDR). Tr (DNA: RG 59, MLR); endorsed by Lear. Report was transmitted in TJ to the Speaker of the House of Representatives, 14 Nov. 1791 (PrC in DLC).

On 3 Nov. 1791 the House of Representatives read and referred to TJ a petition from William How of Shrewsbury Mass., "praying that, as he became an American citizen at the commencement of the late war with Great Britain, entered into the service of the United States, and has continued to be a citizen thereof since that time, he may be relieved against the operation of certain proceedings of a court of law in Nova Scotia, under the dominion of Great Britain, which has been lately had against him, contrary, as he conceives, to the provisions contained in the fourth article of the treaty of peace between the United States and Great Britain" (JHR, I, 447; attested copy by John Beckley of House resolution on How of 3 Nov. 1791, DNA: RG 59, MLR). This article of the peace treaty concerned the collection of private debts contracted by citizens of one country with those of the other.

TJ strongly opposed How's effort to induce the House of Representatives to intercede in his case because he feared that it would set a precedent for further legislative encroachments on the President's authority to conduct foreign affairs and encourage other citizens to seek legislative assistance in matters over which the executive branch of government properly exercised jurisdiction. TJ consulted with James Madison before he submitted his report to the House of Representatives, arguing that in order to avoid even the semblance of legislative interference with executive authority the legislators should do nothing more than permit How to withdraw his petition; if they themselves referred it to the President, they would simply inspire others seeking executive assistance "to avail themselves of the weight of so powerful a sollicitor" (TJ to Madison, 11 Nov. 1791). Madison obviously concurred with this view, because after reading the report this day the House approved his motion giving How leave to withdraw his petition (JHR, I, 453; Gazette of the United States, 16 Nov. 1791). No evidence has been found that How subsequently submitted his petition to the President.

Report on Petition of Charles Colvill

The Secretary of State, to whom was referred, by the House of Representatives, the Petition of Charles Colvill, praying to be paid the Amount of his Ransom from the Algerines, and of his Travelling Expenses, and that Measures be taken for procuring the Ransom of his late Fellow-Captives, with Instructions to examine the same, and report his Opinion thereon, has had the same under Examination, and thereupon

REPORTS

That, as to so much of the Petition as prays that Measures may be taken for procuring the Ransom or Relief of Captains Obrian and Stevens, with their respective Crews, now at Algiers, he begs Leave to refer the House to his two Reports, laid before Congress at their last Session, on the Subject of those Captives, and of the Trade of the United States in the Mediterranean; wherein he stated as fully as was, or is now in his Power, the Situation of those Captives, the different Means, which might be adopted for their Liberation, leaving to the Wisdom of Congress to decide between these Means; since which, no Event of Consequence has come to the Knowledge of the Secretary of State, except that of the Death of the then Dey, and Succession of one of his Ministers to his place, the Effect of which Event, on the Practicability of liberating the Captives, is not known.

And as to so much of the Petition, as prays that the Petitioner may be paid the Amount of his Ransom, together with his Expenses in returning from Algiers to Philadelphia, it is submitted to the Consideration of the House, whether this Precedent might not be considered as authorizing the Friends of the Captives, or other private Persons, or Societies, to enter into Treaty for our Captives, separately, and to bid without Restraint, on the Presumption that the Public were to repay the Price; and whether this would not have the precise Effect of establishing a high Tariff for our future Captives, and thereby attracting piratical Expeditions against them of Preference, which has hitherto been so much the Obstacle to the Ransom of our unfortunate Countrymen: but the Secretary of State is of Opinion that whensoever they shall be ransomed at a Price which the Government shall approve, that then a corresponding Sum ought to be allowed by the United States for reimbursing the Ransom of this Petitioner: and that, in the meantime, such Sum might be advanced to the Petitioner, on Account thereof, as may relieve his present Necessities.   TH: JEFFERSON
Nov. 14. 1791.

PrC (DLC); in clerk's hand, except for date and signature; on verso in clerk's hand: "Recorded and Examined." FC (DNA: RG 59, SDR). Tr (DNA: RG 59, MLR); endorsed by Lear. Report was transmitted in TJ to Speaker of the House of Representatives, 14 Nov. 1791 (PrC in DLC).

On 4 Nov. 1791 the House of Repre-

sentatives and the Senate both read petitions from Charles Colvill of Philadelphia, who had been captured by Algerian pirates in 1785 while serving on the *Dauphin* and ransomed from captivity five years later through the efforts of relatives who raised about $1,700 to secure his release (see Richard O'Bryen to TJ, 12 July 1790). Colvill's petition to the Senate requested reimbursement for the money his brothers had expended to redeem him from captivity, and his petition to the House asked that he be paid "the amount of his ransom from slavery among the Algerines, together with his expenses in travelling from Algiers to Scotland, and from thence to America; as, also, that measures may be taken for procuring the ransom, or relief from slavery, of Captains O'Brian and Stevens, with their respective crews, being citizens of the United States, and now in slavery at Algiers." The Senate referred the petition it received from Colvill to a committee considering the plight of American captives in Algiers, while the House submitted its copy of the petition to TJ with a request that he report on it to that body (Petition of Charles Colvill to Congress, 4 Nov. 1791, DNA: RG 59, MLR; JHR, I, 449; JS, I, 336; attested copy by John Beckley of House resolution on Colvill of 4 Nov. 1791, DNA: RG 59, MLR).

The House and the Senate continued to consider Colvill's petitions even after the submission of TJ's report, but in the end they evidently accepted the wisdom of TJ's contention that acceding to these solicitations would merely encourage the Algerians to demand more exorbitant ransoms in order to secure the release of any Americans they captured. None of the Philadel-

phian's requests for money were granted; indeed, Colvill was still petitioning the House as late as 1796 to recompense him for the expenses incurred by his redemption (JHR, I, 453, 580, 581, 586, 587, II, 515, 523; JS, I, 349, 354, 394).

Colvill's call for additional measures to redeem his former shipmates in Algiers enjoyed greater success. Within less than a month after TJ's report was submitted to the House of Representatives, the Senate committee to which Colvill's petition had been referred asked the Secretary of State to devise a plan for negotiating a treaty of peace with Algiers and ransoming the American captives. TJ promptly complied with this request, and several months later the American government officially adopted such a plan (see Pierce Butler to TJ, 2 Dec. 1791; TJ to Pierce Butler, 2 Dec. 1791; TJ to John Paul Jones, 1 June 1792).

The TWO REPORTS cited by TJ are printed as Documents III and IV in group of documents on reports on Mediterranean trade and Algerine captives, under 28 Dec. 1790. In preparation for his report on Colvill, TJ wrote a brief letter to Tobias Lear on 9 Nov. 1791, requesting "a copy of the Resolution of Senate [he believes of Feb. 1. 1791] advising the redemption of our captives at Algiers" (RC in DLC: William W. Corcoran Papers; see also JEP, I, 72).

Report on Petition of John Mangnall

The Secretary of State, to whom was referred by the Senate of the United States, the petition of John Mangnall, has had the same under consideration, and thereupon makes the following REPORT.

HE finds that Congress, on the application of the petitioner, resolved on the 27th. day of September, 1780, that the profit of the capture of the Dover cutter should be divided among the captors, and that the honorable Mr. Jay, their minister plenipotentiary at the Court of Madrid, should be instructed to endeavor to obtain for the said captors, the benefit intended by their resolve of October 14th. 1777.

THAT such instructions were accordingly sent by the Committee for foreign Affairs to Mr. Jay, who continued, during his residence there, to press the settlement of this claim, under very varying prospects, as to the result.

THAT after he came to the direction of the office for foreign affairs, he continued to press the same subject through our Chargé des Affaires at Madrid; and it has been since resumed, and urged in the strongest terms by the Secretary of State.

THAT as yet no information is received of what has been done, or is likely to be done.

THAT the circumstances of the country where this business has been to be transacted, have rendered the transmission and receipt of letters at all times difficult and precarious, and latterly in a remarkable degree: but still, that there will be no remission of endeavors to obtain justice for the petitioner and his associates.

As to so much of the said petition as prays, that the petitioner may be allowed a pension from the public until his claim shall be decided at the Court of Madrid, the Secretary of State observes, that in times of war, questions are continually arising on the legitimacy of capture, on Acts of piracy, on Acts of violence at sea, and in times of peace, on seizures for contraband, regular and irregular, which draw on discussions with foreign nations, always of long continuance, and often of results in which expedience, rather than justice, renders acquiescence adviseable; that some such cases are now depending between the governments of the United States, and of other countries; that a great number of applications might be made for pensions on the same ground with the present, both now and hereafter; that it is not known that the claims are just 'till they are heard and decided on, and even when decided to be just, the government from which it is due, is alone responsible for the money: and he is therefore of opinion, that such pension ought not to be granted.[1]

Th: Jefferson

Nov. 14. 1791.

PrC (DLC); in clerk's hand, except for signature and date; on verso in clerk's hand: "Recorded and Examined"; report transmitted with TJ to the Senate, 14 Nov. 1791 (PrC in DLC); at foot of text: "The Vice president of the U.S. President of the Senate." FC (DNA: RG 59, SDR); preceded by text of Senate resolution, attested by Samuel A. Otis, reading: "In Senate, November 3d: 1791. Ordered, That the petition of John Manghnal, this day presented and read, be referred to the Secretary of State, to report to the Senate thereon." TJ submitted this report to Washington on 10 Nov. 1791, marking out the paragraph mentioned in textual note below (RC

in DNA: RG 59, MLR; FC in DNA: RG 59, SDC: letter only, with note at foot: "NB. The Report above mentioned was on the petition of John Mangnall, and is filed with the Reports from the Secretary of State"). Lear acknowledged the receipt of the report on 11 Nov. 1791 stating that "the President conceives the Secretary's Report on the Petition of John Mangnall contains what is right and proper on that subject" (PrC in same; FC in DNA: RG 59, SDC).

The Senate read a petition from John Mangnall on 2 Nov. 1791 asking for "compensation for certain losses sustained in the sea service during the late war" and on the following day asked TJ to report on it. TJ's recommendation that Mangnall's request for the payment of a pension be denied met with the approval of the Senate, which read the Secretary of State's report this day and then ordered Mangnall's petition to be tabled (JS, I, 336, 340; Petition of John Mangnall to Senate and House of Representatives, 1 Nov. 1791, DNA: RG 59, MLR).

For an explanation of the *Dover* case, see TJ to William Carmichael, 11 Apr. 1791.

[1] In the report to the President on 10 Nov. 1791, TJ first wrote and then deleted a different version of the final paragraph: "As to so much of the petition as prays that a pension may be allowed him until the adjustment of his claim, it will rest with the wisdom of the Senate to decide on it's reasonableness. The precedent will indeed be new, and may bring on other applications in similar cases to which the irregular conduct of officers, military and civil, have given rise, and will perpetually give rise. But if they shall percieve that the measure is right, the consequence that it will lead to repetitions in other cases equally right ought to be met."

To George Washington

The Secretary of state, to whom has been referred by the President of the United States, the Report of the proceedings in the Executive department of the North Western territory, for the month of July 1791. made by the Secretary of the said territory, thereupon REPORTS

That the letter of July 12. 1791. therein entered, having been already communicated to the legislature of the United states, there is nothing else in the said Report which requires any thing to be done on the part of the President of the United States.

TH: JEFFERSON
Nov. 14. 1791.

RC (DNA: RG 59, MLR); signature and date clipped off. PrC (DLC); includes signature and date in TJ's hand; on verso in clerk's hand: "Recorded and Examined." Tr (DNA: RG 59, SDC). FC (DNA: RG 59, SDR). Not recorded in SJL, but under 14 Nov. 1791 in SJPL TJ recorded four reports sent to the President: "Report Th:J. on Petition of William How. indemnification from England.
do.   Charles Colvill.   refund ransom.
do.   Mangnall.   Dover cutter.
do.   on proceedings of Executive of N.W. territory."

The REPORT OF THE PROCEEDINGS was sent by Lear to TJ, 14 Nov. 1791 (RC in DLC; endorsed by TJ as received the same day). Lear had sent TJ a letter from the Secretary of the territory and the records of the governor on 9 Nov. 1791 (PrC in DNA: RG 59, MLR; FC in DNA: RG 59, SDC).

Winthrop Sargent transmitted a copy of the executive proceedings of Governor Arthur St. Clair in the Northwest Territory for the month of July 1791 with a covering letter to President Washington, dated 1 Aug. 1791, in which he explained that he had decided not to wait until the end of the year to forward this segment of the executive record so as to avoid "detaining it beyond the next Sessions of Congress, when some Questions and Applications upon the Subject of Lands in this Country may make a reference thereto, proper and necessary" (Carter, *Terr. Papers*, II, 348-9). The July records dealt extensively with St. Clair's opposition to Judge John Cleves Symmes' efforts to settle land beyond the eastern boundaries of his patent in the Ohio country, a subject that was obviously germane to TJ's 8 Nov. 1791 Report on Public Lands, and included as well the text of the 12 July 1791 letter from St. Clair to Symmes alluded to by TJ in the present report (same, III, 349-52). TJ had already persuaded Washington to submit the issue of Symmes' disputed boundary to Congress (TJ to Washington, 10 Nov. 1791).

From J. P. P. Derieux

Charlottesville, 15 Nov. 1791. He has received TJ's of 25 Oct. and the letter from Mde. Bellanger enclosed in it. He has read with appreciation Mr. Fenwick's efforts to interest M. LeRoy to his advantage, and he supposes that it was at Paris, and not at Bordeaux, that M. LeRoy died. Mde. Bellanger informed him of LeRoy's death as early as April and she now gives the names of the three executors of his will, all merchants at Bordeaux. She is astonished that he has not received any news of the bequest made for him and his two brothers. He quotes from her letter dated last July 16: she is surprised that he has not yet received her two last letters of April 14 and May 31 and that the executors of the will of M. LeRoy have not written to him, which should have been at the moment of his death in April. New taxes are excessive and they live only by assignats; they no longer recognize the constitution and while only a year ago at the Federation they swore loyalty to the nation, the law, and the king, now she fears the people wish to remove the king. Honest people do not want a republic and happily that is the wish of the great majority of the National Assembly. The Jacobins say it is the Club which is the master of France; it keeps the king prisoner and wants to put him on trial.—If the United States were no further away than England is to France she would make the effort to visit him, but her health and age make that too unreasonable.—She has made a deposit of 4,000 livres for his use while waiting for the 15,000 to come to him.

He sends TJ that part of her letter that credit may be obtained with the bank of Philadelphia for a loan of 4,000 so he can meet some contractual commitments of long standing. Otherwise he would find himself very embarrassed. He apologizes for all the embarrassment he continually gives TJ, and asks him to send the attached letter to Mde. Bellanger.

RC (MHi); 4 p.; in French; endorsed by TJ as received 10 Dec. 1791 and so recorded in SJL. Enclosure not found.

To William Short

SIR   Philadelphia Nov. 16. 1791.

The bearer hereof, Majr. Mountflorence, proposing to visit France on his lawful affairs, I take the liberty of recommending him to your attention and good offices. He is a citizen of the state of North Carolina, and of the profession of the law there, and his merits in every respect will do justice to any civilities or services you can render him, and which will at the same time be esteemed an obligation on, Sir, your most obedt & most humble servt,

TH: JEFFERSON

PrC (MHi); at foot of text: "Mr. Short Chargé des affairs of the U.S. at Paris."

To Jean Baptiste Ternant

SIR   Philadelphia November 16th. 1791.

I have the honor to transmit you the inclosed papers on the subject of the Sloop Jane the property of certain merchants of the Town of Baltimore, commanded by Captn. Woodrough, said to have been taken from him with her cargo as she was passing the Island of Martinique, by Captn. la Riviere Commanding the ship of war of your Nation called la Firme of 74 Guns, and disposed of with her cargo without legal trial or form, and without any satisfaction made to the master or owners. They are now about to send an agent to Martinique to apply for indemnification, and I am to ask the favor of you to give them your letter or letters to Monsieur Betagne Governor of the Island, Captn. la Riviere, or any other persons you may think best, recommending to them an examination into the case of the sufferers, and that justice to which they may be found entitled. I have only to add that a vessel is waiting with the Agent on board until you will have the goodness to favor me with your letters.—I have the honor to be with sentiments of the most perfect esteem and respect, Sir your most obedient and most humble Servant.

PrC (DLC); in clerk's hand, unsigned. FC (DNA: RG 360, DL); letter only. Enclosure: Certified copy of protest made 19 Feb. 1791 by captain and crew of sloop *Jane* before notary public at St. Eustatius stating in detail what TJ summarized above.

The AGENT TO MARTINIQUE: Thomas Darlington. See Samuel Smith to TJ, 5 Nov. 1791.

From George Muter

SIR   Kentucky, Woodford County, Novr. 17th 1791

Knowing that your time must be necessarily taken up by business of great importance, and having nothing of importance to communicate, I have, hitherto, forborne writing to you, other, than acknowledging the receipt of your letter to me, covering the Acts of Congress respecting Kentucky: but, the present situation of the Western country in general and this district in particular, compells me to trouble you with some ideas of mine, and I hope, will plead my excuse.

The militia of this country are, generally, averse to serving with regulars; and as a very great proportion of them are very poor people, being called frequently to perform militia duty, at a considerable distance from home, is to all of them very injurious, and to many, absolutely ruinous. Would it not therefore, be better, to raise in this district, two or more battallions, on a plan, somewhat similar, to that, of the minute battallions in the late war? I have no doubt, but that two battallions, might be raised in Kentucky, with great ease, and very expeditiously; consisting principally, if not entirely, of young men, who coud go into service immediately upon being ordered, and might continue in it for a considerable time, without inconvenience. Great care however, ought to be taken, in the appointment of officers, to get such men as would be fit to command, and likely to be able to raise the men. I apprehend no great difficulty, that, would attend that business; because there are a great many men in Kentucky, that, have served in the late war, some of them with reputation; enough for the higher offices; and many spirited young fellows, who would, with a little experience, make excellent subalterns. I can, at present, see no reason to doubt, such men's being of more real service, than draughts from the militia; and I think too, that they would be, fully as cheap to government: and I am well assured, the people would thereby, be greatly eased, and much more contented.

It would perhaps be of importance, in the present situation of affairs in the Western Country, to appoint an officer to succeed to General Buttler's command, who possesses, in some degree, the confidence of the people of this Country. I mean the western country in general. I think I can assure you that Genl. Wilkinson's appointment, would most probably give general satisfaction. I have not a doubt of his abilities; and from what I have heard of the manner of his resignation (which will be found among the records of the former Congress) I think, it may be considered that, even the present Government, are, in some degree bound to pay particular attention to him.—I have the honour to be with the highest respect Sir your most hble servt,   GEORGE MUTER

RC (DLC); endorsed by TJ as received 24 Dec. 1791 and so recorded in SJL.

TJ's letter transmitting ACTS relating to Kentucky is dated 28 Feb. 1791 and is printed as Document v in Editorial Note and group of documents on the admission of Kentucky and Vermont to the union, at 4 Mch. 1791. General Richard Butler, the militarily incompetent second-in-command of Arthur St. Clair's ill-fated expedition against the Indians in the Northwest Territory, was killed during the crushing defeat the Indians administered to St. Clair's force near the Wabash on 4 Nov. 1791. On WILKINSON'S APPOINTMENT, see Harry Innes to TJ, 30 Sep. 1791.

To William Short

DEAR SIR   Philadelphia Nov. 17. 1791.

Mr. Morris, eldest son of Mr. Robert Morris being about to visit Europe, and to make a considerable tour through it, I trouble him with this line to you, in order to renew your former acquaintance with him, and also to ask the favour of you to procure for him such letters as may be useful to him in those parts of Europe to which he may go.—I know he will receive from you personally the attentions and good offices you can render him, and have therefore only to repeat assurances of the sentiments of esteem & respect with which I am Dear Sir your friend & servt,   TH: JEFFERSON

PrC (MHi).

To Samuel Smith

SIR   Philadelphia Nov. 17. 1791.

Your favor of the 13th. came to hand the night before last. I sent the papers to the French minister, from whom I have this moment recieved the letter now inclosed for the Governor of Martinique. Mr. Skipwith has been detained here by sickness, but will set out in tomorrow's stage, and consequently will be in Baltimore Saturday night.

Supposing that a line from yourself to Mr. Short, to prevent Capt. Woodrough from doing anything amiss, would be more authoritative than one from me, I take the liberty of recommending to you to write to him.—I am Sir your very humble servt,

TH: JEFFERSON

PrC (DLC). FC (DNA: RG 360, DL).

Smith's FAVOR of 13 Nov. 1791 is not recorded in SJL and has not been found. TJ recorded receipt of a 17 Nov. 1791 letter from Ternant in SJL but it also has not been found. Ternant wrote a letter to Montmorin on 19 Nov. 1791 explaining that in order to promote harmonious relations between the United States and France he had forwarded the papers relating to the case of the sloop *Jane* to M. de Behague, the governor of Martinique, and had personally assured TJ that if the facts set forth therein were true he was convinced the governor would redress the grievances of which complaint was made (Turner, *CFM*, p. 76).

From Caspar Wistar, Jr.

Novr. 17th. 1791.

Dr. Wistar offers respectful compliments to Mr. Jefferson. He thinks the Statement perfectly proper and hopes it will excite attention to a Circumstance that promises to be of use in every kind of distillation where boiling is necessary. He has intended for some time to make an experiment with a vessel which should unite Fitch and Voights and Poissonnieres idea of a fire place in the water, with Irvings pipe; and hopes to be able to do it before the business is finished. He will thank Mr. Jefferson for communicating any ideas that occur to him on the subject.

RC (MHi). Not recorded in SJL.

The STATEMENT was a text of TJ's report on Jacob Isaacks' proposed method for desalinating sea water, printed below at 21 Nov. 1791, and for which TJ made use of Wistar's own experiments. Wistar, at TJ's request, had subjected Isaack's proposal to scientific testing (See Editorial Note and group of documents on experiments in desalination of sea water to test the claims of Jacob Isaacks, at 26 Mch. 1791).

From James Hutchinson

November 18th. 1791

Doctor Hutchinson returns Mr. Jefferson his report on Isaacks Petition. It is so carefully, ably, and accurately drawn, that Dr. Hutchinson cannot suggest any alterations for the better or in fact any alteration at all.—Dr. Hutchinson will turn his attention to the subject, and will speedily furnish Mr. Jefferson with such hints as may occur to him, which may be of use to an ignorant seaman in the Operation of distilling.

RC (DLC). Not recorded in SJL.

From David Campbell

SIR   City Tavern Philadelphia Novr. 19th. 1791

To morrow I leave the City. I feel myself quite tired of *fumum strepitumque Romæ.*

I cannot depart without returning you my acknowledgments for the List of Books you furnished me with.

I should have waited personally upon you; but knowing you were so engaged in public business at this time, that you have not a moment to spare, I beg you to accept my sincere thanks and believe me to be with the purest sentiments of Esteem & Regard, your obt. Servt.,   DAVID CAMPBELL

RC (DLC); endorsed by TJ as received 20 Nov. 1791 and so recorded in SJL. FUMUM STREPITUMQUE ROMAE: "fumes and clatter of Rome." The LIST OF BOOKS was enclosed in TJ's letter of 10 Nov. 1791.

From Francis Eppes

DR. SIR   Novr. 19th 1791

This will be handed to you by my Friend Colo. Bird, who coming to Philadelphia I have taken the liberty of introducing to your acquaintance. There are few people whom I should presume to give a letter of this kind, however, from Colo. Bird's knon good character as a Gentleman and Patriot I flater myself this introduction will meet with your approbation.

I have the pleasure to inform you that the Family are well. Betsey is perfectly recoverd and in a fair way to recover her good looks. She as well as the rest of the Family desire to join with me in wishing you and Polly every good this world affords. I am Dr Sir Your Friend   FRANS. EPPES

RC (MHi); endorsed by TJ as received 7 Dec. 1791 and so recorded in SJL. A letter Eppes wrote TJ on 8 Nov. 1791, recorded in SJL as received 10 Nov. 1791, has not been found.

From John Ettwein

SIR   Bethlehem 19. Nov. 1791.

I hope You will pardon the Liberty I take in troubling You with this Letter and representing to You that Your Report to the Presid. of the Unit. States of 8. inst. respecting the Quantity and Situation of the Lands not claimed, gave me some Uneasiness on Account of what is therein reported concerning the Land granted to the Christian Indians on Muskingum River, Vizt: "The Indians however for whom the Reservation was made, have chosen to emigrate beyond the Limits of the United States so that the Lands reserved for them, still remain to the Un. States."

As those 12000. Acres of Land were to be vested in the Society of the Unit. Brethren for propagating the Gospel among the Heathen in Trust and for the Uses expressed in the Ordinances of May 20. 1785. and July 27. 1787., I must beg Leave humbly to remonstrate, that the Emigration of the Christian Indians cannot be construed as making void the Grant of Congress, And I flatter myself, the Honorable Secretary of State, by perusing the simple State of Fact, will be convinced that the Emigration of the said Indians was not by Choice but the most urgent Necessity.

Permit me, Sir, to relate to You the Situation of these Christian Indians since the Year 1785.—When in that Year the said Indians living then on Huron River, above Lake Sinclair, were informed, that the Honorble Congress had reserved the 3. forsaken Towns with 10000 Acres of Land for them and their Children, they prepared themselves to repossess it, and in the Spring 1786. they came on their Return as far as Cajahaga River, but by terrifying Reports of the determined resistance of the white People on the Ohio, against their Return to their old Towns, they were induced to stop at Cajahaga and planted there that Summer; In the Course of which they found that the Land, where they soujourned was given to the Connecticut People and that a Fort was to be built there, and were therefore constrained to move again in the Spring 1787.—Their full Intention was to take Possession of the Land on Muskingum: But being informed by the Superintendant of Indian Affairs and their Friends at Pittsburg, that a lawless Crew threathened them another bloody Visit, if they should venture to settle on Muskingum and the Indian Chiefs at the same time bidding them to come to Sandusky, which they durst not disobey, they came on their Journey as far as Pettquotting or Huron River on this side the Lake, about 30. Miles from Sandusky, in that Place they lived 4. Years in undisturbed Peace. Many of the strayed Sheep, who had left them after the Massacre on Muskingum, returned and a Number of others, among them Gelelemind, al. Kilbuck with his Family joined them. After the Affair on Miami in October 1790, their Peace, by the Confederation of their neighbouring Indian Nations, was intierly interrupted. The Delaware Captain, the Wiondot and Tawa Chiefs, ordered them to prepare for a Removal from Pettquotting, if they would not be treated again as they were treated on Muskingum, where they were plundered, their Cattle killed, and they as Prisoners carried to Sandusky River.—As the Tawa Chief pretended to be a Friend of the Christian Indians and had several times declared, that in Case a War should be determined on, he would provide a safe Place for them, as he knew they would not go to War, they sent a Message, to hear where they should find an Asylum, but receiving no Answer and fearing they might loose the Time for planting and seeing no Hope of Protection from the Western Government, one of the Missionaries was sent to Detroit, to petition the Brittish Government for Leave to come to the East Side of Lake Erie and to lend them some Land, where they could plant and live on until Peace should be restored.—The Commandant of Detroit and Mr. McKee the Indian Agent endeavoured to persuade them not to fly but to remain this Year at Pettquotting, where they would not be in such Danger from the Militia as they feared, and that McKee would use all his Influence with the Indian Warriors, not to disturb them.—But when a Number of friendly Indians were killed on Beaver Creek in March last, two of the killed being of their Fold, and hearing that some of the Militia were seen near Cajahaga, Anxiety and Fear seized the Women and Children that they were ready to run away from Pettquotting and the Missionaries saw no other way to keep their Flock together, but by leaving their fine Settlement and to retire under the Brittish Government, where on a second Application, some Land on the East side of Detroit River was lent them and Protection promised.

This simple Narrative of the Circumstances of these Christian Indians, which is strictly true, will, I am sensible convince Your Honor, that it was not Choice, which made this Congregation forsake their Settlement and the Improvements, which had cost them so much Labour, and of which they had but begun to enjoy the Fruits, to emigrate beyond the Limits of the Unit. States, but that it was the most urgent Necessity and the Conviction that in their Situation they could not be protected.

By the Last Accounts from the Missionaries, their present Situation is not agreable to those Christian Indians, the Land and everything else is displeasing to them, and as soon as they can return without the Risque of their Lives, at least the greatest Part will return.

But, Honored Sir, Permit me to represent this Case also in another Light: The Resolve of Congress was to vest the said 12000. Acres of Land in the Society for propagating the Gospel among the Heathen, in Trust for the Use and Benefit of said Christian Indians. This

Society has received the Ordinance for Surveying the 3. Tracts of Land therein mentioned, before the Land adjoining, called the Army Land, could be surveyed.—Accordingly 2. different Attempts were made to survey the same, and at each time proper Persons were sent by the Society, at considerable Expence to be present and assist at the Survey, but both the Attempts were frustrated on Account of the Difficulties and Dangers from the Indians. Besides these Expences the Return of the Indian Congregation in the Year 1786 has been a great Charge to the Society, and now the necessary Assistance in the Transport as well of the Missionaries, as the Widows, the Orphans, the sick, the blind and the halt of the Indian Congregation in April last, has brought the Missionaries to the Necessity of drawing on the Society for a considerable Sum. I humbly hope therefore, also on this Account, the Honorable Congress will confirm the Grant, according to the Resolve of Sept. 3. 1788. to the Society of the United Brethren for Propagating the Gospel among the Heathen, which has been incorporated by the Legislatures of the States of Pennsylvania and New Jersey.—This Society has determined to let as many of said Indians as shall please (as soon as Circumstances will permit) to live and farm on the said 12000. Acres, as long as they choose, without any Rent, and as soon as possible to rent out the Remainder, to reap some Benefit by it, for the Support of the Society in providing Teachers for said Christian Indians and their Descendants or other Christian Indians in Connexion with the United Brethren.

Not having the Honor to be personally known to You, Sir, I hope the Consciousness of my Duty as Presidt. of the Society of the Brrn. for propagatg. &c., to give a full account of the Case in Question to the Secretary of State will be accepted as an Apology for troubling You with this long Letter.—The Endeavours of the Brethren for a Series of Years, under the greatest Difficulties, to bring the North American Indians to the Knowledge of Christianity and at the same time to civilize them, and the Success they have had under divine Providence, cannot perhaps be known to Your Honor, so as it is known to many worthy Gentlemen of this State.—In Order to give You some Idea of the said Society and of the Method of the Brethren in their Missions among the Heathen in General, I take the Liberty to present to Your Honor the Rules of the said Society and a small Treatise of the Method of the Brethren &c.—With Sentiments of the greatest Respect I have the Honor to be Sir Your most obedt. Servt.,   J. ETTWEIN

FC (PBM); at head of text: "Copy" and "No. 47." Dft (same); at head of text: "Thomas Jefferson Esqr. Secretary of State"; differs from FC in that several portions were expanded therein; unsigned. Recorded in SJL as received 23 Nov. 1791.

Apparently, TJ never replied to this letter from John Ettwein, the noted Indian missionary and bishop of the Moravian Church of North America, who had taken the lead in reviving the Society of the United Brethren for Propagating the Gospel among the Heathen in 1787. Ettwein's efforts to secure restitution from the government for the losses the Christian Indians had sustained in March 1782 at the hands of a group of American militiamen during the infamous massacre at Gnadenhütten finally achieved success in 1798 (Kenneth G. Hamilton, *John Ettwein and the Moravian Church during the Revolutionary Period* [Bethlehem, Pa., 1940], p. 198-208). The enclosed SMALL TREATISE was probably a work by the German Moravian bishop, August Gottlieb Spangenberg, entitled *An Account of the Manner in which the Protestant Church of the Unitas Fratrum, or United Brethren, preach the Gospel, and carry on their Missions among the Heathen* (London, 1788); Sowerby, No. 1544.

From Thomas Barclay

Lisbon, 20 Nov. 1791. He has hired a vessel to take him to Tangier and expects to leave in five or six days. The Portuguese government first ordered passage for him on one of their vessels and then inexplicably rescinded the order.—He has written to the Basha of Tangier, the Emperor's secretary [Francisco] Chiappe, and the Venetian consul at Tangier. He is anxious to leave Lisbon because of reports that the Emperor's vessels are cruising in the Atlantic and that an American vessel which left Madeira on 29 Sep. is missing. An armed Moroccan ship was seen in the track between Madeira and Lisbon in the beginning of October.

RC (DNA: RG 59, CD); 2 p.; endorsed by TJ as received 7 Jan. 1792 and so recorded in SJL.

To Thomas Mann Randolph, Jr.

DEAR SIR   Philadelphia Nov. 20. 1791.

I now inclose you, and shall continue to do so, Fenno's and Freneau's papers. The latter in two papers a week will contain at least as much good matter as Bache's six papers a week, and will be a relief to the post. Those I send you will enable our neighbors to judge whether Freneau is likely to answer their expectation. I have not given in Colo. Bell's list of subscribers, because I do not know whether the post from Richmd. to Staunton is yet commenced. I observe that one fourth of the annual price is to be paid at the end of the first quarter. Consequently they may as well send it on at once.—This city is really in distress from the daily fires happening in it. For three or four weeks past they have scarcely been 24. hours without one. While writing the present I have been called off by a cry of fire. Nobody doubts it to be the work of some incendiary, and nobody knows but it will fall on himself next. There are constant and increased patroles, but as yet to no effect. You will see by the papers that the revolution of France has wound up gloriously.—We are in hourly expectation of Stratton whom we know to have sailed for this place. Maria is well and joins me in affection to you all. Adieu, My dear Sir, yours sincerely, TH: JEFFERSON

RC (DLC); addressed "Thomas Mann Randolph junr. esq. at Monticello. by the Richmond post"; franked.

Thomas Bell's LIST OF SUBSCRIBERS is

in Bell to TJ, 16 Mch. 1792, printed as Document VIII in Editorial Note and group of documents on Jefferson, Freneau, and the founding of the *National Gazette*, at 4 Aug. 1791.

To the Commissioners of the Federal District

GENTLEMEN   Philadelphia Nov. 21. 1791.

A Mr. Blodget has a scheme in contemplation for purchasing and *building* a whole street in the new city, and any one of them which you may think best. The magnitude of the proposition occasioned it to be little attended to in the beginning. However, great as it is, it is believed by good judges to be practicable. It may not be amiss therefore to be ready for it. The street most desireable to be built up at once, we suppose to be the broad one (the avenue) leading from the President's house to the Capitol. To prepare the squares adjoining to that, on both sides, in the first place, can do no harm: because if Mr. Blodget's scheme does not take effect, still it is part of a work done, which was to be done: if his scheme takes effect, you will be in readiness for him, which would be desireable. The President therefore desires me to suggest to you the beginning at once on that avenue, and when all the squares on that shall be laid off, they may go on laying off the rest of the squares between that and the river, from Georgetown to the Eastern branch, according to an idea he has suggested to you in a letter not long since. This however is but a suggestion for the good of the undertaking, on which you will decide as you think proper. I have the honour to be Gentlemen your mo. obedt. & mo. hble servt, TH: JEFFERSON

PrC (DLC); at foot of text: "Messrs. Johnson, Stewart & Carrol." FC (DNA: RG 360, DL). Tr (DNA: RG 42, DCLB).

The President had suggested that the lots between the BROAD ONE (later Pennsylvania Ave.) and the Potomac be laid out in a letter to one of the commissioners the previous day. Washington attributed the suggestion for assigning priority to that area to "intelligent and well informed men, now in this City, who are friends to the measure" (George Washington to David Stuart, 20 Nov. 1791, in Fitzpatrick, *Writings*, XXXI, 442). It is likely that Samuel BLODGET was one of them (See Commissioners of the Federal District to TJ, 10 Dec. 1791). Actually, TJ had "repeated" this suggestion to Washington in his letter of 6 Nov. 1791.

From Sharp Delany

SIR   Customhouse Philada 21st Nov. 1791

I was not in the Office when your Note of this day came to hand.— I would wish therefore to advise You, that by Law when an Owner or Master clearing out a Vessell demands a Clearance without a specification of the Cargo it runs as follows—"Goods Wares and Merchandize as per Manifest filed in this Office,"—otherwise every article is included in the Clearance. The above information may perhaps be necessary. At least my duty and the respect I owe you will excuse this trouble.—I am Sir with great respect your Obedient humble Servt,   SHARP DELANY

RC (DLC); endorsed by TJ as received 21 Nov. 1791 and so recorded in SJL. TJ's note to Delany, the collector of customs at Philadelphia, is not recorded in SJL and has not been found.

To Andrew Ellicott

Dear Sir   Philadelphia Nov. 21. 1791.

It is excessively desireable that an extensive sale of lots in Washington should take place as soon as possible. It has been recommended to the Commissioners to have all the squares adjacent to the avenue from the President's house to the Capitol, on both sides, and from thence to the river, through the whole breadth of the ground between Rock creek and the Eastern branch, first laid off. The object of the present is to ask your *private* opinion of the earliest time at which this portion of the work can be compleated? Which I will beg the favor of you to communicate to me by letter. In order that the sale may not be delayed by the engraving, it is hoped that by communicating what is executed from time to time, the engraver may nearly keep pace with you.—I am with great esteem Dear Sir your most obedt servt,   TH: JEFFERSON

PrC (DLC). FC (DNA: RG 59, DL).

To Lafayette

My dear Sir   Philadelphia Nov. 21. 1791.

Mr. Trumbull proposing to have his paintings of the principal actions of the American war engraved, by subscription, and supposing that some sets may be subscribed for in France, knows too well the value of your patronage there not to be ambitious of obtaining it. But he knows so little his own value, and your sense of it, as to believe that my recommendations to you may be of service to him. You know him my dear friend, the subjects he treats, and his manner of treating them, and this will ensure your services to him, in that way and to that extent, which your position will permit. This is all he and I ask, assuring you we wish you to stop exactly where it would be painful, or awkward, or improper for you to go further. God bless you my dear friend, and prosper those endeavors about which I never write to you because it would interrupt them, but for the success of which, and for your own happiness no body prays more sincerely than Your affectionate friend & servt,

Th: Jefferson

PrC (DLC).

From William Short

Dear Sir   Paris Nov. 21. 1791

The last letter which I have had the honor of recieving from you was dated July 28. Those written by the Secretary of the treasury Sep. 2. and Oct. 3. have been recieved. The newspapers of this place say that succours of men were sent from the U. S. to S. Domingo immediately on the deputies from that island arriving there. The account is said to be received by a commercial house at Havre in a letter from Philadelphia. Since the publication of this article I have been repeatedly applied to for information respecting it. I have been obliged always to answer that I had recieved no letters from America since the arrival of their deputies there; which I learned through foreign newspapers. I observed also that as to the disposition of the U. S. to succour their allies there could be no doubt, that only volunteers however could be sent out of the country and of course that immediate assistance of that sort must be considered as precarious, not depending on the will of government. There is such a disposition here to believe that troops have been sent agreeably to the Newspaper account that few doubts are entertained respecting it. I am exceedingly sorry not to be able to reduce this matter to some kind of certainty. The last letter from the Secretary of the treasury although of a date sufficiently recent says nothing of it of course.

The last accounts recieved here from S. Domingo are of the 9th. of October. It appears from them that the troops and armed citizens though nearly exhausted by fatigue had continued superior in force to the slaves, many of whom were disposed to submit. The colonial committee are to make their report on the subject of these disturbances the 1st. of next month. The merchants and colonists unite in accusing the society *des Amis des noirs*, and they on the contrary accuse the colonial committee of the late assembly and the ministry, and add the cruel treatment of the slaves by the colonists.

It is said also that alarming accounts have been just recieved of disorders prevailing in some of the other French islands, not between master and slave but between the different parties of the white inhabitants. The principal cause of all these disturbances is probably the inadequacy of Government to punish turbulent spirits and of course the impunity with which crimes have been for some time past committed there. I do not find that the suspicions mentioned to you in my last as being entertained by some people here gain ground. I have not omitted proper opportunities of touching on the subject as stated in your letter of July 28. page 4th. and 5th. A milder and more willing ear is given to such insinuations of course under present circumstances. Until a government shall be established here however or something which may have the force of government, everything of the sort must be vain and even useless.

Nothing decisive has as yet taken place with respect to the threats of the Dey of Algiers towards this country as mentioned in my last. One of his demands has been already complied with, the restitution of some Algerine slaves confined at Genoa. The French minister has procured their liberty and sent them on board of a vessel freighted for the purpose, to Algiers.

The Dey seems disposed also to quarrel with Sweden and threatens, without giving any reason for it, to order the capture of the vessels of that nation after the expiration of a short term which he has prescribed. I know not what will be the issue.

I have sent you under a blank cover by the way of Havre several letters received from Algiers by the way of Marseilles.

Since my last in proportion as answers have been recieved to the King's notification from the rest of the European powers they have been communicated to the assembly by M. de Lessart who has the Portefeuille of foreign affairs. Russia and Sweden have not yet answered. The latter refused to receive the notification under pretence of the King's want of liberty. Orders have been sent to the French chargé des affaires to leave Stockholm if the court persist longer in the refusal. The event is not yet known.

It is certain that Russia and Sweden desire the fulfillment of the convention of Pilnitz which is considered as void by the principal of those who signed it. They have entered into a new alliance, all the articles are not yet public. It is supposed it is connected with the affairs of France, and believed that Russia subsidizes Sweden and guarantees the present form of government of that country. This will be soon known with more certainty as the ratification is daily expected from Petersburg.

In the meantime the Princes have a Minister residing at Stockholm who is publicly acknowledged there in that character. They have received also very lately plentiful supplies of money insomuch as to have refused a loan of a million of livres lately offered to them. They have fixed the pay of their followers, officers and soldiers and since their late supplies (supposed to be from Russia) it has been regularly recieved. Some private soldiers of the French army, though in small numbers, have gone to join their officers. You will see in the papers sent by the way of Havre the letters of the King to his brothers to induce their return. They proceed on the principle of his not being free to exercise his will and of course will pay no attention to any act of his which they consider as forced on him by those who surround him.

He has lately negatived by his veto a law passed against the emigrants and particularly severe against the Princes. This is the first time the veto has been exercised and is considered by all here as a proof of his liberty. The assembly submitted to it with patience because they wished to have from the Throne such an attestation of the free exercise of Royal will. It is not yet known what the Princes and their adherents will alledge in future. But as it is certain their opposition is not from mere personal attachment to the King, they will unquestionably continue it notwithstanding his orders and even entreaties to the contrary.

The King is now forming his guard, which is to consist of twelve hundred infantry and six hundred cavalry. They will be ready for the beginning of the next year. An incident which has lately taken place in his appartment renders this circumstance desirable. One of the corporals of the national guard taking it into his head that the

King intends again to escape from Paris ordered the sentinel of his appartment not to let him pass after nine o'clock at night and the order was so faithfully executed that the King was stopped in going out as well as those who desired to enter his appartment, so that he was a prisoner for some hours. The sentinel and corporal have been since imprisoned, and I know not whether any or what proceedings will be had in consequence thereof. The friends of the revolution accuse the enemies of it of being the authors of this circumstance in order that it may be still alleged that the King is in captivity notwithstanding the late exercise of the veto. This accusation however is certainly ill founded.

The Minister of foreign affairs is not yet named. Several have been spoken of. It will be probably M. de Lessart and some other person in that case will be put in his place. The Ambassador to London is not yet appointed. M. de Segur, de Moustier and Berthelemi, at present chargé des affaires and Minister Plenipotentiary there, sollicit the place.

The election of the Mayor of Paris has lately come in. The contest lay between M. de la fayette and M. Pethion, a member of the former assembly and one of the chiefs of the party called Republicans. M. de la fayette was absent and many of his friends said he would not accept, which possibly had some influence on the election. There were about ten thousand voters and M. Pethion had a very considerable majority. There are more than 80,000 who have a right to vote at Paris, yet on this as on former occasions only a small part exercised this right, which may be considered as an unaccountable mark of indifference at a time when there is such an appearance of patriotic enthusiasm. The choice of M. Pethion as Mayor and of two or three others of the same party to fill important places in the corporation of Paris, shews that the Parisians are not as hostile to the principles they profess as has been imagined. This disposition must necessarily excite uneasiness and distrust in the breast of the King, whom it is important to tranquilize and attach by that means to the constitution.

I have already mentioned to you Drost's declining to go to America for the present. I am more disposed every day to believe that he entertained doubts himself as to the practicability of his scheme. I find many here who are convinced that his machine cannot answer for money coinage and give good reasons for it.

I have had a good deal of conversation on that subject lately with a friend of Mr. Bolton. He is an enemy however to Drost and of course what he says must be received with caution. I told him that

Drost declining to go for the present left the field open and that I wished Mr. Bolton would submit to you the terms on which he would erect a mint in America, adding at the same time that I had no authority to desire it and therefore that it was simply my wish as an individual. I think you will receive propositions from him, on which you may rely with much more safety than on those made by Drost, as he has already coined considerable sums of copper and is able to answer, I should imagine, for any engagement he may take.

The dye for the diplomatick medal has again failed under the press. It resisted only so as to take the first impression in silver. The chains are ready and waiting only for the medal. It is promised in a month. I have explained to M. de Montmorin and M. de Moustier the causes of the delay. The dyes which I had had lodged at Mr. Grand's were in danger of rusting. I have put them into Dupre's hands to take care of them until this is finished and then they will be all, five in number, sent to you.—I shall leave this place in two or three days for Antwerp and Amsterdam and shall be absent about a month.—I inclose a letter for the Secretary of the treasury, & am, my dear Sir, most sincerely Yours,   W: SHORT

PrC (DLC: Short Papers); at head of text: "No. 91"; at foot of text: "Thomas Jefferson Secretary of State Philadelphia." Tr (DNA: RG 59, DD). Recorded in SJL as received 9 Feb. 1792. Enclosure: Short to Hamilton, 22 Nov. 1791 (printed in Syrett, *Hamilton*, IX, 522-4).

Hamilton's letters to Short of 2 Sep. 1791 and 3 Oct. 1791 are printed in Syrett, *Hamilton*, IX, 158-62, 272. The SUSPICIONS alluded to by Short involved French fears that Great Britain was conspiring to bring about the independence of the French West Indies (Short to TJ, 8 Nov. 1791).

From Fulwar Skipwith

DEAR SIR   Baltimore 21 Novr 1791

Agreeably to your request I have called on Colo. Smith and afforded him all the information which, I am possessed of, respecting the seisure of the Sloop Jane.—I now do myself the pleasure to subjoin the names of the few citizens of the U. States, who at present reside in the french W. Islands.

Say.   Geo. Patterson, St. Pierre M/que from Balto., brother of Mr. Patterson Director of the Bank.

Saml. Hopkins, mercht. Castrée, St. Lucie, a young man of merit, from Balto.—has resided about two years in St. Lucie.

Nathl. Barrell jr.—Fort-Royal M/que from New-Hampshire.

Hollingsworth and Wilson whom I mentioned as Residents of Guadalupe I find have returned to America, and I do not know of or believe that another American of character is to be found in the Island.

Permit me my Dr Sir again to solicit your notice should any office under the Union present itself unfilled and to which my slender worth and talents may fit me, and which may afford some support to one who is most sincerely Yrs, FULWAR SKIPWITH

RC (DNA: RG 59, CD); addressed: "Tho Jefferson Esquire Secretary of State U. States Philadelphia"; endorsed by TJ as received 24 Nov. 1791 and so recorded in SJL; beneath endorsement TJ wrote: "names of Americans residing within his Consulship, in the West Indies."

To the Speaker of the House of Representatives

SIR   Philadelphia Nov. 21. 1791.
I have now the honour to inclose you a Report on the petition of Jacob Isaacs, referred to me at the last session of the late Congress, with instruction to report thereon. The reference was made a week only before the rising of Congress, and as a compliance with it required that seawater should be procured, and experiments be made on it, it was not practicable to make the report to that session. I also inclose a blank permit with a copy of the report printed on the back of it, in order to shew that the proposition I have therein taken the liberty of making is perfectly practicable. I have the honour to be with sentiments of the most perfect esteem & respect, Sir, Your most obedt. & most humble servt,   TH: JEFFERSON

PrC (DLC). At foot of letter: "The Speaker of the H. of Representatives." Tr (DNA: RG 59, SDR). TJ wrote a similar letter to Washington, omitting the explanation of the time required in completing the report and enclosing a blank ship's permit with printed report on verso (RC of letter in Munson-Williams-Proctor Institute; printed report in DNA: RG 59, MLR; endorsed by Lear; other copies of letter: PrC in DLC; Tr in DNA: RG 59, SDC; Tr in DNA: RG 360, DL).

ENCLOSURE

Report on Desalination of Sea Water

Novemr. 21. 1791
The Secretary of state, to whom was referred by the H. of Representatives the petition of Jacob Isaacks of Newport in Rhode island, has examined into

the truth and importance of the allegations therein set forth and makes thereon the following report.

The petitioner sets forth that by various experiments, with considerable labor and expence, he has discovered a method of converting salt water into fresh, in the proportion of 8 parts out of 10. by a process so simple that it may be performed on board of vessels at sea by the common iron Cabouse with small alterations, by the same fire; and in the same time which is used for cooking the ships provisions, and offers to convey to the government of the U.S. a faithful account of his art or secret to be used by or within the U.S. on their giving to him a reward suitable to the importance of the discovery and in the opinion of government adequate to his expences, and the time he has devoted to the bringing it into effect.

In order to ascertain the merit of the petitioner's discovery, it becomes necessary to examine the advances already made in the art of converting salt water into fresh.

Ld. Bacon, to whom the world is indebted for the first germs of so many branches of science, had observed that with a heat sufficient for distillation salt will not rise in vapour, and that salt water distilled is fresh. And it would seem that all mankind might have observed that the earth is supplied with fresh water chiefly by exhalation from the sea, which is in fact an insensible distillation effected by the heat of the sun. Yet this tho' the most obvious, was not the first idea, in the essays for converting salt water into fresh. Filtration was tried in vain, and congelation could be resorted to only in the coldest regions and seasons. In all the earlier trials by distillation some mixture was thought necessary to aid the operation by a partial precipitation of the salt and other foreign matters contained in sea water. Of this kind were the methods of Sr. Richd. Hawkins in the 16th. century, of Glauber, Hauton, and Lister in the 17th. and of Hales, Appleby, Butler, Chapman, Hoffman and Dove in the 18th. Nor was there any thing in these methods worthy noting on the present occasion except the very simple still contrived extempore by capt. Chapman, and made from such materials as are to be found on board every ship great or small. This was a common pot, with a wooden lid of the usual form, in the center of which a hole was bored to receive perpendicularly a short wooden tube made with an inch and half auger, which perpendicular tube received at it's top and at an acute angle another tube of wood also, which descended till it joined a third of pewter made by rolling up a dish and passing it obliquely thro a cask of cold water. With this simple machine he obtained 2 quarts of fresh water an hour, and observed that the expence of fuel would be very trifling, if the still was contrived to stand on the fire along with the ship's boiler.

In 1762. Dr. Lind, proposing to make experiment of several different mixtures, first distilled rain water, which he supposed would be the purest, and then Sea water, without any mixture, which he expected would be the least pure, in order to arrange between these two supposed extremes the degree of merit of the several ingredients he meant to try. To his great surprise as he confesses, the sea water distilled without any mixture was as pure as the rain water. He pursued the discovery and established the fact that a pure and potable fresh water may be obtained from salt water by simple distillation without the aid of any mixture for firing or precipitating it's foreign contents. In 1767. he proposed an extempore still which in fact was Chapman's, only substituting a gun barrel instead of Chapman's pewter tube, and the hand pump of the ship to be cut in two obliquely and joined again at an acute angle instead of Chapman's wooden tubes bored express; or instead of the wooden lid and upright tube he proposed a teakettle (without it's lid or handle) to be joined bottom upwards over the mouth of the pot, by way of still head, and a wooden tube leading from the spout to a gun barrel passing thro a cask of water the whole luted with equal parts of chalk and meal moistened with salt water.

With this apparatus of a pot, teakettle and gun barrel the Dolphin a 20. gun ship in her voyage round the world in 1768. from 56 galls. of sea water, and with 9. lb. of wood and 69. lb. of pit coal made 42. galls. of good fresh water at the rate of 8. galls. an hour. The Dorsetshire, in her passage from Gibraltar to Mahon made 19. quarts of pure water in 4. hours with 10 lb. of wood. And the Slambal in 1773. between Bombay and Bengal with the hand pump, gun barrel and a pot of 6. galls. of sea water made 10 quarts of fresh water in 3. hours.

In 1771. Dr. Irving putting together Lind's idea of distilling without a mixture, Chapman's still, and Dr. Franklin's method of cooling by evaporation, obtained a premium of £5000. from the British parliament. He wet his tube constantly with a mop instead of passing it through a cask of water. He enlarged it's bore also in order to give a freer passage to the vapour and thereby increase it's quantity by lessening the resistance or pressure on the evaporating surface. This last improvement was his own. It doubtless contributed to the success of his process: and we may suppose the enlargement of the tube to be useful to that point at which the central parts of the vapour passing thro it would begin to escape condensation.[1] Ld. Mulgrave used his method in his voyage towards the North Pole in 1773. making from 34. to 40. gallons of fresh water a day, without any great addition of fuel as he says.

M. de Bougainville in his voyage round the world used very succesfully a still which had been contrived in 1763 by Poyssonier, so as to guard against the water being thrown over from the boiler into the pipes by the agitation of the ship, in which one singularity was that the furnace or fire box was in the middle of the boiler so that the water surrounded it in contact. This still however was expensive and occupied much room.

Such were the advances already made in the art of obtaining fresh from salt water when Mr. Isaacks the petitioner suggested his discovery.

As the merit of this could be ascertained by experiment only the Secretary of state asked the favor of Mr. Rittenhouse President of the Amer. Ph. soc. of Dr. Wistar professor of Chemistry [in the college of Philadelphia,] and Doctor Hutchinson professor of chemistry in the University be present at the experiments. Mr. Isaacks fixed the pot of a small Cabouse, with a tin cap, and strait tube of tin passing obliquely through a cask of cold water. He made use of a mixture the composition of which he did not explain and from 24. pints of sea water taken up about 3. miles out of the capes of Delaware at flood tide he distilled 22. pints of fresh water in 4. hours with 20. lb. of seasoned pine which was a little wetted by having lain in the rain.

In a 2d experiment of the 21st. of March performed in a furnace and 5. gallon still at the College, from 32. pints of sea-water he drew 31. pints of fresh water in 7. H. 24. M. with 51 lb. of hiccory which had been cut about 6. months. In order to decide whether Mr. Isaacks mixture contributed in any and what degree to the success of the operation, it was thought proper to repeat his experiment under the same circumstances exactly, except the omission of the mixture. Accordingly on the next day the same quantity of sea water was put into the same still, the same furnace was used and fuel from the same parcel. It yielded as his had done 31. pints of fresh water, in 11' more of time and with 10. lb. less of wood.

On the 24th. of March Mr. Isaacks performed a 3d. experiment. For this, a common iron pot of 3 1/2 galls. was fixed in brickwork, and the flue from the hearth wound once round the pot spirally, and then passed off up a chimney. The cap was of tin and a straight tin tube of about 2. I. diam. passing obliquely through a barrel of water served instead of a worm. From 16. pints of sea-water he drew off 15. pints of fresh water in 2 H. 55' with 3 lb. of dry hiccory and 8 lb. of seasoned pine. This experiment was also repeated the next day, with the same apparatus, and fuel from the same parcels, but without the mixture. 16. pints of sea water yeilded in like manner 15. pints of fresh in 1' more of time and with 1/2 lb. less of wood. On the whole it was evident that Mr. Isaacks mixture produced no advantage either in the process or result of the distillation.

The distilled water in all these instances was found on experiment to be as pure as the best pump water of the city: it's taste indeed was not as agreeable; but it was not such as to produce any disgust. In fact we drink in common life in many places and under many circumstances and almost always at sea a worse tasted, and probably a less wholesome water.[2]

The obtaining fresh from salt water was for ages considered as an important desideratum for the use of Navigators. The process for doing this by simple distillation is so efficacious, the erecting an extempore still with such utensils as are found on board of every ship is so practicable, as to authorize the assertion that this desideratum is satisfied to a very useful degree. But tho' this has been done for upwards of 30. years, tho it's reality has been established by the actual experience of several vessels which have had recourse to it, yet neither the fact nor the process is known to the mass of seamen, to whom it would be the most useful, and for whom it was principally wanted. The Secretary of state is therefore of opinion that, since the subject has now been brought under observation, it should be made the occasion of disseminating it's knowlege generally and effectually among the sea-faring citizens of the U.S. The following is one of the many methods which might be proposed for doing this. Let the Clearance for every vessel sailing from the ports of the U.S. be printed on a paper on the back whereof shall be a printed account of the essays which have been made for obtaining fresh from salt water, mentioning shortly those which have been unsuccesful, and more fully those which have succeeded; describing the methods which have been found to answer for constructing extempore stills of such implements as are generally on board of every vessel, with a recommendation, in all cases where they shall have occasion to resort to this expedient for obtaining water, to publish the result of their trial in some gazette on their return to the U.S. or to communicate it for publication to the office of the Secretary of state in order that others may, by their success be encoraged to make similar trials, and may be benefited by any improvements or new ideas which may occur to them in practice.

MSS (MHi and DLC); the MS from MHi comprises the entire report with the exception of the long, last paragraph, which was carefully penned by TJ at a different time and dated by a clerk as 21 Nov. 1791. The report was probably begun in the spring of 1791 after much research on the subject, as the five pages of references to experiments and sources attest (see note 2 below). Tr (DNA: RG 59, SDR). PrC of Tr (DLC).

The history of this report is discussed in Editorial Note and group of documents on experiments in desalination of sea water to test the claims of Jacob Isaacks, at 26 Mch. 1791. TJ sent a printed copy of his report to Isaacks on 23 Nov. 1791 (letter printed as Document xi).

Upon receipt of the report, the House of Representatives read and tabled it on 22 Nov. 1791, thereby signifying its agreement with TJ's assessment of Isaack's lack of scientific originality. Then on 8 May 1792 it passed a resolution in words almost identical to the last sentence of the report instructing the Secretary of the Treasury to provide U.S. collectors with printed clearance forms, one side of which should contain descriptions of desalination methods (JHR, I, 459, 604-5). This resolution was immediately approved by the Senate and the President (JS, I, 443, 444).

¹ The previous two sentences were copied and inserted by TJ from a note he wrote on the verso of an undated memorandum from Caspar Wistar (RC in MHi).
² The MS at MHi ends here, but is followed by five pages of notes on related sources and experiments in TJ's hand. Although it is not among those listed, TJ probably made use of Caspar Wistar's "Experiments and Observations on Evaporation in Cold Air," a paper read before the American Philosophical Society in September 1787 and printed in the Society's *Transactions* in 1793. TJ's undated detailed notes on this experiment are in MHi, docketed by him: "Evaporation by Dr. Wistar."

From David Humphreys

Lisbon, 22 Nov. 1791. Since his last letter of 28 Oct. he has received certain information that the Dey of Algiers has declared war on Sweden. A Swedish ship which was loading here for a Mediterranean voyage has consequently been unloaded.—Public business "is often done slowly in this Country." He had to write four or five notes or memoires and wait more than three months before he finally succeeded in persuading the Portuguese government to validate Pintard's commission as consul at Madeira.—Street, the consul at Fayal, has revealed that he wishes to become consul at Lisbon. He is personally unacquainted with Street but is slightly familiar with Street's cousin, Mr. Street D'Arriaga, a wealthy and respectable gentleman in Lisbon whose ample fortune will probably be inherited by Street. Since "many things in business are effected in this Country by influence and connections," there is some reason to consider Street's pretensions. He must add, however, that he believes consular business is well handled presently by Messrs. Dohrman & Harrison.—There is more need for a consul at Oporto where a greater number of vessels from America than usual has arrived this year. He encloses a letter from Dominick Browne, the French consul in Oporto, requesting the office of vice-consul for his son, Bernard Clamouse Browne. He recommends this appointment because upon careful investigation he finds that the elder Browne has been invariably helpful to Americans and that the son is a promising young man who is well suited to hold consular office. "But in case of that appointment, it may be necessary to signify to this Government officially, that the Government of the U.S. grants permission to their Citizens to act in a Consular capacity for her Most Faithful Majesty: as M. de Pinto informed me, without such permission it would be improper to accord a similar indulgence here. I assured him that practice was permitted by the U. S. in favour of other nations; and that I was persuaded there could be no objections to prevent the Portuguese Government from employing Citizens of the U. S. in a Consular character: especially as we are sincerely disposed to give every facility to promote an extensive and beneficial intercourse between the two Nations."—Thomas Barclay has engaged passage to Morocco and announced his coming in letters to the governor of Tangier and the secretary of the Emperor. With the assistance of the secretary of the late Portuguese embassy in Morocco, Barclay has purchased everything he thinks he may need. He encloses Barclay's receipt for 32,175 current guilders, which represents the total of his authorized expenditure in this business. He touched not a farthing of this sum. He gave draughts for this amount of money to Willink, Van Staphorst & Hubbard, and Barclay received the money from John Bulkeley & Son, "my Bankers here." He asks TJ to acknowledge receipt of the voucher as soon as possible, promises to send a duplicate with his next letter, and states that he will retain a third copy in case any are lost.—He encloses "several public Papers" received since the date of his last letter.

RC (DNA: RG 59, DD); 6 p.; at head of text: "(No. 39)"; at foot of text: "The Secretary of State"; endorsed by TJ as received 17 Mch. 1792 and so recorded in SJL. Enclosures: Dominick Browne to Humphreys, 1 Oct. 1791; and Receipt from Barclay, 10 Nov. 1791. Tr (same).

From La Rochefoucauld

[Paris, 22 Novembre 1791]

Je ne m'arrêterai pas, Monsieur, à excuser mon long Silence. Vous avez, malgré ma taciturnité, rendu justice à mes regrets d'y avoir été condamné par l'assiduité du travail qui étoit mon devoir, et vous avez été persuadé que cette cause impérieuse étoit la Seule qui pût me priver de me rappeller moi même à votre Souvenir. Voilà notre Constitution terminée, mais en quittant les fonctions Législatives, j'ai été appellé à celles d'Administrateur du Département de Paris, et je m'y livre avec zèle. Elles exigent dans ce moment encore une grande Suite, parce que le Conseil est assemblé pour sa session annuelle, et que le Directoire marche toujours, mais cette session ne dure qu'un mois, et, comme après sa cloture, il ne me restera, en qualité [. . .][1] bonne volonté au Directoire, je Serai un peu [. . .][1] mes amis, et j'en profiterai quelquefois pour causer avec vous. Je le ferai même très brievement aujourd'hui, parce que j'ai de l'occupation encore, et parce que je veux envoier ma lettre à M. Short avant son départ.

Il vous a tenu au courant de notre état; nous avons eu, depuis votre départ, bien des crises, nos travaux ont éprouvé mille obstacles produits par des causes bien differentes; La fermentation révolutionnaire a été prolongée par des hommes bien coupables, qui ont cru Servir leurs interêts particuliers en provoquant l'anarchie, et qui ont pris le masque du patriotisme, comme le plus propre à seconder leurs desseins criminels; ces hommes ont été démasqués, mais ils n'ont été punis que par l'opinion publique, et d'autres hommes, non moins coup[ables . . .]² leurs vols, mais on commence à les démasq[uer.]

Cependant, au milieu de ces agitations, l'esprit National se montre pour vouloir l'ordre et le rétablissement de la paix, et cette volonté triomphera de toutes les especes de factieux.

J'ai bien regretté que nous aions été détournés par des interêts ou préjugés mercantiles de contracter avec les Etats Unis des liaisons que la nature des choses Sembloit amener naturellement; mais nous nous éclairerons aussi sur ce point, et nos deux pais s'uniront par un attrait réciproque.

M. de la fayette a rempli l'engagement qu'il avoit pris; à la fin de l'Assemblée Constituante, il a quitté sa place, il n'en a voulu accepter aucune; il est actuellement, et pour tout l'hiver, à Chavaniac, et vous pouvez dire à M. Washington que son éleve, constamment digne de son amitié, après [. . .]² et après avoir été honoré de tous les genres [. . .]² de l'estime méritée de tous les amis de la Liberté, de la Constitution et des Loix.

Je ne finirai pas sans vous remercier des excellens *Reports* que vous avez bien voulu m'envoier; le tems me manque pour vous en parler plus au long. Ma famille, que j'ai quitté ces jours-ci à la campagne, vous dit mille choses. Nous voudrions bien vous tenir encore ici, mais votre Patrie a besoin de vous. Adieu, Monsieur, soiez toujours bien persuadé, je vous prie, du bien sincere attachement dont je suis pénétré pour vous.   LA ROCHEFOUCAULD

RC (DLC); mutilated, so that some words are lost at the top of pages 2, 3, and 4, including the dateline; endorsed by TJ as received 9 Feb. 1792 and so recorded in SJL, where the place and date of the letter are established.

¹ Large tear at top of first page has obliterated several words on the verso.
² A similar, larger tear at top of second page has obliterated several words from both recto and verso.

To Tobias Lear

[22 Nov. 1791]

Th: Jefferson presents his compliments to Mr. Lear and informs him he has recieved from Mr. Short a statement of the cost of the

Champagne imported this year for the President, to wit 1680. livres. He sends him a statement of the whole, exact, except of the proceeds of the sterling money at Paris, which Mr. Short has not yet informed him of. He thought he should have had money enough in Mr. Short's hands to have answered the present demand of 30. dozen bottles of Champagne for the President: but on revising his accounts with Mr. Short, he finds himself mistaken. This article, with the under-valuation on the former Champagne, will probably be something upwards of 2000 livres. If Mr. Lear therefore can furnish a bill for that it will probably cover the two demands: or rather a bill on Amsterdam for 800. florins, as bills on Paris are perillous on account of the Assignats.

RC (Estate of Charles William Whipple, New York, 1945); undated; addressed: "Mr. Lear"; endorsed: "From Mr. Jefferson with acct. of Wine 22d Nov. 1791." PrC (MHi). Enclosed in RC was TJ's calculation of the account:
"1790. 1791. Th: Jefferson's disbursements for the wines of the President.

		₶
Frontignan from Dr. Lambert. 2 cases.		
G.W. No. 23.	120.bottles	155– 0
carriage from Frontignan to Bordeaux		44–11
Sauterne from Mde. de Luz-Saluce.		
7 cases	350.bottles	525– 0
packages for do.		28– 0
Bordeaux de la Fite. from Mr. Fenwick.		
5 cases.	240.bottles	720– 0
charges on do.		30– 0
his charges for postage of lres. on the subject.one half		10– 5
do. for entries, shipping, commission &c		195– 8
Freight of all the above from Bordeaux to Charleston to		
Capt. Tilden ½.		88– 0
Champagne from M. d'Orsai. 4. hampers. 45 l.bottles. to		
Mr. Short		1680– 0
transportn. & other charges from Paris to Havre, to		
do. for La Motte		226–18
freight of do. from Havre to Philada. 71. cub. feet @		
1/ sterl.		84–10
		3787–12

Credit
By Warder's excha. on Warder & co. London.£131–5 sterl.
the proceeds in livres not yet known.
Note. No account of the duties on the wines from Bordeaux payable in the U.S. has been ever presented to Th: J. Those on the Champagne were paid here by Mr. Lear."

The bill for CHAMPAGNE FOR THE PRES-IDENT was transmitted in William Short to TJ, 17 July 1791, which TJ had received on 22 Oct. 1791. See also Short to TJ, 6 Oct. 1791.

On Nov. 23 TJ sent a receipt to Lear for Mordecai Lewis' bill for "800 currt. gilders on account of wine" payable to Van Staphorst & Hubbard (RC from Mrs. Henry M. Sage, Albany, N.Y., 1954).

From Thomas Barclay

Lisbon, 23 Nov. 1791. He wrote on the 20th that he had hired a vessel for Tangier. The weather has been very boisterous but he hopes to sail for Tangier in five or six days. Yesterday he received the enclosed letter from Francis Chiappe, who is on his way to Madrid with peace propositions from the Emperor. He hopes to meet Chiappe in Tangier and will prolong his stay there to do so.

RC (DNA: RG 59, CD); 2 p.; endorsed by TJ as received 4 Feb. 1792 and so recorded in SJL. Enclosure not found.

To Alexander Donald

DEAR SIR   Philadelphia [Nov. 23. 1791.]

I recieved duly with yo[ur favor Lackington's ca]talogue, and now in consequence thereof[, seize a moment by] Mr. Morris to send you the inclosed [list, with a prayer that] you will send it to Lackington, re[ceive the books, and forward] them to me at this place. He will [pack them. The amount] would be about 12 guineas, were he to [have the whole un]sold. But it has usually happened, e[ven when I was at] Paris, that before his catalogue could [get to me, and my let]ter in answer to him, one half of what [I wanted would be] gone. Therefore I do not know what lesser [amount they] will come to; but whatever it is I will a[sk the favor of you] to pay it for me, and the moment I know [the sum I will] either replace it to Mr. Brown, or remit you [a bill at your] option.—You will be surprised to be told [that at the late] election of a Governor of Virginia, where the [candidates were] Colo. H. Lee, Colo. Harvie, Genl. Wood, that Mr. Ha[rvie had but] 20. odd votes, Wood 50. odd, and Colo. Lee a majority of the w[hole.] Mr. Harvie's friends had believed there was not the leas[t doubt] of his election.—Our funds here are become stationary; [even] the scrip. Imagination is at work to create some new paper [to] indulge the gamblers with as long as it may last, and so from t[ime] to time to find some new aliment for that precious spirit.—[We] have had two succesful expeditions [against the Indians] this summer, in which they have lost [about 150. and we 4 or] 5. These have proved the superiority [of militia for Indian] expeditions.—Mr. Hammond has [arrived here,[1] and pro]duced his credentials of Minister [plenipotentiary. A] minister in exchange will immed[iately be sent to] London.—I am with great & sincere [attachment] Your friend,   TH: JEFFERSON

PrC (DLC: TJ Papers, 69:11951-2); mutilated, so that line endings on right margins of both pages are lost; missing portions supplied from Tr (DLC: TJ Papers, 67:11681), in 19th century hand (incomplete, so that missing words for the end of text have been conjecturally supplied after point noted in note 1 below).

Donald's FAVOR was dated 6 July 1791 and had arrived 23 Aug. 1791.

[1] Remainder of transcript missing from this point.

ENCLOSURE

Lackington's Catalogue for 1792.

£ s d		
0– 4–6	859.	Keith's hist. of the Brit. plantns. in Virga. with maps neat. gilt. scarce. 4to.
3– 0–0	1843.	Hume's H. of Eng. 8.v. new. in a curious & very elegt. bindg. inlaid wth. maroc. silk headbands, registers &c. 8.V. 8vo. 1790[1]
2–0	2147.	Locke's Collection of pieces. good copy. 8vo.
2–6	2149.	Locke's familr. lres h. b. uncut. 1737. 8vo.
2–3	2150.	Locke's posthumous works. neat. 8vo.
6–3	2253.	Matthews's voyage to Sierra Leone. new. boards. 8vo. 91.[2]
–6	3944.	Locke on tolern. 12mo. 1790
1–0	3957.	Locke on coins. 12mo.
9–0	4421.	Plut's li. 7.v. cuts. h.b. not uniform. 12mo. 1762.
6–6	4795.	Sparman's voyage. 2.v. 12mo. new in calf. elgly. gilt. 89.
1– 6–	6762.	Eucl's elem. in Arabic. fair. fol. Rom. 1594.
19–6	6763.	Euclidis elementa. Gr. Lat. Gregorii. nited. fol. 1703.
12–0	7494.	Newton's Matheml. princ. of Nat. ph. by Motte. 2.v. 8vo. 1729. or 7495. id. or 18007. id.
6–6	9137.	Dacosta's Conchology. 8vo.[3]
4–6	11334.	Elemens de la langue Russe. 8vo. or 12mo. Petsbg 1768.
1–6	11383.	Grammar in the Russn. language. 8vo. or 12mo. 1777
4–3	11392.	Hadley on the dialect of Indostan. 8vo. or 12mo.
1–6	11532.	Privileges of Englishmen in Portugal. 8vo. 12mo. 1736.
3–6	11840	Photii epistolae. Gr. Lat. fol. Lond. 1651.
⟨3–0	12407.	*Aristeae historia* LXXII *interpretation. Gr. Lat. 8vo.*⟩[4]
1–6	12416.	Athenagorae opera. Gr. Lat. 12mo. Ox. 1682.
2–6	12425.	Antoninus. Gr. Lat. Foul. 12mo. 1744.
1–3	12494.	Eutropius. Gr. Lat. 12mo.[5]
10–0	12859.	Maupertius. oeuvres de. 4. torn. 8vo. Lyon. 1756.
2–0	12950.	Noticias de las inquisitiones de Españe y Portugal 8vo
1–11–6	12987.	Bibliotheque des sciences et des beaux arts from the begg. Jan. 1754. to Sep. 1769. 63.v. 12mo.
1–6	14146.	Origenis dial. contre Marcionitas. Gr. Lat. 4to. 1674.
3–	14150.	Origene contre Celse. par Bouhereau. 4to. 1700
1–6	14152.	Polycarpii et Ignatii epistolae. Gr. Lat. 4to. Ox. 1644

4–0	16143.	Common prayer in Manks language 8vo. 1775.
2–3	16177.	Grabe's Spicilegium SS. patrum. 2.V. 8vo. Gr. Lat.[6]
10–6	17432.	Bible in Irish. 12mo. Lond. 1690.
6	17512.	Virgilius Evangelians. 12mo. 1769.
2–6	17818.	Bancroft's Guiane. 8vo.
2–6	18160.	Relation of the Nile 8vo. 1791.
1– 1–0	18344.	Acta Eruditorum Lipsiensa. ab 1682. ad 1740. 7.v. 4to.

MS (DLC: TJ Papers, 80:13877). TJ's retained list, given above, contains fuller titles and descriptions, as well as catalogue numbers and prices; next to the caption he added: "Wrote to A. Donald Nov. 23. 91." The list he actually enclosed, headed: "Books for Th: Jefferson from Lackington's catalogue for 1792." contained brief titles, together with catalogue numbers and prices; at the foot of the list he added: "where the particular number here mentioned, happens to be sold, if there should be another copy of the same book at nearly the same price, Mr. Lackington is desired to send it." The list bears marks indicating which books were and were not sent (see list and textual notes). On the verso, the list is addressed, in an unidentified hand, to Messrs. Donald & Burton at their London address; when the list was returned to TJ, perhaps with Donald's letter of 15 Feb. 1792 transmitting Lackington's bill, TJ endorsed it and added: "bot of Lackington" (MS in same, 80:13880).

[1] On copy sent to Donald TJ added: "or 1841. Hume's £2-14.—or 1842. Hume's £3." On bill from Lackington, the catalogue number is 1842 and TJ added: "Russia leather."
[2] 2253 and the following items were not sent and are not listed on Lackington's bill: 3957, 4421, 6763, 7494, 11334, 11383, 11392, 11532, 11840, 12416, 12950, 14146, 14152, 16177, 17818, 18344.
[3] 9137 was replaced by no. 7000 on Lackington's bill and the price changed to 7-3.
[4] This lined out entry is not on the copy sent to Donald nor on Lackington's bill.
[5] 12494 is listed on Lackington's bill as Delectus, but TJ crossed it out and gave title as above, adding "et Delectus."
[6] 16177 is crossed out on the list sent to Donald and does not appear on Lackington's bill, but it is included in Sowerby (no. 1592) and presumably was received at another time.

To William Short

DEAR SIR   Philadelphia Nov. 24. 1791.

My last to you was of Aug. 29. acknowledging the reciept of your Nos. 67. 68. 69. 70. 71. and informing you I was about setting out to Virginia, and should not again write to you till my return. Only one vessel has sailed from hence to Havre since my return and my notice of her departure was so short that I could not avail myself of it. Your Nos. 72. 73. 74. 75. 78. came here during my absence, and 79. 80. were recd. Oct. 28. The numbers 76. and 77. seem to be missing.

You mention that Drost wishes the devices of our money to be sent to him, that he may engrave them there. This cannot be done, because not yet decided on. The devices will be fixed by the law which shall establish the mint. M. de Ternant tells me he has no instructions to propose to us the negociation of a commercial treaty, and that he does not expect any. I wish it were possible to draw that negociation to this place.—In your letter of July 24. is the following paragraph. 'It is published in the English newspapers that war is inevitable between the U.S. and Spain, and that preparations are making for it on both sides. M. de Montmorin asked me how the business stood at present, and seemed somewhat surprised at my telling him that I knew nothing later than what I had formerly mentioned to him.—I have in more than one instance experienced the inconvenience of being without information. In this it is disagreeable, as it may have the appearance with M. de Montmorin, of my having something to conceal from him, which not being the case it would be wrong that he should be allowed to take up such an idea.—I observed that I did not suppose there was any new circumstance, as you had not informed me of it.'—Your observation was certainly just. It would be an Augean task for me to go through the London newspapers and formally contradict all their lies, even those relating to America. On our side, there have been certainly no preparations for war against Spain, nor have I heard of any on their part but *in the London newspapers*. As to the progress of the negociation, I know nothing of it but from you; having never had a letter from Mr. Carmichael on the subject. Our best newspapers are sent you from my office, with scrupulous exactness, by every vessel sailing to Havre, or any other convenient port of France. On these I rely for giving you information of all the facts possessed by the public; and as to those not possessed by them, I think there has not been a single instance of my leaving you uninformed of any of them which related to the matters under your charge.—In Freneau's paper of the 21st. inst. you will see a small essay on population and emigration, which I think it would be well if the newswriters of Paris would translate and insert in their papers. The sentiments are too just not to make impression.

Some proceedings of the assembly of St. Domingo have lately taken place, which it is necessary for me to state to you exactly that you may be able to do the same to M. de Montmorin. When the insurrection of their Negroes assumed a very threatening appearance the assembly sent a deputy here to ask assistance of military stores and provisions. He addressed himself to M. de Ternant, who (the President being then in Virginia, as I was also) applied to the Secretaries of the Treasury and at war. They furnished 1000. stand of arms, other military stores, and placed 40,000. dollars in the Treasury subject to the order of M. de Ternant, to be laid out in provisions, or otherwise, as he should think best. He sent the arms and other military stores; but the want of provisions did not seem so instantaneous, as to render it necessary, in his opinion, to send any at that time. Before the vessel arrived in St. Domingo, the assembly, further urged by the appearance of danger, sent two deputies more, with larger demands; viz 8000. fusils and bayonets, 2000 mousquetons, 3000 pistols, 3000 sabres, 24000 barrels of flour, 400,000₶ worth of Indian meal, rice, peas and hay, and a large quantity of plank, &c. to repair the buildings destroyed. They applied to M. de Ternant, and then, with his consent, to me; he and I having previously had a conversation on the subject. They proposed to me 1. that we should supply those wants from the money we owed France: or 2. for bills of exchange which they were authorised to draw on a particular fund in France: or 3. that we would guarantee their bills, in which case they could dispose of them to merchants, and buy the necessaries themselves. I convinced them the two latter alternatives were beyond the powers of the Executive, and the 1st. could only be done with the consent of the Minister of France. In the course of our conversation I expressed to them our sincere attachment to France and all it's dominions, and most especially to them who were our neighbors, and whose interests had some common points of union with ours, in matters of commerce: that we wished therefore to render them every service they needed; but that we could not do it in any way disagreeable to France: that they must be sensible that M. de Ternant might apprehend that jealousy would be excited by their addressing themselves directly to foreign powers, and therefore that a concert with him in their applications to us was essential. The subject of independence and their views towards it having been stated in the public papers, this led our conversation to it; and I must say they appeared as far from these views as any persons on earth. I expressed to them freely my opinion that such an object was neither desireable on their part nor attainable: that as to ourselves there was one case which would be peculiarly alarming to us, to wit, were there a danger of their falling under any other power: that we conceived it to be strongly our interests that they should retain their connection with the mother country: that we had a common interest with them in furnishing them the necessaries of life in exchange for sugar and coffee for our own consumption, but that I thought we might rely on the justice of the mother country towards them, for their obtaining this privilege: and on the whole let them see that nothing was to be done but with the consent of the minister of France. I am convinced myself that their views and their application to us are perfectly innocent; however M. de Ternant, and still more M. de la Forest are jealous. The deputies on the other hand think that M. de Ternant is not sensible enough of their wants. They delivered me sealed letters to the President, and to Congress. That to the President contained only a picture of their distresses and application for relief. That to Congress I know no otherwise than thro' the public papers. The Senate read it and sent it to the Representatives, who read it and have taken no other notice of it. The line of conduct I pursue is to persuade these gentlemen to be contented with such moderate supplies from time to time as will keep them from real distress, and to wait with patience for what would be a surplus till M. de Ternant can receive instructions from France which he has reason to expect within a few weeks: and I encourage the latter gentleman even to go beyond their absolute wants of the moment, so far as to keep them in good humour. He is accordingly proposing to lay out 10,000 dollars for them for the present. It would be ridiculous in the present case to talk about forms. There are situations when form must be dispensed with. A man attacked by assassins will call for help to those nearest him, and will not think himself bound to silence till a magistrate may come to his aid. It would be unwise in the highest degree that the colonists should be disgusted with either France or us: for it might then be made to depend on the moderation of another power whether what appears a chimaera might not become a reality. I have thought it necessary to go thus fully into this transaction, and particularly as to the sentiments I have expressed to them, that you may be enabled to place our proceedings in their true light.

Our Indian expeditions have proved succesful. As yet however they have not led to peace.—Mr. Hammond has lately arrived here as Minister Plenipotentiary from the court of London, and we propose to name one to that court in return.—Congress will probably establish the ratio of representation by a bill now before them at one representative for every 30,000 inhabitants. Besides the newspapers as usual, you will recieve herewith the Census lately taken by towns and counties as well as by states.—I am with great & sincere esteem, Dear Sir Your most obedient & most humble servt.,

TH: JEFFERSON

PrC (DLC). FC (DNA: RG 59, DCI).

The essay on POPULATION AND EMIGRATION was the work of James Madison (*National Gazette*, 21 Nov. 1791; Rutland, *Madison*, xiv, 117-22).

TJ provided Short with such a careful explanation of American policy toward ST. DOMINGO to reassure the French government that, notwithstanding the suspicions of American intentions recently expressed by Ternant, the United States favored the continuance of French rule in the colony (Ternant to Montmorin, 17, 24 Nov. 1791, Turner, *CFM*, p. 72-9. See also Timothy M. Matthewson, "George Washington's Policy Toward the Haitian Revolution," *Diplomatic History*, III [1979], 321-36).

Antoine René Charles Mathurin DE LA FOREST was the French consul-general in Philadelphia. Washington made no written response to the 13 Oct. 1791 SEALED LETTER he received from J. Poncignon, the president of the Saint-Domingue General Assembly, setting forth the distressed situation of the beleaguered French colony (DNA: RG 59, MLR). Poncignon's letter of the same date to Congress, which requested congressional support for the French planters and announced that Americans who died while defending Saint-Domingue would be exempted from the droit d'aubaine, that Sylvanus Bourne's consular credentials had been registered, and that a

recent embargo on foreign shipping had been lifted, was translated into English and published in the 24 Nov. 1791 issue of the *National Gazette*. TJ offended Ternant by failing to consult him before transmitting Poncignon's letter to Congress (Ternant to Montmorin, 24 Nov. 1791, Turner, *CFM*, p. 76-7; see also JS, I, 341; JHR, I, 456). M. Payan-Boisneuf and Ambroise Marie François Joseph Palisot, Baron de Beauvois, were the TWO DEPUTIES of the General Assembly who brought these letters to Philadelphia. In a brief note of 26 Nov. 1791, they accepted TJ's invitation to dine with him on 2 Dec. (RC in DNA: RG 59, MLR). M. Roustan was the agent from Saint-Domingue Ternant had dealt with the previous September. For an earlier statement of U.S. policy regarding a favorable posture for furnishing the French colonies the NECESSARIES OF LIFE, see TJ to Short, 26 Aug. 1790.

From C. W. F. Dumas

The Hague, 25 Nov. 1791. Acknowledges TJ's letter of 30 Aug. 1791 and takes pleasure in the favorable news it contains of conditions in the U.S. He has published some of this news in a supplement to the *Leyden Gazette* of this date and plans to make similar use of the work by Mr. Coxe that TJ sent him.—He rejoices in the success of "l'Expédition contre les Sauvages" and hopes that it will make "ces brutes" immune to "les perfides insinuations de vos voisins."—TJ should have received his account through 3 June. One for the last six months of the year will soon follow.—He regrets the expense to the United States of the decaying embassy in which he gratefully resides and recommends that it be sold. If Congress accepts this recommendation, it will be necessary to entrust the sale to him acting in conjunction with Willink, Van Staphorst, and Hubbard.—The governor of the Cape of Good Hope, who is here to answer charges of financial irregularities, has presented the Prince with a handsome service of "la plus précieuse porcelaine des Indes." His suit is in good hands.—There are rumors that the Provinces will be called upon to reimburse a "certaine Dame" for the last trip she made to Berlin for her son's marriage.—He has warned the French minister of reports that the emigrés are trying to buy 3,000 horses and to enlist as many young Hollanders as they can find.—The news that the U.S. has sent aid to Saint-Domingue has been received with great pleasure.—The Prince has set out for Gelderland to seek approval of a revision in the "ancienne constitution" that would make it possible to pass "resolutions de l'Union" with the votes of a majority of four Provinces rather than with the unanimous consent of all seven. If he succeeds, he can then pursue his favorite plan of augmenting the size of the army.—He refers TJ to the newspapers for the latest accounts of European affairs. Therein TJ can read about the mad exploits of that "singe moderne de son Charles XII" and his emigré cohorts. [P.S.] *3 Dec.* The Prince has returned from Gelderland reportedly without accomplishing his objective.

FC (Dumas Letter Book, Rijksarchief, The Hague; photostats in DLC); 2 p.; at head of text: "No. 85." Recorded in SJL as received 5 Apr. 1792.

The SINGE MODERNE was King Gustavus III of Sweden, an ardent opponent of the French Revolution.

To William Short

DEAR SIR   Philadelphia Nov. 25. 1791.

I wrote you a private letter on the 9th. inst. but the vessel was gone before it was ready. Therefore it goes now, and I have nothing to add on that subject, but that nothing more has past thereon. My last private letters before that were of Sep. 1. and Nov. 9.[1]

Tho it is long since I received your's of Nov. 7. 1790. and Dec. 29. on the subject of our accounts, yet it is never till now that I have had as much time as would allow me to take up that subject. I have now done it, and find them right. I have reduced them into one from your several papers, and inclose a copy. I send also a continuation of the account as far as I am able to collect it from your subsequent letters. I have thrown into it all the articles of credit I may have either in your hands, Mr. Grand's or the Van Staphorsts, not knowing in which they might be.—I am now to desire you to send the President 30. dozen bottles more of Champagne non mousseux from M. Dorsay. Take care if you please that he be warned that it should be of first quality, and fit for *present* use; and get it to Havre as quick as possible that it may come during cold or cool weather. Apply to this object my monies in your own, Mr. Grand's or the V. Staph's hands as you please.—I am to acknolege the receipt of your private letters of June 7. and July 17. also.—I am uneasy that your public account from July 1. 1790. to July 1. 1791. is not yet come, as Congress expect I should lay before them at the beginning of their session the account of the application of the foreign fund. I cannot do this yet for want of your's and that of the Willinks & V. Staph.—I mentioned to you in a former letter that I thought you should charge your *travelling* expences to, at, and from Amsterdam, considering your salary running on as a satisfaction for your time, clothes, and houshold remaining at Paris if any.—You will see in my statement of our private account that I have separated those articles which were *public*. I will be obliged to you to make a statement of them by themselves, and acknolege satisfaction from me at the foot of them, that I may use it as a voucher for my account without being obliged to produce our whole private account, which is at present the only voucher I have for the public articles.—I put off applying to Bartram to make me up the seeds desired by the Dutchess Danville till a vessel should be sailing at this season when seeds are fresh. Unfortunately he has not been able to furnish the whole. I now send such as can be procured, and have taken effectual measures to have the rest for the ensuing season. Such is the avidity for Maple sugar, that it is engaged in the country before it comes to market. I have not been able this year to buy a pound for myself; and could not have sent Mde. Danville even a sample of it, had not the President possessed[2] a little of which he spared me enough to answer as a sample. It is only single refined, as none of the double refined is to be found. When double refined it is equal to the double refined of the Cane, and a like equality exists in every state of it. There is no doubt but that were there hands enough in the Sugar-maple country, there are trees enough not only to supply the U. S. but to carry a great deal to Europe and undersell that of the cane. The reason why it may be cheaper, is that it is the work of women and children only, in a domestic way, and at a season when they can do nothing in the farm. The public attention is very much excited towards it, and the high price of W. India sugars will draw these forth. Express my sincere affection to Mde. Danville and M. and Mde. de la Rochefoucault, of whose friendship I shall ever retain the most cordial remembrance. I cannot as yet gratify the Duke's desire as to engrafted peach trees. The Peach of Pennsylvania is not that which is to be offered as of first quality, and in Virginia you know we have attended chiefly to the clingstone peach; and moreover have never engrafted either kind. I must therefore desire a friend to chuse the ensuing season a tree of the best soft peaches at Monticello, and engraft from it the ensuing spring. This will occasion delay; but what is delayed is not therefore lost.—My daughter complains that her Cabinet des modes does not come.—You will have been doubtless informed by your friends of the death of Mr. Edmunds, also of a daughter of his (Eliza) a son of your brother Peyton's, and your sister Sally. Your sisters Eliza and Jenny are gone with your brother to Kentucky. Remember me in the most friendly terms to M. and Mde. de la Fayette, the two Abbés par excellence & to all others who may enquire, as if they were named, & be assured of the cordial esteem & attachment of Dear Sir your affectionate friend & servt,   TH: JEFFERSON

RC (ViW); at head of text: "Private"; endorsed by Short as received 17 Jan. 1792. PrC (DLC); first two pages only (see note 2 below). Enclosure: Summary of account with Mr. Short, Mr. Grand, and Messrs. Willink, Van Staphorst, & Hubbard showing as charges the same entries recorded on the account sent in Short to TJ, 17 July 1791, with the following additions: 85₶ for "Froullé for Desgodetz and other books," 360₶ for "Chanterot a Pendule," and unspecified amounts for "repairing a watch," and "Piranese's designs of the Pantheon (not yet recd.)." Credits amounting to the same 9,994₶-6 as of 7 Sep. 1790 are increased by one of 16 July 1791, "To Warder's Excha. to Mr. Short on Warder & co. Lond. for £131 5s sterl.," and one of 21 Nov. 1791, "To Lewis's excha. to Messrs. Van Stap. on Willinks for 800. flor. courant." At the foot of text, Short wrote: "Mr. Jefferson owes me still for books including Desgodetz as mentioned above—85₶," and "for 50. batons Vanille sent him by his order—50," for a total of "135₶ pd. when exch. was 44½ per écu. Other articles purchased for him and the bills he sent me to be found in the acct. of N. & J. Van Staphorst and Hubbard with *him*." Endorsed by Short: "Papers relative to Acct. with Jefferson.—*NB*. That I might not be obliged to keep a particular acct. with Mr. Jefferson, posterior to that which I transmitted to him, I placed all the cash he had and the bill he remitted me, in the hands of M. Van Staphorst and Hubbard, as he desired me—and drew on those gentlemen to pay for such articles as he desired me to purchase for him so that their acct. with Mr. Jefferson should exempt me from having to account with him if they have kept the acct. as I desired them" (RC in DLC: Short Papers).

[1] TJ's mention of the second letter was inadvertent, inasmuch as he enclosed it herein.

[2] Second page of letter ends here.

To John Adams

SIR   Philadelphia Nov. 26. 1791.

Supposing that the first Consular convention agreed on with France, and not ratified by Congress, may explain as well as account for some articles in that which was last agreed on and ratified, I take the liberty of inclosing, for the members of the Senate, copies of the two conventions as they were printed side by side, to shew where they differed. These differences are not as great as were to be wished, but they were all which could be obtained. I have the honour to be with the most profound respect and esteem, Sir, Your most obedient & most humble servt,   TH: JEFFERSON

PrC (DLC); at foot of text: "The Vice-president of the U.S. Presidt. of the Senate." FC (DNA: RG 360, DL).

At this time the Senate was considering passage of two closely related bills. The first, which had already been approved by the House of Representatives in March 1791, concerned the role of various federal officials in enforcing the terms of the consular convention negotiated by TJ with the government of France in 1788 and ratified by the Senate in the following year, and the second, which had been passed by the House as early as July 1790, dealt with the organization of the American consular service. Three days after TJ wrote this letter to the Vice-President, the Senate, having combined the two bills into one, passed the revised legislation and sent it to the House for approval. At length on 14 Apr. 1792 Washington approved a version of this bill which contained a number of amendments that were made by the House and accepted by the Senate, the most notable of which were the designation of Louis XVI as "King of the French" instead of "his Most Christian Majesty" and the deletion of a clause that would have enabled American consular officials to own ships or vessels "and be entitled to all the privileges and advantages in regard to such ships or vessels, as if such consuls or vice consuls, owning said ships or vessels, actually resided within the United States, any law to the contrary notwithstanding" (JS, I, 187, 189, 194, 231, 232, 236, 311, 340, 341, 343-5, 424-6; Annals, III, 1360-3). TJ's letter to Adams was almost certainly designed to hasten the passage of the two consular bills then before the Senate, a goal he had been striving to achieve for almost a year (see TJ's draft of items for the President's message to Congress, 29 Nov. 1790).

A text of the unratified 1784 consular convention between France and the United States is in JCC, XXXI, 725-35. The texts of the consular agreement TJ concluded with France are printed as Documents XV and XVI in group of documents on the Consular Convention of 1788, under 14 Nov. 1788.

From George Hammond

Philadelphia November 26. 1791.

The undersigned, his Britannic Majesty's Minister Plenipotentiary to the United States of America, has the honor of laying before the Secretary of State the following brief abstract of the case of Thomas Pagan, a subject of his Britannic Majesty, now confined in the prison of Boston, under an execution issued against him out of the supreme judicial court of Massachusets Bay. To this abstract, the undersigned has taken the liberty of annexing some observations, which naturally arise out of the statement of the transaction, and which may perhaps tend to throw some small degree of light on the general merits of the case.

In the late war, Thomas Pagan was agent for, and part owner of a privateer called the Industry, which on the 25th March 1783 off Cape Ann captured a Brigantine called the Thomas, belonging to Mr. Stephen Hooper of Newport. The brigantine and cargo were libelled in the Court of Vice-Admiralty in Nova Scotia, and that Court ordered the prize to be restored.—An appeal was however moved for by the captors, and regularly prosecuted in England before the Lords of Appeals for Prize Causes, who, in Feby 1790, reversed the decree of the Vice-Admiralty Court of Nova Scotia, and condemned the Brigantine and Cargo as good and lawful prize. In December 1788 a Judgment was obtained by Stephen Hooper in the Court of Common Pleas for the County of Essex in Massachusets against Thomas Pagan for £3500 lawful money for money had and received to the Plaintiff's use.—An appeal was brought thereon in May 1789 to the supreme judicial Court of the Commonwealth of Massachusets, held at Ipswich for the county of Essex, and on the 16 June 1789 a verdict was found for Mr. Hooper, and damages were assessed at £3009.2.10, which sum is "for the Vessel, called the brigantine Thomas, her cargo, and every article found on board." After this verdict, and before entering the judgment, Mr. Pagan moved for a new trial, suggesting that the verdict was against law, because the merits of the case originated in a question, whether a certain brigantine, called the Thomas, with her cargo, taken on the high seas by a private ship of war, called the Industry, was prize or no prize, and that the Court had no authority to give judgment in a cause, where the Point of a resulting or implied Promise arose upon a question of this sort. The supreme judicial Court refused this Motion for a new trial, because it appeared to the Court, that in order to a legal Decision it is not necessary to enquire, whether this prize and her Cargo were prize or no prize, and because the case did not in their opinion involve a question relative to any matter or thing necessarily consequent upon the capture thereof; it was therefore considered by the Court, that Hooper should receive of Pagan £3009.2.10. lawful money.—Damages, and taxed Costs £16.2.10.—From this judgment Pagan claimed an appeal to the supreme judicial Court of the United States of America, for these reasons—that the judgment was given in an action brought by Hooper, who is, and at the time of commencing the action was, a citizen of the Commonwealth of Massachusets one of the United States, against Pagan, who at the time when the action was commenced, was, and ever since has been, a subject of the King of Great Britain residing in, and inhabiting, his province of New Brunswick. This claim of appeal was not allowed, because it was considered by the Court, that this Court was the supreme judicial Court of the Commonwealth of Massachusets, from whose judgments there is no appeal, and further because there does not exist any such Court within the United States of America, as that to which Pagan has claimed an appeal from the judgment of this Court.—Whereupon execution issued against Pagan on the 9th October 1789, and he has been confined in Boston prison ever since.

It is to be observed that in August 1789 Mr. Pagan petitioned the supreme judicial Court of Massachusets for a new trial, and after hearing the arguments of Counsel a new trial was refused.—1st Jany 1791 his Britannic Majesty's Consul at Boston applied for redress on behalf of Mr. Pagan to the Governor of Massachusets Bay, who in his letter of the 28th Jany 1791 was pleased to recommend this matter to the serious attention of the Senate and House of Representatives of that state.—On the 14th. Feby 1791 the British

Consul memorialized the Senate and House of Representatives on this subject. On the 22nd Feby a committee of both houses reported a resolution that the memorial of the Consul and Message from the Governor with all the papers be referred to the consideration of the Justices of the supreme judicial Court, who were directed, as far as may be, to examine into, and consider, the circumstances of the case, and if they found that by the force and effect allowed by the law of Nations to foreign Admiralty Jurisdictions &c. Hooper ought not have recovered judgment against Pagan, the Court was authorized to grant a review of the Action.—10 June 1791 the British Consul again represented to the Senate and House of Representatives, that the Justices of the supreme judicial Court had not been pleased to signify their Decision on this subject referred to them by the resolution of the 22nd Feby.—This representation was considered by a Committee of the Senate and of the House of Representatives, who concluded that one of them should make inquiry of some of the Judges to know their determination, and upon being informed that the Judges intended to give their opinion with their reasons *in writing*, the Committee would not proceed any farther in the business.—27th June 1791 Mr. Pagan's Counsel moved the Justices of the supreme judicial Court for their opinion in the case of Hooper and Pagan referred to their consideration, by the resolve of the General Court, founded on the British Consul's Memorial. Chief Justice and Justice Dana being absent, Justice Paine delivered it as the unanimous opinion of the Judges absent as well as present, that Pagan was not entitled to a new trial for any of the Causes mentioned in the said resolve, and added that the Court intended to put their reasons upon paper, and to file them in the cause— "that the sickness of two of the Court had hitherto prevented it, but that it would soon be done."

It is somewhat remarkable, that the supreme judicial Court of Massachusets should alledge that this case did not necessarily involve a question relative to Prize or no Prize, when the very Jury, to whom the Court referred the decision of the Case, established the fact—their verdict for £3009.2.10 Damages, which sum is for the Vessel, called the brigantine Thomas, her cargo, and every thing found on board. Hence it is evident that the case *did* involve a Question of Prize or no Prize and having received a formal Decision by the only Court competent to take Cognizance thereof (viz. the high Court of Appeals for Prize Causes in England) every thing, that at all related to the Property in Question or to the Legality of the Capture, was thereby finally determined. The legality of the Capture being confirmed by the high Court of appeals in England cannot, consistently with the principles of the law of Nations, be discussed in a foreign Court of law, or at least if a foreign Court of Common Law is, by any local regulations, deemed competent to interfere in matters relating to Captures, the Decisions of Admiralty Courts or Courts of Appeal should be received and taken as conclusive Evidence of the legality or illegality of captures; by such Decisions property is either adjudged to the Captors or restored to the Owners; if adjudged to the Captors, they obtain a permanent property in the captured goods, acquired by the rights of war, and this principle originates in the wisdom of nations, and is calculated to prevent endless litigation.

The proceedings of the supreme judicial Court of Massachusets Bay are in direct violation of the rules and usages that have been universally practised among nations in the determination of the validity of Captures, and of all collateral questions that may have reference thereto. The General Court of Massachusets Bay, among other things, kept this point in view, when they referred the case of Mr. Pagan to the consideration of the Justices of the supreme judicial Court, and authorized the Court to grant a review of the action, if it should be found that, by the Force and Effect allowed by the law of Nations to foreign Admiralty Jurisdictions, Mr. Hooper ought not to have recovered judgment against Mr. Pagan; but the supreme judicial Court have not only evaded this material consideration, upon which the whole question incontestably turns, but have assumed a fact in direct contradiction to the truth of the case viz. that the case did not involve a question of prize or no prize.— Moreover they have denied Mr. Pagan the benefit of Appeal to that Court which is competent to decide on the force of Treaties, and which Court, by the constitution of the United States, is declared to possess *appellate* jurisdiction, both as to law and fact, in all cases of controversy between citizens of the United States and subjects of foreign countries to which class this case is peculiarly and strictly to be referred.

From the foregoing abstract of the case of Thomas Pagan, it appears that he is now detained in prison in Boston, in consequence of a judgment given by a Court, which was not competent to decide upon his case, or if competent, did not admit the only evidence that ought to have guided its decision, and that he is denied the means of appealing to the highest Court of Judicature known in these states, which Court, in the very organization of the constitution of the United States, is declared to possess appellate jurisdiction in all cases of a nature similar to the present.

For these reasons the undersigned begs leave respectfully to submit the whole matter to the consideration of the Secretary of state, and to request him to take such measures, as may appear to him the best adapted to the purpose of obtaining for the said Thomas Pagan such speedy and effectual redress, as the merits of his case may seem to require. GEO. HAMMOND.

RC (DNA: RG 59, NL); edges frayed, so that some words and parts of words are lost, which have been taken from the Tr in DLC; endorsed by TJ as received 29 Nov. 1791 but not recorded in SJL. Tr (same). Another Tr (same); at head of text: "(Copy)"; PrC of this Tr (DLC).

The case of Thomas Pagan and Stephen Hooper preoccupied TJ and Hammond more than any diplomatic issue save questions of neutral rights and the disputed provisions of the Treaty of Paris. A legacy of the American Revolution, the case was considerably more complicated than the British minister's account of it suggests. Pagan and his brothers Robert and William were Loyalist merchants from Scotland who in 1780 began to engage in privateering from their base of operations in British-occupied Penobscot, Maine, to make up for the loss of over thirty merchant vessels to the Americans. In accordance with this strategy, one of their privateers, the *Industry*, captured the *Thomas*, an American brigantine owned by the Newburyport, Mass., merchant Stephen Hooper, off Cape Ann on 25 Mch. 1783.

Unbeknownst to Captain Zebedee Hammond of the *Industry*, however, the British government and the American peace commissioners in Paris had already agreed on terms for a cessation of hostilities that provided for the restoration of all "vessels and effects" captured by either side one month after 3 Feb. 1783 "from the Channel and the North seas as far as the Canary Islands inclusively, whether in the ocean or the Mediterranean" and two months after that date "from the said Canary Islands as far as the equinoctial line or equator" (Declaration for Suspension of Arms between Great Britain and United States, 20 Jan.

1783; George III's Proclamation on Cessation of Hostilities, 14 Feb. 1783; American Commissioners' Proclamation on Cessation of Hostilities, 20 Feb. 1783, all in Francis Wharton, *Diplomatic Correspondence of the American Revolution*, VI, 223-4, 252, 257-8). Thus, after Captain Hammond filed a libel in the Vice-Admiralty Court at Halifax, Nova Scotia, contending that the *Thomas* and her cargo constituted a lawful prize under the terms of the Prohibitory Act, Hooper countered with a claim that the *Thomas* was an unlawful prize because she had been captured after 3 Mch.

The Vice-Admiralty Court agreed with Hooper and on 2 June 1783 ordered the vessel and cargo to be restored to him. Captain Hammond, who still maintained that the *Thomas* was a valid prize, immediately obtained an appeal to the Lords Commissioners of Prize Appeals in England, a standing committee of the Privy Council that was authorized to review the decisions of vice-admiralty courts in America. Refusing to return the captured brigantine and cargo to Hooper while the appeal proceeded, Robert Pagan agreed with a representative of the Massachusetts merchant to sell both at public auction, subject to the stipulation that "this sale of Vessel and cargo shall not in the least be construed to a determination of the property either in favor of the prosecution or the claimants." Almost seven years later, in February 1790, the Lords Commissioners reversed the Nova Scotia court's decision strictly on the basis of a procedural technicality—namely Hooper's failure to respond to their summonses to appear before them and answer Captain Hammond's appeal (Claims and Statements of Robert Pagan, 9 and 12 Mch. 1787, PRO: AO 12/11, f. 71-80; Industry v. Thomas, Nova Scotia Vice-Admiralty

Court Records, New Court House, Boston, Court Files, Suffolk, Vol. 661; Decree of Lords Commissioners of Prize Appeals, 12 Feb. 1790, same; Harrison G. Otis to Massachusetts Supreme Judicial Court, n.d., same, Vol. 839; E. Alfred Jones, *The Loyalists of Massachusetts: Their Memorials, Petitions and Claims* [London, 1930], p. 227-8; the Editors gratefully acknowledge the assistance of the staff of the Documentary History of the Supreme Court project for making available photostats of the Massachusetts court record in the case of Pagan v. Hooper).

The legal triumph of the Pagan brothers in England was offset by setbacks in Massachusetts. After the British evacuation of Penobscot, the brothers, still loyal to the crown, moved to New Brunswick, where Robert and William held various public offices while Thomas confined himself to mercantile pursuits. During a business trip to Massachusetts in April 1788 Thomas Pagan was served a writ of attachment that Hooper had obtained against all three Pagan brothers, charging them with repeatedly violating a promise they allegedly made in 1783 to pay him "on demand" the sum of £3,500, the estimated value of the *Thomas* and her cargo. After failing to arbitrate the dispute, Hooper brought suit for trespass against the Pagan brothers in the Essex County Court of Common Pleas in September 1788, claiming that their failure to keep the aforementioned promise had cost him £3,500 in damages.

Thomas Pagan, the only one of the defendants to appear before this court, maintained that he and his brothers had "never promised in manner and form" as Hooper asserted, but the jury rejected this defense and awarded Hooper damages amounting to "£3374 lawful money." Both litigants appealed to the Supreme Judicial Court of Massachusetts, which in June 1789 reaffirmed the lower court's verdict while reducing the damages to which Hooper was entitled by £365 and specifying that they were for the *Thomas* as well as her cargo and every other article on board at the time of her capture. Pagan's counsel then moved for a new trial on the ground that the Supreme Judicial Court had no authority to decide a case in which the real issue was whether the *Thomas* was a lawful prize. But the court rejected this motion after deciding that the issue of the legality of the *Thomas'* capture was immaterial to the case. It then authorized Hooper to recover from Pagan the damages assessed by the jury, whereupon the latter's counsel moved for an appeal to the Supreme Court of the United States because the case involved a dispute between citizens of two different nations. The Supreme Judicial Court rejected this motion as well, claiming that it was the court of last resort in Massachusetts and denying (apparently because Congress had not yet passed the Judiciary Act of 1789) that the court to which Pagan sought to appeal existed. Pagan unsuccessfully appealed for a new trial in August 1789 and was imprisoned in October of that year for non-payment of damages to Hooper.

The ruling of the Lords Commissioners for Prize Appeals in February 1790 that the *Thomas* was a lawful prize inspired Pagan to apply to the Supreme Judicial Court for a new trial in May 1790, but the court rejected this application. Next, after being asked by the state legislature to reconsider the case in light of an appeal for Pagan's release from Thomas MacDonough, the British consul in Boston, the court ruled in June 1791 that Pagan was not entitled to a new trial (Writ of Attachment to Sheriff of Suffolk County, 11 Apr. 1788, New Court House, Boston, Court Files, Suffolk, Vol. 661; Decree of Essex Court of Common Pleas in Pagan v. Hooper, 30 Sep. 1788, same; Decree of Massachusetts Supreme Judicial Court in Pagan v. Hooper, 16 July 1789, same; Deposition of Theophilus Parsons in Pagan v. Hooper, [1789], same; Thomas Pagan to Massachusetts Supreme Judicial Court, 18 May 1790, same; Thomas MacDonough to Governor John Hancock, 1 Jan. 1791, and to the Massachusetts Legislature, 14 Feb. 1791, same, Vol. 839).

George Hammond decided to make Thomas Pagan's case the subject of his first official communication to TJ for several reasons. He was under instructions from the king to support all British subjects "who may have any Suits or just pretensions depending" in the United States, he was genuinely moved by the spectacle of a subject of the crown languishing in an American prison, and he firmly believed that the Supreme Judicial Court of Massachusetts had violated the American Constitution by denying Pagan's request for an appeal to the U.S. Supreme Court and had flouted international law by refusing to accept the Lords Commissioners' decision legitimating the *Thomas*' capture. At first Hammond simply asked TJ to take such steps as would obtain redress for Pagan; but by the end of 1791 he insisted, in response to direct instructions from Lord Grenville, that the American government do whatever was necessary to release Pagan from prison and to compensate him for any injuries resulting from his confinement (George III's instructions to Hammond, 2 Sep. 1791, Mayo, *British Ministers*, p. 3; Grenville to Hammond, 5 Oct. 1791, same, p. 19; Hammond to Grenville, 6 Dec. 1791, PRO: FO 4/11, f. 224; Hammond to TJ, 28 Dec. 1791).

TJ promptly responded to Hammond's representation on Pagan's behalf. He discussed the British minister's letter with Washington, who instructed him to submit it to Attorney General Edmund Randolph to ascertain whether the facts alleged therein required any action by the federal government. After having TJ obtain a transcript of the Massachusetts court records, Randolph notified him on 27 Jan. 1792 that, although he was unable to form "a mature opinion" about Pagan's case, he believed that Pagan's best hope for legal redress was to apply to the Supreme Court for a writ of error under the terms of section 25 of the Judiciary Act of 1789. Among other things, that provision authorized the Supreme Court to reexamine, reverse, or affirm any decision by the highest court in a state that involved the validity of an international treaty to which the United States was a party. TJ immediately apprised Hammond of this advice, but the British minister declined to follow it; instead, he expressed determination "to await the decision of the general government."

TJ met privately with Hammond on 15 Feb. 1792 and sought to convince him that the executive branch of government would not intervene on Pagan's behalf before all judicial remedies had been exhausted and that a writ of error was the only legal method of bringing the case before the Supreme Court. But Hammond still hesitated because he doubted that a Supreme Court justice would grant a writ of error in a case

that had originated in a state court before the establishment of the federal judiciary or that Pagan would be able to find anyone in Boston willing to act as security for his appeal. TJ finally overcame Hammond's doubts by sending him an official legal opinion by Randolph that reemphasized the need for Pagan to apply for a writ of error and noted that "the usage of sovereigns is, not to interfere in the administration of justice, until the foreign subject, who complains, has gone with his case to the dernier resort." TJ also personally assured the British minister that only if Pagan's application were rejected would he be "at the end of the ordinary course of law, at which term alone it is usual for nations to take up the cause of an individual and to enquire whether their judges have refused him justice." Convinced that TJ's remarks amounted to a pledge that the U.S. government would intercede on Pagan's behalf if he failed to obtain legal redress from the Supreme Court, Hammond at last instructed Pagan to apply for a writ of error (TJ to Randolph, 5 Dec. 1791; Randolph to TJ, 5 Dec. 1791, 27 Jan. 1792, 22 Feb. 1792; TJ to Christopher Gore, 13 Dec. 1791; Gore to TJ, 1, 4 Jan. 1792; TJ to Hammond, 28 Jan., 25 Feb. 1792; Hammond to TJ, 30 Jan., 18 Feb. 1792; Hammond to Grenville, 2 Feb., 6 Mch. 1792, PRO: FO 4/14, DLC photostats. Randolph prepared a long summary of this case in May 1792, but there is no evidence that he ever sent it to TJ ["Rough to Secretary of State," May 1792, in DNA: RG 76, British Spoiliations]).

Pagan's application to the Supreme Court for a writ of error did not bring him the judicial relief he sought. Edward Tilghman, the noted Philadelphia attorney Pagan retained to represent him before the Supreme Court, at first believed there was nothing in the Massachusetts court record to justify even a request for such a writ. Tilghman reluctantly decided to apply for one only after Attorney General Randolph personally interceded with him and intimated that such an application would be highly desirable since Pagan's case was under discussion by the Secretary of State and the British minister. Tilghman's request for the writ, submitted to Justice James Wilson, was accompanied by only a partial transcript of the court record. Wilson initially refused to grant the writ, but agreed to reconsider the matter after Randolph intervened again and gave him a complete transcript. In August 1792, having consulted with his fellow justices, he issued a writ of error on Pagan's behalf.

The Supreme Judicial Court, however, declined to obey the writ, since it was incorrectly directed to the "supreme court" of Massachusetts, though the court did assure Chief Justice John Jay of its willingness to take into consideration a properly corrected writ. The Supreme Court considered the Massachusetts court's action on 16 Feb. 1793 and reached a decision that could not have been more displeasing to Pagan. Tilghman moved for the issuance of another writ of error, but when asked by Chief Justice Jay if "there appeared any thing on the record to give the Supreme Court jurisdiction" in Pagan's case, he responded in the negative. Despite a plea by Randolph to consider the international ramifications of the legal dispute between Pagan and Hooper before deciding whether to take cognizance of it, the Supreme Court accepted Tilghman's opinion about its lack of jurisdiction and unanimously rejected his motion for a new writ of error (Randolph to TJ, 30 June, 26 Aug. 1792, 13 Mch. 1793; TJ to Hammond, 2, 12 July 1792; Hammond to TJ, 12, 13 July 1792; Randolph to TJ, 26 Aug. 1792, 13 Mch. 1793; Edward Tilghman to Randolph, 19 Mch. 1793, enclosed with Randolph to TJ, 12 Apr. 1793; Edwin C. Surrency, ed., "The Minutes of the Supreme Court of the United States 1789-1806," *American Journal of Legal History*, v [1961], 181).

The Supreme Court's action moved the case of Pagan and Hooper back into the realm of international diplomacy. Hammond asked TJ on 12 Mch. 1793 what steps the U.S. government planned to take now that Pagan had exhausted all available judicial remedies. TJ immediately requested Randolph to examine the case again to ascertain whether Pagan had been the victim of "that degree of gross and palpable injustice . . . by the national tribunals, which would render the nation itself responsible for their conduct." Randolph reported to TJ that the *Thomas* had unquestionably been captured in violation of the Anglo-American agreement on the cessation of hostilities in North American waters and

that the British government had no reason to complain of Pagan's treatment by American courts. TJ agreed with this analysis and informed Hammond on 18 Apr. 1793 that the federal government planned to refrain from further involvement in the Pagan affair because it "does not appear then to be one of those cases of gross and palpable wrong ascribable only to the wickedness of the heart, and not to error of the head, in the judges who have decided on it, and founding a claim of national satisfaction."

Hammond predictably rejected TJ's assessment of the matter. After a delay of four months caused by the neutrality crisis of 1793, he sought once again to make Pagan's release the subject of negotiation with TJ, arguing that under international law American courts were bound by the original ruling of the Lords Commissioners. TJ remained unmoved. Armed with yet another opinion from Randolph contending that Pagan had been treated fairly by the American judicial system, TJ notified Hammond on 13 Sep. 1793 that the U.S. government could do nothing more for Pagan because his case bore no marks of that "partiality and willful injustice . . . which render a nation responsible for the decisions of its Judges and which the United States would have been perfectly disposed to rectify." This announcement ended the negotiations between TJ and Hammond over Pagan's fate (TJ to Randolph, 13 Mch. 1793; Randolph to TJ, 13 Mch., 12 Apr., 5 Sep. 1793; Hammond to TJ, 9 Apr. 1793, 19 Aug. 1793; TJ to Hammond, 9, 18 Apr., 13 Sep. 1793).

Embittered by his failure to persuade TJ of the justice of Pagan's cause, Hammond submitted a long report on the case to Grenville in October 1793, accompanied by copies of his pertinent correspondence with TJ as well as Randolph's legal opinions. He charged that "in the whole course of its proceedings, the American federal administration, either through a reluctance to involve itself in a dispute with the state of Massachusetts, or through some other less justifiable motive, has evinced no other disposition than that of procrastination, and of shifting from itself as long as it was possible the necessity of a decision." Ironically, Hammond's report made an unexpected impression on Grenville. After reviewing the course of the long legal dispute between Pagan and Hooper, Grenville instructed Hammond in January 1794 to disengage himself from the case until he received further orders from England, as "persons the best qualified to judge on the subject here entertain great doubts whether there is in fact any just ground of complaint against that decision." But before Grenville could decide upon a new course of action, he learned early in the following month that Pagan had finally secured his release from prison through a settlement with Hooper, thereby ending an episode that had irritated Anglo-American relations for several years (Hammond to Grenville, 12 Oct. 1793, PRO: FO 5/1, DLC transcript; Grenville to Hammond, Jan. 1794, 6 Feb. 1794, Mayo, *British Ministers*, p. 51-2).

To George Washington

Questions to be considered of.

I. As to France.

Shall it be proposed to M. de Ternan, to form a treaty, ad referendum, to this effect. 'The citizens of the U. S. and of France, their vessels, productions and manufactures shall be received and considered, each in all the dominions of the other, as if they were the native citizens, or the ships; productions or manufactures of that other. And the productions of the sea shall be received in all the dominions of each as if they were the productions of the country by the industry of whose citizens they have been taken or produced from the sea. Saving only as to the persons of their citizens, that they shall continue under those incapacities for office, each with the other, which the Constitution of France, or of the U.S. or any of them, have or shall establish against foreigners of all nations without exception.'

If not, Shall a treaty be proposed to him, ad referendum, in which the conditions shall be detailed on which the persons ships, productions and manufactures of each shall be received with the other, and the imposts to which they shall be liable be formed into a tariff?

Shall the Senate be consulted in the beginning, in the middle, or only at the close of this transaction?

II. As to England.

Shall Mr. Hammond be *now* asked Whether he is instructed to give us any explanations of the intentions of his court as to the detention of our Western posts, and other infringements of our treaty with them?

Shall he be now asked whether he is authorised to conclude, or to negotiate, any commercial arrangements with us?

TH: JEFFERSON
Nov. 26. 1791

RC (DNA: RG 59, MLR); addressed: "The President of the U. S."; docketed by Washington: "Questions to be considered of in the Negotiations with the French and British Ministers"; noted in SJPL: "[1791. 26 Nov.] heads of consultn. treaty with France.—do. Engld." PrC (DLC). Tr (DNA: RG 59, SDC).

The question of whether to begin negotiations with the British and French ministers on commercial treaties was yet another part of the continuing struggle between TJ and Alexander Hamilton to direct the course of American foreign policy. Hamilton initiated this phase of the conflict on 7 Oct. 1791 by discussing commercial relations between France and the United States with Ternant while the Secretary of State were absent from the nation's capital. Hamilton noted America's interest in expanding its trade with the French West Indies and sought to ascertain whether the French minister was authorized to carry out a 2 June 1791 decree of the National Assembly calling for the negotiation of a new treaty of commerce with the United States. Ternant, who lacked such authority, drew Hamilton's attention to the considerable commercial concessions France had already made to the United States in the West Indies and then repeated familiar complaints about the unfairness of American tonnage duties to French shipping. Hamilton defended the tonnage duties, but noted that all commercial difficulties between the two countries could be eliminated through a new trade treaty, an objective he ardently professed to favor. After Ternant pointedly observed that continued American adherence to the French alliance was an essential precondition for a new commercial treaty, the Secretary of the Treasury brought the conversation to a close by assuring the French minister that the United States would never agree to a treaty of commerce with Great Britain unless it received a share of the carrying trade with the British West Indies (Ternant to Montmorin, 9, 24 Oct. 1791, Turner, *CFM*, p. 57-62).

Having thus laid the groundwork for commercial negotiations with the French minister, Hamilton met with the President after his return to Philadelphia and convinced him that TJ and Ternant should arrange the terms of a new treaty of commerce with France and then submit them to the French government. TJ strongly disagreed with Hamilton's proposed course of action, arguing that it would bind the United States while leaving France free to accept or reject the American terms, but Washington overruled him and ordered him to proceed with the projected treaty. The President then sent him the following brief note: "As the meeting proposed to be held (at nine o'clock tomorrow morning) with the heads of the Great Departments, is to consider important subjects belonging (more immediately) to the Department of State—The President desires Mr. Jefferson would commit the several points on which opinions will be asked to Paper, and in the order they ought to be taken up." TJ thereupon prepared the draft treaty contained in the letter printed above, which was designed to grant a reciprocal right of naturalization to American and French citizens with respect to trade (Washington to TJ, 25 Nov. 1791; RC in DLC; not recorded in SJL; FC in DNA: RG 59, MLR; headed: "To the Secretary of ⟨*the Treasury*⟩ State"; Tr in DNA: RG 59, SDC; see also TJ to John Adams, with enclosure, 28 July 1785, for a similar plan of treaty; Memoranda of Conversations with President, 11 Mch.-9 Apr. 1792).

Although TJ's draft was approved during a cabinet meeting held on this day, he was also instructed to add a section to the treaty dealing more specifically with trade duties and manufacturing bounties. TJ thus prepared a somewhat modified version of his original treaty proposal; as he noted several months later, it called for "exchanging the privileges of native subjects, and fixing all duties forever as they now stood." TJ's proposal aroused the opposition of Hamilton, who maintained that these duties were already too low. As a result, the Secretary of the Treasury submitted a new tariff of duties to Washington that proposed significant increases in the rates on French goods (Memoranda of Conversations with President, 11 Mch.-9 Apr. 1792; Tariff of duties, undated, but written before 9 Dec. 1791; DLC: Hamilton Papers; text in Syrett, *Hamilton*, XIII, 409-10; an undated summary by TJ of Hamilton's tariff is in DLC: TJ Papers, 72: 12597; see also Washington to TJ, 9 Dec. 1791).

TJ sharply disagreed with Hamilton's suggested increases during a discussion of the tariff at a cabinet meeting in the middle of December 1791. He remarked later that their adoption would have been equivalent to asking the French "to give us the privileges of native subjects, and we, as a compensation, were to make them pay higher duties" (Memoranda of Conversations with President, 11 Mch.-9 Apr. 1792). But TJ was even more offended when Hamilton went on to suggest that, in addition to negotiating a new treaty of commerce with Ternant, TJ also begin negotiations with George Hammond for a commercial treaty with Great Britain. Although Washington at first favored this suggestion, TJ resolutely opposed it. He suspected that Hamilton wanted to maneuver him into offering less favorable terms to Ternant than to Hammond so as to frustrate his negotiations with the French and thus pave the way for the conclusion of a commercial treaty with Great Britain that would inevitably destroy the American alliance with France. Nor was TJ's suspicion unjustified. Unbeknownst to him, Hamilton had told George Beckwith in February 1791 that an Anglo-American treaty of commerce would definitely lead to the dissolution of the French alliance, and in December 1791 he revealed to Hammond that he was at work on a report designed to demonstrate that Britain's system of commercial regulations was more favorable to the United States than that of France (Conversation with George Beckwith, 16 Feb. 1791; Conversation with George Hammond, 15-16 Dec. 1791; View of the Commercial Regulations of France and Great Britain, [1792-1793], Syrett, *Hamilton*, VIII, 43, x, 374, XIII, 411-36).

Ultimately, TJ prevailed upon Washington by the end of 1791 to reject Hamilton's proposal for simultaneous commercial negotiations with Ternant and Hammond and to rely instead on the American minister in Paris to solicit overtures from the French government for a new commercial treaty—the position TJ had favored all along. Hamilton did not object. He had failed to elicit any assurance from Hammond that the British government was prepared to grant the United States a share of the British West Indian carrying trade, a concession Hamilton regarded as a sine qua non of any Anglo-American commercial agreement (TJ to William Short, 24 Nov. 1791, 5 Jan. 1792; Proposed Treaty of Commerce with France, [26 Nov. 1791]; TJ to Hamilton, 23 Dec. 1791; TJ to Washington, 23 Dec. 1791; Conversation with George Hammond, 1-8 Jan. 1792, Syrett, *Hamilton*, x, 495-6; TJ to Gouverneur Morris, 10 Mch. 1792; Memoranda of Conversations with President, 11 Mch.-9 Apr. 1792; George F. Zook, "Proposals for a New Commercial Treaty between France and the United States, 1778-1793," *South Atlantic Quarterly*, VIII [1909], 267-83).

Proposed Treaty of Commerce with France

[26 Nov. 1791]

The citizens of the U.S. and of France and of their dominions, their vessels, productions and manufactures, as well those raised by their industry from the sea, as from the soil shall be received and treated, each in all the dominions of the other, as if they were the native citizens, or the home built vessels, or the productions, or manufactures of the other.

Saving that the duties payable on the productions or manufactures of either country or it's dominions, imported into the other or it's dominions, may remain as at present, where they do not exceed

per cent on the value of the article at the port of $\frac{\text{ex-}}{\text{im-}}$ portation; in which case of excess they are hereby, ipso facto, reduced to that measure: and where they shall be hereafter reduced by either party, on any article, in favor of any other nation, they shall stand ipso facto reduced on the same article, in favor of the other party, yeilding the like equivalent only where the reduction has been for an equivalent. And that this beneficial restraint of duties on the industry of either may not be defeated by premiums on that of the other, it is agreed that every premium for any production or manufacture of either country shall be extended on the same condition by the party giving it, to the like production or manufacture of the other.[1]

Saving also as to the persons of their citizens mutually, that they shall continue under those incapacities of office and suffrage, each with the other, which the Constitutions or laws of France, or of the U.S. or any of them, or of any of their dominions, have or shall establish against foreigners of all nations without exception.

MS (DLC: TJ Papers, 72: 12596). Dft (DLC: TJ Papers, 67: 11694).

[1] The Dft consists of a variant version of the preceding paragraph:

"It is to be understood however that either party may lay duties on productions or manufactures provided they do not exceed   per cent. ad valorem on manufactures and   per cent. ad valorem on raw materials, nor what shall be paid by any other the most favored nation. The value to be estimated as at the port of shipment.

vessel or suffrage

No premium shall be given directly or indirectly on the manufactures or productions of either country carried into the other. To be considerd of productions of the sea e: gr.

whether of their own soil, or raised by them from the sea as from the soil

'And Saving also that the duties payable on the productions or manufactures of the dominions of either country imported into those of the other may remain as at present where they do not exceed   per cent on the value of the article at the port of exportation in which case of excess they are hereby ipso facto reduced to that measure and where they shall be hereafter reduced by either party on any article in favor of any other nation, they shall stand ipso facto reduced on the same article in favor of the other party; yeilding the like equivalent only where the reduction has been for an equivalent.'

And in order that the beneficial restraint of duties may not be defeated by premiums, it is agreed that every premium for any production or manufacture of either country shall be extended by the party giving it to the production or manufacture of the other party complying with the same conditions."

To Thomas Mann Randolph, Jr.

DEAR SIR   Philadelphia Nov. 27. 1791.

By a letter recieved from Prince, I find that he has forwarded to the care of Mr. Brown in Richmond 4. bundles of trees for me, numbered as on the next leaf. I have written to Mr. Brown to forward them, and with this may get in time for you to understand the numbers before you plant them.—I have heard nothing of our post yet, tho' I presume it began on the 15th. inst. as Mr. Davies notified me.—Capt. Stratton is at length arrived here. I have not yet seen him. We shall now be able to send on the things for the house-servants.—We have had very cold weather here. The thermometer was yesterday morning at 27. and had been as low a few days before. In fact the winter set in on the 17th. of October with the North East storm thro' which we came, and has continued with now and then a mild day. I have engaged Mr. Rittenhouse to furnish Freneau with his meteorological observations, once a week, so you will have in every other paper what is to be relied on in that way. My love to my dear Martha, and am with sincere affection Dear Sir your friend & servt,   TH: JEFFERSON

RC (DLC); addressed: "Thos. M. Randolph junr. Monticello." Enclosure: TJ's list of the contents of the four bundles, practically identical to that in William Prince to TJ, 8 Nov. 1791, except TJ omitted the prices and referred to item 10 as "Moor park" apricots and item 29, "Monthly" trees, as "Monthly honey suckle." TJ also omit-

ted item 33 from his list. PrC (MHi); letter only.

Augustine Davis failed to inform TJ whether the POST contract and bond were executed by 15 Nov. as he expected them to be when he wrote on 17 Oct. 1791.

To James Brown

SIR   Philadelphia Nov. 28. 1791.

By a letter just recieved from Prince, the Nurseryman of Long island, I learn he has forwarded 4. bundles of trees for me to Richmond addressed to your care. The object of the present letter is to ask the favor of you to send them to Albemarle by my own waggon, if it is plying between that and Richmond at present. If not, then by any careful waggoner who will deliver them either at my house or Colo. Lewis's. The only danger is in their freezing on the way, which can be prevented either by burying the roots of a night, or covering the whole plant well under straw.—I am with great esteem Sir Your most obedt. humble servt,   TH: JEFFERSON

RC (Robert C. Norton, Cleveland, Ohio, 1951); addressed: "Mr. James Brown Merchant Richmond"; franked; postmarked: "28 NO" and "FREE"; endorsed. PrC (MHi).

To William Carmichael

SIR   Philadelphia Nov. 29. 1791.

I wrote you on the 6th. instant by the way of Cadiz, sending the newspapers as usual. With the present we forward them to the present day, as also a pamphlet by Mr. Coxe in answer to Ld. Sheffeild, and a printed copy of the Census, now in the press, should it be ready in time. I wish it were possible to get for us the two Census's taken in Spain by the Count d'Aranda and Count de Florida Blanca. A very formidable insurrection of the negroes in French St. Domingo has taken place. From 30. to 50,000 are said to be in arms. They have sent here for aids of military stores and provisions, which we furnish just so far as the French minister here approves: Mr. Hammond is arrived here as Minister Plenipotentiary from Great Britain, and we are about sending one to that court from hence.—The legislature have before them a bill for allowing one representative for every 30,000 persons, which has past the Representatives, and is now with the Senate. Some late enquiries into the condition of our domestic manufactures, give a very flattering result. Their extent is great and growing through all the states. Some manufactories on a large scale are under contemplation.—In my last I wrote you how sorely the affair of the Dover cutter was pressing. Lest that should miscarry I repeat it here, and that I have no letters from you yet. I am with great esteem, Sir, your most obedient & most humble servant,   TH: JEFFERSON

PrC (DLC). FC (DNA: RG 59, DCI).

A revised and enlarged edition of Tench Coxe's *A Brief Examination of Lord Sheffield's Observations on the Commerce of the United States* was published in Philadelphia on 17 Nov. 1791. See Sowerby, No. 3268. George Hammond was convinced that the publication of Coxe's anti-mercantilist work at this time was deliberately contrived to spur Congress to pass discriminatory commercial legislation against Great Britain (Hammond to Grenville, 17 Nov. 1791, PRO: FO 4/11, f. 162).

From Nathaniel Cutting

SIR   Cape François, Isle of St. Domingo Novr. 29th. 1791.

This Evening hearing that a Vessel will take her departure for Philadelphia early to morrow morning, I take the liberty to acquaint you with my arrival here about three weeks since.

Doubtless you have been particularly inform'd of the horrid devastation that has lately desolated the richest part of this flourishing colony. Therefore I shall not intrude a new detail on that subject. I will only observe that the damages are estimated at upwards of one milliard tournois.—The unparrallelled distress wherein this Colony is involved, seems only to be the necessary consequence of those unhappy dissentions whereof I gave you some account last year. Permit me now to acquaint you that I am very apprehensive the Ravages of the Insurgents will not be confin'd by the boundaries of the Northern District of St. Domingue. Dispatches were yesterday received by an express Boat from Port-au-Prince, stating that the utmost confusion and alarm prevails there. The People of Colour have recently declared that they will never submit to the Decree of the national assembly of France of the 24th. Sept. ulto. which guarantees to the white Colonists the *Initiative* that they have been so long struggling for.—A Body of Mulattoes to the number of one thousand, a few days since marched into Port-au-Prince in Battle array. This reinforcement to their Class, gives it an immense superiority in point of Force in that City.—Those Gentry declare that sooner than submit to the Decree beforemention'd, they will join their forces to that of the Revolted Negroes and deliver the whole Country North of Port-au-Prince to Fire and Sword.—In addition to the painful apprehensions which this threat inspires in the breasts of the Planters, another circumstance gives them infinite uneasiness.—The ancient maroon negroes who have for many years past eluded the vigilance of all pursuers, have formed a junction with the Brigands who have recently scatter'd firebrands and death on this side the mountains. A strong Party of them are reported to have dashed through a part of the Spanish territory and are now hovering on the borders of the fertile, wealthy but defenceless Plantations on the banks of the Artibonite. The distrest Inhabitants have not force sufficient to oppose the incursions of this savage banditti; they are moreover apprehensive that their own Slaves will greedily participate the work of destruction.—In fine, this peerless Colony is apparently on the verge of total Ruin!

Yesterday the *Commissaries Civile* who have been so long and so anxiously expected here, arrived after a passage of 31 days from France. No accounts of the Revolt of the Slaves had reach'd that Kingdom the 27th. Octo., though their Ravages commenced the 21st. Augt.

A Member of the Assembly general, now sitting in this City, call'd on me this morning and inform'd me that the Commissaries, immediately on landing were conducted to the assembly, where the President addrest them in a speech of considerable length, in the course whereof he styled the Colonists *La nation Creole*, and the Inhabitants of France *Nos alliés*.—The instant the president concluded, the Assembly formally and explicitly disavow'd the principles which those expressions might seem to indicate. Such a *sottise* may possibly make a bad impression on the minds of the Commissaries.—In reply to the address they observed that they consider'd themselves at present only as private Citizens who rejoiced to find themselves in the midst of an assembly of their brethren; and that when the Powers wherewith they were invested were recognized and promulgated, they should be happy to coopperate with the assembly in promoting the well-being and tranquility of the Colony.—They Dine this day with M. Blanchelande in order to communicate their Credentials, &c. And to morrow, I understand, their quality will be publicly announced.—I have the honor to be with the greatest Respect, Sir, your most obedt. huml. Servt,

NAT. CUTTING.

RC (DNA: RG 59, MLR); endorsed by TJ as received 4 Jan. 1792 and so recorded in SJL. Dft (MHi: Cutting Papers); varies from RC in phraseology.

The descriptions of the Saint-Domingue slave revolt that Cutting supplied TJ over the next several months were not those of an impartial observer. During his stay on the island he was actively involved in helping the French planters defend a guardhouse just outside Le Cap François against the insurgents (Timothy M. Matthewson, "George Washington's Policy Toward the Haitian Revolution," *Diplomatic History*, III [1979], 325).

From Joseph Fay

SIR   Bennington 29th Novr. 1791

I have been absent a number of weeks attending our fall Session of the Legisture, during which time I left orders with our post Master to enclose you our papers.—I am much disappointed in not being able to obtain any from Quebec. I learn from my friends that more than usual care is Taken to prevent their circulation to this Country.—I am sorry to inform you that not a single seed of the Maple has come to maturity this year in all this Northern Country. I have made diligent inquiry thro' the State; wheather this is owing to the Worms, or a General blast is uncertain. The Great Scarcity and high price of sugars (owing to the Insurecions in the Islands) occasions the Greatest preparations for improving the Maple in this quarter, every providential circumstance seems to Conspire to promote this usefull branch.

I saw in one of your papers, a small Sketch said to be the plan which the National Assembly had formed in case the Uropean powers invaded them, which was not to give quarter to any officer from the *General* to the *Corporal* that should be taken in Arms, but to Treat the Soldiers with the Greatest Humanity. This plan wheather true or false is (in my opinion) a good one, and would be a greater Security to the Nation then 200,000 men in the field. I mention this from the Anxiety which I feel for their Success. Never was the Cause of Humanity more deeply Interested in any one Event.

We have not been able to learn much of your proceedings the present Session, I find however that our members have made their entrance and I hope they will faithfully discharge their trust. I hope to be at Philadelphia in the Course of the Winter.—Please to accept the warmest wishes and friendly Sentiments of Dear Sir Your most obedient Humble Servant,   JOSEPH FAY

RC (DLC); endorsed by TJ as received 16 Dec. 1791 and so recorded in SJL.

To George Hammond

SIR   Philadelphia Nov. 29. 1791.

In recalling your attention to the Seventh article of the Definitive Treaty of Peace between the United States of America, and his Britannic majesty, wherein it was stipulated that 'His Britannic majesty should, with all convenient speed, and without causing any destruction, or carrying away any negroes or other property of the American inhabitants, withdraw all his Armies, garrisons and fleets from the said United States, and from every post, place, and harbour within the same,' I need not observe to you that this article still remains in a state of inexecution, nor recapitulate what, on other occasions, has past on this subject. Of all this I presume you are fully apprized. We consider the friendly movement lately made by the Court of London, in sending a minister to reside with us, as a favorable omen of it's dispositions to cultivate harmony and good will between the two nations, and we are perfectly persuaded that these views will be cordially seconded by yourself, in the ministry which you are appointed to exercise between us. Permit me then, Sir, to ask whether you are instructed to give us explanations of the intentions of your court as to the execution of the article above quoted?

With respect to the Commerce of the two Countries, we have supposed that we saw in several instances, regulations on the part of your government, which, if reciprocally adopted, would materially injure the interests of both nations.

On this subject too, I must beg the favor of you to say whether you are authorized to conclude, or to negociate arrangements with us which may fix the Commerce between the two Countries on principles of reciprocal advantage?—I have the honor to be, with sentiments of the most perfect Esteem and respect, Sir, Your most obedient and most humble servt,   TH: JEFFERSON

Tr (DLC). FC (DNA: RG 59, SDR).

To David Humphreys

DEAR SIR   Philadelphia Nov. 29. 1791.

My last to you was of Aug. 23. acknoleging the reciept of your Nos. 19. 21. and 22. Since that I have recieved from 23. to 33. inclusive. In mine I informed you I was about setting out for Virginia and consequently should not write to you till my return. This opportunity by Capt. Wicks is the first since my return.

The party which had gone at the date of my last, against the Indians North of the Ohio, were commanded by Genl. Wilkerson, and were as successful as the first, having killed and taken about 80 persons, burnt some towns and lost, I believe, not a man. As yet however it has not produced peace.—A very formidable insurrection of the negroes in French St. Domingo has taken place. From 30. to 50,000 are said to be in arms. They have sent here for aids of military stores and provisions, which we furnish just so far as the French minister here approves. Mr. Hammond is arrived here as Minister Plenipotentiary from Great Britain, and we are about sending one to that court from hence.—The Census, particular as to each part of every state is now in the press; if done in time for this conveyance, it shall be forwarded. The legislature have before them a bill for allowing one representative for every 30,000 persons, which has passed the Representatives and is now with the Senate.—Some late enquiries into the state of our domestic manufactures give a very flattering result. Their extent is great and growing through all the states. Some manufactories on a large scale are under contemplation.—As to the article of Etrennes enquired after in one of your letters, it was under consideration in the first instance, when it was submitted to the President to decide on the articles of account which should be allowed the foreign ministers in addition to their salary; and this article was excluded, as every thing was meant to be which was not in the particular enumeration I gave you. With respect to foreign newspapers, I recieve those of Amsterdam, France and London, so regularly and so early, that I will not trouble you for any of them: but I will thank you for those of Lisbon and Madrid, and in your letters to give me all the information you can of Spanish affairs, as I have never yet recieved but one letter from Mr. Carmichael, which you I believe brought from Madrid.—You will recieve with this a pamphlet by Mr. Coxe in answer to Ld. Sheffeild, Freneau's and Fenno's papers. I am with great & sincere esteem Dr. Sir Your most obedient & most humble servt,

TH: JEFFERSON

RC (NjP); endorsed. PrC (DLC). FC (DNA: RG 59, DCI).

Humphreys had raised the question of whether he was authorized to include New Year's gifts—ETRENNES—to Portuguese officials in his diplomatic expense account in his 1 July 1791 letter to TJ.

To Thomas Leiper

SIR   Philadelphia Nov. 29. 1791

I was in hopes Capt Stratton would have brought the 6. hhds. of my tobo. which still remain at Richmond. But he is come without them. I had waited supposing that on his arrival I might have settled the whole purchase with you. I shall immediately order them by the first vessel without waiting for Stratton. For the present however I must ask the favor of you to furnish me with a thousand dollars, cash, or a discountable note, as shall be most convenient to you. I am Sir Your very humble servt,   TH: JEFFERSON

PrC (MHi).

From Thomas Pinckney

SIR   Charleston 29th. Novr. 1791

If the nomination and appointment mentioned to me in your favor of the 6th of this Month should take place I will endeavor to execute the duties of the mission to the best of my ability.

In thus explicitly declaring my acquiescence in the honor conferred by this mark of confidence I fear I have rather complied with my desire of being useful, than consulted the means of being so;

and I trust I shall be acquitted of affected diffidence when I add that a doubt of my fitness for the charge was the only consideration which could have influenced me to withhold my service: but a recollection of the discernment manifested in the appointments already made under the Constitution, my ignorance of the particular objects of the mission, and the very encouraging manner in which you express your confidence in my executing the trust reposed in me with propriety, have convinced me that I ought not in a business of this importance, to be determined only by my own feelings.

As I am but just arrived in Charleston and the mail will be immediately closed, I will defer till the next opportunity, entering into some particulars on what I had intended to write; only adding that a long absence from Europe prevents me from being a proper judge of the pecuniary arrangements but that I have an unbounded confidence that they will be adequate to the purpose.—With sentiments of the most perfect respect and Esteem I have the honor to be Sir Your most obedient & most humble Servant,

THOMAS PINCKNEY

RC (DNA: RG 59, DD). Recorded in SJL as received 14 Dec. 1791.

On the following day Pinckney explained that the PARTICULARS to which he alluded "relate to the eventual preparations for my departure"; that he would be unable to leave South Carolina for at least two months because "I have not only affairs of my own to settle but have the concerns of several near connections as well as the business of the Estates of some deceased friends to put into a train of arrangement"; and that he hoped to sail for England from Philadelphia or New York so that "I should thereby have the benefit of conferring with you on the subjects to be committed to my charge; for altho' instructions are given in writing and mine I am certain will be ample and explicit, yet I conceive that personal communications, especially to one who has not been in the habits of public negociation, must be of considerable advantage" (Pinckney to TJ, 30 Nov. 1791, RC in DNA: RG 59, DD; endorsed by TJ as received 14 Dec. 1791 and so recorded in SJL). At the same time he wrote a brief note informing TJ that with "Two vessels intending to sail at the same time for Philadelphia I avail myself of the opportunity of complying as fully as possible with your

request of an immediate answer" (Pinckney to TJ, 30 Nov. 1791, RC in DNA: RG 59, DD; recorded in SJL as received 14 Dec. 1791).

Upon receiving TJ's letter, Pinckney described his motives for deciding to serve as American minister to Great Britain at greater length in a letter to his friend and political supporter, Edward Rutledge: "Your favor by Jack was delivered to me a couple of hours ago, covering a letter from Mr. Jefferson informing me (agreeably to your Northern intelligence) that he had it in charge from the President to ask whether it would be agreeable that he should nominate me to the Senate as minister plenipotentiary to the court of London. Your departure from town on Saturday has precipitated my determination, upon less consideration than I ought to give it; but my desire to give you and my brother [Charles Cotesworth Pinckney] information of it has induced me to think as fully on the subject as the shortness of the time will admit, and the result is my acquiescence in the appointment. Almost every private consideration appears to be against this determination, but every public one (my inability excepted) in favor of it. In short, all my plans, projects, private interest, and indolence must give way to my sense of the importance of such an office being in the hands of one of our way of thinking" (Thomas Pinckney to Edward Rutledge, 24 Nov. 1791, Charles C. Pinckney, *Life of General Thomas Pinckney* [Boston and New York, 1895], p. 99-101; see also Pinckney to Washington, 29 Nov. 1791; RC in DLC: Washington Papers, and duplicate in DNA: RG 59, DD).

From Andrew Ellicott

DEAR SIR   George Town Novr. 30th 1791

Yours of the 21st. has come safe to hand, but I defered answering it immediately, expecting Major L'Enfant's return from Virginia, whom I should have consulted on the subject, which you submitted to my opinion; but as he is yet absent, and the time of his return uncertain, a longer delay might perhaps be improper.—I shall have every thing in my power done between the Presidents-House, and the Capitol; but as soon as the ground becomes compleatly frozen, we shall be under the necessity of quitting.—I do not think that it will be possible to have another sale, before the last of June next, to answer the two valuable purposes, of shewing the plan to advantage on the ground; and increasing the funds, in the greatest ratio possible.

This will be handed to you, by Mr. Francis Cabot, a Gentleman not only of information; but likewise a zealous friend to the City of Washington. Being sensible, that he will receive your polite attention, it will be unnecessary to recommend him particularly to your notice.—I have the Honour to be with much esteem Your real Friend,   ANDREW ELLICOTT

RC (DNA: RG 59, MLR); endorsed by TJ as received 6 Dec. 1791 and so recorded in SJL.

From George Hammond

SIR   Philadelphia 30th November 1791.

I have the honor of acknowledging the receipt of your letter of yesterday.

With respect to the non-execution of the seventh article, of the definitive treaty of peace between his Britannic Majesty and the United States of America, which you have recalled to my attention, it is scarcely necessary for me to remark to you, Sir, that the King my master was induced to suspend the execution of that article on his part, in consequence of the non-compliance, on the part of the

United States, with the engagements, contained in the fourth, fifth and sixth articles of the same treaty. These two objects are therefore so materially connected with each other, as not to admit of separation, either in the mode of discussing them, or in any subsequent arrangements, which may result from that discussion.

In stating to you, Sir, this indispensable consideration, I must at the same time assure you that, in the confidence of experiencing a similar disposition in the government of the United States, it is his Majesty's desire to remove every ground and occasion of misunderstanding, which may arise between the two countries: And in conformity to that disposition in his Majesty, I can add that—I am instructed to enter into the discussion of all such measures, as may be deemed the most practicable and reasonable for giving effect to those stipulations of the definitive treaty, the execution of which has hitherto been delayed, as well by the government of this country, as by that of Great-Britain.

In answer to your question on the subject of the commerce of Great Britain and the United States, I can also inform you, Sir, that the King is sincerely disposed to promote and facilitate the commercial intercourse between the two countries, and that I am authorized to communicate to this government his Majesty's readiness to enter into a negociation for establishing that intercourse upon principles of reciprocal benefit.

Before I conclude this letter, I cannot omit mentioning the sense I entertain of the obliging expressions of personal regard, which you, Sir, have been pleased to employ, relative to my appointment to the station, which I hold in this country. I can venture to assure you, with the greatest sincerity, that it affords me the warmest satisfaction to be the medium of communicating to the United States the actual good dispositions of my sovereign and nation towards them—and I trust I may be permitted to add, that it would be the highest object of my ambition, to be the humble instrument of contributing, in any manner, to fix upon a permanent basis the future system of harmony and good understanding between the two Countries.—I have the honor to be, with every sentiment of respect and esteem, Sir, your most obedient and most humble Servant,

GEO. HAMMOND.

RC (DNA: RG 59, NL); endorsed by TJ as received 30 Nov. 1791 and so recorded in SJL; TJ also docketed the letter as follows: "Hammond George. His powers as to treaty of peace, commerce." PrC of "(Copy)" (DLC). Tr (DNA: RG 59, NL). Another Tr (DNA: RG 59, SDR).

Hammond believed that TJ had an ulterior purpose in asking him to reveal whether he was authorized to negotiate a commercial treaty with the United States. He was convinced that TJ wanted to elicit an admission that he lacked such authority so that he could include a statement on the "supposed disinclination in the British Government to form a commercial arrangement with the United States" in his anticipated report to Congress on the state of American commerce. Such a statement, Hammond feared, would strengthen the position of those in Congress who favored discriminatory measures against British trade and shipping—hence the British minister's eagerness to assure TJ that he was empowered to discuss the subject of a commercial treaty (Hammond to Grenville, 6 Dec. 1791, PRO: FO 4/11, f. 183-5; see also Hammond to TJ, 6, 14 Dec. 1791). In reality, TJ raised this issue in response to a presidential instruction to pursue the possibility of concluding commercial treaties with France and Great Britain (see note to TJ to Washington, 26 Nov. 1791). The rather limited commercial concessions Hammond was authorized to offer the United States are set forth in the relevant sections of his instructions from Lord Grenville, which were heavily influenced in turn by Lord Hawkesbury's highly mercantilistic 28 Jan. 1791 report to the Privy Council on the state of Anglo-American trade (Mayo, *British Ministers*, p. 9-13). It may have been about this time that TJ began to prepare for commercial negotiations with Hammond by taking an extensive set of notes on one of his copies of Hawkesbury's report (Notes on Hawkesbury; MS in DLC: TJ Papers, 69: 11898-9).

From George Washington

MY DEAR SIR   Wednesday 30th. Novr. 1791

Mr. L'Enfants letter of the 19th. of Octr. to Mr. Lear—Mr. Lear's answer of the 6th. instt. (the press copy of which is so dull as to be scarcely legible), in which I engrafted sentiments of admonition, and with a view also to feel his pulse under reprehension—His reply of the 10th. to that letter together with the papers I put into your hands when here will give you a full view of the business; and the Majrs. conduct; and will enable you to judge from the complexion of things how far he may be spoken to in decisive terms without loosing his services; which, in my opinion would be a serious misfortune.—At the same time *he must know*, there is a line beyond which he will not be suffered to go.—Whether it is zeal, an impetuous temper, or other motives that leads him into such blameable conduct I will not take upon me to decide, but be it what it will, it must be checked; or we shall have no Commissioners.—I am always Yr. Obed. & Affecte.,   GO: WASHINGTON

RC (DLC: District of Columbia Papers); addressed: "Mr. Jefferson"; docketed by Washington: "To Thos. Jefferson Esq. 30th. Novr. 1791." FC (DLC: Washington Papers). Not recorded in SJL. The enclosures have not been found, but a draft of L'Enfant to Lear, 19 Oct. 1791, is in DLC: Digges-L'Enfant-Morgan Papers; partial text printed in Elizabeth S. Kite, *L'Enfant and Washington* (Baltimore, 1929), p. 75-8.

A Bill to Promote the Progress of the Useful Arts

[1 Dec. 1791]

Be it Enacted by the Senate and Representatives of the United States of America in Congress assembled, that when any person shall have invented any new and useful art, machine, or composition of matter, or any new and useful improvement on any art, machine, or composition of matter, and shall desire to have an exclusive property in the same, he shall pay into the Treasury of the United States the sum of   dollars, whereof he shall take a receipt from the Treasurer indorsed on the warrant of the Secretary of the Treasury in the usual form, and shall produce the same to the Secretary of State, in whose office he shall then deposit a description of the said inventions in writing and of the manner of using or process for compounding the same in such full, clear, and exact terms, as to distinguish the same from other things before known and to enable any person skilled in the art or science of which it is a branch, or with which it is most nearly connected to make, compound and use the same; and he shall accompany it with drawings and written references and also with exact models made in a strong and workmanlike manner where the nature of the case admits of drawings or models, and with specimens of the ingredients, and of the composition of matter, sufficient in quantity for the purpose of experiment, where the invention is of a composition of matter: and he shall be entitled to receive from the Secretary of State a certificate thereof under the seal of his office wherein shall be inserted a shorter and more general description of the thing invented to be furnished by the applicant himself, in terms sufficient to point out the general nature thereof, and to warn others against an interference therewith, a copy of which certificate as also of the warrant of the Secretary of the Treasury and Treasurer's receipt he shall file of record in the Clerks office of every District Court of the United States, and shall publish three times in some one Gazette of each of the said Districts. After which it shall not be lawful for any person without the permission of the owner of the said invention or of his agents to make or sell the thing so invented and discovered, for the term of fourteen years from the date of the Treasurer's receipt.

And be it further Enacted that it shall be lawful for the said inventor to assign his title and interest in the said invention at any time before or after the date of the Treasurer's receipt, and the assignee, having recorded the said assignment in the offices of the Secretary of State and of the Clerks of the District Courts, and published the same three times in some one Gazette of each District, shall thereafter stand in the place of the original inventor, both as to right and responsibility, and so the assignees of assignees to any degree. And any person making or selling the thing so invented without permission as aforesaid shall be liable to an action at law, and to such damages as a jury shall assess, unless he can shew that the same thing was known to others before the date of the Treasurer's receipt, and can shew such probable grounds as the nature of a negative proof will admit that that knowledge was not derived from any party from, through or in whom the right is claimed, or unless he can shew on like grounds that he did not know that there existed an exclusive right to the said invention, or can prove that (the same is so unimportant and obvious that it ought not to be the subject of an exclusive right, or that) the description, model, specimen or ingredients deposited in the office of the Secretary of State do not contain the whole matter necessary to possess the public of the full benefit thereof after the expiration of the exclusive right, or that they contain superfluous matter intended to mislead the public, or that the effect pretended to cannot be produced by the means inscribed. Provided that where any State before it's accession to the present form of Government, or the adoption of the said form by nine-States, shall have granted an exclusive right to any invention, the party claiming that right shall not be capable of obtaining an exclusive right under this act, but on relinquishing his right in and under such particular State, so as that obtaining equal benefits he may be subject to equal restrictions with the other Citizens of the United States, and of such relinquishment his obtaining an exclusive right under this Act shall be sufficient evidence.

Provided also that the persons whose applications for Patents were on the 1st. day of February in this present year, depending before the Secretary of State, Secretary at war, and Attorney General, according to the Act of 1790 for promoting the progress of useful arts, on complying with all the conditions of this act except the payment to the Treasurer herein before required, and instead of that payment obtaining from the said Secretary of State, Secretary at War and Attorney General, or any two them, a certificate of the date of his application, and recording and publishing the said certificate instead of the warrant and receipt of Treasury shall be within the purview of this act as if he had made such payment and his term of fourteen years shall be counted from the said date of his application.

And be it further Enacted that after the expiration of any exclusive right to an invention, the public shall have reasonable and sufficient access to the descriptions, drawings, models, and specimens, of the same, so as to be enabled to copy them; and moreover that the Secretary of State shall cause the said descriptions and drawings to be printed, engraved and published, on the best terms he can, to the expences of which the monies paid as before directed in to the Treasury shall be appropriated in the first place, and the balance to the purchase of books to form a public library at the seat of Government, under the direction of such persons as the President of the United States for the time being shall appoint.

And be it Enacted that the Act passed in the year 1790 intituled "An Act to promote the progress of the useful Arts," be and is hereby repealed.

PrC (DLC: TJ Papers, 69:11931-7); entirely in hand of Blackwell; at head of text: "A Bill to promote the progress of the useful arts"; entry in SJPL: "draught of bill for promotion of useful arts."

This bill to alter the patent system has hitherto been assigned to the period before 7 Feb. 1791 because of Paul L. Ford's assertion that it was identical to a bill introduced in the House of Representatives on that date by Alexander White of Virginia (Ford, v, 278-80; JHR, I, 371, 374). A comparison of the text of White's bill (*A Bill to amend an Act, intituled, "An act to promote the Progress of Useful Arts"* [Philadelphia, 1791]; see Evans, No. 23848), apparently unknown to Ford, and TJ's proposal indicates that they cannot be the same and that TJ's bill came later. His was a heavily compressed version of the White bill and sought to minimize even more than the latter the role played by the Secretary of State in the issuance of patents. The conclusive reason for assigning 1 Dec. 1791 to the bill printed above is that TJ used that date when he recorded the draft of such a bill in SJPL. No record appears in SJPL for one prior to that date.

Under the terms of the Patent Act of 1790, the Secretary of State, the Secretary of War, and the Attorney General were responsible for examining applications for patents for new inventions. Owing to his strong scientific interests, TJ quickly became the leading member of the Board of Arts, as these three officials were collectively called when they gathered on the last Saturday of each month to examine specifications and models of inventions before deciding whether they were deserving of patents. By the time TJ drafted the bill printed above, he and his colleagues had reviewed more than a hundred applications and granted almost forty patents. Despite his interest in promoting the growth of American science and technology, however, TJ regretted that Congress had assigned this responsibility to his office because the conduct of his other duties left him with insufficient time to examine properly the growing number of applications for patents. Of all the functions he was obliged to perform as head of the Department of State, he later complained, this was the one that "cuts up his time into the most useless fragments and gives him from time to time the most poignant mortification" because it compelled him "to give crude and uninformed opinions on rights often valuable, and always deemed so by the authors" (TJ to Hugh Williamson, 1 Apr. 1792; P. J. Federico, "Operation of the Patent Act of 1790," *Journal of the Patent Office Society*, XVIII [1936], 237-51).

TJ sought to remedy this situation by abolishing the examination requirement and making the issuance of patents by the Secretary of State essentially a matter of clerical routine. But what he did with his bill after drafting it is uncertain. Presumably he showed it to Congressman Hugh Williamson of North Carolina, the chairman of a committee charged with preparing a new patent law, who had consulted TJ on this subject during the preceding month and was to do so again in the following April (TJ to Williamson, 13 Nov. 1791, 1 Apr. 1792). In any event, though there are few points of similarity between them, the revised patent law passed by Congress in February 1793 achieved the primary goals of TJ's draft bill (Federico, "Outline of the History of the U.S. Patent Office," same, p. 77-83).

From Augustine Davis

HONORED SIR   Richmond, Decemr. 1st. 1791

Yesterday an express arrived here with the following melancholy account, contained in a letter from Harry Innes, Esqr. to Col. James Innes, dated the 13th. Novr. 1791, and which I take the liberty to communicate to you, least the particulars should not reach Philadelphia before this arrives.

"This letter by your fellow soldier Colo. Gist, will probably give you the first information of the defeat of General St. Clair, on the 4th instant, within 15 miles of the Miami village, and 98 of fort Washington, his point of departure from the Ohio. The loss upon this occasion is about 600 killed and wounded (nearly equal to Braddock's defeat) with 7 pieces of artillery, and all the stores.— St. Clair, it is said, had about 1200 men, had reasons to expect an attack, kept his men under arms all night, drawn up in a square. The attack commenced about the dawn of day on all the lines, but principally on the rear line, which was composed of the militia. The Indians gave one fire, and rushed on Tommahawk in hand. The militia gave way to the Centre, and before the artillery could be brought into action, the matrosses were all killed, and it fell into the hands of the enemy. It was soon retaken, but remained useless for the want of men to manage the pieces. The action continued obstinately until 9 o'Clock, when our army gave way. St. Clair rallied his men and brought them off in tolerable order, with most of the wounded, to fort Jefferson, 30 miles in the rear of the action, where, we are informed, they remain closely cooped, and almost starved, living on poor pack horses. The enemy pursued 5 miles.—An effort is now making to go from this district to the relief of fort Jefferson, which I fear will fall into the hands of the enemy, before we can effect the plan; it is from this place 160 miles, we must carry provision. We have to fit ourselves with Clothes on account of the advanced season of the year, which will require two or three days.— A number of our respectable characters are stepping forth upon this occasion. And so great is the impulse, that I shall go as a private, confident of the good effect the example will have. It will be a trip of 15 or 18 days, but will not move from the Ohio unless we are at least 1000 strong; for the enemy having taken 100 bullocks and a great quantity of flour may remain in the neighbourhood of fort Jefferson, expecting a reinforcement to come forward, and if they should be in sufficient strength, give them battle.—The return of the officers killed and wounded is as follows: General Butler, 1 Lieutenant Colonel, 4 Majors, 11 Captains, 10 Lieutenants, 9 Ensigns, 1 Surgeon, Total 37.—Wounded, 2 Lieutenant Colonels, 1 Major, 11 Captains, 6 Lieutenants, 6 Ensigns, 1 surgeon, Total 27.—Among the wounded, Col. Gibson, supposed mortally, also Col. Darke. General St. Clair had many escapes. It is said he had 8 balls through his Clothes."—I have the Honor to be Sir, Yr Obt. Servant, AUGUSTINE DAVIS

RC (DLC); endorsed by TJ as received 8 Dec. 1791 and so recorded in SJL.

From Thomas Pinckney

SIR   Charleston 1st. Decr. 1791

The apprehension of appearing in an improper point of view to those whose esteem I earnestly desire to conciliate, occasions my giving you this trouble, in addition to the dispatches of a public nature forwarded by this opportunity.—A Paragraph has this morning appeared in a daily print of this City mentioning my intended mission.

I have only to assure you that no trifling indiscretion of mine has given rise to this report, which I found circulating on my arrival in Charleston four days after the receipt of your favor.—It is in itself a matter of small consequence, but it may give rise to impressions the apprehension of which I own gives me more uneasiness than perhaps it deserves.—With sentiments of sincere esteem & great respect I have the honor to be Sir, Your most obedient & most humble Servant, THOMAS PINCKNEY

RC (DNA: RG 59, DD); at head of text: "(private)"; endorsed by TJ as received 27 Dec. 1791 and so recorded in SJL.

Plan of a Bill concerning Consuls

[1 Dec. 1791]

The matter of the bill will naturally divide itself as follows.

I. Foreign Consuls residing within the U.S. under a Convention.
II. Consuls of the U.S. residing in foreign countries under a Convention.
III. Provision for future conventions, and cases where there is no Convention.

Preliminary observation. Nothing should be inserted in the bill which is fully and adequately provided for by the Convention with France; because weak magistrates may infer from thence that the parts omitted were not meant by the legislature to be enforced. Are not the 1st. 2d. 3d. sections of the printed bill objectionable in this view? The instructions of the Executive to their Consuls will of course provide for the notification directed in the 2d. clause.

I.   For carrying into full effect the Convention between his most Christian majesty and the U.S. of America entered into for the purpose of defining and establishing the functions and privileges of their respective Consuls and Vice Consuls, be it enacted by the Senate and H. of Repr. of the U.S. of America that where in the 7th. article of the sd. convention it is agreed that when there shall be no Consul or Viceconsul of his most Christian king[1] to attend to the saving of the wreck of any French vessel stranded on the coasts of the U.S. or that the residence of the sd. Consul or Viceconsul (he not being at the place of the wreck) shall be more distant from the sd. place than that of the competent judge of the country, the latter shall immediately proceed to perform the office therein prescribed, the nearest [here name the officer][2] shall be the competent judge designated in the said article and it shall be incumbent on him to perform the office prescribed in the sd. article, and according to the tenor thereof.' Go on to direct who, in conjunction with the Consul or Vice consul (if there be one) shall ascertain the abatement of duties on the damaged goods stipulated in this article.

    Art. 9. allows the Consuls of the most Xn. king to arrest and imprison deserted captns. officers, mariners, seamen and all others being part of a ship's crew. For which purpose they are to address themselves to the courts, judges, and officers competent, who are to aid in arresting the deserter, and to confine him in the prisons of the country. Say who are the 'competent courts, judges and officers" to whom he is to apply, and what prisons they shall use.

[364]

This clause confines the term of imprisonment to 3. months. The French Consuls represent that in many ports of the U.S. no opportunity of reconveying, by a French ship, occurs within that term and they ask a longer. Suppose it be referred to the Federal district judge, on application by the French consul, and on his shewing good cause, to prolong the term, from time to time, not exceeding three months additional in the whole.

Art. 12. it is necessary to authorize some officer to execute the sentences of the Consul, *not extending to life, limb, or liberty.* Will it be best to require the marshal, residing at the port, to do it (and to make it the duty, where none resides, to appoint a deputy residing there) or to allow the Consul to constitute some person of his nation an officer for the purpose? If it should be thought indifferent to us, it might be well to pay the French the compliment of asking their minister here which he would prefer, and it would shield us from complaints of delinquencies in the executing officer.

II. Art. 12. Say by what law the Consul of the U.S. residing in the French dominions, shall decide the cases whereof he has jurisdiction viz. by the same law by which the proper federal court would decide the same case.

Direct appeals from Consular sentences to the proper Federal court, and save defects of formality in proceedings, where the matter is substantially stated.

Art. 4. Declare what validity the authentication under the Consular seal, of any instrument executed in foreign countries, shall have in the courts of the U.S.

Duties not prescribed in the Convention.

To subsist shipwreckt or wandering seamen till an opportunity offers of sending them back to some port of the U.S. and to oblige every master of an American vessel homeward bound, to recieve and bring them back in a certain proportion, they working, if able.

Where a ship is sold in a foreign port, oblige the master to send back the crew, or furnish wherewithal to do it, on pain of an arrest by the consul on his ship, his goods, and his person (if the laws of the land permit it) until he does it.

Oblige all American masters (on pain of arrest, till compliance, of their vessel, cargo, or person, or such other pain as shall be thought effectual) on their arrival in any foreign port within the jurisdiction of a Consul or Vice-consul of the U.S. to report to him or his Agent in the port, their ship's name and owners, burthen, crew, cargo and it's owners, [from] what port of the U.S. they cleared, and at what ports they have touched. [Also?][2] to report to the Consul &c. the cargo they take in and the port or ports of destination, and to take his certificate that such report has been made, on like pain.

Allow certain fees to Consuls, where none are already allowed, for the same services, by the laws of the country in which they reside.

Allow salaries, not exceeding 3000 D. to one Consul in each of the Barbary states.

III. Where there are Consuls of the U.S. residing in foreign countries, with which we have no Convention, but whose governments indulge our Consuls in the exercise of functions, extend the provisions of this bill, or such of them as such government permits, to such Consuls of the U.S. residing with them.

Also where any Consular Convention shall hereafter be renewed with the same, or entered into with any other nation, with stipulations corresponding to those provided for in this bill, extend the provisions of the bill, respectively, to the Consuls on both sides.

PrC (DLC: TJ Papers, 69: 11938-41); at head of text: "[Plan] of a Bill concerning Consuls." Entry in SJPL: "⟨draught⟩ Plan of bill concerning Consuls."

On 29 Nov. 1791, the Senate approved a bill entitled An Act Concerning Consuls and Vice-Consuls, the primary objects of which were to specify the responsibility of federal officials in enforcing certain provisions of the 1788 Consular Convention between France and the United States and to define the functions of American consular officers (see JS, I, 343-5, for text of the bill). The House of Representatives read the bill on the following day and ordered it to be taken up in committee of the whole on 6 Dec. 1791. TJ, who was obviously dissatisfied with the Senate bill, drew up these observations in anticipation of the forthcoming meeting of the committee of the whole and almost certainly intended them for the use of the House during its deliberations on the consular bill. As the above recommendations suggest, TJ was disappointed by the failure of the Senate

bill to be more precise about the enforcement responsibilities of federal officials, the official duties of American consuls, and the bearing of its provisions on countries with whom the United States had no consular agreements. Yet apart from the absence of the original MS of this document, there is no evidence that TJ ever showed it to any member of the House, which delayed consideration of the bill regarding consuls until April 1792. Moreover, the Consular Act that Congress finally approved and the President signed into law in that month did not contain a single revision favored by the Secretary of State (JHR, I, 465, 571; JS, I, 340, 341, 424, 425, 426; Annals, III, 1360-3). For further information on TJ's wish to implement the 1788 Consular Convention in order to strengthen the ties between France and the United States, see Editorial Notes and groups of documents on the consular convention, at 14 Nov. 1788, . and on consular problems, at 21 Feb. 1791.

[1] Substituted for "majesty," deleted.
[2] TJ's brackets.

To James Somerville

SIR Philadelphia Dec. 1. 1791

I am to acknolege the receipt of your favour covering one of Keith's pamphlets on Weights and measures, which contains a great deal of information on the subject. With my thanks be pleased to accept assurances of the regard with which I have the honor to be Sir Your most obedt. humble servt, TH: JEFFERSON

PrC (MHi).

Somerville's letter of 22 Nov. 1791, recorded in SJL as received 22 Nov. 1791, has not been found. George Skene KEITH'S PAMPHLET: *Tracts on Weights, Measures,*

and Coins (London, 1791). See Sowerby, No. 3766. TJ subsequently disparaged this work, critical of his advocacy of the rod pendulum as a standard of measure, as vague and imprecise (TJ to David Rittenhouse, 8 June 1792).

To George Washington

Dec. 1. 1791.

Th: Jefferson presents his respects to the President and sends him a draught of letters to Majr. L'Enfant and the Commissioners, prepared on a conference with Mr. Madison. Perhaps the former may be too severe. It was observed however, that tho' the president's sentiments conveyed to him thro' Mr. Lear, were serious and ought to have produced an effect on him, he gave them the go-by in his letter in answer, and shews that he will not regard correction unless it be pointed.

PrC (DLC). Entry in SJPL reads: "Th:J. to G.W. on [L'Enfant]."

ENCLOSURES

I

George Washington to Commissioners of the Federal District

GENTLEMEN Philadelphia Dec. 1. 1791.

I recieve with real mortification the account of the demolition of Mr. Carrol's house by Majr. L'Enfant, against his consent, and without authority from yourselves, or any other person: for you have done me but justice in asserting he had no such authority from me. My letter of the 28th. ult. to Mr. Carrol of Duddington will prove this. I now inclose you one[1] to Majr. L'Enfant, in which you will see what I say to him on this subject, and will then be so good as to deliver it to him.—You are as sensible as I am, of his value to us. But this has it's limits, and there is a point beyond which he might be overvalued. If he is saved from the notice of the law on the present occasion, I would chuse he should owe it entirely to yourselves, and that he be made sensible that there will be no interference from me on his behalf.[2]

PrC of Dft (DLC); entirely in TJ's hand; entry in SJPL reads: "[draught of letter for G.W.] to Commrs. [Carrol's house]."

Washington sent this letter to the Commissioners with only minor additions (see textual notes below), enclosing one to Daniel Carroll of Duddington dated 2 Dec. 1791 concerning the "unlucky dispute" with L'Enfant, "whose zeal in the public cause has carried him too fast," and suggesting that he quash the injunction he had brought against L'Enfant. See Fitzpatrick, *Writings*, XXXI, 432-3; and Editorial Note on fixing the seat of government, Vol. 20: 48 n. 134.

[1] In the text of the letter sent, Washington added "the copy of" before this word.

[2] Washington added: "The enclosed for Mr. Carrol, of Duddington you may either deliver or destroy as it shall seem best to you. With very great esteem &c."

II

George Washington to Pierre Charles L'Enfant

SIR   Philadelphia Dec. 1. 1791.

I have recieved with sincere concern the information from yourself as well as others, that you have proceeded to demolish the house of Mr. Carrol of Duddington, against his consent, and without authority from the Commissioners, or any other person. In this you have laid yourself open to the laws, and in a country where they will have their course. To their animadversion will belong the present case.—In future I must strictly enjoin you to touch no man's property, without his consent, or the previous order of the Commissioners. I wished you to be employed in the arrangements of the federal city. I still wish it: but only on condition that you can conduct yourself in subordination to the authority of the Commissioners,[1] to the laws of the land, and to the rights of it's citizens.

PrC of Dft (DLC); entirely in TJ's hand; entry in SJPL reads: "draught of letter for G.W. to L'Enfant. Carrol's house."

For additional information on this letter, see Editorial Note on fixing the seat of government, Vol. 20: 47.

[1] In his letter of 2 Dec. 1791 to L'Enfant, Washington inserted "to whom by law the business is entrusted and who stand between you and the President of the United States" at this point. He also added two additional paragraphs: "Your precipitate conduct will, it is to be apprehended, give serious alarm and produce disagreeable consequences. Having the beauty, and regularity of your plan only in view, you pursue it as if every person and thing were *obliged* to yield to it; whereas the Commissioners have many circumstances to attend to, some of which perhaps, may be unknown to you, which evinces in a strong point of view the propriety, the necessity, and even the safety of your acting by their directions.

"I have said, and I repeat it to you again, that it is my firm belief, that the Gentlemen now in office have favorable dispositions towards you; and in all things reasonable and proper will receive, and give full weight to your opinions—and ascribing to your Zeal the mistakes that have happened, I persuade myself under this explanation of matters that nothing in future will intervene to obstruct the harmony which ought to prevail in so interesting a Work" (DLC: Washington Papers; Fitzpatrick, *Writings*, XXXI, 434-5).

From Pierce Butler

SIR   Philadelphia December the 2d. 1791

A Committee of Senate to whom the petition of Charles Colvill was refered; together with sundry papers on the subject of a Treaty with the Alegerines, and the redemption of the American Citizens in Captivity at Algiers, have directed me to ask You to Draft a Bill, Authorising the President of the United states, by and with the advice and Consent of senate, to appoint a proper person to treat with the Dey of Algiers for a peace, the Condition—Annual stipend; and also for the redemption of the Prisoners on the best terms that can be obtained, the redemption, if possible to be Connected with the Treaty; but if no treaty can be had untill the Prisoners are ransomed, then to Authorise the President to adjust the Redemption on the best possible terms.—I am with sentiments of real Esteem and regard Sir Yr Most Obedt. Servant,   P. BUTLER
                                                                    CHAIRMAN

RC (DLC); endorsed by TJ as received 2 Dec. 1791 but recorded in SJL erroneously under 1 Dec.

To Pierce Butler

Dec. 2. 1791.

Th: Jefferson presents his compliments to Mr. Butler, and incloses him the rough draughts of resolutions, believing Mr. Butler can better settle according to his own mind the manner of furnishing the money, either from his own reflection or on consultation with the Secy. of the Treasury.

PrC (DLC). Entry in SJPL reads:
"[Dec.] 2. Th:J. to Pierce Butler:
         draught of Resolution of Senate
                 for ransom and peace
                 with Barbary.
         do.   of both houses."

ENCLOSURES

I

Draught of a Secret resolution of the Senate

Resolved by the Senate of the U.S. that if the President of the U.S. shall think proper to enter into any treaty or convention for the purpose of ransoming the citizens of the U.S. now in captivity at Algiers at an expence not exceeding [40,000] dollars, or for the preservation of peace in future with that power, and with Tunis or Tripoli or both, at an expence not exceeding [40,000] dollars to be annually paid for   years the Senate will advise and consent to the ratification thereof.

Ransom.		D
The ransom lately agreed on by persons unauthorised and unknown		34,792
Clothes and passage of 14. persons @ 100. D. each		1 400
expences of Negotiator &c.	suppose about	3 000
		39 192

Should the attempt be made and fail it will probably cost		5 000.
Peace.		D
The Dutch, Danes, Swedes, and Venetians pay from 24,000 to annly.		30,000
France, as is said, besides presents from time to time pays annly.		100,000
England it is supposed expends one year with another		280,000.

PrC (DLC); brackets in original.

II
Draught of a Secret resolution of both houses.

Resolved by the Senate and House of Representatives of the U.S. in Congress assembled, that if the President of the U.S. by and with the advice and consent of the Senate, shall think proper to enter into any treaty or convention for the purpose of ransoming the citizens of the U.S. now in captivity at Algiers at an expence not exceeding [40,000] dollars, or for the preservation of peace in future with that power, and with Tunis or Tripoli or both at an expence not exceeding [40,000] dollars to be annually paid for   years, the Congress of the U.S. will provide for the same: and that they will provide for the expences of any measures which he shall take for accomplishing these objects, tho' such measures should not succeed, provided such expences exceed not [5000] dollars.

Then should follow a resolution for furnishing the money beforehand &c.

PrC (DLC); brackets in original.

The Senate once again turned its attention to American relations with Algiers and the plight of the captive seamen in the fall of 1791 as a result of two new developments. First was the accession to power in July 1791 of a new Dey of Algiers, Ali Hassan, who was reported to be more favorably disposed toward the United States than his predecessor. Second was the Senate's reception of Charles Colvill's petition.

It was in his capacity as chairman of the Senate committee considering Colvill's petition that Butler wrote to TJ. In response, TJ promptly drafted the resolutions printed above. Despite TJ's previous preference for the use of naval power against Algiers, he may have been willing to cooperate with Butler at this time because he believed Congress' failure earlier in the year to authorize the creation of an American navy left no alternative to ransoming the captives.

Butler's committee made selective use of TJ's draft resolutions. Butler's report, submitted to the Senate on 6 Dec. 1791, disregarded TJ's emphasis on the need for a joint resolution of both houses of Congress and changed his estimate of the cost of the proposed treaties with the three Barbary states, but otherwise remained generally faithful to the main thrust of the Secretary of State's suggested resolves. The committee recommended that the Senate agree to ratify "any treaty or convention for the purpose of establishing and preserving peace with the Regency of Algiers and with Tunis and Tripoli, 'at an expense not exceeding one hundred thousand dollars annually,' for such a term of years as shall be stipulated, and for the purpose of ransoming the citizens of the United States in captivity with the Algerines, 'at an expense not exceeding forty thousand dollars for the said ransom' "; that if such an agreement could not be negotiated with Algiers "the sum of two thousand four hundred dollars annually shall be distributed among the said captives or their families, as they may prefer, in such manner and in such proportion as the President of the United States shall order and direct during their captivity"; and that in order to finance the negotiation of the projected agreements with the three Barbary states the President should "be authorized and empowered to draw on the Treasury of the United States for the sum of one hundred and forty-five thousand dollars" (*Compilation of Reports of the Committee on Foreign Relations, United States Senate*, 8 vols. [Washington, D.C., 1901], VIII, 6; ASP, *Foreign Relations*, I, 133; JS, I, 349).

The Senate considered and debated various forms of the report six times in the three months after its original submission, but it soon became apparent that there was little senatorial support for negotiating with Tripoli and Tunis or for granting financial aid to the captive seamen. Yet the Senate did favor a peace treaty with Algiers and the redemption of the captives, though initially it was reluctant to ask the House of Representatives to agree beforehand to appropriate money for these purposes (Memoranda of Consultations with President, 11 Mch.-9 Apr. 1792; Memorandum of President's Meeting with Senate Committee, 12 Mch. 1792, DLC: Washington Papers). Accordingly, on 7 Mch. 1792, after

defeating a motion to postpone further consideration of Butler's report until the next session of Congress, the Senate appointed a committee to confer with Washington in an effort to persuade him to bypass the House and dispatch an envoy to Algiers with funds drawn directly from the Treasury or borrowed from private creditors solely on the authority of a vote by the Senate (Washington to TJ, 10 Mch. 1792; Memorandum of Conference with President on Treaty with Algiers, 11 Mch. 1792; JEP, I, 91, 92, 100, 106; JS, I, 349, 354, 394).

The appointment of this committee forced TJ to focus his attention once more on the question of relations with Algiers. Having been informed in advance by Ralph Izard of the committee's objective, Washington met with TJ on 11 Mch. 1792 to discuss the position he planned to take during his forthcoming conference. Though by this time TJ was resigned to the necessity of ransoming the captured mariners, he was still less inclined than Washington to pay tribute to the government of Algiers. Indeed, he soon sought without success to persuade Washington again of the merits of employing naval force against the Algerians (TJ to Washington, 1 Apr. 1792). Despite their differences on this point, the President and the Secretary of State remained convinced that it would be prudent to obtain prior financial authorization for the proposed mission to Algiers from both branches of Congress, since in the end the House would have to appropriate the money needed to pay for any agreement that might be reached with the Algerian government. Thus, when Washington met with the members of the Senate committee on 12 Mch. 1792, he informed them that he would not attempt to ransom the captives "without previous authority from *both branches* of the legislature" (Memorandum of President's Meeting with Senate Committee, 9 Apr. 1792, enclosed in TJ to Madison, 17 Apr. 1796; Memorandum of Conference with President on Treaty with Algiers, 11 Mch. 1792; see Memorandum of President's Meeting with Senate Committee, 12 Mch. 1792, DLC: Washington Papers, for a somewhat different version of Washington's remarks).

At first, however, not even this clear expression of presidential opinion was enough to overcome lingering senatorial doubts about the possibly undesirable constitutional and diplomatic implications of applying to the House to fund the projected mission to Algiers. As a result, Washington was finally obliged to send a written message to the Senate on 8 May 1792 asking whether it would agree to approve treaties to ransom the captives and to establish peace with Algiers by paying an annual tribute (JEP, I, 122-3). In response, the Senate not only resolved that it would ratify such agreements between the United States and Algiers but also added a carefully worded amendment to an otherwise routine appro-priations bill which, without specifically describing the purpose for which the money was to be spent, was designed to authorize the President to spend up to $50,000 on negotiations with Algiers. The House immediately approved the Senate's amendment, thereby giving Washington the full legislative authorization he had sought and paving the way for the appointment soon thereafter of John Paul Jones as special envoy to Algiers (JEP, I, 123; JS, I, 442-3; JHR, I, 604-5; *Annals*, III, 1386-7; TJ to John Paul Jones, 1 June 1792; TJ, Report on Algiers and Morocco, 16 Dec. 1793).

From Charles Willson Peale

SIR   [After 3 Dec. 1791]

Was I under a mistake in expecting the favor of your sitting at One O'clock this day?[1] You will oblige me in appointing the time that will be most convenient, to yourself. I have a great desire to exert my abilities in this portrait, and your indulgence will grately obligate Honored Sir your very Humble Servt.,   C W PEALE

FC (PPAP: Peale Letter Book); in Peale's hand; undated, but the letter immediately preceding the above is dated 3 Dec. 1791 and the one following it is the note to TJ that is dated only "Tuesday Morng" and is tentatively assigned the date of 13 Dec. 1791 (see note there).

Peale was painting his famous portrait of TJ (illustrated in this volume), the date of which is determined largely from this and a subsequent letter of 13 Dec. 1791 in Peale's Letter Book (Alfred L. Bush, *The Life Portraits of Thomas Jefferson* [Charlottesville, Va., 1962], p. 31-3).

[1] Peale first wrote "I expected the favor of your sitting at One O'clock this day. Please inform me at what time it will be convenient to oblige me in this business," but altered it to read as above.

From James Brown

DEAR SIR   Richmond 4th: Decem 1791

I was duely favored with Your letters of the 13 and 28 ulto. The former I have communicated to Mr. Short at same time wrote him I should purchase in Ten Shares Bank Stock for him and rest it with him to say on Receipt of my letter that the purchase should be on his or my own account. Yesterday your four Bundles of Tree[s] came to hand from New York. They shall be taken care of and forwarded as you point out.—With much Respect I am Sir Your Ob. Hble. Servt,   JAMES BROWN

RC (MHi); endorsed by TJ as received 10 Dec. 1791 and so recorded in SJL. TJ's letter of 13 Nov. 1791 is recorded in SJL but has not been found.

From Nathaniel Cutting

SIR   Cape Francois, 4th. Decer. 1791.

I took the liberty to write you under the 29th. ulto. mentioning the disagreable intelligence that had recently been received from Port-au-Prince. The fears I then had that new mischief would speedily ensue, have proved but too justly founded. A terrible affray has taken place at Port-au-Prince between the *Mulattoes* and *whites* wherein many lives were sacrificed. Fire was set to the Town in several places and twenty-seven squares out of forty-four whereof it consisted, are totally consumed. The street called Rue des Capitaines, where the principal magazines of Provisions and marchandises were situated, fell a prey to the devouring flames. In fine, we are told that only four *merchants' Houses* have escaped the conflagration. I have seen extract of a Letter to one of the first Commercial Houses in this City which states the loss at 500[1] millions of livres.

The mulattoes immediately retreated to their Camp at Croix-des-Bouquets and we are told that the Commandant of the Western District, M. Coutard, is with them.—The flame of civil discord seems to rage in this climate with a degree of inveteracy unknown in other Countries. Nothing seems to satisfy a Partizan but the sacrifice of his opponents life and property. The work of destruction having thus commenced anew, Omniscience only can tell where it will terminate. Advices received last Evening from *Les Cayes*, state that one or two *chiefs* of the *Mulattoes* at Croix-des-Bouquets, have past into the southern district, have spirited up their Party in the vicinity of *Cayes*, taken possession of several Batteries, and threaten the Town of Les Cayes itself. The *Planters* in that quarter it should seem have taken refuge in the Town.—The victorious mulattoes proclaim that unless *they* depart immediately, each to his habitation and surrender the Town, they will deliver it and its Inhabitants to fire and Sword.

What a distressing situation!

It is difficult, I find, to determine who is right and who is wrong in the first principles of this Tragical business;—doubtless there is blame on all sides;—I fear the result will be the ruin of the Colony!— I have the honor to be, most respectfully, Sir, Your most obedt. & very huml. Serv.   NAT. CUTTING

RC (DNA: RG 59, MLR); endorsed by
TJ as received 29 Dec. 1791 and so recorded in SJL. Dft (MHi: Cutting Papers); varies in phraseology from RC. Text

printed in *National Gazette*, 2 Jan. 1792,
with a few minor alterations of wording.

¹ Thus in MS: Dft reads "50 millions."

To John Dobson

SIR   Philadelphia Dec. 4. 1791

The credit which I was obliged to give on the sale of my tobo. of the year 1790. having put it out of my power to make any payment from that resource till now, I have reserved till now also the taking a review of our affairs. The assignment to yourself of my bond to Farrell & Jones for £500. sterl. principal and int. payable July 19. 1791. has added that demand to the former one you had against me as assee. of my bill of exchange from Tabb for £300 sterl. equal to £375. currency for current money furnished when the legal exchange was 25. per cent, and not 33 ⅓ to which it has been since changed. I presume that no alteration of the denomination of money subsequent to a contract, is to affect that contract, and consequently that this is to be considered originally as a debt of £375. currency. I have no exact statement of the paiments made on this bill. I conjecture only that there is still upwards of £100. due on it; and on the bill and bond together with interest, upwards of £700 currency: for paiment whereof the following is the only provision I can make at this moment.

1. An order now inclosed on Mr. James Wilson for the balance still in his hands.

2. An order on Mr. Pope for the balance which will be in his hands of the money in suit against Woodson & Lewis, after a particular deduction made. In these orders I have named *the balance* in general terms, without specifying particular sums, which could not be done but on a final settlement. The balances however are known to be very nearly as estimated below.

3. I now remit 650. Dollars equal to £195. currency, recieved here for my tobo. of 1790.

4. I shall remit you 150. Dollars equal to £45. more on the arrival of the last part of my tobo. of the same year, expected by the first vessel from Richmond to this port.

5. According to the estimate of my crop of tobacco of this year's growth (1791.) I can appropriate about £200. worth of that to your debt as soon as it can be converted into money. These sums taken together will be nearly as follows.

	£
1. Wilson's balance	about 26–16–3
2. Pope's order with interest till recovered	about 110– 0–0
3. The Present remittance from tobo. of 1790.	195– 0–0
4. Remittance from do. to be made on arrival of tobo.	45– 0–0
5. Paiment to be made from tobo. of 1791.	200– 0–0
	Total will be about 576–16–3

which will leave a balance due to you of perhaps £200, for which I cannot at this moment make specific provision, nor say with certainty that it can be paid before the produce of the ensuing year can be converted into money. One possibility only occurred, and I left orders to avail you of it, to wit. I have directed about 40 slaves to be sold on a certain credit, but allowing a proper discount for[1] ready money. Of any ready money which may be received I have desired Colo. Lewis to £70. in the first place for another purpose, and your balance out of the rest, if so much should be received. Nothing further than this is in my immediate power.

I am sorry to see from a letter of yours to Colo. Lewis that you are about to[2]

PrC (ViU); incomplete, text being supplemented in part by Tr (ViU), also incomplete (see notes 1 and 2 below). For additional information on this letter, see TJ to Dobson, 5 Dec. 1791.

[1] Remainder of text from Tr.
[2] Tr ends at this point.

From David Humphreys

Lisbon, 4 Dec. 1791. He sends a duplicate receipt from Barclay for the 32,175 current guilders "destined for the services with which he is charged at Morocco," the first copy of the receipt having been transmitted in his letter of 22 Nov.—Before sailing from Gibraltar last Wednesday Barclay received a letter from Francisco Chiappe in Morocco and "forwarded the Original to the Office of foreign Affairs; from which (if it shall have arrived) you will perceive the complexion of affairs rather seems to promise a good result."—The war between Algiers and Sweden mentioned in his last seems likely to expand into a war between Algiers and France as well. The Swedish agent at Gibraltar has applied to the commander of the Portuguese squadron at that garrison to dispatch a frigate to the entrance of the Mediterranean to assist Swedish vessels. The folly of the Algerines may yet "bring about a change of conduct in the maritime Powers toward them. On this subject, this Country has for several years set an example worthy of imitation."—The Queen has recovered somewhat from her illness but fears that the appearance of "some dropsical symptoms" presages the approach of death. She is also made uneasy by "seeing the Royal family without succession." It is much to be feared that "designing men will take advantage of her facility of temper and zeal for religion to disturb that tranquility and prosperity which have so happily prevailed for some years past. Indeed, I think it is visible a new system in some respects is taking place."—He dined

two days ago at Mr. Walpole's with the diplomatic corps and the entire Portuguese ministry, "but no news or Politics were spoken of."

RC (DNA: RG 59, DD); 4 p.; at head of text: "(No. 40)"; endorsed by TJ as received
4 Feb. 1792 and so recorded in SJL. Enclosure: Duplicate of receipt by Barclay, in his
hand (same). Tr (same).

From Adam Lindsay

DEAR SIR   Norfolk. 4th Decemr. 1791.
I received your favour dated 15th. Septr. and should have answered it long before this, but had it not in my power to comply
with your request. The person who makes the Candles has been
sick, so that I was under the necessity of waiting his recovery and
he cannot at present supply me entirely.

I have sent you by the Sloop Alexander Hamilton of Norfolk
Captn. Johnston—Three Boxes of Myrtle wax mould'd Candles, 5.
to the lib.-weight 141 ℔ at 1 sh. and Boxes 2/. each, and in about
10 days will ship you of the same 110 ℔. of ⅟4 moulded.—You need
not trouble yourself to remit until I send the whole of your order.
Respecting the Cyder, I have not found any to my mind, but shall
keep a good look-out as this is the proper season.

There is nothing particular here, the Harbour very full of Shipping, trade good, and the town rising fast. We only want houses
for our new inhabitants who arrive daily.—A few days since arrived,
between 30. and 40. useful Mechanics from Shelburne N.S. and
were well received.

I think next summer will draw some Hundreds from thence to
this place. Our Canal subscription is almost full and if practicable
will be put in execution next Spring.—I remain with much respect,
Dr Sir Yr very hble St.,   ADAM LINDSAY

RC (MHi); endorsed by TJ as received 13 Dec. 1791 and so recorded in SJL.

To Martha Jefferson Randolph

MY DEAR DAUGHTER   Philadelphia Dec. 4. 1791.
We are well here, tho' still without news from Mr. Randolph or
yourself, tho' we have been eight weeks from Monticello. Maria was
to have written to you to-day, but she has been so closely engaged
in pasting paper together in the form of a pocket book that she has

not been able. She has been constantly getting colds since she came here. I have put on board Capt Stratton a box with the following articles for your three house-maids.

36. yds. callimanco
13 1/2 hds. calico of different patterns
25. yds. linen
9. yds. muslin
9. pr. cotton stockings
thread.

I put into the same box for you la Cuisiniere Bourgeoise and the following books which Mr. Randolph wished to see. Ginanni del grano—Duhamel, maniere de conserver le grain, Duhamel de l'insecte de l'Angoumois.—Mr. Randolph sees by the papers sent him what is the price of wheat here. Perhaps he might think it worth while to send his Varina wheat here. He could always have the money in Richmond within a fortnight from the arrival of the wheat. I shall be very ready to have it received and disposed of for him on the best terms, if he chuses. So as to corn or any thing else. My affectionate love attends you all. Adieu my dear dear daughter,

Th: Jefferson

RC (NNP); date changed by overwriting from "Dec. 5." to "Dec. 4." PrC (MHi).

The books on agricultural topics of interest to Randolph were GINANNI, *Delle Malattie del Grano in Erba* (Pesaro, 1759; Sowerby, No. 740), DUHAMEL du Monceau, *Traité de la Conservation des Grains* (Paris, 1754; Sowerby, No. 737), and Duhamel du Monceau and Mathieu Tillet, *Histoire d'un Insecte qui devore les Grains de l'Angoumois* (Paris, 1762; Sowerby, No. 738).

To John Cleves Symmes

Sir   Philadelphia Dec. 4. 1791.

Your favor of Sep. 17. has been duly recieved and laid before the President. He does not concieve that the constitution has given him any controul over the proceedings of the Judges, and therefore that his permission or refusal of absence from your district would be merely nugatory.—In the report which I made to the President on the subject of the public lands, and which he laid before the legislature, I took the liberty of suggesting the establishment of a proper judicature for deciding speedily all land controversies between the public and individuals. As yet nothing is done on the subject.—I have the honour to be Sir Your most obedt. humble servt,

Th: Jefferson

PrC (DLC). FC (DNA: RG 360, DL). Symmes' letter of 17 Sep. 1791, recorded in SJL as received 23 Nov. 1791, has not been found.

To John Dobson

SIR   Philadelphia Dec 5. 1791.

The preceding letter was written when I was in Virginia and was taking the best measures in my power to make paiments to you. Blanks were left in it for the date and the sum to be remitted to you from hence, to be filled up on my arrival here, in October, when I expected to have found all my tobo. of 1790. arrived here. In this I was disappointed, but expecting it daily, I put off writing. Your letter of the 16th of Nov. came to my hands a week ago, and this is the first moment it has been in my power to answer it. Instead of waiting to remit the whole 800 dollars together, I have concluded to send now the 650. dollars which are in hand and the remaining 150. Doll. on the arrival of the rest of the tobo. (about 5. or 6. hhds.). Be assured, Sir, it has not been in my power to do any thing more, and that I have been faulty in nothing but in not informing you of the cause of my delay. For this you would excuse me were you to see how every hour of my time is employed. It is moreover known to you that these bonds to Farrell & Jones were given in arrangement of an old affair, and under special expectations and contracts which subjected them to delays of paiment. I am sincerely sorry for any inconvenience they may have brought on you. You shall hear from me on the receipt of my tobo. You know of course that the inclosed bank post bill will be paid by the Collector at Richmond. I am with much esteem, Sir, your mo. obedt. hbl. servt,

TH: JEFFERSON

PrC (MHi). Dobson's letter of 16 Nov. 1791 is recorded in SJL as received 23 Nov. 1791, but has not been found. THE PRECEDING LETTER: TJ to Dobson, 4 Dec. 1791.

To George Hammond

SIR   Philadelphia Dec. 5. 1791.

Your favor of Nov. 30. remains still unanswered because the clerks are employed in copying some documents on the subject of the treaty of peace which I wish to exhibit to you with the answer.

In the meantime, as to that part of your letter which respects matters of commerce, the fear of misunderstanding it induces me to mention my sense of it and to ask if it be right. Where you are pleased to say that 'you are authorised to communicate to this government his majesty's readiness to enter into a negociation for establishing that intercourse [of commerce][1] upon principles of reciprocal benefit' I understand that you are not furnished with any commission or express powers to arrange a treaty with us, or to make any specific propositions on the subject of commerce; but only to assure us that his Britannic majesty is ready to concur with us in appointing persons, times and places for commencing such a negotiation. Be so good as to inform me if there be any misapprehension in this, as some steps on our part may be necessary in consequence of it.—I have the honour to be with the most perfect esteem Sir Your most obedient & most humble servt,

TH: JEFFERSON

PrC (DLC); at foot of text: "The Minister Plen. of Gr. Britain." FC (DNA: RG 360, DL).

[1] Thus in MS.

To Daniel L. Hylton

DEAR SIR   Philadelphia Dec. 5. 1791.

I find that Capt. Stratton is arrived without bringing the residue of my tobo. of last year's growth, which therefore delays the settlement and paiment for the whole crop. I must entreat you my dear Sir to send off this residue by the first vessel coming to this port, as the early setting in of the winter gives reason to expect the river will be soon blocked up, and it would be a serious catastrophe on me not to recieve it. It will be some comfort to you too that it will close this troublesome job I was obliged to put on you. Having nothing new to communicate, I conclude with respectful compliments to Mrs. Hylton & assurances of sincere esteem to yourself from Dear Sir Your friend & servt,   TH: JEFFERSON

PrC (MHi).

To Edmund Randolph

DEAR SIR   Philadelphia Dec. 5. 1791.

The inclosed memorial from the British minister on the case of Thomas Pagan, containing a complaint of injustice in the dispensations of law by the courts of Massachusets to a British subject, the President approves of my referring it to you to report thereon your opinion of the proceedings, and whether any thing, and what, can or ought to be done by the government in consequence thereof.— I am with great & sincere esteem Dear Sir Your most obedient & most humble servt.,   TH: JEFFERSON

PrC (DLC); at foot of text: "The Attorney General of the U.S." FC (DNA: RG 360, DL). Enclosure: George Hammond to TJ, 26 Nov. 1791.

From Edmund Randolph

SIR   Philadelphia December 3 [i.e. 5] 1791.

I have perused the abstract of the case of Thomas Pagan, which I received from you this morning.

Altho' I cannot entertain a momentary doubt of the facts, therein asserted; yet am I compelled by the rules of official responsibility, to request a copy of the record, from which those facts are derived, before I give an opinion on the subject. In procuring this record no time ought to be lost. For the supreme court of the United States will sit on the first Monday of february next; and if it should appear upon a more mature examination, that they can and ought to interpose, some preparatory notices may probably be necessary.—I have the honor, Sir, to be with true esteem your mo. ob. serv.,

EDM: RANDOLPH

RC (DNA: RG 59, NL); although clearly dated "December 3," this letter was undoubtedly written on 5 Dec. 1791, the date on which its receipt is recorded in SJL and endorsed on it by TJ and the date on which TJ transmitted the document here acknowledged.

From George Hammond

SIR   Philadelphia 6th December 1791

As I am extremely solicitous to avoid any misapprehension of my letter of the 30th ulto., I have now the honor of stating to you, in explanation of that part of it, to which you have adverted in yours of yesterday, that, although (as I formerly mentioned, in my first conversations with you, after my arrival in this country) I am not as yet empowered to *conclude* any definitive arrangement, with respect to the commercial intercourse between the two countries, I still meant it to be understood that I am fully authorized to *enter* into a negociation for that purpose, and into the discussion of such principles as may appear best calculated to promote that object, on a basis of reciprocal advantage. I am farther authorized to receive any propositions, which this government may be pleased to make to me upon this subject.—I have the honor to be, with every sentiment of respect and esteem, Sir, your most obedient and most humble Servant,   GEO. HAMMOND.

RC (DNA: RG 59, NL); endorsed by TJ as received 6 Dec. 1791 and so recorded in SJL; also docketed by him: "Hammond George powers as to treat of Commerce." Tr (DNA: RG 59, NL).

Memorandum of Conversation with José de Jaudenes

[Philadelphia] Dec. 6. 1791

Don Joseph Jaudenes communicates verbally to the Secretary of State that his Catholic majesty has been apprised through the channel of the Court of Versailles of our sollicitude to have some arrangements made respecting our free navigation of the Missisipi, and a port thereon convenient for the deposit of merchandize of export and import for lading and unlading the sea and river vessels: and that his Majesty will be ready to enter into treaty thereon *directly* with us whensoever[1] we shall[2] send to Madrid a proper and acceptable person duly authorized to treat on our part.

MS (DNA: RG 59, NL); in TJ's hand, with corrections approved by Jaudenes (see notes 1 and 2 below, and TJ to Joseph Jaudenes and Joseph Viar, 26 Jan. 1792); added at bottom of text: note of conversation with Jaudenes of 27 Dec. 1791. PrC (DLC); enclosed in TJ to Jaudenes and Viar, 26 Jan. 1792; entirely in TJ's hand. Tr (DNA: RG 360, DL).

The historical background of Spain's decision to resume negotiations with the United States at this time is discussed in Editorial Note on threat of disunion in the West, at 10 Mch. 1791. Although TJ was initially under the impression that Spain wished to confine the new negotiations to the navigation of the Mississippi, he subsequently learned from Jaudenes that the Spanish government wished to resolve all of its principal diplomatic differences with the United States (see Memorandum of Conversation with Jaudenes, 27 Dec. 1791;

Jaudenes and Viar to TJ, 25, 27 Jan. 1792; TJ to Jaudenes and Viar, 26 Jan. 1792). The changes in TJ's diplomatic strategy toward Spain resulting from Jaudenes' clarification of Spanish intentions can be seen most clearly by contrasting the limited goals he set forth in his 22 Dec. 1791 report to Washington with the far more ambitious objectives he sought to achieve in the instructions to the American commissioners to Spain contained in his 7 and 18 Mch. 1792 letters to Washington.

[1] TJ first wrote "between the two nations, whenever" but altered it to read as above.
[2] The remainder of the sentence was revised several times; it appears that TJ first wrote "[name?] duly authorized any person to do the same on our part at Madrid." He crossed this out and interlined the above wording.

From Jonathan Dayton

SIR   Wednesday Decemr. 7th. 1791

The Committee appointed by the House of Representatives to consider, and report upon, the petition of the Canadian refugees, wish to be possessed of a list of the persons falling under that description. A return was made to the former Congress, and I am informed is at this time on the files in your office. If this be the case Sir, I will thank you to direct a copy of it to be immediately made out and sent to me. If you are in possession of any list or return of the refugees from Nova Scotia, be so good as to transmit a copy of that also.—I am Sir your very hum. servt.,   JONA: DAYTON

RC (DNA: RG 59, MLR); endorsed by Remsen as received 7 Dec. 1791. Not recorded in SJL.

Jonathan Dayton, a maverick Federalist who had recently been elected to the first of four consecutive terms in the House of Representatives from New Jersey, was chairman of a committee to which on 29 Nov. 1791 the House had referred a petition from some Canadian refugees, "praying compensation for losses and injuries sustained in their persons and property, by adhering to the American cause, during the late war" (JHR, I, 465). Both of the lists of refugees requested by Dayton were ac-

tually in the office of Secretary of War Knox (Dayton, "Report to House of Representatives," 19 Feb. 1793, ASP, *Public Lands*, I, 28). The problem of compensating the several hundred Canadian and Nova Scotian refugees for the losses they had suffered in consequence of their service in the Continental Army or their political support for the American cause during the Revolutionary War is discussed in Allan S. Everest, *Moses Hazen and the Canadian Refugees in the American Revolution* (Syracuse, N.Y., 1976), p. 113-41; and in Carl Wittke, "Canadian Refugees in the American Revolution," *Canadian Historical Review*, III (1922), 320-33.

George Washington to Beverley Randolph

SIR   Philadelphia Dec. 7. 1791.

I have recieved your letter of Nov. 18. covering a resolution of the legislature of Virginia of Nov. 14. and a Memorial of sundry citizens of that commonwealth on the subject of their property carried away by the British, contrary, as they suppose, to the stipulations of the treaty of peace. A regular channel of communication with that government being now open, I shall not fail to pay due attention to this subject.—I have the honor to be with due consideration Yr. Excellency's Most Obedt. Sr.

Dft (DNA: RG 59, MLR); in TJ's hand except for complimentary close added by Lear; at foot of text TJ wrote "The Gov-

ernor of Virginia," to which Lear prefixed the words: "His Excellency." PrC (DLC); without Lear's additions. Entry in SJPL reads: "[draught] of letter from G.W. to Govr. of Virga. on property carried away."

Governor Randolph had transmitted to Washington a resolve of the Virginia General Assembly requesting the federal government to "enforce due execution of the [seventh] Article" of the treaty of peace and to help obtain compensation for the slaves lost to the British during the war (Beverley Randolph to Washington, 18 Nov. 1791, with enclosed 26 Aug. 1791 memorial to and 14 Nov. 1791 resolve of Virginia General Assembly, DNA: RG 59, MLR). TJ had already brought this issue to the attention of the British minister (TJ to Hammond, 29 Nov. 1791).

From Tench Coxe

Decemr. 8th. 1791

Mr. Coxe has the honor to inclose to Mr. Jefferson an abstract from the general imports, intended to exhibit the quantum of manufactured supplies, which each foreign nation has the benefit of selling to the United States. The estimate is formed on a presumption that all the *ad valorem* articles from Europe and the E. Indies are Manufactures. This is almost universally true, and if it varies in regard to one nation, it will be proportionally variant as to all the rest. *The Scale* therefore will be correct.

RC (DLC); endorsed by TJ as received 8 Dec. 1791 but not recorded in SJL.

The enclosed ABSTRACT, which has not been found, was undoubtedly for use in TJ's Report on American Commerce, 16 Dec. 1793.

To John Adams

SIR   Philadelphia Dec. 9. 1791.

The inclosed information relative to ransom and peace with the Algerines, being newly come to hand, I take the liberty of communicating it to you, and through you to the Senate. It concurs in some facts and opinions with what we had before learnt thro other channels, and differs in some others, so as, on the whole, to leave us still in considerable uncertainty as to interesting points.—I have the honor to be with sentiments of the most perfect respect, Sir, Your most obedient & most humble servant,   TH: JEFFERSON

PrC (DLC); at foot of text: "The Vice-President of the U.S. President of the Senate." Entry in SJPL reads: "Th:J. to Pres. of Senate. Ransom and peace, letter from W.S." Enclosure: Extracts from Short to TJ, 24 Aug. 1791.

After reading TJ's letter and enclosure, the Senate referred both documents to the committee on Algerian affairs chaired by Pierce Butler (JEP, I, 91). For a discussion of TJ's relations with this committee, see notes to TJ to Pierce Butler, 2 Dec. 1791.

To Thomas Barclay

DEAR SIR   Philadelphia Dec. 9. 1791.

An opportunity offering by a vessel bound to Mogadore, I avail myself of it to send you a collection of the gazettes of the last three months. To these I add herein a passage from a paper of this morning giving news, which arrived in town last night, of the defeat of Genl. Sinclair by the Indians. This of course will oblige us to another campaign.—As nothing has happened since your departure relative to the objects committed to you I have nothing to say on that head.— Your family was well about 6. weeks ago, when I was in Virginia. I have not been in the way of hearing of them since.—I am with sincere esteem, Dear Sir your most obedt. humble servt,

TH: JEFFERSON

PrC (DLC); at foot of text: "Mr. Barclay at Morocco." FC (DNA: RG 59, DCI). On the same day, TJ instructed Henry Remsen to send William Short an account of St. Clair's defeat, but not to send the usual compliment of newspapers because "the postage will come too high from Bourdeaux to Paris" (Remsen to Short, 9 Dec. 1791; RC in DLC: Short Papers; endorsed by Short as received 28 Jan. 1792).

Report on the Petition of Samuel Breck and Others

The Secretary of State, to whom was referred by the House of Representatives the Petition of Samuel Breck and others, Proprietors of a sail-cloth Manufactory in Boston, praying that they may have the exclusive Privilege of using particular Marks for designating the Sail-Cloth of their Manufactory, has had the same under Consideration and thereupon REPORTS,

That it would, in his Opinion, contribute to Fidelity in the Execution of Manufactures to secure to every Manufactory an exclusive Right to some Mark on it's Wares, proper to itself.

That this should be done by general Laws extending equal Right to every Case to which the Authority of the Legislator should be competent.

That these Cases are of divided Jurisdiction, Manufactures made and consumed within a State being subject to State Legislation, while those which are exported to foreign Nations, or to another State, or into the Indian Territory, are alone within the Legislation of the General Government.

That it will, therefore, be reasonable for the General Legislature to provide in this Behalf by Law for those Cases of Manufacture generally, and those only, which relate to commerce with foreign Nations, and among the several States, and with the Indian Tribes.

And that this may be done by permitting the owner of every Manufactory, to enter in the Records of the Court of the District wherein his Manufactory is, the Name with which he chuses to mark or designate his Wares, and rendering it penal in others to put the same Mark to any other Wares.   TH: JEFFERSON

Dec. 9. 1791.

PrC (DLC); in clerk's hand, except for signature and date; endorsed in clerk's hand: "Recorded and Examined." FC (DNA: RG 59, SDR); preceded by text of House resolution of 28 Nov. 1791, attested by John Beckley, referring to Secretary of State for examination and report the petition of Samuel Breck and others "praying that they may have the exclusive privilege of using the particular marks for the designation of the sail cloth of their manufactory, and that others may be prohibited from imitating the same, under reasonable penalties." This report was transmitted to Speaker of House of Representatives by TJ on 9 Dec. 1791 (PrC in DLC; entirely in TJ's hand). Entry in SJPL reads: "Report Th:J. on Breck's petition. Marks on manufactures."

The petition of Breck and associates was one part of a broader effort to secure competitive advantages for a business firm that was then facing the prospect of serious economic problems. Breck, a Boston merchant, was co-proprietor of the Boston Duck or Sail Cloth Manufactory, a firm whose work force of "about 200 Women & Girls together with about 50 Men" employed 30 looms to produce an average of 45 to 50

pieces of duck a week. The firm's margin of profit was heavily dependent on a bounty for the production of duck from the government of Massachusetts that was due to expire in December 1791. Without this bounty, which was necessary to meet the high cost of flax, Breck was convinced that his firm would either have to raise the price it charged for duck, in which case merchants would probably buy cheaper "Russian Canvas" instead, or discontinue its manufacture. Thus, in addition to asking for the exclusive privilege of using a special mark to distinguish his product from those of his competitors, Breck also hinted to Alexander Hamilton that it would be advisable for the national government to provide a bounty to encourage the manufacture of duck in the United States. Unfortunately for Breck, the House simply tabled TJ's report after reading it on this date, and Congress ignored Hamilton's recommendation in favor of a bounty for domestically produced sail cloth in his Report on Manufactures (JHR, I, 464, 470; Breck to Hamilton, 3 Sep. 1791; Nathaniel Gorham to Hamilton, 13 Oct. 1791; Hamilton, Report on Manufactures, 5 Dec. 1791, Syrett, *Hamilton*, IX, 162-3, 372-3, X, 327).

From Daniel Smith

"*Southwestern Territory, At Mr. Cobbs,*" 9 Dec. 1791. In Blount's absence, acknowledges receipt of TJ's to him of 22 Aug. 1791, "which was so much delayed on its passage that it never came to hand 'till 8th. Nov. last."—The information requested about Davidson county claims amount to 407,780 acres, which includes all allowable under the law of North Carolina except a few remaining preemption and soldier's claims not yet entered. The final total may amount to 410,000.—He has obtained no additional census information since that transmitted by Gov. Blount.—"The Muscle Shoal party make no noise at present in this Country. I hope they have abandoned the scheme."

RC (DNA: RG 59, SWT, M-471/1); 1 p.; endorsed by TJ as received 5 Jan. 1792 and so recorded in SJL. Full text in Carter, *Terr. Papers*, IV, 105.

From George Washington

DEAR SIR   Friday Morning [9 Dec. 1791]
   Yesterday afternoon Colo. Hamilton was desired, as soon as the Tariff was ready, to let it be known.—Enclosed is his answer.—Say whether the meeting shall be tomorrow, or on Monday morning?— Yours sincerely,   GO: WASHINGTON

RC (DLC); addressed: "Mr. Jefferson"; endorsed by TJ as received 9 Dec. 1791 and so recorded in SJPL, in which entry reads: "G.W. to Th:J. tariff of duties with France."

The subject of this letter is discussed in note to TJ to Washington, 26 Nov. 1791. Hamilton's proposed TARIFF is printed in Syrett, *Hamilton*, XIII, 409-10, from an un-dated manuscript in DLC: Hamilton Papers. His ANSWER to Washington has not been found.

From Sylvanus Bourne

Sir   Philadelphia Decr 10th 1791
   The aggregate result of that investigation, which I have made of the sentiments of the members of Congress relating to the Consular System, of this Country, tends to weaken my expectations of ever returning again to the West Indies, and the more especially as the present state of Hispaniola renders still more precarious than before, every pursuit of a mercantile nature:—but faint as my expectations from a tenure of my present Commission may be, they are more than I possess from any other source, or I should e'er this have resigned that Charge, which I was induced to accept from a false association of Ideas, cherished by my aspiring hopes, but which has brought on me the weight of accumulated expences, dissappoint-ment and Chagrin.
   If I have ventured to reiterate my Desire for a birth in the employ of Govt. view me not on that account as a Parasite at Court, but place it to an ingenuous effort for restoring myself and family to that Rank and Situation in life of which the late war deprived us by the sacrifice of a fortune of £10,000. sterlg but perhaps the energy of my wishes in this respect have led me to a false conception of my

capacity to accomplish the object of them in any situation comporting with public Benefit, and were it not for the strong impulse of filial and fraternal Obligations I would not consent again to add my name to the long Catalogue of claimants which ever burthen the Presidents Cabinet rendering his dispensation of offices a task equally delicate and painful—but would hope in a retreat to obscurity, to derive some solace for the want of personal care in contemplating the progressive happiness of that Country to whose best Interests I feel the strongest attachment.

I am sensible that the pleas of losses by the late war or those of present necessity lose their force by their general application, and that those whose Stations expose them to such like solicitations are obliged to guard every avenue to the heart lest it betrays the judgment; it is therefore with diffidence that I submit to your acquaintance of my Character and Pretensions what claim I may have for any future vacancy in the Foreign or Domestic service of the U.S. If in my personal or epistolary Communications with you, I have discovered any want of that manly confidence which is becoming, it is to be attributed to a mind depressed by a long series of misfortunes, challenging the utmost efforts of Philosophy to their support, and only rendered tolerable by the influence of conscious rectitude. I have the honour to be with all possible Respect sir your most Obedt Humble servt,   Sylva: Bourne

PS. I have taken the liberty to inclose a collection of a few general observations on the political state of this Country, which (at the request of Mr. Fenno and in order to beguile a few tedious hours), I ventured to commit to the press on opening of the new Govt— they were many of them wrote in great haste and mutilated by typographical errors—if you should do me the honour of perusing them, you will veil the eye of criticism while you open that of Candour.

RC (DLC: Washington Papers); endorsed by TJ as received 10 Dec. 1791 and so recorded in SJL.

The enclosed OBSERVATIONS consisted of a series of political essays entitled "A Sketch of the Political State of America" that Bourne wrote under the pseudonym "Americanus," published in twenty-three installments in John Fenno's Gazette of the United States between 22 Apr. and 12 Aug. 1789. Bourne's "Sketch" covered three general subjects. In the first five essays Bourne traced the political history of the United States from 1776 to 1787, emphasizing the achievement of American independence, the weaknesses of the Articles of Confederation, and the resultant need for the adoption of the federal constitution. In the next three essays he analyzed the constitution drawn up by the Philadelphia Convention, praising it for creating an energetic form of government while still preserving the liberties of the people. And in the remaining essays he set forth an agenda for the new federal government, laying special emphasis on the need to create an efficient and equitable system of taxation, to pay the public debt and establish a national bank, to promote American commerce overseas, and to foster a spirit of American nationalism through the establishment of a federal university where college graduates from all sections of the country would be instructed in the arts of legislation and jurisprudence. TJ, who praised Bourne's essays, was probably favorably impressed by the anti-British tone of Bourne's work. In addition to attributing the American Revolution to British tyranny and the economic problems of the Confederation to British restrictions on American trade, Bourne also called for the passage of retaliatory legislation against British trade and shipping in order to make the United States economically independent of the former mother country—a goal TJ also sought to achieve. See also TJ to Bourne, 30 Dec. 1791.

From the Commissioners of the Federal District

SIR   George Town Decr. 10th. 1791

Immediately on the receipt of your letter of the 21st Ultimo, we gave directions to Mr. Ellicott, to lay out Squares in the Places mentioned.—The inclosed letter will inform you of the progress he has made. From the opportunities we have had of acquiring any Knowledge on this subject, we think it will be of Importance that some Squares on the most eligible situations on Navigation, should be in readiness by the next Sale.—We are inclined to think, from our conversation with Major L'Enfant, and Mr. Ellicott, that it will not be advisable to have a Sale, sooner than the Middle of June.

Mr. Blodgett has not yet arived. It would certainly be very desireable to form a contract of Such magnitude with him. We fear, from some Ideas thrown out by a Mr. Welsh, who (we understand) is to be concerned with him in the contract, that he rates the Importance of it to the City, so highly, as to expect to get the Ground at a low rate.—We should be happy in case of an offer from him, to be favored with the Presidents Ideas respecting the terms which might be acceded to; In so great a purchase as Mr. Blodgett contemplates, it would certainly be wrong to take our late Sales as the only guide or standard: but how far short of what they averaged per acre would it be proper to stop?

The circumstances respecting Mr. Carrolls House, we have already laid before the President and recieved his late communications on the Subject. As the House was nearly Demolished before the Chancellors Injunction arived; Mr. Carroll did not think it worth while to have it served, trusting perhaps, that our directions expressly forbiding their further proceedings in it, would have been attended to. We are sorry to mention, that the Major who was absent at the time we issued them, paid no attention to them, but compleatly Demolished it on his return. His Conduct in this instance, has given fresh alarm; as the Proprietors had flattered themselves, that in any Instances in which they might concieve themselves injured, they should be able to obtain relief from the Commissioners. As we have already more than once, from our high opinion of his talents, sacrifised to our feelings to our Zeal, we have done it again.

The Major has indeed done us the Honour of Writing us a Letter, Justifying his conduct. We have not noticed it, and believe as we are likely to get every thing Happily adjusted between Mr. Carroll and him, it will be most prudent to drop all explanations. We expect you will see the Major in Philadelphia in a Short time. We can not conclude, without expressing our Sanguine hopes, from the Train in which all matters are now, respecting this unhappy affair, that however reprehensible it may have been in the mode of conducting it, that it will prove Ultimately Salutary.—We are Sir with great respect Yr Most obt Svts.,   DD: STUART

DANL. CARROLL

RC (DLC: District of Columbia Papers); endorsed by TJ as received 13 Dec. 1791 and so recorded in SJL. Enclosure: Andrew Ellicott to Carroll and Stuart, dated "City of Washington December 10th. 1791" and reading: "The squares on the diagonal between George-Town, and the Presidents House, are generally compleat; but there yet remains about one week's work, to finish the squares on the diagonal, between the Presidents House, and Capitol.—The squares on the diagonal between the Capitol, and the eastern branch ferry, will be compleated early in the spring" (same). FC (DNA: RG 42, DCLB); dated 8 Dec. 1791 and varies in minor points of phraseology from RC.

To Thomas Mann Randolph, Jr.

DEAR SIR   Philadelphia Dec. 11. 1791.

We are still without any letters from Monticello since our departure. I received one yesterday from Mr. De Rieux of Nov. 15. in which however he does not mention the family at Monticello. I suppose that some irregularity of the post occasions this. I have never failed to write once a week, and Maria has written several times. Stratton did not sail till yesterday, so that by the time you get this he will probably be at Richmond, with the box of servants clothes.—Mr. Brown writes me word that the 4. bundles of trees from Prince are safe arrived there, so that I am in hopes you have recieved them. The late calamity to the Westward has produced great sensation here. I am in hopes it will have the effect of preventing the enlarging our army of regulars, and inducing us to confide more in Militia operations. Affairs in France seem very happily terminated, and there seems little reason to apprehend foreign interference. Present my kisses to my dear Martha, & little Anne and beleive me to be Dear Sir Your's most affectionately,

TH: JEFFERSON

RC (DLC); addressed: "Thos. M. Randolph junr. esq. Monticello"; franked. PrC (MHi). Under this date TJ recorded in SJL a letter written to Mrs. Randolph, but obviously this is an erroneous entry intended for the above letter, which is not recorded. The fact that Mary had written SEVERAL TIMES is revealing: her record as a correspondent under TJ's immediate tutelage stands in strong contrast to that of the preceding period.

To George Washington

DEAR SIR   Philadelphia Dec. 11. 1791.

I have given you the trouble of more reading on the subject of Major Lenfant's letter, than you perhaps intended. I have done it from an apprehension that your mind might not be thoroughly satisfied whether he was not equally justifiable in the demolition of Mr. Carrol's house, as in the demolition of trees and other obstacles, which he urges in his own justification. The truth is that without orders he was justifiable in neither: and he certainly never had orders to pull down houses.—I am with the most perfect respect & attachment Sir Your most obedt. & most humble servt,

TH: JEFFERSON

PrC (DLC); at foot of text: "The President of the U.S."; entry in SJPL under 11 Dec. 1791 reads: "[Th:J. to G.W.] Letter on [L'Enfant's letter]." See note to enclosure.

ENCLOSURE

Observations on L'Enfant's Letter

Observations on Majr. L'enfant's letter of Dec. 7. 1791. to the President, justifying his demolition of the house of Mr. Carrol of Duddington.

He says that 'Mr. Carrol erected his house partly on a main street, and altogether on ground to which the public had a more immediate title than himself could claim.' When blaming Mr. Carrol then he considers this as a street; but when justifying himself he considers it not yet as a street. For, to account for his not having pointed out to Carrol a situation where he might build, he says 'the President had not yet sanctioned the plan of distribution for the city, nor determined if he would approve the situation of the several areas proposed to him in that plan for public use, and that I would have been highly to be blamed to have anticipated his opinion thereon.' This latter exculpation is solid; the first without foundation. The plan of the city has been not yet definitively determined by the President. Sale to individuals or partition decide the plan as far as these sales or partitions go. A deed with the whole plan annexed, executed by the President and recorded, will ultimately fix it. But till a sale or partition, or deed, it is open to alteration. Consequently there is as yet no such thing as a street except adjacent to the lots actually sold or divided; the erection of a house in any part of the ground cannot as yet be a *nuisance* in law. Mr. Carrol is tenant in common of the soil, with the public, and the erection of a house by a tenant in common on the common property is no nuisance. Mr. Carrol has acted imprudently, intemperately, foolishly; but he has not acted illegally. There must be an establishment of the streets before his house can become a nuisance in the eye of the law. Therefore till that establishment neither Majr. Lenfant, nor the Commissioners would have had a right to demolish his house without his consent.

The Majr. says he had as much right to pull down a house, as to cut down a tree.

This is true, if he has received no authority to do either. But still there will be this difference. To cut down a tree or to demolish a house in the soil of another is a trespass. But the cutting a tree in this country is so slight a trespass, that a man would be thought litigious, who should prosecute it: if he prosecuted civilly, a jury would give small damages; if criminally, the judge would not inflict imprisonment, nor impose but a small fine. But the demolition of a house is so gross a trespass, that every man would prosecute it; if civilly, a jury would give great damages; if criminally, the judge would punish heavily by fine and imprisonment. In the present case, if Carrol was to bring a civil action the jury would probably punish his folly by small damages: but if he were to prosecute criminally, the judge would as probably vindicate the insult on the laws and the breach of the peace by heavy fine and imprisonment. So that if Majr. Lenfant is right in saying he had as much authority to pull down a house as to cut down a tree, still he would feel a difference in the punishment of the law.

But is he right in saying he had as much authority to pull down a house as cut down a tree? I do not know what have been the authorities given him *expressly* or by *implication*. But I can very readily conceive that the authorities which he has recieved, whether from the President or from the Commissioners, whether verbal, or written, may have gone to the demolition of trees, and not of houses. I am sure that he has received no authority either from the President or Commissioners, either expressly or by implication, to pull down houses. An order to him to mark on the ground the lines of the streets and lots, might imply an order to remove trees or *small* obstructions *where they insuperably prevented his operations*; but a person must know little of geometry, who could not, in an open feild, designate streets and lots, even where a line passed through a house, without pulling the house down.

In truth the blame on Majr. Lenfant, is for having pulled down the house of his own authority, and when he had reason to beleive he was in opposition to the sentiments of the President[1]: and his fault is aggravated by it's having been done to gratify private resentment against Mr. Carrol, and most palpably not because it was necessary: and the style in which he writes the justification of his act, shews that a continuation of the same resentment renders him still unable to acquiesce under the authority from which he has been reproved.

He desires a line of demarcation between his office and that of the Commissioners.

What should be this line? And who is to draw it? If we consider the matter under the *act of Congress* only, the President has authority only to name the Commissioners, and to approve or disapprove certain proceedings of theirs. They have the whole executive power, and stand between the President and the subordinate agents. In this view, they may employ or dismiss, order and countermand, take on themselves such parts of the execution as they please, and assign other parts to subordinate agents. Consequently, under the *act of Congress* their will is the line of demarcation between subordinate agents, while no such line can exist between themselves and their agents.—Under the deed from the Proprietors to the President, his powers are much more ample. I do not accurately recollect the tenor of the deed; but I am pretty sure it was such as to put much more ample power into the hands of the President, and to commit to him the whole execution of whatever is to be done under the deed. And this goes particularly to the laying out the town. So that as to this, the President is certainly authorised to draw the line of demarcation between L'enfant and the Commissioners. But I believe there is no necessity for it. As far as I have been able to judge, from conversations and consultations with the Commissioners, I think they are disposed to follow implicitly the will of the President whenever they can find it out. But Lenfant's letters do not breathe the same moderation or acquiescence: and I think it would be much safer to say to him 'the orders of the Commissioners are your line of demarcation,' than, by attempting to define his powers, to give him a line where he may meet with the commissioners foot to foot, and chicane and raise opposition to their orders whenever he thinks they pass his line.

I confess, that on a view of Lenfant's proceedings and letters latterly, I am thoroughly persuaded that to render him useful, his temper must be subdued; and that the only means of preventing his giving constant trouble to the President is to submit him to the unlimited controul of the Commissioners. We know the discretion and forbearance with which they will exercise it.

Th: Jefferson
Dec. 11. 1791.

PrC (DLC); entirely in TJ's hand. Although this document is dated 11 Dec. 1791, entry in SJPL is under 9 Dec. 1791 and reads: "Th:J. to G.W. Observations on L'Enfant's letter." This, together with the fact that the entry precedes that for the covering letter, which is correctly recorded under 11 Dec. 1791, suggests that TJ may have drafted the observations and then held the document for two days, possibly for the purpose of consulting Madison or perhaps in order to reflect further upon the prudence of dispatching so vigorous an opinion. A draft of L'Enfant's letter of 7 Dec. is in DLC: Digges-L'Enfant-Morgan Papers; partial text printed in Elizabeth S. Kite, *L'Enfant and Washington* (Baltimore, 1929), p. 89-91; see also Vol. 20: 48-50.

[1] TJ originally wrote "& Commissioners" after this word and then erased it.

From Richard Bruce

SIR   Albemarle 12th Decr. 1791
Having repeatedly Experienced favors of this kind from you it Emboldens me still to intrude further on your goodness.—David Owings and David Woods have got some military Claim sent on by the Assembly to Congress to have them settled—And they have wrote to Mr. Madison to lay them seperately before Congress. And as I was in some measure the Instigation of their not being paid as you will see by the papers therefore beg you to be so good as to try to get them settled when they Come to hand and write me word their fate. I am sir your most Obt. servt,   RICH BRUCE

RC (DLC); endorsed by TJ and noted in SJL as received 29 Dec. 1791; beneath endorsement TJ wrote: "Th:J. must trouble Mr. Remsen to enquire at the proper office relative to the inclosed."

Owings and Woods, two former members of the Virginia Line who lived in TJ's home county of Albemarle, were each issued a certificate of registered debt for $14.36, with interest thereon from 1 Mch. 1779, by the Department of the Treasury on 25 July 1792 under the terms of an act of March 1792 providing for the payment of members of the Continental Army and Navy for services rendered the United States (ASP, *Claims*, p. 389). In the letter to James Madison entreating him to support their claims, Owings and Woods noted that Bruce "manages the matter for us" (Owings and Woods to Madison, 12 Dec. 1791, Rutland, *Madison*, XIV, 148; see also Madison to TJ, 5 Mch. 1792).

From Daniel Carroll

SIR   George Town Decr. 12th. 1791
I do myself the honor of transmitting herewith, a copy of the Act, passed last Saturday, by the General Assembly, entitled an Act concerning the Territory of Columbia and the City of Washington. It is not from a certified copy. I believe however correct. The Bill propos'd that the Willfull shou'd be under the same circumstances with the Minors &ca. but it was thought proper in that case to proceed by condemnation as in the Law. This was the most essential alteration.—I am Sir with great respect yr most obt. & Hble Sert.,
                                                    DANL. CARROLL

P.S. The Law passd finally on Saturday, but time wou'd not allow to gett a Copy with *the last endorsement by the Clerk.*

RC (DLC); endorsed by TJ as received 16 Dec. 1791 and so recorded in SJL.

The ACT ceding territory in Maryland for the District of Columbia acknowledged the agreements whereby certain people had already given land for the purpose, but because others had not reached similar agreements, "from imbecility and other causes," provided for the legal condemnation of the land within the district of "minors, persons absent out of the state, married women, or persons *non compis mentis*, or lands the property of this state" (*Votes and Proceedings of the House of Delegates of the State of Maryland*, 10 Dec. 1791, p. 81, and *Votes and Proceedings of the Senate of the State of Maryland*, 10 Dec. 1791, p. 26, in Jenkins, *Records*; text of act is in *Laws of Maryland*, Chap. xlv, in same; see also Bryan, *National Capital*, i, 170-1).

To George Hammond

SIR   Philadelphia Dec. 12. 1791.

I take the liberty of inclosing you an extract of a letter from a respectable character, giving information of a Mr. Bowles lately come from England into the Creek country, endeavouring to excite that nation of Indians to war against the United States and pretending to be employed by the government of England. We have other testimony of these his pretensions and that he carries them much farther than is here stated. We have too much confidence in the justice and wisdom of the British government to believe they can approve of the proceedings of this incendiary and impostor, or countenance for a moment a person who takes the liberty of using their name for such a purpose; and I make the communication merely that you may take that notice of the case which in your opinion shall be proper.—I have the honour to be with great & sincere esteem Sir Your most obedient & most humble servant,

TH: JEFFERSON

PrC (DLC); at foot of text: "Mr. Hammond M.P. of G.B." FC (DNA: RG 360, DL). FC (PRO: FO 4/11, f. 260-1); enclosure appended.

ENCLOSURE

Extract of Letter concerning
W. A. Bowles

A vessel arrived here from New Providence with certain accounts of a Mr. Bowles being there, having lately arrived from London in company with five Indians, and British goods to amount of upwards thirty thousand pounds sterling, said to be delivered as presents (by Bowles) to the Indians in this quarter from the goverment of Great Britain. That the said Bowles was actually to sail four days after this vessel from Providence for the coast of Florida, with a principal part of his cargo of goods, and that Indian river, about 100 miles South of Augustine, was to be his first rendezvous; there to be met by large bodies of Indians attached to his views. It is said that he has a very large quantity of arms and ammunition with him; and that he intends establishing a strong post about the head of Indian river and in the province of East Florida, for the purpose of keeping open a communication between Britain and the Creeks, Choctaws, Chickasaws, and other tribes of Indians. This Bowles is the same person who made an attempt to establish a post in Florida about two years past, under the auspices of Lord Dunmore and others in Providence; but the people (about fifty in number) which had with him, described him soon after his landing, by which his scheme for that time proved abortive. Soon after he went with some five Indians he has now with him to Providence, from thence to Canada, and from thence was sent to England at the expence of that government, and whilst in England maintained at a very great expence.

It is confidently asserted that this man is sent out by the British government, tho' not openly avowed by them. I saw some Gentlemen who came passengers from Providence in the vessel that brought those accounts, who informed me that it was generally believed there, that the British government had equipped Bowles, that Govr. Dunmore and all the Officers of government in the Bahamas paid Bowles great attention, though formerly a very low character. Certain it is, that Bowles could not have credit for the amount of five pounds on his own account, in any country where he is known.

FC (PRO: FO 4/11, f. 260-1).

William Augustus Bowles had returned to America in the autumn of 1791 and prevailed upon his Indian supporters to elect him "Director of Affairs" of the Creek and Cherokee nations. In this capacity and mendaciously intimating that he was acting under British authority, he denounced the Treaty of New York concluded between the Creeks and the United States in 1790 and urged several tribes assembled at the Creek town of Coweta to cooperate with the northern Indians in order to se-

cure better terms from the American government (J. L. Wright, Jr., *William Augustus Bowles: Director General of the Creek Nation* [Athens, Ga., 1967], p. 36-70). In addition to the intelligence contained in the enclosure described above, TJ was probably also impelled to write to Hammond by the recent arrival in Philadelphia of a report from Maj. Richard Call, the commander in charge of American troops in Georgia, describing Bowles' activities at Coweta (George Beckwith to Lord Dorchester, 2 Dec. 1791, PRO: FO 4/11, f. 181-2).

Report on Matters for Negotiation with Great Britain

The discussions which are opening between Mr. Hammond and our government, have as yet looked towards no objects but those which depend on the treaty of peace. There are however other matters to be arranged between the two governments, some of which do not rest on that treaty. The following is a statement of the whole of them.

1. The Western posts.
2. The Negroes carried away.
3. The debt of their bank to Maryland, and perhaps to Rho. island.

4. Goods taken from the inhabitants of Boston, while the town was in their possession and compensation promised.

5. Prizes taken after the dates at which hostilities were to cease.

6. Subsistence of prisoners.

7. The Eastern boundary.

Which of these shall be taken into the present discussion?

Which of them shall be left to arrangement through the ordinary channels of our ministers, in order to avoid embarrassing the more important points with matter of less consequence?

On the subject of Commerce, shall Mr. Hammond be desired to produce his powers to treat, as is usual, before conferences are held on that subject?

Th: Jefferson

Dec. 12. 1791.

MS (DLC). PrC (DLC). Entry in SJPL reads: "Subjects of discussion with Mr. Hammond."

The exact purpose of this document is not altogether clear. The care with which TJ drafted it and the subject matter with which it deals indicates that he probably prepared it for Washington's use in order to solicit the President's guidance on the course he should pursue during his forthcoming negotiations with George Hammond. But there is also evidence suggesting that it might have been considered by the cabinet as well as by the President. Hammond reported, apparently on the basis of information supplied by the Secretary of the Treasury, that at about this time TJ discussed the subject of the British minister's authority to negotiate a commercial treaty with the United States during what Hammond was pleased to describe as a meeting of the "council" (Hammond to Grenville, 19 Dec. 1791, PRO: FO 4/11, f. 255-9). Yet whether this report was considered by the President alone or in conjunction with the cabinet, it is instructive to note that within three days after drawing up this document TJ had concluded that the third through the sixth points enumerated therein were "smaller matters" which were inappropriate for the Secretary of State to discuss with the British minister and decided instead to focus his attention on the rest of the issues mentioned in the report (TJ to Hammond, 15 Dec. 1791).

Maryland's effort to regain control of the stock it had acquired in the Bank of England before the Revolutionary War was a minor irritant in Anglo-American relations for over two decades until it was finally resolved during TJ's first term as President (Jacob M. Price, "The Maryland Bank Stock Case: British-American Financial and Political Relations before and after the American Revolution," Aubrey C. Land, Lois G. Carr, and Edward C. Papenfuse, eds., Law, Society, and Politics in Early Maryland [Baltimore, 1977], p. 3-40).

From José Ignacio de Viar

Sir   Philadelphia December 12th. 1791.

Don Joseph Torino, mercht. of Madrid, having sollicited the interposition of the King my master to recover a debt which the Ct. de Espilly assigned to him of 15960 rials of vellon (or 798 dollars) due from the U.S. or their Chargé des affaires at that court, his majesty has commanded me to lay before the U.S. this sollicitation to obtain so legitimate a payment.

In pursuance of his royal orders, and convinced at the same time that the transactions which created the debt claim most justly the acknowledgemt. of the U.S. and their punctual paimt. I take the liberty of stating them to you in the following terms, in joint accord[1] with Don Joseph de Jaudenes, equally Commissioned with myself by his majesty to the U.S.

When in Septemb. 85 the Ct. de Expilly went to Algiers with a commission from his Majesty Mr. Wm. Carmichael who was informed that the Algerines had taken two American crews, recommended his countrymen to his care as far as should be in his power. The Ct. de Expilly gave him his word accordingly and when he arrived at Algiers he attended to their assistance, taking them from chains and labor, and furnishing a small sum which the slaves pay to the regency that they may not go to the public works, giving moreover his assurance that he would pay the price they require in case of flight. He became security also for the two Captains and pilots who were released from labor, and he did not permit them to remain in the prison, nor in the house of the English Consul, where they were obliged to perform the lowest offices, and where, the more to humiliate the Americans, they made them wait at the table where the English captains eat who happened to be in the port. He bought them clothes and beds, and put them in a lodging where he administered to them daily what had been agreed on with Mr. Carmichael before his departure.

In the meantime came, in a Brigantine under Spanish colours, Mr. John Lamb and Paul Randal with a lre. of recommendation from Mr. Carmichael to the Count de Espilly, who seeing that they were not permitted to come ashore, remonstrated and obtained permission for them immediately.

In consequence of what was written by the English Consul at Barcelona, the Regency seised the Brigantine which brought Messrs. Lamb and Randall, because she was of American construction, and half her crew composed also of Americans, and in consequence they would have remained slaves and lost the 10,000 Dollars which they carried if the Ct. de Espilly had not taken the measure of embarking Randall for Genoa in a Brigantine of his Majesty and Lamb in a French vessel which was bound to Spain, and of sending to Tunis the brigantine in which they came.

Mr. Lamb's journey from Alicant to Madrid and the quarantine he performed in that port, were also defrayed on acct. of the Ct. de Expilly. He made use of the brigantine beforementioned when she came back[2] from Tunis, to return to Spain, and at Alicant he paid the seamens wages, and a good gratification to the Captain for the time he had been employed in his Majesty's service.

After Mr. Lamb had left Algiers, the Ct. de Espilly exerted himself so much, in his last voyage, for the Americans, that, to save them from the pest of the year 87. he got them a house and placed them in it furnishing them with necessaries.

Agreeably to what I have stated in the preceding narration the Ct. de Espilly presented his acct. in the year 88. to Mr. Carmichael, and having produced to him his vouchers, they settled the debt at 15960 reals of vellon (or 798 dollars) in favor of the Ct. de Espilly who afterwards transferred the debt to Don Joseph Torino beforementd. now the lawful creditor of the sd. sum.

The delay which he has experienced in the payment of this debt, which was contracted by doing such repeated favors to the citizens of the U.S. and the not having received to this moment the slightest hint of acknowledgement from them, induces me to believe that the U.S. have not been thoroughly apprised of it's circumstances, and the same consideration has encouraged me to state them to you.

I flatter myself that when you shall have been well apprised of them,[3] you will be sensible of the justice of the present application and that, communicating it to the U.S. you will contribute with your influence to their discharge of the debt with all possible dispatch.—In this belief I remain &c.,

JOSEPH IGNATIUS DE VIAR

Tr (DNA: RG 59, NL); English translation of RC in TJ's hand; at foot of text: "To Mr. Thos. Jefferson Secretary of state and of the Department of foreign affairs for the U.S. of America." RC (same); in Spanish; in clerk's hand except for signature. Not recorded in SJL or SJPL. Tr of TJ's translation (DLC); in Remsen's hand; contains slight variations in spelling from TJ's translation.

[1] TJ first translated this as "in concurrence of," then corrected it to read as above.
[2] First translated as "returned."
[3] Preceding seven words first translated as "shall have well understood them."

From Thomas Barclay

Gibraltar, 13 Dec. 1791. He was compelled to put in here on 4 Dec. by contrary winds and hopes to resume his journey to Tangier today. He does not know where he will meet the Emperor, who by last accounts had apparently set out from Larach to Mequinez.

RC (DNA: RG 59, CD); 1 p.

To Christopher Gore

SIR   Philadelphia, December 13th. 1791.

Having received from the British Minister here, a Memorial on the Case of Thomas Pagan, a British Subject, supposed to have been wrongfully condemned and imprisoned by Authority of the Courts of Massachusetts, I take the liberty of asking you to procure for me a complete Copy of the Record of Proceedings in this Case. I understand there has been something done by the Legislature and Executive, as well as judiciary. I enclose you a Copy of the Memorial, that you may be enabled from that to see what Records will be necessary to give complete Information, and will thank you for a return of it, without having made any such Communication of it as might let any Part get into the public Papers. I must beg the Favor of you to hasten the sending on these Records, as the Attorney General supposes it possible that it may be necessary to bring the Matter before the ensuing Supreme Court. If you can communicate any important Facts, not appearing on the Record, I will thank you for them. On your being so[1] good as to note to me the Cost of the Record, it shall be remitted to you.—I am, with great Esteem, Sir, Your most obedient humble Servant,

PrC (DLC); in clerk's hand except for following in TJ's hand at foot of text: "Christopher Gore Atty. for the U.S. at Boston." FC (DNA: RG 360, DL).

[1] The first four words of this sentence, being almost obliterated by water damage, are supplied from the FC.

To George Hammond

SIR   Philadelphia Dec. 13. 1791.

I have laid before the President of the United States the letters of Nov. 30. and Dec. 6. with which you honored me, and in consequence thereof, and particularly of that part of your letter of Dec. 6th. where you say that you are fully authorised to enter into a negociation for the purpose of arranging the commercial intercourse between the two countries, I have the honour to inform you that I am ready to recieve a communication of your full powers for that purpose at any time you shall think proper, and to proceed immediately to their object.—I have the honor to be with sentiments of the most perfect esteem & respect Sir, Your most obedient & most humble servant,   TH: JEFFERSON

PrC (DLC); at foot of text: "Mr. Hammond M.P. of G.B." FC (DNA: RG 360, DL).

To David Humphreys

DEAR SIR   Philadelphia December 13th. 1791

I enclose you the copy of a Letter received from Don Joseph de Viar one of his Catholic Majesty's commissioners here, stating the claim of Don Joseph Torino for a sum of money paid by the Count de Espilles for our captives at Algiers, and on account of our Commissioner Mr. Lamb who was sent there. You will be pleased to consider this as a part of the debt, which in my letter of July 13th. of the present year I desired you to settle and pay. You will of course ask information of Mr. Carmichael on the subject, as he is particularly acquainted with it, and pay immediately what shall appear to be due.—I am with great esteem Dear Sir Your most obedient & most humble Servant,   TH: JEFFERSON

RC (NjP); in Remsen's hand, except for signature; endorsed. PrC (DLC); unsigned. FC (DNA: RG 59, DCI).

From Charles Willson Peale

SIR   Tuesday Morng [13? Dec. 1791]

Your favor of sitting today will oblige Your very Hble Servt.,
                                    C W PEALE

FC (PPAP: Peale Letter Book); in Peale's hand; undated except as above, but the letter succeeding this one was written after an illness and apparently after some lapse of time on 12 Jan. 1792. The one immediately preceding it is the note to TJ printed at 3 Dec. 1791. Neither Peale's two notes nor TJ's presumed replies are recorded in SJL. It is possible that the above inquiry was sent on 6, 13, 20, or 27 Dec. but, given all the circumstances, the 13th seems the more plausible date.

To José Ignacio de Viar

SIR   Philadelphia December 13th. 1791

I was not unapprised that monies had been advanced by the government of Spain, or some of it's Officers, for our captives at Algiers, nor had I been inattentive to it: but no account, nor any specific demand on that subject had come to my knowlege; and finding for some time past the utter impossibility of getting letters either to or from Mr. Carmichael, I had been obliged to adopt a circuitous channel of getting this matter settled through Col. Humphreys, our Minister resident at Lisbon. I had accordingly desired him to get the sum ascertained, and had authorized him to draw for it on our Bankers in Holland. In consequence of this he wrote a letter September 24th. 1791 to Mr. Carmichael, of which I send you an extract. By this, Sir, you will perceive, that in consequence of orders already given, the demand of Don Joseph Jorino,[1] which you have been pleased to apply for, will be there paid on his presenting it duly proved; and that Coll. Humphreys may not be induced by the application here, to consider this matter as withdrawn from his charge, and in a course of settlement here, I have the honor to enclose you a letter to him on that subject, which you will be so good as to transmit to him with the demand. I beg you to be assured, that we are thoroughly sensible of the friendship which your Government has displayed towards these United States in the present as well as other instances, and that we shall avail ourselves with sincere pleasure of every occasion of manifesting to his Catholic Majesty, our dispositions to reciprocate the offices of good friends and neighbours.—I have the honor to be with great and sincere esteem Sir Your most obedient & most humble Servant.

PrC (DLC); in Remsen's hand. FC (DNA: RG 360, DL). Enclosure: extract of a letter from Humphreys to Carmichael, 24 Sep. 1791, a copy of which Humphreys sent to TJ with his letter of 27 Sep. 1791.

Viar and and his fellow Spanish agent, Jaudenes, enclosed TJ's letter of this date to David Humphreys with a letter of their own to the American minister in Portugal of 17 Dec. 1791, which elicited the following reply: "By some uncommon delay I only received a few days ago, by the same vessel that carries this letter, the papers which you did me the honour to enclose to me on the 17th of Decem. of last year. I lost no time in writing to Mr. Carmichael, that he would procure Don Joseph Torino to send his orders to receive the money due to him from the United States of America on account of advances made by the Compte d'Espilly for their Prisoners and Commissioners at Algiers. Be assured as soon as the requisite orders arrive the money shall be paid; and in the meantime that I embrace, with great satisfaction, the occasion

of assuring you with how great consideration and esteem, I have the honour to be, Gentlemen, Your most obedient & Most humble Servant" (Humphreys to Viar and Jaudenes, 26 Nov. 1792, Humphreys, *Humphreys*, II, 132-3).

Before sending the present letter to Viar, TJ first requested Washington to read it as well as two related letters, writing to the President on 14 Dec. 1791: "Th: Jefferson has the honour to submit to the President a letter from Mr. de Viar, with the answer he has prepared to it, and a letter in consequence for Colo. Humphreys" (RC in DNA: RG 59, MLR; FC in DNA: RG 59, SDC; not recorded in SJL or SJPL). Washington made no written response to TJ's note, but he evidently approved TJ's letters of this date to Humphreys and Viar, judging from the fact that the Spanish agent had both in hand by the 17th of December.

[1] Remsen habitually wrote Torino as Jorino, even when transcribing the name from a draft wherein TJ had correctly spelled it.

To George Washington

Dec. 13. 1791

Th: Jefferson presents his respects to the President of the U.S. and sends him the letter he has prepared for Mr. Hammond relative to his Commercial commission.

He also incloses the rough draught of the one he has prepared on the subject of the treaty of peace, with the documents he proposes to communicate in support of the facts. The 1st. of these (the Substance of the Conference &c.) is communicated because Carleton was more explicit in that conversation, than in his letter of May 12. as to the magnitude of the first embarcation and that the negroes then embarked were property of the U.S. Yet this peice of evidence does not seem essentially necessary, and Th:J. asks the opinion of the President on the subject. He will wait on him to-day a quarter before three on these subjects.

RC (DNA: RG 59, MLR); endorsed by Washington: "From The Secretary of State 13th. Decr. 1791 respecting his Corrispondence with the British Minister." FC (DNA: RG 59, SDC). Not recorded in SJL or SJPL. Enclosures: TJ to Hammond, 13 Dec. and 15 Dec. 1791.

From George Hammond

SIR   Philadelphia 14th December 1791.

In answer to your letter of yesterday, I can only repeat what I have before stated, in my first conversations with you after my arrival, and subsequently in my letter of the 6th. of this month; viz, that I have no special Commission, empowering me to *conclude* any *definitive* arrangement upon the subject of the commercial intercourse between Great Britain and the United States: But that I conceive myself fully competent to enter into a negociation with this government for that purpose, in the discussion of the principles, which may serve as the basis, and constitute the stipulations, of any such definitive arrangement.

This opinion of my competency is founded, upon my instructions, inasmuch as they are to regulate my personal conduct, and upon the conviction, that the letter of credence from his Majesty, investing me with a general *plenipotentiary* character, which I had the honor of presenting to the President of the United States, and his consequent recognition of me in that character, are authorities decidedly adequate to the commencement of a preliminary negociation.—I have the honor to be, with sentiments of great respect, Sir, your most obedient and most humble Servant,   GEO. HAMMOND.

RC (DNA: RG 59, NL); endorsed by TJ: "powers to treat of commerce"; also endorsed by him as received 14 Dec. 1791 and so recorded in SJL; slightly mutilated so that some letters and punctuation have been lost and are supplied from Tr (DNA: RG 59, NL).

From George Hammond

SIR   Philadelphia 14th December 1791

I have the honor of acknowledging the receipt of your letter of the 12th of this month, which did not reach me until yesterday evening.

With respect to Bowles, I have no knowledge of any circumstance whatever relative to him, except that of his actual visit to England. His name was never mentioned to me in any manner, directly or indirectly by any of his Majesty's ministers: And I therefore cannot easily believe, if it were their intention to afford him support and countenance, in commencing or prosecuting hostilities against the United States, that I should be left in total ignorance of such an intention.

Upon another subject however of this nature, I have it in express command from my superiors, to disclaim, in the most unequivocal manner, the imputation that the King's government in Canada has encouraged or supported the measures of hostility, taken by the Indians in the Western Country.

From analogy therefore I infer that as the King's government has not countenanced the hostile measures of those Indians, in whose existence and preservation, his Majesty might naturally be supposed to take some degree of interest, from considerations of commerce as well as of local vicinity to his province of Canada, the same motives, which prevented interference in that instance, would more forcibly induce his government not to encourage the hostile views of other Indian tribes, greatly remote in regard, to situation, and to any objects of common interest.

For these reasons I can feel no hesitation in expressing to you, Sir, the strongest personal conviction, that Bowles has no kind of authority for asserting, that he is either employed or countenanced, by the government of England, in inciting the Indians to war against the United States.

Before I conclude, you will I trust permit me to add, that the

[403]

extract of the private letter, which you have done me the honor of communicating to me, exhibits pretty clear internal evidence of prejudice and prepossession, existing in the writer of it; and consequently it is presumable that the accounts, he has received, are not a little exaggerated.—I have the honor to be, with great respect, Sir, your most obedient, humble Servant,   GEO. HAMMOND.

RC (DNA: RG 59, NL); at foot of text: "Mr. Jefferson &c. &c. &c."; endorsed by TJ as received 14 Dec. 1791 and so recorded in SJL; also docketed by him: "Hammond George . . . Disavowal of aid to Indians." Tr (same).

In an obvious effort to allay southern apprehensions about William Augustus Bowles' machinations, TJ made the contents of Hammond's letter known to James Madison, who immediately passed the information on to Gov. Henry Lee of Virginia and Edmund Pendleton (Madison to Lee and to Pendleton, 18 Dec. 1791, Rutland, *Madison*, XIV, 154-7).

Hammond correctly surmised that Bowles was not an agent of the British government. In response to an earlier letter from Hammond on this subject, Lord Grenville made the following observations: "I think it highly necessary to lose no time in informing You, in Answer to what is mentioned respecting Mr. Bowles in your Letter No. 7 and its Inclosure, and also in a letter from Lieut. Colonel Beckwith, which I have received from Lord Dorchester, that the Assertions said to have been made by

Mr. Bowles, of his having received Powers from the British Government, to conclude a Treaty with the Creeks, of his having received Encouragement to take Measures for a Revocation of the late Treaty with the United States, or of his having been furnished by this Government, with Arms, Ammunition or Cannon, are entirely without Foundation. The Particulars of his having any Sort of Commission from this Government, either as Agent or Superintendent of Indians, or in any other Character, or of his having been authorized to promise to the Creeks on the Part of this Country, the Re-establishment of their old Boundary with Georgia, or to hold out to them any Expectation of an English Reinforcement in the Spring, are also wholly groundless" (Hammond to Grenville, 6 Dec. 1791, PRO: FO 4/11, f. 207-8; Grenville to Hammond, 3 Jan. 1792, Mayo, *British Ministers*, p. 20-1; see also George Beckwith to Lord Dorchester, 2 Dec. 1791, PRO: FO 4/11, f. 181-2). Hammond promptly conveyed the substance of Grenville's reassurances to TJ (Hammond to TJ, 30 Mch. 1792).

From George Washington

DEAR SIR   Phila. Decr. 14th. 1791

I am very glad to find that matters, after all that has happened, stand so well between the Commissioners and Majr. L'Enfant.—I am sorry, however, to hear that the work is not in a more progressive State.

Yesterday afternoon I wrote a letter, of which the enclosed is the copy to Majr. L'Enfant, and receiving his of the 10th. added the Postscript thereto.—I hope the two will have a good effect.—I am always with great regard yr. affectionate,   GO: WASHINGTON

RC (DLC); addressed: "Mr. Jefferson"; endorsed by TJ as received 14 Dec. 1791 and recorded in SJPL as: "G.W. to Th:J. Letter relative to Commissioners and Lenfant."

Washington's letter to L'Enfant of YES-TERDAY AFTERNOON was his formal response to the latter's 7 Dec. 1791 defense of his actions in pulling down Carroll's house (see TJ's observations on that letter in enclosure to TJ to Washington, 11 Dec. 1791; Fitzpatrick, *Writings*, XXXI, 442-4; and Vol. 20: 51).

To Nathaniel Barrett

DEAR SIR   Philadelphia Dec. 15. 1791.

In answer to your favor of the 6th. inst. I take the liberty of mentioning to you that the consulates of Lisbon and Cadiz, have both of them been for some time otherwise destined, tho' not yet named to; and consequently that Mr. Appleton cannot be appointed to either. I had not answered his letters on this subject, because were I to answer one, I must answer every application of this nature and you will readily conceive to what this would lead, and consequently that it has been a matter of necessity to establish it as a general rule to give no answers to the parties except where the appointment takes place.—I am with great esteem Dr. Sir your most obedt humble servt,   TH: JEFFERSON

PrC (DLC).

Barrett, who had just returned from Europe, had written TJ on 6 Dec. at the request of Thomas APPLETON, although he did not mention Cadiz (RC in DNA: RG 59, CD; endorsed by TJ as received 13 Dec. 1791 and so recorded in SJL). Appleton had applied for the Lisbon post in letters to TJ of 12 Dec. 1790 and 10 July 1791, and his father had recently supported his application in a letter to the President (Nathaniel Appleton to Washington, 3 Dec. 1791, DLC: Washington Papers). For the candidates who were currently under consideration for consular appointments in Lisbon and Cadiz, see TJ to Washington, 22 Dec. 1791.

From Tench Coxe

Decr. 15th. 1791

Mr. Coxe has the honor to inform Mr. Jefferson that the Charges on the Sally at Port au Prince are in colonial livres of which 8 are equal to a dollar nearly, tho not precisely.

Mr. Coxe will transmit some fuller papers than those sent, which it was hoped in the interim might be of use.

He has ascertained that *Tar* pays in G. Britain a duty of 11d. Sterling, and expects hourly further information in regard to naval Stores, furs &ca.

The inclosed extract from Ld. Sheffields book on the Irish Trade may be useful to Mr. Jefferson.

Turpentine pays 2/3d. ℔ Cwt. I therefore think the books of rates to be relied on as to all Naval Stores.

RC (DLC); enclosure in Remsen's hand: lists of port charges from various ports, endorsed by TJ: "Port charges from Mr. Coxe." Not recorded in SJL or SJPL.

Two days later TJ received a similar report from Philadelphia merchant Walter Stewart that detailed charges for other vessels in the West Indies. In the margin TJ wrote questions about the currency and the size of the vessels, and apparently returned the letter to Stewart, who then filled in answers, added a postscript describing what he had done, and returned the letter to TJ (Walter Stewart to TJ, 17 Dec. 1791, RC in DLC; endorsed by TJ: "Port charges from Genl. Stewart"; not recorded in SJL or SJPL).

Coxe received a letter from a John Evans in Philadelphia on 16 Dec. giving him information on English duties on fur (RC in DLC; docketed by Coxe, and also by TJ: "Furs. English duties on."). Coxe passed along the necessary information to TJ in his note of "Sunday Evening" [18 Dec.]: "Mr. Coxe has the honor to inform Mr.

Jefferson that pitch is certainly 11/ ℔ 112 to. i.e. dutied to exclusion as a manufacture—Tar 11d. ℔ barrl. and turpentine 2/3d. ℔ Cwt.—Mr. Remsen's copy of Mr. Coxe's very rough minutes, corrected, is inclosed—also the accot. of the fur duties in England equal to 15 ad 20 ℔ Ct. ad valorem at the medium prices.—[P.S.] Mr. Coxe will not fail to send the Return of Exports the Moment Mr. Hamilton shall have done with it" (RC in DLC: TJ Papers, 69:11999; not recorded in SJL). He enclosed additional lists of port charges in Remsen's hand, with some corrections by himself, and endorsed by TJ: "Port charges from Mr. Coxe." For the use to which TJ put this information, see the table on American trade with France and Great Britain printed as an enclosure to TJ to Washington, 23 Dec. 1791.

The INCLOSED EXTRACT was from Lord Sheffield's *Observations on the Manufactures, Trade, and Present State of Ireland* (London, 1785), which TJ returned to Coxe on 16 Dec.

To the Governors of Georgia and South Carolina

SIR   Philadelphia December 15th. 1791

I have the honor to enclose you an authenticated copy of the Articles agreed on between the Governor of East Florida and Mr. Seagrove acting for the United States by order of the President, on the subject of fugitive negroes; and to be with sentiments of the most perfect esteem and respect Your Excellency's Most obedient & most humble Servt.

PrC (DLC); in Remsen's hand; at foot of text: "His Excellency the Governor of the State of Georgia." PrC of the letter to the governor of South Carolina, identical with the foregoing, is also in DLC. FC (DNA: RG 360, DL); at head of text: "To the Governors of South Carolina and Georgia."

The historical background of the enclosed agreement between James Seagrove and Governor Quesada on the return of fugitive slaves is described in Editorial Note to group of documents on threat of disunion in the West, at 10 Mch. 1791.

I

James Seagrove to Juan Nepomuceno de Quesada

St. Augustine in Florida Augt. 2. 1791.

The following is delivered by James Seagrove Commissioner on the part of the United States, to his Excellency Don Juan Nepomuceno de Quesada, Governor of the Province of East Florida &c. &c. for his concurrence.

That in order to prevent fugitive Slaves from the United States, taking shelter in Florida, his Excellency the Governor will be pleased to issue his Proclamation, ordering all Officers civil and military within this colony, but particular those on the River St. Mary's, to stop all such fugitive Slaves, and without delay convey them to the Spanish Post on Amelia Island; there to be detained until a person, properly authorized by the United States, shall there call and receive them. Paying at same time a reasonable price for their maintainance, and also expence of conveying from the place where taken to the place of confinement. The sum to be agreed on by Excellency and the Commissioner.

That notice be given as soon as possible, by the Officer Commanding at Amelia, to the Commanding officer at the American Post on St. Mary's, when any fugitive Slaves from the United States are under his care.

That his Excellency would be pleased to issue severe orders against any person harbouring or concealing such fugitive Slaves; but that they be obliged to make them prisoners, and deliver them without delay to the nearest Spanish Post, and from thence to be conveyed to the general place for receiving them at Amelia.

That his Excellency will be pleased to order that all fugitive Slaves belonging to the United States, who have taken shelter in Florida since the date of his Catholic Majesty's order on that head, be immediately restored on the preceding terms.

The Commissioner is ready to confer on, and explain any matter relative to the preceding, being with all possible respect his Excellency's devoted very humble Servant,   ✦ Js. SEAGROVE.

PrC (DLC); in Remsen's hand. FC (DNA: RG 360, DL).

II

Juan Nepomuceno de Quesada to James Seagrove

St. Augustine in Florida August 6th. 1791.

The following is a translation of Governor Quesada's reply to the preceding.

The Governor of East Florida answers as follows to what has been proposed by James Seagrove Esquire (authorized for the purpose by a credential letter from his Excellency Thomas Jefferson, Secretary of State to the United States of America) regarding the negro Slaves, who may escape from said Nation to this Province.

Immediately on the receipt of the royal Schedule ordering that the freedom that used to be granted to runaway Negroes should cease, the necessary Proclamation was issued and the proper directions forwarded to the River St. Mary's.

It is not for the present convenient that the deposit of such runaways should be at Amelia Island, I think that this Town is the securest and most proper place.

It remains at the option of the Gentleman Commissioner whether said runaways shall be employed in the public works (in which case nothing will be charged for their maintenance) or he appoint an attorney here to take charge of them, their labour, substance,[1] and remitment to the owners, in any manner he may think proper; But if the aforesaid Commissioner wishes that the runaways should be kept in prison, without working, the owners must pay for the maintenance administered, and likewise allow a reasonable gratification to the soldiers or Sailors which Government, if required, will furnish to conduct them to the frontiers.

Every claimer must prove his property in the negroes reclaimed, either by a certificate of the Government, or by other documents, sufficiently proving his lawful right.

An order will be issued fixing a penalty on any inhabitant who will harbour a fugitive Slave.

There is no account of even a single Slave being in the Province, who fled from the United States, within the term that passed from the date of the royal Schedule in question to the promulgation of it in Florida; But even in case there were such fugitives, it is the opinion of Government, that they ought not to be restored, nor can it be agreed to without an express order from the King.

(signed) JUAN NEPOMUCENO DE QUESADA

PrC (DLC); in Remsen's hand. FC (DNA: RG 360, DL).

[1] TJ noted in margin of FC: "supposed *subsistance*."

III
Agreement on Fugitive Slaves

St. Augustine in Florida August 7th. 1791.

The beforementioned Commissioner on the part of the United States is of opinion,

That[1] as the Government of East Florida does not chuse to be responsible for any fugitive Slaves from the United States, which in future may shelter themselves in this Province, it will be for the interest of their owners, that immediately on discovery they be confined in prison, there to remain until properly applied for.

In[2] order to give as little trouble as possible to Government on this occasion, the Commissioner have agreed with George Fleming Esqr. of this City, to furnish such fugitive Slaves as may be confined in prison, with the usual allowance of provisions.

It[3] is also understood by the Commissioner that in case any assistance should be required from the Soldiers or Sailors of this Government in conveying such Slaves to the frontier on the River St. Mary's, there to be delivered up; that a reasonable gratification be allowed and paid by the person receiving them.

JS. SEAGROVE

PrC (DLC); in Remsen's hand. FC (DNA: RG 360, DL).

¹ "agreed to by Government" written in margin.
² "agreed." noted in margin.
³ "agreed." noted in margin.

To George Hammond

SIR   Philadelphia Dec. 15. 1791.

I am to acknolege the honor of your letter of Nov. 30. and to express the satisfaction with which we learn that you are instructed to discuss with us the measures which reason and practicability may dictate for giving effect to the stipulations of our treaty yet remaining to be executed. I can assure you on the part of the United States, of every disposition to lessen difficulties, by passing over whatever is of smaller concern, and insisting on those matters only which either justice to individuals, or public policy render indispensable. And in order to simplify our discussions by defining precisely their objects, I have the honor to propose that we shall begin by specifying, on each side, the particular acts which each considers to have been done by the other in contravention of the treaty. I shall set the example.

The Provisional and Definitive treaties, in their vɪɪth. article, stipulated that 'his Britannic majesty should with all convenient speed, and without causing any destruction, or *carrying away any negroes or other property* of the American inhabitants, *withdraw all his armies, garrisons and fleets from the sd. United States* and from every port, place and harbour within the same.'

But 1. the British garrisons were not withdrawn with all convenient speed nor have ever yet been withdrawn from
Michillimackinac, on Lake Michigan:
Detroit on the streight of Lakes Erie and Huron;
Fort Erie, on Lake Erie;
Niagara ⎫
Oswego ⎬ on Lake Ontario;
Oswegatchie, on the river St. Laurence;
Point au fer, and ⎫
Dutchman's point ⎬ on Lake Champlain.
2. The British officers have undertaken to exercise a jurisdiction over the country and inhabitants in the vicinities of those forts; and 3. they have excluded the citizens of the United States from navigating even on our side of the middle line of the rivers and lakes established as the boundary between the two nations.

By these proceedings we have been intercepted entirely from the Commerce of furs with the Indian nations to the Northward: a commerce which had ever been of great importance to the United states, not only for its intrinsic value, but as it was the means of cherishing peace with those Indians, and of superseding the necessity of that expensive warfare, we have been obliged to carry on with them, during the time that these posts have been in other hands.

On withdrawing the troops from New York, 1. a large embarcation of negroes, of the property of the inhabitants of the U.S. took place, before the Commissioners, on our part, for inspecting and superintending embarcations had arrived there, and without any account ever rendered thereof. 2. Near three thousand others were publicly carried away by the avowed order of the British commanding officer, and under the view and against the remonstrances of our Commissioners: 3. a very great number were carried off in private vessels, if not by the express permission, yet certainly without opposition on the part of the commanding officer, who alone had the means of preventing it, and without admitting the inspection of the American commissioners: and 4. of other species of property carried away, the commanding officer permitted no examination at all. In support of these facts I have the honour to inclose you documents, a list of which will be subjoined: and in addition to them, I beg leave to refer to a roll, signed by the joint commissioners, and delivered to your Commanding officer for transmission to his court, containing a description of the negroes publicly carried away by his order as beforementioned, with a copy of which you have doubtless been furnished.

A difference of opinion too having arisen, as to the river intended by the Plenipotentiaries to be the boundary between us and the dominions of Great Britain, and by them called the St. Croix, which name, it seems, is given to two different rivers, the ascertaining of this point becomes a matter of present urgency. It has heretofore been the subject of applications from us to the government of Great Britain.

There are other smaller matters between the two nations, which remain to be adjusted, but I think it would be better to refer these for settlement through the ordinary channel of our ministers, than to embarrass the present important discussions with them. They can never be obstacles to friendship and harmony.

Permit me now, Sir, to ask from you a specification of the particular acts, which, being considered by his Britannic majesty as a noncompliance on our part with the engagements contained in the ivth. vth. and vith. articles of the treaty induced him to suspend the execution of the viith. and render a separate discussion of them inadmissible. And accept assurances of the high respect & esteem with which I have the honor to be, Sir, Your most obedient & most humble servant, TH: JEFFERSON

PrC (DLC); at foot of text: "George Hammond esq. M.P. of G.B."; TJ also listed at the end of the letter the "Documents referred to and inclosed." Enclosures: (1) Sir Guy Carleton to Gen. Washington (Extract), 12 May 1783. (2) American Commissioners to Sir Guy Carleton, 24 May 1783. (3) Mr. Morgann (for Sir Guy Carleton) to American Commissioners, 29 May 1783. (4) American Commissioners to Sir Guy Carleton, 9 June 1783. (5) American Commissioners to General Washington, 14 June 1783. (6) American Commissioners to Sir Guy Carleton (Extract), 17 June 1783. (7) American Commissioners to General Washington, 18 Jan. 1784. FC (DNA: RG 59, SDR). Tr (DNA: RG 360, DL).

TJ copied the list of British occupied GARRISONS in the U.S. from a letter written him by Henry Knox, probably at TJ's request (Knox to TJ, 2 Dec. 1791, RC in DLC).

Hammond was caught off guard by TJ's decision to raise the issue of the American slaves carried off by the British Army and that of the northeastern boundary between the United States and Canada. Consequently, when the minister transmitted a copy of the present letter and its supporting documentation to England, he noted in an accompanying dispatch to the British secretary for foreign affairs: "Your Lordship will perceive from the papers two points, to which no reference is made in my instructions, viz. the claim of the negroes carried away at the time of evacuating New York and the ascertainment of the boundary by fixing the true position of the St. Croix. With respect to the first point, whenever the discussion shall take place, it is my intention, in addition to the arguments, which were alleged by Lord Dorchester, to treat the matter upon principles somewhat more extended. With this view, I shall state that the letter (and I

firmly believe the spirit) of the treaty of peace cannot be supposed to apply to any other description of Negroes than such as were the actual property of the inhabitants of the United States, at the period of the cessation of hostilities—that, of the Negroes, carried away from New York, under the permission and protection of Lord Dorchester, part may be presumed to have been captured during the war, and were consequently booty acquired by the rights of war: But that the principal part of them had fled to the British lines, in consequence of proclamations issued by the British Commanders in Chief (who were at the time in the exercise of legal authority in the country) which promised to them freedom upon their joining the British army— and that this description of Negroes, thus emancipated, had acquired indefeasible rights of personal liberty, of which the British government was not competent to deprive them, by reducing them again to a state of slavery, and to the domination of their ancient masters.—In regard to the second point (the ascertainment of the true position of the river St. Croix) I shall refer—to one of the negotiators of the treaty (Mr. Adams) who, I am privately informed, has expressed much uncertainty upon the subject—to the belief and knowledge of the inhabitants bordering upon that river—and (if it can be procured) to an authentic record, existing in the archives of Massachusets Bay, which is said to establish our interpretation of the boundary beyond the possibility of dispute" (Hammond to Grenville, 19 Dec. 1791, PRO: FO 4/11, f. 255-9).

TJ's preliminary statement of alleged British violations of the Treaty of Paris was undercut from an unexpected quarter. Unbeknownst to the Secretary of State, Hammond conveyed the substance of TJ's letter to Alexander Hamilton. In the Secretary's opinion it was imperative for Great Britain to evacuate the western posts in accordance with its treaty obligations, but he assured the British minister that "it might perhaps still be possible to grant to his Majesty's subjects such privileges and immunities in the respective posts as would protect and secure them in the undisturbed prosecution of the Fur Trade"; that he personally did not attach as much importance as "other members of this government" to the issue of slave compensation; and that he believed that the British position on the northeastern boundary would "be found accurate" (Conversation with George Hammond, [1-8 Jan. 1792], Syrett, *Hamilton*, x, 493-4). This proved to be the first in a long series of secret efforts by Hamilton to interfere in the ongoing negotiations between TJ and Hammond.

From Edward Church

Bordeaux, 16 Dec. 1791. Although he has only considered the matter for two days, he feels impelled by rapidly changing conditions in France to suggest the propriety and expediency "of improving this critical opportunity, to make the present substitute for money, now circulating in France under the denomination of *Assignats*, an instrument in the hands of his Excellency the President of the United States, for liquidating their debt due to France."—A French livre in assignats, "the only currency here," has depreciated to 6½d sterling in bills of exchange on London, Amsterdam, and Hamburg as a result of France's unfavorable balance of trade with England and Holland "and the consequent necessity of remitting the ballance in bills of Excha. or hard money." This circumstance offers the U.S. an opportunity, by placing funds in England or Holland, to pay their debt to France "with a saving of seven parts in twenty; and it may probably be done in a few months to much greater advantage." French citizens are selling bills at this rate to public agents for the use of government, and the French government is glad to receive assignats in the public treasury at par. Were it not for his doubts about the inability of the U.S. to place funds in Europe at this time, he would undertake to prove that it is in the nation's interest to reduce its debt to France in this fashion. The assignat's rate of depreciation, though not so great "when we compare a livre in paper to the former fixed prices of certain manufactures, and other produce of this Country," is still supposed to be 25%.

The sources of currency depreciation in France are many and varied. They include the "amount of assignats now in circulation, said to be fourteen hundred millions of livres; a recent decree for the immediate emission of five hundred millions more; the great, and increasing exigencies of the State, and comparative impotence of the revenues; the large sums in the hands of Individuals; the facility and rapidity with which they are accumulated; the extreme avidity of the Possessors to transmute them; the doubts and fears of some Individuals of their ultimate success, or rather of an event, on the fortunate issue of which, they suppose, their validity depends; the want of a vent, or outlet, to reduce the excess; the total disappearance of every species of gold and silver; the prospect of an invasion the ensuing Spring." The same causes that have deflated the value of assignats will continue to operate until the "uncontested triumph of liberty, that can tend to appreciate them."

The U.S. should not hesitate to take advantage of these financial conditions to reduce the burden of their debt to France. "The unappropriated Stock, or Funds of the U.S., if there are any such, is the object, which, under the present promising prospect, and universal favorable impression of the solidity of the American Funds, I have conceived might be commuted for Assignats, greatly to the advantage of the U.S., with the Merchants, Bankers, Brokers, and Speculators, in this Country, who possess more of that kind of property than they can employ to advantage, and wou'd eagerly seize the opportunity of dividing it, rather than risk all in one bottom." There is no need to fear that this plan would enable foreign investors to exercise undue influence over the American government because they would be too far away "to form cabals, or plots against the State." Assignats exchanged by foreign purchasers of American "Stock, or other publick property," should be immediately paid into the French Treasury "on account of the debt due from the United States. They are at this time eagerly received into the Treasury at Par, nor is it easy to conceive that a property funded upon immovable, and acknowledged ample security, will ever be offered to, or received by the Government, at a reduced value; the loss which Govt. may be supposed to sustain by receiving any quantity, more or less, in a depreciated State, is merely ideal, for many cogent reasons, which your superiour understanding, as well as past experience, will readily furnish." This plan will also lessen the French government's need to emit more assignats and thus stabilize the currency, preventing "the murmurs and discontents of the people, which never fail to break out with every new emission."—If in future assignats are not receivable at the French Treasury except at a depreciated rate, it would still be in the interest of the French government to accept them at more than the prevailing market rate. Such debt payments would benefit France during the current crisis and "be a pleasing reflection to the Citizens of America, that they had contributed to support a glorious struggle for liberty, and at the same time had cancelled a debt, which, if they had not done, must hereafter have been paid to some Tyrant." He presumes his plan would encounter no opposition in France but has been careful to disclose it to no one else lest the Legislative Assembly adopt it "and thus become themselves the Creditors of the United States." He thinks the plan would have special appeal for the many monied men here who "seem totally at a loss where or how to place their paper." If only the U.S. could place funds in Holland, Hamburg, or England and purchase assignats with bills of exchange, "the operation and the advantages are simple and evident; nor is there a doubt of equal or greater advantages 6 months hence, i.e. that the debt due from the U.S. to France, might then be reduced, or discharged, with a certain advantage of present purpose."

He is willing to serve wherever he might be considered useful and asks that this be brought to the attention of the President. In the event of war, Bordeaux will be more quiet and secure than many other parts of France.—"The people, at least those whom I have seen of every class, and description, discover great zeal in the cause, but it seems to border on enthusiasm, and it may perhaps not be difficult to assign a probable cause of the different effects of liberty upon Frenchmen, and the Americans when in somewhat similar circumstances. There was no period anteriour to the American revolution, in which the Americans did not justly consider themselves a free people, and when their rights were invaded, they soberly united to repel the Invaders. It was not to obtain freedom, but to preserve their birthright. They therefore were taught by nature and habit to support liberty with moderation, decency, and dignity. The French were born Slaves, and having just gained that first, and greatest blessing,

Liberty, the sudden possession of this invaluable treasure seems to have elevated and transported them to such a degree as to render them incapable of supporting their happy reverse of fortune with tolerable temperance:—Some excesses have been the effects of this ebullient ardour, but generally, tho' not in all cases, they have been of the venial kind; their *vif* savours too much of the extravagant; how it may operate in a Camp remains yet to be proved; it will doubtless be necessary to appoint Officers of great experience, abilities, equanimity, address, firmness, and sincere attachment to the cause in which they are engaged, to conciliate, subdue, organize, and transform into good soldiers, such an heterogeneous, and combustible compound."

By express from Paris he has just learned that the king appeared before the Legislative Assembly and proposed to raise an army of 150,000 men to subdue the emigré forces led by his brothers and cousins. The king also assured the Legislative Assembly that the emigrés could expect no support from the Emperor or any other crowned head. This news raised the exchange rate by 2½%, but it is doubtful that this improvement will continue unless the threat of war disappears. The Legislative Assembly has published an estimate of the value of the clerical estates pledged for the redemption of the assignats, by which it appears that "the Amount of the value of the Estates transcends the amount of the Assignats, fourteen hundred millions of Livres; and the valuation may be considered very moderate, as the Estates hitherto sold, have in general far exceeded the appraisement, frequently 40 or 50 per Cent."—He has received TJ's letter of 13 May and is pleased by its flattering description of conditions in the U.S. J. Vernes plans to write TJ by this opportunity. "He is a leading Patriot in this City."

RC (DNA: RG 59, CD); 14 p. Not recorded in SJL.

Church's suggestion that the United, States pay its debt to France in depreciated assignats was ill-calculated to appeal to TJ, since he had already expressly assured the French minister that the government of the United States was opposed to such an expedient (TJ to Ternant, 1 Sep. 1791).

To Tench Coxe

Dec. 16. 91.

Th: Jefferson presents his compliments to Mr. Coxe and returns him his book with thanks, finding it is the same which he already possessed.—The account of port charges at Port-au-Prince on the Sally of Philada., cannot be used in comparison, because her tonnage is not mentioned.—There is no account of charges in any port of the English West Indies.—Also, in stating those in the French W. Indies, is it not in the *Colonial* livre? Does Mr. Coxe know exactly what that is? Th:J. cannot recollect it with certainty.

RC (NjP); addressed: "Mr. Coxe." Not recorded in SJL or SJPL.

To George Washington

Dec. 16. 1791.

Th: Jefferson presents his respects to the President and sends a sketch of such a message as he thinks might accompany the statement from the Secretary at war. He does not know whether the President intended that an estimate of the next years operations should accompany it. But he thinks it a proper occasion to bring forward the preparations for the next year, and that it forms the safest ground for making the present communication.

RC (DNA: RG 59, MLR); endorsed by Washington: "Proposed Message to Accompany a Report from the Secy of War's Statement 16th Decr. 1791." PrC (DLC).

Tr (DNA: RG 59, MLR). Entry in SJPL reads: "Th:J. to G.W. Letter and draught of message for Secy. at War."

E N C L O S U R E

Draft Message on Western Defense

GENTLEMEN OF THE SENATE

The pacific measures which were adopted for establishing peace between the U.S. and the North Western Indians, having proved ineffectual, and the military operations which thereon became necessary, tho' successful in the first instances, being otherwise in the last as was stated to you in my communication of   instant, it behoves us to look forward in time to the further protection of our Western citizens.

I see no reason to doubt that operations of force must still be pursued. I have therefore instructed the Secretary at war to prepare, for your information, a statement of the transactions of his department material to this object. These are now laid before you. While they serve to shew that the plan which was adopted for employing the public force and wealth was such as promised reasonably a more effectual issue, they will enable you also to judge of the provision which it may be now be expedient to make for the ensuing year. An estimate of the Secretary at war on this subject is now laid before you.

PrC of Dft (DLC); entirely in TJ's hand.

When news of Arthur St. Clair's stunning defeat at the hands of the Miami and the Wabash on 4 Nov. 1791 reached Philadelphia on 8 Dec. 1791, it touched off a heated public debate over the Washington administration's policy toward the Indians in the Northwest Territory. Washington officially notified Congress on 12 Dec. 1791 of this shocking debacle, in which 900 members of St. Clair's 1,400-man force of regulars and militia were either killed or wounded; and he promised to make a "further communication . . . of all such matters as shall be necessary to enable the Legislature to judge of the future measures which it may be proper to pursue" (Fitzpatrick, *Writings*, XXXI, 442). In accordance with this promise, Secretary of War Henry Knox drew up two statements for submission to Congress, both dated 26 Dec. 1791. The first described the preparations made by the administration for St. Clair's expedition, and the second set forth a new plan of operations that called for increasing the size of the regular army from two to five regiments as well as negotiating with the disaffected tribes. After discussing these statements with TJ and other members of his cabinet, Washington submitted them to Congress on 11 Jan. 1792 with a covering letter that reflected the spirit, though not the exact substance, of the draft message by TJ printed above.

The administration's proposal to increase the size of the army to five regiments gave rise to a spirited exchange of views in the House of Representatives that divided the members along sectional lines. New England representatives opposed the projected increase, denouncing the Indian war in the Northwest as unjust, pointing to encroachments by white settlers on tribal lands as the cause of hostilities, and calling for negotiations with the Indians. In response, congressmen from the middle and southern states attributed the war to unjustified Indian attacks on innocent white settlers, advocated the resumption of hostilities with the Miami and the Wabash, and thus favored the proposed increase. Opponents of the administration also argued that regular troops were far inferior to militia as Indian fighters, while supporters retorted that militia troops were too undisciplined to wage an effective campaign against the Indians. Despite opposition arguments, the House passed a bill on 1 Feb. 1792 authorizing the President to raise five regiments of regulars. The Senate followed suit later in the month only after Washington agreed to change the army high command and enter into peace negotiations with the Indians before embarking on another campaign (Washington to TJ, 18 and 27 Dec. 1791; ASP, *Indian Affairs*, I, 139-202; *Annals*, III, 337-54; Richard H. Kohn, *Eagle and Sword: The Federalists and the Creation of the Military Establishment in America, 1783-1802* [New York, 1975], p. 111-26).

TJ was deeply disappointed by this turn of events. Upon first learning of St. Clair's defeat, he expressed the wish that this set-back would lead to a major change in the administration's approach to the war with the western tribes (TJ to Thomas Mann Randolph, Jr., 11 Dec. 1791). TJ's hope that henceforth Washington would rely less on the regular army and more on the militia in waging war against the Indians stemmed not only from his belief that militiamen were more skillful Indian fighters than regulars but also from his conviction that a large standing army was a potential threat to American liberties and his apprehension that such a force would swell the public debt and thus contribute to the perpetuation of the Hamiltonian fiscal policies to which he was now so ardently opposed (see TJ to Charles Carroll, 15 Apr. 1791; TJ to James Monroe, 17 Apr. 1791). Yet, perhaps out of deference to the far greater military experience of the President and the Secretary of War, TJ never openly opposed the military plans of Washington and Knox in the official councils of government. In private, however, he was less restrained. "You think that a regular, disciplined, military force is proper for the defence of this Country," an anonymous Federalist who was apparently acquainted with TJ wrote to Washington shortly after the President had submitted Knox's plan for an enlarged army to the House of Representatives. "Every man who understands the interest of this Country thinks so too. When you ask the S[ecretary] of S[tate], he affects great humility, and says he is not a judge of military matters. Behind your back he reviles wth. the greatest asperity your military measures and ridicules the idea of employing any regular Troops. Militia he says ought alone to be depended on" (Anonymous to Washington, ca. 20 Jan. 1792, DLC: Washington Papers). Thus, TJ's dissatisfaction with the federal government's military tactics in the Northwest Territory was but one more reflection of the deepening political fissures in the cabinet as Washington's first administration entered its final year.

From Thomas Barclay

Gibraltar, 18 Dec. 1791. He wrote to TJ on the 12th [i.e., 13th] and expected to reach Tangier on the 12th but was unable to sail because of unfavorable weather conditions. Several letters from Morocco arrived three days ago that enable him to give an accurate account of recent events in that land.

Sometime before the late Emperor's death on 11 Apr. 1790 he ordered Muley Slema, a younger son, to invest a sanctuary near Tetuan whither an older son, Muley Yezid, had fled to escape his father's anger. After the Emperor died at Saffy, Muley Yezid left the sanctuary and was proclaimed his successor in the north as well as in the cities of Fez, Mequinez, and Morocco. To escape his brother's wrath, Muley Slema took refuge in the sanctuary and remains there still.—Assuming the title of Mahomet El Mehedy El Yezid, the new Emperor appeared at Fez and Mequinez to put down a revolt against his rule and then returned to the north. When the people of the city of Morocco grew impatient at the Emperor's absence, the governor of it proclaimed Muley Ischem, another son of the late Emperor, in his place. But Muley Ischem has since withdrawn from competion with his brother, lacking either civil or military ability, "and the only Event of Consequence that attended his momentary elevation, was the plundering of Morocco by the Mountaineers who appeared in Suport of his interest."

The new Emperor held two audiences with foreign consuls at Tetuan shortly after leaving the sanctuary. On 21 Apr. 1790 he informed them that he intended to make war on all Christians except the English and the Russians and ordered the consuls of all other nations to leave in four months. Then on the following day he declared that he would remain at peace with all Christians except the Spaniards but added that peace with them was possible if they sent an ambassador to him, paid 250,000 dollars in duties on wheat that his father had allowed the Spanish consul general Mr. Salmon to export, and delivered 100 quintals of cochineal in accordance with a pledge made to the late Emperor. At the same time he put to death Attal, a Jewish financial agent for his father; the Talb Haudrania, a confidant of his father; L'Abbas, the commander of the force that had invested the sanctuary; Hassan, the Spanish vice-consul at Tetuan; and the Effendi—"and to shew his great detestation of the Spaniards, he ordered the hand of their great friend the Effendi to be nailed on the Door of the Consul's house at Tangier, but the order was evaded and the hand nailed on a board that was placed near the [house]." Mr. Salmon arrived in the Bay of Tangier in a ship of war on 12 Aug. 1790, having been appointed Spanish minister to Morocco and bearing money and presents for the Emperor. After trying for six weeks to extract a pledge from the Emperor that he could return to his ship safely if peace negotiations between them failed, Salmon announced on 22 Sep. that he was sending ashore a boat "loaded with Some bulky items of Little value." In the meantime, however, Salmon's brother, the Spanish vice-consul, and the Fathers of Redemption residing in Tangier made their way to Salmon's ship whereupon this ship and all Spanish vessels in the harbor set sail, driving one Moroccan cruiser ashore and capturing two others in full view of the Emperor. Salmon defended his actions by claiming that he already knew Spain had declared war on Morocco, but others allege that "Several people of great influence had been concerned in the Exportation of the wheat, and if the Duties had been actually paid by the Court of Spain, it would have brought about a restoration of property and other explanations of a very disagreeable nature."—The Emperor immediately had the Basha of Tangier beheaded and replaced by Tahar Feunis. He then besieged Ceuta with 32,000 men but raised the siege on 17 Nov. after Spain disavowed Salmon's conduct and restored the captured cruisers. Thereafter he journeyed to Rabat "where he renewed most of the treaties made by his father, and dispatched Benothman to Madrid as ambassador with propositions of establishing peace upon certain conditions."— As a result of Benothman's mission, Spain shipped 84,000 dollars worth of naval stores to Tangier in July 1791. But this fell so far below the Emperor's expectations that he renewed the siege of Ceuta on 18 Aug., causing Benothman to remain in Spain as a pensioner of the king. The siege was raised on 14 Sep., after which the governors of Ceuta and Tetuan agreed to a boundary line "between the Ceuta and the foot of Abila, beyond which neither the Spaniards or Moors Should pass on any pretence whatever." Six weeks ago, the governor of Teutan having complained that this line was improperly drawn, the Emperor ordered him to demand an explanation from the Spanish. Accompanied by a party of horsemen, the governor held a meeting with a party of Spaniards in the course of which he shot and beheaded Captain Mendoça, a Spanish officer who had served as interpreter during the original boundary negotiations. Consequently, it is now believed that Spain will support Muley Slema's "pretentions to the Crown" with money and vessels, "and an apprehension of this happening has induced the Emperor to send Francisco Chiappe to Spain."

RC (DNA: RG 59, CD); 4 p.; in clerk's hand, except for complimentary close, signature, and following notation at end of text, all in Barclay's hand: "Honble Mr. Jefferson Duplicate. Original by way of Cadiz. Duplicate to Lisbon. (No. 1)." Recorded in SJL as received 4 Apr. 1792.

To Thomas Mann Randolph, Jr.

DEAR SIR   Philadelphia Dec. 18. 1791.

I am obliged to trouble you in the following affair. Doctor Walker, in his account against my father's estate, omitted to credit a sum of £200. paid him Aug. 31. 1766. by Kippen & co. on account of the estate, and debited in their account against the estate. It appeared that he had credited the estate another sum of £200. from Kippen & co. as received 1761. March. and it was suggested that perhaps these might be the same sums, with only a mistake of dates. This suggestion became strengthened by Mr. Francis Walker's applying to James Lyle to know if it appeared in Kippen & co's books that they had made any such paiment as that of £200 in 1761. to Dr. Walker for the estate, and his answering that he found no such payment in their acct. against the estate. If these were the same sums, it followed either that Dr. Walker had credited £200. by prophecy 5. years before he received it, or that McCaul had not charged it to the estate till 5. years after he had paid it. Yet Mr. Lyle said he could establish the payment of 1766. as it stood on their books both as to sum and time: so that it remained to us to establish that which Dr. Walker had credited as £200. paid Mar.

1761.—On turning to the Account book of the estate as kept by Mr. Harvie (one of the executors and a most exact accountant) I found in his own handwriting the estates account against Dr. Walker wherein is a charge in these words '1762. To cash in account with Mr. Mc.Caul £199-18-1' and again in a settled account with Mr. Mc.Caul in the same book is a credit in these words '1762. Dec. 25 by cash paid per orders from Thomas Walker £199-18-1.' Here then is not only a proof concurring with Dr. Walker's own account, but a correction of the sum, to wit £199-18-1 which Dr. Walker had entered in round numbers, and which had he entered fractionally, the difference in sum from the paiment of 1766. would have prevented all suspicion of their identity: and a correction also of the date to 1762. instead of 1761. Indeed in Dr. Walker's account this credit (dated March) follows one of Apr. 1761. Consequently the March after April 1761. must have been in 1762. and the entrance of the year in the margin omitted by inadvertence. Notwithstanding these proofs, it seemed necessary to get over the objection that the estate did not appear to have paid this sum of £199-18-1 to Kippen & co. consequently that it had not a right to a credit of two such paiments.—I had Kippen & co's acct. from 1764. downwards, but not from my father's death Aug. 17. 1757. till 1764. I therefore wrote to Mr. Lyle in Nov. 1790. to have the first 7. years of it copied for me against my return to Virginia in the fall of 1791. that I might then be enabled to search the acct. myself and get the matter settled: but he failed to do it. I wrote again in Nov. 1791. and in consequence he has had it copied, and sent it here to me, and in the very first glance on it, discover the payment of Dec. 1762. charged by Kippen & co. to the estate in the following words.

	£	s	d
'1762. Dec.24. To Richard Randolph	68	18	1
1763. Jan.17. To cash pd. Capt. Meriwether	29	10	–
22. To do. pd. Walker's orders	101	10'	

Adding these articles together they make exactly the £199-18-1 credited between Mr. Harvie and Mc.Caul as 'pd. per orders from Thomas Walker.' To render this proof incontrovertible it will be well for me to prove (because this account does not express) that the £68-18-1 paid to Richd. Randolph was paid on account of Dr. Walker, and it is to obtain this proof that I ask your assistance. Whenever you shall be at Presque-isle be so good as to engage Mr. David Randolph to examine his father's papers and see whether in 1762 Dr. Walker was indebted to him? Whether my father's estate was indebted to him? (I know it was not). Whether about 1762. Dec. 24. his father recd. £68-18-1 from Kippen & co.? Did he recieve it on Dr. Walker's account, or on my father's account? Or for what?

It would not have been necessary, my dear Sir, to have troubled you with this long detail, merely to enable you to obtain this proof for me: but, in case any accident should happen to me, I wished to leave a statement of this matter, because after a lapse of 30. years, 200£ are become 500£. and consequently a very serious demand. If I obtain proof that the money pd. to R.R. was for Dr. Walker, it will be presumed that that paid to Capt. Meriwether was, because of the near connection and mutual transactions known to have taken place between Dr. Walker and Meriwether.

We have no news yet from Monticello since we left it. I cannot account for this. I take for granted you have written. Present my best love to my dear daughter, & believe me to be Dear Sir Your's affectionately,   TH: JEFFERSON

RC (DLC). PrC (MHi); consisting of pages 1 and 2, the third page being in ViU, and the fourth page not found.

For TJ's letter to James Lyle of NOV. 1790, see TJ to Richard Hanson, 7 Nov.

1790. His second letter to Lyle was dated 7 Oct. 1791 rather than in Nov.; Lyle's response of 28 Nov. 1791, quoted above and noted in SJL as received 10 Dec. 1791, has not been found.

From George Washington

Sunday 18th. Decr 1791

The P____ requests that Mr. J____ would give the letter and statement herewith sent from the S____y of War a perusal, and return it to him in the course of the day, with his opinion as to the propriety of the manner of making the communication to Congress; and whether it ought not, at any rate, to be introduced in some such way as this (if it is to pass through him to Congress) "Pursuant to directions I submit" &ca. or (if it is to go immediately from the War department to that body) "I lay before Congress by direction from[1] the P____ of the U.S. the following statement" &ca.

RC (DLC); endorsed by TJ as received 18 Dec. 1791; entry in SJPL reads: "[Letter from G.W. to Th:]J. on statement from Secy at War for Congress." Dft (DNA: RG 59, MLR); written on verso of address-leaf of one of TJ's letters to the President; docketed by Washington: "To Mr. Jefferson & Colo. Hamilton." Tr (DNA: RG 59, SDC);

caption reads: "To Mr. Jefferson and Mr. Hamilton." As these documents indicate, Washington sent an identical letter to the Secretary of the Treasury.

The Dft was incorrectly printed in Vol. 18: 144 under the conjectural date "Before 8 Dec. 1790."

Washington sent TJ a preliminary version of Secretary of War Knox's proposed report on the federal government's preparations for St. Clair's ill-fated expedition against the western Indians. This report was accompanied by a brief covering letter from Knox stating: "I beg leave to submit for your consideration the draft of the proposed statement, and upon which I will request your opinion on Monday morning.

It is to be understood, that all the most material papers are to accompany the statement" (Knox to Washington, 17 Dec. 1791, DLC: Washington Papers). Knox submitted his final report on 26 Dec. 1791, accompanied by another on recommended measures to be taken (See Washington to TJ, 27 Dec. 1791).

[1] "of" in Dft.

From Delamotte

Le Havre, 19 Dec. 1791. He last wrote to TJ on 27 Nov. and enclosed four letters from Short in Holland.—France was gratified by recent reports that the U.S. had sent 1,800 men to Saint-Domingue. Even after Frenchmen realized that these reports could not be true because the U.S. lacked a sufficiently large standing army, they continue to take pleasure in the news of shipments of American arms, ammunition, and provisions to Saint-Domingue.—The French government is sending massive reinforcements to Saint-Domingue. Five ships with 1,000 to 1,200 soldiers have already left France and another 8,000 will soon follow. In the meantime reports have arrived claiming that the rebellious slaves have laid down their arms and returned to their plantations. "Vous savés assés, Monsieur, combien il est interessant pour la France que le Commerce de St. Domingue, L'aliment le plus salutaire de celui de la Métropole, ne soit point intérompu. Cette Insurrection a influé, peutêtre au delà de ce qu'elle devoit faire, sur le prix des denrées de nos Colonies. Elle a nui à notre crédit dans L'Etranger et nos Assignats se sont dépréciés d'autant. Alors on a recherché la denrée, non seulement pour sa rareté, mais aussi comme un échange de valeur réelle contre l'assignat. Les Sucres Brut, qui valoient 75₶ Le quintal avant la nouvelle du desastre de St. Domingue, valent aujourd'huy 130₶. Nos changes avec l'Etranger suivent cette proportion désespérante, celui sur Londres se cotte 20d. Sterling pour un écu de 3₶, et si ce discrédit avoit continué avec la même rapidité qui se manifestoit depuis 10. ou 12. Jours, on ne peut pas dire dans quel desordre nous serions tombés."—The threat of an attack on France by the emigrés in Germany has prompted the French government to take decisive action. It has warned the emigrés to desist from their preparations for hostilities and decided to attack them with three armies if they refuse.—France faces a subsistence shortage. The government has ordered large amounts of supplies from Ireland and will probably place similar orders in the U.S.—"Les tabacs ne se sont pas encore beaucoup senti de l'augmentation de tous les objets d'une valeur intrinseque. Les premieres qualités se Vendent 40. á 44₶."

RC (DNA: RG 59, CD); 3 p.; endorsed by TJ as received 14 Apr. 1792 and so recorded in SJL.

From George Hammond

SIR   Philadelphia 19th December 1791

I have the honor, of acknowledging the receipt of your letter of the 15th curt., and of expressing my perfect approbation of, and concurrence in, the mode, you have suggested, of discussing the several particulars, relative to the nonexecution of the definitive treaty of peace.

In conformity to your example, I am now preparing an abstract of the circumstances that appear to me contraventions, on the part of the United States, of the fourth, fifth and sixth articles of that Treaty. This abstract I intend to present to you, Sir, with as little delay as the extensive nature of the subject under consideration will admit.—I have the honor to be, with sentiments of great respect and consideration, Sir, your most obedient humble Servant,

GEO. HAMMOND.

RC (DNA: RG 59, NL); endorsed by TJ as received 19 Dec. 1791 and so recorded in SJL; also docketed by TJ: "Hammond George . . . on receiving my assignment of breaches." Tr (DNA: RG 59, NL).

TJ had to wait for almost three months before Hammond completed his ABSTRACT of alleged American violations of the Treaty of Paris (Hammond to TJ, 5 Mch. 1792).

From Martin de Villeneuve

                                       chez Mr. john Codeman
MONSIEUR   boston 19. Xbre 1791

Permettez moi de rappeller à votre souvenir l'audience que vous eutes la bonté de me donner Lors de votre Cejour à paris sous la recommendation du Comte de Montmorin, et la visite que j'ai eu L'honneur de vous faire Lors de mon passage dans votre bonne ville accompagné de Mr. J. FitzSimon, pour vous prier, Monsieur, de m'assurer Si l'article XIII. de la Convention Consulaire entre Le roi et Les etats unis, que vous avez Signé Le 14 novembre 1788. Laisse aucun doute pour accorder entre deux negotiant françois la liberté de traduire Leurs différents dans aucune Cour de Ce pays, Comme Le pretend defendre ici, Mr. Le Consul de france avec Lequel je suis en difficulté à Cet Egart, pour avoir fait Saisir le depart d'un batiment appartenant à un françois sans son authorité et par la voix judiciaire americaine. Cependant il est prouvé que Mr. Le Consul de France c'est trouvé present à des jugemens rendus devant la Cour de Cette province entre Sujets françois.—Je suis avec respect Monsieur Votre très humble et très obeissant Serviteur,

MARTIN DE VILLENEUVE

RC (DNA: RG 59, MLR); endorsed by TJ as received 27 Dec. 1791 and so recorded in SJL.

This letter was an outgrowth of a dispute between Villeneuve and Michel Barriou, two French merchants from Bordeaux who were then residing in Boston. The dispute began a week before the present letter was written when Villeneuve sought payment for goods that Barriou had sold on his account. After rejecting an offer by Barriou to refer the matter to Philippe de Létombe, the CONSUL DE FRANCE in Boston, Villeneuve obtained an order from the Suffolk County Court of Common Pleas that summoned Barriou to appear before it to answer charges that he owed Villeneuve the sum in question and that authorized Villeneuve to seize a brigantine owned by Barriou as security for the latter's appearance in court. Barriou protested to Létombe that Villeneuve's resort to the Massachusetts court violated a 1778 edict of the king governing the authority of French consuls in foreign lands as well as Article XII of the 1788 consular convention between France and the United States, both of which, he claimed, required disputes between French citizens in a foreign country to be settled by a French consul. Létombe accepted

Barriou's contention and ordered Villeneuve to bring his complaint against Barriou before the French consular court in Boston. Villeneuve refused to obey Létombe's order, claiming that the royal edict and the article of the Franco-American consular convention cited by Létombe did not give French consuls jurisdiction over purely commercial disagreements between French subjects, and sought to elicit TJ's support for his claim. But TJ, who with respect to Article XII had long since accepted the view that "for the encouragement of commerce it is become usual to permit, by Convention, foreign merchants of the same country to refer their disputes to a judge of their own," scrupulously refrained from answering either this letter or one on the same subject that Villeneuve wrote him three days later, thereby tacitly expressing his support for Létombe's jurisdiction in this case (TJ, Observations on the Contre-Projet, [ca. 16 Sep. 1788], Document XIII in group of documents on the consular convention of 1788, at 14 Nov. 1788; Villeneuve to TJ, 22 Dec. 1791; see also Létombe to Bertrand, 31 Dec. 1791; same to Thevenard, 31 Dec. 1791; same to La Coste, [June 1792], all in Arch. Aff. Etr., Corres. Consul., B I, 210/476-504, 518-26).

Report on Sale of Lands on Lake Erie

The Secretary of state, to whom was referred, by the President of the United States, a letter from the Governor of Pennsylvania with the documents therein mentioned, on the subject of certain lands on Lake Erie, having had the same under consideration, thereupon REPORTS

That Congress, by their resolution of June 6. 1788. directed the Geographer general of the United States to ascertain the quantity of land belonging to the United States between Pennsylvania and Lake Erie, and authorized a sale thereof:

That a sale was accordingly made to the commonwealth of Pennsylvania:

That Congress by their resolution of Sep. 4. 1788. relinquished to the sd. Commonwealth all their right to the government and jurisdiction of the sd. tract of land; but the right of soil was not transferred by the resolution:

That a survey of the sd. tract has been since made and the amount of the purchase money been settled between the Comptrollers of the United states and of the sd. Commonwealth, and that the Governor of Pennsylvania declares in the said letter to the President of the United states that he is ready to close the transaction on behalf of the sd. Commonwealth:

That there is no person at present authorised by law to convey to the sd. Commonwealth the right of soil in the sd. tract of land.

And the Secretary of state is therefore of opinion that the sd. letter and documents should be laid before the legislature of the United States to make such provision by law for conveying the sd. right of soil as they in their wisdom shall think fit.   TH: JEFFERSON
Dec. 19. 1791.

PrC (DLC). Entry in SJPL reads: "[Report of?] Th:J. on sale of lands on L. Erie to Pensva."

The task of completing Pennsylvania's purchase of a portion of the public domain lying along the shores of Lake Erie was one of the last legacies of the Continental Congress to the new federal government. When the boundary of New York was finally settled after the cession of the western land claims of New York and Massachusetts to the United States, the Continental Congress discovered that there was still left over a tract of land of about 200,000 acres bounded by New York, Pennsylvania, and Lake Erie. Since this part of the public domain was cut off from the Northwest Territory by the Connecticut Reserve, the cession of which was not then expected, the Continental Congress decided on 6 June 1788 to survey it and offer it for sale at not less than 75¢ an acre. Pennsylvania, which wanted to expand its frontage along Lake Erie, thereupon contracted with the Board of Treasury to buy this tract for 75¢ an acre, and the Continental Congress transferred to the state "all their right, title and claim to the Government and Jurisdiction"

over the land on 6 Sep. 1788. But before further action could be taken the Continental Congress passed out of existence. After Comptroller General John Nicholson of Pennsylvania and the Department of the Treasury agreed on the terms of payment in the fall of 1791, however, according to which Pennsylvania undertook to pay the federal government $151,640.25 for 202,187 acres, Governor Thomas Mifflin wrote a letter to Washington on 15 Dec. 1791 in which he asked the President to lay a number of enclosed documents relating to the purchase before Congress so that it could authorize the actual transfer of the land. Following TJ's advice, Washington submitted Mifflin's letter and enclosures and TJ's report thereon to Congress on 20 Dec. 1791. Within eight days Congress approved an act authorizing the President to issue letters patent conveying the Lake Erie tract to Pennsylvania that Washington signed into law on 3 Jan. 1792 (JCC, XXXIV, 203, 499-500; Syrett, *Hamilton*, VIII, 325-7, 412, IX, 92, 239; *Pennsylvania Archives*, 9th ser., I, 301; JHR, I, 478-81; JS, I, 357-8, 360; Payson J. Treat, *The National Land System 1785-1820* [New York, 1910], p. 63-4).

To Adam Lindsay

SIR   Philadelphia Dec. 20. 1791.

Your favor of the 4th. inst. came duly to hand as did also the 3. boxes of candles by capt. Johnston. I shall, as you desire, await the remaining 110 ℔ to remit you the cost of the whole in one bill. I shall thank you to keep in mind my request for the Hughes's crab cyder of the best quality. It is in high esteem here.

I rejoice to hear of the daily increase of Norfolk, being satisfied that every place on the waters of the Chesapeake and Albemarle sound must, by a law of nature, become secondary and subordinate to it. An accidental circumstance has thrown it into the rear of the race, and the advantages gained in the mean time by other places, will assist to keep them the longer ahead. But in the long run, natural advantages must prevail over those which are merely acquired.—I am with much esteem Sir Your very humble servt.,

TH: JEFFERSON

Tr (DLC); in the hand of Virginia Randolph.

To George Washington

Dec. 20. 1791.

Th: Jefferson having obtained a copy of the statement of the affair between Pennsylva. and Virginia as made by the delegates in the Virginia assembly from the county where it happened, has the honor to inclose it to the President.

RC (DNA: RG 59, MLR); endorsed by Washington: "From The Secy of State 20th. Decr. 1791 State of the dispute between Virginia and Pennsylvania." Not recorded in SJL or SJPL.

ENCLOSURE

Statement of Conflict between Pennsylvania and Virginia

A statement of facts concerning the proclamation of Governor Mifflin issued against Francis McGuire, Baldwin Parsons, and Absalom Wells, as attested by the two Representatives from the County of Ohio.

A Mr. Davies formerly of Maryland, removed into Virginia, and settled near the Pennsylvania line as it was then supposed to run. He brought with him a negroe who was born and bred up in his family. Some years after his removal, Commissioners were appointed to ascertain the Boundary line between the two

States, and in running it, this Mr. Davies was thrown into the State of Pennsylvania. Shortly afterwards he was advertised of a law in Pennsylvania, which would deprive him of his property after the expiration of six months, and *fine* and *punish* him into the bargain.

In order to avoid these unexpected calamities, he sent his negroe a few miles from him across the line into Virginia, where he hired him to a Mr. Miller. A certain club, called by way of derision the "Negroe club," and said to be an arm of the *"Pennsylvania society for the abolition of slavery,"* seduced this negroe back again into Pennsylvania, where, after indenting him for 6 or 7 years as a *compensation* to themselves for their *humanity*, according to their constant custom, he was to have the benefit of the Pennsylvania Law and be free. Mr. Miller fearing that he should be liable to pay Mr. Davies for the negro, advertised him. Mr. McGuire, Mr. Parsons and Mr. Wells, gentlemen of the most unexceptionable characters, of great respectability and of independent property, roused with indignation at the nefarious practices of this negroe club, and importuned by their neighbours to step forth in defence of their property, went out in search of the negroe, found him and brought him home. For this, they are branded with infamy by the proclamation of Pennsylvania, and are charged moreover with having *fled* from justice; when the fact is, that they have never removed from their usual places of abode in Virginia, or attempted in any way to elude justice. They have been into Pennsylvania, and into the very County of Washington where they were indicted, and at the very Court House of that County when the people were assembled, not once but frequently since, and always unmolested.

The facts concerning the proclamation issued against Francis McGuire and Samuel Brady, attested by the same gentlemen, are as follows.

A Mr. Ryley's family in February or March last, consisting of 7 persons, were attacked by a party of indians: Two of them were taken prisoners, and the remaining five murdered: The people armed and pursued them, but in vain: They returned, and sent out spies to watch their motions and to discover their tracks if possible: Their tracks were discovered: A letter was dispatched to Capt. Wells of the Pennsylvania militia to join the Virginia party: He did so: They went out again in pursuit of the indians (Capt. Brady an old continental and distinguished officer attending as a volunteer under Capts. Wells and McGuire) and they were overtaken some where near Big Beaver creek in Pennsylvania: four of them were killed: Capt. Wells killed one with his own hands, and scalped him: Capt. Brady did not even fire his gun: But yet Capt. Brady, the *Virginian* and a *volunteer*, is branded and proclaimed, whilst Capt. Wells the *Pennsylvanian*, who took the command in conjunction with McGuire is uncensured and unnoticed.

MS (DNA: RG 59, MLR); entirely in Remsen's hand. Not recorded in SJL or SJPL. PrC of MS (DLC); docketed by TJ: "Virginia and Pennsylvania." FC (DNA: RG 59, SDC).

The enclosure is a copy of a 20 Nov. 1791 statement made to Governor Beverley Randolph by William McMachen and Benjamin Biggs, representatives from the COUNTY OF OHIO in the Virginia House of Delegates. The statement itself is an incomplete and sometimes inaccurate account of a highly complex dispute that was a significant episode in the history of the young American republic because it provided the impetus for the passage of the first Fugitive Slave Act. The controversy between Pennsylvania and Virginia over the issue of extradition stemmed in the first instance from the murder by Virginians of some Delaware Indians in Pennsylvania in retaliation for the murder of some Ohio County, Virginia, settlers. Governor Thomas Mifflin's demands for the extradition of the suspected culprits from Virginia under terms of the fourth article of the U.S. Constitution were not honored by Governor Randolph (CVSP, V, 289-94, 298-9, 301-2, 306, 314-8; ASP, *Indian Affairs*, I, 174; *Pennsylvania Archives*, 9th ser., I, 57).

This dispute was further exacerbated by Pennsylvania's closely related effort to secure the extradition from Virginia of the kidnappers of the NEGROE John, two of whom were also implicated in the Indian murders. John's first Pennsylvania owner had leased him to an Ohio County slaveholder in order to avoid having to free him under the 1780 PENNSYLVANIA LAW for the gradual abolition of slavery; but John had escaped back into his state, only to be kidnapped back to Virginia, where he was sold. Mifflin asked for the return of John

and the extradition of his three kidnappers, a request ignored by Virginia's governor because of the failure of the federal Constitution and Virginia law to prescribe how such persons were "to be arrested for delivery."

Both matters were brought to Washington's attention, and he finally referred them to Congress in October 1791. This step eventually quelled the controversy and led to the passage in 1793 of the first Fugitive Slave Act, setting forth specific procedures for obtaining the return of fugitives from justice as well as fugitive slaves (CVSP, V, 320-1, 326-9, 340-50, 421, VI, 70-1, 83-7; ASP, *Miscellaneous*, I, 39-43; Paul Finkleman, *An Imperfect Union: Slavery, Federalism, and Comity* [Chapel Hill, N.C., 1981], p. 44-8; William R. Leslie, "A Study in the Origins of Interstate Rendition: The Big Beaver Creek Murders," AHR, LVII [1951-1952], 63-76). There is no evidence that the President made any use of these statements.

To José Ignacio de Viar and José de Jaudenes

GENTLEMEN   Philadelphia Dec. 21. 1791.

The bearer hereof Kenneth Thompson, a citizen of the United States, proposing to go down the Missisipi to New-Orleans on business, wishes to obtain a passport from you to that place, for his greater safety. He brings me letters from Maryland assuring me of his being a person of merit and good deportment; on these assurances I take the liberty of presenting his application to you, only asking you to do for him what is within the regular line of your ordinary proceedings, in like cases, and begging you to understand that if there would be any thing contrary to rule in granting his request, I do not in that case interest myself in it at all, nor wish to lay you under any embarrasment.—I have the honour to be with much esteem and respect, Gentlemen Your most obedt. & most humble servt,   TH: JEFFERSON

PrC (DLC); at foot of text: "Messieurs Viar and Jaudenes Commissioners of his Catholic majesty." FC (DNA: RG 360, DL).

Overton Carr of Maryland and William Hunter, Jr. of Virginia had written TJ letters of recommendation for Thompson. Carr noted that Thompson was "a young

Gentleman" whose "Adventurous spirit has prompted him to seek his fortune upon the Banks of the Ohio, where He has been for Some time Settled in the Capacity of a Merchant; and is desirous of Opening an intercourse with new Orleans, where Business has been heretofore carried on to very great advantage. But the jealousy of the Spanish Government, now Extremely watchful in consequence of the French Revolution, has rendered the Communication more hazardous and difficult than formerly. Numbers however still enjoy the privilidge of trading there, by means of Pasports and He is now on his way to Philadelphia in order to obtain something of this kind" (Carr to TJ, 4 Dec. 1791; RC in DLC; endorsed by TJ as received 20 Dec. 1791 and so recorded in SJL). Hunter gave substantially the same account of Thompson in his letter (Hunter to TJ, 8 Dec. 1791; RC in DNA: RG 59, MLR; endorsed by TJ as received 20 Dec. 1791 and so recorded in SJL).

Viar and Jaudenes replied that they had no power to issue a passport but they would happily write a letter of endorsement to the Governor of New Orleans (Viar and Jaudenes to TJ, 22 Dec. 1791; RC in DNA: RG 59, NL; endorsed by TJ as received 22 Dec. 1791 and so recorded in SJL).

To Jonathan N. Havens and Sylvester Dering

GENTLEMEN   Philadelphia Dec. 22. 1791.

I return you thanks for your letter of Nov. 1. with the valuable information it contained on the subject of the Hessian fly. They throw peculiar light on the generations of that insect, which other information had placed under much confusion. If further observations should confirm the fact that there are but two generations a year, it may lead perhaps to a remedy. As the Committee of the Philosophical society will probably continue their enquiries thro' another year, any further observations which you may make will be thankfully recieved and communicated to them by, Gentlemen Your most obedt. & most humble servt,   TH: JEFFERSON

RC (PPAP); addressed: "Messrs. Havens & Dering in Shelter island"; franked; endorsed; enclosed in TJ to Ezra L'Hommedieu, 22 Dec. 1791. PrC (DLC).

From Daniel L. Hylton

DEAR SIR   Richmond Virga: Decr: 22th. 1791

Your favour of 5th. instant came to hand a few days past and expected until the receipt thereof Capt. Stratton had long since carryed the whole of your crop of tobacco, having left orders with the inspectors whenever he apply'd to deliver the balance of your crop in their Warehouse. Only two hhds. now remains which would have been shipt at the same time he carryed the last, had they not been damaged in coming down the river which obligd me to have them repackd and put in new hhds. I have made every exertion to get them sent on, but cannot find a Vessle who will venture to go to Philadelphia at this season for fear of being block'd up in the delaware. I am truly concern'd you should experience any inconvenience for want of only the two hhds. now remaining and the gentleman with whom you have made the contract must be ungenerous to the last degree to withold payment from you for those he has already received on that Score. Inclos'd you have the account of the whole expences balance in your favour 63/6, please to inform me how you will have it appropriated. Mrs. Hylton with Mr. Eppes daughter Betsey left this today to spend their Xmas at eppington. Please to inform Mr. J. W. E. the family were very well; whenever an opportunity presents itself of rendering you any service here I beg youll ever take that liberty with me and will at all times give me pleasure to execute it. Mrs. H. joins with me in our best Wishes for the happiness of you and yours am Dr Sir Yr. Sincere fd. & st,

DANL. L. HYLTON

RC (MHi); endorsed by TJ as received 31 Dec. 1791 and so recorded in SJL.

To Ezra L'Hommedieu

SIR   Philadelphia Dec. 22. 1791.

Be pleased to accept my thanks for your favor of Sep. 10. and the valuable information procured thro' your means. I am confident it will be found to throw more light on the subject of the Hessian fly, than any thing I have before seen. The committee appointed for that purpose will probably find it necessary to continue their enquiries and observations through another year. I take the liberty of putting under your cover a letter to Messrs. Dering and Havens, & am with great esteem Sir Your most obedt. humble servt,

TH: JEFFERSON

RC (Andrew Fiske, Shelter Island, N.Y., 1973). PrC (DLC).

To Archibald McCalester

SIR   Philadelphia Dec. 22. 1791.

I am favoured with yours of the 1st. of November and recollect with pleasure our acquaintance in Virginia. With respect to the schools of Europe, my mind is perfectly made up, and on full enquiry. The best in the world is Edinburgh. Latterly too, the spirit of republicanism, has become that of the students in general and of the younger professors; so that on that account also it is eligible for an American. On the continent of Europe no place is comparable to Geneva. The sciences are there more modernised than any where else. There too the spirit of republicanism is strong with the body of the inhabitants: but that of aristocracy is strong also with a particular class; so that it is of some consequence to attend to the class of society in which a youth is made to move. It is a cheap place. Of all these particulars Mr. Kinloch and Mr. Huger of So. Carolina can give you the best account, as they were educated there, and the latter is lately from thence. I have the honour to be with great esteem, Sir Your most obedient humble servt, TH: JEFFERSON

PrC (DLC).

McCalester's sudden demise at the age of thirty-four on 23 Feb. 1792 prevented him from acting on TJ's advice regarding the schooling of his stepson ("Marriage and Death Notices from the City Gazette," *South Carolina Historical and Genealogical Magazine*, XXI [1920], 122-3; Caroline T. Moore, comp., *Abstracts of Wills of Charleston District South Carolina . . . 1783-1800* [Columbia, S.C., 1974], p. 267-8).

To Eliphalet Pearson

SIR   Philadelphia Dec. 22. 1791.

I am to acknolege the reciept of your favor of July 4th. covering a copy of Judge Lowell's eulogy on the late worthy President of the Academy of arts and sciences. I sincerely wish that my situation in life permitted me to contribute my mite to the labours of the society for the advancement of science, and to justify the honor they did me in placing my name on their roll. But however wedded by affection to the objects of their pursuit, I am obliged to unremitting attentions to others less acceptable to my mind, and much less attaching. I read with pleasure whatever comes from the society, and am happy in the occasion given me of assuring them of my respects and attachment and yourself of the sentiments of esteem with which I have the honor to be Sir Your most obedient humble servt, TH: JEFFERSON

PrC (DLC).

From Martin de Villeneuve

Boston, 22 Dec. 1791. He recalls with pleasure his visit with TJ in Paris with the recommendation of Comte de Montmorin and in the company of Mr. J. Fitzsimons. He wishes to know whether Article XII of the 14 Nov. 1788 Consular Convention between the United States and France governs the settlement of differences between French citizens or whether Article XIII allows French merchants in the U.S. to have their differences settled by an American court without the consent of the local French consul. He has transferred a dispute between himself and another French merchant over the seizure of a vessel to the local Court of Common Pleas, not only because this tribunal renders justice promptly, but also because he has learned that the French consul here has been present at cases heard by this court involving French subjects. He excuses himself for writing a second letter on this subject and notes that the French consul also awaits TJ's reply.

RC (DNA: RG 59, MLR); 2 p., in French. Not recorded in SJL.

Note on the Subject of Vacant Consulships

Lisbon. Candidates. Edward Church. His case is known to the President. John Telles of Philadelphia. His papers inclosed. Samuel Harrison. See Colo. Humphrey's lre. to the President. John Cowper. (Virginia) Recommended by Josiah Parker.

Cadiz. The former candidates not approved, and no new offer. It is very desireable we should have a consul there. Should Mr. Church not be appointed to Lisbon, he would be proper for Cadiz. There are good perquisites to the former; but I do not know that there are any to the latter.

Bristol. Elias Vanderhorst of So. Carolina, recommended by Majr. Butler. It is a port where we have a good deal of commerce, and as this is the first application for a Consulship for a Carolinian, and Vanderhorst is highly spoken of, I am of opinion it is expedient to nominate him.

When the President shall be pleased to fix on the persons for the above ports, a nomination shall be prepared with a description of their districts.

Th: Jefferson
Dec. 22. 1791.

RC (DNA: RG 59, MLR); addressed: "The President of the United States"; endorsed by Lear. PrC (DLC). FC (DNA: RG 59, SDC). Entry in SJPL reads: "[Nomination of Consu]ls."

After reading this report Washington evidently asked TJ to prepare a message nominating Edward Church consul at Lisbon and Elias Vanderhorst consul at Bristol, a draft of which he completed on 24 Dec. 1791 (PrC in DLC). Washington delayed submitting these nominations to the Senate until 3 May 1792, whereupon that body approved both nominations after some debate over Church (JEP, I, 121-2). Washington did not fill the consular vacancy at Cadiz until 20 Feb. 1793, when the Senate confirmed his nomination of Joseph Yznardi, "a native of Spain," to serve there (same, I, 130-1).

John Telles' unsuccessful quest for the Lisbon consulship is described in Editorial Note on consular problems, at 21 Feb. 1791. David Humphreys' 12 May 1791 letter to Washington on behalf of Samuel Harrison is summarized at length in notes to Humphreys to TJ, 3 May 1791. Josiah Parker recommended John Cowper in a letter to TJ of 8 Aug. 1790.

Report on Negotiations with Spain

THE SECRETARY OF STATE

REPORTS

to the President of the United States that one of the Commissioners of Spain, in the name of both, has lately communicated to him verbally, by order of his court, that his Catholic majesty, apprised of our sollicitude to have some arrangements made respecting our free navigation of the river Missisipi, and the use of a port thereon, is ready to enter into treaty thereon at Madrid.

The Secretary of state is of opinion that this overture should be attended to without delay, and that the proposal of treating at Madrid, tho' not what might have been desired, should yet be accepted; and a commission plenipotentiary made out for the purpose.

That Mr. Carmichael, the present Chargé des affaires of the United States at Madrid, from the local acquaintance which he must have acquired with persons and circumstances, would be an useful and proper member of the commission: but that it would be useful also to join with him some person more particularly acquainted with the circumstances of the navigation to be treated of.

That the fund appropriated by the act providing the means of intercourse between the United States and foreign nations will insufficiently furnish the ordinary and regular demands on it, and is consequently inadequate to the mission of an additional Commissioner express from hence:

That therefore it will be adviseable on this account, as well as for the sake of dispatch, to constitute some one of the Ministers of the United States in Europe, jointly with Mr. Carmichael, Commissioners plenipotentiary for the special purpose of negotiating and concluding, with any person or persons duly authorised by his Catholic majesty, a convention or treaty for the free navigation of the river Missisipi by the citizens of the United States, under such accomodations with respect to a port and other circumstances, as may render the sd. navigation practicable, useful, and free from dispute; saving to the President and Senate their respective rights as to the ratification of the same; and that the said negociation be at Madrid or such other place in Spain as shall be desired by his Catholic majesty.

TH: JEFFERSON
Dec. 22. 1791.

RC (DNA: RG 59, MLR); endorsed by Lear. PrC (DLC). FC (DNA: RG 59, SDC). Entry in SJPL: "[Repor]t Th:J. proposing to open negociation with Spain."

The OVERTURE communicated verbally is printed above as Memorandum of Conversation with Jaudenes, 6 Dec. 1791. Washington concurred with the recommendations TJ made in this report and on 11 Jan. 1792 submitted a copy of this document to the Senate with an accompanying message nominating William Carmichael and William Short "Commissioners Plenipotentiary" to negotiate with Spain on the navigation of the Mississippi. In his letter to the Senate, Washington incorporated TJ's draft nomination (PrC in DLC: TJ Papers, 80: 13881; entry in SJPL after 3 Jan. and before 10 Jan. reads: "Nominations of Carmichael and Short to treat with Spain"; JEP, I, 95-6). Two days earlier the Spanish agents in Philadelphia had written TJ a brief note requesting "some reply (if possible) to the official Communication" of Spain's willingness to resume diplomatic negotiations with the U.S. (Jaudenes and Viar to TJ, 9 Jan. 1792, RC in DNA: RG 59, NL; endorsed by TJ as received 9 Jan. 1792 and so recorded in SJL). On 24 Jan. 1792, the Senate approved both nominations, eight days after it had narrowly voted in favor of Washington's nomination of Short as minister resident to The Hague (JEP, I, 97, 98, 99; see also Lear to TJ, 24 Jan. 1792, RC and Lear's retained draft in DNA: RG 59, MLR; Tr in DNA: RG 59, SDC). TJ recommended Carmichael for this appointment despite a warning from one of the Spanish agents that he was unacceptable to the Spanish minister for foreign affairs, Floridablanca (Bemis, *Pinckney's Treaty*, p. 160-1). Short had been involved in diplomatic efforts to resolve the Mississippi question since the time of the Nootka Sound crisis (TJ to Short, 10 Aug. 1790, Document VI in group of documents on the war crisis of 1790, at 12 July 1790; TJ to Short, 12, 19 Mch. 1791, Documents VII and X in group of documents on threat of disunion in the West, at 10 Mch. 1791). For the subsequent expansion of the objectives of the Carmichael and Short mission to Spain, see TJ to Jaudenes and Viar, 26 Jan. 1792.

To Alexander Hamilton

Dec. 23. 1791.

Th: Jefferson presents his respectful compliments to the Secretary of the treasury and incloses him the copy of a letter and table which he has addressed to the President of the United States, and which being on a subject whereon the Secretary of the Treasury and Th:J.

have differed in opinion, he thinks it his duty to communicate to him.

RC (DLC: Hamilton Papers). For the letter and table see TJ to Washington, 23 Dec. 1791. The subject on which TJ and Hamilton differed was that of the proposed commercial treaty with France (see note, TJ to Washington, 26 Nov. 1791).

From David Humphreys

Lisbon, 23 Dec. 1791. He takes advantage of this opportunity by Capt. Stobo to advise TJ that in his letters of 22 Nov. and 4 Dec. he enclosed receipts from Thomas Barclay for 32,175 current guilders for Barclay's Moroccan mission. He has been attentive to the request in TJ's 11 Apr. letter for information about Brazil, though his efforts have been constrained by the Portuguese government's jealousy of its colonies. From casual conversations with people acquainted with Brazil, and especially from one long discussion initiated by M. de Pinto he is able to make certain general observations about that colony, starting with the fact that it has a population of about 1,600,000 people.

"The real Riches and Resources of the Inhabitants are encreasing in some kind of Ratio to the diminution of the Produce of the Mines. Instead of giving a certain proportion of the precious metals to Government, they were obliged (a few years ago) to furnish a specific sum. This caused uneasiness, remonstrance, a change of system, and eventually a great substitution of Agriculture, for labour in the Mines. Hence the vast augmentation of the imports from Brazil to the mother Country; particularly in the articles of Cotton, Sugar, Rice and Tobacco. Mr. Pinto informed me, he believed the value of the Cotton imported from Brazil was equal to that of all other articles brought from thence. I told him, I had heard many of the last ships, from Portugal to Brazil, had carried Money as a remittance for the productions of that Country. He replied, he had no doubt it was very true. From these circumstances you will naturally conclude, the Merchants and Planters must be very wealthy. Their wealth is undoubtedly daily encreasing. Few now transfer their property, or come to reside in the mother Country. The ties of attachment are weakening. The Merchants, instead of consigning their Cargoes, as formerly, to Merchants in Portugal, have, within a short time, established Factors and Agents here. Manufactures of several kinds are also growing rapidly in the Colonies. Those in wood and iron, especially as applied to shipbuilding, have acquired the same degree of improvement as in the mother Country. The ships built by the Portuguese, are on the English Model, and inferior to no others in Europe.

"The Natives of Portugal are by no means deficient in point of genius. Notwithstanding the depression and embarrassment under which it labours, recent facts exist to prove, that Individuals have an uncommon portion of it. Yet the Brazillians are allowed to be a more shrewd and penetrating People. They are generally, like the Inhabitants of most warm Climates, indolent. Still they have more books, more instruction, and particularly more knowledge on the subject of Government, than the People of Portugal.

"Some troubles, though not extending to insurrections, have happened within a year past in Brazil. Now a pretty good share of tranquility prevails. The Colonists have however many causes of complaint; and the Government at home of apprehension, that a seperation must one day inevitably take place."

He will continue to seek further information about Brazil. He has not heard lately from William Carmichael but the Portuguese ambassador to Spain hints that the Spanish government favors negotiations with the U.S. He is inclined to believe that this hint is well founded because of one or two articles in French Gazettes mentioning the U.S. wish for a port at the mouth of the Mississippi and its peremptory demand for free navigation of that river. He encloses the Gazettes he received since his last letter.—P.S. He just received a letter from Gibraltar dated 5 Dec. announcing the arrival of Barclay and conjecturing that Barclay would want to remain there until he learned the outcome of the civil war in Morocco.

RC (DNA: RG 59, DD); 8 p.; at head of text: "(No. 41)"; at foot of text: "The Secry of State"; endorsed by TJ as received 16 Mch. 1792 and so recorded in SJL. Tr (same).

Humphreys also wrote a brief letter to TJ on 24 Dec. 1791, quoting the following extract of an 8 Dec. 1791 letter Thomas Barclay had written to him from Gibraltar: "On Sunday we got into the Mouth of the Streights, but it blew so violently from the Southwest, that after several attempts to get into the Bay of Tangier, we were obliged to push for this place; where we remain for a change of wind, the first of which we shall embrace to cross over to Africa" (RC in DNA: RG 59, DD; at head of text: "(No. 41)"; endorsed by TJ as received 16 Mch. 1792 and so recorded in SJL. Tr in same). Immediately after receiving this note, TJ sent it and Humphreys' dispatch No. 41 to the President (TJ to Washington, 16 Mch. 1792, RC in DNA: RG 59, MLR; addressed: "The President of the U.S."; endorsed by Lear. Tr in DNA: RG 59, SDC; not recorded in SJL or SJPL).

To Archibald Stuart

DEAR SIR   Philadelphia Dec. 23. 1791.

I received duly your favor of Octob. 22. and should have answered it by the gentleman who delivered it, but that he left town before I knew of it.

That it is really important to provide a constitution for our state cannot be doubted: as little can it be doubted that the ordinance called by that name has important defects. But before we attempt it, we should endeavor to be as certain as is practicable that in the attempt we should not make bad worse. I have understood that Mr. Henry has always been opposed to this undertaking: and I confess that I consider his talents and influence such as that, were it decided that we should call a Convention for the purpose of amending, I should fear he might induce that convention either to fix the thing as at present, or change it for the worse. Would it not therefore be well that means should be adopted for coming at his ideas of the changes he would agree to, and for communicating to him those which we should propose? Perhaps he might find ours not so distant from his but that some mutual sacrifices might bring them together.

I shall hazard my own ideas to you as hastily as my business obliges me. I wish to preserve the line drawn by the federal constitution between the general and particular governments as it stands at present and to take every prudent means of preventing either from stepping over it. Tho' the experiment has not yet had a long enough course to shew us from which quarter incroachments are most to be feared, yet it is easy to foresee from the nature of things that the incroachments of the state governments will tend to an excess of liberty which will correct itself (as in the late instance) while those of the general government will tend to monarchy, which will fortify itself from day to day, instead of working it's own cure, as all experience shews. I would rather be exposed to the inconveniencies[1] attending too much liberty than those attending too small a degree of it. Then it is important to strengthen the state governments: and as this cannot be done by any change in the federal constitution, (for the preservation of that is all we need contend for,) it must be done by the states themselves, erecting such barriers at the constitutional line as cannot be surmounted either by themselves or by the general government. The only barrier in their power, is a wise[2] government. A weak one will lose ground in every contest. To obtain a wise and an able government, I consider the following changes as important. Render the legislature a desireable station by lessening the number of representatives (say to 100) and lengthening somewhat their term, and proportion them equally among the electors: adopt also a better mode of appointing Senators. Render the Executive a more desireable post to men of abilities by making [him] more independant of the legislature. To wit, let him be chosen by other electors, for a longer time, and ineligible for ever after. Responsibility is a tremendous engine in a free government. Let him feel the whole weight of it then by taking away the shelter[3] of his executive council. Experience both ways has already established the superiority of this measure. Render the Judiciary respectable by every possible means, to wit, firm tenure in office, competent salaries, and reduction of their numbers. Men of high learning and abilities are few in every country; and by taking in those who are not so, the able part of the body have their hands tied by the unable. This branch of government will have the weight of the conflict on their hands, because they will be the last appeal of reason.—These are my general ideas of amendments. But, preserving the ends, I should be flexible and conciliatory as to the means. You ask whether Mr. Madison and myself could attend on a convention which should be called? Mr. Madison's engagements as a member of Congress will probably be from October to March or April in every year. Mine are constant while I hold my office, and my attendance would be very unimportant. Were it otherwise, my office should not stand in the way of it. I am with great & sincere esteem Dr. Sir, your friend & servt,   TH: JEFFERSON

PrC (DLC).

¹ TJ first wrote "dangers" but crossed it out and then wrote this word.
² Preceding two words substituted for "an able," deleted.
³ This word inserted for another, crossed out and illegible.

To George Washington

SIR   Philadelphia, December 23rd. 1791.

As the conditions of our commerce with the French and British Dominions, are important, and a moment seems to be approaching when it may be useful that both should be accurately understood, I have thrown a representation of them into the form of a table, shewing at one view, how the principal articles interesting to our agriculture and navigation stand in the European and American Dominions of these two powers. As to so much of it as respects France, I have cited under every article the law on which it depends; which laws, from 1784 downwards, are in my possession.

Port-charges are so different according to the size of the Vessel, and the dexterity of the Captain, that an examination of a greater number of Port-bills might, perhaps, produce a different result. I can only say that that expressed in the table is fairly drawn from such bills as I could readily get access to, and that I have no reason to suppose it varies much from the truth, nor on which side the variation would lie. Still I cannot make myself responsible for this Article. The Authorities cited will vouch the rest.—I have the Honor to be, with the most perfect respect and attachment Sir, Your most obedient and Most humble Servant

RC (DNA: RG 59, MLR); in a clerk's hand; signature clipped; endorsed by Washington: "Comparison of the Trade between France & G. Britn." Tr (NNC). Tr (DNA: RG 59, SDC). Tr (DLC: Hamilton Papers); letter only; docketed by Hamilton: "very *important.*" PrC of Tr in Hamilton Papers (DLC) includes Notes and Table. Entry in SJPL reads: "[Th:J. to G.W. Tab]le of commerce with France and England."

Report on Commerce

Footing of the Commerce of the United States, with France & England; and with the French & English american Colonies.

	France	Grt. Britn: & Ireland		French Ama.	English Ama:
Wheat, Flour &c.	Free(a.).	Prohibited till it is 6/3 a Bushel	Wheat, Flour &c.	Prohibited by(g) a genl. Law, Free by Suspensions from Time to Time.	Free by Proclamaton
Rice	Free(a.)	7/4 sterlg. the Kent.	Rice	1. pr. Cent(c.)	Free by Proclamatn.
Salted fish	8₶ Kental(b.)	Prohibited	Salted fish	1 pr. C. + 3₶ K.(h.)	Prohibited
Salted beef	5.₶ K.(c.)	Prohibited	Salted beef	1 pr. C. + 3₶ K.(a.)	Prohibited
Salted pork	5.₶ K(d.) in some Ports. prohibited in others	44/9 K.			
Furs	Free(a.)	15 to 20 pr C.			
Indigo	5₶ K(e.)	Free			
Whale oil	7₶ 10s Barrel(a.) of 520 lbs.	£18-3 Ton			
Tar, pitch, Turpentine	2½ pr.(a.) Ct.¹	11.d 11/ 2/3 B.			
Ships	free(a.) for naturalizat.	Prohibd. naturalizat.			
Port fees(i.)	Cents Bordeaux .23 the ton } average .18 Havre .14 the ton	London .76 Liverpool .61 } Dol 1.09 Bristol 1.43 Hull 1.57 } Average		Cape Franc .96 Port au Pr. .40 } .55 Martinique .18	Jamaica .76 Antigua .42 Barbadoes .42 } .44 average St Kitts .43

Exports to[f.]	1,384,246 D.	[k.]6,888,978 D.	Exports to	3,284,656 D.	2,357,583 D.
Imports from[f.]	155,136 D.	13,965,464 D.	Imports from	1,913,212 D.	1,319,964 D.
Freightd. in their[f.] Vessels	9,842 Tons	119,194 Tons	Freighted in their Vessels	3,959 tons	107,759 tons
Freighted in our[f.] Vessels	19,173 Tons	39,171 Tons	Freighted in our Vessels	97,236 Tons	Prohibited

The following Articles, being on an equal footing in both Countries, are thrown together.

Tobacco	Free of Duty, but under Monopoly	1/3 the lb.	Corn Indian	1 pr. C.[c.]	Free by Proclamation
Wood	Free[a.]	Free	Wood	1 pr. C.[c.]	Free by Proclamat.
Pot & Pearl Ash	Free[a.]	Free	Salted Pork	Prohibited[c.]	Prohibited
Flax seed	Free[a.]	Free	Horses & Mules	Free[c.]	Free by Proclamat.
			Live Provisions	1 pr. C.[c.]	Free by Proclamat.
			Tar, pitch, Turpentine	1 pr. C.[c.]	Free by Proclamat.
			Imports allowed	Rum, Molasses, generally Sugar & all other Commodities till Augt. 1st. 1794.	Rum, Molasses, Sugar, Coffee, Cocoanuts, Ginger, Pimento, by Proclamation.

Notes

(a.) by Arret of Dec. 29. 1787.

(b.) by Arret of 1763.

(c.) by Arret of Aug. 30. 1784.

(d.) by Arret of   1688.

(e.) by Arret of   1760.

(f.) taken from the Custom House Returns of U.S.

(g.) there is a general Law of France prohibiting foreign Flour in their Islands, with a suspending Power to their Governors in Cases of Necessity. An Arret of May 9, 1789, by their Governor makes it free till 1794, Aug. 1. and in fact is generally free there.

(h.) The Arret of September 18. 1785, gave a Premium of 10₶ the Kental on Fish brought in their own Bottoms, for 5 Years so that the Law expired Sep. 18. 1790. Another Arret, past a week after, laid a Duty of 5.₶ the Kental on fish brought in foreign Vessels, to raise money for the Premium beforementioned, this last Arret was not limited in Time; yet seems to be understood as only commensurate with the other. Accordingly an Arret of May. 9. 1789. has made fish in foreign Bottoms liable to 3.₶ the K. only till Aug. 1. 1794.

(i.) The Port charges are estimated from Bills collected from the Merchants of Philadelphia. They are different in different Ports of the same Country, and different in the same Ports on Vessels of different Sizes. Where I had several Bills of the same Port, I averaged them together. The Dollar is rated at 4/4½ Sterl. in England, at 6/8 in the British West Indies at 5₶ 12s. in France, and at 8₶ 5s. in the french West Indies.

Several Articles stated to be *free* in France do in Fact pay one eighth of a per Cent which was retained merely to oblige an Entry to be made in their Custom House Books. In like manner several of the Articles stated to be *free* in England, do in Fact pay a light Duty. The English Duties are taken from the Book of Rates.

		Dollars
(k.) The Exports to Gr. Britain & Ireland are		6,888,978.50

How much they consume I know not. They certainly reexport the following—

Grain. the whole since the Law of the last Parliamt.	1,093,885	
" Tobacco ⅚ according to Sheffeild's Tables	2,295,411	
" Rice ⅝ according to same	552,750	
" Indigo ⅓ according to same	315,887	
Furs, probably one Half	17,950	
Ginseng, the whole	32,424	
Mahogany ⎱ not being of our Productions	16,724	
Wine ⎰ should also be deducted	4,425	4,329,456
Remainder, including their Consumption, and the unknown		2,559,522

re-exportations; the reexportations certainly known then are ⅝ of the whole.

RC (DNA: RG 59, MLR); in a clerk's hand. PrC of Dft in TJ's hand (MoSHi: Bixby Collection). Tr (NNC). Tr (DNA: RG 59, SDC). PrC of Tr in Hamilton Papers (DLC). MS (DLC, TJ Papers: 46:7768); an earlier rough draft in TJ's hand; undated.

[1] In Tr (NNC) and PrC in DLC, "5 sous the K. by new Tariff" appears below this entry.

To William Blount

SIR   Philadelphia Dec. 24. 1791.

I have the honor to acknolege the receipt of your favor of Sep. 19. with the schedule it contained, and now to inclose you a printed copy of the Census of the whole of the United states, and one of my report on the lands belonging to them.

Congress have at present under their consideration the Post office bill, and we are endeavoring to get a post established from Richmond to Staunton and from thence along the road towards your government as far as the profits of the post office will justify it, and I hope it will be done. This communication with you, as well as with Kentuckey, has been much wanted for every purpose of government.—I have the honour to be with great respect Sir Your most obedient & most humble servt,   TH: JEFFERSON

PrC (DLC); at foot of text: "Governor Blount." FC (DNA: RG 360, DL). Enclosures: (1) *Return of the Whole Number of Persons within the Several Districts of the United States* (Philadelphia, 1791). (2) TJ's Report on Public Lands, 8 Nov. 1791.

A bill to establish a post office and post roads had been presented on 29 Nov. 1791 and the House had debated its merits throughout most of December. After the House approved a bill on 10 Jan. 1792, the Senate adopted a revised version on 30 Jan. A compromise measure was finally approved on 3 Feb. and the President signed the measure on 20 Feb. 1792 (JHR, I, 465, 469, 470, 475, 478, 479, 480, 481, 482, 483, 486, 487-8, 490, 499, 501, 502, 505, 507, 511; U.S. Statutes at Large, I, 211-9; and Wesley E. Rich, *The History of the United States Post Office to the Year 1829* [Cambridge, Mass., 1924], p. 71).

From Joseph Fenwick

SIR   Bordeaux 24 Decmr. 1791.

Herewith is a copy of my last respects mostly on the Subject of the depreciation of the Assignats, since they have continued to fall and all the foreign Exchanges, and coins, also that of the country are at least one third better than the Assignats. Indeed Dollars are now selling for eight Livres, and exchange on London is under 6½ d. Stg. ℔ Livre. The progress of this uncertain value, and the restoration of confidence, will depend on the management of the finances, and the issue of an almost certain War with Emigrants. How that will terminate depends on too many causes to permit a prediction. An opinion may be hazarded on given circumstances. Shoud they be supported by the Emperor and King of Prussia or either of them, an uncertain and disastrous war must follow, if not they cannot long remain an object of disquietude to this Country. The joint resolution of the Executive and Legislative Bodys of France of declaring the Electors of Mayance and Treves ennemies to the french Nation, unless they expelled from their Territory the hostile Assemblies of the french Emigrants by the 15th. Jany. next, will discover the misterious sentiments of the neighbouring powers toward the affairs of France.

The minds of the people in this quarter appear much agitated. The commercial interest very sensibly effected by the insurrection in Hispaniola, as well as by the low exchange, which with other bad tendencies has that of keeping up the price of grain, now realy scarce and high. The political opinions more divided than ever, in three visible parties—one for a republican government composing the different Clubs, another for the present Constitution, and a third, the friends to the former. In this situation a war appears a popular and desirable event to unite the two former parties against the latter, and I think woud augment the public confidence and better the actual situation of affairs, unless attacked with imposing success by a formidable enemy.

There are no preparations making here either for the army or Navy, the regular national guard (not the militia) are pretty well equipped and disposed to march wherever ordered.

I have seen in a Richmond newspaper some reflections on my conduct toward several American vessels that arrived here last summer with Tobacco that cleared for England. I sent you the 25 Sepr. a copy of a letter I wrote Mr. Short on the subject, that explained my conduct on the occasion, which I am so far from thinking was reprehensible, that was it to do over again I shoud persue the same. I was displeased at seeing your name refered to in the Advertisement being conscious that I gave no room for it. I told the Gentlemen who were interested in the affair, in order to remove every air of personallity that I acted under the orders of the Minister of my own government.

My interferance in the situation of a vessel now here, may again expose me to some newspaper censure by the parties interested in her. A Brigg† from Charleston loaded with Tobacco and Rice, said to belong to Boston, to support which she has a Register granted by the District of Dartmouth in 1785. and no other paper whatever to justify her pretentions to the American Flagg. Therefore I have on the presumption of her being English, and conviction of not being American under the laws of the present Government, informed the Director of the Customs here that the vessel coud not

† Triton, Capt. Barrel.

be recognised as belonging to the United States of America. Indeed the Captain avows that he was regarded as a foreigner in the ports of America, but that he has never had any other Register and was always admitted as an American in Europe, and that his Brigg belongs in fact to a British subject residing in America.

I here take the occasion to observe, that I think it woud be prudent to have different forms of Clearances for American and foreign vessels in the Custom Houses in America. The State of Virginia is the only one that I have observed has adopted a different form. But from the other States, the Clearances for American and foreign vessels seem to run indiscriminately in the same manner.

All american produce now sells very readily and nominally higher in our Market. The late short crops here keeps up the prices of grain and Rice and speculations in Tobacco supports also its price. But such is the uncertainty of the value of paper, that it is impossible to make any good quotations of the real value of the actual prices, or how they will rule in future.

I am desired by the Club national of Bordeaux to send you an examplaire of their proces verbal of a feast given to the Americans, English, and Poles which I herewith inclose.—With highest consideration I have the honor to be Sir Your most Obd. & most Humble St., JOSEPH FENWICK

RC (DNA: RG 59, CD). Recorded in SJL as received 27 Mch. 1792.

The 12 Oct. 1791 issue of the *Virginia Gazette and General Advertiser* was the RICHMOND NEWSPAPER that printed a series of letters concerning Fenwick's refusal, in accordance with a recently passed decree of the National Assembly, to certify that three tobacco-laden ships from Virginia could land in Bordeaux because they lacked clearance papers for France.

The CLUB NATIONAL—Club du Café national—of Bordeaux held a civic feast on 11 Dec. 1791 featuring "an inauguration of the united flags of France, England, the United States of America, and Poland"; an address by the president of the club extolling the accomplishments of the French Revolution and calling for eternal peace and friendship among the French, British, American, and Polish people; a reply by Fenwick expressing gratitude for French aid during the American Revolution and hope for the continued progress of constitutional liberty in France; and the offering of forty-one toasts expressive of various revolutionary sentiments (*National Gazette*, 2 Apr. 1792).

To Daniel L. Hylton

DEAR SIR   Philadelphia Dec. 24. 1791.

Since mine to you of the 5th. yours of Nov. 12th. came to hand exactly a month after it was written. I have got the gentleman who purchased my tobacco to examine whether there was any which from it's marks or other circumstances might not be mine. He says he was careful not to receive any but what was under my mark, that he has manufactured a part, and consequently cannot now re-examine the hhds in which that was, but he has re-examined all the hhds. now remaining, which is the greatest part, and they are all under my mark. Possibly Mr. Randolph's overseer may have still continued my mark as being that of the plantation as before used. In this or any case if it appears that any of Mr. Randolph's tobo. has come instead of mine, either let it be replaced out of mine remaining there, or, if he chuses it, let it all still come on, and he shall recieve it's neat proceeds here, at his election. I am anxious to know how much of mine of the growth of 1790. is still to come on, tho' I am sorry to be so troublesome to you. I am with great esteem Dear Sir Your friend & servt, TH: JEFFERSON

PrC (MHi).

To Henry Mullins

DEAR SIR   Philadelphia Dec. 24. 1791.

Mr. James Strange who acts for Donald Scot & co. having sent me an account in which no credit was given for the £70. which you were to pay Richard Anderson for me, I wrote to him claiming the credit. He writes me in answer that no such entry has been made by Mr. Anderson to my credit, and that you are not debited any sum on my account. I must beg the favor of you to take measures to establish this payment, and to enable me to place myself on safe ground. The first time you go to Richmond be so good as to carry your proofs and accounts &c. to Mr. Strange, and get the matter settled. He is candid and will do in it whatever is just: but let me pray you not to let it be omitted.—I am with much esteem Dear Sir Your friend & servt., TH: JEFFERSON

PrC (MHi). For the correspondence with STRANGE, see TJ to Strange, 7 Oct. 1791, and note.

To Daniel Smith

SIR   Philadelphia Dec. 24. 1791.

I have to acknolege the receipt of your favors of Sep. 1. and Octob. 4. together with the report of the Executive proceedings in the South Western government from March 1. to July 26.

In answer to that part of yours of Sep. 1. on the subject of a seal for the use of that government, I think it extremely proper and necessary, and that one should be provided at public expence.

The opposition made by Governor Blount and yourself to all attempts by citizens of the U.S. to settle within the Indian lines without authority from the General government is approved, and should be continued.

There being a prospect that Congress, who have now the post office bill before them, will establish a post from Richmond to Stanton, and continue it thence towards the S.W. government a good distance, if not nearly to it, our future correspondence will be more easy, quick and certain.—I am with great esteem Sir Your most obedt. & most humble servt, TH: JEFFERSON

PrC (DLC). FC (DNA: RG 360, DL).

Notes on Conversation on Rufus King

Dec. 25. 1791.

Colo. Gunn (of Georgia) dining the other day with Colo. Hamilton said to him, with that plain freedom he is known to use, 'I wish Sir you would advise your friend King, to observe some kind of consistency in his votes. There has been scarcely a question before Senate on which he has not voted both ways. On the Representation bill, for instance, he first voted for the proposition of the Representatives, and ultimately voted against it.' 'Why' sais Colo. H. 'I'll tell you as to that Colo. Gunn, that it never was intended that bill should pass.' Gunn told this to Butler, who told it to Th:J.

MS (DLC); entirely in TJ's hand. Entry in SJPL reads: "[No]te. King and Hamilton as to Representation bill." Included in the "Anas."

Senator James Gunn's perplexity in trying to account for Rufus King's votes on the bill to reapportion congressional representation in accordance with the census of 1790 is understandable. Between 7 and 20 Dec. 1791 King alternately favored and opposed the House proposal to award each state one representative for every 30,000 inhabitants as well as a Senate amendment to change the ratio to one representative for every 33,000 inhabitants, a curious voting pattern that even his most recent biographer is at a loss to explain (JS, I, 342, 351, 354, 358; Robert Ernst, *Rufus King: American Federalist* [Chapel Hill, N.C., 1968], p. 170). For a discussion of reapportionment, see TJ's Opinion on the Bill for Apportioning Representation, 4 Apr. 1792.

To Martha Jefferson Randolph

MY DEAR DAUGHTER   Philadelphia Dec. 25. 1791.

Your's of Nov. 29. and Mr. Randolph's of Nov. 28. came to hand five days ago. They brought us the first news we had received from Monticello since we left it. A day or two after, Mr. Millar of Charlottesville arrived here and gave us information of a little later date, and particularly of Colo. Lewis and Mrs. Gilmer's illness. His account of Mrs. Gilmer was alarming, and I am anxious to hear it's issue. Our feelings on little Anne's danger as well as her escape were greatly excited on all your accounts. These alarms and losses are the price parents pay for the pleasure they recieve from their children. I hope her future good health will spare you any more of them.—We are likely to get a post established through Columbia, Charlottesville, and Staunton, on a permanent footing, and consequently a more regular one. This I hope will remove all precariousness in the transportation of our letters. Tho I am afraid there is one kind of precariousness it will not remove; that in the writing of them, for you do not mention having written before the 29th. of Nov. tho' we had then left Monticello near seven weeks: I have written every week regularly. Present me affectionately to Mr. Randolph. Kiss dear Anne for me, and believe me to be your's with tender love.   TH: JEFFERSON

RC (NNP). PrC (CSmH). Accompanying this letter was one from Maria Jefferson to Thomas Mann Randolph, Jr., saying: "You nor my sister niether mention'd what had become of the box that had our things in it. I am in great want of them particularly my music. I am to stay with Papa as long as the holydays last which is a week" (Maria Jefferson to Thomas Mann Randolph, Jr., 25 Dec. 1791; RC in DLC). Neither Martha Jefferson Randolph's letter of 29 Nov. 1791 nor her husband's of 28 Nov. 1791, both recorded in SJL as received 22 Dec. 1791, has been found.

From George Washington

25th. Decr. 1791

The P__ returns Mr. Muters letter, and gives Mr. J__ an opportunity of reading one from Judge Innes on the same subject. The latter, commences his operations *from* the point, *to* which we have not *yet* been able to get, namely, established Posts in the Indian Country—the primary object of the Campaign, after the accomplishment of which, every thing else would be easy.

RC (DLC); addressed: "Mr. Jefferson"; endorsed by TJ as received 25 Dec. 1791. Entry in SJPL reads: "[G.]W. to Th:J. Innes's and Muter's letters on Indian war."

George Muter's letter is that of 17 Nov. 1791, which TJ had received only the day before. Before returning it to TJ, Washington allowed Secretary of War Knox to read the letter (Knox to Washington, 25 Dec. 1791, DLC: Washington Papers). Harry Innes' letter has not been found.

From George Washington

MY DEAR SIR   25th. Decr. 1791

You will find by the enclosed that our troubles in the Federal City are not yet at an end.—I pray you to give the letters a consideration and inform me of the result, to morrow, or next day.—Yours affectly. & sincerely,   GO: WASHINGTON

RC (DLC); addressed: "Mr. Jefferson"; endorsed by TJ as received 25 Dec. 1791. Entry in SJPL reads: "G.W. to Th:J. Federal city."

The Commissioners had written to Washington, enclosing a copy of a memorial from the proprietors, and expressing pessimism about settling the problem of L'Enfant's destruction of the house of Daniel Carroll of Duddington, which they felt more optimistic about when they had written TJ eleven days earlier (Commis-

sioners to Washington, 21 Dec. 1791, DNA: RG 42; Robert Peter and others to Commissioners, 21 Dec. 1791, DNA: RG 42, PC; Commissioners to TJ, 10 Dec. 1791). TJ probably discussed this matter with Washington on the 27th, whereupon the President wrote the Commissioners that he would seek the opinion of the Attorney General (Washington to Commissioners, 27 Dec. 1791, DNA: RG 42. See Editorial Note on fixing the seat of government, Vol. 20: 52).

From Thomas Barclay

Gibraltar, 26 Dec. 1791. The Emperor of Morocco has no ships at sea, Spanish cruisers having blockaded Salice and Larach. Internal dissensions and inadequate supplies of naval stores from Spain have made it impossible for him to carry out his boast that he would equip twenty sail from Larach.—The Spanish court is very hostile to Morocco. A Spanish cruiser has seized a ship from Amsterdam carrying gunpowder to Mogadore, and Spanish fleets here and at Almeria are said to be destined for Tangier, "which I think very doubtful as the Season for Such an Expedition is far advanced." The Basha is fortifying Tangier by land and sea, and three consuls have applied to the Emperor for permission to return home, their apprehension increased by Spain's refusal to permit Francisco Chiappe to go to Madrid.

The Emperor met Muley Slema at the sanctuary but failed to persuade him to join him. After this visit the Emperor found that the main body of his army of 7,000 men had gone to Mequinez, leaving him with only a few personal adherents. He went to Rabat and from thence sent his son to the troops, "who complained much of their want of pay and absolutely demanded the distribution of Some money which was made to the amount of one dollar nearly to each man, but this distribution proving very unsatisfactory The troops remain at Mequinez and the Emperor at Rabat."—Last month the Emperor was further embarrassed. Upon learning that Abderhaman Benasser had been fortifying Saffy and raising men without his orders, he sought to arrange his execution at the hands of Rachmania, a person of consequence in the city of Morocco who enjoyed the Emperor's confidence. But Benasser learned of this plot and is now in the field at the head of 30,000 men, "but his views are not Known, whether he intends to Support Muley Slema, or attempt a revolution in his own favor is doubtful." Benasser has been in communication with Muley Slema, and his men have reportedly seized the revenues at Mogadore.—Muley Slema declares that he will never leave the sanctuary until he is proclaimed Emperor. Another brother, Muley Abderhaman, has displayed pretensions to part of the territories south of Atlas.—He has received information from the minister of Holland, who has just returned from renewing a treaty with Morocco. He encloses copies of letters he wrote to the Basha of Tangier and Francisco Chiappe, together with the Basha's reply.

RC (DNA: RG 59, CD); 2 p.; at foot of text: "(No. 2)"; entirely in clerk's hand, except for following at foot of text in Barclay's hand: "Mr. Jefferson—This by way of Lisbon Duplicate to Boston Triplicate to Cadiz"; endorsed by TJ as received 4 Apr. 1792 and so recorded in SJL. Enclosures: (1) Barclay to Basha Tahar Fennis, 20 Dec. 1791. (2) Barclay to Francis Chiappe, 20 Dec. 1791. (3) Translation of letter from Basha Tahar Fennis to Barclay, 23 Dec. 1791.

From William Blount

"*Territory of the United States of America South of the river Ohio, at Mr. Cobb's,*" *26 Dec. 1791.* He has learned that Virginia has "passed a law extending their government over that space of country which lays between the lines run by the Virginia and North-Carolina Commissioners, commonly called Walker's and Henderson's lines. I have before informed you that I had thought it my duty to claim on the part of the United States to Henderson's, as that was the line North-Carolina claimed to, and actually held, and exercised jurisdiction to at the time she passed the cession act. I should be glad of instructions on this head."

RC (DNA: RG 59, SWT, M-471/1); 1 p.; endorsed by TJ as received 18 Jan. 1792 and so recorded in SJL; full text in Carter, *Terr. Papers*, IV, 107.

Virginia and North Carolina had taken steps in 1779 to survey their common boundary west of the Allegheny Mountains along the parallel 36° 31'. The commissioners, however, could not agree on the location of the line and therefore ran two parallel lines two miles apart. The northern line, claimed by North Carolina, was known as Henderson's line, and the southern line, claimed by Virginia, was called Walker's line. Following the cession to the U.S. of both states' western lands,

the question of the remaining boundary between them was resolved when Virginia's "Act concerning the Southern boundary of this State" became law on 7 Dec. 1791. This act was meant to recognize North Carolina's designation of Walker's line as the official boundary between the two states (Hening, XIII, 258). Blount was concerned about the effect of this on determining the southern extent of his jurisdiction in the Southwest Territory. This issue was further complicated by the impending admission of Kentucky to the union, which led TJ to advise Blount that settlement of the question would have to include representatives of that state (TJ to Blount, 6 June 1792). In the fall of 1792, TJ collected relevant papers and sent them to the President, who turned the matter over to Congress (TJ to Washington, 2 Nov. 1792, and enclosures). The extended boundary was finally established when Virginia and Tennessee compromised in 1803 on a line down the middle of the parallel lines drawn in 1779, about one mile north of Walker's line, and when Kentucky and Tennessee decided in 1820 to follow Walker's line to determine their common border. These issues are summarized in Edward M. Douglas, "Boundary Areas, Geographic Centers and Altitudes of the United States and the Several States . . .," U.S. Geological Survey, *Bulletin 689* (Washington, 1923), p. 126, 161-2.

From Lewis Littlepage

DEAR SIR   Warsaw 26th. December 1791.

I have recieved with infinite satisfaction your letter of the 29th. July last, and thank you for the trouble you were kind enough to take to inform yourself of, and let me know, the fate of my letter to the President:—I should not have written to him at all, had I known at the time that you had accepted the American Ministry.

The Definitive Treaty between Russia, and the Porte, must be by this time concluded; as the circumstances preceding it have entirely changed the Systems of the North, you will not perhaps think I trespass upon your time in giving you a short, *historical*, account of them.

England, having been prevented by the Spanish Armament, from sending a fleet to the Baltic, in 1790, Russia found no great difficulty (particularly after the affair of Biorko Bay) in forcing the King of Sweden to conclude a Separate Peace:—She then felt her *defensive* superiority over Great Britain, but being still embarrassed by a most expensive, though successful, Turkish war, no longer seconded by Austria, apprehensive of an irruption of the Prussians, and perhaps Poles, into Livonia, and White Russia, and above all of some subsequent perfidy in the King of Sweden; she still held a moderate, but firm language, and even offered peace to the Turks (provided they would treat *with her alone*) upon better conditions, she declared, than they were to expect from the mediation of their Ally, and Friends: viz:—the absolute *Status in quo*, (as I informed you in my letter from Paris) with only a proviso of "*the demolition of Oczakow.*"

These overtures were rejected principally from the intrigues of England: she began to be seriously alarmed at the maritime strength of Russia upon the Baltic; still more at the prospect of Peace, without her having obtained the object which had induced her to *excite* the war, viz: a Treaty of Commerce upon her own conditions with Russia.

The consequence was, that she not only engaged the Porte to persevere in hostile measures, but came forward herself with an armament, called upon Prussia, and offered 1500-000 £. sterling to the King of Sweden to recommence a war:—it was too late; the Empress had found the weak side of the King of Sweden: she first frighten[ed him] with the idea of a counter-revolution in his own country by placing his Brother Prince Charles of Sweden, Duke of Sudermania, at the head of the long crushed, but not extinct, Patriotic Party:—On the other hand she offered, in case he became her friend, 1. "peace at home, protection, and a *subsidy*": 2. (knowing his Quixotical character) "to make him Chief of a counter-revolution *in France*"; and lastly, instead of taking away his own crown (from him who would wish to remain a *King*, if only of "shreds and patches") she promised "to secure to him, or his Brother, the reversion of that of Poland": He was secured.

As to the King of Prussia, he is a *brave*, not a *military*, character; the first quality he recieved from Nature, the second she refused, and rendered it impossible to be acquired from his physical composition, that is to say, an unweildy Bulk, much eating, more sleeping, and, notwithstanding, an inordinate desire of women, joined to uncommon venereal powers.

He had consented to take the field in 1790, on account of the death of his favorite Mistress, and besides being obliged to go into Silesia to assist at his reviews, he is a man of that sort, that it was a matter of perfect indifference to him, to go a few miles further, and see his cannon fired with ball against the Austrians, or to stay within his frontier and see them fired with only powder at the parade.

He is however at bottom (when you can get to it) a man of sound sense, and, most undoubtedly, the purest, *personal*, probity:—As to political ideas, he never had but *two*, viz: whether he should believe Hertzberg or Bishopswerder, between whom he was situated like one of Voltaire's Romantic characters, between *Topaz* and *Ebene*, or his good, and evil, genius.

Hertzberg was *warlike* (in council) that is to say a *Tool* of England, and the Princess of Orange. Bishopswerder was *pacific*, that is to say a tool of nobody, but very desirous of preserving the time, and money, of his Master, for more private, and innocent, uses. The latter, although a German, and a Soldier, had however acquired (or rather been capable of *repeating*) a tolerably good political lesson. He was taught to know, and say, That *Austria* always had been, and sooner, or later, must be, the bulwark of England in Germany, and upon the Continent in general.

1. Because she neither has, nor can have, any *maritime force*.

2. Because she is, and must be, notwithstanding marriages, alliances, and temporary engagements, the *natural Enemy* of *France*, and the Bourbons.

3. That the connection between England and Prussia, first arose, and still continues, more from the *domineering position* of the latter over the Electorate, and consequently *Elector*, of Hanover, than from any real and common interest between the King, and Kingdom, of Prussia, and the King and Kingdom of England.

4. and lastly. That it was the Court of England which had proposed, and *insisted* upon, the *Status in quo* at Reichenbach, in order to enable the King of Prussia to turn his arms against Russia; in other words, had prevented him from engaging in a war, which in all human probability would have almost crushed the power of his most dangerous Rival, in order to plunge him into another, where he had every thing to lose, nothing but blows to gain; the whole advantage of which would be *to England*, whose grand, and *avowed*, object, was, a final *reconciliation*, and *treaty*, with the Power she meant to attack by the sword of Prussia; which *treaty* would in fact be equally detrimental to both, as the object of it was to render Great Britain *mistress of the commerce of the Baltic*, in the *liberty* of which commerce Prussia is as much interested as Russia.

It so happened that I arrived in Berlin the very day on which an English Courrier brought the final decision of his Court *to arm*. Borghese also recieved, upon my arrival, the orders of his Cabinet to propose once more, not the *mediation* (the Empress having always objected to that word) but "good offices" of Spain; the basis of which was; "That Oczakow should be *demolished*, and the whole of the *Yedsan*, or *Nogay*, *Tartary*, that is the territory between the *Bog*, and the *Dniester*, from the frontier of the Polish Ucraine, to the Black Sea, to remain *unoccupied*, or *terrein neutre*."

A grand Council was summoned at Potsdam, composed of Hertzberg, Schulembourg, and Mollendorff: Bishopswerder in the mean time (properly *instructed*) played his cards.

Schulembourg, and Mollendorff, gave it pointedly as their opinion, that "Any *hostile measure* against Russia would be unadvised, and perhaps, fatal in it's consequences, because 1. Austria had reserved all doors open to herself, by not concluding *definitively* with the Turks at Szistowe. If the war between Prussia, and Russia, should be successful to the *first*, Leopold, it was to be expected, would at last be compelled to come forward, to prevent his Rival from becoming the Arbiter of the North:—If the *contrary*, he would not miss so favorable an opportunity to *crush* the House of Brandenbourg.

2. From the exposed situation of the coasts of Pomerania, and West Prussia, the difficulty of marching a Prussian Army into Livonia, on account of the passage of the Divina, and the indispensable siege of the important and strong fortress of Riga, defended by a numerous garrison, and covered by an army of *50,000* of the best troops of Russia, inured to fatigue, and fire, in the Turkish, and Swedish, wars, and commanded by one of their most successful, and daring, Generals (*Schonwarow*).

3. From the extreme *uncertainty* of the Decisions of Sweden, and Poland."

It will be necessary to observe to you, that Hertzberg was already not a little disconcerted by the peremptory stile of the Court of England, which (as he was neither prepared for, nor warned of, such measures) he now percieved regarded him rather as the *instrument* of it's designs, than *mobile* of it's councils.

He therefore proposed, by way of *Mezzo Termine*, not to *accept* (that would derogate from the dignity of an *armed mediation*) but to *father* the *Spanish propositions*, and that by the simple operation of scratching out the name of *Florida Blanca*, and inserting that of *Hertzberg;* in other words to propose, as *ab origine*, from Frederic William II. to Russia, the propositions of Charles IV of Spain! (which propositions by the bye, were *previously* known, and discussed, both at Vienna, and Petersbourg!)

The King, upon this occasion, flew into a passion worthy of his greatness (I mean *size*), told Hertzberg "that he was *corrupted*" (in which he was right), "that he was a *fool*" (in which he was wrong).

Hertzberg, at first only dumb-founded, at last, upon hearing the word *Spandau* articulated, actually fell into a fit, and was brought back to Berlin in a state of convulsive insensibility.

Schulembourg drew up the answer to England, the purport of which was, "That the King would always be ready to fulfill his engagements for restoring the Peace, and preserving the equilibrium, of Europe; but could not think of adopting *hostile measures* against Russia, until *he should see* an English Fleet in the Baltic, capable of protecting the coasts of Pomerania, and West Prussia."

The British Cabinet here found themselves at a *non plus*:—a violent opposition at home, lukewarm collusion in their principal Ally, and, by this time, a certainty of the King of Sweden's being gained over to Russia; at last determined them to *change their lan-*

guage, and Fawkener was sent to Petersbourg with orders to lay aside the *Roman*, and adopt quite the *modern*, stile and method, of negociation.

I arrived in Warsaw (after only three weeks residence in Berlin) on the 27th. of April:—On the 3d. of May following the Revolution took place, by which the *Hereditary Succession* was established in the House of Saxony. As the secret causes, concomitant, and even succeeding, circumstances of that Revolution, are not, (unfortunately) to be considered as *past events*, but are yet most critically important, and *dubious* (as to their final result) you will excuse me from touching upon them, only so far as they regard the *general system*.

The Revolution of the 3d. May was preceded by a declaration of the Polish Diet to "observe an *Armed Neutrality*, in case of a rupture between Russia, and Prussia."

This was another great obstacle to the Allies, in the prosecution of *warlike measures*, as from the geographical situation of Poland, in case of a war between her and Russia, it was evident that Potemkin's Army in Moldavia must be obliged to retrograde beyond, at least the Dniester, or risk being placed between *two fires*, and having all their communications with, and supplies from, their own country, *cut off*.

Russia now saw her own consequence; she raised her language, *disavowed* Denmark, *rejected* Spain; and claimed (as her ultimatum, sword in hand) "the absolute *cession to her* of the *Nogay Tartary*, with the right of *fortifying at pleasure* the banks of the Dniester."

England, and Prussia, temporized, threatened, soothed, almost supplicated;—it was too late:—the season was too far advanced to begin a Campaign in the North; in the South, Russia pushed her conquests with such rapidity that Leopold himself was more than once upon the point of *retracting* his Convention of Reichenbach; he *quibbled* at Szistowe, and affected to consider the *Status in quo*, not as what *was*, but as what *should be*, or *have been*:—He was mistaken;—Russia worked for *herself*, not for a *timid Ally*.

The Storming of Anapa, (the key of North Natolin) with a slaughter equal to that of Oczakow, or Ismahil; Repnin's passage across the Danube and victory of Maczyn, joined to an action between the Russian, and Ottoman, Fleets, upon the Euxine, in which the latter were torn to pieces, and pursued within view of the Bosphorus;— at last overcame the obstinacy of the Sultan;—he demanded Peace, and the Preliminaries were signed, in the heart of his Empire, upon the *last mentioned conditions* (accepted *in toto*) nearly at the time that England, and Prussia, had consented to give up their *mediation* at Petersbourg.

I must however own that these conditions are highly *detrimental to Poland*:—Russia, enraged at the Revolution of the 3d. May, and at our long negociated, (though finally *renounced*) defensive, and *commercial*, Treaty with the Porte, insisted upon them merely in the view of *shutting us out from the Black Sea*, and reducing us as much to *her* dependance on that side, as we are, unfortunately, in *that of Prussia*, on the side of *the Baltic*.

God knows what may follow. I hope, and labour, for the best:—Potemkin's death saved us from an *immediate war*, and has (for the moment) disconcerted all the *external* systems of Russia. I again repeat (and you must concieve) that this situation is too delicate to become the subject of literary, and distant, discussion.

I once more give you a general review of the present state of European Politics, in the North.

The Chasm, or *vacuum*, produced in the *Rights of Kings*, by the Revolution of France, has, as you know, attracted all the *atoms* of Despotism towards it, in order to *fill it up*, instead of which, may they all tumble in together, and there, as was very near happening to the *Father of Politics* (according to Milton) may they *fall for ever*, without meeting with one friendly cloud of Discord, or corruption, to puff them up again!!!

To begin with the most considerable of them, *Austria*: Leopold is a dangerous, dissimulating, and perfidious, character:—The *finesse* of Italy, and Florence, grafted upon the cold, but capacious, stock, of a Lorrain, and German, has flourished with exuberance. You are not to rely upon any thing *ostensible* from him, either respecting the affairs of France, or others:—his view is *to decieve*, and *success* the greatest, and *only* merit, he proposes to himself. As to his *Neroism*, you may judge of it from Reichenbach, where, instead of drawing his sword, and throwing away the scabbard, he broke the blade, and threw away even the hilt.

I confess that, in consequence, he *"re-established his affairs"* (according to Kaunitz's own words) *"upon a fundamental footing"* (which, I apprehend, may mean *in English*, a *kicking in the a-r-s-*!!!)

But, jesting apart, his *Policy* has really served him more than the most *successful war* could have done:—he has secured to himself the Imperial Crown, without opposition; not only recovered Brabant, but quenched the flame of sedition in Hungary, Gallicia, the Milanese, and even Austria; lastly, he has compleatly *gulled* the King of Prussia, as it is morally certain, that the interview of Pilnitz (although favorable to the present system of *this country*) has sealed the ruin of the Prussian Monarchy.

Frederic William, and Leopold, are perfect Antipodes to each other, in every mental, and physical, quality; but the two extremes have met:—they were both *pacific*; the *first* from *indolence*, and *dissipation*; the *latter* from *cowardice*, and *avarice*. Being most apprehensive of each other, they, with equal eagerness, agreed to *coalesce*.

The truth is, they both rejoice at what has happened *in France*, provided they can keep the contagion from reaching them, and if they do go to war (for the sacrifice of a few thousand *Automats* is nothing in these countries) under pretext of supporting the King of the French, it will only be in the view of more compleatly ruining in the end both King, and Nation.

Their more immediate view, is to keep the great Northern Bear from prowling near their own Dens; which is their reason for supporting *us* at present, in order to form a barrier against Russia.

In short, the probable result of this Union will be, that the Prussian will *squander*, the Austrian *accumulate*; the *first*, if he lives many years, may die at last plain *Marquis of Brandenbourg*; the second, if he survives the Empress of Russia, will die *the Arbiter of Europe*.

Russia is highly *discontented*, both at the establishment of *Hereditary Succession* in Poland, and at the co-alition between Leopold, and Frederic William. If things remain upon their present footing, she is reduced (*continentally*) almost to the condition of an *Asiatic Power*. Every effort therefore is to be expected on her part that can tend to produce *a change*. How far her *means* may correspond with her wishes, is problematical.

The late war, 'though glorious to her arms, has however produced but little real advantage, and it's consequences are ruinous:—No less than *380,000 Recruits* have been raised in Russia, during the last four years, to replace *lost men*.

Potemkin, although he really had not enriched himself, as all Europe believed, and Mirabeau affirmed, in his letters upon the Court of Berlin, (he died more in debt than he was worth) has notwithstanding left the finances of the Empire in a most disordered state.

These reasons, *it is to be hoped*, will induce the Empress to employ herself, at least for some time, in the arrangement of her internal affairs. Besides, it may be calculated, that the loss, and impossibility of, at least for some time, *replacing*, an all-powerful Minister, and whom she had rendered so from policy, in order that he might be the Aegis of her declining years, must alarm, and disconcert her. She was dressed for a Ball of great ceremony when the news of his death arrived, upon receiving which she retired, without betraying the least emotion, summoned the Ministers of the different Departments to bring their *Portefeuilles* and deposit them in her Cabinet, where she remained, without even taking off her *gala* suit, for fifteen hours, and, for as many days afterwards, only slept and ate, irregularly, during which she successively dispatched orders, in her own hand writing, to all parts of her Empire, and has since continued to transact every thing herself.

Potemkin *believed himself* poisoned, and would take nothing during his illness: the truth is he died of a mortification in his bowels, occasioned by an overflowing of the bile, as he would take nothing to carry it off.

His primary political object, at the time of his death, was to excite a *Confederation* in Poland, against the Constitution of the 3d. May, and to support it by all the power of Russia:—he despised Leopold, and calculated that even the King of Prussia, after having finally turned off Hertzberg, renounced all his grand systems, sacrificed the Turks &c &c., and who, by the way, was not *consulted* upon the Polish Revolution, which, consequently (however he might *approve*) he was not *bound to support;* would in his turn consent to a *Status in quo* in Poland, rather than come at last to blows. How far his calculation was just cannot be precisely determined; but for my own part I think it fortunate for Poland that the experiment was not made.

Potemkin's more *general* System, was to regain the entire preponderance of Russia in the North, by *embroiling the South;* pursuant to which the Empress came forward with all her florid, and "magnanimous," declarations, to the French Princes, and *olim* Nobility, in the view of exciting a Royal Crusade against France:—Nobody really gave into it, except the Swedish Maker, and *unmaker*, of Revolutions, and the King of Spain. As for Leopold, he at once penetrated into her motives, which he pronounced to be "more *artful*, than *magnanimous*."

Our worthy friend Frederic William, I confess, did not see quite so far; he only concieved her conduct to be "very *pretty*, but very *nonsensical*."

Whether these projects ended with Potemkin, or whether they are still reserved, in petto, by Russia, for some future explosion, time only can discover, but I am convinced that the two systems are inseparably connected, and that the first gun fired against France (on the side of Germany) will very soon be re-echoed from the frontiers of Lithuania, and the Ucraine.

To conclude this little sketch, I once more recur to England.

She was displeased at the King of Prussia's non-chalence, in the winding up of their *Dis*-armed Mediation; but she had more reason to be so, when she saw him, soon after, entirely break her shackles, disgrace her creature Hertzberg, and, instead of remaining a *Grenadier*, ready to march, at her orders, either into the Bogs of Holland, or the forrests of Livonia, presume to *act* (I dare not say *think*) for *himself!*—His connection with Austria gave the last blow to the hopes and influence, of England:—Ewart was recalled from Berlin, and Hailes (who has always been subordinate to Ewart and Hertzberg) is shortly to leave this Court.

The English Ministry, in the course of this year, have been most dolefully, and lamentably, baffled in all their views: when they first percieved the King of Sweden, after all his vapouring, to be paying court to the Empress, they began, and have ever since continued, to labour assiduously at detaching Denmark from Russia; but as there appears little probability of success in that quarter, I should not be surprised if they at last swallow the pill (bitter as it is) of making the *first advances* towards a reconciliation with Russia, and a Treaty of commerce upon terms of *equality*, and *reciprocity*.

This is merely *speculative*, and may not take place soon; but I think the union between Austria, and Prussia, points out a similar conduct to their respective Allies, whom they have mutually disgusted, viz: Russia, and England.

I shall always be happy to hear from you; every thing respecting America is interesting to me. Be assured, my Dear Sir, that I shall esteem honored in corresponding with you, as a *Friend;* as Minister of my Country, I think it as much my duty to give you every information in my power (consistent with my own situation) as if I was employed by you. If you can even find any means of conveying a Cypher to me, perhaps you may have reason to be satisfied with my correspondence.

I have presented your compliments to your Friends, who most affectionately desire theirs in return:—Piattoli is particularly sensible of your condescension, and presents his respects to you.

The King, with whom I read, during our residence at his country seat, last summer, great part of your notes upon Virginia, and to whom I communicated your last letter, desires me to assure you of "his highest regard."—I have the honor to be, with great esteem and respect, Dear Sir, your most obedient humble Servant,

L. LITTLEPAGE.

RC (DLC); at head of text: "(No. 2)"; at foot of text: "T. Jefferson Esquire Minister, and Secretary of State of the United States"; endorsed by TJ as received 5 May 1792 and so recorded in SJL. Enclosed in William Short to TJ, 24 Jan. 1792.

Littlepage was a twenty-nine year old native of Virginia who was then a chamberlain and diplomatic agent in the service of Stanislas II Augustus, the last king of Poland. His LETTER FROM PARIS was written to TJ on 5 Mch. 1791. The REVOLUTION of 3 May 1791 was the *coup d'état* whereby King Stanislas and the Patriotic

Party induced a rump session of the Polish Diet to approve a liberal written constitution (Norman Davies, *God's Playground: A History of Poland*, 2 vols. [Oxford, England, 1981], I, 533-5). The work in question by MIRABEAU was Honoré Gabriel Riqueti, Comte de Mirabeau, *Histoire Secrete de la Cour de Berlin, ou Correspondance d'un Voyageur françois, depuis le 5 Juillet 1786 jusqu'au 19 Janvier 1787* ([Paris], 1789; Sowerby, No. 281). TJ had sent greetings to the Abbé Scipione Piatolli, an adviser of King Stanislas whom he met during his mission in Paris, in his letter to Littlepage of 29 July 1791.

From James Currie

Richmond, 27 Dec. 1791. This letter will be delivered by Alexander Campbell, U.S. attorney in Richmond, and a man "well deserving of your politeness and attention, if convenient or agreeable to you to show him any." Unable to visit Monticello while TJ was there, he wrote a letter "to be left at Colo. Bell's in Charlottes Ville and forwarded to Monticello, which I hope you receivd." He fears the business with John Griffin has become desperate, and hopes TJ will send a note by Campbell if the situation is otherwise. He has heard nothing from Griffin since September. That unfortunate man has seen the sheriff sell his servants and furniture to relieve some of his securities. Thomas Mann Randolph visited recently. The family at Monticello is well. Your observations about Henry & Johnston in the matter he asked about were perfectly accurate, and he dropped the matter. He told him as a "particular friend" of his inclination to begin reading law "if that matter could have been brought to bear to enable me to affect it with propriety and decency: The practice of Physic is not so pleasing or profitable to me as formerly and my inclinations the same as when we parted." He hopes he may sollicit advice if anything comes up in Richmond "in which you can be effective from your situation." *Richmond 26 Feb. 1792.* P.S. In order to expedite the post, Campbell had sent the above and several other letters forward, but recalled them when his trip to Philadelphia was cancelled. Would TJ mind having them delivered now? It is said that Griffin is here, but is unavailable. He hopes TJ's efforts have secured his debt by now, and he desires a short letter from TJ about the business.

RC (DLC); 4 p.; addressed: "The Hble. Thomas Jefferson Esq Secretary of State Philadelphia"; with note: "Hond. by Mr. Campbell"; endorsed by TJ as received 3 Mch. 1792 and so recorded in SJL.

Memorandum of Conversation with José de Jaudenes

[Philadelphia] Dec. 27 [1791]

Don Joseph Jaudenes (at a dinner at the city tavern) told me he had received new instructions from his court to express to us the king's dispositions to settle every thing on the most friendly footing, and to express his uneasiness at having recd. the communication of our sentiments thro' the Chargé des affaires of France, while a direct communication was open between us, the matter having been only suspended but not broken off since the departure of Mr. Gardoqui: and to express his pleasure also at the polite reception the President had given to his Commissioners here.

MS (DNA: RG 59, NL); entirely in TJ's hand; at top of text: notes on conversation with Jaudenes, 6 Dec. 1791. PrC (DLC); enclosed in TJ to Jaudenes and Viar, 26 Jan. 1792. Tr (DNA: RG 360, DL).

From George Washington

MY DEAR SIR   Tuesday Afternoon [27 Dec. 1791]

I have just received, and scarcely had time to read the enclosed.— [I wan]t to see you, and the heads of the [oth]er Departments to morrow morning at nine Oclock on business of the War Department.—Yrs. Affectly,   GO: WASHINGTON

RC (DLC); addressed: "Mr. Jefferson"; endorsed by TJ as received 27 Dec. 1791. Entry in SJPL reads: "[G.W. to Th:J.] proposing consultation."

Washington enclosed copies of Secretary of War Knox's 26 Dec. 1791 reports on the events leading up to the defeat of Ar-thur St. Clair's expedition against the Indians and the measures the federal government ought to take to retrieve the situation in the Northwest Territory. Knox had submitted these reports to Washington the previous day (Knox to Washington, 26 Dec. 1791, DLC: Washington Papers; ASP, *Indian Affairs*, I, 139-202).

From Nathaniel Cutting

SIR   Cape François, Isle of St. Domingo, 28th. Decer. 1791.

Since I did myself the honor to write you from hence under date 4th. current, affaires have remain'd in pretty much the same state throughout the northern district of this Colony; I mean with respect to the ravages of the Insurgents. The southern and western Districts have been obliged to take copious draughts from the cup of bitterness. Should I attempt to recite the melancholly accounts which have presented themselves from day to day during my residence here, you might probably find the detail uninteresting and it would certainly be prolix. Permit me to acquaint you simply, that since the terrible conflagration at Port-au-Prince on the 21st. ultimo. M. Coutard, the Gouverner of the Western District, and M. Jumecourt, the second in command, have taken up their quarters with the People of Colour at their Camp in the Parish of Croix-des-Bouquets. Those two Gentlemen were of high military rank under the ancient Government, and have several hundred *white* adherents now with them. The mulattoes, it is said, look up to M. Coutard as to their God, and all their manœuvres are directed by him.—If he has the power of controlling the opperations of that vindictive race, its excesses should be carried to his accompt;—and whatever plausible pretexts he might place on the debit side, the ballance would appear infinitely against him. The people of colour assembled at Croix-des-Bouquets lately sent a Deputation to the Colonial Assembly and to the *Comissaries Civils* to state their demands;—they not only insist on the exact observance of the Concordat and subsequent Treaty of Peace, enter'd into sometime since in the western District, but also that all the *Guardes nationaux soldées* of the Colonie and the two Regiments of Artois and Normandy shall be immediately sent to France.—And that every *white man*, be his occupation what it may, who is not in possession of a plantation or other effective property in the Colony to the amount of £50,000, shall depart the Colony forthwith. You may naturally suppose that such extravagant demands will never be complied with.—Those mal-contents have not committed such general and indiscriminate ravages in the South and west as the Insurgents have done on this side the Island; but they have been guilty of much more bloodshed.—They have disarmed the *whites* in almost every Parish from St. Marc southward, Port-au-Prince excepted. They have afterwards in the most cruel manner murder'd in cool blood great numbers of those whom they had thus render'd defenceless. Their savage barbarity has spared neither age nor sex. I heard a letter read yesterday which states that at Leogane they have basely murder'd sixty Persons, who were in the Hospital. Other accounts of their treatment of Matrons, Virgins and Infants, would make a Nero blush. Is it possible that the French Aristocrates can be the stimulators and abettors of all the horrid proceedings which have deluged this Colony in blood and brought it to the brink of ruin, in the illusory hope of thereby effecting a Counter Revolution in France? Many circumstances go far to prove the affirmative; but for the honor of Human nature and of a polished nation I would fain persuade myself that these infernal transactions are only the ebullitions of uncultivated spirits which have made a sudden transition from the extreme of ignorance and despotic restraint, to certain mistaken ideas of the Rights of Man and that unbridled licentiousness consequent thereto.

While new Clouds appear to be enveloping the other parts of the Colony, and threaten a fresh inundation of misery, the aspect of the political hemisphere in this quarter appears more serene than for months past. The Chiefs of the Brigands here have taken advantage of the general amnesty recently proclaimed by Les Commissaries Civils from France, to make overtures to the Colonial Assembly for causing their deluded followers to surrender their arms and return to their duty, and for liberating the *whites* whom they now hold as Prisoners. It was on the 8th. current that two Deputies from the Insurgents presented themselves at the Bar of the assembly with the proclamation in their hands and a well-written Letter from John François. No other answer was given than for those Emissaries to retire to their Camp and return at the end of eight days to receive the determination of the assembly respecting the propositions contained in the Letter. Accordingly on the 16th. the same Emissaries returned, when the President of the Assembly addrest them in a firm tone to the following effect;—"That it was inconsistent with the dignity of the Colonial assembly to treat with revolted Slaves—that whenever they returned to their duty, all the indulgence should be shewn them which could be expected from the known clemency of their Proprietors and consistent with the nature of their case; but the makers and Guardians of the Laws could not think of holding any intercourse with those who were actually in arms contrary to all principles of law and order." He then order'd them instantly to retire. The next day a new deputation from the Brigands arrived with a very submissive address, proposing as a proof of their sincere desire of returning to their duty, that they would immediately release all the *whites* whom they hold as Prisoners;—they solicited a conference with Les Commissaries Civils in order to engage their intercession with Government. This application was so favorably received that on Thursday the 22d. current Messieurs Les Commissaries Civils, attended by a strong escort of Patriotic Cavalry gave John François a Rendezvous at the Habitation call'd St. Michel, near Petit Ance on the side of the Bay opposite to this City. That Chief threw himself on his knees before the Commissaries and begg'd that he might be admitted to take advantage of the general Amnesty. He

likewise supplicated that the same privilige might be extended to
his Wife who for some time past has been confined in the Prison of
this City. He promised that he would cause his Partizans to send
in the whites who were held as Prisoners, as soon as they could
possibly be convey'd from the different places where they were
confined, and that he would likewise cause all his followers to surrender their arms as expeditiously as possible and return to their
duty upon the plantations to which they respectively belonged.—
Several white Prisoners have since been sent in, but I do not learn
that any arms have yet been surrender'd. The assembly remain firm
in their resolution not to hold any correspondence with the Brigands,
except on the base of unconditional submission. On the 18th. current
The Frigate La Fine, arrived here in 33 days from Brest, with a
Detachment of the Regiment of Provence on board, and brought
the animating intelligence that great preparations were making in
France to dispatch a very respectable force in order to reestablish
this valuable Colony. Yesterday M. de Blanchelande communicated
to the President positive intelligence which he has received—though
the Public do not know by what route—that 18,000 Troops have
actually sail'd from France destined for this Colony. Their arrival
here is ardently wished and momentarily expected. The Brigands
have always had accurate intelligence of everything that passes in
this City;—Nay, they must have had some secret friends and abettors
in the Legislative or Administrative assemblies here, since it has
been proved that they have been speedily acquainted with what has
past even in a *secret Committee.*—Thus, as they cannot entertain a
doubt of the formidable preparations that are making against them,
their Chiefs are apparently convinced that they cannot extricate
themseives or their deluded followers from that Labarinth of misery
into which their Crimes have driven them. He who arrogated to
himself the Title of *King* now humbly supplicates the clemency of
those against whom he has been the principal instrument of com-
mitting every species of outrage which the most deprav'd imagination could suggest. How far it may be politic to accord grace to
him and his principal adherents I will not pretend to say; if to obtain
a mitigation of deserved punishment they should be induced to
discover the prime instigators and abettors of the Revolt wherein
this same John François has acted so conspicuous a part, it might
open such a field of recrimination as would give room for unquiet
spirits to martial all the forces of ingenious malice in battle array,
so that by artful skirmishing they could for a long time prevent the
return of that concord and reciprocal confidence which alone can

restore the Colony to its former flourishing state. On this consideration it may be best that the names of the original Conspirators should still remain conceal'd and to draw the veil of oblivion over all crimes and misdemeanors that have been the offspring of their nefarious machinations. The alternative of total extirpation or unconditional submission which is all that is now left for the Insurgents, seems to be a guarantee for the continuance of that tranquility which begins to dawn in the northern district. This is, however, a very critical moment. Those who "are so far advanced in crimes that it is more difficult to return than to proceed," doubtless wish to put the finishing stroke to the work of destruction before the arrival of the expected Force from France shall blast their malignant hopes forever.

Many are firmly persuaded that there are Emissaries from the Mal-contents now concealed in this City who are determined, if possible, to display the same scene here which was lately exhibited at Port-au-Prince.—For several days past reports have been circulated that a collection of combustibles was discover'd in one place, private conversation respecting the plan for burning the City was overheard in another, and suspected persons were arrested in a third. I suppose it has been observed by the principal guardians of the public safety that the Citizens are too apt to relax in their vigilance where they do not apprehend immediate danger; therefore, whether a report like the above is founded on fact, or merely fabricated, it is good policy to give an alarm now and then to make people more alert in their duty.—More evil is still to be apprehended from the inveterate enmity that exists between certain individuals among the *whites themselves* and from that unparrallelled degree of insubordination which pervades every department of Government, than from anything that Slaves or the intermediate class can opperate. Through the unhappy division of the whites, the people of colour are absolute masters in all the Country adjacent to Port-au-Prince and have long had the power of perpetrating infinite mischief with impunity. They have uniformly declared that if the ships in the Road fired on them they would instantly set fire to the neighbouring habitations. To prevent this impending destruction M. Grimouard, Captain of the Borée Seventy four and Commandant on that station, had very prudently temporized in the expectation that such force would speedily arrive as would give one party or the other a decided preponderance.—Recent advices from that quarter state that on the 17th. current The inferior officers and Crews of the Borée and a Frigate which lay before Port-au-Prince, commenced a Cannonade upon a Post occupied by the Mulattoes, not only against the advice, but contrary to the express commands of the Commandant and other Commission'd officers. The Mulattoes immediately proceeded to put their previous threats in execution, and the superb Habitations which were situated on the Plain of Port-au-Prince now present to the enquiring eye but so many heaps of Ruins!—When the latest accounts came away, on the 18th., the flames were perceived as far as the sight could reach toward Leogane. A Rumour prevail'd here yesterday that the Equipage of the Borée have massacred M. Grimouard their Captain.—I hope this intelligence is premature, for I cannot find anyone who knows how it came. All intercourse by Land between this and Port-au-Prince having been long cut off, we are dependent upon the variable elements for our communications; and at this season the winds are generally unfavorable to a Vessel coming from thence to this Port; this accounts for our not having received later advices from that quarter than the foregoing.

It is exceedingly unfortunate for this Colony that ever since the commencement of the Revolution all confidence between the Legislative and Executive Bodies has been annihilated. There is almost as much coolness subsisting between the present Colonial Assembly and M. de Blanchelande, as there formerly was between the assembly of St. Marc and M. de Penier.—As is asserted respecting the *natural*, so in the *political System* it is apparently true that there are bodies possest of certain repulsive qualities which cause them mutually to recede from each other, to the great detriment of that order and harmony which is so essential to general felicity. Some do not scruple to assert that so many discordant particles have enter'd into the composition of the present Legislative Body of this Colony as must accellerate its dissolution. Some there are who pretend to such a superior degree of sagacity that they can percieve in the intrigues of certain members of the Colonial Assembly the detestable source of all the evils which have afflicted this Colony. Others pretend that as the fourteen Parishes of the Western District lately recall'd all their Deputies, the present assembly, where they continue to sit, is not legally constituted. Not to enter into the merits of this question, one thing is evident even to a superficial observer like myself—that is, the Assembly does not act as if it had great confidence in its own abilities. Its debates are generally desultory, diffuse and indecisive. Mere words more than the essence of things seem to occupy its attention.—The discussion of the question whether the assembly should style itself "*Generale*" or "*Coloniale*," lately occupied it four days, notwithstanding the same *important* subject had been much agitated by the same body at Leogane last Summer.

From observations similar to the foregoing, many judicious men are of opinion that the Inhabitants of this Colony are not capable of Legislating for themselves, but that it is necessary some superior independent power should decide all their political controversies. The friends of Peace and good order apparently place their ultimate hopes for the re-establishment of the Colony, upon the firmness and unanimity of the Civil Commissaries and of the Forces momentarily expected here. If they act in concert for the general good without leaning to one Party or the other, or listening to the sinister suggestions of such who would sacrifice the Public welfare to their private interest or revenge, tranquility may speedily be restored and the wealth and happiness of this *unique* Colony may, like the Phœnix, be resuscitated from its own ashes with increasing brilliance.—I have the honor to be with the greatest respect, Sir, Your most obedt. & very huml. Servt.,   NAT. CUTTING

RC (DNA: RG 59, MLR); endorsed by TJ as received 5 Feb. 1792 and so recorded in SJL. FC (MHi: Cutting Papers).

FRANÇOIS: Jean François, a maroon who had adopted the title of "Grand Admiral and Commander in Chief," and at this time the principal leader of the slave revolt in the North Province of Saint-Domingue

(Ralph Korngold, *Citizen Toussaint* [Boston, 1944], p. 74-5). M. DE BLANCHE-LANDE: Philebert François Rouxel de Blanchelande, the governor of Saint-Domingue, who had replaced the Comte de Peynier in 1790 (Herbert I. Priestley, *France Overseas through the Old Régime: A Study of European Expansion* [New York, 1939], p. 329).

From Nicholas Forster

SIR   Richmond 28th. Decr. 1791

Mr. Thos. M: Randolph having inform'd me it was your intention to rent on a lease your tract of land in Gouchland County call'd Elk hill; wanting such a place I have been to see it, and beg leave to offer myself as your tenant, provided the term of the lease and the rent answer the idea Mr. Randolph has given me. As the mode of cultivation I propose pursuing may have an influence on these, it is my intention to adhere to the English sistem of agriculture as near as the climate of Virginia will admit or the markets allow. Wheat, Sheep, and Stock are my principle objects.

Your various avocations in a publick line may have call'd off your attention from such a small object. This Sir will be my excuse for dweling a moment on the present situation of the plantation. The dweling house will require much repair. The out houses are in a very ruinous state and the plantation almost entirely destitute of fencing.

As the season is advancing fast for commencing work, I beg to know for what term you will grant a lease and what annual rent you will require as soon as you conveniently can.

Being a stranger in this county should you be inclined to make any enquiry respecting me Mr. T: M: Randolph or Mr. David M: Randolph of Presq: Isle can answer any questions you may be desireous of making.—I am Sir Your most Obedt. Hle. Sert.,

NICH: FORSTER

RC (MHi); endorsed by TJ as received 5 Jan. 1792 and so recorded in SJL.

Apparently Thomas Mann Randolph misunderstood TJ's intentions with respect to Elkhill when the former tenant failed to renew his lease. TJ had decided to sell this property in order to apply the proceeds to his inherited debt to Farrell & Jones; he therefore declined a long-term lease (TJ to Thomas Mann Randolph, Jr., 8 Jan. 1792).

From George Hammond

SIR   Philadelphia 28th. December 1791.

Since I had the honor of addressing to you (on the 26th of November) a memorial on the case of Mr. Thomas Pagan, I have received from my Court some farther information upon the subject. I therefore flatter myself, Sir, that you will permit me, to recall this affair to your attention, and to express the solicitude, which I must naturally feel, to learn some determination with regard to it. My firm confidence in the justice of this government leaves me no reason to doubt that that determination will fully meet the expectations of my Court and of Mr. Pagan, and lead to the adoption of such measures as may procure for him, liberation from prison, and a reasonable compensation for the injury he has sustained, as well in his property as person, in consequence of his long and unjust confinement.—I have the honor to be, with sentiments of the greatest respect and consideration, Sir, your most obedient and most humble Servant,   GEO. HAMMOND

RC (DNA: RG 59, NL); at foot of text: "Mr. Jefferson &c. &c. &c."; endorsed by TJ as received 28 Dec. 1791 and so recorded in SJL; also docketed by TJ: "Hammond George . . . Pagan's case." Hammond wrote this after receiving a letter from the British secretary for foreign affairs that enclosed additional papers concerning the case of Thomas Pagan and instructed him "to press this Matter in the strongest Manner, with the American Government, in order to procure the Release of Mr. Pagan, if he should be still in Confinement, and a just Compensation for the Losses he may have sustained by the Proceedings against him" (Grenville to Hammond, 5 Oct. 1791, Mayo, *British Ministers*, p. 19).

To George Hammond

Sir   Philadelphia Dec. 28. 1791.

I have duly received your favor of to-day on the subject of Mr. Pagan. His case arises on the proceedings of the supreme court of justice of Massachusets, and requires of course to be considered by the Attorney General of the United States, who calls for a sight of the record of those proceedings. I have accordingly written to Massachusets to have a copy of the record of the judiciary proceedings, as also of those of the legislature and Executive. As soon as they are received they will be submitted to the Attorney general, and you may be assured of being informed of the sentiments of our government on the subject, as soon as he shall have reported thereon.—I have the honor to be with the most perfect respect & esteem Sir Your most obedt & most humble servt,   TH: JEFFERSON

PrC (DLC); at foot of text: "Mr. Hammond M.P. of G.B." FC (DNA: RG 360, DL). TJ's letter TO MASSACHUSETS is to Christopher Gore, 13 Dec. 1791.

From Robert R. Livingston

Dr Sir   New York 28th. Decr 1791

My Brother is this moment departing for Philadelphia and has requested a letter of introduction to you. I find a pleasure in complying with his request not only on his account, but because it affords me an opportunity of intimating that I am not ignorant of, or ungratful for, your late acts of friendship & of assuring you of the sincere esteem & respect with which Dr Sir I have the honor to be Your Most Ob Hum: Servt,   RBT. R LIVINGSTON

RC (ViW); endorsed by TJ as received 2 Jan. 1792 and so recorded in SJL.

From Sylvanus Bourne

Sir   Philadelphia Decr. 29 1791

At the time I had the honour of addressing you last, I was in expectation of forming such a mercantile connection, as would have induced me to return to the west Indies; but the late repeated bad news from that quarter, has discouraged the Person who contemplated this connection with me from any further pursuit of it. I now therefore beg leave (agreably to your advice as to the mode of returning my Commn. to the President) to inclose it to your care, accompanied by some papers committed to my charge the object of which I had no opportunity to effect, but which may possibly be taken up hereafter. I feel the conviction of error in having called your attention to those Pieces signed Americanus and fear you have viewed it as the result of self approbation and assumed merit, an effect of all others I should wish to have avoided.

Should my apprehensions be well founded Permit me to indulge the hope that you will not cherish an opinion so contrary to my feelings and unfavourable to my Character, for be persuaded Sir that I am sincerely emulous of your Esteem and in any situation of life it would be a source of real pleasure to me to know that I possessed it. I have the honour to be With the greatest Respect your most obedt humble servt,   Sylva: Bourne

RC (DLC: Washington Papers); endorsed by TJ as received 30 Dec. 1791 and so recorded in SJL.

When it was rumored early in the month that Bourne might resign, aspirants wasted no time in seeking the appointment as U.S. consul in Saint-Domingue (Samuel Wall to TJ, 15 Dec. 1791, RC in DLC: Washington Papers; endorsed by TJ as received 15 Dec. 1791 and so recorded in SJL; docketed by TJ: "to be Consul St. Domingo"; and Payan to TJ, 22 Dec. 1791, RC in same; endorsed by TJ as received 22 Dec. 1791 and so recorded in SJL; docketed by TJ: "for St. Domingo").

To Sylvanus Bourne

Dec. 30. 91.

Th: Jefferson presents his compliments to Mr. Bourne, and acknoleges the receipt of his letter of yesterday. He was far from receiving in a disadvantageous light Mr. Bourne's note on the subject of the peices in Fenno's paper. On the contrary he has felt himself indebted to him for having drawn his attention to publications which he finds filled with good sense and loyalty to his country. He wishes him sincerely success in whatever may be his undertakings, and shall always be happy to befriend them if in his power.

RC (DLC: Rare Books); addressed to: "Mr. Bourne late Consul for the U.S. in St. Domingo." Apparently TJ forwarded Bourne's letter of resignation and commission to George Washington. Tobias Lear returned them this day (Lear to TJ, 30 Dec. 1791; RC in DLC; endorsed by TJ as received 30 Dec. 1791; FC in DNA: RG 59, MLR; Tr in same, SDC).

From William Short

DEAR SIR   Amsterdam Dec. 30. 1791.

My last was written a few days previous to my leaving Paris for this place, whither I have supposed it proper I should come on account of the loans negotiating here and at Antwerp. Notwithstanding the inclement and disagreeable season I did not think myself authorized to dispense with the journey, as from the tenor of your and Mr. Hamilton's letters of the last year, I took it for granted you would expect it from the novelty of the business at Antwerp and its situation here—the state of affairs in Paris also being such as to render my presence there by no means essential at that time. Not supposing it necessary I did not appoint a secretary there, conforming therein to your abovementioned letter of last year.— The inclosed letter to the Secretary of the Treasury will shew the present prosperous situation of the business confided to my care here. It requiring no longer my presence at this place I shall set out on wednesday next the 4th. of Jany. for Paris.

A very short time before I left it M. de Lessart was confirmed in the department of foreign affairs and M. de Gerville, a lawyer of Paris, succeeded him as *Ministre de l'interieur.*—M. de Narbonne has also succeeded M. Duportail as Minister of war.—He has begun his administration with a good deal of zeal and activity which has gained him much favour.

The King went lately to the assembly and announced to them his determination to force the German Princes to withdraw the protection they give to the French emigrants assembled in an hostile manner on the frontiers. To support the measures three armies are to be assembled under Messrs. Luckner, Rochambeau and de la fayette. This brings matters to a crisis which is probably the intention of the Minister of war who rightly calculates that it gives a chance for the revival of government, whereas the continuance of the present state is although a slow yet certain destruction.

The Emperor in his Regal capacity seems to be the most moderate sovereign in Europe towards the French revolution, as he is certainly the most influential.—As head of the Empire he has ratified the *conclusion* of the Diet for insisting on the nullity of the acts of the assembly with respect to the possessions in Alsace and Lorraine, of some of the members of the Germanic body.—He has lately written to the King of France exacting formally the restitution of the lesions occasioned by those acts and an indemnity for the injuries already sustained thereby. It is certainly not in the power of the King of France to comply therewith.

Russia, Sweden and Spain are the powers which take the most active parts in favour of the French Princes. I learn here however that the King of Sweden who was considered as the Agamemnon of the league has declined a loan lately offered him at this place on good terms, which proves to me he does not intend acting in an hostile manner for the present.—The determinations and actions of foreign powers will necessarily be decided eventually by the situation of the internal affairs of France.

The Dey of Algiers has granted a continuance of peace to that country. The presents of Sweden having been sent will probably appease him also, but as yet there is no public notification of his having altered the hostile dispositions he announced to the Swedish Consul.

The newspapers which have been forwarded to you from Paris since my departure will have informed you of the proceedings of the assembly. The taxes not coming in they have been obliged to augment the emission of assignats. Their depreciation of course continues.—You will see also that a considerable reform has taken place in the *corps diplomatique*.—Those who were most conspicuously hostile to the revolution have been displaced.—M. de Choiseul Greffier goes from Constantinople to London; de Moustier succeeds him at Constantinople; Berthelemi, the minister at London, goes Ambassador to Switzerland, and M. de Segur, the Ambassador at Rome, goes on a particular commission to Berlin. Several young men never before employed are appointed Ministers Plenipotentiary to different courts.

Lord Cornwallis's American fortune seems to have pursued him to the East Indies. Seasons and rivers are constantly against him and what he calls a signal victory does not prevent his being immediately forced to make a painful and precipitate retreat.

The true situation of S. Domingo seems not yet to be fully known in France. You will have seen the different discussions in the assembly relative thereto, and the account rendered by the deputy who was sent to sollicit succour in America.—I mentioned to you in my last the numberless questions I was asked on this subject and my absolute ignorance of every thing respecting it.—I subjoin here a state of the letters which I have had the honor of receiving from you during the present year, by which you will see that your last was in July.

March 23. received your letter dated	Jan.	23.
May. 28	March.	8
do.	do.	12
do.	do.	15
do.	do.	19
June 11	April.	25
July. 7	May.	10
Sep. 26	July.	28.

I have the honor to be with sentiments of the most perfect respect & attachment, Dear Sir, your most obedient humble servant,

W: SHORT

PrC (DLC: Short Papers); at head of text: "*No. 92*"; at foot of text: "Thomas Jefferson Secretary of State, Philadelphia." Tr (DNA: RG 59, DD). Recorded in SJL as received 28 Mch. 1792. Short's letter to Hamilton, 30 Dec. 1791, is printed in Syrett, *Hamilton*, x, 485-90.

From Thomas Barclay

Gibraltar, 31 Dec. 1791. He encloses copies of his letters of 18 and 26 Dec.— His letters to the Basha of Tangier and Francis Chiappe were designed to inform them that he would not arrive in Morocco until it became safe to do so. The sons of L'Abbas have taken the field to avenge their father's death. Muley Yezid's prospects look gloomy. He is as attached to the English as Muley Slema is to the Spaniards.—"The first day on which I think there will be any prospect of fulfilling my Mission I shall endeavor to Cross over, and this may be Very soon, for should the Emperor be able to put himself at the head of any Considerable number of Troops, it is more than probable he may appear at Tangier or Tetuan, in which case it might be Very improper for me to remain here, unless something material should arise in the meantime, I must however be governed by Circumstances."—Yesterday Admiral Peyton sent a frigate to Tangier to collect intelligence.

RC (DNA: RG 59, CD); 3 p.; at foot of text: "(No. 3)." Dupl (same); with slight variations; at foot of text: "Duplicate to Cadiz. Original to Boston." Recorded in SJL as received 4 Apr. 1792.

From Thomas Barclay

Gibraltar, 31 Dec. 1791. He encloses three letters from the American prisoners at Algiers received by [James] Simpson, the Russian consul here, who has established a correspondence with them. These letters reveal two facts of importance. "One is that Mr. Lamb in the Name of the United States made an absolute agreement for the Ransom of these people, the other that liberty has been offered to them if they will enter into the service of the Dey of Algiers." He thinks that it might be in the interest of the U.S. to fulfill Lamb's engagement and at the same time declare that "no future Redemptions would be made."—He also thinks consideration should be given to permitting the prisoners to accept the terms offered by the Dey.—He encloses a description of Algerian and Tunisian naval forces as of July. The regency of Algiers declared war on Sweden on 26 Oct. but so far Algiers does not seem to have taken any prizes. "The Tripolitines have no Cruisers at Sea, nor is there any danger of the Algerines getting into the Atlantic, while the Portuguese fleet of which I send you the particulars remains in this bay."

RC (DNA: RG 59, CD); 3 p.; endorsed by TJ as received 5 May 1792 and so recorded in SJL.

The American captives' mistaken belief that John Lamb had concluded an ABSOLUTE AGREEMENT for their ransom during his mission to Algiers in 1786 was based on what the Dey of Algiers had told them about their meeting rather than on what appear to be the facts in this matter. The Dey told the captives that Lamb had agreed to pay the sum of $50,000 rather than the low figure authorized by TJ and John Adams, but that he had then broken his word. It seems clear that in reality Lamb undertook to do nothing more than apprise TJ and Adams of the Algerian ransom demands. It is impossible to determine whether the Dey had misunderstood Lamb or whether he deliberately misled the captives (Supplementary Instructions to John Lamb, 1-11 Oct. 1785, Document III in Editorial Note and group of documents pertaining to the mission of Barclay and Lamb to the Barbary States, at 11 Oct. 1785; Lamb to the American Commissioners, 20 May 1786; Richard O'Bryen to TJ, 12 July 1790). For a contrary interpretation of Lamb's dealings with the Dey, based on the 8 June 1786 letter to TJ from Richard O'Bryen and Others that does not even mention Lamb's alleged acceptance of the Algerian ruler's terms, see H. G. Barnby, *The Prisoners of Algiers* (London, 1966), p. 81.

The enclosed table of naval force reads:

"Naval force of Algier, July 1791.
1—44 gun frigate launched in June, built at Algiers by a Spanish Carpenter and the Masts supplied from Carthage
1—24 Gun frigate given 2 years ago by France.
3—Xebecs from 14 to 20 guns each
1—Half Galley, 2 guns in her prow
6—Xebecs from 24 to 30 guns each which had been lent to the Grand Seignior but are returned
1—Xebec of 24 guns and several small vessels, on the stocks
The Bay of Mascara has one half Galley with 2 guns in her prow.
Force of Tunis, July 1791
Their Cruisers are reduced to about 6 small Xebecs and Row Boats from 2 to 8 guns each which are Employed in making depredations on several of the Italian States.
Portuguese Squadron in the Bay of Gibraltar the 31 Decr. 1791.
The Medusa of   74 guns
Two Frigates of   40 each
Four Brigantines of 20 each"

From William Barton

SIR   Market street, Dec. 31st. 1791.

The sheets which compose the Pamphlet, herewith inclosed, will be comprized in the third Volume of the Philosophical Society's Transactions, now in the press. Being favored by the Printer with a few copies of this part (with the addition of a Title-page) I beg, Sir, your Acceptance of one.

If some additional Observations on the same subject, resulting from the Census, which have been read in the Society, should be deemed worthy of a place in their Transactions, I shall take the liberty of sending You a Copy, when printed.—I have the Honor to be, With great Respect, Sir, Your Most Obedt. And very Hble. Servt.,   W. BARTON

RC (DLC); endorsed by TJ as received 31 Dec. 1791 and so recorded in SJL.

On Barton's enclosed pamphlet, see TJ to David Rittenhouse, 19 Mch. 1791. His ADDITIONAL OBSERVATIONS, which were read before the Society on 2 Dec. 1791, were printed in the American Philosophical Society *Transactions*, III (1793), 134-7. Barton sent TJ a copy of this supplement on 10 Aug. 1792 (RC in DLC; endorsed by TJ as received 25 Aug. 1792 and so recorded in SJL).

From C. W. F. Dumas

The Hague, 31 Dec. 1791. The great powers of Europe are in chaos because of the impact of the French and Polish Revolutions. They fear and hate each other and dread "l'exemple que la nation françoise a donné aux autres." Lafayette goes from Paris to Metz to raise men and supplies from the emigrés, beginning with Ettenheim.—The embassy must be sold because its physical condition is deteriorating at the same time that the taxes imposed on it are rising.—TJ will see in "le Supplement 103 de Mr. Luzac" the first of his letters and a promise to publish similar pieces. Luzac's readers prefer bickerings, mischief, and fighting more than accounts of "un peuple heureux," however.—[P.S.] He encloses a poem he has dedicated to Lafayette and a copy of a letter recently received from him.

FC (Dumas Letter Book, Rijksarchief, The Hague; photostats in DLC); 1 p.; at head of text: "No. 86." RC (missing) is recorded in SJL as received 8 May 1792. Enclosures not found.

From Joshua Johnson

London, 31 Dec. 1791. Enclosing the quarterly accounts through today of American ships touching in this port. Also enclosed is an account of disbursements for the same quarter which total £61.3.2 when added to those formerly transmitted, "and to which I beg your attention."

RC (DNA: RG 59, CD); 1 p.; in clerk's hand except for signature. Enclosures not found.

INDEX

INDEX

Favorite (ship): mentioned, 123
Favras, Marquis de: execution of, 260
Fawkener, William: British envoy to Russia, 453
Fay, Joseph: letter to, 102-3; letters from, 18, 150-1, 351-2; and maple sugar, 18, 351-2; sends newspapers to TJ, 18, 103, 150, 351-2; on French Revolution, 150-1, 352; on *Rights of Man*, 150
Fayal, Azores: U.S. consul in, 273, 322
Federal District: map of, 47-8, 77, 136, 244, 312; sale of land in, 47-8, 73, 88, 94-5, 136, 207, 220, 233, 263, 312, 356, 388; and Banneker, 52, 98; funds for, 58, 73, 85n, 88, 89n, 136; Capitol, 90, 263, 311, 312, 356, 388; streets in, 90; name of, 91, 136; postal service, 91; President's house, 136, 263, 311, 312, 356, 388; laying out of streets in, 263, 311, 312, 388; conflict between L'Enfant and Commissioners, 358, 367-8, 388-9, 390-2, 404, 447; destruction of Carroll's house, 367-8, 388-9, 390-2, 447; land cession by Md., 393
Federal District Commissioners: letters to, 88-9, 311; letter from, 388-9; funds for, 58, 85, 89n; meeting at Georgetown, 88, 91, 94-5, 136; queries for, 89-91; letter to Washington quoted, 89n; correspondence with Washington cited, 94, 447n; discontinue land sales, 220; conflict with L'Enfant, 263, 358, 367-8, 388-9, 390-2, 404, 447n; and sale of land, 263; and Samuel Blodget, Jr., 311; and laying out of streets, 312; letter from Washington, 367-8; letter from Ellicott quoted, 389n
Federalist, The: distribution in Portugal, 111
Fendel, Capt.: petition of, 142
Fenno, John: prints *Gazette of the United States*, 62, 310-11, 354; *Gazette of the United States* sent to TJ, 122; prints "Americanus" essays, 387, 468
Fenwick, Joseph: letter to, 103-4; letters from, 108-9, 166, 181, 238, 441-3; and Derieux's legacy, 31-2, 103-4, 181, 232; account with Short, 103-4; correspondence with cited, 103-4, 118; and TJ's wine, 103-4, 117, 119n, 122n, 325; compensation for, 166; on French Revolution, 166, 239, 441; on U.S. trade with France, 166, 239; letter to Short cited, 166n, 442; letter

from quoted, 232; and Mrs. Ollivier's inheritance, 238; mentioned, 30
Fersen, Axel: and flight to Varennes, 59
Fessenden, Thomas Greene: criticizes TJ, 54n
Fez, Morocco: in Moroccan civil war, 417
Finnie, Col. William: accounts, 184
First Part of the Institutes of the Laws of England (Sir Edward Coke): mentioned, 259
fish: exported to Denmark, 87; in Anglo-Portuguese trade, 111; import duties on, 438-9 (table)
Fisher, Daniel: health, 17
fisheries: TJ's report on praised by Rutledge, 13
Fitch, John: and desalination of sea water, 305
Fitzgerald, Edward: and U.S. relations with Spain, 22; British ambassador to France, 68, 183
FitzSimons, J.: visits TJ, 422, 431
FitzSimons, Thomas: letter from, 61; and Report on Commerce, 61
Flahaut, Mme de: procures vanilla for TJ, 191
Flanders: manufactures, 158; linen, 166
flaxseed: import duties on, 438-9 (table)
Fleming, George: and fugitive slaves, 408
Flint, Royal: proposed land purchase, 4, 6n, 282
Florida, East: agreement on rendition of fugitive slaves from, 7, 406-8; and fugitives from justice, 266-8
Floridablanca, José Monino y Redondo, Conde de: soothes British ambassador, 138; and French Revolution, 218; census of Spain, 349; relations with Russia, 452
flour: price, 123; import duties on, 189, 438-9 (table); export to France, 215; sale of, 238; for Saint-Domingue, 330
Folger, Benjamin: applies for patent, 264
Forest, Antoine René Charles Mathurin de la: suspicions of TJ, 331
Forrest, Uriah: letter to, 41; letter from, 220-1; and Federal District, 220
Forster, Nicholas: letter from, 465-6; wishes to lease Elkhill, 465-6
Fort Erie: retention by British, 409
Fort McIntosh, Treaty of: boundaries under, 279, 283
FRANCE: mentioned, 11, 16, 22, 47, 164, 314

[485]

Gist, Col. Mordecai: and St. Clair's defeat, 362-3
Glasgow, James: letter from cited, 285n; and Report on Public Lands, 285n, 286n
glass: manufacture in Portugal, 218
Glauber, Johann Rudolf: and desalination of sea water, 319
Gnadenhutten, Ohio: township, 282
gold: shipped to Great Britain, 218
Gore, Christopher: letters to, 15-16, 399; TJ requests Mass. records from, 15-16; and Pagan v. Hooper, 399
Grabe, John Ernest: *Spicilegium SS. Patrum*, 328
grain: price, 166, 443; exported to France, 215; circulation in France, 270; reexported from Great Britain, 440
Grand, Ferdinand: conflict with Droz, 22, 70, 213; TJ's account with, 191, 215-16, 333, 335n; draft on Willink, Van Staphorst & Hubbard, 229-31
Grant, Mr.: mentioned, 220
GREAT BRITAIN: mentioned, 14, 26, 326

Economy
trade with Denmark, 87; trade with Portugal, 111, 218; and Hessian fly, 139-40; importation of foreign wheat forbidden, 144, 290; manufactures, 159; linen, 166; trade with France, 215, 412; demand for cotton, 218

Foreign Relations
and Russo-Turkish war, 11, 21, 46; with Russia, 55, 107, 132, 139, 149, 254-5, 449, 453, 457; with Algiers, 69, 255; with northern Europe, 110; with France, 113, 214, 273; and fugitives from justice, 266; with French West Indies, 317n; with Morocco, 417; with Prussia, 450-1, 457; with Sweden, 450, 457; with Denmark, 457

Newspapers
unreliability of, 329

Parliament
passes corn law, 72; meeting of, 125; and desalination of sea water, 320

Politics and Government
Fay comments on, 150

Society
criticism of, 254

U.S. Relations with
fear of U.S. territorial ambitions, 26; appointment of minister to U.S., 33, 71, 75, 131, 132, 142, 149, 174, 183, 233; U.S. consuls in, 93; Short's assessment of, 113; loan to U.S., 114; appointment of U.S. minister to, 174, 242, 261-3, 288, 289n, 326, 332, 353, 354-6, 363; policy toward Indians, 403-4

U.S. Trade with
U.S. commercial retaliation against, 13, 74, 202, 225, 388n; access to Guernsey and Jersey restricted, 33, 59, 142-3, 144n; regulation of, 61n; U.S. share of carrying trade, 290; duties on, 405, 438-9; port charges, 438-9; reexports, 440
Great Miami, Treaty of: boundaries under, 279, 283
Greene, Nathanael: land grant for, 278, 287n, 288n
Greene co., Tenn.: boundary, 276; land grants in, 278, 286n
Greenleaf, Thomas: letter from, 41
Greenock, England: U.S. ship seized at, 33
Grenville, William Wyndham, Lord: and Auldjo's consular commission, 132; instructions to Hammond, 235n, 358n; letters from Hammond quoted, 285n, 411n; and Pagan v. Hooper, 342n, 343n, 466-7n; disavows Bowles, 404n
Griffin, John Tayloe: financial affairs, 99, 116, 183, 458
Griffith, Capt.: petition of, 105n
Grimouard, M. (master of *Borée*): reportedly murdered by crew, 463
Guadeloupe, W.I.: discontent in, 164
Guernsey, Channel Island: U.S. trade with restricted, 33, 54n, 142, 143n, 144n
Guilford, Conn.: and Hessian fly, 139-40
Gunn, James: and reapportionment bill, 445
Gustavus III, King of Sweden: and French Revolution, 20, 59, 163, 333n, 456, 470; peace with Russia, 449-50, 452, 457

Hadley, George: *Compendious Grammar of the Current Corrupt Dialect of the Jargon of Hindostan*, 327
Hague, The: U.S. embassy in, 297, 332

INDEX

JEFFERSON, THOMAS (cont.)

Scientific Interests

unit of measure, 55-6, 118; threshing machine, 57; odometer, 119n; Hessian fly, 139-40, 244-52, 428, 429; reform of patent system, 295, 359-61; desalination of sea water, 305, 318-22; meteorological observations, 348; weights and measures, 367; regrets lack of time to pursue, 430; human longevity and demographic growth, 473

Secretary of State

and Northwest Territory, 8-9, 62-3, 291, 300-1, 377; and Southwest Territory, 27-8, 29-30, 45-6, 441, 444-5; receives French minister, 32-3; procures state laws, 42; and Federal District, 47-8, 58, 77, 88-91, 94-5, 112, 136, 263-4, 311, 312, 367-8, 390-2; relations with Banneker, 49-54, 97-8; and National Gazette, 62, 294, 310-11; and commercial treaty with Britain, 72-3, 105, 344-6, 353, 378-9, 395-6, 399, 402, 433-4, 437; policy toward Britain, 73-4; seeks support for Republican cause, 74-5; and impressment of Hugh Purdie, 92, 94; and consular system, 93, 100, 104, 335, 364-6, 405, 431; seeks text of Hawkesbury's report, 93-4; criticizes French trade restrictions, 96-7, 100, 103; criticizes Spanish immigration policy, 96-7; favors commercial treaty with France, 96, 101, 103, 329, 344-6, 433-4, 437; and navigation of Mississippi, 96-7, 258-9, 381; and U.S. Mint, 96, 328-9; and U.S. debt to France, 109, 110, 119-20; and postal service, 147, 441; suggestions for President's annual address, 225; receives British minister, 241-3; and case of Dover cutter, 258-9, 298-9, 349; policy on furnishing U.S. laws to states, 260; and appointment of minister to Britain, 261-3, 288, 349; and appointment of minister to France, 262-3, 288; and appointment of minister to Netherlands, 262, 288; advice on correspondence between President and state governors, 263; and Saint-Domingue, 264n, 294, 329-31, 349, 353; and rendition of fugitives, 266-7, 425-6; and case of Jane, 288-9,

302, 304-5; and redemption of captives in Algiers, 295-6, 369-72, 383-4; and reform of patent system, 295, 359-61; and violations of Treaty of Paris, 295-6, 352, 382, 395-6, 402, 409-12; denounces British newspapers, 329; and relations with Spain, 329, 381, 432-3; and Short's accounts, 333-4; and case of Thomas Pagan, 340-4, 379-80, 399, 467; conflict with Hamilton over commercial treaties, 344-6; Hammond's suspicions of, 357-8n; and relations with Algiers, 369-72, 383-4; and compensation for slaves taken by British, 382, 402, 410, 411-12n; and Barclay's mission to Morocco, 384; and trademarks for manufacturers, 384-5; and St. Clair's defeat, 389-90; suspicions of Bowles, 394-5; and U.S. debt to Expilly, 400-1; and agreement with governor of East Florida on fugitive slaves, 406-8; and British retention of western posts, 409-10; and U.S. boundary with Canada, 410, 411n; negotiations with Hammond frustrated by Hamilton, 411-12n; and relations with Western Indians, 415-16; and dispute between Va. and Pa., 425-6

Virginia Estate

dispute over Elkhill, 165, 186-7; trees for, 268-9, 348

Writings

"Anas", x-xi, xxxviii, 33-8 (editorial note), 246 (illus.), 445; Report on Census, xxxviii-xxxix, 227-8, 246 (illus.); Summary Journal of Public Letters, ix; Notes on the State of Virginia, 52-3n, 54n, 68, 457; Report on Public Lands, 274-88; Report on Petition of William How, 295-6; Report on Petition of Charles Colvill, 296-8; Report on Petition of John Mangnall, 298-9; Report on Desalination of Sea Water, 318-22; Proposed Treaty of Commerce with France, 346-7; Bill to Promote Progress of Useful Arts, 359-61; Plan of Bill concerning Consuls, 364-6; Report on Petition of Samuel Breck, 384-5; Report on Sale of Lands on Lake Erie, 423-4; Report on Vacant Consulships, 431; Report on Negotiations with Spain, 432-3

McDonald, Alexander: *The Youth's Assistant*, 15n
MacDonough, Thomas: and Pagan v. Hooper, 336-40, 341n
McGillivray, Alexander: opposes Cox, 30n
McGuire, Francis: kidnaps slave from Pa., 425-6; and Big Beaver Creek massacre, 426
McHenry, James: letter from, 224-5; seeks appointment as minister to Netherlands, 224-5
McKee, Alexander: and Christian Indians, 308
McKinsey, Capt. (master of *Mary*): mentioned, 94n
McKnight, Dr. Charles: and Fisher's health, 18n
McMachen, William: statement to Randolph, 426n
Maczyn, battle of: mentioned, 453
Madeira: U.S. consul in, 322
Madison, James: letters to, 48-9, 77, 291-2; letter from, 17; visits Va., 11, 56, 91-2; and relations with Great Britain, 13; criticizes speculation, 17; and Federal District, 77, 88, 94, 112, 136, 263, 367; and U.S. debt to France, 120n; and ministry to France, 174; and reform of Va. constitution, 223-4, 436; and ministry to Netherlands, 225; and case of William How, 291, 296n; and military claims, 393; and Bowles, 404n; mentioned, 18, 147
Mafra, Portugal: convent in, 7
mahogany: reexported from Great Britain, 440
Maine: census, 227
Mainz, Elector of: and émigrés, 442
Malaga, Spain: U.S. consul in, 137
Malta: navy, 125
Mandrillon, Joseph: *Mémoires pour servir à l'histoire de la révolution de Provinces Unies en 1787*, 234
Mangnall, John: and case of *Dover*, 258, 298; TJ's report on, 298-9; request for pension denied by Senate, 300n
manufactures: in S.C., 154-9; in Flanders, 158; in Netherlands, 158; in Great Britain, 159; Hamilton's inquiries about, 159n; in Portugal, 218; in U.S., 349, 353-4; U.S. imports of, 383; in Brazil, 434
maple sugar: in Vt., 18, 351-2; popularity in U.S., 102, 334; in Canada, 110
maps: Tatham's plans for, 80-3

Marbois, François Barbé de: assaulted by Longchamps, 267-8n
Maria I, Queen of Portugal: dedicates convent, 7; receives Humphreys, 170; reported loan to Russia, 241; health, 375; succession to, 375; mentioned, 163
Marie Antoinette, Queen of France: relations with Leopold II, 20; and triumvirate, 106; status, 130; attends National Assembly, 145; attends opera, 160
maroons: in Saint-Domingue, 350
Marseilles: U.S. consul in, 123; U.S. shipping deterred from by piracy, 123; and American captives in Algiers, 241
Marshall, John: *Life of George Washington*, 34; and Wayles estate debt, 127
Martin, Alexander: land grant for, 278, 287n, 288n; and Report on Public Lands, 284n, 286n
Martin (Francis Eppes' slave): mentioned, 226
Martinique, W.I.: U.S. consul in, 40, 180; port charges, 278; *Jane* seized at, 302
Mary (ship): mentioned, 94n
Maryland: and Bill of Rights, 16n; and commercial relations with Great Britain, 151; census, 227; cedes land to Federal District, 393-4; stock in Bank of England, 395
Maryland Society for the Abolition of Slavery: and Banneker, 53n
Mascara, Bey of: and cession of Oran, 214
Mason and Dixon line: survey of, 83
Massachusetts: and Bill of Rights, 15; census, 227; land cessions to U.S., 424n
Massachusetts General Court: and Pagan v. Hooper, 336-42
Massachusetts Supreme Judicial Court: and Pagan v. Hooper, 336-44, 467
masts: for Algiers, 240
Mathematical Principles of Natural Philosophy (Sir Isaac Newton): ordered by TJ, 327
Matthews, John: *Voyage to the river Sierra-Leone*, 327
Maupertius, Pierre Louis Moreau de: *Oeuvres*, 327
Maury, James: letter to, 104; letters from, 59, 144, 290; on European diplomacy, 59; letter from Charles Long cited, 59n; U.S. consul in Liverpool,

Piatolli (Piattoli), Scipione, Abbé: mentioned, 457

Pickering, Timothy: mentioned, 147

Piébot (grocer): mentioned, 191

Pierce, John: and Va. specific tax, 184

Pilnitz, Declaration of: mentioned, 161, 162-3n, 315, 455

pimento: import duties on, 438-9 (table)

Pinckney, Charles: letter to, 406-8; seeks appointment as minister to Great Britain, 262n; and convention with Spain on fugitives, 266-8; letter to Washington quoted, 267-8n; letter to Washington cited, 267n; and fugitive slaves, 406-8

Pinckney, Charles Cotesworth: and relations with Great Britain, 13; TJ seeks support of, 74; and Thomas Pinckney's appointment as minister, 355n

Pinckney, Thomas: letter to, 261; letters from, 354-5, 363; portrait by Trumbull, xxxviii, 246 (illus.); TJ seeks support of, 74; appointed minister to Great Britain, 261-3, 288, 354-5, 363; criticism of, 263n; letters from quoted, 355n; letter to Rutledge quoted, 355n

Pine, Mary (Mrs. Robert Edge Pine): educates Mary Jefferson, 233, 294

Pine, Robert Edge: death of, 233n

Pinto de Sousa Coutinho, Luis, Chevalier de: and Street's consular commission, 273-4; and Portuguese consular policy, 322-3; provides Humphreys with information on Brazil, 433-4

Piranese, Giovanni Battista: drawings of Pantheon, 335n

pitch: for Algiers, 240; import duties on, 406n, 438-9 (table)

Pitt, William: relations with Russia, 107

plague: in Algiers, 124

plank: for Algiers, 240

Pleasants, James: TJ's debt to, 198n

Pleasants, Thomas, Jr.: letter from, 237; declines federal appointment, 237; letter to cited, 237

Plumard de Bellanger, Mme: and Derieux's legacy, 31-2, 301; mentioned, 164

Plutarch: *Lives*, 327

Pointe-au-Fer: retention by British, 409

Poissonier, Pierre: and desalination of sea water, 305

Poland: throne offered to Elector of Saxony, 21, 67; defensive plans, 67; revolution in, 151, 297, 453, 458n; rela-

tions with Austria, 163; relations with Prussia, 163, 452; relations with Saxony, 163; relations with Russia, 453, 455; succession to throne, 453, 455; constitution, 456, 458n; Patriotic Party, 458n

Poland, King of. *See* Stanislas II Augustus

Polly (ship): mentioned, 92, 131

Polycarp, St.: *Epistolae*, 327

Polycarpi et Ignatii Epistolae (SS. Polycarp and Ignatius): ordered by TJ, 327

Pombal, Sebastien José de Carvalho e Mello, Comte d'Oeyras, Marquis de: economic policies, 219

Pomerania, Prussia: mentioned, 452

Poncignon, J.: and Saint-Domingue slave revolt, 332n

Poole, England: U.S. consul in, 132-3n

Pope, Nathaniel: letter to, 201; as attorney for TJ, 165, 187, 199, 201, 374-5; letter to quoted, 204n

pork: for French navy, 143, 162; import duties on, 438-9 (table)

Port-au-Prince, Saint-Domingue: port charges, 278, 405; and Saint-Domingue slave revolt, 373, 460, 463

port charges: Tench Coxe's information on, 405, 406n, 414; Walter Stewart's information on, 406n; in British W.I., 438-9, 440; in France, 438-9, 440; in French W.I., 438-9, 440; in Great Britain, 438-9, 440; in Ireland, 438-9, 440

Portugal: political situation in, 7; agriculture, 47, 139; and French Revolution, 59, 110; trade with U.S., 61n; clergy favorable to U.S., 110; Inquisition, 110; trade with Great Britain, 110-11, 218; relations with Algiers, 124, 240, 241; climate, 139; minister to U.S., 164; colonies, 218; crime in, 218; government, 218; manufactures, 218; exports wine, 219; and U.S. consuls, 273, 322; transaction of public business in, 322; succession to throne, 375; national character, 434; relations with Brazil, 434; navy, 472n

Portugal, Queen of. *See* Maria I

postal service: in Va., 11, 14, 44, 84, 147, 170, 219, 224, 348, 441, 445, 446; in Southwest Territory, 14, 44, 56-8, 84, 170-1, 207, 219; in France, 70; in Ky., 84; in Federal District, 91

WASHINGTON, GEORGE (*cont.*)

Other Correspondence

with Church cited, 30; with Federal District Commissioners quoted, 89n; with George Walker cited, 89n; with Arthur Young cited, 93-4, 97; with Daniel Carroll cited, 94; with Federal District Commissioners cited, 94, 447n; with Samuel Vaughan cited, 97, 97n; with Tubeuf cited, 141n; with Short cited, 223n; with Charles Pinckney cited, 263, 267n; with Charles Pinckney quoted, 267-8n; with Littlepage cited, 284; with Lansdowne quoted, 289n; with David Stuart cited, 311-12n; with Daniel Carroll of Duddington cited, 367; with Federal District Commissioners, 367-8; with L'Enfant, 368; with Beverley Randolph, 382; with Hamilton cited, 386, 421n; with L'Enfant cited, 404; with Nathaniel Appleton cited, 405n

Personal Affairs

health, 11; visits Va., 11, 23, 62, 329; and Ebenezer Stevens, 23; observes threshing machine, 57; wine for, 103-4, 325, 333; recommends Daniel Horry, 222; and Lafayette, 324

President

and St. Clair-Symmes dispute, 10, 14; approves Blount's leave of absence, 45, 57-8; and Federal District, 47, 58, 77, 88, 94-5, 136, 311, 358, 367-8, 390-2, 404, 447; and Chipman's commission, 137-8; proposed appointment of Stevens, 146; and postal service in Va., 147; and appointment of Randolph as U.S. marshal in Va., 189; message to Congress, 225, 233, 258, 259; and lighthouses in N.C., 235-6; correspondence with governors, 263; sent Report on Public Lands, 274; and Symmes' land purchase, 291; signs Consular Act, 366n; disclaims authority over judges, 377; and Pa.'s purchase of Lake Erie tract, 423-4; and dispute between Va. and Pa. over fugitives, 425-6

Washington co., Tenn.: boundary, 276; land grants in, 277, 286n

Washington Court House, Va.: postal service, 84

watches: workmen for, 118; repair of, 335n

Waters, Esther (Hetty) Rittenhouse: visits Mary Jefferson, 294

Wayles, John: and Harrison's debt to Isaac Coles, 188

Wayles estate debt: TJ's settlement of, 127, 186, 374-5, 378

Wayne, Anthony: victory over Indians, 285n

weather: Rittenhouse's observations of, 348; TJ's comments on, 348

weights and measures: discussed by Rittenhouse, 55-6; unit of measure adopted by National Assembly, 98; Gouverneur Morris' views on, 265-6; Keith's pamphlet on, 367

Wells, Absalom: kidnaps slave from Pa., 425-6; and Big Beaver Creek massacre, 426

Welsh, Mr.: and Federal District, 388

western posts: retention by British, 202, 352, 395, 409-10

West Indies, British: trade with U.S., 255, 346n, 438-9; port charges, 405-6, 414, 438-9; trade duties, 438-9

West Indies, Danish: trade with Denmark, 87; commercial regulations, 117; trade duties, 117; commerce, 189

West Indies, French: carrying trade, 132; discontent in, 161-2; amnesty for, 172; U.S. policy toward, 173n; pamphlet on commerce of, 207; disorders in, 314; suspected British designs on, 317n; trade with U.S., 345n, 438-9; port charges, 405-6, 414, 438-9; trade duties, 438-9

West Prussia: mentioned, 452

whale fisheries: statement on procured by Johnson, 92

whale oil: exported to Denmark, 87; price, 123; restrictions on exportation to France, 166n; manufacture of, 264; import duties on, 438-9 (table)

wheat: price, 3, 123, 377; demand for in Portugal, 47; harvest in U.S., 62, 63-4, 104, 105; harvest in France, 123; and Hessian fly, 139-40, 244-52; import into Great Britain, 144, 290; sale of, 210, 231; import duties on, 417, 438-9 (table)

White, Alexander: and patent reform bill, 361n